Frequently Asked Questions

SO-AAC-952

The chapter titles on the left list the book's main topics. Across from the titles are questions commonly asked about the topics. Follow either a chapter title or a question to the appropriate page in the book. Or go to the appropriate tabbed divider, which contains a more detailed outline of that part of the book.

From the Clark College English Department *iva*

Preface for students *v*

Inside back cover: ⟨ CULTURE & LANGUAGE ⟩ Guide
Complete Contents
Editing Symbols

To access **MyCompLab** within your **Blackboard** course, you must first register online.

Before you begin, you will need:

a computer running Windows® or Mac OS® with an internet connection and web browser

a valid email address that you check regularly

Blackboard course URL, username, and password

a MyCompLab access code (beneath the pull tab)

LSCLBW-CINHK-WHEEL-SIDON-PETRI-VIRES

Your instructor's online media has been customized specifically to the learning objectives of your course. Your instructor has carefully selected the content and tailored it to help you earn the best grade possible while using the latest technology.

You will need a computer running Windows® or Mac OS® that has an internet connection and a web browser. To take advantage of all the available resources in this course, you may also need to install some browser plug-ins, such as the Macromedia® Flash™ player.

1. Log in to Blackboard:

Course URL: _____

Username: _____

Password: _____

To access your Blackboard site, consult your instructor for your Blackboard course URL (web address), username, and password, recording them in the spaces provided. When prompted, you will need your username and password to access your Blackboard resources.

Visit your course URL and locate your course. You may arrive at your custom course page immediately, or you may arrive at a page that directs you to a list of courses. From the choices available, select your course title and begin!

2. Log in to MyCompLab:

Within your Blackboard course, follow the on screen instructions to locate your link to **MyCompLab**.

When registering for **MyCompLab** as a first-time user, provide your access code and additional registration information to create a unique login name and password.

You will need your login name and password each time you log in to access your **MyCompLab** resources; record them in the spaces provided:

Login name: _____

Password: _____

The Little, Brown

Compact
Handbook

JANE E. AARON

With Additional Content

Custom Edition for Clark College

Taken from:

The Little, Brown Compact Handbook with Exercises, Sixth Edition
by Jane E. Aaron

The Brief Penguin Handbook, Second Edition
by Lester Faigley

PEARSON
Custom
Publishing

PEARSON
Longman

Taken from:

The Little, Brown Compact Handbook with Exercises, Sixth Edition
by Jane E. Aaron
Copyright © 2007 Pearson Education, Inc.
Published by Longman
Boston, Massachusetts 02116

The Brief Penguin Handbook, Second Edition
by Lester Faigley
Copyright © 2006 Pearson Education, Inc.
Published by Longman

Printed in the United States of America

10 9 8 7 6 5 4 3 2 1

ISBN 0-536-29722-3

2006240374

TB

Please visit our web site at *www.pearsoncustom.com*

PEARSON CUSTOM PUBLISHING
75 Arlington Street, Suite 300, Boston, MA 02116
A Pearson Education Company

Dear Clark Student:

All of us at Clark College would like to welcome you to our campus. We have selected this custom edition of *Little, Brown* for its flexibility, as coming to know it will aid you in all of your academic endeavors and beyond. Honestly, the greater the extent to which you make use of this book, that is, the more familiar you are with its content and organization, the more you can customize your learning and ensure your success as a student. Answers to questions of any kind can be found here; this is an opportunity to take charge of your own education.

We ask that you keep this book throughout the English composition sequence, as all instructors will use it for English 101 and 102; it will also be invaluable for English 098, our literature classes, and writing across the disciplines. While you may sell other books back to the bookstore at the end of the term, this is an exception: you will need this book throughout your education here at Clark.

In the front of your new handbook you'll find an access code that admits you to MyCompLab 2.0. This is an online workshop that your instructor may use for diagnostic quizzes, achievement tests, in-class games or plain old homework. It's tied to an electronic gradebook that your instructor may use to track your progress and suggest improvements, so this access code belongs to you and is part of the text you bought. This code is all yours for two years; however, if you sell or lose your book, you may have to purchase a new access code in order to keep up with your instructor's requirements. We hope you and your instructor will take full advantage of MyCompLab as you explore the demands of academic writing together.

We've also included in these preliminary pages some information specific to Clark that we hope you'll find helpful, so please take a moment to familiarize yourself with these references and services. To begin, Clark provides many on-campus resources to ensure your success. Here is a very brief list of frequently used services and their telephone contact information. For a more detailed list, please consult http://www.clark.edu/student_services.

- Tutoring and Writing Center: 992-2253
- Cannell Library: 992-2151
- Computer Lab Help Desk: 992-2562
- Financial Aid: 992-2153
- Disability Support Services: 992-2314
- Displaced Homemakers: 992-2321

Once again, welcome to Clark. We're glad to have you.

Sincerely,

The English Department

English Department Composition Outcomes

These student learning outcomes (SLOs) delineate the skills around which Clark English faculty design their courses. Please make note of the exit skills for your particular course.

	097	098	101	102
SLO 1 Design and execute thorough searches for information	Students should be able to complete the library self-guided tour, obtain a library card, and locate current magazines, newspapers, and books in the stacks.	Students should be able to use the book catalog to find specialized encyclopedias, atlases, almanacs, and dictionaries.	Students should be able to use databases and the World Wide Web to find sources relevant to a particular topic. They should evaluate and consider reliability (including considerations of academic vs. popular sources) when deciding how to use sources in a paper.	Students should be able to design and execute a thorough search, choosing appropriate tools to find information for a specific, complex project. They should know when and how to seek help from librarians as well as be able to use Clark's library to access other library collections, subject-specific databases, trade publications, and initiate interlibrary loans.

	097	098	101	102
SLO 2 Describe, paraphrase, and summarize college-level material accurately.	Students should be able to summarize a magazine article of several paragraphs, giving appropriate credit.	Students should be able to summarize the main points college level material, using their own words and giving appropriate credit	Students should be able to summarize the main points from an academic or professional essay. They should be able to paraphrase 3–5 sentences from an academic or professional essay. They should be able to apply MLA documentation standards.	Students should be able to summarize and paraphrase a range of materials, including academic or professional articles, within a single essay. Formal documentation standards apply.
SLO 3 Analyze and use a variety of college-level material to both identify areas for investigation and to develop ideas to communicate	Students should be able to write a paragraph answering questions about the content of a variety of material, including two to three page articles.	Students should be able to critically engage with a college-level text, answer questions about it, and discuss it.	Students should be able to pose questions and develop critical responses to academic and professional essays. They should be able to use their own questions and responses to develop a thesis for an essay using three or more sources.	Students should be able to use a range of sources and references to generate topics, create questions to focus research, develop an effective note-taking system, and ultimately write research papers that use at least 10 sources. They should be able to integrate researched material smoothly into the essay, subordinating sources to a thesis.

097	098	101	102
SLO 5	Students should be able to:	Students should be able to:	Students should be able to:
Understand and apply the principles of effective communication when writing and speaking:	■ Develop and organize 500–750 word essays unified by a central idea.	■ Develop and organize 1000–1500 word essays unified by a central idea.	■ Develop and organize a 2500–3000 word essay unified by a central idea requiring systematic, substantial research (10 or more authoritative sources).
a) develop and organize around one central idea	■ Support the ideas in short essays with sufficient detail and evidence.	■ Support ideas with sufficient detail and evidence. In at least one essay, show ability to provide evidence from multiple sources (evidence that goes beyond personal experience). Students should be able to identify and defend the assumptions that underlie their positions and use rhetorical strategies in their writing.	■ Support ideas with sufficient detail and evidence based on extensive research.
b) support central and related ideas with detail and evidence	■ Use introductions, conclusions, and transition words and sentences to maintain clarity and connection to the thesis.		■ Create an effective essay organization, subordinating sources to a thesis.
c) create an easy to follow organization	■ Write complete sentences consistently with few fragments and run-ons; maintain a consistent point of view and tense; write complex and well as simple and compound sentences; choose language that is accurate and free from slang and cliche. Remaining problems should be manageable	■ Make the purpose, main idea, and direction of thought clear to a reader, using a variety of methods in several types of writing.	■ Edit and proofread to follow the conventions of standard English.
SLO 5 (Develop and organize paragraphs to support clearly focused topic sentences.)			

097 (continued)

Students should be able to:

■ Develop and organize paragraphs to support clearly focused topic sentences.

■ Distinguish between general ideas and supporting detail and write well supported paragraphs.

■ In a paragraph, tie development to a topic sentence and use transitions to keep paragraph unified.

■ Demonstrate an understanding of what makes a sentence. Simple and compound sentences should be easy to read and understand. Word choices should be accurate. Students should have demonstrated clear improvement in this area during the class.

d) use verbal skills such as precise word choice and correct grammar

	097	098	101	102
		enough for a 101 teacher's comments and advice to be helpful. Students should demonstrate clear improvement in this area during the class.	■ Show increased ability to edit and proofread; there may be occasional problems in syntax, grammar, and punctuation but no multiple or chronic errors should occur.	
SLO 6 Adapt to a variety of audiences and occasions	Students should be able to understand what audience and voice mean.	Students should be able to adapt their writing in voice and tone and edit essays to make the language appropriate to a particular audience.	Students should be able to adapt diction, voice, tone, and evidence to various audiences.	Students should be able to adapt diction, voice, tone, and evidence to an academic audience. They should be able to create a consistent voice when using a variety of sources.
SLO 7 Communicate in ethical ways (documentation, avoid deceptive language, expect this from others)	Students should be able to use basic signal phrases and quotation marks as techniques for using resource material ethically and accurately.	Students should be able to: ■ use basic signal phrases and quotation marks, as well as in-text citation and Works Cited in essays using a source. ■ write without deceptive or inflammatory language.	Students should be able to: ■ use accurate MLA documentation in completed essays ■ present a reasoned and fair argument without deceptive or inflammatory language.	Students should be able to: ■ synthesize MLA citation techniques in lengthy manuscripts ■ present a reasoned and fair argument without deceptive or inflammatory language. ■ evaluate other writers' credibility and authority.

SLO 8

(Work collaboratively by expressing opinions with tact, listening to others, and shouldering an appropriate share of the workload) Students should be able to:

- Listen and contribute pertinent comments to class discussion without dominating the conversations
- Prepare for peer response activities
- In peer response, use the language of academic writing to talk about papers (thesis, organization, transitions, etc.) and articulate strengths and weaknesses in peers' writing with specific references to peers' papers.
- In small groups, stay focused on work at hand, offer input that is helpful and insightful, not distract by socializing, and occasionally record and report.

SLO 9

(Improve communication by practicing self-assessment, set goals, seek and use feedback, revise and edit for excellence, practice self-discipline and persistence, and apply skills in new contexts) Students should be able to:

- Consistently work to meet deadlines.
- Seek out instructor feedback and advice or seek out assistance at the College Writing Center.
- Come prepared for conferences or tutoring sessions
- Use instructor and peer feedback to make improvement in writing.
- Experiment with the different stages of the process.
- Use revision to strengthen elements such as thesis, organization, and supporting evidence.
- Use editing to eliminate grammatical errors.
- Assess own papers for revision and editing.
- Apply learned skills to each new assignment as the quarter progresses

Marjorie Sandbloom
ENGL 101
Sandra Woodward
15 March 2006

Truckers and Biodiesel

Rolling down the interstate highway and blowing clouds of black smoke into the air, fleets of semi trucks traverse America day and night to deliver various commodities to business industries. Semi trucks are the vital connecting link between shipping ports and railway lines and are heavily relied on to move freight. If semi trucks were to stop operating, commerce would come to a standstill, and the economy would suffer. Keeping the avenues of trade up and running in the transportation industry takes fuel, and the demands on America's supply are constantly increasing. As truck and automobile drivers have become complacent and accustomed to the accessibility of fuel at gas stations, they may not recognize that petroleum could become unavailable. Facing the possibility of such a serious crisis, the United States government should fund and continue to support research for biodiesel to keep the trucking fleets moving.

The issue of oil shortages was abruptly brought into focus when terrorists attacked the United States on 9/11. No one knew whether that day would permanently change the way Americans live. Two Gulf Wars have made the situation even more precarious, with uncertain outcomes that could determine access to world oil. Internal civil strife or external conflicts could affect any one of the Middle Eastern oil producing countries. Embargoes could be put into place. At any given time, the doors could close and the steady supply of oil reserves America has come to depend on could end. Saudi Arabia is viewed as a vast country with the potential to produce unlimited amounts of reserves for any nation willing to buy. Yet the Saudi's oil fields are rapidly becoming saturated with water, as suggested by Mark Simmons in his book, Twilight in the Desert (Sickinger C2). In fact, it's clear that oil is a finite commodity. According to Ken Deffeyes, a former Shell Oil geologist, professor emeritus of geosciences at Princeton University and author, the oil companies aren't addressing the issue of shortages: "They're not drilling, they're not building new pipelines and not building new refineries," which puts the U.S. in a precarious position (Sickinger C2). Without the resources of additional oil, the trucking industry can't keep transporting commodities indefinitely.

Though we have come this far from 9/11, no one knows what the future will bring because the situation in the Middle East is so unstable. If that worry isn't enough, any type of natural catastrophe such as the recent flooding from Hurricane Katrina in New Orleans, could affect oil refineries situated in the path of disaster. Living on the edge moment to moment is not preparing for the unexpected. Without a solid back-up plan and a follow-through agenda, the U.S. is left without fuel reserves to fill the needs and demands. Amy Myers Jaffe, Director of the Energy Forum at the James A. Baker III Institute for Public Policy in Houston, suggests that the United States "should mandate that every oil company keep 5 to 10 percent of its average sales of gasoline, heating oil, and natural gas on reserve for use in emergency, as is done in Europe."

The concern and need for additional sources of alternative fuel is evident. President Bush signed The Energy Policy Act of 2005 to "help diversify the nation's fuel supply by renewing incentives for producers and suppliers of renewable fuels, such as biodiesel and ethanol" (Guerrero). Biodiesel, a relatively new fuel source, is a blend of diesel and vegetable oils or animal fats formulated and produced for commercial trucks. The method is to take sustainable crops and process the oils after crushing or grinding them. Soybean is the primary crop used for production in the United States. Different manufacturers vary the percentage ratio of diesel (as the base) to the added biodiesel. The diesel is the larger percentage, and biodiesel is the smaller percentage mixed and added to it. Certain classifications are used to distinguish the different levels of biodiesel blends added to conventional fuel. For example, B20 is "a blend of 20% biodiesel with 80% conventional fuel" (Schulz).

Currently, several states are using biodiesel in their trucking fleets. Kevin Brink, the Vice President of Business Development for Norrenberns Truck Service, located in Nashville, Illinois, "switched the company's 162 tractors to biodiesel," because "diesel fuel prices kept going higher and higher, and we were looking for ways to cut fuel costs." He also said, "It's good for the environment, good for the economy, and good for farmers," referring to the change (qtd. in Guerrero). Illinois gives a tax break in conjunction with the federal government to the fueling stations that sell biodiesel and to those that purchase it. Minnesota is the first state to enforce a mandate of "2% biodiesel" blend after processing plants in the state were built to support the venture (Fischer). An article from the Oregonian reports that legislation has been introduced in the state of Washington that "would require all diesel sold in the state to contain 2 percent biodiesel by Dec. 1, 2008" (Webley B1). The state of Oregon is watching to see what happens with the legislation in Washington before reintroducing legislation requiring a biodiesel standard (Webley B4). Plants for biodiesel are also being built in Iowa and Missouri (Fischer).

Even though biodiesel has been reported to burn cleaner fuel and produces cleaner exhaust, which is 48 percent less carbon monoxide than the standard un-blended diesel, questions remain as to the effect it will have on the engines (Web-ley). The loudest complaint comes from John Hausladen, President of the Minnesota Trucking Association. Biodiesel is known to gel faster than diesel and at higher temperatures which has the ability to clog the fuel filters in the engines, particu-larly in the frigid Minnesota winters. As a result, it can incapacitate the trucks and force the semi drivers to sit idle. Wages are lost to both the company and drivers which becomes a big financial concern, not to mention the cost of repairs on the fleet (Fischer). Fuel filters have to be changed twice as often when using biodiesel, but advocates say it is worth the cost compared to the savings and incentives (Schulz).

Another major problem is engine warranties. Bob Martin, spokesman for Mack Trucks, one of the largest manufacturers of diesel trucks in the United States, says "the company waives warranties for alternative fuel blends higher than 5%" (Guer-rero). There is a debate over the quality and purity of biodiesel if the government doesn't regulate what goes into the blend. So many different oils can be used from a variety of sources that the issue becomes one of quality control. The major manu-facturers of diesel engines are sufficiently concerned that they allow only low per-centage mixes of the diesel to be used under warranty. Jim Dugan, spokesman for Caterpillar Inc., a manufacturer of earth moving equipment and machinery says, "Caterpillar neither endorses nor prohibits the use of biodiesel fuels in our ma-chines and with our engines, . . . and it is the responsibility of the user to utilize the correct fuel as recommended by the manufacturer and as allowed by the Envi-ronmental Protection Agency and other regulatory agencies" (Schulz). To help avoid warranty tangles, the National Biodiesel Board "recommends that truckers buy biodiesel only from suppliers approved by the American Society for Testing Materi-als" (Schulz). For now, adhering to correct use of warranty requirements is a prob-lem the purchasers must solve.

Besides saving costs for trucking firms, the producers of biodiesel hope to change the amount of black smoke emitted into the environment, a huge pollutant. One report indicates that "using biodiesel substantially reduces the amount of un-burnt hydrocarbons, carbon monoxide and particulate matter." The chemists also found that biodiesel has "10% built-in oxygen that helps it to burn fully," and that "handling of biodiesel is safer compared to petroleum diesel due to its higher flash point," which means it doesn't ignite as fast. Another positive result of biodiesel is "the high level of lubricity," which makes "excellent lubricants for the injection systems," a plus for the hard wear and tear on heavy duty engines (Biodiesel: Clean). One interesting twist is the change of odor of the blend used. When used cooking oil has been rendered for fuel use, biodiesel can smell "like popcorn or French fries," a long stretch from the acrid smell of straight diesel billowing out of the exhaust stacks as the semi thunders down the highway (Fischer).

More research needs to be done in two areas before the trucking companies and the EPA will know how useful biodiesel may finally turn out to be. First, the National Biodiesel Board and the Department of Energy are working on an extensive, "testing program . . . to see how 20% and lesser blends match up to the Environmental Protection Agency's cleaner-diesel emission rules," which is a good indicator that the issue of clean air is important and being taken seriously (Schulz). Also, current figures aren't in yet comparing fuel mileage of trucks with or without the use of biodiesel, and if companies are getting better mileage results with biodiesel. Additional research also needs to be done to ensure biodiesel blends won't damage engines that are produced by companies such as Mack and Caterpillar. The trucking and engine industries are more likely to support a biodiesel mandate without reservation if proven standards are established.

Even with incomplete reports, it makes sense to continue to develop the properties of biodiesel into an efficient fuel for the commercial trucking industry and continue research until satisfactory results are achieved. According to Ralph Groschen, an agriculture marketing specialist for the Minnesota Department of Agriculture, "other states will be watching to see what effect the Minnesota law will have on transportation and commerce" (Schulz). Engineers and some trucking organizations do not want to see the government, state or federal, interfere and enforce mandates like those in Minnesota, or the legislation proposed in Washington, especially if quality testing is still ongoing to improve biodiesel fuel.

The U.S. government should be actively involved in the research, development and production of biodiesel as an alternative fuel source. If what Ken Deffeyes says is true that "we've found 94% of all the oil we're ever going to find," then it is imperative to find ways to solve the problem (Sickenger C2). Blindly depending on the Middle East for an endless quantity of oil is clearly not the answer. Without the necessary supply of fuel, the trucking fleets would roll to a stop. If that should ever happen, the economy of the United States would freeze. Biodiesel is one resource that will become the accepted fuel of the future once testing has been completed and quality standards put in place.

Works Cited

"Biodiesel: Clean Fuel of the Future." <u>Hydrocarbon Processing</u> Feb 2005: 1. <u>Research Library Complete</u>. ProQuest. Lewis D. Cannell Library, Vancouver, WA. 27 Feb 2006.

Fischer, Andrea. "Truckers Concerned about Minnesota's New 2% Biodiesel Mandate." <u>Transport Topics</u> 10 Oct. 2005: 5. <u>Research Library Complete</u>. ProQuest. Lewis D. Cannell Library, Vancouver, WA. 27 Feb 2006.

Guerrero, Thelma. "Illinois Fleet Jumps Aboard the Soybean Bandwagon." <u>Transport Topics</u> 12 Sept. 2005: S1. <u>Research Library Complete</u>. ProQuest. Lewis D. Cannell Library, Vancouver, WA. 27 Feb 2006.

Jaffe, Amy Myers. "Seven Ways to Fix the Oil Crisis." <u>Esquire</u> Dec. 2005: 217. <u>Research Library Complete</u>. ProQuest. Lewis D. Cannell Library, Vancouver, WA. 22 Feb 2006.

Schulz, John D. "Will Fuel Prices Make the Option More Attractive?" <u>Transport Topics</u> 12 Sept. 2005: S1. <u>Research Library Complete</u>. ProQuest. Lewis D. Cannell Library, Vancouver, WA. 27 Feb 2006.

Sickenger, Ted. "Oil Expert: Output Downhill from Here." <u>The Oregonian</u> 27 Feb 2006, sunrise ed., C1-C2.

Webley, Kayla. "The State Considers Proposal to Mandate Alternative Fuel" <u>The Sunday Oregonian</u> 5 Feb 2006, sunrise ed., B1.

Citing Sources Using MLA
From *The Little, Brown Compact Handbook*

This guide provides an overview for common bibliographic references. For more detailed information, see "Writing in the Disciplines, MLA," which begins on page 432 of this text.

- **Consult** your instructor for specific guidelines for composing a Works Cited list.
- ***Avoid Plagiarism!*** Plagiarism is using someone's work without giving credit. It is academic dishonesty and may result in disciplinary action. To avoid plagiarizing, see "Research Writing: Avoiding Plagiarism and Documenting Sources," which begins on page 418.

Print Sources

NOTE: This guide single spaces citations to conserve space. Remember to double space your Works Cited!

Book with one author:
Tan, Amy. The Bonesetter's Daughter. New York: Putnam, 2001.

Book with two authors:
Eggins, Suzanne, and Diane Slade. Analysing Casual Conversation. London: Cassell, 1997.

Book with an editor:
Powell, Kevin, ed. Step into a World: A Global Anthology of the New Black Literature. New York: Wiley, 2000.

Encyclopedia article without an author: (abbreviated format for well-known encyclopedia)
"Sonata." The American Heritage Dictionary of the English Language. 4th ed. 2000.

Article in a reference book:
Moch, Leslie Page. "Migration." Encyclopedia of European Social History: From 1350 to 2000. 6 vols. Ed. Peter N. Stearns. Detroit: Scribner's, 2001.

Book with two or more volumes:
Holmes, Kenneth L., ed. Covered Wagon Women: Diaries & Letters from the Western Trails, 1840-1890. 8 vols. Glendale, CA: Clark, 1983-1993.

Article in an Opposing Viewpoints volume:
Bracey, Gerald W. "The Quality of Public Education Has Not Declined." Education: Opposing Viewpoints. Detroit: Greenhaven Press, 2005. Rpt. of "What Crisis?" Washington Post National Weekly Edition May 13–19, 2002: 23.

Previously published article in a collection:
Roberts, Sheila. "A Confined World: A Rereading of Pauline Smith." World Literature Written in English 24 (1984): 232–38. Rpt. in Twentieth-Century Literary Criticism. Ed. Dennis Poupard. Vol. 25. Detroit: Gale, 1988. 399–402.

Article from a scholarly journal paginated by volume:
Ryan, Katy. "Revolutionary Suicide in Toni Morrison's Fiction." African American Review 34 (2000): 389–412.

Article from scholarly journal paginated by issue:
Wood, Michael. "Broken Dates: Fiction and the Century." Kenyon Review 22.3 (2000): 50–64.

Article from a popular magazine:
Lord, Lewis. "There's Something about Mary Todd." U.S. News and World Report 19 Feb. 2001: 53.

Article in daily newspaper:
Wilford, John Noble. "In a Golden Age of Discovery, Faraway Worlds Beckon." New York Times 9 Feb. 1997, late ed., sec. 1: 1+.

Electronic Sources
(other examples at: www.dianahacker.com/resdoc)

(Frequently, online articles do not have page numbers. If so, include the total number of pages, paragraphs or other sections, if they are numbered.)

Magazine article from EBSCOhost database:
Lord, Lewis. "There's Something About Mary Todd." U.S. News and World Report 19 Feb. 2001: 53. Academic Search Premier. EBSCOhost. Cannell Library, Vancouver, WA. 12 June 2006.

Journal article from EBSCOhost database:
Fitzgerald, Jill. "How Will Bilingual/ESL Programs in Literacy Change in the Next Millenium?" Reading Research Quarterly 35.4 (2000):520. Academic Search Premier. EBSCOhost. Cannell Library, Vancouver, WA. 12 June 2006.

Magazine article from ProQuest Direct database:
Thompson, Mark. "Grounded in Kosovo." Time 31 May 1999: 60–62. Research Library Complete. ProQuest. Cannell Library, Vancouver, WA. 4 Apr. 2001.

Journal article from ProQuest Direct database:
Sarhar, Sahotra. "Wilderness Preservation and Biodiversity Conservation—Keeping Divergent Goals Distinct." <u>BioScience</u> 49 (1999): 405–12. <u>Research Library Complete</u>. ProQuest. Cannell Library, Vancouver, WA. 4 Feb. 2002.

Newspaper article from ProQuest Direct database:
Hays, Kristen. "Enron Whistleblower Watkins to Resign." <u>Columbian</u> 16 Nov. 2002. <u>Research Library Complete</u>. ProQuest. Cannell Library, Vancouver, WA. 4 Dec. 2002.

Gale Virtual Reference Library database:
Long, Thomas. "Utopia." <u>Encyclopedia of Community</u>. Eds. Karen Christensen and David Levinson. Thousand Oaks: Sage, 2003. 1437–42. <u>Gale Virtual Reference Library</u>. Thomson Gale. Cannell Library, Vancouver, WA. 12 June 2006.

Reference article from Literature Resource Center database:
Williams, Aubrey L. "Alexander Pope." <u>Eighteenth Century British Poets, First Series</u>. Ed. John Sitter. Dictionary of Literary Biography. Vol. 95. Detroit: Gale, 1990. <u>Literature Resource Center</u>. Thomson Gale. Cannell Library, Vancouver, WA. 1 Mar. 2005.

CQ Researcher online:
Hosansky, David. "Food Safety." <u>CQ Researcher</u> 1 Nov. 2002. <u>CQ Researcher Online</u>. Cannell Library, Vancouver, WA. 7 Feb. 2003.

World WideWeb site:
basic format:
Author. "Title of Short Work." <u>Title of Site</u>. Date site was posted or updated (if available). Sponsor of the site (if not named as the author). Date you accessed the site <URL>.
example:
"Media Giants." <u>The Merchants of Cool</u>. 2001. <u>PBS Online</u>. 7 Mar. 2001 <http://pbs.org/wgbh/ pages/frontline/shows/cool/giants>.

WWW site version of an article from a print journal:
Cox, Caroline. "Toward Healthy Eating." <u>Journal of Pesticide Reform</u> 15.4 (1995). Ecological Agriculture Projects. McGill University. 2 Mar. 2005. <http://www.eap.mcgill.ca/ MagRack/JPR/JPR_23.htm>.

How Books Are Organized

■ The Library of Congress Classification System

A GENERAL WORKS

AC	Collections. Series. Collected works
AE	Encyclopedias (General)
AG	Dictionaries;general reference books
AI	Indexes (General)
AM	Museums (General); Collecting (General)
AN	Newspapers
AP	Periodicals (General)
AS	Academics and learned societies (General)
AY	Yearbooks. Almanacs. Directories
AZ	History of scholarship and learning. The humanities; Popular errors, delusions, superstitions

B PHILOSOPHY. PSYCHOLOGY. RELIGION

B	Philosophy (General)
BC	Logic
BD	Speculative philosophy
BF	Psychology
BH	Aesthetics
BJ	Ethics. Social usages. Etiquette
BL	Religions. Mythology. Rationalism
BM	Judaism
BP	Islam. Bahaism. Theosophy, etc.
BQ	Buddhism
BR	Christianity
BS	The Bible
BT	Doctrinal theology
BV	Practical theology
BX	Christian denominations

C AUXILIARY SCIENCES OF HISTORY

C	Auxiliary sciences of history (General)
CB	History of civilization
CC	Archaeology (General)
CD	Diplomatics. Archives. Seals
CE	Technical chronology. Calendar
CJ	Numismatics
CN	Inscriptions. Epigraphy
CR	Heraldry
CS	Genealogy
CT	Biography

D HISTORY: GENERAL AND OLD WORLD

D	History (General)
DA	Great Britain
DB	Austria. Liechtenstein. Hungary. Czechoslovakia
DC	France, Andorra, Monaco
DD	Germany
DE	The Mediterranean. Greco-Roman World
DF	Greece
DG	Italy
DH	Netherlands. (Low Countries)
DJ	Netherlands (Holland)
DJK	Eastern Europe
DK	Soviet Union
DL	Northern Europe. Scandinavia
DP	Spain. Portugal
DQ	Switzerland
DR	Balkan Peninsula
DS	Asia
DT	Africa
DU	Oceania (South Seas)
DX	Gypsies

E–F HISTORY: AMERICA

E 11–29	America (General)
E 31–46	North America
E 51–99	Indians. Indians of N. America
E 101–135	Discovery of Am.; early explor
E 151–169.12	United States (General)
E 171–183.9	United States (History)
E 184–185.98	Elements in the population
E 184.5–185.98	Afro-Americans
E 186–199	Colonial history
E 201–298	Revolution
E 301–453	Revolution to the Civil War
E 351–364.9	War of 1812
E 401–415.2	War with Mexico
E 441–453	Slavery
E 456–655	Civil War
E 482–489	Confederate States of America
E 660–738	Late nineteenth century
E 714–735	Spanish-American War
E 740–	Twentieth century

F 1–975	United States local history
F 1001–1140	British America. Canada
F 1201–2191	Mexico. Latin America, Central America, West Indies
F 2201–3799	South America

G GEOGRAPHY (GENERAL) ATLASES. MAPS
GA   Mathematical geography. Cartography
GB   Physical geography
GC   Oceanography
GE   Environmental Studies
GF   Human ecology. Anthropogeography
GN   Anthropology
GR   Folklore
GT   Manners and customs (General)
GV   Recreation. Leisure

H SOCIAL SCIENCES
H   Social sciences (General)
HA   Statistics
HB   Economic theory. Demography
HC–HD   Economic history and conditions
HE   Transportation and communications
HF   Commerce
HG   Finance
HJ   Public finance
HM   Sociology (General and theoretical)
HN   Social history/problems/reform
HQ   The family. Marriage. Women
HS   Societies: Secret, benevolent, etc. Clubs
HT   Communities. Classes. Races
HV   Social pathology/public welfare. Criminology
HX   Socialism. Communism. Anarchism

J POLITICAL SCIENCE
J   General legislative and executive papers
JA   Collections and general works
JC   Political theory
JF   General works
JK   United States
JL   British America. Latin America
JN   Europe
JQ   Asia. Africa. Australia. Oceania
JS   Local government
JV   Colonies and colonization. Emigration and immigration
JX   International law. International relations

K LAW
(Most K divisions, see full schedule)
K 1–7720   Law (General)
KDZ 0–4999 America. North America

L EDUCATION
L   Education (General)
LA   History of education
LB   Theory and practice of education
LC   Special aspects of education

LD	Schools: United States
LE	Schools: America, except United States
LF	Schools: Europe
LG	Schools: Asia. Africa. Oceania
LH	College and school magazines and papers
LJ	Student fraternities and societies, U.S.
LT	Textbooks

M MUSIC AND BOOKS ON MUSIC

M	Music
ML	Literature of music
MT	Musical instruction and study
N	Fine Arts

N VISUAL ARTS (GENERAL)

NA	Architecture
NB	Sculpture
NC	Drawing. Design. Illustration
ND	Painting
NE	Print media
NK	Decorative & Applied arts
	Decoration and ornament
NX	Arts in general

P LANGUAGE AND LITERATURE

P	Philology and linguistics (General)
PA	Classical languages and literatures
PB	Modern European languages
PC	Romance languages
PD	Germanic languages
PE	English
PF–PM	Other languages
PN	Literature
PQ	Romance literature
PR	English literature
PS	American literature
PT	Germanic literatures
PZ	Juvenile belles letters

Q SCIENCE

Q	Science (General)
QA	Mathematics
QB	Astronomy
QC	Physics
QD	Chemistry
QE	Geology
QH	Natural history (Gen.). Biology (Gen.)
QK	Botany
QL	Zoology
QM	Human anatomy

QP	Physiology
QR	Microbiology

R MEDICINE

R	Medicine (General)
RA	Public aspects of medicine
RB	Pathology
RC	Internal medicine. Practice of medicine
RD	Surgery
RE	Ophthalmology
RF	Otorhinolaryngology
RG	Gynecology and obstetrics
RJ	Pediatrics
RK	Dentistry
RL	Dermatology
RM	Therapeutics. Pharmacology
RS	Pharmacy and materia medica
RT	Nursing
RV	Botanic, Thomsonian, and eclectic med.
RX	Homeopathy
RZ	Other systems of medicine

S AGRICULTURE

S	Agriculture (General)
SB	Plant culture
SD	Forestry
SF	Animal culture
SH	Aquaculture. Fisheries. Angling
SK	Hunting

T TECHNOLOGY

T	Technology (General)
TA	Engineering (Gen.). Civil eng. (Gen.)
TC	Hydraulic engineering
TD	Environmental tech. Sanitary engineering
TE	Highway eng. Roads and pavements
TF	Railroad engineering and operation
TG	Bridge engineering
TH	Building construction
TJ	Mechanical engineering and machinery
TK	Electrical eng. Electronics. Nuclear eng.
TL	Motor vehicles. Aeronautics. Astronautics
TN	Mining engineering. Metallurgy
TP	Chemical technology
TR	Photography
TS	Manufactures
TT	Handicrafts. Arts and crafts
TX	Home economics

U–V MILITARY SCIENCE; NAVAL SCIENCE

Z BIBLIOGRAPHY. LIBRARY SCIENCE

Clark College English Department Statement on Plagiarism

Much of your college education will involve learning what others have written and then integrating those ideas into your own thinking. But in academic writing, any ideas or language not credited to another are assumed to be that of the author. The problem of plagiarism comes in when you fail to give credit for those ideas that are not originally yours. The word *plagiarism*, which comes from the Latin word for "kidnapping," refers to the unacknowledged use of another's words, ideas, or information. Your instructor will introduce you to strategies to avoid plagiarism, the conventions for using and acknowledging sources, and good note-taking procedures. Your instructor will also help you to gain confidence in your own writing so that you do not feel a need to borrow the words of others. The following is a guide to help you avoid plagiarism.

■ What you need not acknowledge

Anything that is written entirely in your own words AND meets one of the following two criteria:

1. **Common knowledge.** If most people know something without having to do research on it, you need not cite it. However, if you quote someone's explanation of information that is common knowledge, it must be cited as a direct quote.
2. **Your own ideas and reasoning.**

■ What you should acknowledge in order to show that you have done research and that you are indebted to particularly useful sources of widely available information

Anything that is written entirely in your own words AND meets one of the following criteria:

1. Facts available from a wide variety of sources.
2. Facts widely available but especially well addressed in a particular source.

■ What you must acknowledge

1. **Any direct quotation,** even if it contains common knowledge or information widely available.
2. **Paraphrases and summaries of sources that provide background information, facts, and even common knowledge if you present that information in a way that is informed by a particular source.**

3. **Arguable assertions.** If an author presents an assertion that may or may not be true, you must cite the source.
4. **Statistics, charts, tables, and graphs from any source.** You must credit all graphic material, even if you yourself create the graph.

The purchase of research papers or the employment of a person or agency to prepare such papers is considered by the English Department to be plagiarism. You may get help in writing your paper, but there are limits to the amount of help you can honestly receive. For instance, if your instructor so prescribes, others may read your paper and point out weaknesses, but they must not rewrite the paper for you. Your instructor will define other uses and limitations of outside help as he or she deems appropriate.

We members of the English Department cannot overemphasize the fact that plagiarism is an extremely serious violation of academic honesty and that it can lead to most serious consequences.

The standard departmental penalty for plagiarism discovered in any English course will be failure of that course. Please see *The Clark College Code of Student Conduct* to note that the Dean of Students can authorize additional penalties for "Academic cheating or plagiarism or aiding or abetting cheating or plagiarism."

Also note that the English faculty will also consider it an act of dishonesty to resubmit or to rewrite any paper that you have accomplished in any earlier or concurrent course for a new grade without gaining the explicit permission of your instructor. Discovery of your having done so will also result in failure of the course.

(Adopted from BGSU GSW Dept.)

Preface for Students

The Little, Brown Compact Handbook with Exercises contains the basic information you'll need for writing in and out of school. Here you can find out how to get ideas, use commas, search the Internet, cite sources, craft an argument, and write a résumé—all in a convenient, accessible package.

This book is mainly a reference for you to dip into as needs arise. You probably won't read the book all the way through, nor will you use everything it contains: you already know much of the content anyway, whether consciously or not. The trick is to figure out what you *don't* know—taking cues from your own writing experiences and the comments of others—and then to find the answers to your questions in these pages. On most topics, you'll find exercises for practice as well.

Using this book will not by itself make you a good writer; for that, you need to care about your work at every level, from finding a subject to spelling words. But learning how to use the handbook and the information in it can give you the means to write *what* you want in the *way* you want.

■ Reference aids

You have many ways to find what you need in the handbook:

- **Use a directory.** "Frequently Asked Questions" (inside the front cover) provides questions in everyday language that are commonly asked about the book's main topics. "Contents" (inside the back cover) provides an overview of the entire book.

- **Use a tabbed divider.** At each tab, a detailed outline directs you to the material covered in that part of the book.

- **Use the glossary.** "Glossary of Usage" (Gl pp. 553–66) clarifies more than 275 words that are commonly confused and misused.

- **Use the index.** The extensive index includes every term, concept, and problem word or expression mentioned in the book.

- **Use a list.** Two helpful aids fall at the back of the book. "CULTURE LANGUAGE Guide" (just before "Contents") pulls together all the material for students using standard American English as a second language or a second dialect. And "Editing Symbols" (inside the back cover) explains abbreviations often used to mark papers.

- **Use the elements of the page.** As shown in the following illustration, each page of the handbook tells you where you are and what you can find there.

The handbook's page elements

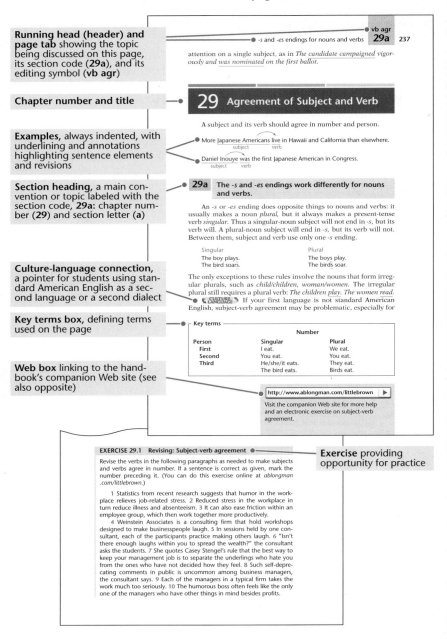

Running head (header) and page tab showing the topic being discussed on this page, its section code (**29a**), and its editing symbol (**vb agr**)

-s and *-es* endings for nouns and verbs ‎ **vb agr 29a** 237

attention on a single subject, as in *The candidate campaigned vigorously and was nominated on the first ballot.*

Chapter number and title

29 Agreement of Subject and Verb

A subject and its verb should agree in number and person.

Examples, always indented, with underlining and annotations highlighting sentence elements and revisions

More Japanese Americans live in Hawaii and California than elsewhere.
subject — verb

Daniel Inouye was the first Japanese American in Congress.
subject — verb

Section heading, a main convention or topic labeled with the section code, **29a:** chapter number (**29**) and section letter (**a**)

29a The *-s* and *-es* endings work differently for nouns and verbs.

An *-s* or *-es* ending does opposite things to nouns and verbs: it usually makes a noun *plural,* but it always makes a present-tense verb *singular.* Thus a singular-noun subject will not end in *-s,* but its verb will. A plural-noun subject will end in *-s,* but its verb will not. Between them, subject and verb use only one *-s* ending.

Singular	Plural
The boy plays.	The boys play.
The bird soars.	The birds soar.

The only exceptions to these rules involve the nouns that form irregular plurals, such as *child/children, woman/women.* The irregular plural still requires a plural verb: *The children play. The women read.*

Culture-language connection, a pointer for students using standard American English as a second language or a second dialect

CULTURE LANGUAGE If your first language is not standard American English, subject-verb agreement may be problematic, especially for

Key terms box, defining terms used on the page

┌─ Key terms ─────────────────────

	Number	
Person	**Singular**	**Plural**
First	I eat.	We eat.
Second	You eat.	You eat.
Third	He/she/it eats.	They eat.
	The bird eats.	Birds eat.

Web box linking to the handbook's companion Web site (see also opposite)

http://www.ablongman.com/littlebrown ▶

Visit the companion Web site for more help and an electronic exercise on subject-verb agreement.

EXERCISE 29.1 Revising: Subject-verb agreement

Revise the verbs in the following paragraphs as needed to make subjects and verbs agree in number. If a sentence is correct as given, mark the number preceding it. (You can do this exercise online at *ablongman.com/littlebrown.*)

1 Statistics from recent research suggests that humor in the workplace relieves job-related stress. 2 Reduced stress in the workplace in turn reduce illness and absenteeism. 3 It can also ease friction within an employee group, which then work together more productively.
4 Weinstein Associates is a consulting firm that hold workshops designed to make businesspeople laugh. 5 In sessions held by one consultant, each of the participants practice making others laugh. 6 "Isn't there enough laughs within you to spread the wealth?" the consultant asks the students. 7 She quotes Casey Stengel's rule that the best way to keep your management job is to separate the underlings who hate you from the ones who have not decided how they feel. 8 Such self-deprecating comments in public is uncommon among business managers, the consultant says. 9 Each of the managers in a typical firm takes the work much too seriously. 10 The humorous boss often feels like the only one of the managers who have other things in mind besides profits.

Exercise providing opportunity for practice

■ **Companion Web site**

The companion Web site offers many resources to help you use the book and improve your writing. You can use the site on your own (it is not password protected), or your instructor may direct you to portions of it as part of his or her course assignments.

Go to *ablongman.com/littlebrown,* and click on *The Little, Brown Compact Handbook with Exercises.* You'll see further directions to the following:

- Downloadable checklists and other material from the book.
- The book's exercises in electronic format.
- More than a thousand additional electronic exercises.
- Video tutorials that supplement the book's explanations.
- Hundreds of links to other Web sites providing help on the book's topics.
- Sample research papers from various academic disciplines.
- Usage flashcards allowing you to test yourself on tricky words and phrases.

Preface for Instructors

The Little, Brown Compact Handbook with Exercises provides writers with an accessible reference, one that helps them find what they need and then use what they find. Combining the authority of its parent, *The Little, Brown Handbook*, with a briefer and more convenient format, the *Compact Handbook* addresses writers of varying experience, in varying fields, answering common questions about the writing process, grammar and style, research writing, and more.

This new edition improves on the handbook's strengths as a clear, concise, and accessible reference, while keeping pace with rapid changes in writing and its teaching. In the context of the handbook's many reference functions, the following pages highlight as New the most significant additions and changes.

■ A reference with built-in exercises

New The sixth edition comes in two versions, one with and one without exercises. The two are identical except that the one you are holding includes more than 150 sets of exercises on usage, grammar, punctuation, and mechanics as well as rhetorical concerns such as thesis statements and paraphrasing. The exercises are in connected discourse, and their subjects come from across the academic curriculum.

■ A reference for writing in and out of college

New Two groups of chapters greatly expand the handbook's range. The first, Part 2, gives students the tools for analyzing and composing in many different writing situations:

- ■ New A chapter on academic writing introduces purpose, audience, language, and other elements.
- ■ New A chapter on study skills provides practical tips for managing time, reading for comprehension, and preparing for exams.
- ■ Two chapters detail techniques of critical reading and argument.
- ■ New Three chapters cover online writing (including e-mail and Web composition), oral presentations (including *PowerPoint*), and public writing (including writing for business and for community work).

Part 8 then offers a strong introduction to writing in the disciplines:

- New A chapter treats the goals and requirements common to writing in all academic disciplines.
- New Complementing the chapter on writing about literature, a chapter discusses the emphases and methods of writing in other humanities, the social sciences, and the natural and applied sciences.
- Extensive, specially tabbed sections cover documentation and format in MLA, APA, Chicago, and CSE styles.

A reference for research writing

The handbook always attends closely to research writing, keeping pace with changes in its methods and challenges.

- The discussion emphasizes using the library as Web gateway, managing information, evaluating and synthesizing sources, integrating source material, and avoiding plagiarism.
- New Guidelines and an example explain how to prepare an annotated bibliography.
- New Library subscription services receive even greater emphasis. In addition to a detailed, annotated sample search, the text now provides help with choosing databases.
- New Web logs are covered as possible sources requiring careful evaluation and documentation.
- New A section introduces images as research sources and provides URLs for image banks.
- New An expanded discussion of evaluating Web sites includes tips for distinguishing scholarly, personal, commercial, and other kinds of sites.
- New MLA documentation now includes annotated sample pages from key source types, showing students how to find the bibliographical information needed to cite each type.
- New The extensive coverage of documentation in four styles—MLA, APA, Chicago, and CSE—reflects each style's latest version and includes more electronic sources, such as Web logs and multimedia.

A guide to visual literacy

The handbook helps students process visual information and use it effectively in their writing.

- New An expanded section on using illustrations includes annotated examples.
- New An expanded discussion of viewing images critically uses diverse examples to demonstrate identifying and analyzing visual elements.

- New A section on reading and using visual arguments focuses on images' claims, evidence, assumptions, appeals, and fallacies.
- New Illustrations in most of the handbook's student papers show various ways in which visual information can support written ideas.

■ A reference on the writing process

The handbook takes a concise, practical approach to assessing the writing situation, generating ideas, writing the thesis statement, revising, and other elements of the writing process.

- Numerous examples, including a student work-in-progress on Internet communication, illustrate every stage.
- New Using spelling and grammar/style checkers is now integrated into the discussion of editing.

■ A reference for culturally and linguistically diverse writers

At notes and sections labeled ⟨ CULTURE LANGUAGE ⟩, the handbook provides extensive rhetorical and grammatical help for writers whose first language or dialect is not standard American English.

- Fully integrated coverage, instead of a separate section, means that students can find what they need without having to know which problems they do and don't share with native SAE speakers.
- New "⟨ CULTURE LANGUAGE ⟩ Guide," just before the back endpapers, orients students with advice on mastering SAE and pulls all the integrated coverage together in one place.

■ A reference on usage, grammar, and punctuation

The handbook's core reference material continues to be reliable and accessible.

- Concise text explains all basic concepts and common errors.
- Annotated examples from across the curriculum represent college writers and writing.

■ An accessible reference

The handbook is an open book for students, with many features to help them navigate and use its contents.

- A convenient lay-flat binding and tabbed dividers make the book easy to use.
- "Frequently Asked Questions" (front endpapers) invites students in through questions commonly asked about the book's topics.

- A unique approach to terminology facilitates reference and reading. Headings in the text and tables of contents avoid or explain terms. And "Key terms" boxes in the text provide essential definitions, dramatically reducing cross-references and page flipping.
- New When cross-references are needed, divider numbers in color now send students directly to the appropriate divider section—for instance, "See 3 pp. 130–32."
- New Dictionary-style headers in the index make it easy to find entries.
- An unusually accessible organization groups related problems.
- A preface just for students details the book's reference aids and explains its page layout.

■ An integrated text and Web site

At the start of every handbook chapter, a Web box links students to the book's companion Web site, a powerful online resource for students and teachers.

- New Most of the handbook's exercises can be downloaded and completed electronically or on paper. A cross-reference to the Web site appears in the instruction of each dual-format exercise.
- More than a thousand additional self-study questions, keyed to the handbook, provide immediate feedback for every answer.
- Many of the handbook's checklists are available for students to download and use in generating ideas and revising their work.
- More than thirty video tutorials provide explanations, examples, and tips to help students understand concepts and techniques.
- Hundreds of Web links direct students to helpful sites on the writing process, critical thinking, argument, grammar, research, writing in the disciplines, and more.
- Ten documented student research papers provide examples of writing across the curriculum.
- Usage flashcards allow students to test their knowledge and practice usage.
- The "Instructor's Resources" section provides answers to the handbook's exercises, lists and summaries from the book in transparency and *PowerPoint* format, and links to Web sites useful to writing teachers.

■ Supplements

In addition to the companion Web site, an extensive package of supplements accompanies *The Little, Brown Compact Handbook with Exercises* for both students and instructors.

For students

An asterisk precedes every supplement that is free to students when it is packaged with *The Little, Brown Compact Handbook with Exercises*.

- *MyCompLab* with the E-book of *The Little, Brown Compact Handbook with Exercises* offers comprehensive online resources in grammar, writing, and research in one dynamic, accessible place:

    Grammar resources include *ExerciseZone*, with more than three thousand self-grading practice questions on sentences and paragraphs; and *ESL ExerciseZone*, with more than seven hundred self-grading questions.

    Writing resources include a hundred writing activities involving videos, images, and Web sites; guided assistance through the writing process, with worksheets and exercises; and an extensive collection of sample papers from across the disciplines.

    Research resources include *ResearchNavigator*, which provides help with the research process, the *AutoCite* bibliography maker, and access to *ContentSelect* by EBSCOhost and the subject-search archive of the *New York Times*; and *Avoiding Plagiarism*, which offers tutorials in recognizing plagiarism, paraphrasing, documenting sources in MLA or APA style, and other topics.

    Other student features of *MyCompLab* include *Grade Tracker*, a system for tracking work on the site, and access to *Longman's English Tutor Center*, offering live help from qualified writing teachers.

- *Developmental Exercises to Accompany The Little, Brown Compact Handbook* provides practical activities in workbook format for developmental writers. An answer key is available.

- *ESL Worksheets*, by Jocelyn Steer and Dawn Schmid, provides nonnative speakers with extra practice in typical problem areas.

- *Longman Grammar and Documentation Study Card* is a laminated eight-page guide to key writing skills.

- Many supplements help students in and out of writing courses: *10 Practices of Highly Successful Students; *The Longman Writer's Portfolio and Student Planner; *The Longman Writer's Journal; *The Longman Researcher's Journal; *Peer-Evaluation Manual; *Analyzing Literature: A Guide for Students; *Visual Communication;* and the Literacy Library, consisting of *Academic Literacy, *Workplace Literacy,* and *Public Literacy.*

- Four references are available: *The New American Webster Handy College Dictionary; *The Oxford American Desk Diction-

ary and Thesaurus; *The Oxford Essential Thesaurus; and *The Oxford American College Dictionary.*

- Two programs provide resources at deep discounts: any Penguin title can be packaged with the handbook; and *Newsweek* magazine is available to students in twelve-week subscriptions.

For instructors

All of the following supplements are free to confirmed adopters of *The Little, Brown Compact Handbook with Exercises.*

- *MyCompLab* offers a wealth of teaching resources:

  MyCompLab Faculty Teaching Guide helps instructors make the most of this extensive resource.

  Online course-management versions of *MyCompLab* are available in *CourseCompass, Blackboard,* and *WebCT.*

  MyDropBox, a leading online plagiarism detection service, is available to instructors who adopt the handbook in a Value Pack.

- The answer key to *The Little, Brown Compact Handbook with Exercises* includes answers to all of the book's exercises.

- *Diagnostic and Editing Tests and Exercises* are cross-referenced to the handbook and are available on reproducible sheets or on CD.

- *Longman's Teaching Resource Library* includes works on both theory and practice.

Acknowledgments

The Little, Brown Compact Handbook stays fresh and useful because instructors talk with Longman's sales representatives and editors, answer questionnaires, write detailed reviews, and send me personal notes.

For the sixth edition, I am especially grateful to the many instructors who communicated with me directly or through reviews, drawing on their rich experience to offer insights into the handbook and suggestions for its improvement: Michael Burke, Southern Illinois University, Edwardsville; Daniel Compora, University of Toledo; Stephen Ferruci, Eastern Connecticut State University; Virginia K. Freed, Bay Path College; James Grabill, Clackamas Community College; Robert T. Koch, Jr., Gordon College; Karla Saari Kitalong, University of Central Florida; Patricia Kramer, Rock Valley College; Eleanor Latham, Central Oregon Community College; John P. LoVecchio, Elmira College; Sandra D. Lynn, New Mexico State University, Carlsbad; Amy Martin, Pace University; Rich Miller, Suffolk University; Jennifer P. Nesbitt, Pennsylvania State University, York; David Sharpe, Ohio University; James R. Sodon,

St. Louis Community College, Florissant Valley; David J. Sorrells, Lamar State College, Port Arthur; Katherine C. Wood, Texas A&M University; Janet Wright Starner, Wilkes University; Wayne Stein, University of Central Oklahoma; and John Ziebell, Community College of Southern Nevada.

In responding to the ideas of these thoughtful critics, I had the help of many creative people. Carol Hollar-Zwick, development editor and sine qua non, is every author's ideal for can-do attitude, smart thinking, and gentle encouragement. Brooke Hessler, Oklahoma City University, was an invaluable consultant on visual literacy and research writing. Caroline Crouse, University of Minnesota, served as a guide through the labyrinth of the contemporary library. Susan Smith Nash, Excelsior College, helped with disabilities issues and new technologies. And Sylvan Barnet, Tufts University, continued to lend his expertise in the chapter "Reading and Writing About Literature," which is adapted from his *Short Guide to Writing About Literature* and *Introduction to Literature* (with William Burto and William E. Cain).

A superb team helped me make this book. At Longman, Brandon Hight, the book's sponsor, offered perceptive insights into instructors' and students' needs. He and Rebecca Gilpin, editorial assistant, responded enthusiastically to my many needs. Megan Galvin-Fak, marketing manager, provided helpful ideas at key moments in development. Donna DeBenedictis applied a long view and a sharp eye to overseeing production. At Nesbitt Graphics, Jerilyn Bockorick created both the striking new design and the clear page layouts, and Susan McIntyre worked her now-customary miracles of scheduling and management to produce the book. I am grateful to all these collaborators.

PART 1

The Writing Process

PART **1**

The Writing Process

1 The Writing Situation

Like most writers (even very experienced ones), you may find writing sometimes easy but more often challenging, sometimes smooth but more often halting. Writing involves creation, and creation requires freedom, experimentation, and, yes, missteps. Instead of proceeding in a straight line over a clear path, you might start writing without knowing what you have to say, circle back to explore a new idea, or keep going even though you're sure you'll have to rewrite later.

As uncertain as the writing process may be, you can bring some control to it by assessing your writing situation, particularly your subject, audience, and purpose.

1a   Assessing the writing situation

Any writing you do for others occurs in a context that both limits and clarifies your choices. You are communicating something about a particular subject to a particular audience of readers for a specific reason. You may need to conduct research. You'll probably be up against a length requirement and a deadline. And you may be expected to present your work in a certain format.

These are the elements of the **writing situation,** and analyzing them at the very start of a project can tell you much about how to proceed.

Context

- **What is your writing for?** A course in school? Work? Something else? What do you know of the requirements for writing in this context?
- **Will you present your writing on paper, online, or orally?** What does the presentation method require in preparation time, special skills, and use of technology?
- **How much leeway do you have for this writing?** What does the stated or implied assignment tell you?

Subject (pp. 5–6)

- **What does your writing assignment require you to write about?** If you don't have a specific assignment, what subjects might be appropriate for this situation?

http://www.ablongman.com/littlebrown ▶

Visit the companion Web site for more help and electronic exercises on the writing situation.

- **What interests you about the subject?** What do you already know about it? What questions do you have about it?
- **What does the assignment require you to do with the subject?**

Audience (pp. 6–7)

- **Who will read your writing?**
- **What do your readers already know and think about your subject?** Do they have any characteristics—such as educational background, experience in your field, or political views—that could influence their reception of your writing?
- **What is your relationship to your readers?** How formal or informal should your writing be?
- **What do you want readers to do or think after they read your writing?**

Purpose (pp. 6–8)

- **What aim does your assignment specify?** For instance, does it ask you to explain something or argue a point?
- **Why are you writing?**
- **What do you want your work to accomplish?** What effect do you intend it to have on readers?
- **How can you best achieve your purpose?**

Research (7 pp. 369–429)

- **What kinds of evidence will best suit your subject, audience, and purpose?** What combination of facts, examples, and expert opinions will support your ideas?
- **Does your assignment require research?** Will you need to consult sources of information or conduct other research, such as interviews, surveys, or experiments?
- **Even if research is not required, what additional information do you need to develop your subject?** How will you obtain it?
- **What style should you use to cite your sources?** (See 7 pp. 425–26 on source documentation in the academic disciplines.)

Deadline and length

- **When is the assignment due?** How will you apportion the work you have to do in the available time?
- **How long should your writing be?** If no length is assigned, what seems appropriate for your topic, audience, and purpose?

Document design

- **What organization and format does the assignment require?** (See pp. 53–54 on format in the academic disciplines and 2 pp. 127–38 on format in public writing.)

- How might you use margins, headings, and other elements to achieve your purpose? (See pp. 55–61.)
- How might you use graphs, photographs, or other illustrations to support ideas and interest readers? (See pp. 61–65 and 2 pp. 104–10 on using illustrations in writing.)

1b   Finding your subject

A subject for writing has several basic requirements:

- **It should be suitable for the assignment.**
- **It should be neither too general nor too limited** for the length of paper and deadline assigned.
- **It should be something you care about.**

When you receive an assignment, study its wording and its implications about your writing situation to guide your choice of subject:

- **What's wanted from you?** Many writing assignments contain words such as *discuss, describe, analyze, report, interpret, explain, define, argue,* or *evaluate.* These words specify the way you are to approach your subject, what kind of thinking is expected of you, and what your general purpose is. (See p. 8.)
- **For whom are you writing?** Many assignments will specify or imply your readers, but sometimes you will have to figure out for yourself who your audience is and what it expects of you. (For more on analyzing your audience, see pp. 6–7.)
- **What kind of research is required?** Sometimes an assignment specifies the kinds of sources you are expected to consult, and you can use such information to choose your subject. (If you are unsure whether research is required, check with your instructor.)
- **Does the subject need to be narrowed?** To do the subject justice in the length and time required, you'll often need to limit it. (See below.)

Answering questions about your assignment will help set some boundaries for your choice of subject. Then you can explore your own interests and experiences to narrow the subject so that you can cover it adequately within the space and time assigned. Federal aid to college students could be the subject of a book; the kinds of aid available or why the government should increase aid would be a more appropriate subject for a four-page paper due in a week. Here are some guidelines for narrowing broad subjects:

- **Break your broad subject into as many specific subjects as you can think of.** Make a list.

- **For each specific subject that interests you and fits the assignment, roughly sketch out the main ideas.** Consider how many paragraphs or pages of specific facts, examples, and other details you would need to pin those ideas down. This thinking should give you at least a vague idea of how much work you'd have to do and how long the resulting paper might be.
- **Break a too-broad subject down further,** repeating the previous steps.

The Internet can also help you limit a general subject. On the Web, browse a directory such as *BUBL LINK* (*bubl.ac.uk/link*). As you pursue increasingly narrow categories, you may find a suitably limited topic.

1c Considering your audience

The readers likely to see your work—your **audience**—may influence your choice of subject and your definition of purpose. Your audience certainly will influence what you say about your subject and how you say it—for instance, how much background information you give and whether you adopt a serious or a friendly tone.

For much academic and public writing, readers have specific needs and expectations. You still must make many choices based on audience, but the options are somewhat defined. (See **2** pp. 69–74 and **8** pp. 433–56 on academic writing and **2** pp. 127–38 on public writing.) In other writing situations, the conventions of structure and presentation are vaguer and the choices are more open. The box on the facing page contains questions that can help you define and make these choices.

1d Defining your purpose

Your **purpose** in writing is your chief reason for communicating something about your subject to a particular audience of readers. It is your answer to a potential reader's question, "So what?"

Most writing you do will have one of four main purposes. Occasionally, you will *entertain* readers or *express yourself*—your feelings or ideas—to readers. More often you will *explain* something to readers or *persuade* readers to respect and accept, and sometimes even act on, your well-supported opinion. These purposes often overlap in a single essay, but usually one predominates. And the dominant purpose will influence your particular slant on your subject, the details you choose, and even the words you use.

Questions about audience

Identity and expectations

- Who *are* my readers?
- What are my readers' expectations for the kind of writing I'm doing? Do they expect features such as a particular organization and format, distinctive kinds of evidence, or a certain style of documenting sources?
- What do I want readers to know or do after reading my work? How should I make that clear to them?
- What is my relationship to my readers? How formal or informal will they expect me to be? What role and tone should I assume? What role do I want readers to play?

Characteristics, knowledge, and attitudes

- What characteristics of readers are relevant for my subject and purpose? For instance:

  Age and sex
  Occupation: students, professional colleagues, etc.
  Social or economic role: subject-matter experts, voters, car buyers, potential employers, etc.
  Economic or educational background
  Ethnic background
  Political, religious, or moral beliefs and values
  Hobbies or activities

- How will the characteristics of readers influence their attitudes toward my subject?
- What do readers already know and *not* know about my subject? How much do I have to tell them?
- How should I handle any specialized terms? Will readers know them? If not, should I define them?
- What ideas, arguments, or information might surprise, excite, or offend readers? How should I handle these points?
- What misconceptions might readers have of my subject and/or my approach to it? How can I dispel these misconceptions?

Uses and format

- What will readers do with my writing? Should I expect them to read every word from the top, to scan for information, or to look for conclusions? Can I help by providing a summary, headings, illustrations, or other aids? (See pp. 53–66 on document design.)

You can download these questions from *ablongman.com/littlebrown*. Duplicate the list for each writing project, write appropriate answers, and print a copy for reference as you compose.

Many writing assignments narrow the purpose by using a signal word, such as the following:

- **Report:** Survey, organize, and objectively present the available evidence on the subject.
- **Summarize:** Concisely state the main points in a text, argument, theory, or other work.
- **Discuss:** Examine the main points, competing views, or implications of the subject.
- **Compare and contrast:** Explain the similarities and differences between two subjects. (See also pp. 48–49.)
- **Define:** Specify the meaning of a term or a concept—distinctive characteristics, boundaries, and so on. (See also p. 47.)
- **Analyze:** Identify the elements of the subject, and discuss how they work together. (See also pp. 47 and **2** pp. 87–88.)
- **Interpret:** Infer the subject's meaning or implications.
- **Evaluate:** Judge the quality or significance of the subject, considering pros and cons. (See also **2** pp. 88–89.)
- **Argue:** Take a position on the subject, and support your position with evidence. (See also **2** pp. 95–104.)

You can conceive of your purpose more specifically, too, in a way that incorporates your particular topic and the outcome you intend:

To explain how Annie Dillard's "Total Eclipse" builds to its climax so that readers appreciate the author's skill

To explain the methods of an engineering study so that readers understand and accept your conclusions

To explain the steps in a new office procedure so that staffers will be able to follow it without difficulty

To argue against additional regulation of health-maintenance organizations so that readers will perceive the disadvantages for themselves

2 Invention

Writers use a host of techniques to help invent or discover ideas and information about their subjects. **Whichever of the following techniques you use, do your work in writing, not just in your head.** Your ideas will be retrievable, and the very act of writing will lead you to fresh insights.

http://www.ablongman.com/littlebrown ▶

Visit the companion Web site for more help with invention.

CULTURE LANGUAGE The discovery process encouraged here rewards rapid writing without a lot of thinking beforehand about what you will write or how. If your first language is not standard American English, you may find it helpful initially to do this exploratory writing in your native language or dialect and then to translate the worthwhile material for use in your drafts. This process can be productive, but it is extra work. You may want to try it at first and gradually move to composing in standard American English.

2a Keeping a journal

A **journal** is a diary of ideas kept on paper or on a computer. It gives you a place to record your thoughts and can provide ideas for writing. Because you write for yourself, you can work out your ideas without the pressure of an audience "out there" who will evaluate logic or organization or correctness. If you write every day, even just for a few minutes, the routine will loosen your writing muscles and improve your confidence.

You can use a journal for varied purposes: perhaps to confide your feelings, explore your responses to movies and other media, practice certain kinds of writing (such as poems or news stories), think critically about what you read, or pursue ideas from your courses. In the example following, Sara Ling responded to an experience:

> Had an exchange today on the snowboarding forum with a woman who joined the forum a while ago. She says she signed on at first with a screen name that didn't give away her gender, and she didn't tell anyone she was a woman. She was afraid the guys on the forum might shout her down. She waited until she'd established herself as an experienced snowboarder. Then she revealed her gender, and no one reacted badly. She asked me about my experiences, since my screen name says Sara. Had to admit I'd had problems of the what-does-a-girl-know sort. Wish I'd taken her approach.

(Further examples of Ling's writing appear on p. 11 and in the next three chapters.)

CULTURE LANGUAGE A journal can be especially helpful if your first language is not standard American English. You can practice writing to improve your fluency, try out sentence patterns, and experiment with vocabulary words. Equally important, you can experiment with applying what you know from experience to what you read and observe.

2b Observing your surroundings

Sometimes you can find a good subject or good ideas by looking around you, not in the half-conscious way most of us move from place to place in our daily lives but deliberately, all senses alert. On a bus, for instance, are there certain types of passengers? What seems to be on the driver's mind? To get the most from observation, you should have a notepad and pen or a handheld computer handy for taking notes and making sketches. Back at your desk, study your notes and sketches for oddities or patterns that you'd like to explore further.

2c   Freewriting

■ Writing into a subject

Many writers find subjects or discover ideas by **freewriting:** writing without stopping for a certain amount of time (say, ten minutes) or to a certain length (say, one page). The goal of freewriting is to generate ideas and information from *within* yourself by going around the part of your mind that doesn't want to write or can't think of anything to write. You let words themselves suggest other words. *What* you write is not important; that you *keep* writing is. Don't stop, even if that means repeating the same words until new words come. Don't go back to reread, don't censor ideas that seem dumb or repetitious, and above all don't stop to edit: grammar, punctuation, spelling, and the like are irrelevant at this stage.

If you write on a computer, try this technique for moving forward while freewriting: turn off your computer's monitor, or turn its brightness control all the way down so that the screen is dark. The computer will record what you type but keep it from you and thus prevent you from tinkering with your prose. This **invisible writing** may feel uncomfortable at first, but it can free the mind for very creative results.

CULTURE LANGUAGE Invisible writing can be especially helpful if you are uneasy writing in standard American English and you tend to worry about errors while writing. The blank computer screen leaves you no choice but to explore ideas without regard for their expression. If you choose to write with the monitor on, concentrate on *what* you want to say, not *how* you're saying it.

■ Focused freewriting

Focused freewriting is more concentrated: you start with your subject and write about it without stopping for, say, fifteen minutes or one full page. As in all freewriting, you push to bypass mental blocks and self-consciousness, not debating what to say or editing what you've written. With focused freewriting, though, you let the physical act of writing take you into and around your subject.

An example of focused freewriting can be found in the work of Sara Ling, whose journal entry appears on p. 9. In a composition course Ling's instructor had distributed "Welcome to Cyberbia," an essay by M. Kadi about communication on the Internet. The instructor then gave the following assignment:

> M. Kadi's "Welcome to Cyberbia" holds that the Internet will do little to bridge differences among people because its users gravitate toward other users who are like themselves in most respects. More than a decade later, do Kadi's concerns seem valid? Can the Internet serve as a medium for positive change in the way people of diverse backgrounds relate to each other? If so, how? If not, why not? In an essay of 500–700 words, respond to Kadi's essay with a limited and well-supported opinion of your own. The first draft is due Monday, October 31, for class discussion.

On first reading Kadi's essay, Ling had been impressed with its tight logic but had found unconvincing its pessimistic view of the Internet's potential. She reread the essay and realized that some of Kadi's assertions did not correspond to her own experiences on the Internet. This discovery prompted the following focused freewriting:

> Kadi says we only meet people like ourselves on the Internet, but I've met lots who have very different backgrounds and interests—or "turned out to have" is more like it, since I didn't know anything about them at first. There's the anonymity thing, but Kadi ignores it. You can be anyone or no one. I can pose as a man if I want (probably should have, to avoid rejection on the snowboarding forum). No one has to know I'm female or Asian American or a student. We're not stuck in our identities. Not hampered by them in expressing our views and getting those views accepted. Communication without set identity, especially physical appearance. This could make for more tolerance of others, of difference.

(We will continue to follow Ling's work in this and the next three chapters.)

2d Brainstorming

A method similar to freewriting is **brainstorming**—focusing intently on a subject for a fixed period (say, fifteen minutes), pushing yourself to list every idea and detail that comes to mind. Like freewriting, brainstorming requires turning off your internal editor so that you keep moving ahead. (The technique of invisible writing on a computer, described opposite, can help you move forward.)

Here is an example of brainstorming by a student, Johanna Abrams, on what a summer job can teach:

```
summer work teaches—
        how to look busy while doing nothing
        how to avoid the sun in summer
        seriously: discipline, budgeting money, value of money
    which job? Burger King cashier? baby sitter? mail-room clerk?
    mail room: how to sort mail into boxes: this is learning??
```

how to survive getting fired—humiliation, outrage
Mrs. King! the mail-room queen as learning experience
the shock of getting fired: what to tell parents, friends?
Mrs. K was so rigid—dumb procedures
initials instead of names on the mail boxes—confusion!
Mrs. K's anger, resentment: the disadvantages of being smarter than your boss
The odd thing about working in an office: a world with its own rules for how to act
what Mr. D said about the pecking order—big chick (Mrs. K) pecks on little chick (me)
a job can beat you down—make you be mean to other people

2e   Clustering

Like freewriting and brainstorming, **clustering** also draws on free association and rapid, unedited work. But it emphasizes the relations between ideas by combining writing and nonlinear drawing. When clustering, you radiate outward from a center point—your topic. When an idea occurs, you pursue related ideas in a branching structure until they seem exhausted. Then you do the same with other ideas, continuously branching out or drawing arrows.

The example below shows how a student used clustering for ten minutes to expand on a topic he arrived at through freewriting: writing as a means of disguise.

Clustering

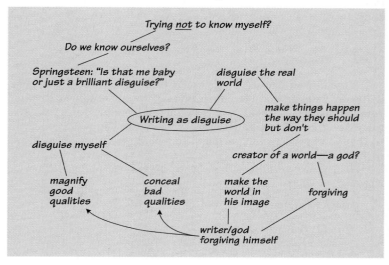

2f Asking questions

Asking yourself a set of questions about your subject—and writing out the answers—can help you look at the topic objectively and see fresh possibilities in it.

1 Journalist's questions

A journalist with a story to report poses a set of questions:

- Who was involved?
- What happened, and what were the results?
- When did it happen?
- Where did it happen?
- Why did it happen?
- How did it happen?

These questions can also be useful in probing an essay subject, especially when you are telling a story or examining causes and effects.

2 Questions about patterns

We think about and understand a vast range of subjects through patterns such as narration, classification, and comparison and contrast. Asking questions based on the patterns can help you view your topic from many angles. Sometimes you may want to develop an entire essay using just one pattern.

- How did it happen? (Narration)
- How does it look, sound, feel, smell, taste? (Description)
- What are examples of it or reasons for it? (Illustration or support)
- What is it? What does it encompass, and what does it exclude? (Definition)
- What are its parts or characteristics? (Division or analysis)
- What groups or categories can it be sorted into? (Classification)
- How is it like, or different from, other things? (Comparison and contrast)
- Why did it happen? What results did or could it have? (Cause-and-effect analysis)
- How do you do it, or how does it work? (Process analysis)

For more on these patterns, including paragraph-length examples, see pp. 45–49.

3 Thesis and Organization

Shaping your raw material helps you clear away unneeded ideas, spot possible gaps, and energize your subject. The two main operations in shaping material are focusing on a thesis (below) and organizing ideas (p. 17).

3a   Conceiving a thesis statement

Your readers will expect your essay to be focused on and controlled by a main idea, or **thesis.** In your final draft you may express this idea in a **thesis statement,** often at the end of your introduction.

1   Functions of the thesis statement

As an expression of the thesis, the thesis statement serves three crucial functions and one optional one:

The thesis statement

- The thesis statement **narrows your subject** to a single, central idea that you want readers to gain from your essay.
- It **claims something specific and significant** about your subject, a claim that requires support.
- It **conveys your purpose,** your reason for writing.
- It often concisely **previews the arrangement of ideas.**

All of the following thesis statements fulfill the first three functions listed in the box (the nature of the claim is highlighted in brackets). Examples 4 and 5 also fulfill the fourth function, previewing organization.

Subject	Thesis statement
1. Direct distribution of music to consumers via the Web	Because artists can now publish their music directly via the Web, consumers have many more choices than traditional distribution allows. [**Topic:** consumers. **Claim:** have many more choices.]

http://www.ablongman.com/littlebrown ▶

Visit the companion Web site for more help and an electronic exercise on thesis and organization.

Subject	Thesis statement
2. Federal aid to college students	As an investment in its own economy, the United States should provide a tuition grant to any college student who qualifies academically. [**Topic:** United States. **Claim:** should provide a tuition grant to any college student who qualifies academically.]
3. Abraham Lincoln's delay in emancipating the slaves	Lincoln delayed emancipating any slaves until 1863 because his primary goal was to restore and preserve the Union, with or without slavery. [**Topic:** Lincoln's delay. **Claim:** was caused by his goal of preserving the Union.
4. Preventing juvenile crime	Juveniles can be diverted from crime by active learning programs, full-time sports, and intervention by mentors and role models. [**Topic:** juveniles. **Claim:** can be diverted from crime in three ways.]
5. The effects of strip-mining	Strip-mining should be tightly controlled in this region to reduce its pollution of water resources, its destruction of the land, and its devastating effects on people's lives. [**Topic:** strip-mining. **Claim:** should be tightly controlled for three reasons.]

CULTURE LANGUAGE In some cultures it is considered rude or unnecessary for a writer to state his or her main idea outright. When writing in standard American English for school or work, you can assume that readers expect a clear and early idea of what you think.

2 Development of the thesis statement

A thesis will not usually leap fully formed into your head: you will have to develop and shape the idea as you develop and shape your essay. Still, trying to draft a thesis statement early can give you a point of reference when changes inevitably occur.

While you are developing your thesis statement, ask questions about each attempt:

Checklist for revising the thesis statement

- How well does the **subject** of your statement capture the subject of your paper?
- What **claim** does your statement make about your subject?
- What is the **significance** of the claim? How does it answer "So what?" and convey your purpose?
- How can the claim be **limited** or made more **specific**? Does it state a single idea and clarify the boundaries of the idea?
- How **unified** is the statement? How does each word and phrase contribute to a single idea?

Here are examples of thesis statements revised to meet these requirements:

Original	Revised
This new product brought in over $300,000 last year. [A statement of fact, not a claim about the product: what is significant about the product's success?]	This new product succeeded because of its innovative marketing campaign, including widespread press coverage, in-store entertainment, and a consumer newsletter.
People should not go on fad diets. [A vague statement that needs limiting with one or more reasons: what's wrong with fad diets?]	Fad diets can be dangerous when they deprive the body of essential nutrients or rely excessively on potentially harmful foods.
Televised sports are different from live sports. [A general statement that needs to be made more specific: how are they different, and why is the difference significant?]	Although television cannot transmit all the excitement of a live game, its close-ups and slow-motion replays reveal much about the players and the strategy of the game.
Seat belts can save lives, but now carmakers are installing air bags. [Not unified: how do the two parts of the sentence relate to each other?]	If drivers had used lifesaving seat belts more often, carmakers might not have needed to install air bags.

EXERCISE 3.1   Evaluating thesis statements

Evaluate the following thesis statements, considering whether each one is sufficiently limited, specific, and unified. Rewrite the statements as necessary to meet these goals. (You can do this exercise online at *ablongman.com/littlebrown*.)

1 Aggression usually leads to violence, injury, and even death, and we should use it constructively.
2 The religion of Islam is widely misunderstood in the United States.
3 One evening of a radio talk show amply illustrates both the appeal of such shows and their silliness.
4 Good manners make our society work.
5 The poem is about motherhood.
6 Television is useful for children and a mindless escape for adults who do not want to think about their problems.
7 I disliked American history in high school, but I like it in college.
8 Drunken drivers, whose perception and coordination are impaired, should receive mandatory suspensions of their licenses.
9 Business is a good major for many students.
10 The state's lenient divorce laws undermine the institution of marriage, which is fundamental to our culture, and they should certainly be made stricter for couples who have children.

3b Organizing your ideas

Most essays share a basic pattern of introduction (states the subject), body (develops the subject), and conclusion (pulls the essay's ideas together). Introductions and conclusions are discussed on pp. 50–53. Within the body, every paragraph develops some aspect of the essay's main idea, or thesis. See pp. 34–36 for Sara Ling's essay, with annotations highlighting the body's pattern of support for the thesis statement.

CULTURE LANGUAGE If you are not used to reading and writing American academic prose, its pattern of introduction-body-conclusion and the particular schemes discussed on the next page may seem unfamiliar. For instance, instead of introductions that focus quickly on the topic and thesis, you may be used to openings that establish personal connections with readers or that approach the thesis indirectly. And instead of body paragraphs that first emphasize general points and then support those points with specific evidence, you may be used to general statements without support (because writers can assume that readers will supply the evidence themselves) or to evidence without explanation (because writers can assume that readers will infer the general points). When writing American academic prose, you need to take into account readers' expectations for directness and for the statement and support of general points.

1 The general and the specific

To organize material for an essay, you need to distinguish general and specific ideas and see the relations between ideas. **General** and **specific** refer to the number of instances or objects included in a group signified by a word. The following "ladder" illustrates a general-to-specific hierarchy:

Most general
 ↑ life form
 plant
 rose
 ↓ Uncle Dan's prize-winning American Beauty rose
Most specific

As you arrange your material, pick out the general ideas and then the specific points that support them. Set aside points that seem irrelevant to your key ideas. On a computer you can easily experiment with various arrangements of general ideas and supporting information: save your master list of ideas, duplicate it, and then use the Cut and Paste functions to move material around or (a little quicker) drag selected text to where you want it.

2 Schemes for organizing essays

An essay's body paragraphs may be arranged in many ways that are familiar to readers. The choice depends on your subject, purpose, and audience.

- **Spatial:** In describing a person, place, or thing, move through space systematically from a starting point to other features—for instance, top to bottom, near to far, left to right.
- **Chronological:** In recounting a sequence of events, arrange the events as they actually occurred in time, first to last.
- **General to specific:** Begin with an overall discussion of the subject; then fill in details, facts, examples, and other support.
- **Specific to general:** First provide the support; then draw a conclusion from it.
- **Climactic:** Arrange ideas in order of increasing importance to your thesis or increasing interest to the reader.
- **Problem-solution:** First outline a problem that needs solving; then propose a solution.

3 Outlines

It's not essential to craft a detailed outline before you begin drafting an essay; in fact, too detailed a plan could prevent you from discovering ideas while you draft. Still, even a rough scheme can show you patterns of general and specific, suggest proportions, and highlight gaps or overlaps in coverage.

There are several different kinds of outlines, some more flexible than others.

■ Scratch or informal outline

A scratch or informal outline includes key general points in the order they will be covered. It may also suggest the specific evidence for them.

Here is Sara Ling's scratch outline for her essay on Internet communication:

Thesis statement
By lowering the barriers of physical appearance, the unique anonymity of Internet communication could build diversity into community.

Scratch outline
No fear of prejudgment
    Physical attributes unknown—age, race, gender, etc.
    We won't be shut out because of appearance
Inability to prejudge others
    Assumptions based on appearance
    Meeting of minds only
    Finding shared interests and concerns

■ Tree diagram

In a tree diagram, ideas and details branch out in increasing specificity. Unlike more linear outlines, this diagram can be supplemented and extended indefinitely, so it is easy to alter. Johanna Abrams developed the following example from her brainstorming about a summer job (pp. 11–12):

Thesis statement
Two months working in a large agency taught me that an office's pecking order should be respected.

Tree diagram

Mail-room work		Mrs. King's behavior	

Confusion | Inefficient, arbitrary procedures | Anger and resentment | Self-protection

Initials on mail | Coffee breaks | Delivery times | Cold-ness | Mean-ness | Rigidity | Desperation

My behavior — Busybody, Arrogant (Critical, Questioning, Rude, No sympathy)

Office/barnyard pecking order — Sequence of pecking, Effects on lowest chicken (Low self-esteem, Self-protection, Need for power)

A tree diagram or other visual map can be especially useful for planning a project for the Web. The diagram can help you lay out the organization of your project and its links and then later can serve as a site map for your readers. (For more on writing for the Web, see **2** pp. 118–23.)

■ Formal outline

A formal outline not only lays out main ideas and their support but also shows the relative importance of all the essay's elements. On the basis of her scratch outline (facing page), Sara Ling prepared the following formal outline for her essay on the Internet.

Thesis statement
By lowering the barriers of physical appearance, the unique anonymity of Internet communication could build diversity into community.

Formal outline

I. No fear of being prejudged
  A. Unknown physical attributes
    1. Gender
    2. Age
    3. Race
    4. Style
  B. Freer communication
  C. No automatic rejection
II. Inability to prejudge others
  A. No assumptions based on appearance
    1. Body type
    2. Physical disability
    3. Race
  B. Discovery of shared interests and concerns
    1. Sports and other activities
    2. Family values
    3. Political views
  C. Reduction of physical bias

This example illustrates several principles of outlining that can ensure completeness, balance, and clear relationships:

- **All parts are systematically indented and labeled:** Roman numerals (I, II) for primary divisions; indented capital letters (A, B) for secondary divisions; further indented Arabic numerals (1, 2) for supporting examples. (The next level down would be indented further still and labeled with small letters: a, b.)
- **The outline divides the material into several groups.** A long list of points at the same level should be broken up into groups.
- **Topics of equal generality appear in parallel headings,** with the same indention and numbering or lettering.
- **All subdivided headings break into at least two parts.** A topic cannot logically be divided into only one part.
- **All headings are expressed in parallel grammatical form**—in the example, as phrases using a noun plus modifiers. This is a topic outline; in a sentence outline all headings are expressed as full sentences (see **8** p. 499).

Note Because of its structure, a formal outline can be an excellent tool for analyzing a draft before revising it. See p. 25.

4   Unity and coherence

Two qualities of effective writing relate to organization: unity and coherence. When you perceive that someone's writing "flows well," you are probably appreciating these qualities.

To check an outline or draft for **unity,** ask these questions:

- Is each section relevant to the main idea (thesis) of the essay?
- Within main sections, does each example or detail support the principal idea of that section?

To check your outline or draft for **coherence**, ask the following questions:

- Do the ideas follow a clear sequence?
- Are the parts of the essay logically connected?
- Are the connections clear and smooth?

See also pp. 39–45 on unity and coherence in paragraphs.

EXERCISE 3.2 Organizing ideas

The following list of ideas was extracted by a student from freewriting he did for a brief paper on soccer in the United States. Using his thesis statement as a guide, pick out the general ideas and arrange the relevant specific points under them. In some cases you may have to infer general ideas to cover specific points in the list. (You can do this exercise online at *ablongman.com/littlebrown*.)

Thesis statement

Soccer will probably never be the sport in the United States that it is elsewhere because both the potential fans and the potential backers resist it.

List of ideas

Sports seasons are already too crowded for fans.
Soccer rules are confusing to Americans.
A lot of kids play soccer in school, but the game is still "foreign."
Sports money goes where the money is.
Backers are wary of losing money on new ventures.
Fans have limited time to watch.
Fans have limited money to pay for sports.
Backers are concerned with TV contracts.
Previous attempts to start a pro soccer league failed.
TV contracts almost matter more than live audiences.
Failure of the US Football League was costly.
Baseball, football, hockey, and basketball seasons overlap.
Soccer fans couldn't fill huge stadiums.
American soccer fans are too few for TV interest.

4 Drafting

Drafting is an occasion for exploration. Don't expect to transcribe solid thoughts into polished prose: solidity and polish will come with revision and editing. Instead, while drafting let the very act of writing help you find and form your meaning.

4a   Starting to draft

Beginning a draft sometimes takes courage, even for seasoned professionals. Procrastination may actually help if you let ideas for writing simmer at the same time. At some point, though, you'll have to face the blank paper or computer screen. The following techniques can help you begin:

- **Read over what you've already written**—notes, outlines, and so on—and immediately start your draft with whatever comes to mind.
- **Freewrite** (see p. 10).
- **Skip the opening and start in the middle.** Or write the conclusion.
- **Write a paragraph.** Explain what you think your essay will be about when you finish it.
- **Start writing the part that you understand best.** Using your outline, divide your essay into chunks—say, one for the introduction, another for the first point, and so on. One of these chunks may call out to be written.

4b   Maintaining momentum

Drafting requires momentum: the forward movement opens you to fresh ideas and connections. To keep moving while drafting, try one or more of these techniques:

- **Set aside enough time for yourself.** For a brief essay, a first draft is likely to take at least an hour or two.
- **Work in a quiet place.**
- **If you must stop working, write down what you expect to do next.** Then you can pick up where you stopped with minimal disruption.

http://www.ablongman.com/littlebrown ▶

Visit the companion Web site for more help with drafting.

- **Be as fluid as possible.** Spontaneity will allow your attitudes toward your subject to surface naturally in your sentences.
- **Keep going.** Skip over sticky spots; leave a blank if you can't find the right word; put alternative ideas or phrasings in brackets so that you can consider them later without bogging down. If an idea pops out of nowhere but doesn't seem to fit in, quickly jot it down on a separate sheet, or write it into the draft and bracket or boldface it for later attention.
- **Resist self-criticism.** Don't worry about your style, grammar, spelling, punctuation, and the like. Don't worry about what your readers will think. These are very important matters, but save them for revision.
- **Use your thesis statement and outline.** They can remind you of your planned purpose, organization, and content. However, if your writing leads you in a more interesting direction, follow.

If you write on a computer, frequently save the text you're drafting—at least every five or ten minutes and every time you leave the computer.

4c Examining a sample first draft

Sara Ling's first draft on Internet communication appears below. As you read the draft, mark the thesis statement and each key idea developing the thesis. Note places where you think the ideas could be clearer or better supported.

Title?

In "Welcome to Cyberbia," written in 1995, M. Kadi predicts that the Internet will lead to more fragmentation in society because people just seek out others like themselves. But Kadi fails to foresee how the unique anonymity of Internet communication could actually build diversity into community by lowering the barriers of physical appearance.

Anonymity on the Internet. It's one of the best things about technology. Most people who communicate online use an invented screen name to avoid revealing personal details such as age, gender, and ethnic background. No one knows whether you're fat or thin or neat or sloppy. What kind of clothes you wear. (Maybe you're not wearing clothes at all). People who know you personally don't even know who you are with an invented screen name.

We can make ourselves known without first being prejudged because of our physical attributes. For example, I participate in a snowboarding forum that has mostly men. I didn't realize what I was getting into when I used my full name as my screen name. Before long, I had received unfriendly responses such as "What does a girl know?" and "Why don't you go back to knitting?" I guess I had run into a male prejudice against female snowboarders. However, another woman on the forum had no such problems. At first she signed on with a screen name that did not reveal her gender, and no one responded negatively to her messages. When she had contributed for a while, she earned respect from the other snowboarders. When she revealed that she was a woman at that point, no one responded negatively in the way I had experienced. She posed at first as someone different from who she really was and could make herself heard.

We also cannot prejudge others because of their appearance. Often in face-to-face interaction we assume we know things about people just because of the way they look. Assumptions prevent people from discovering their shared interests and concerns, and this is particularly true where race is concerned. The anonymity of the Internet makes physical barriers irrelevant, and only people's minds meet. Because of this, the Internet could create a world free of physical bias.

Logged on to the Internet we can become more tolerant of others. We can become a community.

5 Revising and Editing

During revision—literally "re-seeing"—you shift your focus outward from yourself and your subject toward your readers, concentrating on what will help them respond as you want. It's wise to revise in at least two stages, one devoted to fundamental meaning and structure (here called **revising**) and one devoted to word choice, grammar, punctuation, and other features of the surface (here called **editing**). Knowing that you will edit later gives you the freedom at first to look beyond the confines of the page or screen to the whole paper.

5a Revising the whole essay

To revise your writing, you have to read it critically, and that means you have to create some distance between your draft and yourself. One of the following techniques may help you see your work objectively.

http://www.ablongman.com/littlebrown ▶

Visit the companion Web site for more help with revising and editing.

- **Take a break after finishing the draft.** A few hours may be enough; a whole night or day is preferable.
- **Ask someone to read and react to your draft.** If your instructor encourages collaboration among students, by all means take advantage of the opportunity to hear the responses of others. (See pp. 36–37 for more on collaboration.)
- **Type a handwritten draft.** The act of transcription can reveal gaps in content or problems in structure.
- **Outline your draft.** Highlight the main points supporting the thesis, and convert these sentences to outline form. Then examine the outline you've made for logical order, gaps, and digressions. A formal outline can be especially illuminating because of its careful structure (see pp. 19–20).
- **Listen to your draft.** Read the draft out loud to yourself or a friend or classmate, record and listen to it, or have someone read the draft to you.
- **Ease the pressure.** Don't try to re-see everything in your draft at once. Use the checklist below, making a separate pass through the draft for each item.

Checklist for revision

Purpose

What is the essay's purpose? Does it conform to the assignment? Is it consistent throughout the paper? (See pp. 6–8.)

Thesis

What is the thesis of the essay? Where does it become clear? How well do thesis and paper match: Does the paper stray from the thesis? Does it fulfill the commitment of the thesis? (See pp. 14–16.)

Structure

What are the main points of the paper? (List them.) How well does each support the thesis? How effective is their arrangement for the paper's purpose? (See pp. 17–21.)

Development

How well do details, examples, and other evidence support each main point? Where, if at all, might readers find support skimpy or have trouble understanding the content? (See pp. 6–7, 45–49.)

Tone

What is the tone of the paper? How do particular words and sentence structures create the tone? How appropriate is it for the purpose, topic, and intended readers? Where is it most and least successful?

(continued)

Checklist for revision
(continued)

Unity
What does each sentence and paragraph contribute to the thesis? Where, if at all, do digressions occur? Should these be cut, or can they be rewritten to support the thesis? (See pp. 20–21, 39–40.)

Coherence
How clearly and smoothly does the paper flow? Where does it seem rough or awkward? Can any transitions be improved? (See pp. 20–21, 40–44.)

Title, introduction, conclusion
How accurately and interestingly does the title reflect the essay's content? (See below.) How well does the introduction engage and focus readers' attention? (See pp. 50–51.) How effective is the conclusion in providing a sense of completion? (See pp. 51–53.)

You can download this checklist from *ablongman.com/littlebrown*. Make a copy for each writing project, and insert answers to each question with your ideas for changes.

1 Revising on a word processor

When you revise on a computer, take a few precautions to avoid losing your work and to keep track of your drafts:

- **Save your work every five to ten minutes.**
- **After doing any major work on a project, create a backup version of the file.**
- **Work on a duplicate of your latest draft.** Then the original will remain intact until you're truly finished with it. On the duplicate you can use your word processor's Track Changes function, which shows changes alongside the original text and allows you to accept or reject alterations later.
- **Save each draft under its own file name.** You may need to consult it for ideas or phrasings.

2 Titling your essay

The revision stage is a good time to consider a title because attempting to sum up your essay in a phrase can focus your attention sharply on your topic, purpose, and audience. The title should tell the reader what your paper is about, but it should not restate the assignment or the thesis statement. Most titles fall in one of these categories:

- **A *descriptive title* announces the subject clearly and accurately.** Such a title is almost always appropriate and is usually expected for academic writing. Sara Ling's final title—"The Internet: Fragmentation or Community?"—is an example.

- A *suggestive title* **hints at the subject to arouse curiosity.** It is common in popular magazines and may be appropriate for writing that is somewhat informal. Ling might have chosen a suggestive title such as "What We Don't Know Can Help Us" or "Secrets of the Internet."

For more information on essay titles, see **MLA** p. 497 (MLA format), **APA** p. 523 (APA format), and **6** p. 358 (capitalizing words in a title).

5b   Examining a sample revision

In revising her first draft, Sara Ling had the help of her instructor and several of her classmates, to whom she showed the draft as part of her assignment. Based on the revision checklist, she thought that she wanted to stick with her initial purpose and thesis statement and that they had held up well in the draft. But she also knew without being told that her introduction and conclusion were too hurried, that the movement between paragraphs was too abrupt, that the example of the snowboarding forum went on too long, and that the fourth paragraph was thin: she hadn't supplied enough details to support her ideas and convince her readers.

Ling's readers confirmed her self-evaluation. Several, however, raised points that she had not considered, reflected in these comments by classmates:

Comment 1

Why do you say (par. 2) that most people use invented screen names? I don't, and I know other people who don't either. Do you have evidence of how many people use invented names or why they do?

Comment 2

I would have an easier time agreeing with you about the Internet if you weren't quite so gung-ho. For instance, what about the dangers of the Internet, as when adults prey on children or men prey on women? In par. 3, you don't acknowledge that such things can and do happen. Also, is a bias-free world (par. 4) really such a sure thing? People will still meet in person, after all.

At first Ling was tempted to resist these comments because the writers seemed to object to her ideas. But eventually she understood that the comments showed ways she could make the ideas convincing to more readers. The changes took some time, partly because Ling decided to conduct a survey of students in order to test her assumption about people's use of invented screen names.

The first half of Ling's draft appears on the following pages, showing the survey results and other changes explained in annotations.

Ling used the Track Changes function on her word processor, so that deletions are crossed out and additions are in blue.

The Internet: Fragmentation or Community?

~~Title?~~

We hear all sorts of predictions about how the Internet will enrich our lives and promote equality, tolerance, and thus community in our society. But are these promises realistic? In her 1995 essay "Welcome to Cyberbia," M. Kadi argues that they are not. Instead, she~~In "Welcome to Cyberbia," written in 1995, M. Kadi~~ predicts that the Internet will lead to more fragmentation, not community, ~~in society~~ because users merely ~~people just~~ seek out others ~~like themselves~~ with the same biases, needs, and concerns as their own. The point is an interesting one, ~~B~~but Kadi fails to foresee ~~that~~ how the unique anonymity of Internet communication could actually build diversity into community by lowering the barriers of physical appearance.

Internet communication can be anonymous on at least two levels. ~~Anonymity on the Internet. It's one of the best things about technology. Most people who communicate online use an invented screen name to avoid revealing personal details such as age, gender, and ethnic background. No one knows~~ The people who communicate with you do not know your age. ~~w~~Whether you're fat or thin or neat or sloppy. What kind of clothes you wear. (Maybe you're not wearing clothes at all). Or anything else about physical appearance. ~~People who know you personally don't even know who you are with an invented screen name.~~ If you use an invented screen name instead of your real name, readers don't even know whatever your name says about you, such as gender or ethnic background.

Internet anonymity seems a popular option, judging by the numbers of invented user names seen in online forums. But I thought it would be a good idea to determine the extent of invented user names as well as the reasons for them, so I surveyed seventy-eight students with two questions: (1) Do you ever write with an invented user name when contributing to chat rooms, newsgroups, blogs, and so on? (2) If yes, why do you use an invented name: to protect your privacy, to avoid revealing personal information, or for some other reason? Fig. 1 shows that most of the students do use invented names online. And most do so to protect their privacy or to avoid revealing personal details.

Margin annotations:

Descriptive title names topic and forecasts approach.

Expanded introduction draws readers into Ling's question and summarizes Kadi's essay.

New transition relates paragraph to thesis statement and smoothes flow.

Blanket assertion is deleted in favor of survey results added later.

Addition clarifies use of invented screen names.

Largest revision presents results of survey conducted to support use of invented screen names.

New pie graph presents survey results in an easy-to-read format.

Fig. 1. Use of invented screen names among seventy-eight Internet users.

5c Editing the revised draft

After you've revised your essay so that all the content is in place, then turn to the important work of removing any surface problems that could interfere with a reader's understanding or enjoyment of your ideas.

1 Strategies for editing

Try these approaches to discover what needs editing:

- **Take a break.** Even fifteen minutes can clear your head.
- **Read the draft slowly, and read what you actually see.** Otherwise, you're likely to read what you intended to write but didn't.
- **Read as if you are encountering the draft for the first time.** Put yourself in the reader's place.
- **Have a classmate, friend, or relative read your work.** Make sure you understand and consider the reader's suggestions, even if eventually you decide not to take them.
- **Read the draft aloud or, even better, record it.** Listen for awkward rhythms, repetitive sentence patterns, and missing or clumsy transitions.
- **Learn from your own experience.** Keep a record of the problems that others have pointed out in your writing. When editing, check your work against this record.

In your editing, work first for clarity and a smooth movement among sentences and then for correctness. Use the questions in the checklist on the next page to guide your editing, referring to the page numbers in parentheses as needed.

2 A sample edited paragraph

The second paragraph of Sara Ling's edited draft appears on p. 31. One change Ling made throughout the essay shows up in this editing: she resolved an inconsistency in references to *you, people,*

Checklist for editing

Clarity

How well do words and sentences convey their intended meanings? Which if any words and sentences are confusing? Check especially for these:

Exact language (3 pp. 167–75)
Parallelism (3 pp. 152–55)
Clear modifiers (4 pp. 271–77)
Clear reference of pronouns (4 pp. 256–59)
Complete sentences (4 pp. 278–82)
Sentences separated correctly (4 pp. 283–87)

Effectiveness

How well do words and sentences engage and focus readers? Where does the writing seem wordy, choppy, or dull? Check especially for these:

Emphasis of main ideas (3 pp. 141–50)
Smooth and informative transitions (pp. 43–45)
Variety in sentence length and structure (3 pp. 156–59)
Appropriate language (3 pp. 160–66)
Concise sentences (3 pp. 177–82)

Correctness

How little or how much do surface errors interfere with clarity and effectiveness? Check especially for these:

Spelling (6 pp. 345–51)
Verb forms, especially -s and -ed endings and correct forms of irregular verbs (4 pp. 210–24)
Verb tenses, especially consistency (4 pp. 225–31)
Agreement between subjects and verbs, especially when words come between them or the subject is *each, everyone,* or a similar word (4 pp. 237–42)
Pronoun forms (4 pp. 244–50)
Agreement between pronouns and antecedents, especially when the antecedent contains *or* or it is *everyone, person,* or a similar word (4 pp. 251–54)
Sentence fragments (4 pp. 278–82)
Commas, especially with comma splices (4 pp. 283–87) and with *and* or *but,* with introductory elements, with nonessential elements, and with series (5 pp. 298–308)
Apostrophes in possessives but not plural nouns (*Dave's/witches*) and in contractions but not possessive personal pronouns (*it's/its*) (5 p. 327)

You can download this checklist from *ablongman.com/littlebrown.* Make a copy for each writing project, and insert answers along with notes on specific changes to make.

and *we*, settling on a consistent *we*. In addition, Ling corrected several sentence fragments in the middle of the paragraph.

Internet communication can be anonymous on at least two levels. The people we~~you~~ communicate with do not know our~~your~~ age~~.~~, ~~W~~whether we're~~you're~~ fat or thin or neat or sloppy~~.~~, ~~W~~what kind of clothes we~~you~~ wear~~.~~ ~~(Maybe you're not~~ if we're wearing clothes at all)~~.~~, ~~Ө~~or anything else about physical appearance. If we~~you~~ use ~~an~~ invented screen names instead of our~~your~~ real names, readers don't even know whatever our~~your~~ names may reveal or suggest ~~says~~ about us~~you~~, such as gender or ethnic background.

3 Editing on a word processor

When you work on a word processor, consider these additional approaches to editing:

- **Don't rely on your word processor's spelling or grammar and style checker to find what needs editing.** See the discussion of these checkers below.

- **If possible, work on a double-spaced paper copy.** Most people find it much harder to spot errors on a computer screen than on paper.

- **Use the Find command to locate and correct your common problems**—certain misspellings, overuse of *there is*, wordy phrases such as *the fact that*, and so on.

- **Resist overediting.** The ease of editing on a computer can lead to rewriting sentences over and over, stealing the life from your prose. If your grammar and style checker contributes to the temptation, consider turning it off.

- **Take special care with additions and omissions.** Make sure you haven't omitted needed words or left in unneeded words.

4 Working with spelling and grammar/style checkers

The spelling checker and grammar and style checker that may come with your word processor can be helpful *if* you work within their limitations. The programs miss many problems and may even flag items that are actually correct. Further, they know nothing of your purpose and your audience, so they cannot make important decisions about your writing. Always use these tools critically:

- **Read your work yourself to ensure that it's clear and error-free.**

- **Consider a checker's suggestions carefully, weighing each one against your intentions.** If you aren't sure whether to accept a checker's suggestion, consult a dictionary, writing handbook, or other source. Your version may be fine.

Using a spelling checker

Your word processor's spelling checker can be a great ally: it will flag words that are spelled incorrectly and usually suggest alternative spellings that resemble what you've typed. However, this ally can also undermine you because of its limitations:

- **The checker may flag a word that you've spelled correctly** just because the word does not appear in its dictionary.

- **The checker may suggest incorrect alternatives.** In providing a list of alternative spellings for your word, the checker may highlight the one it considers most likely to be correct. You need to verify that this alternative is actually what you intend before selecting it. Consult an online or printed dictionary when you aren't sure of the checker's recommendations.

- **Most important, a spelling checker will not flag words that appear in its dictionary but you have misused.** The jingle in the following screen shot has circulated widely as a warning about spelling checkers (we found it in the *Bulletin of the Missouri Council of Teachers of Mathematics*).

Spelling checker

A spelling checker failed to catch any of the thirteen errors in this jingle. Can you spot them?

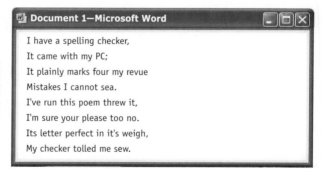

Document 1—Microsoft Word

I have a spelling checker,

It came with my PC;

It plainly marks four my revue

Mistakes I cannot sea.

I've run this poem threw it,

I'm sure your please too no.

Its letter perfect in it's weigh,

My checker tolled me sew.

Using a grammar and style checker

Word processors' grammar and style checkers can flag incorrect grammar or punctuation and wordy or awkward sentences. However, these programs can call your attention only to passages that *may* be faulty. They miss many errors because they are not yet capable of analyzing language in all its complexity (for instance, they can't accurately distinguish a word's part of speech when there are different possibilities, as *light* can be a noun, a verb, or an adjective). And they often question passages that don't need editing, such as an appropriate passive verb or a deliberate and emphatic use of repetition.

You can customize a grammar and style checker to suit your needs and habits as a writer. (Select Options under the Tools menu.) Most checkers allow you to specify whether to check grammar only or grammar and style. Some style checkers can be set to the level of writing you intend, such as formal, standard, and informal. (For academic writing choose formal.) You can also instruct the checker to flag specific grammar and style problems that tend to occur in your writing, such as mismatched subjects and verbs, apostrophes in plural nouns, overused passive voice, or a confusion between *its* and *it's*.

5d Formatting and proofreading the final draft

After editing your essay, retype or print it one last time. Follow the wishes of your instructor in formatting your document. Two common formats are discussed and illustrated in this book: MLA (**MLA** pp. 496–98) and APA (**APA** pp. 523–26). In addition, Chapter 7 treats principles and elements of document design.

Be sure to proofread the final essay several times to spot and correct errors. To increase the accuracy of your proofreading, you may need to experiment with ways to keep yourself from relaxing into the rhythm and the content of your prose. Here are a few tricks, including some used by professional proofreaders:

- **Read printed copy,** even if you will eventually submit the paper electronically. Most people proofread more accurately when reading type on paper than when reading it on a computer screen. (At the same time, don't view the printed copy as necessarily error-free just because it's clean. Clean-looking copy may still harbor errors.)
- **Read the paper aloud,** very slowly, and distinctly pronounce exactly what you see.
- **Place a ruler under each line as you read it.**
- **Read "against copy,"** comparing your final draft one sentence at a time against the edited draft.
- **Ignore content.** To keep the content of your writing from distracting you while you proofread, read the essay backward, end to beginning, examining each sentence as a separate unit. Or, taking advantage of a word processor, isolate each paragraph from its context by printing it on a separate page. (Of course, reassemble the paragraphs before submitting the paper.)

5e Examining a sample final draft

Sara Ling's final essay appears on the following pages, typed in MLA format except for page numbers. Comments in the margins point out key features of the essay's content.

Sara Ling

Professor Nelson

English 120A

4 November 2005

Descriptive title

The Internet:

Fragmentation or Community?

Introduction

We hear all sorts of predictions about how the Internet will enrich our individual lives and promote communication, tolerance, and thus community in our society. But are these promises realistic? In her 1995 essay "Welcome to Cyberbia," M. Kadi argues that they are not. Instead, she predicts that the Internet will lead to more fragmentation, not community, because users merely seek out others with the same biases, concerns, and needs as their own. The point is an interesting one, but Kadi fails to foresee that the unique anonymity of Internet communication could actually build diversity into community by lowering the barriers of physical appearance.

Question to be addressed

Summary of Kadi's essay

Thesis statement

Internet communication can be anonymous on at least two levels. The people we communicate with do not know our age, whether we're fat or thin or neat or sloppy, what kind of clothes we wear (if we're wearing clothes at all), or anything else about physical appearance. If we use invented screen names instead of our real names, readers don't even know whatever our names may reveal or suggest about us, such as gender or ethnic background.

Explanation of Internet's anonymity

Internet anonymity seems a popular option, judging by the numbers of invented user names seen in online forums. To determine the extent of invented user names as well as the reasons for them, I surveyed seventy-eight students. I asked two questions: (1) Do you ever write with an invented user name when contributing to chat rooms, newsgroups, Web logs, and so on? (2) If yes, why do you use an invented name: to protect your privacy, to avoid revealing personal information, or for some other reason? The results are shown in fig. 1. A large majority of the students (seventy-eight percent) do use invented names online. And most of them do so to protect their privacy (thirty-seven percent) or to avoid revealing personal details (thirty percent).

Presentation of survey conducted to gauge use of invented screen names

Explanation of survey method

Summary of survey results

Users of the Internet clearly value the anonymity it can give them. This anonymity allows users to communicate freely without being prejudged because of physical attributes. In follow-up interviews, twenty students said that they use invented names to mask personal details because they think the details might work against them in online communication. One

First main point: We are not prejudged by others.

Examples of first point

Do not use invented names (22%)

Use invented names to avoid revealing personal details (30%)

Use invented names for other reasons (11%)

Use invented names to protect privacy (37%)

Fig. 1. Use of invented screen names among seventy-eight Internet users.

said she is able to participate in a physics discussion list without fear of being ignored by the group's professional physicists. Another said he thinks he can contribute more freely to a political forum because no one knows he's African American. I learned the benefits of anonymity myself when I joined a snowboarding forum using my full name and received hostile responses such as "What does a girl know?" and "Why don't you go back to knitting?" I assumed I had run into a male prejudice against female snowboarders. However, another woman on the forum had no such problems when she contributed for a while before revealing her gender.

Granted, concealing or altering identities on the Internet can be a problem, as when adults pose as children to seduce or harm them. These well-publicized occurrences say much about the need to monitor children's use of the Internet and to be cautious about meeting Internet correspondents. However, they do not undermine the value of being able to make ourselves heard in situations where normally (in the real world) we would be shut out.

The Internet's anonymity has a flip side, too: just as we cannot be prejudged, so we cannot prejudge others because of their appearance. Often in face-to-face interaction, we assume we know things about people just because of the way they look. Someone with an athletic build must be unintelligent. Someone who is heavy must be uninteresting. Perhaps most significant, someone of another race must have fixed and contrary views about all kinds of issues, from family values to crime to affirmative action. Assumptions like these prevent us from discovering the interests and concerns we share with people who merely look different. But with the anonymity of the Internet, such physical barriers to understanding are irrelevant.

A world without physical bias may be an unreachable ideal. However, the more we communicate with just our minds, the more likely it is that

Qualification of first point

Conclusion of first point

Second main point: We cannot prejudge others.

Clarification of second point

Examples of second point

Effects of assumptions

Conclusion of second point

Conclusion, summarizing essay

our minds will find common ground and put less emphasis on physical characteristics. Logged on, we can begin to become more accepted and more accepting, more tolerated and more tolerant. We can begin to become a community.

Work cited in MLA style (see MLA p. 468)

Work Cited

Kadi, M. "Welcome to Cyberbia." Utne Reader Mar.-Apr. 1995: 57-59.

5f Revising collaboratively

In many writing courses students work together on writing, most often commenting on each other's work to help with revision. This collaborative writing gives experience in reading written work critically and in reaching others through writing. Collaboration may occur face to face in small groups, via drafts and comments on paper, or on computers.

Whether you collaborate in person, on paper, or on a computer, you will be more comfortable and helpful and will benefit more from others' comments if you follow a few guidelines.

■ Commenting on others' writing

- **Be sure you know what the writer is saying.** If necessary, summarize the paper to understand its content. (See 2 pp. 79–80.)
- **Address only your most significant concerns with the work.** Use the revision checklist on pp. 25–26 as a guide to what is significant. Unless you have other instructions, ignore mistakes in grammar, punctuation, and the like. (The temptation to focus on such errors may be especially strong if the writer is less experienced than you are with standard American English.) Emphasizing mistakes will contribute little to the writer's revision.
- **Remember that you are the reader, not the writer.** Don't edit sentences, add details, or otherwise assume responsibility for the paper.
- **Phrase your comments carefully.** Avoid misunderstandings by making sure comments are both clear and respectful. If you are responding on paper or online, not face to face with the writer, remember that the writer has nothing but your written words to go on. He or she can't ask you for immediate clarification and can't infer your attitudes from gestures, facial expressions, and tone of voice.
- **Be specific.** If something confuses you, say *why*. If you disagree with a conclusion, say *why*.
- **Be supportive as well as honest.** Tell the writer what you like about the paper. Word comments positively: instead of *This*

paragraph doesn't interest me, say *You have an interesting detail here that I almost missed.* Question the writer in a way that emphasizes the effect of the work on you, the reader: *This paragraph confuses me because.* . . . And avoid measuring the work against a set of external standards: *This essay is poorly organized. Your thesis statement is inadequate.*

- **While reading, make your comments in writing.** Even if you will be delivering your comments in person later on, the written record will help you recall what you thought.
- **Link comments to specific parts of a paper.** Especially if you are reading the paper on a computer, be clear about what in the paper each comment relates to. You can embed your comments directly into the paper, distinguishing them with highlighting or color, or you can use the Comment function of a word processor.

Benefiting from comments on your writing

- **Think of your readers as counselors or coaches.** They can help you see the virtues and flaws in your work and sharpen your awareness of readers' needs.
- **Read or listen to comments closely.**
- **Know what the critic is saying.** If you need more information, ask for it, or consult the appropriate section of this handbook.
- **Don't become defensive.** Letting comments offend you will only erect a barrier to improvement in your writing. As one writing teacher advises, "Leave your ego at the door."
- **Revise your work in response to appropriate comments.** Whether or not you are required to act on comments, you will learn more from actually revising than from just thinking about it.
- **Remember that you are the final authority on your work.** You should be open to suggestions, but you are free to decline advice when you think it is inappropriate.
- **Keep track of both the strengths and weaknesses others identify.** Then in later assignments you can build on your successes and give special attention to problem areas.

CULTURE LANGUAGE In some cultures writers do not expect criticism from readers, or readers do not expect to think and speak critically about what they read. If critical responses are uncommon in your native culture, collaboration may at first be uncomfortable for you. As a writer, think of a draft or even a final paper as more an exploration of ideas than the last word on your subject; then you may be more receptive to readers' suggestions. As a reader, allow yourself to approach a text skeptically, and know that your tactful questions and suggestions will usually be considered appropriate.

5g   Preparing a writing portfolio

Your writing teacher may ask you to assemble samples of your writing into a portfolio, or folder, once or more during the course. Such a portfolio gives you a chance to consider all your writing over a period and to showcase your best work.

Although the requirements for portfolios vary, most teachers are looking for a range of writing that demonstrates your progress and strengths as a writer. You, in turn, see how you have advanced from one assignment to the next, as you've had time for new knowledge to sink in and time for practice. Teachers often allow students to revise papers before placing them in the portfolio, even if the papers were submitted earlier. In that case, every paper in the portfolio can benefit from all your learning.

An assignment to assemble a writing portfolio will probably also provide guidelines for what to include, how the portfolio will be evaluated, and how (or whether) it will be weighted for a grade. Be sure you understand the purpose of the portfolio and who will read it. For instance, if your composition teacher will be the only reader and his or her guidelines encourage you to show evidence of progress, you might include a paper that took big risks but never entirely succeeded. In contrast, if a committee of teachers will read your work and the guidelines urge you to demonstrate your competence as a writer, you might include only papers that did succeed.

Unless the guidelines specify otherwise, provide error-free copies of your final drafts, label all your samples with your name, and assemble them all in a folder. Add a cover letter or memo that lists the samples, explains why you've included each one, and evaluates your progress as a writer. The self-evaluation involved should be a learning experience for you and will help your readers assess your development as a writer.

6   Paragraphs

A **paragraph** is a group of related sentences set off by a beginning indention or, sometimes, by extra space. Paragraphs give you and your readers a breather from long stretches of text, and they indicate key steps in the development of your thesis.

http://www.ablongman.com/littlebrown ▶

Visit the companion Web site for more help and electronic exercises on paragraphs.

Checklist for revising paragraphs

- **Is the paragraph unified?** Does it adhere to one general idea that is either stated in a topic sentence or otherwise apparent? (See below.)
- **Is the paragraph coherent?** Do the sentences follow a clear sequence? Are the sentences linked as needed by parallelism, repetition or restatement, pronouns, consistency, and transitional expressions? (See the next page.)
- **Is the paragraph developed?** Is the general idea of the paragraph well supported with specific evidence such as details, facts, examples, and reasons? (See p. 45.)

This chapter discusses the three qualities of an effective body paragraph: unity (below), coherence (next page), and development (p. 45). In addition, the chapter discusses two special kinds of paragraphs: introductions and conclusions (pp. 50 and 52).

CULTURE LANGUAGE ➤ Not all cultures share the paragraphing conventions of American academic writing. In some other languages, writing moves differently from English—not from left to right, but from right to left or down rows from top to bottom. Even in languages that move as English does, writers may not use paragraphs at all. Or they may use paragraphs but not state the central ideas or provide transitional expressions to show readers how sentences relate. If your native language is not English and you have difficulty with paragraphs, don't worry about paragraphing during drafting. Instead, during a separate step of revision, divide your text into parts that develop your main points. Mark those parts with indentions.

6a   Maintaining paragraph unity

An effective paragraph develops one central idea—in other words, it is **unified**. Here is an example:

> Some people really like chili, apparently, but nobody can agree how the stuff should be made. C. V. Wood, twice winner at Terlingua, uses flank steak, pork chops, chicken, and green chilis. My friend Hughes Rudd of CBS News, who imported five hundred pounds of chili powder into Russia as a condition of accepting employment as Moscow correspondent, favors coarse-ground beef. Isadore Bleckman, the cameraman I must live with on the road, insists upon one-inch cubes of stew beef and puts garlic in his chili, an Illinois affectation. An Indian of my acquaintance, Mr. Fulton Batisse, who eats chili for breakfast when he can, uses buffalo meat and plays an Indian drum while it's cooking. I ask you.
>
> —Charles Kuralt, *Dateline America*

Kuralt's paragraph works because it follows through on its central idea, which is stated in the underlined first sentence, the **topic sentence**. After the topic sentence, each of the next four sentences offers an example of a chili concoction. (In the final sentence Kuralt comments on the examples.)

What if instead Kuralt had written his paragraph as follows? Here the topic of chili preparation is forgotten mid-paragraph, as the sentences digress to describe life in Moscow:

> Some people really like chili, apparently, but nobody can agree how the stuff should be made. C. V. Wood, twice winner at Terlingua, uses flank steak, pork chops, chicken, and green chilis. My friend Hughes Rudd, who imported five hundred pounds of chili powder into Russia as a condition of accepting employment as Moscow correspondent, favors coarse-ground beef. He had some trouble finding the beef in Moscow, though. He sometimes had to scour all the markets and wait in long lines. For any American used to overstocked supermarkets and department stores, Russia can be quite a shock.

Instead of following through on its topic sentence, the paragraph loses its way. It is not unified.

A topic sentence need not always come first in the paragraph. For instance, it may come last, presenting your idea only after you have provided the evidence for it. Or it may not be stated at all, especially in narrative or descriptive writing in which the point becomes clear in the details. But always the idea should govern the paragraph's content as if it were standing guard at the opening.

6b   Achieving paragraph coherence

When a paragraph is **coherent**, readers can see how it holds together: the sentences seem to flow logically and smoothly into one another. Exactly the opposite happens with this paragraph:

> The ancient Egyptians were masters of preserving dead people's bodies by making mummies of them. Mummies several thousand years old have been discovered nearly intact. The skin, hair, teeth, finger- and toenails, and facial features of the mummies were evident. One can diagnose the diseases they suffered in life, such as smallpox, arthritis, and nutritional deficiencies. The process was remarkably effective. Sometimes apparent were the fatal afflictions of the dead people: a middle-aged king died from a blow on the head, and polio killed a child king. Mummification consisted of removing the internal organs, applying natural preservatives inside and out, and then wrapping the body in layers of bandages.

The paragraph is hard to read. The sentences lurch instead of gliding from point to point.

The paragraph as it was actually written appears below. It is much clearer because the writer arranged information differently and also built links into his sentences so that they would flow smoothly:

- After stating the central idea in a topic sentence, the writer moves to two more specific explanations and illustrates the second with four sentences of examples.
- Circled words repeat or restate key terms or concepts.
- Boxed words link sentences and clarify relationships.
- Underlined phrases are in parallel grammatical form to reflect their parallel content.

Central idea
The ancient Egyptians were masters of preserving dead people's bodies by making mummies of them. Basically, mummification consisted of removing the internal organs, applying natural preservatives inside and out, and then wrapping the body in layers of bandages. And the process was remarkably effective. Indeed, mummies several thousand years old have been discovered nearly intact. Their skin, hair, teeth, finger- and toenails, and facial features are still evident. Their diseases in life, such as smallpox, arthritis, and nutritional deficiencies, are still diagnosable. Even their fatal afflictions are still apparent: a middle-aged king died from a blow on the head; a child king died from polio.

—Mitchell Rosenbaum (student), "Lost Arts of the Egyptians"

1 Paragraph organization

A coherent paragraph organizes information so that readers can easily follow along. These are common paragraph schemes:

- **General to specific:** Sentences downshift from more general statements to more specific ones. (See the paragraph by Rosenbaum above.)
- **Climactic:** Sentences increase in drama or interest, ending in a climax. (See the paragraph by Mayer on the next page.)
- **Spatial:** Sentences scan a person, place, or object from top to bottom, from side to side, or in some other way that approximates the way people actually look at things. (See the paragraph by Woolf on p. 46.)
- **Chronological:** Sentences present events as they occurred in time, earlier to later. (See the paragraph by LaFrank on pp. 43–44.)

2 Parallelism

Parallelism helps tie sentences together. In the following paragraph the underlined parallel structures of *She* and a verb link all sentences after the first one. Parallelism also appears *within* many of the sentences. Aphra Behn (1640–89) was the first Englishwoman to write professionally.

In addition to her busy career as a writer, Aphra Behn also found time to briefly marry and spend a little while in debtor's prison. <u>She found</u> time to take up a career as a spy for the English in their <u>war</u> against the Dutch. <u>She made</u> the long and difficult voyage to Suriname [in South America] <u>and became</u> involved in a slave rebellion there. <u>She plunged</u> into political debate at Will's Coffee House and defended <u>her</u> position from the stage of the Drury Lane Theater. <u>She</u> actively <u>argued</u> for women's rights to be educated and to marry whom they pleased, or not at all. <u>She defied</u> the seventeenth-century dictum that ladies must be "modest" and wrote freely about sex.

—Angeline Goreau, "Aphra Behn"

3 Repetition and restatement

Repeating or restating key words helps make a paragraph coherent and also reminds readers what the topic is. In the following paragraph note the underlined repetition of *sleep* and the restatement of *adults*.

Perhaps the simplest fact about <u>sleep</u> is that individual needs for it vary widely. Most <u>adults sleep</u> between seven and nine hours, but occasionally <u>people</u> turn up who need twelve hours or so, while some <u>rare types</u> can get by on three or four. Rarest of all are those <u>legendary types</u> who require almost no <u>sleep</u> at all; respected researchers have recently studied three <u>such people</u>. One of them—a healthy, happy woman in her seventies—<u>sleeps</u> about an hour every two or three days. The other two are men in early middle age, who get by on a few minutes a night. One of them complains about the daily fifteen minutes or so he's forced to "waste" in <u>sleeping</u>.

—Lawrence A. Mayer, "The Confounding Enemy of Sleep"

4 Pronouns

Because pronouns refer to nouns, they can help relate sentences to each other. In the paragraph above by Angeline Goreau, *she* works just this way by substituting for *Aphra Behn* in every sentence after the first.

5 Consistency

Consistency (or the lack of it) occurs primarily in the person and number of nouns and pronouns and in the tense of verbs. Any inconsistencies not required by meaning will interfere with a reader's ability to follow the development of ideas.

Key terms

parallelism The use of similar grammatical structures for similar elements of meaning within or among sentences: *The book <u>caused a stir in the media</u> and <u>aroused debate in Congress</u>.* (See also **3** pp. 152–55.)

pronoun A word that refers to and functions as a noun, such as *I, you, he, she, it, we, they: The patient could not raise <u>her</u> arm.* (See **4** p. 189.)

Note the underlined inconsistencies in the next paragraphs:

Shifts in tense

In the Hopi religion, water is the driving force. Since the Hopi <u>lived</u> in the Arizona desert, they <u>needed</u> water urgently for drinking, cooking, and irrigating crops. Their complex beliefs <u>are</u> focused in part on gaining the assistance of supernatural forces in obtaining water. Many of the Hopi kachinas, or spirit essences, <u>were</u> directly concerned with clouds, rain, and snow.

Shifts in number

<u>Kachinas</u> represent the things and events of the real world, such as clouds, mischief, cornmeal, and even death. A <u>kachina</u> is not worshiped as a god but regarded as an interested friend. <u>They</u> visit the Hopi from December through July in the form of men who dress in kachina costumes and perform dances and other rituals.

Shifts in person

Unlike the man, the Hopi <u>woman</u> does not keep contact with kachinas through costumes and dancing. Instead, <u>one</u> receives a small likeness of a kachina, called a *tihu*, from the man impersonating the kachina. <u>You</u> are more likely to receive a tihu as a girl approaching marriage, though a child or older woman may receive one, too.

A grammar checker cannot help you locate shifts in tense, number, or person among sentences. Shifts are sometimes necessary (as when tenses change to reflect actual differences in time). Furthermore, a passage with needless shifts may still consist of sentences that are grammatically correct, as all the sentences are in the preceding examples.

6 Transitional expressions

Transitional expressions such as *therefore, in contrast,* or *meanwhile* can forge specific connections between sentences, as do the underlined expressions in this paragraph:

Medical science has <u>thus</u> succeeded in identifying the hundreds of viruses that can cause the <u>common</u> cold. It has <u>also</u> discovered the most effective means of prevention. One person transmits the cold viruses to another most often by hand. <u>For instance,</u> an infected person covers his

---

┌─ **Key terms** ─────────────────────────────────────

tense The form of a verb that indicates the time of its action, such as present (*I run*), past (*I ran*), or future (*I will run*). (See **4** p. 225.)

number The form of a noun, pronoun, or verb that indicates whether it is singular (one) or plural (more than one): *boy is, boys are.*

person The form of a pronoun that indicates whether the subject is speaking (first person: *I, we*), spoken to (second person: *you*), or spoken about (third person: *he, she, it, they*). All nouns are in the third person.

mouth to cough. He then picks up the telephone. Half an hour later, his daughter picks up the same telephone. Immediately afterward, she rubs her eyes. Within a few days, she, too, has a cold. And thus it spreads. To avoid colds, therefore, people should wash their hands often and keep their hands away from their faces.

—Kathleen LaFrank (student), "Colds: Myth and Science"

Note that you can use transitional expressions to link paragraphs as well as sentences. In the first sentence of LaFrank's paragraph, the word *thus* signals that the sentence refers to an effect discussed in the preceding paragraph.

The box below lists many transitional expressions by the functions they perform.

Transitional expressions

To add or show sequence
again, also, and, and then, besides, equally important, finally, first, further, furthermore, in addition, in the first place, last, moreover, next, second, still, too

To compare
also, in the same way, likewise, similarly

To contrast
although, and yet, but, but at the same time, despite, even so, even though, for all that, however, in contrast, in spite of, nevertheless, notwithstanding, on the contrary, on the other hand, regardless, still, though, yet

To give examples or intensify
after all, an illustration of, even, for example, for instance, indeed, in fact, it is true, of course, specifically, that is, to illustrate, truly

To indicate place
above, adjacent to, below, elsewhere, farther on, here, near, nearby, on the other side, opposite to, there, to the east, to the left

To indicate time
after a while, afterward, as long as, as soon as, at last, at length, at that time, before, earlier, formerly, immediately, in the meantime, in the past, lately, later, meanwhile, now, presently, shortly, simultaneously, since, so far, soon, subsequently, then, thereafter, until, until now, when

To repeat, summarize, or conclude
all in all, altogether, as has been said, in brief, in conclusion, in other words, in particular, in short, in simpler terms, in summary, on the whole, that is, therefore, to put it differently, to summarize

To show cause or effect

accordingly, as a result, because, consequently, for this purpose, hence, otherwise, since, then, therefore, thereupon, thus, to this end, with this object

Note Draw carefully on this list of transitional expressions because the ones in each group are not interchangeable. For instance, *besides*, *finally*, and *second* may all be used to add information, but each has its own distinct meaning.

CULTURE LANGUAGE If transitional expressions are not common in your native language, you may be tempted to compensate when writing in English by adding them to the beginnings of most sentences. But such explicit transitions aren't needed everywhere, and in fact too many can be intrusive and awkward. When inserting transitional expressions, consider the reader's need for a signal: often the connection from sentence to sentence is already clear from the context or can be made clear by relating the content of sentences more closely (see **3** pp. 144–45). When you do need transitional expressions, try varying their positions in your sentences, as illustrated in the sample paragraph on pp. 43–44.

6c   Developing paragraphs

An effective, well-developed paragraph always provides the specific information that readers need and expect in order to understand you and to stay interested in what you say. Paragraph length can be a rough gauge of development: anything much shorter than 100 to 150 words may leave readers with a sense of incompleteness.

To develop or shape an idea in a paragraph, one or more of the following patterns may help. (These patterns may also be used to develop entire essays. See p. 18.)

1 Narration

Narration retells a significant sequence of events, usually in the order of their occurrence (that is, chronologically). A narrator is concerned not just with the sequence of events but also with their consequence, their importance to the whole.

> Jill's story is typical for "recruits" to religious cults. She was very lonely in college and appreciated the attention of the nice young men and women who lived in a house near campus. They persuaded her to share their meals and then to move in with them. Between intense bombardments of "love," they deprived her of sleep and sometimes

threatened to throw her out. Jill became increasingly confused and dependent, losing touch with any reality besides the one in the group. She dropped out of school and refused to see or communicate with her family. Before long she, too, was preying on lonely college students.

—Hillary Begas (student), "The Love Bombers"

2   Description

Description details the sensory qualities of a person, scene, thing, or feeling, using concrete and specific words to convey a dominant mood, illustrate an idea, or achieve some other purpose.

The sun struck straight upon the house, making the white walls glare between the dark windows. Their panes, woven thickly with green branches, held circles of impenetrable darkness. Sharp-edged wedges of light lay upon the window-sill and showed inside the room plates with blue rings, cups with curved handles, the bulge of a great bowl, the crisscross pattern in the rug, and the formidable corners and lines of cabinets and bookcases. Behind their conglomeration hung a zone of shadow in which might be a further shape to be disencumbered of shadow or still denser depths of darkness.   —Virginia Woolf, *The Waves*

3   Illustration or support

An idea may be developed with several specific examples, like those used by Charles Kuralt on p. 39, or with a single extended example, as in the next paragraph:

The language problem that I was attacking loomed larger and larger as I began to learn more. When I would describe in English certain concepts and objects enmeshed in Korean emotion and imagination, I became slowly aware of nuances, of differences between two languages even in simple expression. The remark "Kim entered the house" seems to be simple enough, yet, unless a reader has a clear visual image of a Korean house, his understanding of the sentence is not complete. When a Korean says he is "in the house," he may be in his courtyard, or on his porch, or in his small room! If I wanted to give a specific picture of entering the house in the Western sense, I had to say "room" instead of house—sometimes. I say "sometimes" because many Koreans entertain their guests on their porches and still are considered to be hospitable, and in the Korean sense, going into the "room" may be a more intimate act than it would be in the English sense. Such problems!

—Kim Yong Ik, "A Book-Writing Venture"

Sometimes you can develop a paragraph by providing your reasons for stating a general idea. For instance:

There are three reasons, quite apart from scientific considerations, that mankind needs to travel in space. The first reason is the need for garbage disposal: we need to transfer industrial processes into space, so that the earth may remain a green and pleasant place for our grandchildren to live in. The second reason is the need to escape material impoverishment: the resources of this planet are finite, and we shall not forgo forever the abundant solar energy and minerals and living space that are spread out all around us. The third reason is our spiritual need for an open frontier: the ultimate purpose of space travel is to bring to humanity not only scientific discoveries and an occasional spectacular show on television but a real expansion of our spirit.

—Freeman Dyson, "Disturbing the Universe"

4 Definition

Defining a complicated, abstract, or controversial term often requires extended explanation. The following definition comes from an essay asserting that "quality in product and effort has become a vanishing element of current civilization." Notice how the writer pins down meaning with examples and contrasts.

In the hope of possibly reducing the hail of censure which is certain to greet this essay (I am thinking of going to Alaska or possibly Patagonia in the week it is published), let me say that quality, as I understand it, means investment of the best skill and effort possible to produce the finest and most admirable result possible. Its presence or absence in some degree characterizes every manmade object, service, skilled or unskilled labor—laying bricks, painting a picture, ironing shirts, practicing medicine, shoemaking, scholarship, writing a book. You do it well or you do it half-well. Materials are sound and durable or they are sleazy; method is painstaking or whatever is easiest. Quality is achieving or reaching for the highest standard as against being satisfied with the sloppy or fraudulent. It is honesty of purpose as against catering to cheap or sensational sentiment. It does not allow compromise with the second-rate.   —Barbara Tuchman, "The Decline of Quality"

5 Division or analysis

With division or analysis, you separate something into its elements—for instance, you might divide a newspaper into its sections. You may also approach the elements critically, interpreting their meaning and significance (see also 2 pp. 86–89):

The surface realism of the soap opera conjures up an illusion of "liveness." The domestic settings and easygoing rhythms encourage the viewer to believe that the drama, however ridiculous, is simply an extension of daily life. The conversation is so slow that some have called it "radio with pictures." (Advertisers have always assumed that busy housewives would listen, rather than watch.) Conversation is casual and colloquial, as though one were eavesdropping on neighbors. There is plenty of time to "read" the character's face; close-ups establish intimacy. The sets are comfortably familiar: well-lit interiors of living rooms, restaurants, offices, and hospitals. Daytime soaps have little of the glamour of their prime-time relations. The viewer easily imagines that the conversation is taking place in real time.

—Ruth Rosen, "Search for Yesterday"

6 Classification

When you classify items, you sort them into groups. The classification allows you to see and explain the relations among the items. The following paragraph identifies three groups, or classes, of parents:

> In my experience, the parents who hire daytime sitters for their school-age children tend to fall into one of three groups. The first group includes parents who work and want someone to be at home when the children return from school. These parents are looking for an extension of themselves, someone who will give the care they would give if they were at home. The second group includes parents who may be home all day themselves but are too disorganized or too frazzled by their children's demands to handle child care alone. They are looking for an organizer and helpmate. The third and final group includes parents who do not want to be bothered by their children, whether they are home all day or not. Unlike the parents in the first two groups, who care for their children however they can, these parents seek a permanent substitute for themselves.   —Nancy Whittle (student), "Modern Parenting"

7 Comparison and contrast

Comparison and contrast may be used separately or together to develop an idea. The following paragraph illustrates one of two common ways of organizing a comparison and contrast: **subject by subject,** first one subject and then the other.

> Consider the differences also in the behavior of rock and classical music audiences. At a rock concert, the audience members yell, whistle, sing along, and stamp their feet. They may even stand during the entire performance. The better the music, the more active they'll be. At a classical concert, in contrast, the better the performance, the more *still* the audience is. Members of the classical audience are so highly disciplined that they refrain from even clearing their throats or coughing. No matter what effect the powerful music has on their intellects and feelings, they sit on their hands.
> —Tony Nahm (student), "Rock and Roll Is Here to Stay"

The next paragraph illustrates the other common organization: **point by point,** with the two subjects discussed side by side and matched feature for feature:

> The first electronic computer, ENIAC, went into operation just over fifty years ago, yet the differences between it and today's personal computer are enormous. ENIAC was enormous itself, consisting of forty panels, each two feet wide and four feet deep. Today's notebook PC or Macintosh, by contrast, can fit on one's lap. ENIAC had to be configured by hand, with its programmers taking up to two days to reset switches and cables. Today, the average user can change programs in an instant.

And for all its size and inconvenience, ENIAC was also slow. In its time, its operating speed of 100,000 pulses per second seemed amazingly fast. However, today's notebook can operate at more than 1 billion pulses per second.

—Shirley Kujiwara (student), "The Computers We Deserve"

8 Cause-and-effect analysis

When you use analysis to explain why something happened or what did or may happen, then you are determining causes or effects. In the following paragraph the author looks at the cause of an effect—Japanese collectivism:

The *shinkansen* or "bullet train" speeds across the rural areas of Japan giving a quick view of cluster after cluster of farmhouses surrounded by rice paddies. This particular pattern did not develop purely by chance, but as a consequence of the technology peculiar to the growing of rice, the staple of the Japanese diet. The growing of rice requires the construction and maintenance of an irrigation system, something that takes many hands to build. More importantly, the planting and the harvesting of rice can only be done efficiently with the cooperation of twenty or more people. The "bottom line" is that a single family working alone cannot produce enough rice to survive, but a dozen families working together can produce a surplus. Thus the Japanese have had to develop the capacity to work together in harmony, no matter what the forces of disagreement or social disintegration, in order to survive.   —William Ouchi, *Theory Z*

9 Process analysis

When you analyze how to do something or how something works, you explain a process. The following example identifies the process, describes the equipment needed, and details the steps in the process:

As a car owner, you waste money when you pay a mechanic to change the engine oil. The job is not difficult, even if you know little about cars. All you need is a wrench to remove the drain plug, a large, flat pan to collect the draining oil, plastic bottles to dispose of the used oil, and fresh oil. First, warm up the car's engine so that the oil will flow more easily. When the engine is warm, shut it off and remove its oil-filler cap (the owner's manual shows where this cap is). Then locate the drain plug under the engine (again consulting the owner's manual for its location) and place the flat pan under the plug. Remove the plug with the wrench, letting the oil flow into the pan. When the oil stops flowing, replace the plug and, at the engine's filler hole, add the amount and kind of fresh oil specified by the owner's manual. Pour the used oil into the plastic bottles and take it to a waste-oil collector, which any garage mechanic can recommend.

—Anthony Andreas (student), "Do-It-Yourself Car Care"

6d Writing introductory and concluding paragraphs

1 Introductions

An introduction draws readers from their world into yours.

- **It focuses readers' attention on the topic and arouses their curiosity about what you have to say.**
- **It specifies your subject and implies your attitude.**
- **Often it includes your thesis statement.**
- **It is concise and sincere.**

Numerous options for focusing readers' attention are listed in the box below.

Some strategies for introductions

- Ask a question.
- Relate an incident.
- Use a vivid quotation.
- Create a visual image that represents your subject.
- Offer a surprising statistic or other fact.
- Provide background.
- State an opinion related to your thesis.

- Outline the argument your thesis refutes.
- Make a historical comparison or contrast.
- Outline a problem or dilemma.
- Define a word central to your subject.
- In some business or technical writing, simply state your main idea.

CULTURE LANGUAGE These options for an introduction may not be what you are used to if your native language is not English. In other cultures readers may seek familiarity or reassurance from an author's introduction, or they may prefer an indirect approach to the subject. In academic and business English, however, writers and readers prefer concise, direct expression.

Effective openings

A very common introduction opens with a statement of the essay's general subject, clarifies or limits the subject in one or more sentences, and then asserts the point of the essay in the thesis statement (underlined in the following examples):

> Can your home or office computer make you sterile? Can it strike you blind or dumb? The answer is: probably not. Nevertheless, reports of side effects relating to computer use should be examined, especially in the area of birth defects, eye complaints, and postural difficulties. Although little conclusive evidence exists to establish a causal link

between computer use and problems of this sort, the circumstantial evidence can be disturbing. —Thomas Hartmann,
"How Dangerous Is Your Computer?"

The Declaration of Independence is so widely regarded as a statement of American ideals that its origins in practical politics tend to be forgotten. Thomas Jefferson's draft was intensely debated and then revised in the Continental Congress. Jefferson was disappointed with the result. However, a close reading of both the historical context and the revisions themselves indicates that the Congress improved the document for its intended purpose. — Ann Weiss (student), "The Editing of the Declaration of Independence"

In much business writing, it's more important to tell readers immediately what your point is than to try to engage them. This introduction to a brief memo quickly outlines a problem and (in the thesis statement) suggests a way to solve it:

Starting next month, the holiday rush and staff vacations will leave our department short-handed. We need to hire two or perhaps three temporary keyboarders to maintain our schedules for the month.

Additional effective introductions appear in complete writing samples elsewhere in this book: p. 34, **2** p. 110, **8** pp. 443 and 500.

■ **Openings to avoid**

When writing and revising your introduction, avoid approaches that are likely to bore or confuse readers:

- **A vague generality or truth.** Don't extend your reach too wide with a line such as *Throughout human history . . .* or *In today's world. . . .* You may have needed a warm-up paragraph to start drafting, but your readers can do without it.
- **A flat announcement.** Don't start with *The purpose of this essay is . . .* , *In this essay I will . . .* , or any similar presentation of your intention or topic.
- **A reference to the essay's title.** Don't refer to the title of the essay in the first sentence—for example, *This is a big problem* or *This book is about the history of the guitar.*
- **According to Webster. . . .** Don't start by citing a dictionary definition. A definition can be an effective springboard to an essay, but this kind of lead-in has become dull with overuse.
- **An apology.** Don't fault your opinion or your knowledge with *I'm not sure if I'm right, but I think . . .* , *I don't know much about this, but . . .* , or a similar line.

2 Conclusions

Your conclusion finishes off your essay and tells readers where you think you have brought them. It answers the question "So what?"

■ **Effective conclusions**

Usually set off in its own paragraph, the conclusion may consist of a single sentence or a group of sentences. It may take one or more of the approaches listed in the box below.

Some strategies for conclusions

- Recommend a course of action.
- Summarize the paper.
- Echo the approach of the introduction.
- Restate your thesis and reflect on its implications.
- Strike a note of hope or despair.

- Give a symbolic or powerful fact or other detail.
- Give an especially compelling example.
- Create an image that represents your subject.
- Use a quotation.

The following paragraph concludes the essay on the Declaration of Independence whose introduction appears on the previous page. The writer both summarizes her essay and echoes her introduction.

> The Declaration of Independence has come to be a statement of this nation's political philosophy, but that was not its purpose in 1776. Jefferson's passionate expression had to bow to the goals of the Congress as a whole to forge unity among the colonies and to win the support of foreign nations. —Ann Weiss (student), "The Editing of the Declaration of Independence"

In the next paragraph the author concludes an essay on environmental protection with a call for action:

> Until we get the answers, I think we had better keep on building power plants and growing food with the help of fertilizers and such insect-controlling chemicals as we now have. The risks are well known, thanks to the environmentalists. If they had not created a widespread public awareness of the ecological crisis, we wouldn't stand a chance. But such awareness by itself is not enough. Flaming manifestos and prophecies of doom are no longer much help, and a search for scapegoats can only make matters worse. The time for sensations and manifestos is about over. Now we need rigorous analysis, united effort and very hard work. —Peter F. Drucker, "How Best to Protect the Environment"

■ **Conclusions to avoid**

Several kinds of conclusions rarely work well:

■ **A repeat of the introduction.** Don't simply replay your introduction. The conclusion should capture what the paragraphs of the body have added to the introduction.

- **A new direction.** Don't introduce a subject different from the one your essay has been about.
- **A sweeping generalization.** Don't conclude more than you reasonably can from the evidence you have presented. If your essay is about your frustrating experience trying to clear a parking ticket, you cannot reasonably conclude that *all* local police forces are too tied up in red tape to be of service to the people.
- **An apology.** Don't cast doubt on your essay. Don't say, *Even though I'm no expert* or *This may not be convincing, but I believe it's true* or anything similar. Rather, to win your readers' confidence, display confidence.

7 Document Design

Imaginehowharditwouldbetoreadandwriteiftextlookedlikethis. To make reading and writing easier, we place spaces between words. This convention and many others—such as page margins, paragraph breaks, and headings—have evolved over time to help writers communicate clearly with readers.

7a Designing academic papers and other documents

The design guidelines offered in this chapter apply to all types of documents, including academic papers, Web sites, business reports, flyers, and newsletters. Each type has specific requirements as well, covered elsewhere in this book.

1 Designing academic papers

Many academic disciplines prefer specific formats for students' papers. This book details two such formats:

- **MLA,** used in English, foreign languages, and other humanities (**MLA** pp. 496–98).
- **APA,** used in the social sciences and some natural and applied sciences (**APA** pp. 523–26).

Other academic formats can be found in the discipline style guides listed in **8** pp. 447, 451–52, and 456.

http://www.ablongman.com/littlebrown

Visit the companion Web site for more help with document design.

The design guidelines in this chapter extend the range of elements and options covered by most academic styles. Your instructors may want you to adhere strictly to a particular style or may allow some latitude in design. Ask them for their preferences.

2 Writing online

In and out of school, you are likely to do a lot of online writing—certainly e-mail and possibly Web logs and other Web sites. The purposes and audiences for online writing vary widely, and so do readers' expectations for its design. See **2** pp. 114–23 for the approaches you can take in different online writing situations.

3 Designing business documents and other public writing

When you write outside your college courses, your audience will have certain expectations for how your documents should look and read. Guidelines for such writing appear later in this book:

- **Public writing,** including letters, job applications, reports, proposals, flyers, newsletters, brochures (**2** pp. 127–38).
- **Oral presentations,** including *PowerPoint* slides and other visual aids (**2** pp. 123–27).

7b Considering principles of design

Most of the principles of design respond to the ways we read. White space, for instance, relieves our eyes and helps to lead us through a document. Groupings or lists help to show relationships. Type sizes, images, and color add variety and help to emphasize important elements.

The sample documents shown on pp. 56–57 illustrate quite different ways of presenting a report for a marketing course. Even at a glance, the second document is easier to scan and read. It makes better use of white space, groups similar elements, uses bullets and fonts for emphasis, and more successfully integrates the visual data of the chart.

As you design your own documents, think about your purpose, the expectations of your readers, and how readers will move through your document. Also consider the following general principles, noting that they overlap and support one another:

- **Conduct readers through the document.** Establish **flow,** a pattern for the eye to follow, with headings, lists, and other elements.
- **Use white space to ease crowding and focus readers' attention.** Provide ample margins, and give breathing room to headings, lists, and other elements. Even the space indicating new

paragraphs (indentions or blank lines) gives readers a break and reassures them that ideas are divided into manageable chunks.

- **Group information to show relationships.** Use headings (like those in this chapter) and lists (like the one you're reading) to convey the similarities and differences among parts of a document.

- **Emphasize important elements.** Establish hierarchies of information with type fonts and sizes, headings, indentions, color, boxes, and white space. In this book, for example, the importance of headings is clear from their size and color and from the presence of decorative elements, such as the boxes around 7c and the heading below.

- **Standardize to create and fulfill expectations.** Help direct readers through a document by, for instance, using the same size and color for all headings at the same level of importance. Standardizing also reduces clutter, making it easier for readers to determine the significance of the parts.

7c Using the elements of design

Applying the preceding principles involves margins, text, lists, headings, color, and illustrations. You won't use all these elements for every project, and in many writing situations you will be required to follow a prescribed format (see pp. 53–54 on formats in academic writing). If you are addressing readers who have vision disabilities, consider the additional guidelines discussed on pp. 65–66.

Note Your word processor may provide wizards or templates for many kinds of documents, such as letters, memos, reports, agendas, résumés, and brochures. **Wizards** guide you through setting up and writing complicated documents. **Templates** are preset forms to which you add your own text, headings, and other elements. Wizards and templates can be helpful, but not if they lead you to create cookie-cutter documents no matter what the writing situation. Always keep in mind that a document should be appropriate for your subject, audience, and purpose.

1 Setting margins

Margins at the top, bottom, and sides of a page help to prevent the page from overwhelming readers with unpleasant crowding. Most academic and business documents use a minimum one-inch margin on all sides. Publicity documents, such as flyers and brochures, often use narrower margins, compensating with white space between elements. (See 2 pp. 137–38.)

Original design

Runs title and subtitle together. Does not distinguish title from text.

Crowds the page with minimal margins.

Downplays paragraph breaks with small indentions.

Buries statistics in a paragraph. Obscures relationships with non-parallel wording.

Does not introduce the figure, leaving readers to infer its meaning and purpose.

Overemphasizes the figure with large size and excessive white space.

Presents the figure un-dynamically, flat on.

Does not caption the figure to explain what it shows, offering only a figure number and a partial text explanation.

Ready or Not, Here They Come: College Students and the Internet

College life once meant classrooms of students listening to teachers or groups of students talking over lunch in the union. But the reality today is more complex: students interact with their peers and professors by computer as much as face to face. As these students graduate and enter the workforce, all of society will be affected by their experience.

According to the Pew Internet Research Center (2005), today's college students are practiced computer and Internet users. The Pew Center reports that 20 percent of students in college today started using computers between ages five and eight. By age eighteen all students were using computers. Almost all college students, 86 percent, rely on the Internet, with 66 percent of students using more than one e-mail address. Computer ownership among this group is also very high: 85 percent have purchased or have been given at least one computer.

Students are eager to tap into the Internet's benefits and convenience.

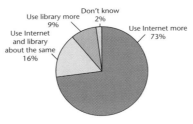

Figure 1

The Internet has eclipsed the library as the site of college students' research, as shown in Figure 1 from the Pew Report. In fact, a mere 9 percent of students

---

2 Creating readable text

A document must be readable. You can make text readable by attending to line spacing, type fonts and sizes, highlighting, word spacing, and line breaks.

■ Line spacing

Most academic documents are double-spaced, with an initial indention for paragraphs, while most business documents are single-spaced, with an extra line of space between paragraphs. Double or triple spacing sets off headings in both types. Web sites and publicity documents, such as flyers and brochures, tend to use more line spacing to separate and group distinct parts of the content.

Revised design

<table>
<tr><td>

Ready or Not, Here They Come
College Students and the Internet

College life once meant classrooms of students listening to teachers or groups of students talking over lunch in the union. But the reality today is more complex: students interact with their peers and professors by computer as much as face to face. As these students graduate and enter the workforce, all of society will be affected by their experience.

According to the Pew Internet Research Center (2005), today's college students are practiced computer users and Internet users.

- They started young: 20 percent were using computers between ages five and eight, and all were using them by age eighteen.
- They rely on the Internet: 86 percent have used the network, and 66 percent use more than one e-mail address.
- They own computers: 85 percent have purchased or have been given at least one computer.

Students are eager to tap into the Internet's benefits and convenience. Figure 1, from the Pew Report, shows that the Internet has eclipsed the library as the site of college students' research.

□16% ▣9% □2% ▣73% ■ Use Internet more
□ Use Internet and library about the same
□ Use library more
□ Don't know

Figure 1. College students' use of the Internet and the library for research

</td><td>

Distinguishes title from subtitle and both from text.

Provides adequate margins.

Emphasizes paragraph breaks with white space.

Groups statistics in a bulleted list set off with white space. Uses parallel wording for parallel information.

Introduces the figure to indicate its meaning and purpose.

Reduces white space around the figure.

Presents the figure to emphasize the most significant segment.

Captions the figure so that it can be read independently from the text.

</td></tr>
</table>

▦ Type fonts and sizes

The readability of text also derives from the type fonts (or faces) and their sizes. For academic and business documents, generally choose a type size of 10 or 12 points, as in these samples:

`10-point Courier`   10-point Times New Roman
`12-point Courier`   **12-point Times New Roman**

These fonts and the one you're reading have **serifs**—the small lines that finish the letters. Serif fonts are suitable for formal writing and are often easier to read on paper. **Sans serif** fonts (*sans* means "without" in French) include this one found on many word processors:

10-point Arial   12-point Arial

Sans serif fonts can be easier to read on a computer screen and are clearer on paper for readers with some vision disabilities (see p. 65). Your word processor probably offers many decorative fonts:

10-point Bodega Sans   10-POINT COMIC
10-POINT STENCIL   *10-point Park Avenue*

Decorative fonts are generally inappropriate for academic and business writing, where letter forms should be conventional and regular. But on some Web sites and in publicity documents, decorative fonts can attract attention, create motion, and reinforce a theme.

Note The point size of a type font is often an unreliable guide to its actual size, as the decorative fonts above illustrate. Before you use a font, print out a sample to be sure it is the size you want.

■ Highlighting

Within a document's text, <u>underlined</u>, *italic*, **boldface**, or even color type can emphasize key words or sentences. Underlining is rarest these days, although it remains called for in MLA style. (See **MLA** p. 468.) Both academic and business writing sometimes use boldface to give strong emphasis—for instance, to a term being defined—and publicity documents often rely extensively on boldface to draw the reader's eye. Neither academic nor business writing generally uses color within passages of text. In Web and publicity documents, however, color may be effective if the color is dark enough to be readable. (See p. 60 for more on color in document design.)

No matter what your writing situation, use highlighting selectively to complement your meaning, not merely for decoration.

■ Word spacing

In most writing situations, follow these guidelines for spacing within and between words:

- **Leave one space between words.**
- **Leave one space after all punctuation, with these exceptions:**

Dash (two hyphens or the so-called em dash on a computer)	book--its	book—its
Hyphen	one-half	
Apostrophe within a word	book's	
Two or more adjacent marks	book.")	
Opening quotation mark, parenthesis, or bracket	("book	[book

- **Leave one space before and after an ellipsis mark.** In the examples below, ellipsis marks indicate omissions within a sentence and at the end of a sentence. See **5** pp. 339–40 for additional examples.

book . . . in   book. . . . The

■ **Line breaks**

Your word processor will generally insert appropriate breaks between lines of continuous text: it will not, for instance, automatically begin a line with a comma or period, and it will not end a line with an opening parenthesis or bracket. However, you will have to prevent it from breaking a two-hyphen dash or a three-dot ellipsis mark by spacing to push the beginning of each mark to the next line.

When you instruct it to do so (usually under the Tools menu), your word processor will also automatically hyphenate words to prevent very short lines. If you must decide yourself where to break words, see **6** pp. 352–53.

3 Using lists

Lists give visual reinforcement to the relations between like items—for example, the steps in a process or the elements of a proposal. A list is easier to read than a paragraph and adds white space to the page.

When wording a list, work for parallelism among items—for instance, all complete sentences or all phrases (see also **3** pp. 154–55). Set the list with space above and below and with numbering or bullets (centered dots or other devices, used in the list below about headings). On most word processors you can format a numbered or bulleted list automatically using the Format menu.

4 Using headings

Headings are signposts: they direct the reader's attention by focusing the eye on a document's most significant content. Most Web and publicity documents use headings both decoratively and functionally, to capture and then direct readers' attention. In contrast, most academic and business documents use headings only functionally, to divide text, orient readers, and create emphasis.

When you use headings in academic and business documents, follow these guidelines:

■ **Use one, two, or three levels of headings** depending on the needs of your material and the length of your document. Some level of heading every two or so pages will help keep readers on track.
■ **Create an outline of your document** to plan where headings should go. Use the first level of heading for the main points (and sections) of your document. Use a second and perhaps a third level of heading to mark subsections of supporting information.
■ **Keep headings as short as possible** while making them specific about the material that follows.

- **Word headings consistently**—for instance, all questions (*What Is the Scientific Method?*), all phrases with *-ing* words (*Understanding the Scientific Method*), or all phrases with nouns (*The Scientific Method*).
- **Indicate the relative importance of headings** with type size, positioning, and highlighting, such as capital letters, underlining, or boldface.

First-Level Heading

Second-Level Heading

Third-Level Heading

Generally, you can use the same type font and size for headings as for the text.

- **Don't break a page immediately after a heading.** Push the heading to the next page.

Note Document format in psychology and some other social sciences requires a particular treatment of headings. See **APA** pp. 523–26.

5 Using color

With a color printer, many word processors and most desktop publishers can produce documents that use color for bullets, headings, borders, boxes, illustrations, and other elements. Web and publicity documents almost always use color, whereas academic and business documents consisting only of text and headings may not need color. (Ask your instructor or supervisor for his or her preferences.) If you do use color, follow these guidelines:

- **Employ color to clarify and highlight your content.** Too much color or too many colors on a page will distract rather than focus readers' attention.
- **Make sure that color type is readable.** For text, where type is likely to be relatively small, use only dark colors. For headings, lighter colors may be readable if the type is large and boldfaced.
- **Stick to the same color for all headings at the same level**—for instance, red for main headings, black for secondary headings.
- **Use color for bullets, lines, and other nontext elements.** But use no more than a few colors to keep pages clean.
- **Use color to distinguish the parts of illustrations**—the segments of charts, the lines of graphs, and the parts of diagrams. Use only as many colors as you need to make your illustration clear.

See also p. 66 on the use of color for readers who have vision disabilities.

7d   Using illustrations

Illustrations can often make a point for you more efficiently than words can. Tables present data. Figures (such as graphs and charts) usually recast data in visual form. Diagrams, drawings, photographs, and clip art can explain processes, represent what something looks like, add emphasis, or convey a theme.

1   Using illustrations appropriately for the writing situation

Academic and many business documents tend to use illustrations differently from publicity documents. In the latter, illustrations generally attract attention, enliven the piece, or emphasize a point, and they may not be linked directly to the document's text. In academic and business writing, however, illustrations directly reinforce and amplify the text. Follow these guidelines for academic and most business writing:

- **Focus on a purpose for your illustration**—a reason for including it and a point you want it to make. Otherwise, readers may find it irrelevant or confusing.
- **Provide a source note for someone else's independent material**—whether data or an entire illustration (see 7 p. 396). Each discipline has a slightly different style for such source notes: those in the illustrations on the next several pages reflect MLA style for English and some other humanities.
- **Number figures, photographs, and other images together:** Figure 1, Figure 2, and so on.
- **Number and label tables separately:** Table 1, Table 2, and so on.
- **Refer to each illustration in your text**—for instance, "See fig. 2." Place the text reference at the point(s) in the text where readers will benefit by consulting the illustration.
- **Determine the placement of illustrations.** The social sciences and some other disciplines require each illustration to fall on a page by itself immediately after the text reference to it (see **APA** pp. 525–26). You may want to follow this rule in other situations as well if you have a large number of illustrations. Otherwise, you can place them on your text pages just after their references.

2   Using tables

Tables usually present raw data, making complex information accessible to readers. The data may show how variables relate to one another, how two or more groups contrast, or how variables change over time. The following table emphasizes the last two functions.

Table

A self-explanatory title falls above the table.

Table 1

Percentage of Young Adults Living at Home, 1960-2000

Self-explanatory head-ings label horizontal rows and vertical columns.

The layout of rows and columns is clear: head-ings align with their data, and numbers align vertically down columns.

	1960	1970	1980	1990	2000
Males					
Age 18-24	52	54	54	58	57
Age 25-34	9	9	10	15	13
Females					
Age 18-24	35	41	43	48	47
Age 25-34	7	7	7	8	8

Source: Data from United States, Dept. of Commerce, Census Bureau, Census 2000 Summary Tables, 1 July 2002 <http:www.census.gov/servlet/QTTTable?_ts=30543101060>.

3 Using figures

Figures represent data or show concepts visually. They include charts, graphs, and diagrams.

■ Pie charts

Pie charts show the relations among the parts of a whole. The whole totals 100 percent, and each pie slice is proportional in size to its share of the whole. Use a pie chart when shares, not the underlying data, are your focus.

Pie chart

Color distinguishes seg-ments of the chart. Use dis-tinct shades of gray, black, and white if your paper will not be read in color.

Segment percentages total 100.

Every segment is clearly labeled. You can also use a key, as in the chart on p. 57.

Self-explanatory caption falls below the chart.

Married (59.5%)   Never married (23.9%)   Divorced (9.9%)   Widowed (6.7%)

Fig. 1. Marital status in 2004 of adults aged eighteen and over. Data from United States, Dept. of Commerce, Census Bureau, Statistical Abstract of the United States, 2004-05 (Washing-ton, GPO, 2005) no. 30.

■ Bar charts

Bar charts compare groups or time periods on a measure such as quantity or frequency. Use a bar chart when relative size is your focus.

Bar chart

Vertical scale shows and clearly labels the values being measured. Zero point clarifies values.

Horizontal scale shows and clearly labels the groups being compared.

Fig. 2. Lifetime prevalence of use of alcohol, compared with other drugs, among twelfth graders in 2004. Data from Monitoring the Future: A Continuing Study of American Youth, U of Michigan, 12 May 2005, 10 Oct. 2005 <http://www.monitoringthefuture.org/data/data.html>.

Self-explanatory caption falls below the chart.

■ Line graphs

Line graphs show change over time in one or more subjects. They are an economical and highly visual way to compare many points of data.

Line graph

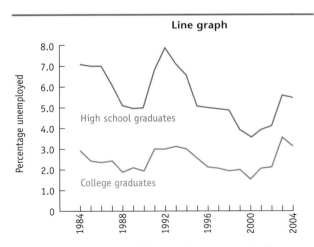

Vertical scale shows and clearly labels the values being measured. Zero point clarifies values.

Color and labels distinguish the subjects being compared. Use dotted and dashed black lines if your paper will not be read in color.

Horizontal scale shows and clearly labels the range of dates.

Fig. 3. Unemployent rates of high school graduates and college graduates, 1984-2004. Data from Antony Davies, The Economics of College Tuition, 3 Mar. 2005, 26 June 2005 <http:// www.mercatus.org/capitalhill/php?id=420>.

Self-explanatory caption falls below the graph.

■ Diagrams

Diagrams show concepts visually, such as the structure of an organization, the way something works or looks, or the relations among subjects. Often, diagrams show what can't be described economically in words.

Diagram

Diagram makes concept comprehensible.

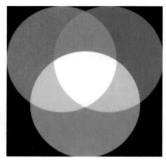

Self-explanatory caption falls below the diagram.

Fig. 4. RGB color theory, applied to televisions and computer monitors, in which all possible colors and white are created from red, green, and blue. From "Color Theory," Wikipedia, 16 July 2005, 2 Aug. 2005 <http://en.wikipedia.org/wiki/Color_theory>.

■ Photographs and other images

Sometimes you may focus an entire paper on an image such as a photograph, painting, or advertisement. But most commonly you'll use images to add substance to ideas or to enliven them. You might clarify a psychology paper with a photograph from a key experiment, add information to an analysis of a novel with a drawing of the author, or capture the theme of a brochure with a cartoon. Images grab readers' attention, so use them carefully to explain, reinforce, or enhance your writing.

One kind of image rarely appears in academic writing: **clip art,** or decorative icons and drawings that may reinforce a theme but do not add substance. Many word processors provide files of clip art, and they are also available from CD-ROMs and Web sites. (Those below come from *Barry's Clipart Server* at *http://www.barrysclipart*

Clip art

Photograph

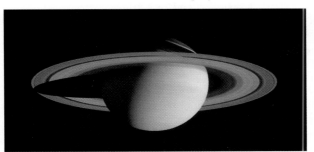

Photograph shows subject more economically and dramatically than words could.

Fig. 5. View of Saturn from the Cassini spacecraft, showing the planet and its rings. From United States, National Atmospheric and Space Administration, Jet Propulsion Laboratory, Cassini-Huygens: Mission to Saturn and Titan, 24 Feb. 2005, 26 Apr. 2005 <http://saturn.jpl.nasa.gov/multimedia/images/image-details.cfm?imageID=1398>.

Self-explanatory caption falls below the image.

.com/index.php.) Be selective in using clip art, even in publicity documents where decoration may be appropriate. The art should be relevant to your theme and content, directing readers' attention to elements you want to stress.

Note When using an image prepared by someone else—for instance, a photograph or an item of clip art downloaded from the Web—you must verify that the source permits reproduction of the image before you use it. In most documents but especially academic papers, you must also fully cite the source of any borrowed image. See 7 pp. 424–25 on copyright issues with Internet sources.

7e Considering readers with disabilities

Your audience may include readers who have low vision, problems with color perception, or difficulties processing visual information. If so, consider adapting your design to meet these readers' needs. Here are a few pointers:

- **Use large type fonts.** Most guidelines call for 14 points or larger.
- **Use standard type fonts.** Many people with low vision find it easier to read sans serif fonts such as Arial than serif fonts (see pp. 57–58). Avoid decorative fonts with unusual flourishes, even in headings.
- **Avoid words in all-capital letters.**

- **Avoid relying on color alone to distinguish elements.** Label elements, and distinguish them by position or size.
- **Use red and green selectively.** To readers who are red-green colorblind, these colors will appear in shades of gray, yellow, or blue.
- **Use contrasting colors.** To make colors distinct, choose them from opposite sides of the color spectrum—violet and yellow, for instance, or orange and blue.
- **Use only light colors for tints behind type.** Make the type itself black or a very dark color.

PART 2

Writing in and out of College

Writing in and out of College

8 Academic Writing

When you write in college, you work within a community of teachers and students who have specific aims and expectations. The basic aim of this community—whether in English, psychology, biology, or some other discipline—is to contribute to and build knowledge through questioning, research, and communication. The differences among disciplines lie mainly in the kinds of questions asked, the kinds of research done to find the answers, and the ways of communicating the answers.

Academic writers communicate using conventional forms, such as case studies, research reports, and reviews of others' writing on a particular subject. Both a discipline's concerns and the kind of writing create the writing situation, which in turn shapes a writer's choice of subject, conception of audience, definition of purpose, choice of structure and content, and even choice of language. This chapter introduces academic writing situations in general. See also **8** pp. 433–56 on the specific goals and expectations of the humanities, the social sciences, and the natural and applied sciences.

8a   Becoming an academic writer

As an academic writer, you participate in a discipline community first by studying a subject, acquiring its vocabulary, and learning to express yourself in its ways. As you gain experience and knowledge, you begin to contribute to the community by asking questions and communicating your answers. In any discipline, making the transition to academic writing will be easier if you practice the strategies outlined in the following box.

Tips for becoming an academic writer

- **Study the syllabus for each course.** This outline lays out the instructor's expectations as well as the course topics, assignments, and deadlines.
- **Do the assigned reading.** You'll gain experience with the discipline's terms and ideas, and you'll become familiar with the kinds of writing expected of you.

(continued)

http://www.ablongman.com/littlebrown ▶

Visit the companion Web site for more help with academic writing.

Tips for becoming an academic writer
(continued)

- **Attend and participate in class.** Make class attendance a priority, whether or not the instructor checks the roll. Listen carefully, take notes (see p. 76 for tips), ask questions, and join in discussions.
- **Ask questions.** Instructors, advisers, tutors, other students—all can help you.
- **Understand the writing situation posed by each assignment.** Knowing your audience, purpose, options for subjects, and other elements of the situation will help you meet the assignment's expectations. (See 1 p. 5 on analyzing assignments.)

8b Analyzing audience

Some of your writing assignments may specify an identifiable group of readers—for instance, fellow students, the city council, or the editors of a newspaper. Such readers' needs and expectations vary widely; the discussion in 1 pp. 6–7 can help you discover what they might be. Many assignments will specify or assume an educated audience or an academic audience. This more general group of readers looks for writing that is clear, balanced, well organized, and well reasoned, among other qualities discussed on the next page. Still other assignments will specify or assume an audience of experts on your subject, readers who look in addition for writing that meets the subject's requirements for claims and evidence, organization, language, format, and other qualities.

Of course, much of your academic writing will have only one reader besides you: the instructor of the course for which you are writing. Instructors fill two main roles as readers:

- **They represent the audience you are addressing.** They may actually be members of the audience, as when you address academic readers or subject experts. Or they may imagine themselves as members of your audience—reading, for instance, as if they sat on the city council. In either case, they're interested in how effectively you write for the audience.
- **They serve as coaches,** guiding you toward achieving the goals of the course and, more broadly, toward the academic aims of building and communicating knowledge.

Like everyone else, instructors have preferences and peeves, but you'll waste time and energy trying to anticipate them. Do attend to written and spoken directions for assignments, of course. But otherwise view your instructors as representatives of the community you are writing for. Their responses will be guided by the community's aims and expectations and by a desire to teach you about them.

8c Determining purpose

For most academic writing, your general purpose will be mainly explanatory or mainly argumentative. That is, you will aim to clarify your subject so that readers understand it as you do, or you will aim to gain readers' agreement with a debatable idea about the subject. (See 1 p. 6 for more on general purposes and pp. 95–114 for more on argument.)

Your specific purpose—including your subject and how you hope readers will respond—depends on the kind of writing you're doing. In a biology lab report, for instance, you want your readers to understand why you conducted your study, how you conducted it, what the results were, and what their significance is. Not coincidentally, these topics correspond to the major sections of a biology lab report. In following the standard format, you both help to define your purpose and begin to meet the discipline's (and thus your instructor's) expectations.

Your specific purpose will be more complex as well. You take a course to learn about a subject and the ways experts think about it. Your writing, in return, contributes to the discipline through the knowledge you uncover and the lens of your perspective. At the same time, as a student you want to demonstrate your competence with research, evidence, format, and other requirements of the discipline.

8d Choosing structure and content

Many academic writing assignments will at least imply how you should organize your paper and even how you should develop your ideas. Like the biology lab report mentioned above, the type of paper required will break into discrete parts, each with its own requirements for content.

No matter what type of paper an assignment specifies, the broad academic aims of building and exchanging knowledge determine features that are common across disciplines. Follow these general guidelines for your academic writing, supplementing them as indicated with others elsewhere in this book:

- **Develop a central idea or claim, called a** *thesis*. Everything in the paper should relate clearly to this claim. For more on theses, see 1 pp. 14–16.
- **State the thesis,** usually near the beginning of the paper.

- **Support the thesis with evidence,** drawn usually from research and sometimes from your own experience. The kinds of evidence will depend on the discipline you're writing in and the type of paper you're doing. For more on evidence in the disciplines, see **8** pp. 436–39 (literature), 444–45 (other humanities), 448 (social sciences), and 452–53 (natural and applied sciences).
- **Interact with sources.** Do not merely summarize sources but evaluate and synthesize them from your own perspective. For more on using sources, see **7** pp. 397–407.
- **Acknowledge sources fully,** using the documentation style appropriate to the discipline. For lists of disciplines' style guides, see **8** pp. 447, 451–52, and 456. For documentation guidelines and samples, see **MLA** pp. 460–95 (English and some other humanities), **APA** pp. 507–22 (social sciences), **CHIC** pp. 533–43 (history, philosophy, and other humanities), and **CSE** pp. 544–50 (natural and applied sciences).
- **Balance your presentation.** Discuss evidence and opposing views fairly, and take a serious and impartial approach.
- **Organize clearly within the framework of the type of writing you're doing.** Develop your ideas as simply and directly as your purpose and content allow. Clearly relate sentences, paragraphs, and sections so that readers always know where they are in the paper's development.

CULTURE LANGUAGE These features are far from universal. In other cultures, for instance, academic writers may be indirect or may not have to acknowledge well-known sources. Recognizing such differences between practices in your native culture and in the United States can help you adapt to US academic writing.

8e   Using academic language

American academic writing relies on a dialect called standard American English. The dialect is also used in business, the professions, government, the media, and other sites of social and economic power where people of diverse backgrounds must communicate with one another. It is "standard" not because it is better than other forms of English, but because it is accepted as the common language, much as the dollar bill is accepted as the common currency.

Standard American English varies a lot, from the formal English of a President's State of the Union address through the middle formality of this handbook to the informal chitchat between anchors on morning TV. Even in academic writing, standard American English allows much room for the writer's own tone and voice, as these passages on the same topic show:

More formal

Using the technique of "color engineering," manufacturers and advertisers can heighten the interest of consumers in a product by adding color that does not contribute to the utility of the product but appeals more to emotions. In one example from the 1920s, manufacturers of fountain pens, which had previously been made of hard black rubber, dramatically increased sales simply by producing the pens in bright colors.

| Two complicated sentences, one explaining the technique and one giving the example |
| Drawn-out phrasing, such as *interest of consumers* instead of *consumers' interest* |
| Formal vocabulary, such as *heighten, contribute,* and *utility* |

Less formal

A touch of "color engineering" can sharpen the emotional appeal of a product or its ad. New color can boost sales even when the color serves no use. In the 1920s, for example, fountain-pen makers introduced brightly colored pens along with the familiar ones of hard black rubber. Sales shot up.

| Four sentences, two each for explaining the technique and giving the example |
| More informal phrasing, such as *Sales shot up* |
| More informal vocabulary, such as *touch, boost,* and *ad* |

As different as they are, both examples illustrate several common features of academic language:

- **It follows the conventions of standard American English for grammar and usage.** These conventions are described in guides to the dialect, such as this handbook.
- **It uses a standard vocabulary,** not one that only some groups understand, such as slang, an ethnic or regional dialect, or another language. (See **3** pp. 160–62 for more on specialized vocabularies.)
- **It creates some distance between writer and reader with the third person (*he, she, it, they*).** The first person (*I, we*) is sometimes appropriate to express personal opinions or invite readers to think along, but not with a strongly explanatory purpose (*I discovered that "color engineering" can heighten . . .*). The second person (*you*) is appropriate only in addressing readers directly (as in this handbook), and even then it may seem condescending or too chummy (*You should know that "color engineering" can heighten . . .*).
- **It is authoritative and neutral.** In the preceding examples, the writers express themselves confidently, not timidly (as in *One possible example of color engineering that might be considered in this case is . . .*). They also refrain from hostility (*Advertisers will stop at nothing to achieve their goals*) and enthusiasm (*Color engineering is genius at work*).

At first, the diverse demands of academic writing may leave you groping for an appropriate voice. In an effort to sound fresh and confident, you may write too casually:

Too casual

"Color engineering" is a great way to get at consumers' feelings. . . .
When the guys jazzed up the color, sales shot through the roof.

In an effort to sound "academic," you may produce wordy and awkward sentences:

Wordy and awkward

The emotions of consumers can be made more engaged by the technique known as "color engineering." . . . A very large increase in the
sales of fountain pens was achieved by the manufacturers of the pens
as a result of this color enhancement technique. [The passive voice in
this example, such as *increase . . . was achieved* instead of *the manufacturers achieved,* adds to its wordiness and indirection. See **4** pp.
234–36 for more on voice.]

A cure for writing too informally or too stiffly is to read academic
writing so that the language and style become familiar and to edit
your writing (see **1** pp. 29–30).

■ CULTURE LANGUAGE ⟩ If your first language is not English or is an English dialect besides standard American, you know well the power of
communicating with others who share your language. Learning to
write standard American English in no way requires you to abandon
your first language. Like most multilingual people, you are probably
already adept at switching between languages as the situation demands—speaking one way with your relatives, say, and another way
with an employer. As you practice academic writing, you'll develop
the same flexibility with it.

EXERCISE 8.1   Using academic language

Revise the following paragraph to make the language more academic
while keeping the factual information the same. (You can do this exercise
online at *ablongman.com/littlebrown.*)

   If you buy into the stereotype of girls chatting away on their cell
phones, you should think again. One of the major wireless companies
surveyed 1021 cell phone owners for a period of five years and—
surprise!—reported that guys talk on cell phones more than girls do. In
fact, guys were way ahead of girls, using an average of 571 minutes a
month compared to 424 for girls. That's 35 percent more time on the
phone! The survey also asked about conversations on home phones, and
while girls still beat the field, the guys are catching up.

9   Study Skills

Academic success depends on active, involved learning. If you haven't already, read the previous chapter on academic writing. Apply the principles there with this chapter's practical tips for managing your time, getting the most from your classes and your reading, and preparing for exams.

9a   Managing your time

Planning and pacing your schoolwork and other activities will help you study more efficiently with less stress.

1   Scheduling your time

One way to organize your time is to use a calendar that divides each day into waking hours. Block out your activities that occur regularly and at specific times, such as commuting, attending classes, and working. Then fill in the other activities (such as exercise, eating, and studying) that do not necessarily occur at fixed times. Be sure to leave time for relaxing: an unrealistic schedule that assigns all available time to studying will quickly prove too difficult to live by.

2   Organizing your workload

Use the syllabuses for your courses to estimate the amount of weekly study time required for each course. Generally, plan on two hours of studying for each hour in class—that is, about six hours for a typical course. Block out study periods using these guidelines:

- **Schedule study time close to class time.** You'll study more productively if you review notes, read assigned material, or work on projects shortly after each class period.
- **Pace assignments.** Plan to start early and work regularly on projects requiring extensive time, such as research papers, so that you will not be overwhelmed near the deadline. (See **7** p. 372 for advice on scheduling research projects.)
- **Adjust the weekly plan as needed to accommodate changes in your workload.** Before each week begins, examine its schedule

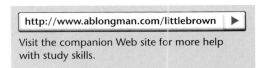

http://www.ablongman.com/littlebrown ▶

Visit the companion Web site for more help with study skills.

to be sure you've built in enough time to study for an exam, finish a paper, or meet other deadlines and commitments.

3   Making the most of study time

When you sit down to study, use your time efficiently:

- **Set realistic study goals.** Divide your study sessions into small chunks, each with a short-term goal, such as previewing a textbook chapter or drafting three paragraphs of a paper. Plan breaks, too, so that you can clear your mind, stretch, and refocus on your goals.
- **Tackle difficult homework first.** Resist any urge to put off demanding jobs, such as working on papers, reading textbooks, or doing math problems. Save easy tasks for when you're less alert.
- **Evaluate how you use your study time.** At the end of each week, ask yourself whether you were as productive as you needed to be. If not, what changes can you make to accomplish your goals for the coming week?

9b   Listening and taking notes in class

When you begin each class, push aside other concerns so that you can focus and listen. Either on paper or on a computer, record what you hear as completely as possible while sorting out the main ideas from the secondary and supporting ones. (See the box below.) Such active note taking will help you understand the instructor's approach to the course and provide you with complete material for later study.

Tips for taking class notes

- **Use your own words.** You will understand and retain the material better if you rephrase it. But use the speaker's words if necessary to catch everything.
- **Leave space in your notes if you miss something.** Ask someone for the missing information as soon as possible after the class.
- **Include any reading content mentioned by your instructor.** Use the notes to integrate all the components of the course—your instructor's views, your own thoughts, and the assigned reading, even if you've already read it.
- **Review your notes shortly after class.** Reinforce your new knowledge when it is fresh by underlining key words and ideas, adding headings and comments in the margins, converting your notes to questions, or outlining the lecture based on your notes.

9c Reading for comprehension

The assigned reading you do for college courses—such as text-books, journal articles, and works of literature—requires a greater focus on understanding and retention than does the reading you do for entertainment or for practical information. The process outlined below may seem time consuming, but with practice you'll become efficient at it.

Note The following process stresses ways of understanding what you read. In critical reading, covered in the next chapter, you extend this process to analyze and evaluate what you read and see.

1 Writing while reading

Reading for comprehension is an *active* process. Students often believe they are reading actively when they roll a highlighter over the important ideas in a text, but truly engaged reading requires more than that. If you take notes while reading, you "translate" the work into your own words and reconstruct it for yourself.

The substance of your reading notes will change as you preview, read, and summarize. At first, you may jot quick, short notes in the margins, on separate pages, or on a computer. (Use the last two for material you don't own or are reading online.) As you delve into the work, the notes should become more detailed, restating important points, asking questions, connecting ideas. (See pp. 85–86 for an example of a text annotated in this way by a student.) For some reading, you may want to keep a reading journal that records both what the work says and what you think about it.

2 Previewing

For most course reading, you should **skim** before reading word for word. Skimming gives you an overview of the material: its length and difficulty, organization, and principal ideas.

- **Gauge length and level.** Is the material brief and straightforward enough to read in one sitting, or do you need more time?
- **Examine the title and introduction.** The title and first couple of paragraphs will give you a sense of the topic, the author's approach, and the main ideas. As you read them, ask yourself what you already know about the subject so that you can integrate new information with old.
- **Move from heading to heading.** Viewing the headings as headlines or as the levels of an outline will give you a feeling for which ideas the author sees as primary and which subordinate.
- **Note highlighted words.** You will likely need to learn the meanings of terms in **bold**, *italic*, or color.

- **Slow down for pictures, diagrams, tables, graphs, and other illustrations.** They often contain concentrated information.
- **Read the summary or conclusion.** These paragraphs often recap the main ideas.
- **Think over what you've skimmed.** Try to recall the central idea, or thesis, and the sequence of ideas.

3 Reading

After previewing a text, you can settle into it to learn what it has to say.

■ First reading

The first time through new material, read as steadily and smoothly as possible, trying to get the gist of what the author is saying.

- **Read in a place where you can concentrate.** Choose a quiet environment away from distractions such as music or talking.
- **Give yourself time.** Rushing yourself or worrying about something else you have to do will prevent you from grasping what you read.
- **Try to enjoy the work.** Seek connections between it and what you already know. Appreciate new information, interesting relationships, forceful writing, humor, good examples.
- **Make notes sparingly during this first reading.** Mark major stumbling blocks—such as a paragraph you don't understand—so that you can try to resolve them before rereading.

CULTURE LANGUAGE If English is not your first language and you come across unfamiliar words, don't stop and look up every one. You will lose more in concentration than you will gain in understanding. Instead, try to guess the meanings of unfamiliar words from their contexts, circle them, and look them up later.

■ Rereading

After the first reading, plan on at least one other. This time read *slowly*. Your main concern should be to grasp the content and how it is constructed. That means rereading a paragraph if you didn't get the point or using a dictionary to look up words you don't know.

Use your pen, pencil, or keyboard freely to highlight and distill the text:

- **Distinguish main ideas from supporting ideas.** Look for the central idea, or thesis, for the main idea of each paragraph or section, and for the evidence supporting ideas.
- **Learn key terms.** Understand both their meanings and their applications.

- **Discern the connections among ideas.** Be sure you see why the author moves from point A to point B to point C and how those points relate to support the central idea. It often helps to outline the text or summarize it (see below).

- **Add your own comments.** In the margins or separately, note links to other readings or to class discussions, questions to explore further, possible topics for your writing, points you find especially strong or weak. (This last category will occupy much of your time when you are expected to read critically. See pp. 82–89.)

4 Summarizing

A good way to master the content of a text is to **summarize** it: reduce it to its main points, in your own words.

Writing a summary

- **Understand the meaning.** Look up words or concepts you don't know so that you understand the author's sentences and how they relate to one another.
- **Understand the organization.** Work through the text to identify its sections—single paragraphs or groups of paragraphs focused on a single topic. To understand how parts of a work relate to one another, try drawing a tree diagram or creating an outline (1 pp. 19–20).
- **Distill each section.** Write a one- or two-sentence summary of each section you identify. Focus on the main point of the section, omitting examples, facts, and other supporting evidence.
- **State the main idea.** Write a sentence or two capturing the author's central idea.
- **Support the main idea.** Write a full paragraph (or more, if needed) that begins with the central idea and supports it with the sentences that summarize sections of the work. The paragraph should concisely and accurately state the thrust of the entire work.
- *Use your own words.* By writing, you re-create the meaning of the work in a way that makes sense for you.

Summarizing even a passage of text can be tricky. Below is one attempt to summarize the following material from an introductory biology textbook.

Original text

As astronomers study newly discovered planets orbiting distant stars, they hope to find evidence of water on these far-off celestial bodies, for water is the substance that makes possible life as we know it here on Earth. All organisms familiar to us are made mostly of water and live in an environment dominated by water. They require water more than any other substance. Human beings, for example, can survive for quite a few weeks without food, but only a week or so without water. Molecules of water participate in many chemical reactions necessary to sustain life. Most cells are surrounded by water, and cells themselves are about 70–95% water. Three-quarters of Earth's surface is submerged in water. Although most of this water is in liquid form, water is also present on Earth as ice and vapor. Water is the only common substance to exist in the natural environment in all three physical states of matter: solid, liquid, and gas.

—Neil A. Campbell and Jane B. Reece, *Biology*

Draft summary

Astronomers look for water in outer space because life depends on it. It is the most common substance on Earth and in living cells, and it can be a liquid, a solid (ice), or a gas (vapor).

This summary accurately restates ideas in the original, but it does not pare the passage to its essence. The work of astronomers and the three physical states of water add color and texture to the original, but they are asides to the key concept that water sustains life because of its role in life. The following revision narrows the summary to this concept:

Revised summary

Water is the most essential support for life, the dominant substance on Earth and in living cells and a component of life-sustaining chemical processes.

Note Do not count on the AutoSummarize function on your word processor for summarizing texts that you may have copied onto your computer. The summaries are rarely accurate, and you will not gain the experience of interacting with the texts on your own.

9d   Preparing for exams

Studying for an exam involves three main steps, each requiring about a third of the preparation time: reviewing the material, organizing summaries of the material, and testing yourself. Your main goals are to strengthen your understanding of the subject, making both its ideas and its details more memorable, and to increase the flexibility of your new knowledge so that you can apply it in new contexts.

Note Cramming for an exam is about the least effective way of preparing for one. It takes longer to learn under stress, and the learning is shallower, more difficult to apply, and more quickly forgotten. Information learned under stress is even harder to apply in stressful situations, such as taking an exam. And the lack of sleep that usually accompanies cramming makes a good performance even more unlikely. If you must cram for a test, face the fact that you can't learn everything. Spend your time reviewing main concepts and facts.

1 Reviewing and memorizing the material

Divide your class notes and reading assignments into manageable units. Reread the material, recite or write out the main ideas and selected supporting ideas and examples, and then skim for an overview. Proceed in this way through all the units of the course, returning to earlier ones as needed to refresh your memory or to relate ideas.

During this stage you should be memorizing what you don't already know by heart. Try these strategies for strengthening your memory:

- **Link new and known information.** For instance, to remember a sequence of four dates in twentieth-century African history, link the dates to simultaneous and more familiar events in the United States.
- **Create groups of ideas or facts that make sense to you.** For instance, memorize French vocabulary words in related groups, such as words for parts of the body or parts of a house. Keep the groups small: research has shown that we can easily memorize about seven items at a time but have trouble with more.
- **Create narratives and visual images.** You may recall a story or a picture more easily than words. For instance, to remember how the economic laws of supply and demand affect the market for rental housing, you could tie the principles to a narrative about the aftermath of the 1906 San Francisco earthquake, when half the population was suddenly homeless. Or you could visualize a person who has dollar signs for eyes and is converting a spare room into a high-priced rental unit, as many did after the earthquake to meet the new demand for housing.
- **Use *mnemonic devices*, or tricks for remembering.** Say the history dates you want to remember are separated by five years, then four, then nine. By memorizing the first date and recalling 5 + 4 = 9, you'll have command of all four dates.

2 Organizing summaries of the material

Allow time to reorganize the material in your own way, creating categories that will help you apply the information in various contexts. For instance, in studying for a biology exam, work to understand a process, such as how a plant develops or how photosynthesis occurs. Or in studying for an American government test, explain the structures of the local, state, and federal levels of government. Other useful categories include advantages/disadvantages and causes/effects. Such analytical thinking will improve your mastery of the course material and may even prepare you directly for specific essay questions.

3 Testing yourself

Convert each heading in your lecture notes and course reading into a question. Answer in writing, going back to the course material to fill in what you don't yet know. Be sure you can define and explain all key terms. For subjects that require solving problems (such as mathematics, statistics, or physics), work out a difficult problem for every type on which you will be tested. For all subjects, focus on the main themes and questions of the course. In a psychology course, for example, be certain you understand principal theories and their implications. In a literature course, test your knowledge of literary movements and genres or the relations among specific works.

When you are satisfied with your preparation, stop studying and get a good night's sleep.

10 Critical Thinking and Reading

Throughout college and beyond, you will be expected to think, read, and write critically. **Critical** here does not mean "negative" but "skeptical," "exacting," "creative." You already operate critically every day as you figure out why things happen to you or what your experiences mean. This chapter introduces more formal methods for reading texts critically (below) and viewing images critically (p. 89).

Note Critical thinking plays a large role in research writing. See **7** pp. 397–405 on evaluating print and online sources and **7** pp. 406–07 on synthesizing sources.

10a Reading texts critically

In college and work, much of your critical thinking will focus on written texts (a short story, a journal article, a Web log) or on visual objects (a photograph, a chart, a film). Like all subjects worthy of critical consideration, such works operate on at least three levels: (1) what the creator actually says or shows, (2) what the creator does not say or show but builds into the work (intentionally or not),

http://www.ablongman.com/littlebrown ▶

Visit the companion Web site for more help and an electronic exercise on critical thinking and reading.

and (3) what you think. Discovering the first of these levels—reading for comprehension—is discussed in the preceding chapter as part of study skills (see pp. 77–80). This chapter builds on the earlier material to help you discover the other two levels.

CULTURE LANGUAGE The idea of reading critically may require you to make some adjustments if readers in your native culture tend to seek understanding or agreement more than engagement from what they read. Readers of English use texts for all kinds of reasons, including pleasure, reinforcement, and information. But they also read skeptically, critically, to see the author's motives, test their own ideas, and arrive at new knowledge.

1 **Previewing the material**

When you're reading a work of literature, such as a short story or a poem, it's often best just to plunge right in. But for critical reading of other works, it's worthwhile to skim before reading word for word, forming expectations and even some preliminary questions. The preview will make your reading more informed and fruitful.

- **What is the work's subject and structure?** Following the steps outlined on pp. 77–78, gauge the length and level, read the title and introduction for clues to the topic and main ideas, read the headings, note highlighted words (defined terms), examine illustrations, and read the summary or conclusion.

- **What are the facts of publication?** Does the date of publication suggest currency or datedness? Does the publisher or publication specialize in a particular kind of material—scholarly articles, say, or popular books? For a Web document, who or what sponsors the site: an individual? a nonprofit organization? an academic institution? a corporation? a government body?

- **What do you know about the author?** Does a biography tell you about the author's publications, interests, biases, and reputation in the field? For an online source, which may be posted by an unfamiliar or anonymous author, what can you gather about the author from his or her words? If possible, trace unfamiliar authors to learn more about them.

- **What is your preliminary response?** What do you already know about the author's topic? What questions do you have about either the topic or the author's approach to it? What biases of your own might influence your reception of the work —for instance, curiosity, boredom, or an outlook similar or opposed to the author's?

Reprinted on the following pages is an essay by Thomas Sowell, an economist, newspaper columnist, and author of many books on economics, politics, and education. Preview the essay using the preceding guidelines, and then read it once or twice, until you think you understand what the author is saying. Note your questions and reactions in writing.

Student Loans

The first lesson of economics is scarcity: There is never enough of anything to fully satisfy all those who want it. 1

The first lesson of politics is to disregard the first lesson of economics. When politicians discover some group that is being vocal about not having as much as they want, the "solution" is to give them more. Where do politicians get this "more"? They rob Peter to pay Paul. 2

After a while, of course, they discover that Peter doesn't have enough. Bursting with compassion, politicians rush to the rescue. Needless to say, they do not admit that robbing Peter to pay Paul was a dumb idea in the first place. On the contrary, they now rob Tom, Dick, and Harry to help Peter. 3

The latest chapter in this long-running saga is that politicians have now suddenly discovered that many college students graduate heavily in debt. To politicians it follows, as the night follows the day, that the government should come to their rescue with the taxpayers' money. 4

How big is this crushing burden of college students' debt that we hear so much about from politicians and media deep thinkers? For those students who graduate from public colleges owing money, the debt averages a little under $7000. For those who graduate from private colleges owing money, the average debt is a little under $9000. 5

Buying a very modestly priced automobile involves more debt than that. And a car loan has to be paid off faster than the ten years that college graduates get to repay their student loans. Moreover, you have to keep buying cars every several years, while one college education lasts a lifetime. 6

College graduates of course earn higher incomes than other people. Why, then, should we panic at the thought that they have to repay loans for the education which gave them their opportunities? Even graduates with relatively modest incomes pay less than 10 percent of their annual salary on the first loan the first year—with declining percentages in future years, as their pay increases. 7

Political hysteria and media hype may focus on the low-income student with a huge debt. That is where you get your heart-rending stories—even if they are not all that typical. In reality, the soaring student loans of the past decade have resulted from allowing high-income people to borrow under government programs. 8

Before 1978, college loans were available through government programs only to students whose family income was below some cut-off level. That cut-off level was about double the national average income, but at least it kept out the Rockefellers and the Vanderbilts. But, in an era of "compassion," Congress took off even those limits. 9

That opened the floodgates. No matter how rich you were, it still paid to borrow money through the government at low interest rates. The money you had set aside for your children's education could be 10 invested somewhere else, at higher interest rates. Then, when the student loan became due, parents could pay it off with the money they had set aside—pocketing the difference in interest rates.

To politicians and the media, however, the rapidly growing loans 11 showed what a great "need" there was. The fact that many students welshed when time came to repay their loans showed how "crushing" their burden of debt must be. In reality, those who welsh typically have smaller loans, but have dropped out of college before finishing. People who are irresponsible in one way are often irresponsible in other ways.

No small amount of the deterioration of college standards has been 12 due to the increasingly easy availability of college to people who are not very serious about getting an education. College is not a bad place to hang out for a few years, if you have nothing better to do, and if someone else is paying for it. Its costs are staggering, but the taxpayers carry much of that burden, not only for state universities and city colleges, but also to an increasing extent even for "private" institutions.

Numerous government subsidies and loan programs make it possi- 13 ble for many people to use vast amounts of society's resources at low cost to themselves. Whether in money terms or in real terms, federal aid to higher education has increased several hundred percent since 1970. That has enabled colleges to raise their tuition by leaps and bounds and enabled professors to be paid more and more for doing less and less teaching.

Naturally all these beneficiaries are going to create hype and hyste- 14 ria to keep more of the taxpayers' money coming in. But we would be fools to keep on writing blank checks for them.

When you weigh the cost of things, in economics that's called 15 "trade-offs." In politics, it's called "mean-spirited." Apparently, if we just took a different attitude, scarcity would go away.

—Thomas Sowell

2 Reading

Reading is itself more than a one-step process. You want to understand the first level on which the text operates—what the author actually says—and begin to form your impressions.

A procedure for this stage appears in the preceding chapter (pp. 78–79). To recap: Read once through fairly smoothly, trying to appreciate the work and keeping notes to a minimum. Then read again more carefully, this time making detailed notes, to grasp the ideas and their connections and to pose questions. In the following example, a student, Charlene Robinson, annotates the first four paragraphs of "Student Loans":

The first lesson of economics is scarcity: There is never enough of anything to fully satisfy all those who want it.

The first lesson of politics is to disregard the first lesson of economics. When politicians discover some group that is being vocal about not

Basic contradiction between economics and politics

having as much as they want, the "solution" is to give them more. Where do politicians get this "more"? They rob Peter to pay Paul. After a while, of course, they discover that Peter doesn't have enough. Bursting with compassion, politicians rush to the rescue. Needless to say, they do not admit that robbing Peter to pay Paul was a dumb idea in the first place. On the contrary, they now rob Tom, Dick, and Harry to help Peter.

biblical
← reference?

ironic and
dismissive
language

The latest chapter in this long-running saga is that politicians have now suddenly discovered that many college students graduate heavily in debt. To politicians it follows, as the night follows the day, that the government should come to their rescue with the taxpayers' money.

politicians=fools?
or irresponsible?

3 Summarizing

Summarizing a text—distilling it to its essential ideas, in your own words—is an important step for comprehending it and is discussed in detail in the previous chapter (pp. 79–80). Here, we'll look at how Charlene Robinson summarized paragraphs 1–4 of Thomas Sowell's "Student Loans." She first drafted this sentence:

Draft summary

As much as politicians would like to satisfy voters by giving them everything they ask for, the government cannot afford a student loan program.

Reading the sentence and Sowell's paragraphs, Robinson saw that this draft misread the text by asserting that the government cannot afford student loans. She realized that Sowell's point is more complicated than that and rewrote her summary:

Revised summary

As their support of the government's student loan program illustrates, politicians ignore the economic reality that using resources to benefit one group (students in debt) involves taking the resources from another group (taxpayers).

Note Using your own words when writing a summary not only helps you understand the meaning but also constitutes the first step in avoiding plagiarism. The second step is to cite the source when you use it in something written for others. See **7** pp. 418–25.

4 Developing a critical response

Once you've grasped the content of what you're reading—what the author says—then you can turn to understanding what the author does not say outright but suggests or implies or even lets slip.

At this stage you are concerned with the purpose or intention of the author and with how he or she carries it out.

Critical thinking and reading consist of four overlapping operations: analyzing, interpreting, synthesizing, and (often) evaluating.

Analyzing

Analysis is the separation of something into its parts or elements, the better to understand it. To see these elements in what you are reading, begin with a question that reflects your purpose in analyzing the text: why you're curious about it or what you're trying to make out of it. This question will serve as a kind of lens that highlights some features and not others.

Analyzing Thomas Sowell's "Student Loans" (pp. 84–85), you might ask one of these questions:

Questions for analysis	Elements
What is Sowell's attitude toward politicians?	References to politicians: content, words, tone
How does Sowell support his assertions about the loan program's costs?	Support: evidence, such as statistics and examples

Interpreting

Identifying the elements of something is of course only the beginning: you also need to interpret the meaning or significance of the elements and of the whole. Interpretation usually requires you to infer the author's **assumptions**—that is, opinions or beliefs about what is or what could or should be. (*Infer* means to draw a conclusion based on evidence.)

Assumptions are pervasive: we all adhere to certain values, beliefs, and opinions. But assumptions are not always stated outright. Speakers and writers may judge that their audience already understands and accepts their assumptions; they may not even be aware of their assumptions; or they may deliberately refrain from stating their assumptions for fear that the audience will disagree. That is why your job as a critical thinker is to interpret what the assumptions are.

Thomas Sowell's "Student Loans" is based on certain assumptions, some obvious, some not so obvious. If you were analyzing Sowell's attitude toward politicians, as suggested earlier, you would focus on his statements about them. Sowell says that they "disregard the first lesson of economics" (paragraph 2), which implies that they ignore important principles (knowing that Sowell is an economist himself makes this a reasonable assumption on your part). Sowell also says that politicians "rob Peter to pay Paul," are "[b]ursting with compassion," "do not admit . . . a dumb idea," are characters in a "long-running saga," and arrive at the solution of spending taxes "as the night follows the day"—that is, inevitably (paragraphs 2–4). From these statements and others, you can infer the following:

> Sowell assumes that politicians become compassionate when a cause is loud and popular, not necessarily just, and they act irresponsibly by trying to solve the problem with other people's (taxpayers') money.

Synthesizing

If you stopped at analysis and interpretation, critical thinking and reading might leave you with a pile of elements and possible meanings but no vision of the whole. With **synthesis** you make connections among parts *or* among wholes. You create a new whole by drawing conclusions about relationships and implications.

The statement below about Thomas Sowell's essay "Student Loans" connects his assumptions about politicians to a larger idea also implied by the essay:

> Sowell's view that politicians are irresponsible with taxpayers' money reflects his overall opinion that the laws of economics, not politics, should drive government.

Synthesis may involve working within the text, as in the preceding example, or it may take you outside the text to the surroundings. (This emphasis is important in research writing, as discussed in 7 pp. 406–07.) The following questions can help you investigate the context of a work:

- **How does the work compare with works by others?** For instance, how have other writers responded to Sowell's views on student loans?
- **How does the work fit into the context of other works by the same author or group?** How do Sowell's views on student loans typify, or not, the author's other writing on political and economic issues?
- **What cultural, economic, or political forces influence the work?** What other examples might Sowell have given to illustrate his view that economics, not politics, should determine government spending?
- **What historical forces influence the work?** How has the indebtedness of college students changed over the past four decades?

Evaluating

Critical reading and writing often end at synthesis: you form and explain your understanding of what the work says and doesn't say. If you are also expected to **evaluate** the work, however, you will go further to judge its quality and significance. You may be evaluating a source you've discovered in research (see 7 pp. 397–405), or you may be completing an assignment to state and defend a judgment, a statement such as *Thomas Sowell does not summon the evidence to support his case.* You can read Charlene Robinson's critical analysis of Thomas Sowell's "Student Loans" at *ablongman.com/littlebrown.*

Evaluation takes a certain amount of confidence. You may think that you lack the expertise to cast judgment on another's work, especially if the work is difficult or the author well known. True, the more informed you are, the better a critical reader you are. But conscientious reading and analysis will give you the internal authority to judge a work *as it stands* and *as it seems to you,* against your own unique bundle of experiences, observations, and attitudes.

10b Viewing images critically

Every day we are bombarded with images—pictures on billboards, commercials on television, graphs and charts in newspapers and textbooks, to name just a few examples. Most images slide by without our noticing them, or so we think. But images, sometimes even more than text, can influence us covertly. Their creators have purposes, some worthy, some not, and understanding those purposes requires critical reading. The method parallels that in the previous section for reading text critically: preview, read for comprehension, analyze, interpret, synthesize, and (often) evaluate.

1 Previewing an image

Your first step in exploring an image is to form initial impressions of the work's origin and purpose and to note distinctive features. This previewing process is like the one for previewing a text (p. 83):

- **What do you see?** What is most striking about the image? What is its subject? What is the gist of any text or symbols? What is the overall effect of the image?

- **What are the facts of publication?** Where did you first see the image? Do you think the image was created especially for that location or for others as well? What can you tell about when the image was created?

- **What do you know about the person or group that created the image?** For instance, was the creator an artist, scholar, news organization, or corporation? What seems to have been the creator's purpose?

- **What is your preliminary response?** What about the image interests, confuses, or disturbs you? Are the form, style, and subject familiar or unfamiliar? How might your knowledge, experiences, and values influence your reception of the image?

If possible, print a copy of the image or scan it into your reading journal, and write comments in the image margins or separately.

2 Reading an image

Reading an image requires the same level of concentration as reading a text. Try to answer the following questions about the image. If some answers aren't clear at this point, skip the question until later.

- **What is the purpose of the image?** Is it mainly explanatory, conveying information, or is it argumentative, trying to convince readers of something or persuade them to act? What information or point of view does it seem intended to get across?

- **Who is the intended audience for the image?** What does the source of the image, including its publication facts, tell about the image creator's expectations for readers' knowledge, interests, and attitudes? What do the features of the image itself add to your impression?

- **What do any words or symbols add to the image?** Whether located on the image or outside it (such as in a caption), do words or symbols add information, focus your attention, or alter your impression of the image?

- **What people, places, things, or action does the image show?** Does the image tell a story? Do its characters or other features tap into your knowledge, or are they unfamiliar?

- **What is the form of the image?** Is it a photograph, advertisement, painting, graph, diagram, cartoon, or something else? How do its content and apparent purpose and audience relate to its form?

The illustration on the facing page shows the notes that a student, John Latner, made on an advertisement for *Time* magazine.

3 Analyzing an image

■ Elements for analysis

As when analyzing a written work, you analyze an image by identifying its elements. The image elements you might consider appear in the box opposite and on p. 92. Keep in mind that an image is a visual *composition* whose every element likely reflects a deliberate effort to communicate. Still, few images include all the elements, and you can narrow the list further by posing a question about the image you are reading, as illustrated on pp. 92–93.

Annotation of an image

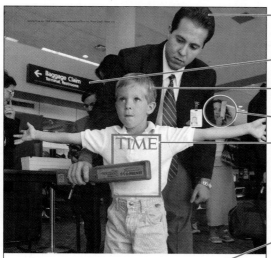

Agent checking boy's body (for weapons?)

Sign = airport security area

Blond kid in preppy clothes = typical American child?

What's she doing?

Red *Time* cover = target
Scanning wand = bull's-eye
Red with boy's clothes = USA

Clearly a story about US airport (+ homeland) security

Interesting question— Treating a boy as a security threat isn't common sense

Author and source both = *Time* mag. Why does *Time* promote itself to people who are already reading it?

At what point do national security and common sense collide?

Join the conversation.

Advertisement appearing in *Time* magazine, October 7, 2002

Elements of images

- **Emphasis:** Most images pull your eyes to certain features: a graph line moving sharply upward, a provocative figure, bright color, thick lines, and so on. The cropping of a photograph or the date range in a chart will also reflect what the image creator considers important.

- **Narration:** Most images tell stories, whether in a sequence (a TV commercial or a graph showing changes over time) or at a single moment (a photograph, a painting, or a pie chart). Sometimes dialog or a title or caption contributes to the story.

- **Point of view:** The image creator influences responses by taking account of both the viewer's physical relation to the image subject—for instance, whether it is seen head-on or from above—and the viewer's assumed attitude toward the subject.

- **Arrangement:** Patterns among colors or forms, figures in the foreground and background, and elements that are juxtaposed or set apart contribute to the image's meaning and effect.

(continued)

Elements of images
(continued)

- **Color:** An image's colors can direct the viewer's attention and convey the creator's attitude toward the subject. Color may also suggest a mood, an era, a cultural connection, or another frame for viewing the image.
- **Characterization:** The figures and objects in an image have certain qualities—sympathetic or not, desirable or not, and so on. Their characteristics reflect the roles they play in the image's story.
- **Context:** The source of an image or the background in an image affects its meaning, whether it is a graph from a scholarly journal or a photo of a car on a sunny beach.
- **Tension:** Images often communicate a problem or seize attention with features that seem wrong, such as misspelled or misaligned words, distorted figures, or controversial relations between characters.
- **Allusions:** An **allusion** is a reference to something the audience is likely to recognize and respond to. Examples include a cultural symbol such as a dollar sign, a mythological figure such as a unicorn, or a familiar movie character such as Darth Vader from *Star Wars*.

- **Question for analysis**

You can focus your analysis of elements by framing your main interest in the image as a question. John Latner posed this question about the *Time* advertisement: *Does the ad challenge readers to view airport security differently, or does it just reinforce common perceptions?* The question led Latner to focus on certain elements of the ad:

Image elements	Responses
Emphasis	The ad foregrounds the boy (especially his eyes looking upward), the security agent, and the *Time* cover over a scanner like a target and bull's-eye.
Point of view	We identify with the boy—so innocent and uncomfortable—and we're positioned at his eye level. The security agent almost hovers over us, too.
Narration	The collision point of the caption ("At what point do national security and common sense collide?") seems to be the bull's-eye—treating a boy as a security threat. The ad's commonsense opinion seems to be that airport security procedures are flawed, unfair. But the caption's question mark and "Join the conversation" imply that there may be other views, too.
Color	The boy is much the brightest figure in the image, and his brightness emphasizes his fairness. His clothes and the *Time* cover are patriotic colors.
Allusions	The familiar *Time* cover and the security checkpoint stand out. Also, is there Christian symbolism in the

boy's outstretched arms, open hands, and upward gaze—like Christ on the cross?

Characterization

The boy is the unlikely terrorist, maybe even a victim. He is the stereotyped all-American kid, blond, blue-eyed, wholesome. The security agent is the boy's "interrogator"—serious, dark, menacing.

Tension

The security agent hovering over the boy is disturbing. So are their actions and the busy scene behind them—bound to evoke a negative response from anyone who's experienced air travel in recent years.

■ **Sample image for analysis**

The following image gives you a chance to analyze elements of a Web page. Try to answer the questions in the annotations.

Elements of a Web page

Narration: What story is being told by the Web page as a whole and by the chart? Who is telling the story, and why?

Arrangement: How are the bars in the chart organized? What does their arrangement contribute to the story?

Point of view: What can you tell about the intended audience? What is the audience's interest in the story?

Context: How do the CNN source and the page's banner and titles affect the story being told by the chart?

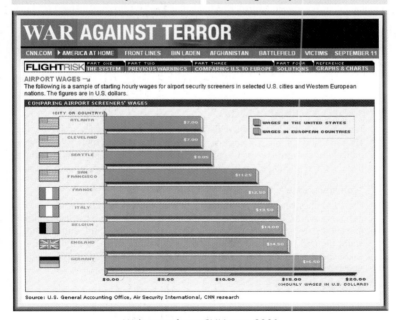

Web page from *CNN.com*, 2001

4 Interpreting an image

The strategies for interpreting an image parallel those for interpreting a written text (pp. 87–88). In this process you look more deeply at the elements, considering them in relation to the image creator's likely assumptions and intentions. You aim to draw reasonable inferences about *why* the image looks as it does, such as this inference about the *Time* advertisement on page 91:

> The creators of the *Time* ad assume that the magazine's readers are concerned about both national security and the treatment of air travelers.

This statement is supported by the ad's text and photograph: the caption specifically mentions national security, and the photograph clearly emphasizes the experience of air travelers.

5 Synthesizing ideas about an image

As discussed on p. 88, with synthesis you take analysis and interpretation a step further to consider how a work's elements and underlying assumptions relate and what the overall message is. You may also expand your synthesis to view the whole image in a larger context: How does the work fit into the context of other works? What cultural, economic, political, or historical forces influence the work?

Placing an image in its context often requires research. For instance, to learn more about the assumptions underlying the *Time* advertisement, John Latner investigated data on the backgrounds and perceptions of the magazine's readers. And to understand the marketing strategies at work in the image, he consulted a book on advertising campaigns that, like the *Time* ad, promote products to people who already use them. The following ideas resulted from his synthesis:

Social and political context
The visual emphasis on the boy plays to two views often held by travelers and Time's readers: airport searches needlessly inconvenience people who are very unlikely to be terrorists, and the better alternative may be profiling, treating people differently based on physical characteristics such as skin and hair color.

"Common sense"
The ad implies certain understandings of readers' "common sense" about national security and airport security: security is a serious issue, many airport procedures are unreasonably broad based and time consuming, and profiling might be used to focus on people who look like terrorists. The ad doesn't challenge these perceptions, but with "Join the conversation" it does suggest that the problem is open to interpretation.

Marketing context
The provocative photograph seems to promise an unconventional perspective on the subject, but the ad mostly reinforces the views assumed to be held by

readers. Time's strategy reflects marketing studies: people are more likely to purchase a product that reflects their own opinions and values, even when they're acquiring the product to broaden their understanding.

6 Evaluating an image

If your critical reading moves on to evaluation, you'll form judgments about the quality and significance of the image: Is the message of the image accurate and fair, or is it distorted and biased? Can you support, refute, or extend the message? Does the image achieve its apparent purpose, and is the purpose worthwhile? How does the image affect you?

You can read John Latner's evaluation of the *Time* advertisement at *ablongman.com/littlebrown*.

11 Argument

Argument is writing that attempts to solve a problem, open readers' minds to an opinion, change readers' own opinions, or move readers to action. Using a variety of techniques, you engage readers to find common ground and narrow the distance between your views and theirs.

CULTURE LANGUAGE The ways of conceiving and writing arguments described here may be initially uncomfortable to you if your native culture approaches such writing differently. In some cultures, for example, a writer is expected to begin indirectly, to avoid asserting his or her opinion outright, to rely for evidence on appeals to tradition, or to establish a compromise rather than argue a position. In American academic and business settings, writers aim for a well-articulated opinion, evidence gathered from many sources, and a direct and concise argument for the opinion.

11a Understanding and using the elements of argument

An argument has four main elements: subject, claims, evidence, and assumptions. (The last three are adapted from the work of the British philosopher Stephen Toulmin.)

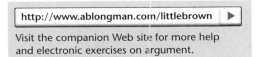

http://www.ablongman.com/littlebrown ▶

Visit the companion Web site for more help and electronic exercises on argument.

1 The subject

An argument starts with a subject and often with an opinion about the subject as well—that is, an idea that makes you want to write about the subject. (If you don't have a subject or you aren't sure what you think, see 1 pp. 8–13 for some invention techniques.) Your initial opinion should meet several requirements:

- **It can be disputed:** reasonable people can disagree over it.
- **It *will* be disputed:** it is controversial.
- **It is narrow enough to research and argue in the space and time available.**

On the flip side of these requirements are several kinds of statements or views that will not work as the starting place of argument: indisputable facts, such as the functions of the human liver; personal preferences or beliefs, such as a moral commitment to vegetarianism; and ideas that few would disagree with, such as the virtues of a secure home.

EXERCISE 11.1 Testing argument subjects

Analyze each subject below to determine whether it is appropriate for argument. Explain your reasoning in each case.

1 Granting of athletic scholarships
2 Care of automobile tires
3 Censoring the Web sites of hate groups
4 History of the town park
5 Housing for the homeless
6 Billboards in urban residential areas or in rural areas
7 Animal testing for cosmetics research
8 Cats versus dogs as pets
9 Ten steps in recycling wastepaper
10 Benefits of being a parent

---

2 Claims

Claims are statements that require support. In an argument you develop your subject into a central claim or **thesis,** asserted outright in a **thesis statement** (see 1 pp. 14–16). This central claim is what the argument is about.

A thesis statement is always an **opinion**—that is, a judgment based on facts and arguable on the basis of facts. It may be one of the following:

- **A claim about past or present reality:**

  In both its space and its equipment, the college's chemistry laboratory is outdated.

  Academic cheating increases with students' economic insecurity.

- **A claim of value:**

    The new room fees are unjustified given the condition of the dormitories.

    Computer music pirates undermine the system that encourages the very creation of music.

- **A recommendation for a course of action,** often a solution to a perceived problem:

    The college's outdated chemistry laboratory should be replaced incrementally over the next five years.

    Schools and businesses can help to resolve the region's traffic congestion by implementing car pools and rewarding participants.

The backbone of an argument consists of specific claims that support the thesis statement. These may also be statements of opinion, or they may fall in two other categories:

- **Statements of *fact*,** including facts that are generally known or are verifiable (such as the cost of tuition at your school) and those that require inference from verifiable facts (such as the monetary value of a college education).

- **Statements of *belief*,** or convictions based on personal faith or values, such as *The primary goal of government should be to provide equality of opportunity for all.* Although seemingly arguable, a statement of belief is not based on facts and so cannot be contested on the basis of facts.

3 Evidence

Evidence demonstrates the validity of your claims. The evidence to support the claim that the school needs a new chemistry lab might include the present lab's age, an inventory of facilities and equipment, and the testimony of chemistry professors.

There are several kinds of evidence:

- **Facts,** statements whose truth can be verified: *Poland is slightly smaller than New Mexico.*

- **Statistics,** facts expressed as numbers: *Of those polled, 22 percent prefer a flat tax.*

- **Examples,** specific instances of the point being made: *Many groups, such as the elderly and the disabled, would benefit from this policy.*

- **Expert opinions,** the judgments formed by authorities on the basis of their own examination of the facts: *Affirmative action is necessary to right past injustices, a point argued by Howard Glickstein, a past director of the US Commission on Civil Rights.*

- **Appeals to readers' beliefs or needs,** statements that ask readers to accept a claim in part because it states something they already accept as true without evidence: *The shabby, antiquated* *chemistry lab shames the school, making it seem a second-rate institution.*

Evidence must be reliable to be convincing. Ask these questions about your evidence:

- **Is it accurate**—trustworthy, exact, and undistorted?
- **Is it relevant**—authoritative, pertinent, and current?
- **Is it representative**—true to its context, neither under- nor overrepresenting any element of the sample it's drawn from?
- **Is it adequate**—plentiful and specific?

4 Assumptions

An **assumption** is an opinion, a principle, or a belief that ties evidence to claims: the assumption explains why a particular piece of evidence is relevant to a particular claim. For instance:

Claim: The college needs a new chemistry laboratory.
Evidence (in part): The testimony of chemistry professors.
Assumption: Chemistry professors are the most capable of evaluating the present lab's quality.

Assumptions are not flaws in arguments but necessities: we all acquire beliefs and opinions that shape our views of the world. Interpreting a work's assumptions is a significant part of critical reading and viewing (see pp. 87–88 and 94), and discovering your own assumptions is a significant part of argument. If your readers do not share your assumptions or perceive that you are not forthright about your biases, they will be less receptive to your argument.

11b Writing reasonably

Reasonableness is essential if an argument is to establish common ground between you and your readers. Readers expect logical thinking, appropriate appeals, fairness toward the opposition, and, combining all of these, writing that is free of fallacies.

1 Logical thinking

The thesis of your argument is a conclusion you reach by reasoning about evidence. Two processes of reasoning, induction and deduction, are familiar to you even if you aren't familiar with their names.

■ Induction

When you're about to buy a used car, you consult friends, relatives, and consumer guides before deciding what kind of car to buy. Using **induction**, or **inductive reasoning**, you make specific observations about cars (your evidence) and you induce, or infer, a **gen-**

eralization that Car X is most reliable. The generalization is a claim supported by your observations.

You might also use inductive reasoning in a term paper on print advertising:

> **Evidence:** Advertisements in newspapers and magazines.
> **Evidence:** Comments by advertisers and publishers.
> **Evidence:** Data on the effectiveness of advertising.
> **Generalization or claim:** Print is the most cost-effective medium for advertising.

Reasoning inductively, you connect your evidence to your generalization by assuming that what is true in one set of circumstances (the evidence you examine) is also true in a similar set of circumstances (evidence you do not examine). With induction you create new knowledge out of old.

The more evidence you accumulate, the more probable it is that your generalization is true. Note, however, that absolute certainty is not possible. At some point you must *assume* that your evidence justifies your generalization, for yourself and your readers. Most errors in inductive reasoning involve oversimplifying either the evidence or the generalization. See pp. 102–03 on fallacies.

■ Deduction

You use **deduction,** or **deductive reasoning,** when you proceed from your generalization that Car X is the most reliable used car to your own specific circumstances (you want to buy a used car) to the conclusion that you should buy a Car X. In deduction your assumption is a generalization, principle, or belief that you think is true. It links the evidence (new information) to the claim (the conclusion you draw). With deduction you apply old information to new.

Say that you want the school administration to postpone new room fees for one dormitory. You can base your argument on a deductive **syllogism:**

> **Premise:** The administration should not raise fees on dorm rooms in poor condition. [A generalization or belief that you assume to be true.]
> **Premise:** The rooms in Polk Hall are in poor condition. [New information: a specific case of the first premise.]
> **Conclusion:** The administration should not raise fees on the rooms in Polk Hall. [Your claim.]

As long as the premises of a syllogism are true, the conclusion derives logically and certainly from them. Errors in constructing syllogisms lie behind many of the fallacies discussed on pp. 101–02.

2 | Rational, emotional, and ethical appeals

In most arguments you will combine **rational appeals** to readers' capacities for logical reasoning with **emotional appeals** to readers' beliefs and feelings. The following example illustrates both: the second sentence makes a rational appeal (to the logic of financial gain), and the third sentence makes an emotional appeal (to the sense of fairness and open-mindedness).

> Advertising should show more physically challenged people. The millions of disabled Americans have considerable buying power, yet so far advertisers have made no attempt to tap that power. Further, by keeping the physically challenged out of the mainstream depicted in ads, advertisers encourage widespread prejudice against disability, prejudice that frightens and demeans those who hold it.

For an emotional appeal to be successful, it must be appropriate for the audience and the argument:

- **It must not misjudge readers' actual feelings.**
- **It must not raise emotional issues that are irrelevant to the claims and the evidence.** See the next two pages on specific inappropriate appeals, such as bandwagon and ad hominem.

A third kind of approach to readers, the **ethical appeal,** is the sense you give of being a competent, fair person who is worth heeding. A rational appeal and an appropriate emotional appeal contribute to your ethical appeal, and so does your acknowledging opposing views (see below). An argument that is concisely written and correct in grammar, spelling, and other matters will underscore your competence. In addition, a sincere and even tone will assure readers that you are a balanced person who wants to reason with them.

A sincere and even tone need not exclude language with emotional appeal—words such as *frightens* and *demeans* at the end of the example about advertising. But avoid certain forms of expression that will mark you as unfair:

- **Insulting words,** such as *idiotic* or *fascist.*
- **Biased language,** such as *fags* or *broads* (see **3** pp. 163–66).
- **Sarcasm,** such as the phrase *What a brilliant idea* to indicate contempt for the idea and its originator.
- **Exclamation points!** They'll make you sound shrill!

3   Acknowledgment of opposing views

A good test of your fairness in argument is how you handle possible objections. Assuming your thesis is indeed arguable, then others can marshal their own evidence to support a different view or views. You need to find out what these other views are and what the support is for them. Then, in your argument, you need to take these views on, refute those you can, grant the validity of others, and demonstrate why, despite their validity, the opposing views are less compelling than your own. (See the sample essay on pp. 110–14 for an example.)

Before you draft your essay, list for yourself all the opposing views you can think of. You'll find them in your research, by talking to friends, and by critically thinking about your own ideas. You can also look for a range of views in a discussion group dealing with your subject. (The archive at *groups.yahoo.com* is a place to start.)

To deal with opposing views, figure out which ones you can refute (do more research if necessary), and prepare to concede those views you can't refute. It's not a mark of weakness or failure to admit that the opposition has a point or two. Indeed, by showing yourself to be honest and fair, you strengthen your ethical appeal and thus your entire argument.

4 Fallacies

Fallacies—errors in argument—either evade the issue of the argument or treat the argument as if it were much simpler than it is.

■ Evasions

An effective argument squarely faces the central issue or question it addresses. An ineffective argument may dodge the issue in one of the following ways:

- **Begging the question:** treating an opinion that is open to question as if it were already proved or disproved.

  The college library's expenses should be reduced by cutting subscriptions to useless periodicals. [Begged questions: Are some of the library's periodicals useless? Useless to whom?]

- **Non sequitur** (Latin: "It does not follow"): linking two or more ideas that in fact have no logical connection.

  She uses a wheelchair, so she must be unhappy. [The second clause does not follow from the first.]

- **Red herring:** introducing an irrelevant issue intended to distract readers from the relevant issues.

  A campus speech code is essential to protect students, who already have enough problems coping with rising tuition. [Tuition costs and speech codes are different subjects. What protections do students need that a speech code will provide?]

- **Appeal to readers' fear or pity:** substituting emotions for reasoning.

  She should not have to pay taxes because she is an aged widow with no friends or relatives. [Appeals to people's pity. Should age and loneliness, rather than income, determine a person's tax obligation?]

- **Bandwagon:** inviting readers to accept a claim because everyone else does.

As everyone knows, marijuana use leads to heroin addiction. [What is the evidence?]

- **Ad hominem** (Latin: "to the man"): attacking the qualities of the people holding an opposing view rather than the substance of the view itself.

One of the scientists has been treated for emotional problems, so his pessimism about nuclear waste merits no attention. [Do the scientist's previous emotional problems invalidate his current views?]

Oversimplifications

In a vain attempt to create something neatly convincing, an ineffective argument may conceal or ignore complexities in one of the following ways:

- **Hasty generalization:** making a claim on the basis of inadequate evidence.

It is disturbing that several of the youths who shot up schools were users of violent video games. Obviously, these games can breed violence, and they should be banned. [A few cases do not establish the relation between the games and violent behavior. Most youths who play violent video games do not behave violently.]

- **Sweeping generalization:** making an insupportable statement. Many sweeping generalizations are **absolute statements** involving words such as *all, always, never,* and *no one* that allow no exceptions. Others are **stereotypes**, conventional and oversimplified characterizations of a group of people:

People who live in cities are unfriendly.
Californians are fad-crazy.
Women are emotional.
Men can't express their feelings.

(See also 3 pp.163–66 on sexist and other biased language.)
- **Reductive fallacy:** oversimplifying (reducing) the relation between causes and effects.

Poverty causes crime. [If so, then why do people who are not poor commit crimes? And why aren't all poor people criminals?]

- **Post hoc fallacy** (from Latin, *post hoc, ergo propter hoc:* "after this, therefore because of this"): assuming that because A preceded B, then A must have caused B.

The town council erred in permitting the adult bookstore to open, for shortly afterward two women were assaulted. [It cannot be assumed without evidence that the women's assailants visited or were influenced by the bookstore.]

- **Either/or fallacy:** assuming that a complicated question has only two answers, one good and one bad, both good, or both bad.

  Either we permit mandatory drug testing in the workplace or productivity will continue to decline. [Productivity is not necessarily dependent on drug testing.]

EXERCISE 11.2   Identifying and revising fallacies

Fallacies tend to appear together, as each of the following sentences illustrates. Identify at least one fallacy in each sentence. Then revise the sentences to make them more reasonable. (You can do this exercise online at *ablongman.com/littlebrown*.)

1 The American government can sell nuclear technology to non-nuclear nations, so why can't individuals, who after all have a God-given right to earn a living as they see fit?
2 A successful marriage demands a maturity that no one under twenty-five possesses.
3 Students' persistent complaints about the grading system prove that it is unfair.
4 People watch television because they are too lazy to talk or read or because they want mindless escape from their lives.
5 Racial tension is bound to occur when people with different backgrounds are forced to live side by side.

11c   Organizing an argument

All arguments include the same parts:

- The *introduction* establishes the significance of the subject and provides background. The introduction may run a paragraph or two, and it generally includes the thesis statement. However, if you think your readers may have difficulty accepting your thesis statement before they see at least some support for it, then it may come later in the paper. (See 1 pp. 50–51 for more on introductions.)
- The *body* states and develops the claims supporting the thesis. In one or more paragraphs, the body develops each claim with clearly relevant evidence. See the next page for more on organizing the body.
- The *response to opposing views* details and addresses those views, either demonstrating your argument's greater strengths or conceding the opponents' points. See the next page for more on organizing this response.

- **The *conclusion* completes the argument,** restating the thesis, summarizing the supporting claims, and making a final appeal to readers. (See 1 pp. 51–53 for more on conclusions.)

The structure of the body and the response to opposing views depends on your subject, purpose, audience, and form of reasoning. Here are several possible arrangements:

The traditional scheme	The problem-solution scheme
Claim 1 and evidence	The problem: claims and evidence
Claim 2 and evidence	The solution: claims and evidence
Claim X and evidence	Response to opposing views
Response to opposing views	

Variations on the traditional scheme

Use a variation if you believe your readers will reject your argument without an early or intermittent response to opposing views.

Response to opposing views	Claim 1 and evidence
Claim 1 and evidence	Response and opposing views
Claim 2 and evidence	Claim 2 and evidence
Claim X and evidence	Response and opposing views
	Claim X and evidence
	Response to opposing views

11d Using visual arguments

In a **visual argument** you use one or more images to engage and convince readers. Advertisements often provide the most vivid and memorable examples of visual arguments, but writers in almost every field—from medicine to music, from physics to physical education—support their claims with images. The main elements of written arguments discussed on pp. 96–98—claims, evidence, and assumptions—appear also in visual arguments.

1 Claims

The claims in an image may be made by composition as well as by content, with or without accompanying words. For instance:

Image   A photograph framing hundreds of chickens crammed into small cages, resembling familiar images of World War II concentration camps.

Claim   Commercial poultry-raising practices are cruel and unethical.

Image   A chart with dramatically contrasting bars that represent the optimism, stress, and heart disease reported by people before and after they participated in a program of daily walking.

Claim   Daily exercise leads to a healthier and happier life.

Following is one of a series of advertisements featuring un-named but well-known people as milk drinkers. The celebrity here is Oscar de la Hoya, a boxing champion. The ad makes several claims both in the photograph and in the text.

Claims in an image

Image claim: Cool, tough men drink milk.

Image claim: Attractive people drink milk.

Image claim: Athletes drink milk.

Text claim: Milk is a good source of nutrition, helping to build muscles.

Advertisement by the Milk Processor
Education Program

2 Evidence

The kinds of evidence offered by images parallel those found in written arguments:

- **Facts:** You might provide facts in the form of data, as in a graph showing a five-year rise in oil prices. Or you might draw an inference from data, as the ad above does by stating that milk provides "high-quality protein for your muscles without the fat."
- **Examples:** Most often, you'll use examples to focus on an in-stance of your argument's claims, as Oscar de la Hoya repre-sents milk drinkers in the ad above.

- **Expert opinions:** You might present a chart from an expert showing a trend in unemployment among high school graduates.
- **Appeals to beliefs or needs:** You might depict how things clearly ought to be (an anti-drug brochure featuring a teenager who is confidently refusing peer pressure) or, in contrast, show how things clearly should not be (a Web site for an anti-hunger campaign featuring images of emaciated children).

To make an image work hard as evidence, be sure it relates directly to a point in your argument, adds to that point, and gives readers something to think about. Always include a caption that provides source information and that explicitly ties the image to your text, so that readers don't have to puzzle out your intentions. Number images in sequence (Fig. 1, Fig. 2, and so on), and refer to them by number at the appropriate points in your text. (See **1** pp. 61–65 for more on captioning and numbering illustrations.)

The images below and opposite illustrate the use of visual evidence in an argument with the following thesis: *Television shows focusing on cosmetic procedures are encouraging women to opt for such procedures in order to conform to a particular standard of beauty.*

Images as evidence

Before and after images showing the effects of cosmetic procedures more emphatically than a description would

Caption explaining the images and the woman's cosmetic treatments, tying the images to the text of the paper.

Fig. 1. Before and after images of a participant on the television show Extreme Makeover. In addition to the change in personal style implied by the change in clothes, hairdo, and body language, this participant also underwent nose surgery, a brow lift, eye surgery, dental work, liposuction, and breast augmentation. Photographs from Walt Disney Internet Group, ABC, Extreme Makeover, 2005, 30 May 2005 <http://abc.go.com/primetime/extrememakeover/index.html>.

Cosmetic Surgery Trends
Surgical and Nonsurgical Cosmetic Procedures: Totals
Source: American Society for Aesthetic Plastic Surgery

Graph from a reputable source demonstrating the overall increase in cosmetic procedures

Fig. 2. Numbers of cosmetic procedures performed in the United States, 1997-2004. In 2004 such procedures increased 44 percent. Graph from American Society for Aesthetic Plastic Surgery, 2004 Cosmetic Surgery National Data Bank: Statistics, 3 June 2005 <http://www.surgery.org/press/statistics-2004.php>.

Caption explaining the graph and highlighting the 2004 increase, the most relevant to the paper's claims

3 Assumptions

Like a written argument, a visual argument is based on assumptions—your ideas about the relation between evidence and claims (p. 98). Look again at the milk ad featuring Oscar de la Hoya (p. 105). The advertiser seems to have assumed that simply stating the benefits of milk drinking would not be convincing and that a celebrity endorsement would strengthen the claims and evidence. In addition, the photograph of de la Hoya emphasizes qualities that the advertiser presumably thought would appeal to readers: toughness, directness, and even (in the robe draped over the boxer's shoulders) patriotism.

As in written arguments, the assumptions in visual arguments must be appropriate for your readers if the argument is to succeed with them. The milk ad originally appeared in sports magazines, so the advertiser could assume that readers knew of and admired de la Hoya. But to readers uninterested in sports or even opposed to boxing, the photograph might actually undermine the ad's effectiveness.

4 Appeals

Images can help to strengthen the rational, emotional, and ethical appeals of your written argument (pp. 99–100):

- **Images can contribute evidence,** as long as they come from reliable sources, present information accurately and fairly, and relate clearly to the argument's claims.

- **Images can appeal to a host of ideas and emotions,** including patriotism, curiosity, moral values, sympathy, and anger. Any such appeal should correctly gauge readers' beliefs and feelings, and it should be clearly relevant to the argument.

- **Images can show that you are a competent, fair, and trustworthy source of information,** largely through their relevance, reliability, and sensitivity to readers' needs and feelings.

To see how appeals can work in images, look at a photograph used in the sample argument paper on p. 111. This image illustrates the writer's claim that television can ease loneliness.

Appeals in an image

Rational appeal: Backs up the writer's claim that TV can ease loneliness: the man appears to live alone (only one chair is visible) and is interacting enthusiastically with the TV

Emotional appeal: Reinforces the benefits of TV watching: the man's isolation may be disturbing, but his excitement is pleasing

Ethical appeal: Conveys the writer's competence through the appropriateness of the image for the point being made

Fig. 1. Television can be a source of companionship for people whose living situations and limited mobility leave them lonely. Photograph by Jean Michel Foujols, Corbis image 42-15243193, 13 June 2005 <http://pro.corbis.com>.

5 Recognizing fallacies

When making a visual argument, you'll need to guard against all the fallacies discussed on pp. 101–03. Here we'll focus on specific visual examples. The first, the milk ad on p. 105, uses Oscar de la Hoya for snob appeal, inviting readers to be like someone they admire. If you drink milk, the ad says subtly, you too may become fit, skillful, and direct (notice that de la Hoya looks unguardedly into the camera). The ad does have some substance in its specific and verifiable claim that milk contains "high-quality protein for your muscles without the fat," but de la Hoya himself, with his milk mustache, makes a stronger claim.

Other examples of visual fallacies appear in the map below, which represents the Electoral College vote in the 2004 US presidential election: red for states won by Republican George W. Bush, blue for states won by Democrat John F. Kerry. The colors represent majority votes and Electoral College, not popular, votes. Still, the colors have been used to characterize the political and social preferences of each state's entire population and to reinforce stereotypes about rural vs. urban, heartland vs. coastal, and conservative vs. liberal citizens.

Fallacies in a visual argument

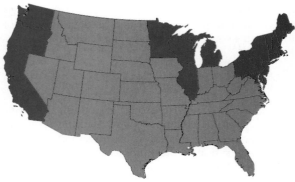

Either/or fallacy: Solid colors implying that all of the voters in each state chose either the Republican or the Democratic candidate, when every state had voters for both candidates and for candidates from other political parties

Sweeping generalization: Strong contrast implying that voters' concerns were unconflicted and were represented by a single vote

The Electoral College vote in the 2004 US presidential election: red states for Bush, blue states for Kerry

6 Choice of images

You can wait until you've drafted an argument before concentrating on what images to include. This approach keeps your focus on the research and writing needed to craft the best argument from sources. But you can also begin thinking visually at the beginning of a project, as you might if your initial interest in the subject was sparked by a compelling image. Either way, ask yourself some basic questions as you consider visual options:

- **Which parts of your argument can use visual reinforcement?** What can be explained better visually than verbally? Can a graph or chart present data compactly and interestingly? Can a photograph appeal effectively to readers' beliefs and values?

- **What are the limitations or requirements of your writing situation?** What do the type of writing you're doing and its format allow? Look through examples of similar writing to gauge the kinds of illustrations readers will expect.
- **What kinds of visuals are readily available on your subject?** As you researched your subject, what images seemed especially effective? What sources have you not yet explored? (See **7** pp. 394–96 for tips on locating images.)
- **Should you create original images tailored to your argument?** Instead of searching for existing images, would your time be better spent taking your own photographs or using computer software to compose visual explanations, such as charts, graphs, and diagrams?

Note Any image you include in a paper requires the same detailed citation as a written source. If you plan to publish your argument online, you will also need to seek permission from the author. See **7** pp. 418–26 on citing sources and obtaining permissions.

11e   Examining a sample argument

The following essay by Craig Holbrook, a student, illustrates the principles discussed in this chapter. As you read the essay, notice especially the structure, the relation of claims and supporting evidence (including illustrations), the kinds of appeals Holbrook makes, and the ways he addresses opposing views.

TV Can Be Good for You

Introduction	Television wastes time, pollutes minds, destroys brain cells,
Identification of prevailing view	and turns some viewers into murderers. Thus runs the prevailing talk about the medium, supported by serious research as well as simple
Disagreement with prevailing view	belief. But television has at least one strong virtue, too, which helps to explain its endurance as a cultural force. It provides replacement
Thesis statement making three claims for television	voices that ease loneliness, spark healthful laughter, and even educate young children.
Background for claim 1: effects of loneliness	Most people who have lived alone understand the curse of silence, when the only sound is the buzz of unhappiness or anxiety inside one's own head. Although people of all ages who live alone can experience intense loneliness, the elderly are especially vulnera-
Evidence for effects of loneliness	ble to solitude. For example, they may suffer increased confusion or depression when left alone for long periods but then rebound when they have steady companionship (Bondevik and Skogstad 329-30).
Evidence for effects of television on loneliness	A study of elderly men and women in New Zealand found that television can actually serve as a companion by assuming "the role

of social contact with the wider world," reducing "feelings of isolation and loneliness because it directs viewers' attention away from themselves" ("Television Programming"). (See fig. 1.) Thus television's replacement voices can provide comfort because they distract from a focus on being alone.

Statement of claim 1

Illustration supporting claim 1

Fig. 1. Television can be a source of companionship for people whose living situations and limited mobility leave them lonely. Photograph by Jean Michel Foujols, Corbis image 42-15243193, 13 June 2005 <http://pro.corbis.com>.

The absence of real voices can be most damaging when it means a lack of laughter. Here, too, research shows that television can have a positive effect on health. Laughter is one of the most powerful calming forces available to human beings, proven in many studies to reduce heart rate, lower blood pressure, and ease other stress-related ailments (Burroughs, Mahoney, and Lippman 172; Griffiths 18). (See fig. 2.) Television offers plenty of laughter: the recent listings for a single Friday night included more than twenty comedy programs running on the networks and on basic cable.

Background for claim 2: effects of laughter

Evidence for effects of laughter

Evidence for comedy on television

A study reported in a health magazine found that laughter inspired by television and video is as healthful as the laughter generated by live comedy. Volunteers laughing at a video comedy routine "showed significant improvements in several immune functions, such as natural killer-cell activity" (Laliberte 78). Further, the effects of the comedy were so profound that "merely anticipating watching a funny video improved mood, depression, and anger as much as two days beforehand" (Laliberte 79). Even for people with plenty of companionship, television's replacement voices can have healthful effects by causing laughter.

Evidence for effects of laughter in response to television

Statement of claim 2

Illustration supporting
healthful effects of
laughter

Fig. 2. According to the Society for Neuroscience, the process of
understanding and being amused by something funny stimulates at
least three main areas of the brain. The society makes no recommendation about TV watching, but other studies show the healthful
effects of the activity. Illustration by Lydia Kibiuk from Society for
Neuroscience, Brain Briefings, Dec. 2001, 12 June 2005 <http://
apu.sfn.org/BrainBriefings/bb_humor.htm>.

Background for
claim 3: educational
effects

Television also provides information about the world. This
service can be helpful to everyone but especially to children, whose
natural curiosity can exhaust the knowledge and patience of their
parents and caretakers. While the TV may be baby-sitting children,
it can also enrich them. For example, educational programs such as
those on the Discovery Channel, the Disney Channel, and PBS offer
a steady stream of information at various cognitive levels. (See fig.
3.) Even many cartoons, which are generally dismissed as mindless
or worse, familiarize children with the material of literature, including strong characters enacting classic narratives.

Evidence for educa-
tional programming
on television

Evidence for educa-
tional effects of
television on children

Two researchers studying children and television found that TV
is a source of creative and psychological instruction, inspiring children "to play imaginatively and develop confidence and skills" (Colman and Colman 9). Instead of passively watching, children "interact
with the programs and videos" and "sometimes include the fictional
characters in reality's in play time" (Colman and Colman 8). Thus television's voices both inform young viewers and encourage exchange.

Statement of claim 3

Anticipation of
objection: harm of
television

The value of these replacement voices should not be oversold.
For one thing, almost everyone agrees that too much TV does no

Fig. 3. Educational television programs such as <u>Sesame Street</u> are an important source of learning for children. Characters such as Elmo (shown here) promote reading, learning, and healthy behaviors. Photograph from United Nations Children's Fund, <u>The State of the World's Children</u>, 2002, 12 June 2005 <http://www.unicef.org/sowc02/feature10.htm>.

one any good and may cause much harm. Many studies show that excessive TV watching increases violent behavior, especially in children, and can cause, rather than ease, other antisocial behaviors (Reeks 114; Walsh 34). In addition, human beings require the give and take of actual interaction. Steven Pinker, an expert in children's language acquisition, warns that children cannot develop language properly by watching television. They need to interact with actual speakers who respond directly to their needs (282). Replacement voices are not real voices and in the end can do only limited good.

Anticipation of objection: need for actual interaction

Qualification of claims in response to objections

But even limited good is something, especially for those who are lonely or neglected. Television is not an entirely positive force, but neither is it an entirely negative one. Its voices stand by to provide company, laughter, and information whenever they're needed.

Conclusion

Works Cited

Bondevik, Margareth, and Anders Skogstad. "The Oldest Old, ADL, Social Network, and Loneliness." <u>Western Journal of Nursing Research</u> 20.3 (1998): 325-43.

Burroughs, W. Jeffrey, Diana L. Mahoney, and Louis G. Lippman. "Attributes of Health-Promoting Laughter: Cross-Generational Comparison." <u>Journal of Psychology</u> 136.2 (2004): 171-81.

Colman, Robyn, and Adrian Colman. "Inspirational Television." <u>Youth Studies in Australia</u> 21.3 (2003): 8-10.

Foujols, Jean Michel. Photograph. Corbis image 42-15243193. 13 June 2005 <http://pro.corbis.com>.

Griffiths, Joan. "The Mirthful Brain." Omni Aug. 1996: 18-19.

Kibiuk, Lydia. Illustration. Society for Neuroscience. Brain Briefings. Dec. 2001. 12 June 2005 <http://apu.sfn.org/BrainBriefings/ bb_humor.htm>.

Laliberte, Richard W. "The Benefits of Laughter." Shape Sept. 2003: 78-79.

Pinker, Steven. The Language Instinct: How the Mind Creates Language. New York: Harper, 1994.

Reeks, Anne. "Kids and TV: A Guide." Parenting Apr. 2005: 110-15.

"Television Programming for Older People: Summary Research Report." NZ on Air. 25 July 2004. 15 Oct. 2005 <http:// www.nzonair.gov.nz/media/oldpeoplesreport.pdf>.

United Nations Children's Fund. Photograph. The State of the World's Children. 2002. 12 June 2005 <http://www.unicef.org/ sowc02/feature10.htm>.

Walsh, Teri. "Too Much TV Linked to Depression." Prevention Feb. 2001: 34-36.

—Craig Holbrook (student)

12 Online Writing

In and out of college, you will write extensively online. Many forms of online writing expand your options as a writer, but they also present distinctive challenges, both conceptual and technical. This chapter discusses some of the options and challenges of e-mail (below), online collaboration (p. 117), and Web composition (p. 118).

12a Using electronic mail

You may be using e-mail every day to converse quickly and casually with friends and family. In college you'll also use e-mail for a host of academic reasons, from collaborating with classmates to conducting research, and you'll want to communicate both purposefully and efficiently. This section covers composing and re-

http://www.ablongman.com/littlebrown ▶

Visit the companion Web site for more help with online writing.

sponding to messages and observing Internet etiquette. For more on using e-mail as a research tool, see **7** p. 393.

1 Composing messages

To use e-mail productively, pause to weigh each element of the message. Consider especially your audience and purpose and how your tone will come across to readers. In the message shown below, the writer knows the recipients well and yet has serious information to convey to them, so he writes informally but states his points and concerns carefully. Writing to the corporation mentioned in the message, the writer would be more formal in both tone and approach. Although e-mail is typically more casual than printed correspondence, in academic settings a crafted message is more likely to achieve the intended purpose. Proofread all but the most informal messages for errors in grammar, punctuation, and spelling.

E-mail message

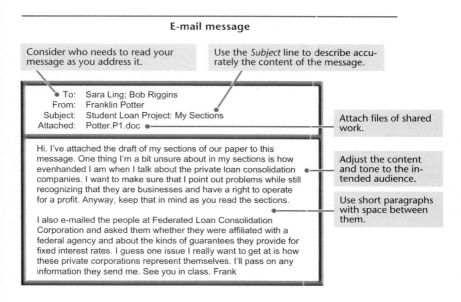

Consider who needs to read your message as you address it.

Use the *Subject* line to describe accurately the content of the message.

To: Sara Ling; Bob Riggins
From: Franklin Potter
Subject: Student Loan Project: My Sections
Attached: Potter.P1.doc

Attach files of shared work.

Hi. I've attached the draft of my sections of our paper to this message. One thing I'm a bit unsure about in my sections is how evenhanded I am when I talk about the private loan consolidation companies. I want to make sure that I point out problems while still recognizing that they are businesses and have a right to operate for a profit. Anyway, keep that in mind as you read the sections.

Adjust the content and tone to the intended audience.

Use short paragraphs with space between them.

I also e-mailed the people at Federated Loan Consolidation Corporation and asked them whether they were affiliated with a federal agency and about the kinds of guarantees they provide for fixed interest rates. I guess one issue I really want to get at is how these private corporations represent themselves. I'll pass on any information they send me. See you in class. Frank

2 Responding to messages

When you respond to a message, consider whom you're addressing and what your readers will see. The Reply function will automatically address the person who wrote you, whereas the Reply All function will address others who may have been sent copies of the original message. The *Subject* line will automatically contain the original subject heading preceded by *Re:* (from Latin, meaning "In reference to"), so change the heading if you change or expand the subject. Many e-mail programs can be set to reprint the entire original message, allowing you to insert your responses where appropriate or just respond to part and delete the rest. If you add more recipients to your response, make sure not to pass on previous private messages by mistake.

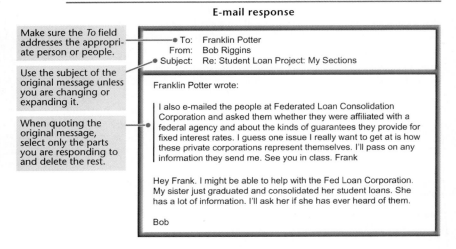

E-mail response

Make sure the *To* field addresses the appropriate person or people.

Use the subject of the original message unless you are changing or expanding it.

When quoting the original message, select only the parts you are responding to and delete the rest.

To: Franklin Potter
From: Bob Riggins
Subject: Re: Student Loan Project: My Sections

Franklin Potter wrote:

I also e-mailed the people at Federated Loan Consolidation Corporation and asked them whether they were affiliated with a federal agency and about the kinds of guarantees they provide for fixed interest rates. I guess one issue I really want to get at is how these private corporations represent themselves. I'll pass on any information they send me. See you in class. Frank

Hey Frank. I might be able to help with the Fed Loan Corporation. My sister just graduated and consolidated her student loans. She has a lot of information. I'll ask her if she has ever heard of them.

Bob

3 Observing netiquette

To communicate effectively online, you'll need to abide by some rules of behavior and simple courtesies. You won't always see others observing this **netiquette,** or Internet etiquette, but you will see that those who do observe it receive the more thoughtful and considerate replies.

Addressing messages

- **Avoid spamming.** With a few keystrokes, you can broadcast a message to many recipients at once—all the students in a course, say, or all the participants in a discussion group. Occasionally you may indeed have a worthwhile idea or important information that everyone on the list will want to know. But flooding whole lists with irrelevant messages—called **spamming**—is rude and irritating.
- **Avoid sending frivolous messages to all the members of a group.** Instead of dashing off "I agree" and distributing the two-word message widely, put some time into composing a thoughtful response and send it only to those who will be interested.

Composing messages

- **Remember that the messages you receive represent individuals.** Don't say or do anything that you wouldn't say or do face to face.

- **Use names.** In the body of your message, address your reader(s) by name if possible and sign off with your own name and information on how to contact you. Your own name is especially important if your e-mail address does not spell it out.
- **Pay careful attention to tone.** Refrain from flaming, or attacking, correspondents. Don't use all-capital letters, which SHOUT. And use irony or sarcasm only cautiously: in the absence of facial expressions, they can be misunderstood. To indicate irony and emotions, you can use **emoticons,** such as the smiley :-). These sideways faces made up of punctuation can easily be overused, though, and should not substitute for thoughtfully worded opinions.
- **Avoid saying anything in e-mail that you would not say in a printed document such as a letter or memo.** E-mail can usually be retrieved from the server, and in business and academic settings it may well be retrieved in disputes over contracts, grades, and other matters.

Reading and responding to messages

- **Be a forgiving reader.** Avoid nitpicking over spelling or other surface errors. And because attitudes are sometimes difficult to convey, give authors an initial benefit of the doubt: a writer who at first seems hostile may simply have tried too hard to be concise; a writer who at first seems unserious may simply have failed at injecting humor into a worthwhile message.
- **Forward messages only with permission.** You may want to send a message you've received to someone else, but do so only if you know that the author of the message won't mind.
- **Avoid participating in flame "wars,"** overheated dialogs that contribute little or no information or understanding. If a war breaks out in a discussion, ignore it: don't rush to defend someone who is being attacked, and don't respond even if you are under attack yourself.

12b Collaborating online

Many instructors integrate online collaboration into their courses, encouraging students to work in groups for discussing ideas and exchanging and commenting on drafts of projects.

1 Participating in discussions

Online conversations in your courses will occur either in real-time chat, which occurs immediately, like a telephone conversation, or in a delayed medium such as e-mail or a Web forum or blog. Chat discussions can be fast-paced and often work better for brainstorming topics and exchanging impressions than for careful articulation of ideas. Delayed conversations allow detailed, thoughtful messages and responses, so they are good places to develop ideas, explore assignments, and respond to others' work. For either type of conversation, observe the netiquette guidelines on pages 116–17.

2 Working on drafts

In writing and other courses, you and your fellow students may be invited to exchange and respond to one another's projects by e-mail or over the Web. To guide your reading of others' work, use the revision checklist in **1** pp. 25–26 and the collaboration tips in **1** pp. 36–37. Focus on the deep issues in others' drafts, especially early drafts: thesis, purpose, audience, organization, and support for the thesis. Hold comments on style, grammar, punctuation, and other surface matters until you're reviewing late drafts, if indeed you are expected to comment on them at all.

12c Creating Web compositions

Creating a Web page or site is sometimes as simple as saving a document in a different format, but more often it means thinking in a new way.

The diagrams on the next page show a key difference between traditional printed documents and Web sites. Most traditional documents are meant to be read in sequence from start to finish. In contrast, most Web sites are intended to be examined in whatever order readers choose as they follow links to pages within the site and to other sites. A Web site thus requires careful planning of the links between pages and thoughtful cues to orient readers.

When you create a composition for the Web, it will likely fall into one of two categories: pages such as class papers that resemble printed documents in being linear and text-heavy and that call for familiar ways of writing and reading (p. 120); or "native" hypertext documents that you build from scratch, which call for screen-oriented writing and reading (p. 121).

Note If you anticipate that some of your readers may have visual, hearing, or reading disabilities, you'll need to consider their needs while designing Web sites. Some of these considerations are covered under document design in **1** pp. 65–66, and others are fundamental to any effective Web design, as discussed in this section. In addition, avoid any content that relies exclusively on images or sound, instead supplementing such elements with text descriptions, and try to provide key concepts both as text and as images and sound. For more on Web design for readers with disabilities, visit the World Wide Web Consortium at *w3.org/tr/wai-webcontent* or the American Council for the Blind at *acb.org/accessible-formats.html*.

Traditional print document

Web site

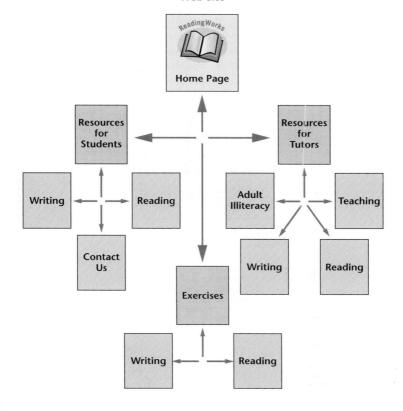

1 Using HTML

Most Web pages are created using hypertext markup language, or HTML, and an HTML editor. The HTML editing program inserts command codes into your document that achieve the effects you want when the material appears on the Web.

From the user's point of view, most HTML editors work much as word processors do, with similar options for sizing, formatting, and highlighting copy and with a display that shows what you will see in the final version. Indeed, you can compose a Web page without bothering at all about the behind-the-scenes HTML coding. As you gain experience with Web building, however, you may want to create more sophisticated pages by editing the codes themselves.

There are many HTML editors on the market. *FrontPage, Go-Live,* and *Dreamweaver* are three of the most popular. The Web site for this book (*ablongman.com/littlebrown*) provides links to free or low-cost HTML editors.

2 Creating online papers

If an instructor asks you to post a paper to a Web site or Web log, you can compose it on your word processor and then use the Save As HTML function available on most word processors to translate it into a Web page. After translating the paper, your word processor should allow you to modify some of the elements on the page, or you can open the translated document in an HTML editor. The illustration below shows the opening screen of a student's project for a composition course.

Paper submitted on the Web

White background providing strong contrast

Standard font for readability

Menu providing links to major sections in the paper

Heading marking major section

ReadingWorks
Springfield Veterans Administration Hospital

Making a Difference: A Service-Learning Project
Alex Ramirez

Illiteracy or low literacy skills among military veterans is a pervasive problem in Springfield County and around the US. Many veterans do not have the literacy skills to find high-paying jobs needed to own a home and support a family. The literacy center at Springfield VA Hospital, where I volunteer as a tutor and completed my service-learning project, aims to provide the education these veterans need to improve their literacy skills.

Literacy rates among military veterans
Tutoring at ReadingWorks
Preparing documents and a Web site for ReadingWorks

Literacy Rates Among Militiary Veterans
Most military veterans have basic literacy skills; very few cannot read or

3 Creating original sites

When you create an original Web site, you need to be aware that Web readers generally alternate between skimming pages for highlights and focusing intently on sections of text. To facilitate this kind of reading, you'll want to consider your site's structure and content, flow, ease of navigation, and use of images, video, and sound.

▪ Structure and content

Organize your site so that it efficiently arranges your content and orients readers:

- **Sketch possible site plans before getting started.** (See p. 119 for an example.) Your aim is to develop a sense of the major components of your project and to create a logical space for each component.

- **Consider how menus on the site's pages can provide overviews of the organization as well as direct access to the pages.** The Web page below includes a menu on the left.

- **Treat the first few sentences of any page as a get-acquainted space for you and your readers.** On the page below, the text hooks readers with questions and then orients them with general information.

- **Distill your text so that it includes only essential information.** Concise prose is essential in any writing situation, of course. But Web readers expect to scan text quickly and, in any event, have difficulty following long text passages on a computer screen.

Original Web site

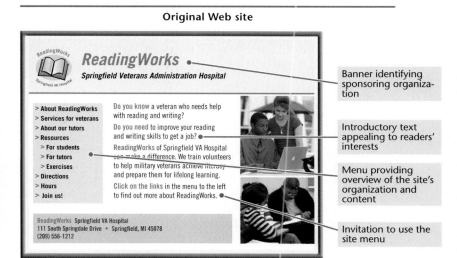

ReadingWorks
Springfield Veterans Administration Hospital

Banner identifying sponsoring organization

> About ReadingWorks
> Services for veterans
> About our tutors
> Resources
> For students
> For tutors
> Exercises
> Directions
> Hours
> Join us!

Do you know a veteran who needs help with reading and writing?

Do you need to improve your reading and writing skills to get a job? ●

ReadingWorks of Springfield VA Hospital can make a difference. We train volunteers to help military veterans achieve literacy and prepare them for lifelong learning.

Click on the links in the menu to the left to find out more about ReadingWorks. ●

Introductory text appealing to readers' interests

Menu providing overview of the site's organization and content

ReadingWorks Springfield VA Hospital
111 South Springdale Drive • Springfield, MI 45078
(209) 556-1212

Invitation to use the site menu

■ **Flow**

Beginning Web authors sometimes start at the top of the page and then add element upon element until information proceeds down the screen much as it would in a printed document. However, by thinking about how information will flow on a page, you can take better advantage of the Web's visual nature. Follow these guidelines:

- **Standardize elements of your design to create expectations in readers and to fulfill those expectations.** For instance, develop a uniform style for the main headings of pages, for headings within pages, and for menus.
- **Make scanning easy for readers.** Focus readers on crucial text by adding space around it. Add headings to break up text and to highlight content. Use lists to reinforce the parallel importance of items. (See 1 pp. 59–60 for more on headings and lists.)

■ **Easy navigation**

A Web site of more than a few pages requires a menu on every page that lists the features of the site, giving its plan at a glance. By clicking on any item in the menu, readers can go directly to a page that interests them.

You can embed a menu at the top, side, or bottom of a page. Menus at the top or side are best on short pages because they will not scroll off the screen as readers move down the page. On longer pages, menus at the bottom prevent readers from reaching a dead end, a point where they can't easily move forward or backward. You can also use a combination of menus.

■ **Images, video, and sound**

Most Web readers expect at least some enhancement of text with multimedia elements—images, video, and sound.

Note See 7 p. 425 on observing copyright restrictions with images, video, and sound.

Images

To use photographs, charts, and other images effectively, follow these guidelines:

- **Use visual elements for a purpose.** They should supplement text, highlight important features, and direct the flow of information. Don't use them as mere decoration.
- **Make the size of your files a central concern** so that readers don't have to wait forever for your site to download. If you are using photographs or other images, try to keep the file size below thirty kilobytes (30k).
- **Compose descriptions of images that relate them to your text.** Don't ask the elements to convey your meaning by themselves.

- **Provide alternative descriptions of images** for readers with disabilities or readers whose Web browsers can't display the images.

Video and sound

Video and sound files can provide information that is simply unavailable in printed documents. For instance, as part of a film review you might show and analyze a short clip from the film. Or as part of a project on a controversial issue you might provide links to sound files containing political speeches.

Video and sound files can be difficult to work with and can be slow to download at the reader's end. Make sure they're worth the time: they should provide essential information and should be well integrated with the rest of your composition.

Sources of multimedia elements

You can use your own multimedia elements or obtain them from other sources:

- **Create your own graphs, diagrams, and other illustrations using a graphics program.** Any graphics program requires learning and practice to be used efficiently but can produce professional-looking illustrations.
- **Incorporate your own artwork, photographs, video clips, and sound recordings.** You may be able to find the needed equipment and software at your campus computer lab.
- **Obtain icons, video, and other multimedia elements from other electronic sources.** Be sure that you have enough space on your hard drive or a disk to hold the file.

13 Oral Presentations

Effective speakers use organization, voice, and other techniques to help their audiences follow and appreciate their presentations.

13a Organizing the presentation

Give your oral presentation a recognizable shape so that listeners can see how ideas and details relate to each other.

http://www.ablongman.com/littlebrown ▶

Visit the companion Web site for more help with oral presentations and *PowerPoint*.

■ The introduction

The beginning of an oral presentation should try to accomplish three goals:

- **Gain the audience's attention and interest.** Begin with a question, an unusual example or statistic, or a short, relevant story.
- **Put yourself in the speech.** Demonstrate your expertise, experience, or concern to gain the interest and trust of your audience.
- **Introduce and preview your topic and purpose.** By the time your introduction is over, listeners should know what your subject is and the direction you'll take to develop your ideas.

Your introduction should prepare your audience for your main points but not give them away. Think of it as a sneak preview of your speech, not the place for an apology such as *I wish I'd had more time to prepare* . . . or a dull statement such as *My speech is about.* . . .

■ Supporting material

Just as you do when writing, you should use facts, statistics, examples, and expert opinions to support the main points of your oral presentation. In addition, you can make your points more memorable with vivid description, well-chosen quotations, true or fictional stories, and analogies.

■ The conclusion

You want your conclusion to be clear, of course, but you also want it to be memorable. Remind listeners of how your topic and main idea connect to their needs and interests. If your speech was motivational, tap an emotion that matches your message. If your speech was informational, give some tips on how to remember important details.

13b Delivering the presentation

■ Methods of delivery

You can deliver an oral presentation in several ways:

- **Impromptu, without preparation:** Make a presentation without planning what you will say. Impromptu speaking requires confidence and excellent general preparation.
- **Extemporaneously:** Prepare notes to glance at but not read from. This method allows you to look and sound natural while ensuring that you don't forget anything.
- **Speaking from a text:** Read aloud from a written presentation. You won't lose your way, but you may lose your audience. Avoid reading for an entire presentation.

- **Speaking from memory:** Deliver a prepared presentation without notes. You can look at your audience every minute, but the stress of retrieving the next words may make you seem tense and unresponsive.

Vocal delivery

The sound of your voice will influence how listeners receive you. Rehearse your presentation several times until you are confident that you are speaking loudly, slowly, and clearly enough for your audience to understand you.

Physical delivery

You are more than your spoken words when you make an oral presentation. If you are able, stand up to deliver your presentation, moving your body toward one side of the room and the other, stepping out from behind any lectern or desk, and gesturing as appropriate. Above all, make eye contact with your audience as you speak. Looking directly in your listeners' eyes conveys your honesty, your confidence, and your control of the material.

Visual aids

You can supplement an oral presentation with visual aids such as posters, models, slides, or videos.

- **Use visual aids to underscore your points.** Short lists of key ideas, illustrations such as graphs or photographs, or objects such as models can make your presentation more interesting and memorable. But use visual aids judiciously: a battery of illustrations or objects will bury your message rather than amplify it.
- **Coordinate visual aids with your message.** Time each visual to reinforce a point you're making. Tell listeners what they're looking at. Give them enough viewing time so they don't mind turning their attention back to you.
- **Show visual aids only while they're needed.** To regain your audience's attention, remove or turn off any aid as soon as you have finished with it.

Many speakers use *PowerPoint* or other software to present visual aids. Preparing screens of brief points supported by data, images, or video, you can use such software to help listeners follow your main points. To use *PowerPoint* or other software effectively, follow the guidelines above and also the following:

- **Don't put your whole presentation on screen.** Select key points, and distill them to as few words as possible. Think of the slides as quick, easy-to-remember summaries.

- **Use a simple design.** Avoid turning your presentation into a show about the software's many capabilities.
- **Use a consistent design.** For optimal flow through the presentation, each slide should be formatted similarly.
- **Add only relevant illustrations.** Avoid loading the presentation with mere decoration.

PowerPoint slides

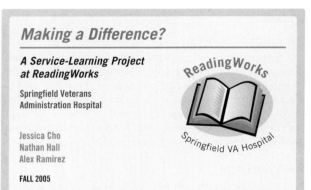

First slide, introducing the project and presentation

Simple, consistent slide design focusing viewers' attention on information, not *PowerPoint* features

Making a Difference?

A Service-Learning Project at ReadingWorks

Springfield Veterans Administration Hospital

Jessica Cho
Nathan Hall
Alex Ramirez

FALL 2005

ReadingWorks
Springfield VA Hospital

Later slide, using brief, bulleted points to be explained by the speaker

Photographs reinforcing the project's activities

Semester goals

- Tutor military veterans
- Research adult literacy
- Keep a journal
- Collaborate on documents for ReadingWorks
- Report experiences and findings

- **Practice**

Take time to rehearse your presentation out loud, with the notes you will be using. Gauge your performance by making an audio- or videotape of yourself or by practicing in front of a mirror. Practicing out loud will also tell you if your presentation is running too long or too short.

If you plan to use visual aids, you'll need to practice with them, too. Your goal is to eliminate hitches (upside-down slides, missing charts) and to weave the visuals seamlessly into your presentation.

▪ Stage fright

Many people report that speaking in front of an audience is their number-one fear. Even many experienced and polished speakers have some anxiety about delivering an oral presentation, but they use this nervous energy to their advantage, letting it propel them into working hard on each presentation. Several techniques can help you reduce anxiety:

- **Use simple relaxation exercises.** Deep breathing or tensing and relaxing your stomach muscles can ease some of the physical symptoms of speech anxiety—stomachache, rapid heartbeat, and shaky hands, legs, and voice.
- **Think positively.** Instead of worrying about the mistakes you might make, concentrate on how well you've prepared and practiced your presentation and how significant your ideas are.
- **Don't avoid opportunities to speak in public.** Practice and experience build speaking skills and offer the best insurance for success.

14 Public Writing

Writing outside of school, such as for business or for community work, resembles academic writing in many ways. It usually involves the same basic writing process, discussed in **1** pp. 3–33: assessing the writing situation, developing what you want to say, freely working out your meaning in a draft, and editing and revising so that your writing will achieve your purpose with readers. It often involves research, as discussed in **7** pp. 371–426. And it involves the standards of conciseness, appropriate and exact language, and correct grammar and usage discussed in **3** through **6**.

But public writing has its own conventions, too. They vary widely, depending on what you're writing and why, whether it's a proposal for your job or a flyer for a community group. This chapter covers several types of public writing: business letters and résumés (next page); memos, reports, and proposals (p. 133); and flyers, newsletters, and brochures for community work (p. 136).

http://www.ablongman.com/littlebrown ▶

Visit the companion Web site for more help with all kinds of public writing.

CULTURE LANGUAGE ◥ Public writing in the United States, especially business writing, favors efficiency and may seem abrupt or impolite compared with such writing in your native culture. For instance, a business letter elsewhere may be expected to begin with polite questions about the addressee or with compliments for the addressee's company, whereas US business letters are expected to get right to the point.

14a Writing business letters and résumés

When you write for business, you are addressing busy people who want to see quickly why you are writing and how they should respond to you. Follow these general guidelines:

- State your purpose right at the start.
- Be straightforward, clear, concise, objective, and courteous.
- Observe conventions of grammar and usage, which make your writing clear and impress your reader with your care.

1 Business letter format

For any business letter, use either unlined white paper measuring 8½″ × 11″ or what is called letterhead stationery with your address printed at the top of the sheet. Type the letter single-spaced (with double spacing between elements) on only one side of a sheet. A common business-letter form is illustrated on the next page:

- The *return-address heading* gives your address and the date. Do not include your name. If you are using stationery with a printed heading, you need only give the date.
- The *inside address* shows the name, title, and complete address of the person you are writing to.
- The *salutation* greets the addressee. Whenever possible, address your letter to a specific person. (Call the company or department to ask whom to address.) If you can't find a person's name, then use a job title (*Dear Human Resources Manager, Dear Customer Service Manager*) or use a general salutation (*Dear Smythe Shoes*). Use *Ms.* as the title for a woman when she has no other title, when you don't know how she prefers to be addressed, or when you know that she prefers *Ms.*
- The *body* contains the substance. Instead of indenting the first line of each paragraph, insert an extra line of space between paragraphs.
- The *close* should reflect the level of formality in the salutation: *Respectfully, Cordially, Yours truly,* and *Sincerely* are more formal closes; *Regards* and *Best wishes* are less formal.

Business letter (job application)

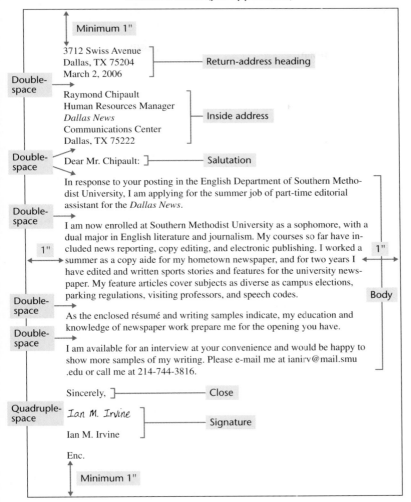

- The *signature* has two parts: your name typed four lines below the close, and your handwritten signature in the space between. Give your name as you sign checks and other documents.
- **Include any additional information below the signature,** such as *Enc.* (indicating an enclosure with the letter) or *cc: Margaret Zusky* (indicating that a copy is being sent to the person named).

Use an envelope that will accommodate the letter once it is folded horizontally in thirds. The envelope should show your name and address in the upper left corner and the addressee's name, title, and address in the center. For easy machine reading, the United States Postal Service recommends all capital letters and no punctuation (spaces separate the elements on a line), as in this address:

RAYMOND CHIPAULT
HUMAN RESOURCES MANAGER
DALLAS NEWS
COMMUNICATIONS CENTER
DALLAS TX 75222-0188

2 Job-application letter

The sample on the preceding page illustrates the key features of a job-application letter:

- **Interpret your résumé for the particular job.** Don't detail your entire résumé, reciting your job history. Instead, highlight and reshape only the relevant parts.
- **Announce at the outset what job you seek and how you heard about it.**
- **Include any special reason you have for applying,** such as a specific career goal.
- **Summarize your qualifications for this particular job,** including relevant facts about education and employment history and emphasizing notable accomplishments. Mention that additional information appears in an accompanying résumé.
- **Describe your availability.** At the end of the letter, mention that you are free for an interview at the convenience of the addressee, or specify when you will be available (for instance, when your current job or classes leave your free, or when you could travel to the employer's city).

3 Résumé

The résumé that accompanies a job application should provide information in table format that allows a potential employer to evaluate your qualifications. The résumé should include your name and address, a career objective, your education and employment history, special skills or awards, and information about how to obtain your references. All the information should fit on one uncrowded page unless your education and experience are extensive. See the sample opposite for writing and formatting guidelines for a résumé that you submit in print.

Some employers may ask for an electronic version of your résumé so that they can add it to a computerized database of appli-

Résumé (print)

Ian M. Irvine	3712 Swiss Avenue Dallas, TX 75204 214-744-3816 ianirv@mail.smu.edu	Name and contact information
Position desired	Part-time editorial assistant.	Career objective stated simply and clearly
Education	*Southern Methodist University*, 2004 to present Current standing: sophomore. Major: English literature and journalism. Journalism courses: news reporting, copy editing, electronic publishing, communication arts, broadcast journalism. *Abilene (Texas) Senior High School*, 2000-04. Graduated with academic, college-preparatory degree.	Education before work experience for most college students
Employment history	2004 to present. Reporter, *Daily Campus*, student newspaper of Southern Methodist University. Write regular coverage of baseball, track, and soccer teams. Write feature stories on campus policies and events. Edit sports news, campus listings, features. Summer 2005. Copy aide, *Abilene Reporter-News*. Assisted reporters with copy routing and research. Summer 2004. Painter, Longhorn Painters, Abilene. Prepared and painted exteriors and interiors of houses.	Headings marking sections, set off with space and highlighting Conventional use of capital letters: yes for proper nouns and after periods; no for job titles, course names, department names, and so on
Special skills	Fluent in Spanish. Proficient in Internet research and word processing.	
References	Available on request: Placement Office Southern Methodist University Dallas, TX 75275	Standard, consistent type font

cants. The employers may scan your printed résumé to convert it to an electronic file, which they can then store in an appropriate database, or they may request that you embed your résumé in an e-mail message. To produce a scannable or electronic résumé, follow the guidelines below and consult the sample on the next page.

- **Keep the design simple for accurate scanning or electronic transmittal.** Avoid images, unusual type, more than one column, vertical or horizontal lines, italics, and underlining.

Résumé (scannable or electronic)

Ian M. Irvine
3712 Swiss Avenue
Dallas, TX 75204
214-744-3816

KEYWORDS: Editor, editorial assistant, publishing, electronic publishing.

OBJECTIVE
Part-time editorial assistant.

EDUCATION
Southern Methodist University, 2004 to present.
Major: English literature and journalism.
Journalism courses: news reporting, copy editing, electronic publishing, communication arts, broadcast journalism.

Abilene (Texas) Senior High School, 2000-04.
Academic, college preparatory degree.

EMPLOYMENT HISTORY
Reporter, Daily Campus, Southern Methodist University, 2004 to present. Writer of articles for student newspaper on sports teams, campus policies, and local events. Editor of sports news, campus listings, and features.

Copy aide, Abilene Reporter-News, Abilene, summer 2005. Assistant to reporters, routing copy and doing research.

Painter, Longhorn Painters, Abilene, summer 2004. Preparation and painting of exteriors and interiors of houses.

SPECIAL SKILLS
Fluent in Spanish.
Proficient in Internet research and word processing.

REFERENCES
Available upon request:
Placement Office
Southern Methodist University
Dallas, TX 75275

Accurate keywords, allowing the employer to place the résumé into an appropriate database

Simple design, avoiding unusual type, italics, multiple columns, decorative lines, and images

Standard font easily read by scanners

Every line aligning at left margin

- **Use concise, specific words to describe your skills and experience.** The employer's computer may use keywords (often nouns) to identify the résumés of suitable job candidates, and you want to ensure that your résumé includes the appropriate keywords. Name your specific skills—for example, the computer programs you can operate—and write concretely with words like *manager* (not *person with responsibility for*) and *reporter* (not *staff member who reports*). Look for likely keywords in the employer's description of the job you seek.

4 Electronic communication

Electronic communication—mainly e-mail and faxes—adds a few twists to business writing. E-mail now plays such a prominent role in communication of all sorts that it is discussed extensively as part of writing online (see pp. 114–17). Generally, the standards for business e-mail are the same as for other business correspondence.

Faxes follow closely the formats of print documents, but there are unique concerns:

- **Consider legibility.** Small type, photographs, horizontal lines, and other elements that look fine on your copy may not be legible to the addressee.
- **Include a cover sheet.** Most faxes require a cover sheet with the addressee's name, company, and fax number; the date, time, and subject; your own name and fax and telephone numbers; and the total number of pages (including the cover sheet) in the fax.
- **Advise your addressee to expect a fax.** Fax transmissions can go astray. The advice is essential if the fax is confidential because the machine is often shared.
- **Consider urgency.** Transmission by fax can imply that the correspondence is urgent. If yours isn't, you may want to use the mail instead.

14b Writing memos, reports, and proposals

1 Memos

Business memorandums (memos, for short) address people within the same organization. Most memos deal briefly with a specific topic, such as an answer to a question or an evaluation.

Both the form and the structure of a memo are designed to get to the point and dispose of it quickly (see the sample on the next page). State your reason for writing in the first sentence. Devote the first paragraph to a concise presentation of your answer, conclusion, or evaluation. In the rest of the memo explain your reasoning or evidence. Use headings or lists as appropriate to highlight key information.

4 Reports and proposals

Reports and proposals are text-heavy documents, sometimes lengthy, that convey information such as the results of research, a plan for action, or a recommendation for change. As with other business correspondence, you will prepare a report or proposal for a specific purpose, and you will be addressing interested but busy readers.

Reports and proposals usually divide into sections. The sections vary depending on the purpose of the document, but usually

Business memo

Heading: company's name, addressee's name, writer's name and initials, date, and subject description

Bigelow Wax Company

TO: Aileen Rosen, Director of Sales
FROM: Patricia Phillips, Territory 12   *PP*
DATE: March 17, 2006
SUBJECT: 2005 sales of Quick Wax in Territory 12

Body: single-spaced with double spacing between paragraphs; paragraphs not indented

Since it was introduced in January 2005, Quick Wax has been unsuccessful in Territory 12 and has not affected the sales of our Easy Shine. Discussions with customers and my own analysis of Quick Wax suggest three reasons for its failure to compete with our product.

1. Quick Wax has not received the promotion necessary for a new product. Advertising—primarily on radio—has been sporadic and has not developed a clear, consistent image for the product. In addition, the Quick Wax sales representative in Territory 12 is new and inexperienced; he is not known to customers, and his sales pitch (which I once overheard) is weak. As far as I can tell, his efforts are not supported by phone calls or mailings from his home office.

2. When Quick Wax does make it to the store shelves, buyers do not choose it over our product. Though priced competitively with our product, Quick Wax is poorly packaged. The container seems smaller than ours, though in fact it holds the same eight ounces. The lettering on the Quick Wax package (red on blue) is difficult to read, in contrast to the white-on-green lettering on the Easy Shine package.

3. Our special purchase offers and my increased efforts to serve existing customers have had the intended effect of keeping customers satisfied with our product and reducing their inclination to stock something new.

People receiving copies

Copies: L. Mendes, Director of Marketing
        J. MacGregor, Customer Service Manager

they include an overview or summary, which tells the reader what the document is about; a statement of the problem or need, which justifies the report or proposal; a statement of the plan or solution, which responds to the need or problem; and a recommendation or evaluation. Consider the following guidelines as you prepare a report or proposal:

- **Do your research.** The standard formats of reports and proposals require you to be well informed, so be alert to where you have enough information or where you don't.

Report

Canada Geese at ABC Institute: An Environmental Problem

Summary

The flock of Canada geese on and around ABC Institute's grounds has grown dramatically in recent years to become a nuisance and an environmental problem. This report reviews the problem, considers possible solutions, and proposes that ABC Institute and the US Fish and Wildlife Service cooperate to reduce the flock by humane means.

The Problem

Canada geese began living at Taylor Lake next to ABC Institute when they were relocated there in 1985 by the state game department. As a nonmigratory flock, the geese are present year-round, with the highest population each year occurring in early spring. In recent years the flock has grown dramatically. The Audubon Society's annual Christmas bird census shows a thirty-fold increase from the 37 geese counted in 1986 to the 1125 counted in 2005.

The principal environmental problem caused by the geese is pollution of grass and water by defecation. Geese droppings cover the ABC Institute's grounds as well as the park's picnicking areas. The runoff from these droppings into Taylor Lake has substantially affected the quality of the lake's water, so that local authorities have twice (2004 and 2005) issued warnings against swimming.

Possible Solutions

The goose overpopulation and resulting environmental problems have several possible solutions:

- Harass the geese with dogs and audiovisual effects (light and noise) so that the geese choose to leave. This solution is inhumane to the geese and unpleasant for human neighbors.
- Feed the geese a chemical that will weaken the shells of their eggs and thus reduce growth of the flock. This solution is inhumane to the geese and also impractical, because geese are long-lived.
- Kill adult geese. This solution is, obviously, inhumane to the geese.
- Thin the goose population by trapping and removing many geese (perhaps 600) to areas less populated by humans, such as wildlife preserves.

Though costly (see figures below), the last solution is the most humane. It would be harmless to the geese, provided that sizable netted enclosures are used for traps. [Discussion of solution and "Recommendations" follow.]

Annotations (right margin):

Descriptive title conveying report's contents

Standard format: summary, statement of the problem, solutions, and (not shown) recommendations

Major sections delineated by headings

Formal tone, appropriate to a business-writing situation

Single spacing with double spacing between paragraphs and around the list

Bulleted list emphasizing alternative solutions

- **Focus on the purpose of each section.** Stick to the point of each section, saying only what you need to say, even if you have additional information. Each section should accomplish its purpose and contribute to the whole.

- **Follow an appropriate format.** In many businesses, reports and proposals have specific formatting requirements. If you are unsure about the requirements, ask your supervisor.

A sample report appears above. For a sample proposal, visit *ablongman.com/littlebrown*.

14c Writing for community work

At some point in your life, you're likely to volunteer for a community organization such as a soup kitchen, a daycare center, or a literacy program. Many college courses involve service learning, in which you do such volunteer work, write about the experience for your course, and write *for* the organization you're helping.

The writing you do for a community group may range from flyers to grant proposals. The two guidelines opposite will help you prepare effective projects like the ones here, for a literacy program.

Flyer

Large type and color focusing a distant reader's attention on important information: what's happening, when, where, and who is invited

White space drawing viewers' eyes to main message and creating flow among elements

Color highlighting only key information

Less important information set in smaller type

FIRST
ANNUAL
AWARDS DINNER

ReadingWorks
Springfield VA Hospital

WHEN
Friday night
May 25
7:30 to 10:30

**For information
contact ReadingWorks
209-556-1212**

WHERE
Suite 42
Springfield VA Hospital

WHO
Students, tutors, and their families are invited to join us for an evening of food and music as we celebrate their efforts and accomplishments.

ReadingWorks of Springfield Veterans Administration Hospital
111 South Springdale Drive
Springfield, MI 45078

- **Craft each document for its purpose and audience.** You are trying to achieve a specific aim with your readers, and the approach and tone you use will influence their responses. If, for example, you are writing letters to local businesses to raise funds for a homeless shelter, bring to mind the person or people who will read your letter. How can you best persuade those readers to donate money?
- **Expect to work with others.** Much public writing is the work of more than one person. Even if you draft the document on your own, others will review the content, tone, and design. Such

---

Newsletter

 ReadingWorks

Springfield Veterans Administration Hospital | **SUMMER 2005**

From the director

Can you help? With more and more learners in the ReadingWorks program, we need more and more tutors. You may know people who would be interested in participating in the program, if only they knew about it.

Those of you who have been tutoring VA patients in reading and writing know both the great need you fulfill and the great benefits you bring to the students. New tutors need no special skills—we'll provide the training—only patience and an interest in helping others.

We've scheduled an orientation meeting for Friday, September 12, at 6:30 PM. Please come and bring a friend who is willing to contribute a couple of hours a week to our work.

Thanks,
Kate Goodman

IN THIS ISSUE

FIRST ANNUAL AWARDS DINNER

A festive night for students and tutors

The first annual Reading-Works Awards Dinner on May 25th was a great success. Springfield's own Golden Fork provided tasty food and Amber Allen supplied lively music. The students decorated Suite 42 on the theme of books and reading. In all, 127 people attended.

The highlight of the night was the awards ceremony. Nine students, recommended by their tutors, received certificates recognizing their efforts and special accomplishments in learning to read and write:

Ramon Berva
Edward Byar
David Dunbar
Tony Garnier
Chris Guigni
Akili Haynes
Josh Livingston
Alex Obeld
B. J. Resnansky

In addition, nine tutors received certificates commemorating five years of service to ReadingWorks:

Anita Crumpton
Felix Cruz-Rivera
Bette Elgen

Kayleah Bortoluzzi
Harriotte Henderson
Ben Obiso
Meggie Puente
Max Smith
Sara Villante

Congratulations to all!

PTSD: New Guidelines

Most of us are working with veterans who have been diagnosed with post-traumatic stress disorder. Because this disorder is often complicated by alcoholism, depression, anxiety, and other problems, the National Center for PTSD has issued some guidelines for helping PTSD patients in ways that reduce their stress.

- The hospital must know your tutoring schedule, and you need to sign in and out before and after each tutoring session.

- To protect patients' privacy, meet them only in designated visiting and tutoring areas, never in their rooms.

- Treat patients with dignity and respect, even when (as sometimes happens) they grow frustrated and angry. Seek help from a nurse or orderly if you need it.

Multicolumn format allowing room for headings, articles, and other elements on a single page

Two-column heading emphasizing the main article

Elements helping readers skim for highlights: spacing, varied font sizes, lines, and a bulleted list

Color focusing readers' attention on banner, headlines, and table of contents

Lively but uncluttered overall appearance

Box in the first column highlighting table of contents

collaboration is rewarding, but it sometimes requires patience and goodwill. See **1** pp. 36–37 for advice on collaborating.

Brochure

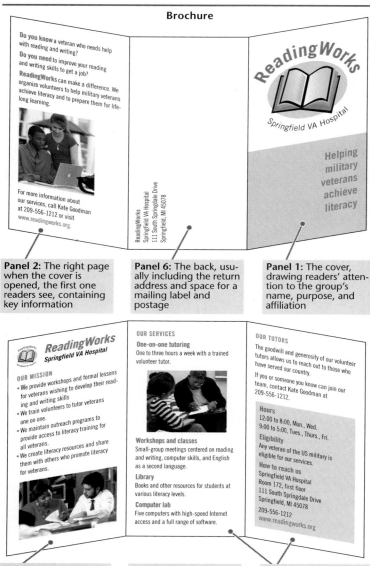

Panel 2: The right page when the cover is opened, the first one readers see, containing key information

Panel 6: The back, usually including the return address and space for a mailing label and postage

Panel 1: The cover, drawing readers' attention to the group's name, purpose, and affiliation

Panel 3: The left page when the cover is opened, reinforcing the message of panel 2

Varied type, color, and photographs, adding visual interest and focusing readers' attention

Panels 4 and 5: The inside panels, containing contact information and other details

Clarity and Style

Clarity and Style

15 Emphasis

Emphatic writing leads readers to see your main ideas both within and among sentences. You can achieve emphasis by attending to your subjects and verbs (below), using sentence beginnings and endings (p. 143), coordinating equally important ideas (p. 146), and subordinating less important ideas (p. 148). In addition, emphatic writing is concise writing, the subject of Chapter 20.

Note Many grammar and style checkers can spot some problems with emphasis, such as nouns made from verbs, passive voice, wordy phrases, and long sentences that may also be flabby and unemphatic. However, the checkers cannot help you identify the important ideas in your sentences or whether those ideas receive appropriate emphasis.

15a   Using subjects and verbs effectively

The heart of every sentence is its subject, which usually names the actor, and its verb, which usually specifies the subject's action: *Children* [subject] *grow* [verb]. When these elements do not identify the key actor and action in the sentence, readers must find that information elsewhere and the sentence may be wordy and unemphatic.

In the following sentences, the subjects and verbs are underlined.

> Unemphatic   The intention of the company was to expand its workforce. A proposal was also made to diversify the backgrounds and abilities of employees.

These sentences are unemphatic because their key ideas do not appear in their subjects and verbs. In the revision on the next page the sentences are not only clearer but more concise.

Key terms

subject Who or what a sentence is about: *Biologists often study animals.* (See 4 pp. 195–97.)

verb The part of a sentence that asserts something about the subject: *Biologists often study animals.* (See 4 pp. 196–97.)

---

http://www.ablongman.com/littlebrown   ▶

Visit the companion Web site for more help and electronic exercises on emphasis.

Revised — The company intended to expand its workforce. It also proposed to diversify the backgrounds and abilities of employees.

The constructions discussed below and opposite usually drain meaning from a sentence's subject and verb.

■ Nouns made from verbs

Nouns made from verbs can obscure the key actions of sentences and add words. These nouns include *intention* (from *intend*), *proposal* (from *propose*), *decision* (from *decide*), *expectation* (from *expect*), and *inclusion* (from *include*).

Unemphatic — After the company made a decision to hire more disabled workers, its next step was the construction of wheelchair ramps and other facilities.

Revised — After the company decided to hire more disabled workers, it next constructed wheelchair ramps and other facilities.

■ Weak verbs

Weak verbs, such as *made* and *was* in the unemphatic sentence above, tend to stall sentences just where they should be moving and often bury key actions:

Unemphatic — The company is now the leader among businesses in complying with the 1990 disabilities act. Its officers make frequent speeches on the act to business groups.

Revised — The company now leads other businesses in complying with the 1990 disabilities act. Its officers frequently speak on the act to business groups.

Forms of *be, have,* and *make* are often weak, but don't try to eliminate every use of them: *be* and *have* are essential as helping verbs (*is going, has written*); *be* links subjects and words describing them (*Planes are noisy*); and *have* and *make* have independent meanings (among them "possess" and "force," respectively). But do consider replacing forms of *be, have,* and *make* when one of the words following the verb could be made into a strong verb itself, as in the following examples.

Unemphatic	Emphatic
was influential	influenced
is a glorification	glorifies

Key terms

noun A word that names a person, thing, quality, place, or idea: *student, desk, happiness, city, democracy.* (See **4** pp. 188–89.)

helping verb A verb used with another verb to convey time, obligation, and other meanings: *was drilling, would have been drilling.* (See **4** p. 191.)

Unemphatic	Emphatic
have a preference	prefer
had the appearance	appeared, seemed
made a claim	claimed

■ **Passive voice**

Verbs in the passive voice state actions received by, not performed by, their subjects. Thus the passive de-emphasizes the true actor of the sentence, sometimes omitting it entirely. Generally, prefer the active voice, in which the subject performs the action. (See also **4** pp. 234–36 for help with editing the passive voice.)

Unemphatic	The 1990 law is seen by most businesses as fair, but the costs of complying have sometimes been exaggerated.
Revised	Most businesses see the 1990 law as fair, but some opponents have exaggerated the costs of complying.

EXERCISE 15.1   Revising: Emphasis of subjects and verbs

Rewrite the sentences in the following paragraph so that their subjects and verbs identify the key actors and actions. (You can do this exercise online at *ablongman.com/littlebrown.*)

1 Many heroes were helpful in the emancipation of the slaves. 2 However, the work of Harriet Tubman, an escaped slave herself, stands above the rest. 3 Tubman's accomplishments included the guidance of hundreds of slaves to freedom on the Underground Railroad. 4 A return to slavery was risked by Tubman or possibly death. 5 During the Civil War she was also a carrier of information from the South to the North. 6 After the war Tubman was instrumental in helping to raise money for former slaves who were in need of support.

15b   Using sentence beginnings and endings

Readers automatically seek a writer's principal meaning in the main clause of a sentence—essentially, in the subject that names the actor and in the verb that usually specifies the action (see p. 141). Thus you can help readers understand the meaning you

┌─ **Key terms** ───────────────────────────────

passive voice The verb form when the subject names the *receiver* of the verb's action: *The house was destroyed by the tornado.*

active voice The verb form when the subject names the *performer* of the verb's action: *The tornado destroyed the house.*

main clause A word group that can stand alone as a sentence, containing a subject and a verb and not beginning with a subordinating word: *The books were expensive.* (See **4** p. 206.)

intend by controlling the information in your subjects and the relation of the main clause to any modifiers attached to it.

■ Old and new information

Generally, readers expect the beginning of a sentence to contain information that they already know or that you have already introduced. They then look to the ending for new information. In the unemphatic passage below, the second and third sentences both begin with new topics, while the old topics appear at the ends of the sentences. The pattern of the passage is A→B. C→B. D→A.

Unemphatic   Education almost means controversy these days, with rising costs and constant complaints about its inadequacies. But the value of schooling should not be obscured by the controversy. The single best means of economic advancement, despite its shortcomings, remains education.

In the more emphatic revision, the old information begins each sentence and new information ends the sentence. The passage follows the pattern A→B. B→C. A→D.

Revised   Education almost means controversy these days, with rising costs and constant complaints about its inadequacies. But the controversy should not obscure the value of schooling. Education remains, despite its shortcomings, the single best means of economic advancement.

■ Cumulative and periodic sentences

You can call attention to information by placing it first or last in a sentence, reserving the middle for incidentals:

Unemphatic   Education remains the single best means of economic advancement, despite its shortcomings. [Emphasizes shortcomings.]

Revised   Despite its shortcomings, education remains the single best means of economic advancement. [Emphasizes advancement more than shortcomings.]

Revised   Education remains, despite its shortcomings, the single best means of economic advancement. [De-emphasizes shortcomings.]

Key term

modifier A word or word group that describes another word or word group: *sweet* candy, *running in the park*. (See **4** pp. 192 and 201.)

A sentence that adds modifiers to the main clause is called **cumulative** because it accumulates information as it proceeds:

Cumulative   Education has no equal in opening minds, instilling values, and creating opportunities.

Cumulative   Most of the Great American Desert is made up of bare rock, rugged cliffs, mesas, canyons, mountains, separated from one another by broad flat basins covered with sun-baked mud and alkali, supporting a sparse and measured growth of sagebrush or creosote or saltbush, depending on location and elevation.   —Edward Abbey

The opposite kind of sentence, called **periodic**, saves the main clause until just before the end (the period) of the sentence. Everything before the main clause points toward it:

Periodic   In opening minds, instilling values, and creating opportunities, education has no equal.

Periodic   With people from all over the world—Korean grocers, Jamaican cricket players, Vietnamese fishers, Haitian cabdrivers, Chinese doctors—the American mosaic is continually changing.

The periodic sentence creates suspense by reserving important information for the end. But readers should already have an idea of the sentence's subject—because it was mentioned in the preceding sentence—so that they know what the opening modifiers describe.

EXERCISE 15.2   Sentence combining: Beginnings and endings

Locate the main idea in each group of sentences below. Then combine each group into a single sentence that emphasizes that idea by placing it at the beginning or the end. For sentences 2–5, determine the position of the main idea by considering its relation to the previous sentences: if the main idea picks up a topic that's already been introduced, place it at the beginning; if it adds new information, place it at the end. (You can do this exercise online at *ablongman.com/littlebrown.*)

Example:
The storm blew roofs off buildings. It caused extensive damage. It knocked down many trees.

Main idea at beginning: The storm caused extensive damage, blowing roofs off buildings and knocking down many trees.

Main idea at end: Blowing roofs off buildings and knocking down many trees, the storm caused extensive damage.

1   Pat Taylor strode into the room. The room was packed. He greeted students called "Taylor's Kids." He nodded to their parents and teachers.

2   This was a wealthy Louisiana oilman. He had promised his "Kids" free college educations. He was determined to make higher education available to all qualified but disadvantaged students.

3 The students welcomed Taylor. Their voices joined in singing. They sang "You Are the Wind Beneath My Wings." Their faces beamed with hope. Their eyes flashed with self-confidence.
4 The students had thought a college education was beyond their dreams. It seemed too costly. It seemed too demanding.
5 Taylor had to ease the costs and the demands of getting to college. He created a bold plan. The plan consisted of scholarships, tutoring, and counseling.

15c Using coordination

Use **coordination** to show that two or more elements in a sentence are equally important in meaning and thus to clarify the relation between them:

■ **Link two main clauses with a comma and a coordinating conjunction,** such as *and* or *but*.

⎯equally important⎯

Independence Hall in Philadelphia is now restored, but fifty years ago it was in bad shape.

■ **Link two main clauses with a semicolon alone or with a semicolon and a conjunctive adverb,** such as *however*.

⎯equally important⎯

The building was standing; however, it suffered from decay.

■ **Within clauses, link words and phrases with a coordinating conjunction,** such as *and* or *or*.

equally
⎯ important ⎯

The people and officials of the nation were indifferent to Indepen-

⎯equally important⎯

dence Hall or took it for granted.

■ **Link main clauses, words, or phrases with a correlative conjunction,** such as *not only . . . but also*.

⎯equally important⎯

People not only took the building for granted but also neglected it.

┌─ **Key terms** ───

main clause A word group that can stand alone as a sentence, containing a subject and a verb and not beginning with a subordinating word: *The books were expensive.* (See **4** p. 206.)

coordinating conjunctions *And, but, or, nor,* and sometimes *for, so, yet.* (See **4** p. 194.)

conjunctive adverbs Modifiers that describe the relation of the ideas in two clauses, such as *hence, however, indeed,* and *thus.* (See **4** p. 286.)

correlative conjunctions Pairs of connecting words, such as *both . . . and, either . . . or, not only . . . but also.* (See **4** p. 194.)

Note Grammar and style checkers may spot some errors in punctuating coordinated elements, and they can flag long sentences that may contain excessive coordination. But otherwise they provide little help with coordination because they cannot recognize the relations among ideas in sentences.

1 Coordinating to relate equal ideas

Coordination shows the equality between elements, as illustrated in the examples opposite. At the same time that it clarifies meaning, it can also help smooth choppy sentences:

Choppy sentences	We should not rely so heavily on oil. Coal and uranium are also overused. We have a substantial energy resource in the moving waters of our rivers. Smaller streams add to the total volume of water. The resource renews itself. Oil and coal are irreplaceable. Uranium is also irreplaceable. The cost of water does not increase much over time. The costs of coal, oil, and uranium rise dramatically.

The revision groups coal, oil, and uranium and clearly opposes them to water (the connecting words are underlined):

Ideas coordinated	We should not rely so heavily on oil, coal, <u>and</u> uranium, <u>for</u> we have a substantial energy resource in the moving waters of our rivers <u>and</u> streams. Oil, coal, <u>and</u> uranium are irreplaceable <u>and</u> thus subject to dramatic cost increases; water, <u>however</u>, is self-renewing <u>and</u> more stable in cost.

2 Coordinating effectively

Use coordination only to express the *equality* of ideas or details. A string of coordinated elements—especially main clauses—implies that all points are equally important:

Excessive coordination	The weeks leading up to the resignation of President Nixon were eventful, and the Supreme Court and the Congress closed in on him, and the Senate Judiciary Committee voted to begin impeachment proceedings, and finally the President resigned on August 9, 1974.

Such a passage needs editing to stress the important points (underlined below) and to de-emphasize the less important information:

Revised	<u>The weeks leading up to the resignation of President Nixon were eventful</u>, as the Supreme Court and the Congress closed in on him and the Senate Judiciary Committee voted to begin impeachment proceedings. <u>Finally, the President resigned on August 9, 1974.</u>

Even within a single sentence, coordination should express a logical equality between ideas:

Faulty   John Stuart Mill was a nineteenth-century utilitarian, and he believed that actions should be judged by their usefulness or by the happiness they cause. [The two clauses are not separate and equal: the second expands on the first by explaining what a utilitarian such as Mill believed.]

Revised   John Stuart Mill, <u>a nineteenth-century utilitarian</u>, believed that actions should be judged by their usefulness or by the happiness they cause.

EXERCISE 15.3   Sentence combining: Coordination

Combine sentences in the following passages to coordinate related ideas in the ways that seem most effective to you. You will have to supply coordinating conjunctions or conjunctive adverbs and the appropriate punctuation. (You can do this exercise online at *ablongman.com/littlebrown*.)

1 Many chronic misspellers do not have the time to master spelling rules. They may not have the motivation. They may rely on dictionaries to catch misspellings. Most dictionaries list words under their correct spellings. One kind of dictionary is designed for chronic misspellers. It lists each word under its common *mis*spellings. It then provides the correct spelling. It also provides the definition.

2 Henry Hudson was an English explorer. He captained ships for the Dutch East India Company. On a voyage in 1610 he passed by Greenland. He sailed into a great bay in today's northern Canada. He thought he and his sailors could winter there. The cold was terrible. Food ran out. The sailors mutinied. The sailors cast Hudson adrift in a small boat. Eight others were also in the boat. Hudson and his companions perished.

15d Using subordination

Use **subordination** to indicate that some elements in a sentence are less important than others for your meaning. Usually, the main idea appears in the main clause, and supporting details appear in subordinate structures:

- Use a subordinate clause beginning with *although, because, if, who* (*whom*), *that, which,* or another subordinating word.

Key terms

main clause A word group that can stand alone as a sentence, containing a subject and a verb and not beginning with a subordinating word: *The books were expensive.* (See **4** p. 206.)

subordinate clause A word group that contains a subject and verb, begins with a subordinating word such as *because* or *who*, and is not a question: *Words can do damage <u>when they hurt feelings</u>.* (See **4** p. 206.)

more important
┌────less important (subordinate clause)────┐ ┌───(main clause)───┐
Although production costs have declined, they are still high.

less important
┌──────(subordinate clause)──────┐
Costs, which include labor and facilities, are difficult to control.
◄────── more important (main clause) ──────►

■ **Use a phrase.**

less important more important
┌──────(phrase)──────┐ ┌──────(main clause)──────┐
Despite some decline, production costs are still high.

┌──────less important (phrase)──────┐
Costs, including labor and facilities, are difficult to control.
◄────── more important (main clause) ──────►

■ **Use a single word.**

Declining costs have not matched prices.
Labor costs are difficult to control.

Note Grammar and style checkers may spot some errors in punctuating subordinated elements, and they can flag long sentences that may contain excessive subordination. But otherwise they provide little help with subordination because they cannot recognize the relations among ideas in sentences.

1 Subordinating to emphasize main ideas

A string of main clauses can make everything in a passage seem equally important:

String of   Computer prices have dropped, and production costs
main clauses   have dropped more slowly, and computer manufacturers
                    have had to struggle, for their profits have been shrinking.

Emphasis comes from keeping the truly important information in the main clause (underlined) and subordinating the less important details:

Revised   Because production costs have dropped more slowly than
                    prices, computer manufacturers have had to struggle
                    with shrinking profits.

2 Subordinating effectively

Use subordination only for the less important information in a sentence.

┌─ **Key term** ───
│ **phrase** A word group that lacks a subject or verb or both: *Words can do*
│ *damage by hurting feelings.* (See **4** p. 201.)
└──

Faulty	Ms. Angelo was in her first year of teaching, although she was a better instructor than others with many years of experience.

The preceding sentence suggests that Angelo's inexperience is the main idea, whereas the writer intended to stress her skill *despite* her inexperience. Reducing the inexperience to a subordinate clause and elevating the skill to the main clause (underlined) gives appropriate emphasis:

Revised	Although Ms. Angelo was in her first year of teaching, <u>she was a better instructor than others with many years of experience.</u>

Subordination loses its power to organize and emphasize when too much loosely related detail crowds into one long, meandering sentence:

Overloaded	The boats that were moored at the dock when the hurricane, which was one of the worst in three decades, struck were ripped from their moorings, because the owners had not been adequately prepared, since the weather service had predicted that the storm would blow out to sea, which they do at this time of year.

The revision stresses important information in the main clauses (underlined):

Revised	Struck by one of the worst hurricanes in three decades, <u>the boats at the dock were ripped from their moorings.</u> <u>The owners were unprepared</u> because the weather service had said that hurricanes at this time of year blow out to sea.

EXERCISE 15.4 Revising: Subordination for emphasis

Emphasize the important information in the following paragraph by giving it in main clauses and subordinating other information. (You can do this exercise online at *ablongman.com/littlebrown*.)

1 During the Civil War, soldiers often admired their commanding officers, and they gave them nicknames, and these names frequently contained the word *old*, but not all of the commanders were old. 2 Confederate General Thomas "Stonewall" Jackson was also called "Old Jack," and he was not yet forty years old. 3 Another Southern general in the Civil War was called "Old Pete," and his full name was James Longstreet. 4 The Union general Henry W. Halleck had a reputation as a good military strategist, and he was an expert on the work of a French military authority, Henri Jomini, and Halleck was called "Old Brains." 5 Well before the Civil War, General William Henry Harrison won the Battle of Tippecanoe, and he received the nickname "Old Tippecanoe," and he used the name in his presidential campaign slogan, "Tippecanoe and

Tyler, Too," and he won the election in 1840, but he died of pneumonia a month after taking office.

EXERCISE 15.5   Sentence combining: Subordination

Combine each of the following pairs of sentences twice, each time using one of the subordinate structures in parentheses to make a single sentence. You will have to add, delete, change, and rearrange words. (You can do this exercise online at *ablongman.com/littlebrown*.)

Example:
During the late eighteenth century, workers carried beverages in brightly colored bottles. The bottles had cork stoppers. (*Clause beginning that. Phrase beginning with.*)
During the late eighteenth century, workers carried beverages in brightly colored bottles that had cork stoppers.

During the late eighteenth century, workers carried beverages in brightly colored bottles with cork stoppers.

1 The bombardier beetle sees an enemy. It shoots out a jet of chemicals to protect itself. (*Clause beginning when. Phrase beginning seeing.*)
2 The beetle's spray is very potent. It consists of hot and irritating chemicals. (*Phrase beginning consisting. Phrase beginning of.*)
3 The spray's two chemicals are stored separately in the beetle's body and mixed in the spraying gland. The chemicals resemble a nerve-gas weapon. (*Phrase beginning stored. Clause beginning which.*)
4 The tip of the beetle's abdomen sprays the chemicals. The tip revolves like a turret on a World War II bomber. (*Phrase beginning revolving. Phrase beginning spraying.*)
5 The beetle defeats most of its enemies. It is still eaten by spiders and birds. (*Clause beginning although. Phrase beginning except.*)

EXERCISE 15.6   Revising: Effective subordination

Revise the following paragraph to eliminate faulty or excessive subordination and thus to emphasize the main ideas. Correct faulty subordination by reversing main and subordinate structures. Correct excessive subordination by coordinating equal ideas or by making separate sentences. (You can do this exercise online at *ablongman.com/littlebrown*.)

1 Genaro González is a successful writer, which means that his stories and novels have been published to critical acclaim. 2 In interviews, he talks about his love of writing, even though he has also earned a doctorate in psychology because he enjoys teaching. 3 González's first story, which reflects his growing consciousness of his Aztec heritage and place in the world, is titled "Un Hijo del Sol." 4 He wrote the first version of "Un Hijo del Sol" while he was a sophomore at the University of Texas-Pan American, which is in the Rio Grande valley of southern Texas, which Gonzáles called "el Valle" in the story, and where he now teaches psychology.

5 Gonzáles, who writes equally well in English and Spanish, received a large fellowship that enabled him to take a leave of absence from his teaching job at Pan American so that for a year he could write full-time.

EXERCISE 15.7 Revising: Coordination and subordination

The following paragraph consists entirely of simple sentences. Use coordination and subordination to combine sentences in the ways you think most effective to emphasize main ideas. (You can do this exercise online at *ablongman.com/littlebrown*.)

Sir Walter Raleigh personified the Elizabethan Age. That was the period of Elizabeth I's rule of England. The period occurred in the last half of the sixteenth century. Raleigh was a courtier and poet. He was also an explorer and entrepreneur. Supposedly, he gained Queen Elizabeth's favor. He did this by throwing his cloak beneath her feet at the right moment. She was just about to step over a puddle. There is no evidence for this story. It does illustrate Raleigh's dramatic and dynamic personality. His energy drew others to him. He was one of Elizabeth's favorites. She supported him. She also dispensed favors to him. However, he lost his queen's goodwill. Without her permission he seduced one of her maids of honor. He eventually married the maid of honor. Elizabeth died. Then her successor imprisoned Raleigh in the Tower of London. Her successor was James I. The king falsely charged Raleigh with treason. Raleigh was released after thirteen years. He was arrested again two years later on the old treason charges. At the age of sixty-six he was beheaded.

---

16 Parallelism

Parallelism is a similarity of grammatical form for similar elements of meaning within a sentence or among sentences.

The air is dirtied by factories belching smoke
                       and
                       cars spewing exhaust.

In this example the two underlined phrases have the same function and importance (both specify sources of air pollution), so they also have the same grammatical construction. Parallelism makes form follow meaning.

Note A grammar and style checker cannot recognize faulty parallelism because it cannot recognize the relations among ideas.

http://www.ablongman.com/littlebrown ▶

Visit the companion Web site for more help and electronic exercises on parallelism.

16a Using parallelism with *and, but, or, nor, yet*

The coordinating conjunctions *and, but, or, nor,* and *yet* always signal a need for parallelism:

The industrial base was <u>shifting</u> and <u>shrinking</u>. [Parallel words.]

Politicians rarely <u>acknowledged the problem</u> or <u>proposed alternatives</u>. [Parallel phrases.]

Industrial workers were understandably disturbed <u>that they were losing their jobs</u> and <u>that no one seemed to care</u>. [Parallel clauses.]

When sentence elements linked by coordinating conjunctions are not parallel in structure, the sentence is awkward and distracting:

Nonparallel	The reasons steel companies kept losing money were <u>that their plants were inefficient</u>, <u>high labor costs</u>, and <u>foreign competition was increasing</u>.
Revised	The reasons steel companies kept losing money were <u>inefficient plants</u>, <u>high labor costs</u>, and <u>increasing foreign competition</u>.
Nonparallel	Success was difficult even for efficient companies because <u>of the shift away from all manufacturing in the United States</u> and <u>the fact that steel production was shifting toward emerging nations</u>.
Revised	Success was difficult even for efficient companies because of the shift <u>away from all manufacturing in the United States</u> and <u>toward steel production in emerging nations</u>.

All the words required by idiom or grammar must be stated in compound constructions (see also **4** p. 176):

Faulty	Given training, workers can acquire the <u>skills</u> and <u>interest</u> in other jobs. [Idiom dictates different prepositions with *skills* and *interest*.]
Revised	Given training, workers can acquire the skills <u>for</u> and interest in other jobs.

16b Using parallelism with *both . . . and, not . . . but,* or another correlative conjunction

Correlative conjunctions stress equality and balance between elements. Parallelism confirms the equality.

Key term

coordinating conjunctions Words that connect elements of the same kind and importance: *and, but, or, nor,* and sometimes *for, so, yet.* (See **4** p. 194.)

It is not <u>a tax bill</u> but <u>a tax relief bill</u>, providing relief not <u>for the needy</u> but <u>for the greedy</u>. —Franklin Delano Roosevelt

With correlative conjunctions, the element after the second connector must match the element after the first connector:

Nonparallel	Huck Finn learns not only <u>that human beings have an enormous capacity for folly</u> but also <u>enormous dignity.</u> [The first element includes *that human beings have;* the second element does not.]
Revised	Huck Finn learns <u>that human beings have</u> not only <u>an enormous capacity for folly</u> but also <u>enormous dignity.</u> [Repositioning *that human beings have* makes the two elements parallel.]

16c Using parallelism in comparisons

Parallelism confirms the likeness or difference between two elements being compared using *than* or *as:*

Nonparallel	Huck Finn proves less <u>a bad boy</u> than <u>to be an independent spirit</u>. In the end he is every bit <u>as determined in rejecting help</u> as he is <u>to leave</u> for "the territory."
Revised	Huck Finn proves less <u>a bad boy</u> than <u>an independent spirit</u>. In the end he is every bit <u>as determined to reject help</u> as he is <u>to leave</u> for "the territory."

(See also **4** pp. 263–64 on making comparisons logical.)

16d Using parallelism with lists, headings, and outlines

The items in a list or outline are coordinate and should be parallel. Parallelism is essential in the headings that divide a paper into sections and in a formal topic outline (See **1** pp. 19–20 and 59–60).

Nonparallel	Revised
Changes in Renaissance England	Changes in Renaissance England
1. Extension of trade routes	1. Extension of trade routes
2. Merchant class became more powerful	2. <u>Increased power</u> of the merchant class

---

Key term

correlative conjunctions Pairs of words that connect elements of the same kind and importance, such as *but . . . and, either . . . or, neither . . . nor, not . . . but, not only . . . but also.* (See **4** p. 193.)

3. The death of feudalism	3. Death of feudalism
4. Upsurging of the arts	4. Upsurge of the arts
5. Religious quarrels began	5. Rise of religious quarrels

EXERCISE 16.1 Revising: Parallelism

Revise the following paragraph as needed to create parallelism for grammar and coherence. Add or delete words or rephrase as necessary. (You can do this exercise online at *ablongman.com/littlebrown*.)

1 The ancient Greeks celebrated four athletic contests: the Olympic Games at Olympia, the Isthmian Games were held near Corinth, at Delphi the Pythian Games, and the Nemean Games were sponsored by the people of Cleonae. 2 Each day the games consisted of either athletic events or holding ceremonies and sacrifices to the gods. 3 Competitors participated in running sprints, spectacular chariot and horse races, and running long distances while wearing full armor. 4 The purpose of such events was developing physical strength, demonstrating skill and endurance, and sharpening the skills needed for war. 5 The athletes competed less to achieve great wealth than for gaining honor both for themselves and their cities. 6 Of course, exceptional athletes received financial support from patrons, poems and statues by admiring artists, and they even got lavish living quarters from their sponsoring cities. 7 With the medal counts and flag ceremonies, today's Olympians sometimes seem to be proving their countries' superiority more than to demonstrate individual talent.

EXERCISE 16.2 Sentence combining: Parallelism

Combine each group of sentences below into one concise sentence in which parallel elements appear in parallel structures. You will have to add, delete, change, and rearrange words. Each item has more than one possible answer. (You can do this exercise online at *ablongman.com/ littlebrown*.)

Example:

The new process works smoothly. It is efficient, too.
The new process works smoothly and efficiently.

1 People can develop post-traumatic stress disorder (PTSD). They develop it after experiencing a dangerous situation. They will also have felt fear for their survival.
2 The disorder can be triggered by a wide variety of events. Combat is a typical cause. Similarly, natural disasters can result in PTSD. Some people experience PTSD after a hostage situation.
3 PTSD can occur immediately after the stressful incident. Or it may not appear until many years later.
4 Sometimes people with PTSD will act irrationally. Moreover, they often become angry.
5 Other symptoms include dreaming that one is reliving the experience. They include hallucinating that one is back in the terrifying place. In another symptom one imagines that strangers are actually one's former torturers.

17 Variety and Details

Writing that's interesting as well as clear has at least two features: the sentences vary in length and structure, and they are well textured with details.

Note Some grammar and style checkers will flag long sentences, and you can check for appropriate variety in a series of such sentences. But generally these programs cannot help you see where variety may be needed because they cannot recognize the relative importance and complexity of your ideas.

17a Varying sentence length

In most contemporary writing, sentences tend to vary from about ten to about forty words. When sentences are all at one extreme or the other, readers may have difficulty focusing on main ideas and seeing the relations among them.

- **Long sentences.** If most of your sentences contain thirty-five words or more, your main ideas may not stand out from the details that support them. Break some of the long sentences into shorter, simpler ones.
- **Short sentences.** If most of your sentences contain fewer than ten or fifteen words, all your ideas may seem equally important and the links between them may not be clear. Try combining them with coordination (p. 146) and subordination (p. 148) to show relationships and stress main ideas over supporting information.

17b Varying sentence structure

A passage will be monotonous if all its sentences follow the same pattern, like soldiers marching in a parade. Try these techniques for varying structure.

1 Subordination

A string of main clauses in simple or compound sentences can be especially plodding.

http://www.ablongman.com/littlebrown ▶

Visit the companion Web site for more help and an electronic exercise on variety and details.

| Monotonous | The moon is now drifting away from the earth. It moves away at the rate of about one inch a year. This movement is lengthening our days. They increase a thousandth of a second every century. Forty-seven of our present days will someday make up a month. We might eventually lose the moon altogether. Such great planetary movement rightly concerns astronomers, but it need not worry us. It will take 50 million years. |

Enliven such writing—and make the main ideas stand out—by expressing the less important information in subordinate clauses and phrases. In the revision below, underlining indicates subordinate structures that used to be main clauses:

| Revised | The moon is now drifting away from the earth <u>about one inch a year</u>. <u>At a thousandth of a second every century,</u> this movement is lengthening our days. Forty-seven of our present days will someday make up a month, <u>if we don't eventually lose the moon altogether</u>. Such great planetary movement rightly concerns astronomers, but it need not worry us. It will take 50 million years. |

2 Sentence combining

As the preceding example shows, subordinating to achieve variety often involves combining short, choppy sentences into longer units that link related information and stress main ideas. Here is another unvaried passage:

| Monotonous | Astronomy may seem a remote science. It may seem to have little to do with people's daily lives. Many astronomers find otherwise. They see their science as soothing. It gives perspective to everyday routines and problems. |

Combining five sentences into one, the revision on the next page is both clearer and easier to read. Underlining highlights the many changes.

Key terms

main clause A word group that contains a subject and a verb and does not begin with a subordinating word: *Tourism is an industry. It brings in over $2 billion a year.* (See **4** p. 206.)

subordinate clause A word group that contains a subject and verb, begins with a subordinating word such as *because* or *who,* and is not a question: *Tourism is an industry <u>that brings in over $2 billion a year</u>.* (See **4** p. 206.)

phrase A word group that lacks a subject or verb or both: *Tourism is an industry <u>valued at over $2 billion a year</u>.* (See **4** p. 201.)

Revised — Astronomy may seem a remote science having little to do with people's daily lives, but many astronomers find their science soothing because it gives perspective to everyday routines and problems.

3 Varied sentence beginnings

An English sentence often begins with its subject, which generally captures old information from a preceding sentence (see p. 143):

The defendant's lawyer was determined to break the prosecution's witness. He relentlessly cross-examined the stubborn witness for a week.

However, an unbroken sequence of sentences beginning with the subject quickly becomes monotonous:

Monotonous — The defendant's lawyer was determined to break the prosecution's witness. He relentlessly cross-examined the witness for a week. The witness had expected to be dismissed within an hour and was visibly irritated. She did not cooperate. She was reprimanded by the judge.

Beginning some of these sentences with other expressions improves readability and clarity:

Revised — The defendant's lawyer was determined to break the prosecution's witness. For a week he relentlessly cross-examined the witness. Expecting to be dismissed within an hour, the witness was visibly irritated. She did not cooperate. Indeed, she was reprimanded by the judge.

The underlined expressions represent the most common choices for varying sentence beginnings:

- **Adverb modifiers,** such as *For a week* (modifies the verb *cross-examined*).
- **Adjective modifiers,** such as *Expecting to be dismissed within an hour* (modifies *witness*).
- **Transitional expressions,** such as *Indeed.* (See **1** pp. 44–45 for a list.)

CULTURE LANGUAGE In standard American English, placing certain adverb modifiers at the beginning of a sentence requires you to alter the normal subject-verb order as well. The most common of these

---

Key terms

adverb A word or word group that describes a verb, an adjective, another adverb, or a whole sentence: *dressed sharply, clearly unhappy, soaring from the mountain.* (See **4** p. 192.)

adjective A word or word group that describes a noun or pronoun: *sweet smile, certain someone.* (See **4** p. 192.)

modifiers are negatives, including *seldom, rarely, in no case, not since,* and *not until.*

          adverb   subject   verb phrase
Faulty   Seldom a witness has held the stand so long.

          adverb   helping verb   subject   main verb
Revised   Seldom has a witness held the stand so long.

4 Varied word order

Occasionally you can vary a sentence and emphasize it at the same time by inverting the usual order of parts:

> A dozen witnesses testified for the prosecution, and the defense attorney barely questioned eleven of them. The twelfth, however, he grilled. [Normal word order: *He grilled the twelfth, however.*]

Inverted sentences used without need are artificial. Use them only when emphasis demands.

17c   Adding details

Relevant details such as facts and examples create the texture and life that keep readers awake and help them grasp your meaning. For instance:

Flat   Constructed after World War II, Levittown, New York, consisted of thousands of houses in two basic styles. Over the decades, residents have altered the houses so dramatically that the original styles are often unrecognizable.

Detailed   Constructed on potato fields after World War II, Levittown, New York, consisted of more than seventeen thousand houses in Cape Cod and ranch styles. Over the decades, residents have added expansive front porches, punched dormer windows through roofs, converted garages to sun porches, and otherwise altered the houses so dramatically that the original styles are often unrecognizable.

EXERCISE 17.1   Revising: Variety

The following paragraph consists entirely of simple sentences that begin with their subjects. Use the techniques discussed in this chapter to vary the sentences. Delete, add, change, and rearrange words to make the paragraph more readable and to make important ideas stand out clearly. (You can do this exercise online at *ablongman.com/littlebrown.*)

The Italian volcano Vesuvius had been dormant for many years. It then exploded on August 24 in the year AD 79. The ash, pumice, and mud from the volcano buried two busy towns. Herculaneum is one.

The more famous is Pompeii. Both towns lay undiscovered for many centuries. Herculaneum and Pompeii were discovered in 1709 and 1748, respectively. The excavation of Pompeii was the more systematic. It was the occasion for initiating modern methods of conservation and restoration. Herculaneum was simply looted of its more valuable finds. It was then left to disintegrate. Pompeii appears much as it did before the eruption. A luxurious house opens onto a lush central garden. An election poster decorates a wall. A dining table is set for breakfast.

18 Appropriate and Exact Language

The clarity and effectiveness of your writing will depend greatly on the use of language that is appropriate for your writing situation (below) and that expresses your meaning exactly (p. 167).

18a Choosing appropriate language

Appropriate language suits your writing situation—your subject, purpose, and audience. In most college and career writing you should rely on what's called **standard American English,** the dialect of English normally expected and used in school, business, the professions, government, and the communications media. (For more on its role in academic writing, see **2** pp. 72–74.)

The vocabulary of standard American English is huge, allowing expression of an infinite range of ideas and feelings; but it does exclude words that only some groups of people use, understand, or find inoffensive. Some of these more limited vocabularies should be avoided altogether; others should be used cautiously and in relevant situations, as when aiming for a special effect with an audience you know will appreciate it. Whenever you doubt a word's status, consult a dictionary (see pp. 167–68).

Note Many grammar and style checkers can be set to flag potentially inappropriate words, such as nonstandard dialect, slang, colloquialisms, and gender-specific terms (*manmade, mailman*). However, the checker can flag only words listed in its dictionary of questionable words. For example, a checker flagged *businessman* as potentially sexist in *A successful businessman puts clients first,* but the checker did not flag *his* in *A successful businessperson listens to*

http://www.ablongman.com/littlebrown ▶

Visit the companion Web site for more help and electronic exercises on appropriate and exact language.

his clients. If you use a checker to review your language, you'll need to determine whether a flagged word is or is not appropriate for your writing situation.

1 Nonstandard dialect ❝ CULTURE LANGUAGE ❞

Like many countries, the United States includes scores of regional, social, and ethnic groups with their own distinct **dialects,** or versions of English. Standard American English is one of those dialects, and so are Black English, Appalachian English, Creole, and the English of coastal Maine. All the dialects of English share many features, but each also has its own vocabulary, pronunciation, and grammar.

If you speak a dialect of English besides standard American English, be careful about using your dialect in situations where standard English is the norm, such as in academic or business writing. Dialects are not wrong in themselves, but forms imported from one dialect into another may still be perceived as unclear or incorrect. When you know standard English is expected in your writing, edit to eliminate expressions in your dialect that you know (or have been told) differ from standard English. These expressions may include *theirselves, hisn, them books,* and others labeled "nonstandard" by a dictionary. They may also include verb forms, as discussed in 4 pp. 214–24. For help identifying and editing nonstandard language, see the "❝ CULTURE LANGUAGE ❞ Guide" just before the back endpapers of this book.

Your participation in the community of standard English does not require you to abandon your own dialect. You may want to use it in writing you do for yourself, such as journals, notes, and drafts, which should be composed as freely as possible. You may want to quote it in an academic paper, as when analyzing or reporting conversation in dialect. And, of course, you will want to use it with others who speak it.

2 Slang

Slang is the language used by a group, such as musicians or computer programmers, to reflect common experiences and to make technical references efficient. The following example is from an essay on the slang of "skaters" (skateboarders):

> Curtis slashed ultra-punk crunchers on his longboard, while the Rube-man flailed his usual Gumbyness on tweaked frontsides and lofty fakie ollies.
> —Miles Orkin, "Mucho Slingage by the Pool"

Among those who understand it, slang may be vivid and forceful. It often occurs in dialog, and an occasional slang expression can enliven an informal essay. But most slang is too flippant and imprecise for effective communication, and it is generally inappropriate for college or business writing. Notice the gain in seriousness and precision achieved in the following revision:

| Slang | Many students start out <u>pretty together</u> but then <u>get weird</u>. |
| Revised | Many students start out <u>with clear goals</u> but then <u>lose their direction</u>. |

3 Colloquial language

Colloquial language is the everyday spoken language, including expressions such as *get together, go crazy, do the dirty work,* and *get along.*

When you write informally, colloquial language may be appropriate to achieve the casual, relaxed effect of conversation. An occasional colloquial word dropped into otherwise more formal writing can also help you achieve a desired emphasis. But most colloquial language is not precise enough for college or career writing. In such writing you should generally avoid any words and expressions labeled "informal" or "colloquial" in your dictionary.

| Colloquial | According to a Native American myth, the Great Creator <u>had a dog hanging around with him</u> when he created the earth. |
| Revised | According to a Native American myth, the Great Creator <u>was accompanied by a dog</u> when he created the earth. |

4 Technical words

All disciplines and professions rely on specialized language that allows the members to communicate precisely and efficiently with each other. Chemists, for instance, have their *phosphatides,* and literary critics have their *motifs* and *subtexts.* Without explanation, technical words are meaningless to nonspecialists. When you are writing for nonspecialists, avoid unnecessary technical terms and carefully define terms you must use.

5 Indirect and pretentious writing

Small, plain, and direct words are almost always preferable to big, showy, or evasive words. Take special care to avoid euphemisms, double talk, and pretentious writing.

A **euphemism** is a presumably inoffensive word that a writer or speaker substitutes for a word deemed potentially offensive or too blunt, such as *passed away* for *died* or *misspeak* for *lie.* Use euphemisms only when you know that blunt, truthful words would needlessly hurt or offend members of your audience.

A kind of euphemism that deliberately evades the truth is **double talk** (also called **doublespeak** or **weasel words**): language intended to confuse or to be misunderstood. Today double talk is unfortunately common in politics and advertising—the *revenue enhancement* that is really a tax, the *peace-keeping function* that is really war making, the *biodegradable* bags that last decades. Double talk has no place in honest writing.

Euphemism and sometimes double talk seem to keep company with **pretentious writing,** fancy language that is more elaborate than its subject requires. Choose your words for their exactness and economy. The big, ornate word may be tempting, but pass it up. Your readers will be grateful.

Pretentious   To perpetuate our endeavor of providing funds for our elderly citizens as we do at the present moment, we will face the exigency of enhanced contributions from all our citizens.

Revised   We cannot continue to fund Social Security and Medicare for the elderly unless we raise taxes.

6 Sexist and other biased language

Even when we do not mean it to, our language can reflect and perpetuate hurtful prejudices toward groups of people. Such biased language can be obvious—words such as *nigger, honky, mick, kike, fag, dyke,* and *broad.* But it can also be subtle, generalizing about groups in ways that may be familiar but that are also inaccurate or unfair.

Biased language reflects poorly on the user, not on the person or persons whom it mischaracterizes or insults. Unbiased language does not submit to false generalizations. It treats people respectfully as individuals and labels groups as they wish to be labeled.

■ Stereotypes of race, ethnicity, religion, age, and other characteristics

A **stereotype** is a generalization based on poor evidence, a kind of formula for understanding and judging people simply because of their membership in a group:

Men are uncommunicative.
Women are emotional.
Liberals want to raise taxes.
Conservatives are affluent.

At best, stereotypes betray a noncritical writer, one who is not thinking beyond notions received from others. In your writing, be alert for statements that characterize whole groups of people:

Stereotype   Elderly drivers should have their licenses limited to daytime driving only. [Asserts that all elderly people are poor night drivers.]

| Revised | Drivers with impaired night vision should have their licenses limited to daytime driving only. |

Some stereotypes have become part of the language, but they are still potentially offensive:

| Stereotype | The administrators are too blind to see the need for a new gymnasium. [Implies that blind people are dense or unperceptive.] |
| Revised | The administrators do not understand the need for a new gymnasium. |

■ **Sexist language**

Among the most subtle and persistent biased language is that expressing narrow ideas about men's and women's roles, position, and value in society. Like other stereotypes, this **sexist language** can wound or irritate readers, and it indicates the writer's thoughtlessness or unfairness. The following box suggests some ways of eliminating sexist language.

Eliminating sexist language

■ **Avoid demeaning and patronizing language:**

Sexist	Dr. Keith Kim and Lydia Hawkins coauthored the article.
Revised	Dr. Keith Kim and Dr. Lydia Hawkins coauthored the article.
Revised	Keith Kim and Lydia Hawkins coauthored the article.

| Sexist | Ladies are entering almost every occupation formerly filled by men. |
| Revised | Women are entering almost every occupation formerly filled by men. |

■ **Avoid occupational or social stereotypes:**

| Sexist | The considerate doctor commends a nurse when she provides his patients with good care. |
| Revised | The considerate doctor commends a nurse who provides good care for patients. |

| Sexist | The grocery shopper should save her coupons. |
| Revised | Grocery shoppers should save their coupons. |

■ **Avoid referring needlessly to gender:**

| Sexist | Marie Curie, a woman chemist, discovered radium. |
| Revised | Marie Curie, a chemist, discovered radium. |

| Sexist | The patients were tended by a male nurse. |
| Revised | The patients were tended by a nurse. |

- **Avoid using *man* or words containing *man* to refer to all human beings.** Here are a few alternatives:

businessman	businessperson
chairman	chair, chairperson
congressman	representative in Congress, legislator
craftsman	craftsperson, artisan
layman	layperson
mankind	humankind, humanity, human beings, humans
manmade	handmade, manufactured, synthetic, artificial
manpower	personnel, human resources
policeman	police officer
salesman	salesperson, sales representative

Sexist   Man has not reached the limits of social justice.

Revised   Humankind [or Humanity] has not reached the limits of social justice.

Sexist   The furniture consists of manmade materials.

Revised   The furniture consists of synthetic materials.

- **Avoid the generic *he*,** the male pronoun used to refer to both genders. (See also 4 pp. 252–54.)

Sexist   The newborn child explores his world.

Revised   Newborn children explore their world. [Use the plural for the pronoun and the word it refers to.]

Revised   The newborn child explores the world. [Avoid the pronoun altogether.]

Revised   The newborn child explores his or her world. [Substitute male and female pronouns.]

Use the last option sparingly—only once in a group of sentences and only to stress the singular individual.

CULTURE LANGUAGE Forms of address vary widely from culture to culture. In some cultures, for instance, one shows respect by referring to all older women as if they were married, using the equivalent of *Mrs.* Usage in the United States is changing toward making no assumptions about marital status, rank, or other characteristics—for instance, addressing a woman as *Ms.* unless she is known to prefer *Mrs.* or *Miss.*

- **Appropriate labels**

We often need to label groups: *swimmers, politicians, mothers, Christians, Westerners, students.* But labels can be shorthand stereotypes, slighting the person labeled and ignoring the preferences of the group members themselves. Although sometimes dismissed as "political correctness," showing sensitivity about labels hurts no one and helps gain your readers' trust and respect.

- Avoid labels that (intentionally or not) disparage the person or group you refer to. A person with emotional problems is not a *mental patient*. A person with cancer is not a *cancer victim*. A person using a wheelchair is not *wheelchair-bound*.

- Use names for racial, ethnic, and other groups that reflect the preferences of each group's members, or at least many of them. Examples of current preferences include *African American* or *black*, *latino/latina* (for Americans and American immigrants of Spanish-speaking descent), and *people with disabilities* (rather than *the handicapped*). But labels change often. To learn how a group's members wish to be labeled, ask them directly, attend to usage in reputable periodicals, or check a recent dictionary.

A helpful reference for appropriate labels is *Guidelines for Bias-Free Writing*, by Marilyn Schwartz and the Task Force on Bias-Free Language of the Association of American University Presses.

EXERCISE 18.1 Revising: Appropriate words

Rewrite the following paragraphs as needed for standard American English, focusing on inappropriate slang, technical or pretentious language, and biased language. Consult a dictionary to determine whether particular words are appropriate and to find suitable substitutes. (You can do this exercise online at *ablongman.com/littlebrown*.)

1 Acquired immune deficiency syndrome (AIDS) is a major deal all over the world, and those who think the disease is limited to homos, druggies, and foreigners are quite mistaken. 2 Indeed, stats suggest that in the United States one in every five hundred American college kids carries the HIV virus that causes AIDS. 3 If such numbers are to be believed, then doctors and public health officials will continue to have a whole lot of HIV and AIDS victims on their hands in the years to come.

4 A person with HIV or a full-blown AIDS sufferer deserves to be treated with respect, like someone with any other disease. 5 He should not be dissed or subjected to exclusionary behavior on the part of his fellow citizens. 6 Instead, each victim has the necessity for all the medical care and financial assistance due those who are in the extremity of illness. 7 Many professionals in the medical and social services communities are committed to helping HIV and AIDS patients. 8 For example, a doctor may help his patients by obtaining social services for them as well as by providing medical care. 9 A social worker may visit an HIV or AIDS victim and determine whether he qualifies for public assistance, since many patients don't have the dough for insurance or drugs. 10 Patients who are very ill may require the ministrations of a home-care nurse. 11 She can administer medications and make the sick person as comfy as possible.

EXERCISE 18.2 Revising: Sexist language

Revise the following paragraph to eliminate sexist language. If you change a singular noun or pronoun to plural, be sure to make any needed changes in verbs or other pronouns. (You can do this exercise online at *ablongman.com/littlebrown*.)

1 When a student applies for a job, he should prepare the best possible résumé, because the businessman who is scanning a stack of résumés will read them all quickly. 2 The person who wants his résumé to stand out will make sure it highlights his best points. 3 A person applying for a job as a mailman should emphasize his honesty and responsibility. 4 A girl applying for a position as a home-care nurse should also emphasize her honesty and responsibility as well as her background of capable nursing. 5 Someone seeking work as a computer programmer will highlight his experience with computers. 6 Students without extensive job experience should highlight their volunteer work. 7 For instance, a student may have been chairman of a campus organization or secretary of her church's youth group. 8 If everyone writing a résumé considers what the man who will read it is looking for, the applicant will know better what he should include and how he should format that information.

18b Choosing exact language

To write clearly and effectively, you will want to find the words that fit your meaning exactly and convey your attitude precisely.

Note A grammar and style checker can provide some help with inexact language. For instance, you can set it to flag commonly confused words (such as *continuous/continual*), misused prepositions in idioms (such as *accuse for* instead of *accuse of*), and clichés. But a checker can't help you at all with inappropriate connotation, excessive abstraction, or other problems discussed in this section.

1 Word meanings and synonyms

For writing exactly, a dictionary is essential and a thesaurus can be helpful.

■ Desk dictionaries

A desk dictionary defines about 150,000 to 200,000 words and provides pronunciation, grammatical functions, history, and other information. The sample on the next page is from *Merriam-Webster's Collegiate Dictionary.*

Good desk dictionaries, in addition to *Merriam-Webster's,* include the *American Heritage College Dictionary,* the *Random House Webster's College Dictionary,* and *Webster's New World Dictionary.* Most of these are available in both print and electronic form (CD-ROM or online). In addition, several Web sites provide online dictionaries or links to online dictionaries. For links visit *ablongman.com/littlebrown.*

Dictionary entry for *reckon*

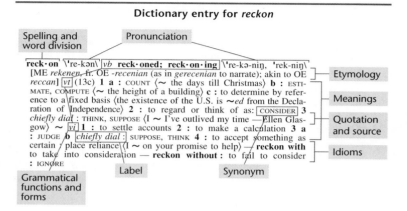

Spelling and word division | Pronunciation | Etymology | Meanings | Quotation and source | Idioms | Label | Synonym | Grammatical functions and forms

⬛ CULTURE LANGUAGE If English is not your native language, you probably should have a dictionary prepared especially for students using English as a second language (ESL). Such a dictionary contains special information on prepositions, count versus noncount nouns, and many other matters. Reliable ESL dictionaries include *COBUILD English Language Dictionary, Longman Dictionary of Contemporary English,* and *Oxford Advanced Learner's Dictionary.*

▪ Thesauruses

To find a word with the exact shade of meaning you intend, you may want to consult a thesaurus, or book of **synonyms**—words with approximately the same meaning. A thesaurus such as *Roget's International Thesaurus* lists most imaginable synonyms for thousands of words. The word *news,* for instance, has half a page of synonyms in *Roget's International,* including *tidings, dispatch, gossip,* and *journalism.*

Since a thesaurus aims to open up possibilities, its lists of synonyms include approximate as well as precise matches. The thesaurus does not define synonyms or distinguish among them, however, so you need a dictionary to discover exact meanings. In general, don't use a word from a thesaurus—even one you like the sound of—until you are sure of its appropriateness for your meaning.

Note For links to online thesauruses, visit *ablongman.com/ littlebrown.* Your word processor may also include a thesaurus, making it easy to look up synonyms and insert the chosen word into your text. But still you should consult a dictionary unless you are certain of the word's meaning.

EXERCISE 18.3 Using a dictionary

Look up five of the following words in a dictionary. For each word, write down (*a*) the division into syllables, (*b*) the pronunciation, (*c*) the grammatical functions and forms, (*d*) the etymology, (*e*) each meaning, and (*f*) any special uses indicated by labels. Finally, use the word in two sentences of your own. (You can do this exercise online at *ablongman.com/littlebrown.*)

1 depreciation	5 assassin	8 steal
2 secretary	6 astrology	9 plain (*adjective*)
3 grammar	7 toxic	10 ceremony
4 manifest		

2 The right word for your meaning

All words have one or more basic meanings (called **denotations**)—the meanings listed in the dictionary, without reference to emotional associations. If readers are to understand you, you must use words according to their established meanings.

- Consult a dictionary whenever you are unsure of a word's meaning.
- Distinguish between similar-sounding words that have widely different denotations:

Inexact   Older people often suffer <u>infirmaries</u> [places for the sick].

Exact   Older people often suffer <u>infirmities</u> [disabilities].

Some words, called **homonyms**, sound exactly alike but differ in meaning: for example, *principal/principle* or *rain/reign/rein*. (See **6** pp. 345–46 for a list of commonly confused homonyms.)

- Distinguish between words with related but distinct meanings:

Inexact   Television commercials <u>continuously</u> [unceasingly] interrupt programming.

Exact   Television commercials <u>continually</u> [regularly] interrupt programming.

In addition to their emotion-free meanings, many words also carry associations with specific feelings. These **connotations** can shape readers' responses and are thus a powerful tool for writers. The following word pairs have related denotations but very different connotations:

pride: sense of self-worth
vanity: excessive regard for oneself

firm: steady, unchanging, unyielding
stubborn: unreasonable, bullheaded

enthusiasm: excitement
mania: excessive interest or desire

A dictionary can help you track down words with the exact connotations you want. Besides providing meanings, your dictionary may also list and distinguish synonyms to guide your choices. A thesaurus can also help if you use it carefully, as discussed on the previous page.

EXERCISE 18.4   Revising: Denotation

Revise any underlined word below that is used incorrectly. Consult a dictionary if you are uncertain of a word's precise meaning. (You can do this exercise online at *ablongman.com/littlebrown*.)

1 The acclaimed writer Maxine Hong Kingston <u>sites</u> her mother's stories about ancestors and ancient Chinese customs <u>as</u> the sources of her first two books, *The Woman Warrior* and *China Men*. 2 One of her mother's tales, about a pregnant aunt who was <u>ostracized</u> by villagers, had a great <u>affect</u> on the young Kingston. 3 The aunt gained <u>avengeance</u> by drowning herself in the village water supply. 4 Kingston made the aunt <u>infamous</u> by giving her <u>immortality</u> in *The Woman Warrior*. 5 Two of Kingston's <u>progeny</u>, her great-grandfathers, are the focal points of *China Men*. 6 Both men led rebellions against <u>suppressive</u> employers: a sugar-cane farmer and a railroad-construction engineer. 7 Kingston's innovative writing <u>infers</u> her opposition to racism and sexism both in the China of the past and in the United States of the present. 8 She was <u>rewarded</u> many prizes for these distinguished books.

EXERCISE 18.5   Considering the connotation of words

Fill in the blank in each sentence below with the most appropriate word from the list in parentheses. Consult a dictionary to be sure of your choice. (You can do this exercise online at *ablongman.com/littlebrown*.)

1 Infection with the AIDS virus, HIV, is a serious health _____. (*problem, worry, difficulty, plight*)
2 Once the virus has entered the blood system, it _____ T-cells. (*murders, destroys, slaughters, executes*)
3 The _____ of T-cells is to combat infections. (*ambition, function, aim, goal*)
4 Without enough T-cells, the body is nearly _____ against infections. (*defenseless, hopeless, desperate*)
5 To prevent exposure to the virus, one should be especially _____ in sexual relationships. (*chary, circumspect, cautious, calculating*)

3 Concrete and specific words

Clear, exact writing balances abstract and general words, which outline ideas and objects, with concrete and specific words, which sharpen and solidify.

- **Abstract words** name qualities and ideas: *beauty, inflation, management, culture, liberal*. **Concrete words** name things we can know by our five senses of sight, hearing, touch, taste, and smell: *sleek, humming, brick, bitter, musty*.
- **General words** name classes or groups of things, such as *birds, weather*, or *buildings*, and include all the varieties of the class. **Specific words** limit a general class, such as *buildings*, by naming a variety, such as *skyscraper, Victorian courthouse*, or *hut*.

Abstract and general words are useful in the broad statements that set the course for your writing.

The wild horse in America has a romantic history.

Relations between the sexes today are more relaxed than they were in the past.

But such statements need development with concrete and specific detail. Detail can turn a vague sentence into an exact one:

Vague   The size of his hands made his smallness real. [How big were his hands? How small was he?]

Exact   Not until I saw his delicate, doll-like hands did I realize that he stood a full head shorter than most other men.

Note You can use your computer's Find function to help you find and revise abstract and general words that you tend to overuse. Examples of such words include *nice, interesting, things, very, good, a lot, a little,* and *some.*

EXERCISE 18.6   Revising: Concrete and specific words

Make the following paragraph vivid by expanding the sentences with appropriate details of your own choosing. Substitute concrete and specific words for the abstract and general ones that are underlined. (You can do this exercise online at *ablongman.com/littlebrown.*)

1 I remember clearly how awful I felt the first time I attended Mrs. Murphy's second-grade class. 2 I had recently moved from a small town in Missouri to a crowded suburb of Chicago. 3 My new school looked big from the outside and seemed dark inside as I walked down the long corridor toward the classroom. 4 The class was noisy as I neared the door; but when I entered, everyone became quiet and looked at me. 5 I felt uncomfortable and wanted a place to hide. 6 However, in a loud voice Mrs. Murphy directed me to the front of the room to introduce myself.

EXERCISE 18.7   Using concrete and specific words

For each abstract or general word below, give at least two other words or phrases that are increasingly specific or concrete. Consult a dictionary as needed. Use the most specific or concrete word from each group in a sentence of your own. (You can do this exercise online at *ablongman.com/littlebrown.*)

Example:

awake, watchful, vigilant
Vigilant guards patrol the buildings.

1 fabric	6 green	11 teacher
2 delicious	7 walk (*verb*)	12 nice
3 car	8 flower	13 virtue
4 narrow-minded	9 serious	14 angry
5 reach (*verb*)	10 pretty	15 crime

4 Idioms

Idioms are expressions in any language that do not fit the rules for meaning or grammar—for instance, *put up with, plug away at, make off with*.

Idiomatic combinations of verbs or adjectives and prepositions can be confusing for both native and nonnative speakers of English. Some of these pairings are listed below. (More appear in **4** p. 224.)

Idioms with prepositions

abide <u>by</u> a rule
abide <u>in</u> a place or state

according <u>to</u>
accords <u>with</u>

accuse <u>of</u> a crime

accustomed <u>to</u>

adapt <u>from</u> a source
adapt <u>to</u> a situation

afraid <u>of</u>

agree <u>on</u> a plan as a group
agree <u>to</u> someone else's plan
agree <u>with</u> a person

angry <u>with</u>

aware <u>of</u>

based <u>on</u>

belong <u>in</u> or <u>on</u> a place
belong <u>to</u> a group

capable <u>of</u>

certain <u>of</u>

charge <u>for</u> a purchase
charge <u>with</u> a crime

concur <u>in</u> an opinion
concur <u>with</u> a person

contend <u>for</u> a principle
contend <u>with</u> a person

dependent <u>on</u>

differ <u>about</u> or <u>over</u> a question
differ <u>from</u> in some quality
differ <u>with</u> a person

disappointed <u>by</u> or <u>in</u> a person
disappointed <u>in</u> or <u>with</u> a thing

familiar <u>with</u>

identical <u>with</u> or <u>to</u>

impatient <u>for</u> a raise
impatient <u>with</u> a person

independent <u>of</u>

infer <u>from</u>

inferior <u>to</u>

involved <u>in</u> a task
involved <u>with</u> a person

oblivious <u>of</u> or <u>to</u> one's
   surroundings
oblivious <u>of</u> something forgotten

occupied <u>by</u> a person
occupied <u>in</u> study
occupied <u>with</u> a thing

opposed <u>to</u>

part <u>from</u> a person
part <u>with</u> a possession

prior <u>to</u>

proud <u>of</u>

related <u>to</u>

rewarded <u>by</u> the judge
rewarded <u>for</u> something done
rewarded <u>with</u> a gift

similar <u>to</u>

sorry <u>about</u> an error
sorry <u>for</u> a person

superior <u>to</u>

wait <u>at</u> a place
wait <u>for</u> a train, a person
wait <u>in</u> a room
wait <u>on</u> a customer

CULTURE LANGUAGE If you are learning standard American English, you are justified in stumbling over its prepositions: their meanings can shift depending on context, and they have many idiomatic uses. In mastering the prepositions of standard English, you probably can't avoid memorization. But you can help yourself by memorizing related groups, such as *at/in/on* and *for/since*.

At, in, or *on* in expressions of time

- Use *at* before actual clock time: *at 8:30.*
- Use *in* before a month, year, century, or period: *in April, in 2007, in the twenty-first century, in the next month.*
- Use *on* before a day or date: *on Tuesday, on August 3, on Labor Day.*

At, in, or *on* in expressions of place

- Use *at* before a specific place or address: *at the school, at 511 Iris Street.*
- Use *in* before a place with limits or before a city, state, country, or continent: *in the house, in a box, in Oklahoma City, in China, in Asia.*
- Use *on* to mean "supported by" or "touching the surface of": *on the table, on Iris Street, on page 150.*

For or *since* in expressions of time

- Use *for* before a period of time: *for an hour, for two years.*
- Use *since* before a specific point in time: *since 1999, since Friday.*

A dictionary of English as a second language is the best source for the meanings of prepositions; see the suggestions on p. 168.

EXERCISE 18.8   Using prepositions in idioms

In the paragraph below, insert the preposition that correctly completes each idiom. Consult the box on the previous page or a dictionary as needed. (You can do this exercise online at *ablongman.com/littlebrown.*)

1 The friend who introduced Nick and Lana was proud _____ his matchmaking. 2 They had fallen _____ love _____ their first date. 3 Nick and Lana soon became so dependent _____ each other that they talked _____ the phone several times every day. 4 Certain _____ their love, Nick and Lana decided to get married. 5 Now, as they waited _____ the justice of the peace, they seemed oblivious _____ the other people in the lobby. 6 But Nick inferred _____ Lana's glance at a handsome man that she was no longer occupied _____ him alone. 7 Angry _____ Lana, Nick charged her _____ not loving him enough to get married. 8 Impatient _____ Nick's childish behavior, Lana disagreed _____ his interpretation of her glance. 9 They decided that if they could differ so violently _____ a minor incident, they should part _____ each other _____ at least a week. 10 They agreed to think _____ their expectations for marriage.

EXERCISE 18.9   Using prepositions in idioms

Complete the following paragraph by filling in the blanks with the appropriate prepositions. (You can do this exercise online at *ablongman.com/littlebrown.*)

1 The Eighteenth Amendment _____ the US Constitution was ratified _____ 1919. 2 It prohibited the "manufacture, sale, or transportation _____ intoxicating liquors." 3 Temperance groups _____ the United States wanted to prevent drinking, but the more striking effect of Prohibition was the boost it gave to organized crime. 4 According _____ legend, the most smuggling and bootlegging occurred _____ Chicago. 5 There, _____ February 14, 1929, Al Capone gained control _____ the Chicago underworld by ordering the execution _____ his rival Bugsy Moran and his men _____ a city parking garage. 6 Though Moran escaped unharmed, Capone ruled Chicago _____ two bloody years before he was convicted of tax evasion _____ 1931.

---

5 Figurative language

Figurative language (or a **figure of speech**) departs from the literal meanings of words, usually by comparing very different ideas or objects:

Literal   As I try to write, I can think of nothing to say.
Figurative As I try to write, my mind is a slab of black slate.

Imaginatively and carefully used, figurative language can capture meaning more precisely and feelingly than literal language. Here is a figure of speech at work in technical writing (paraphrasing the physicist Edward Andrade):

The molecules in a liquid move continuously like couples on an overcrowded dance floor, jostling each other.

The two most common figures of speech are the simile and the metaphor. Both compare two things of different classes, often one abstract and the other concrete. A **simile** makes the comparison explicit and usually begins with *like* or *as:*

Whenever we grow, we tend to feel it, as a young seed must feel the weight and inertia of the earth when it seeks to break out of its shell on its way to becoming a plant.   —Alice Walker

A **metaphor** claims that the two things are identical, omitting such words as *like* and *as:*

A school is a hopper into which children are heaved while they are young and tender; therein they are pressed into certain standard shapes and covered from head to heels with official rubber stamps.
                                                                 —H. L. Mencken

To be successful, figurative language must be fresh and un-strained, calling attention not to itself but to the writer's meaning. Be especially wary of mixed metaphors, which combine two or more incompatible figures:

Mixed   Various thorny problems that we try to sweep under the rug continue to bob up all the same.

Improved   Various thorny problems that we try to weed out continue to thrive all the same.

EXERCISE 18.10   Using figurative language

Invent appropriate similes or metaphors of your own to describe each scene or quality below, and use the figure in a sentence. (You can do this exercise online at *ablongman.com/littlebrown*.)

Example:
The attraction of a lake on a hot day
The small waves like fingers beckoned us irresistibly.

1 The sound of a kindergarten classroom
2 People waiting in line to buy tickets to a rock concert
3 The politeness of strangers meeting for the first time
4 A streetlight seen through dense fog
5 The effect of watching television for ten hours straight

---

6   Trite expressions

Trite expressions, or **clichés,** are phrases so old and so often re-peated that they have become stale. They include the following:

add insult to injury	a needle in a haystack
better late than never	point with pride
crushing blow	pride and joy
easier said than done	ripe old age
face the music	rude awakening
few and far between	shoulder the burden
green with envy	shoulder to cry on
hard as a rock	sneaking suspicion
heavy as lead	stand in awe
hit the nail on the head	strong as an ox
hour of need	thin as a rail
ladder of success	tried and true
moving experience	wise as an owl

To edit clichés, listen to your writing for any expressions that you have heard or used before. You can also supplement your ef-forts with a style checker, which may include a cliché detector. When you find a cliché, substitute fresh words of your own or re-state the idea in plain language.

EXERCISE 18.11 Revising: Trite expressions

Revise the following paragraph to eliminate trite expressions. (You can do this exercise online at *ablongman.com/littlebrown*.)

1 The disastrous consequences of the war have shaken the small nation to its roots. 2 Prices for food have shot sky high, and citizens have sneaking suspicions that others are making a killing on the black market. 3 Medical supplies are so few and far between that even civilians who are sick as dogs cannot get treatment. 4 With most men fighting or injured or killed, women have had to bite the bullet and shoulder the burden in farming and manufacturing. 5 Last but not least, the war's heavy drain on the nation's pocketbook has left the economy in shambles.

19 Completeness

The most serious kind of incomplete sentence is the grammatical fragment (see **4** pp. 278–82). But sentences are also incomplete when they omit one or more words needed for clarity.

Note Grammar and style checkers will not flag most kinds of incomplete sentences discussed in this chapter.

19a Writing complete compounds

You may omit words from a compound construction when the omission will not confuse readers:

Environmentalists have hopes for alternative fuels and [for] public transportation.

Some cars will run on electricity and some [will run] on methane.

Such omissions are possible only when the words omitted are common to all the parts of a compound construction. When the parts differ in any way, all words must be included in all parts.

> ┌─ **Key term** ─────────────────────
>
> **compound construction** Two or more elements (words, phrases, clauses) that are equal in importance and that function as a unit: *Rain fell, and streams overflowed* (clauses); *dogs and cats* (words).

http://www.ablongman.com/littlebrown ▶

Visit the companion Web site for more help and an electronic exercise on complete sentences.

One new car gets eighty miles per gallon; some old cars get as little as five miles per gallon. [One verb is singular, the other plural.]

Environmentalists believe in and work for fuel conservation. [Idiom requires different prepositions with *believe* and *work*.]

19b Adding needed words

In haste or carelessness, do not omit small words that are needed for clarity:

Incomplete	Regular payroll deductions are a type painless savings. You hardly notice missing amounts, and after period of years the contributions can add a large total.
Revised	Regular payroll deductions are a type of painless savings. You hardly notice the missing amounts, and after a period of years the contributions can add up to a large total.

Attentive proofreading is the only insurance against this kind of omission. *Proofread all your papers carefully.* See **1** p. 33 for tips.

⟨ CULTURE LANGUAGE ⟩ If your native language or dialect is not standard American English, you may have difficulty knowing when to use the English articles *a, an,* and *the*. For guidelines see **4** pp. 266–70.

EXERCISE 19.1 Revising: Completeness

Add words to the following paragraph so that the sentences are complete and clear. (You can do this exercise online at *ablongman.com/littlebrown*.)

1 The first ice cream, eaten China in about 2000 BC, was lumpier than modern ice cream. 2 The Chinese made their ice cream of milk, spices, and overcooked rice and packed in snow to solidify. 3 Ice milk and fruit ices became popular among wealthy in fourteenth-century Italy. 4 At her wedding in 1533 to king of France, Catherine de Médicis offered several flavors of fruit ices. 5 Modern sherbets resemble her ices; modern ice cream her soft dessert of thick, sweetened cream.

---

20 Conciseness

Concise writing makes every word count. Conciseness is not the same as mere brevity: detail and originality should not be cut with needless words. Rather, the length of an expression should be appropriate to the thought.

http://www.ablongman.com/littlebrown ▶

Visit the companion Web site for more help and electronic exercises on writing concisely.

Ways to achieve conciseness

Wordy (87 words)

The highly pressured <u>nature</u> of critical-care nursing is <u>due to the fact that</u> the patients have life-threatening illnesses. Critical-care nurses must have possession of steady nerves to care for patients who are critically ill and very sick. The nurses must also have possession of interpersonal skills. They must also have medical skills. It is considered by most health-care professionals that these nurses are essential if there is to be improvement of patients who are now in critical care from that status to the status of intermediate care.

Focus on subject and verb, and cut or shorten empty words and phrases.

Avoid nouns made from verbs.

Cut unneeded repetition.

Combine sentences.

Change passive voice to active voice.

Eliminate *there is* constructions.

Cut unneeded repetition, and reduce clauses and phrases.

Concise (37 words)

Critical-care nursing is highly pressured because the patients have life-threatening illnesses. Critical-care nurses must possess steady nerves and interpersonal and medical skills. Most health-care professionals consider these nurses essential if patients are to improve to intermediate care.

You may find yourself writing wordily when you are unsure of your subject or when your thoughts are tangled. It's fine, even necessary, to grope while drafting. But you should straighten out your ideas and eliminate wordiness during revision and editing.

Note Any grammar and style checker will identify at least some wordy structures, such as repeated words, weak verbs, passive voice, and *there is* and *it is* constructions. But a checker can't identify all potentially wordy structures, nor can it tell you whether a structure is appropriate for your ideas.

CULTURE LANGUAGE As you'll see in the examples that follow, wordiness is not a problem of incorrect grammar. A sentence may be perfectly grammatical but still contain unneeded words that interfere with the clarity and force of your idea.

20a   Focusing on the subject and verb

Using the subjects and verbs of your sentences for the key actors and actions will reduce words and emphasize important ideas. (See pp. 141–43 for more on this topic.)

| Wordy | The reason why most of the country shifts to daylight savings time is that winter days are much shorter than summer days. |
| Concise | Most of the country shifts to daylight savings time because winter days are much shorter than summer days. |

Focusing on subjects and verbs will also help you avoid several other causes of wordiness discussed further on pages 142–43:

Nouns made from verbs

| Wordy | The occurrence of the winter solstice, the shortest day of the year, is an event occurring about December 22. |
| Concise | The winter solstice, the shortest day of the year, occurs about December 22. |

Weak verbs

| Wordy | The earth's axis has a tilt as the planet is in orbit around the sun so that the northern and southern hemispheres are alternately in alignment toward the sun. |
| Concise | The earth's axis tilts as the planet orbits the sun so that the northern and southern hemispheres alternately align toward the sun. |

Passive voice

| Wordy | During its winter the northern hemisphere is tilted farthest away from the sun, so the nights are made longer and the days are made shorter. |
| Concise | During its winter the northern hemisphere tilts away from the sun, making the nights longer and the days shorter. |

See also **4** p. 235 on changing the passive voice to the active voice, as in the example above.

20b Cutting empty words

Empty words walk in place, gaining little or nothing in meaning. Many can be cut entirely. The following are just a few examples:

all things considered	in a manner of speaking
as far as I'm concerned	in my opinion
for all intents and purposes	last but not least
for the most part	more or less

Other empty words can also be cut, usually along with some of the words around them.

┌─ **Key terms** ─────────────────────────

passive voice The verb form when the subject names the *receiver* of the verb's action: *The house was destroyed by the tornado.* (See **4** p. 234.)

active voice The verb form when the subject names the *performer* of the verb's action: *The tornado destroyed the house.* (See **4** p. 234.)

area	element	kind	situation
aspect	factor	manner	thing
case	field	nature	type

Still others can be reduced from several words to a single word:

For	Substitute
at all times	always
at the present time	now, yet
because of the fact that	because
by virtue of the fact that	because
due to the fact that	because
for the purpose of	for
in order to	to
in the event that	if
in the final analysis	finally

Cutting or reducing such words and phrases will make your writing move faster and work harder:

Wordy   As far as I am concerned, because of the fact that a situation of discrimination still exists in the field of medicine, women have not at the present time achieved equality with men.

Concise   Because discrimination still exists in medicine, women have not yet achieved equality with men.

20c Cutting unneeded repetition

Unnecessary repetition weakens sentences:

Wordy   Many unskilled workers without training in a particular job are unemployed and do not have any work.

Concise   Many unskilled workers are unemployed.

Be especially alert to phrases that say the same thing twice. In the examples below, the unneeded words are underlined:

circle around	important [basic] essentials
consensus of opinion	puzzling in nature
cooperate together	repeat again
final completion	return again
frank and honest exchange	square [round] in shape
the future to come	surrounding circumstances

CULTURE LANGUAGE The preceding phrases are redundant because the main word already implies the underlined word or words. A dictionary will tell you what meanings a word implies. *Assassinate,* for instance, means "murder someone well known," so the following sentence is redundant: *Julius Caesar was assassinated and killed.*

20d Reducing clauses and phrases

Modifiers can be expanded or contracted depending on the emphasis you want to achieve. (Generally, the longer a construction, the more emphatic it is.) When editing sentences, consider whether any modifiers can be reduced without loss of emphasis or clarity:

Wordy   The Channel Tunnel, which runs between Britain and France, bores through a bed of solid chalk that is twenty-three miles across.

Concise   The Channel Tunnel between Britain and France bores through twenty-three miles of solid chalk.

20e Cutting *there is* or *it is*

You can postpone the sentence subject with the words *there is* (*there are, there was, there were*) and *it is* (*it was*): *There is reason for voting. It is your vote that counts.* These **expletive constructions** can be useful to emphasize the subject (as when introducing it for the first time) or to indicate a change in direction. But often they just add words and create limp substitutes for more vigorous sentences:

Wordy   There were delays and cost overruns that plagued construction of the Channel Tunnel. It is the expectation of investors to earn profits at last, now that there are trains passing daily through the tunnel.

Concise   Delays and cost overruns plagued construction of the Channel Tunnel. Investors expect to earn profits at last, now that trains pass daily through the tunnel.

CULTURE LANGUAGE When you must use an expletive construction, be careful to include *there* or *it*. Only commands and some questions can begin with verbs.

20f Combining sentences

Often the information in two or more sentences can be combined into one tight sentence:

Wordy   An unexpected problem with the Channel Tunnel is stowaways. The stowaways are mostly illegal immigrants. They are trying to smuggle themselves into England. They cling to train roofs and undercarriages.

Key term

modifier A word or word group that limits or qualifies another word: *slippery* road, cars *with tire chains*.

Concise   An unexpected problem with the Channel Tunnel is stow-
            aways, mostly illegal immigrants who are trying to smug-
            gle themselves into England by clinging to train roofs and
            undercarriages.

20g Rewriting jargon

Jargon can refer to the special vocabulary of any discipline or
profession (see p. 162). But it has also come to describe vague,
inflated language that is overcomplicated, even incomprehensible.
When it comes from government or business, we call it **bureau-
cratese.**

Jargon   The necessity for individuals to become separate entities in
             their own right may impel children to engage in open
             rebelliousness against parental authority or against sibling
             influence, with resultant bewilderment of those being re-
             belled against.

Translation Children's natural desire to become themselves may make
             them rebel against bewildered parents or siblings.

EXERCISE 20.1   Revising: Writing concisely

Make the following paragraph more concise. Combine sentences
when doing so reduces wordiness. (You can do this exercise online at
ablongman.com/littlebrown.)

If sore muscles after exercising are a problem for you, there are some
measures that can be taken by you to ease the discomfort. It is advisable
to avoid heat for the first day of soreness. The application of heat within
the first twenty-four hours can cause an increase in muscle soreness and
stiffness. In contrast, the immediate application of cold will help to reduce inflammation. Blood vessels are constricted by cold. Blood is kept
away from the injured muscles. There are two ways the application of
cold can be made: you can take a cold shower or use an ice pack. Inflammation of muscles can also be reduced with aspirin, ibuprofen, or
another anti-inflammatory medication. When healing is occurring, you
need to take it easy. A day or two after overdoing exercise, it is advisable
for you to get some light exercise and gentle massage.

EXERCISE 20.2   Revising: Conciseness

Make the following paragraph as concise as possible. Be merciless. (You
can do this exercise online at *ablongman.com/littlebrown.*)

At the end of a lengthy line of reasoning, he came to the conclusion
that the situation with carcinogens [cancer-causing substances] should
be regarded as similar to the situation with the automobile. Instead of
giving in to an irrational fear of cancer, we should consider all aspects of

the problem in a balanced and dispassionate frame of mind, making a total of the benefits received from potential carcinogens (plastics, pesticides, and other similar products) and measuring said total against the damage done by such products. This is the nature of most discussions about the automobile. Instead of responding irrationally to the visual, aural, and air pollution caused by automobiles, we have decided to live with them (while simultaneously working to improve on them) for the benefits brought to society as a whole.

PART 4

Sentence Parts and Patterns

Sentence Parts and Patterns

Basic Grammar

Grammar describes how language works, and understanding it can help you create clear and accurate sentences. This section explains the kinds of words in sentences (Chapter 21) and how to build basic sentences (22), expand them (23), and classify them (24).

Note Grammar and style checkers can both offer assistance and cause problems as you compose sentences. Look for the cautions and tips for using such checkers in this and the next part of this book. For more information about style and grammar checkers, see **1** pp. 32–33.

21 Parts of Speech

All English words fall into eight groups, called **parts of speech:** nouns, pronouns, verbs, adjectives, adverbs, prepositions, conjunctions, and interjections.

Note In different sentences a word may serve as different parts of speech. For example:

> The government sent <u>aid</u> to the city. [*Aid* is a noun.]
> Governments <u>aid</u> citizens. [*Aid* is a verb.]

The *function* of a word in a sentence always determines its part of speech in that sentence.

21a Recognizing nouns

Nouns name. They may name a person (*Hillary Duff, Jesse Jackson, astronaut*), a thing (*chair, book, Mt. Rainier*), a quality (*pain, mystery, simplicity*), a place (*city, Washington, ocean, Red Sea*), or an idea (*reality, peace, success*).

The forms of nouns depend partly on where they fit in certain groups. As the following examples indicate, the same noun may appear in more than one group.

- A *common noun* names a general class of things and does not begin with a capital letter: *earthquake, citizen, earth, fortitude, army.*

http://www.ablongman.com/littlebrown ▶

Visit the companion Web site for more help and an electronic exercise on the parts of speech.

- A *proper noun* names a specific person, place, or thing and begins with a capital letter: *Helen Hunt, Washington Monument, El Paso, US Congress.*
- A *count noun* names a thing considered countable in English. Most count nouns add *-s* or *-es* to distinguish between singular (one) and plural (more than one): *citizen, citizens; city, cities.* Some count nouns form irregular plurals: *woman, women; child, children.*
- A *noncount noun* names things or qualities that aren't considered countable in English: *earth, sugar, chaos, fortitude.* Noncount nouns do not form plurals.
- A *collective noun* is singular in form but names a group: *army, family, herd, US Congress.*

In addition, most nouns form the **possessive** by adding *-'s* to show ownership (*Nadia's books, citizen's rights*), source (*Auden's poems*), and some other relationships.

21b Recognizing pronouns

Most **pronouns** substitute for nouns and function in sentences as nouns do: *Susanne Ling enlisted in the Air Force when she graduated.* Pronouns fall into groups depending on their form or function:

- A *personal pronoun* refers to a specific individual or to individuals: *I, you, he, she, it, we,* and *they.*
- An *indefinite pronoun* does not refer to a specific noun: *anyone, everything, no one, somebody,* and so on. *No one came. Nothing moves. Everybody speaks.*
- A *relative pronoun* relates a group of words to a noun or another pronoun: *who, whoever, which, that. Everyone who attended received a prize. The book that won is a novel.*
- An *interrogative pronoun* introduces a question: *who, whom, whose, which, what. What song is that? Who will contribute?*
- A *demonstrative pronoun* identifies or points to a noun: *this, these, that, those,* and so on. *Those berries are ripe. This is the problem.*
- An *intensive pronoun* emphasizes a noun or another pronoun: *myself, himself, itself, themselves,* and so on. *I myself asked that question. The price itself is in doubt.*
- A *reflexive pronoun* indicates that the sentence subject also receives the action of the verb: *myself, himself, itself, themselves,* and so on. *He perjured himself. They injured themselves.*

The personal pronouns *I, he, she, we,* and *they* and the relative pronouns *who* and *whoever* change form depending on their function in the sentence. (See Chapter 30.)

21c   Recognizing verbs

Verbs express an action (*bring, change, grow, consider*), an occurrence (*become, happen, occur*), or a state of being (*be, seem, remain*).

1   Forms of verbs

Verbs have five distinctive forms. If the form can change as described here, the word is a verb:

- The *plain form* **is the dictionary form of the verb.** When the subject is a plural noun or the pronoun *I, we, you,* or *they,* the plain form indicates action that occurs in the present, occurs habitually, or is generally true.

  A few artists <u>live</u> in town today.
  They <u>hold</u> classes downtown.

- The *-s form* **ends in -s or -es.** When the subject is a singular noun, a pronoun such as *everyone,* or the personal pronoun *he, she,* or *it,* the -s form indicates action that occurs in the present, occurs habitually, or is generally true.

  The artist <u>lives</u> in town today.
  She <u>holds</u> classes downtown.

- The *past-tense form* **indicates that the action of the verb occurred before now.** It usually adds *-d* or *-ed* to the plain form, although most irregular verbs create it in different ways (see pp. 210–13).

  Many artists <u>lived</u> in town before this year.
  They <u>held</u> classes downtown. [Irregular verb.]

- The *past participle* **is usually the same as the past-tense form, except in most irregular verbs.** It combines with forms of *have* or *be* (*has <u>climbed</u>, was <u>created</u>*), or by itself it modifies nouns and pronouns (*the <u>sliced</u> apples*).

  Artists have <u>lived</u> in town for decades.
  They have <u>held</u> classes downtown. [Irregular verb.]

- The *present participle* **adds -ing to the verb's plain form.** It combines with forms of *be* (*is <u>buying</u>*), modifies nouns and pronouns (*the <u>boiling</u> water*), or functions as a noun (*<u>Running</u> exhausts me*).

  A few artists are <u>living</u> in town today.
  They are <u>holding</u> classes downtown.

The verb *be* has eight forms rather than the five forms of most other verbs:

Plain form	be
Present participle	being
Past participle	been

	I	*he, she, it*	*we, you, they*
Present tense	am	is	are
Past tense	was	was	were

2 Helping verbs

Some verb forms combine with **helping verbs** to indicate time, possibility, obligation, necessity, and other kinds of meaning: *can run, was sleeping, had been working.* In these **verb phrases** *run, sleeping,* and *working* are **main verbs**—they carry the principal meaning.

Verb phrase

Helping   Main

Artists <u>can</u>   <u>train</u> others to draw.
The techniques <u>have</u>   <u>changed</u> little.

These are the most common helping verbs:

be able to	had better	must	used to
be supposed to	have to	ought to	will
can	may	shall	would
could	might	should	

Forms of *be:* be, am, is, are, was, were, been, being
Forms of *have:* have, has, had, having
Forms of *do:* do, does, did

See pp. 216–20 for more on helping verbs.

EXERCISE 21.1 Identifying nouns, pronouns, and verbs

Identify the words that function as nouns (N), pronouns (P), and verbs (V) in the following paragraph. (You can do this exercise online at *ablongman .com/littlebrown.*)

Example:

    N   N   V   N
Ancestors of the gingko <u>tree</u> <u>lived</u> 175 to 200 million <u>years</u> ago.

1 The gingko tree has another name: it is the maidenhair tree. 2 Gingko trees sometimes grow to over a hundred feet in height. 3 They have fan-shaped leaves about three inches wide. 4 A deciduous tree, the gingko loses its leaves in the fall after they turn bright yellow. 5 Because the gingko shows tolerance for smoke, low temperatures, and low rainfall, it appears in many cities. 6 A shortcoming, however, is the foul odor of its fruit. 7 The fruit looks something like a plum. 8 Inside the fruit lies a large white seed that some Asians value as food. 9 The gingko tree is esteemed in the United States and Europe as an ornamental tree. 10 The male is more common for this purpose because it does not bear fruit.

21d Recognizing adjectives and adverbs

Adjectives describe or modify nouns and pronouns. They specify which one, what quality, or how many.

old city
adjective noun

generous one
adjective pronoun

two pears
adjective noun

Adverbs describe or modify verbs, adjectives, other adverbs, and whole groups of words. They specify when, where, how, and to what extent.

nearly destroyed
adverb verb

too quickly
adverb adverb

very generous
adverb adjective

Unfortunately, taxes will rise.
adverb word group

An -*ly* ending often signals an adverb, but not always: *friendly* is an adjective; *never* and *not* are adverbs. The only way to tell whether a word is an adjective or an adverb is to determine what it modifies.

Adjectives and adverbs appear in three forms: **positive** (*green, angrily*), **comparative** (*greener, more angrily*), and **superlative** (*greenest, most angrily*).

See Chapter 33 for more on adjectives and adverbs.

EXERCISE 21.2 Identifying adjectives and adverbs

Identify the adjectives (ADJ) and adverbs (ADV) in the following paragraph. Mark *a, an,* and *the* as adjectives. (You can do this exercise online at *ablongman.com/littlebrown.*)

Example:

ADV
Stress can hit people when they least expect it.

1 You can reduce stress by making a few simple changes. 2 Get up fifteen minutes earlier than you ordinarily do. 3 Eat a healthy breakfast, and eat it slowly so that you enjoy it. 4 Do your unpleasant tasks early in the day. 5 Carry a book or magazine when you know you'll have to wait in line somewhere. 6 Make promises sparingly and keep them faithfully. 7 Plan ahead to prevent stressful situations—for example, carrying spare keys so you won't be locked out of your car or house. 8 See a doctor and dentist regularly. 9 And every day, do at least one thing you really enjoy.

21e Recognizing connecting words: Prepositions and conjunctions

Connecting words are mostly small words that link parts of sentences. They never change form.

1 Prepositions

Prepositions form nouns or pronouns (plus any modifiers) into word groups called **prepositional phrases:** *about love, down the stairs.* These phrases usually serve as modifiers in sentences, as in *The plants trailed down the stairs.* (See p. 201.)

Common prepositions

about	before	except for	of	throughout
above	behind	excepting	off	till
according to	below	for	on	to
across	beneath	from	onto	toward
after	beside	in	on top of	under
against	between	in addition to	out	underneath
along	beyond	inside	out of	unlike
along with	by	inside of	outside	until
among	concerning	in spite of	over	up
around	despite	instead of	past	upon
as	down	into	regarding	up to
aside from	due to	like	round	with
at	during	near	since	within
because of	except	next to	through	without

CULTURE LANGUAGE The meanings and uses of English prepositions can be difficult to master. See **3** pp. 172–73 for a discussion of prepositions in idioms. See pp. 223–24 for uses of prepositions in two-word verbs such as *look after* or *look up.*

2 Subordinating conjunctions

Subordinating conjunctions form sentences into word groups called **subordinate clauses,** such as *when the meeting ended* or *that she knew.* These clauses serve as parts of sentences: *Everyone was relieved when the meeting ended. She said that she knew.* (See p. 206.)

Common subordinating conjunctions

after	even if	rather than	until
although	even though	since	when
as	if	so that	whenever
as if	if only	than	where
as long as	in order that	that	whereas
as though	now that	though	wherever
because	once	till	whether
before	provided	unless	while

CULTURE LANGUAGE Subordinating conjunctions convey meaning without help from other function words, such as the coordinating conjunctions *and, but, for,* or *so:*

Faulty   Even though the parents are illiterate, but their children may read well. [*Even though* and *but* have the same meaning, so both are not needed.]

Revised   *Even though* the parents are illiterate, their children may read well.

3 Coordinating and correlative conjunctions

Coordinating and correlative conjunctions connect words or word groups of the same kind, such as nouns or sentences.

Coordinating conjunctions consist of a single word:

Coordinating conjunctions

and	nor	for	yet
but	or	so	

Biofeedback or simple relaxation can relieve headaches.
Relaxation works well, and it is inexpensive.

Correlative conjunctions are combinations of coordinating conjunctions and other words:

Common correlative conjunctions

both . . . and	neither . . . nor
not only . . . but also	whether . . . or
not . . . but	as . . . as
either . . . or	

Both biofeedback and relaxation can relieve headaches.
The headache sufferer learns not only to recognize the causes of headaches but also to control those causes.

EXERCISE 21.3 Adding connecting words

Fill each blank in the following paragraph with the appropriate connecting word: a preposition, a subordinating conjunction, or a coordinating conjunction. Consult the lists on p. 193 and above if you need help. (You can do this exercise online at *ablongman.com/littlebrown.*)

Example:

A Trojan priest warned, "Beware _____ Greeks bearing gifts." (*preposition*)

A Trojan priest warned, "Beware of Greeks bearing gifts."

1 Just about everyone has heard the story _____ the Trojan Horse. (*preposition*) **2** This incident happened at the city of Troy _____ was planned by the Greeks. (*coordinating conjunction*) **3** The Greeks built a huge wooden horse; _____ it was a hollow space big enough to hold many men. (*preposition*) **4** At night, they rolled the horse to the gate of Troy _____ left it there before sailing their ships out to sea. (*coordinating conjunction*) **5** _____ the morning, the Trojans were surprised to see the enormous horse. (*preposition*) **6** _____ they were amazed when they saw that the Greeks were gone. (*coordinating conjunction*) **7** _____ they were curious to examine this gift from the Greeks, they dragged the horse into the city and left it outside the temple. (*subordinating conjunction*) **8** In the middle of the night, the hidden Greeks emerged _____ the horse and began setting fires all over town. (*preposition*) **9** _____ the Trojan soldiers awoke and came out of their houses, the Greeks killed them one by one. (*subordinating conjunction*) **10** By the next morning, the Trojan men were dead _____ the women were slaves to the Greeks. (*coordinating conjunction*)

21f Recognizing interjections

Interjections express feeling or command attention. They are rarely used in academic or business writing.

Oh, the meeting went fine.
They won seven thousand dollars! Wow!

22 The Sentence

The **sentence** is the basic unit of expression. It is grammatically complete and independent: it does not serve as an adjective, adverb, or other single part of speech.

22a Recognizing subjects and predicates

Most sentences make statements. First the **subject** names something; then the **predicate** makes an assertion about the subject or describes an action by the subject.

http://www.ablongman.com/littlebrown ▶

Visit the companion Web site for more help and electronic exercises on the sentence.

	Subject	Predicate
	Art	thrives.

The **simple subject** consists of one or more nouns or pronouns, whereas the **complete subject** also includes any modifiers. The **simple predicate** consists of one or more verbs, whereas the **complete predicate** adds any words needed to complete the meaning of the verb plus any modifiers.

Sometimes, as in the short example *Art thrives,* the simple and complete subject and predicate are the same. More often, they are different:

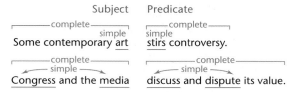

In the second example, the simple subject and simple predicate are both **compound:** in each, two words joined by a coordinating conjunction (*and*) serve the same function.

Note If a sentence contains a word group such as *that makes it into established museums* or *because viewers finally agree about its quality,* you may be tempted to mark the subject and verb in the word group as the subject and verb of the sentence. But these word groups are subordinate clauses, made into modifiers by the words they begin with: *that* and *because.* See pp. 206–07 for more on subordinate clauses.

CULTURE & LANGUAGE The subject of a sentence in standard American English may be a noun (*art*) or a pronoun that refers to the noun (*it*), but not both. (See p. 291.)

| Faulty | Some <u>art</u> <u>it</u> stirs controversy. |
| Revised | Some <u>art</u> stirs controversy. |

Tests to find subjects and predicates

The tests below use the following example:

> Art that makes it into museums has often survived controversy.

Identify the subject.

- **Ask *who* or *what* is acting or being described in the sentence.**

  | Complete subject | art that makes it into museums |

- **Isolate the simple subject by deleting modifiers**—words or word groups that don't name the actor of the sentence but give information about it. In the example, the word group *that makes it into muse-ums* does not name the actor but modifies it.

Simple subject art

Identify the predicate.

- **Ask what the sentence asserts about the subject:** what is its action, or what state is it in? In the example, the assertion about *art* is that it *has often survived controversy.*

Complete predicate   has often survived controversy

- **Isolate the verb, the simple predicate, by changing the time of the subject's action.** The simple predicate is the word or words that change as a result.

Example   Art . . . has often survived controversy.
Present   Art . . . often <u>survives</u> controversy.
Future   Art . . . often <u>will survive</u> controversy.
Simple predicate   has survived

EXERCISE 22.1   Identifying subjects and predicates

Identify the subject and the predicate of each sentence below. Then use each sentence as a model to create a sentence of your own. (You can do this exercise online at *ablongman.com/littlebrown.*)

> *Example:*
>   subject   predicate
> An important scientist / spoke at commencement.
> *Sample imitation:* The hungry family ate at the diner.

1 The leaves fell.
2 October ends soon.
3 The orchard owners made apple cider.
4 They examined each apple carefully before using it.
5 Over a hundred people will buy cider at the roadside stand.

EXERCISE 22.2   Identifying subjects and predicates

In the following sentences, insert a slash between the complete subject and the complete predicate. Underline each simple subject once and each simple predicate twice. (You can do this exercise online at *ablongman.com/littlebrown.*)

> *Example:*
> The <u>pony</u>, the light <u>horse</u>, and the draft <u>horse</u> / <u><u>are</u></u> the three main types of domestic horses.

1 The horse has a long history of serving humanity but today is mainly a show and sport animal. 2 A member of the genus *Equus*, the domestic horse is related to the wild Przewalski's horse, the ass, and the zebra. 3 The domestic horse and its relatives are all plains-dwelling herd

animals. 4 Oddly, the modern horse evolved in North America and then became extinct here after spreading to other parts of the world. 5 It was reintroduced here by the Spaniards, profoundly affecting the culture of Native Americans. 6 The North American animals called wild horses are actually descended from escaped domesticated horses that reproduced in the wild. 7 According to records, horses were hunted and domesticated as early as four to five thousand years ago. 8 The earliest ancestor of the modern horse may have been eohippus, approximately 55 million years ago.

22b   Recognizing predicate patterns

All English sentences are based on five patterns, each differing in the complete predicate (the verb and any words following it).

CULTURE LANGUAGE The word order in English sentences may not correspond to word order in the sentences of your native language or dialect. English, for instance, strongly prefers subject first, then verb, whereas some other languages prefer the verb first.

■ Pattern 1: The earth trembled.

In the simplest pattern the predicate consists only of an **intransitive verb,** a verb that does not require a following word to complete its meaning.

Subject	Predicate
	Intransitive verb
The earth	trembled.
The hospital	may close.

■ Pattern 2: The earthquake destroyed the city.

In pattern 2 the verb is followed by a **direct object,** a noun or pronoun that identifies who or what receives the action of the verb. A verb that requires a direct object to complete its meaning is called **transitive.**

Subject	Predicate	
	Transitive verb	*Direct object*
The earthquake	destroyed	the city.
Education	opens	doors.

CULTURE LANGUAGE Only transitive verbs may be used in the passive voice: *The city was destroyed*. Your dictionary will indicate whether a verb is transitive or intransitive. For some verbs (*begin, learn, read, write,* and others), it will indicate both uses.

▪ Pattern 3: The result was chaos.

In pattern 3 the verb is followed by a **subject complement,** a word that renames or describes the subject. A verb in this pattern is called a **linking verb** because it links its subject to the description following. The linking verbs include *be, seem, appear, become, grow, remain, stay, prove, feel, look, smell, sound,* and *taste.* Subject complements are usually nouns or adjectives.

Subject	Predicate	
	Linking verb	*Subject complement*
The result	was	chaos.
The man	became	an accountant.

▪ Pattern 4: The government sent the city aid.

In pattern 4 the verb is followed by a direct object and an **indirect object,** a word identifying to or for whom the action of the verb is performed. The direct object and indirect object refer to different things, people, or places.

Subject	Predicate		
	Transitive verb	*Indirect object*	*Direct object*
The government	sent	the city	aid.
One company	offered	its employees	bonuses.

A number of verbs can take indirect objects, including *send* and *offer* (preceding examples) and *allow, bring, buy, deny, find, get, give, leave, make, pay, read, sell, show, teach,* and *write.*

CULTURE LANGUAGE Some verbs are never followed by an indirect object—*admit, announce, demonstrate, explain, introduce, mention, prove, recommend, say,* and some others. However, the direct objects of these verbs may be followed by *to* or *for* and a noun or pronoun that specifies to or for whom the action was done: *The manual explains the new procedure to workers. A video demonstrates the procedure for us.*

▪ Pattern 5: The citizens considered the earthquake a disaster.

In pattern 5 the verb is followed by a direct object and an **object complement,** a word that renames or describes the direct object. Object complements may be nouns or adjectives.

┌─ Key term ───
passive voice The verb form when the subject names the receiver of the verb's action: *Bad weather was predicted.* (See p. 234.)
└──

Subject	Predicate		
	Transitive verb	*Direct object*	*Object complement*
The citizens	considered	the earthquake	a disaster.
Success	makes	some people	nervous.

EXERCISE 22.3   Identifying sentence parts

In the following sentences identify the subject (S) and verb (V) as well as any direct object (DO), indirect object (IO), subject complement (SC), or object complement (OC). (You can do this exercise online at *ablongman.com/littlebrown*.)

Example:

         S   V   V   DO
Crime statistics can cause surprise.

1   The number of serious crimes in the United States decreased.
2   A decline in serious crimes occurred each year.
3   The Crime Index measures serious crime.
4   The FBI invented the index.
5   The four serious violent crimes are murder, robbery, forcible rape, and aggravated assault.
6   Auto theft, burglary, arson, and larceny-theft are the four serious crimes against property.
7   The Crime Index gives the FBI a measure of crime.
8   The index shows trends in crimes and the people who commit them.
9   The nation's largest cities showed the largest decline in crime.
10 Smaller cities, where crime did not decrease, proved that the decline in crime is unrepresentative of the nation.

EXERCISE 22.4   Identifying sentence patterns

In the following sentences, identify each verb as intransitive, transitive, or linking. Then identify each direct object (DO), indirect object (IO), subject complement (SC), and object complement (OC). (You can do this exercise online at *ablongman.com/littlebrown*.)

Example:

        transitive
        verb   IO   DO   DO
Children give their parents both headaches and pleasures.

1   Many people find New York City exciting.
2   Tourists flock there each year.
3   Often they visit Times Square first.
4   The square's lights are astounding.
5   The flashing signs sell visitors everything from TVs to underwear.

23 Phrases and Subordinate Clauses

Most sentences contain word groups that serve as adjectives, adverbs, or nouns and thus cannot stand alone as sentences.

- A *phrase* lacks either a subject or a predicate or both: *fearing an accident; in a panic.*
- A *subordinate clause* contains a subject and a predicate but begins with a subordinating word: <u>when</u> *prices rise;* <u>whoever</u> *laughs.*

23a Recognizing phrases

1 Prepositional phrases

A **prepositional phrase** consists of a preposition plus a noun, a pronoun, or a word group serving as a noun, called the **object of the preposition.** A list of prepositions appears on p. 193.

Preposition	Object
of	spaghetti
on	the surface
with	great satisfaction
upon	entering the room
from	where you are standing

Prepositional phrases usually function as adjectives or adverbs.

Life on a raft was an opportunity for adventure.
    adjective phrase   adjective phrase

Huck Finn rode the raft by choice.
                  adverb phrase

With his companion, Jim, Huck met many types of people.
    adverb phrase   adjective phrase

EXERCISE 23.1 Identifying prepositional phrases

Underline the prepositional phrases in the following passage, and name the word that the phrase modifies. (You can do this exercise online at *ablongman.com/littlebrown.*)

http://www.ablongman.com/littlebrown ▶

Visit the companion Web site for more help and electronic exercises on phrases and subordinate clauses.

Example:

After an hour I finally arrived at the home of my professor.

1 On July 3, 1863, at Gettysburg, Pennsylvania, General Robert E. Lee gambled unsuccessfully for a Confederate victory in the American Civil War. 2 Called Pickett's Charge, the battle was one of the most disastrous conflicts of the war. 3 Confederate and Union forces faced each other on parallel ridges separated by almost a mile of open fields. 4 After an artillery bombardment of the Union position, about 12,000 Confederate infantry marched toward the Union ridge. 5 The Union guns had been silent but suddenly roared, mowing the approaching Confederates. 6 Within an hour, perhaps half of the Confederate soldiers lay wounded or dead.

EXERCISE 23.2 Sentence combining: Prepositional phrases

To practice writing sentences with prepositional phrases, combine each group of sentences below into one sentence that includes one or two prepositional phrases. You will have to add, delete, and rearrange words. Some items have more than one possible answer. (You can do this exercise online at *ablongman.com/littlebrown.*)

Example:

I will start working. The new job will pay the minimum wage.
I will start working at a new job for the minimum wage.

1 The slow loris protects itself well. Its habitat is Southeast Asia. It possesses a poisonous chemical.
2 To frighten predators, the loris exudes the chemical. The chemical comes from a gland. The gland is on the loris's upper arm.
3 The loris's chemical is highly toxic. The chemical is not like a skunk's spray. Even small quantities of the chemical are toxic.
4 A tiny dose can affect a human. The dose would get in the mouth. The human would be sent into shock.
5 Predators probably can sense the toxin. They detect it at a distance. They use their nasal organs.

2 Verbal phrases

Certain forms of verbs, called **verbals,** can serve as modifiers or nouns. Often these verbals appear with their own modifiers and objects in **verbal phrases.**

Note Verbals cannot serve as verbs in sentences. *The sun rises over the dump* is a sentence; *The sun rising over the dump* is a sentence fragment. (See p. 279.)

■ Participial phrases

Phrases made from present participles (ending in *-ing*) or past participles (usually ending in *-d* or *-ed*) serve as adjectives.

Strolling shoppers fill the malls.
adjective

They make selections determined by personal taste.
          adjective phrase

Note With irregular verbs, the past participle may have a different ending—for instance, *hidden funds*. (See pp. 211–13.)

CULTURE LANGUAGE For verbs expressing feeling, the present and past participles have different meanings: *It was a boring lecture. The bored students slept*. (See p. 265.)

■ Gerund phrases

A **gerund** is the *-ing* form of a verb when it serves as a noun. Gerunds and gerund phrases can do whatever nouns can do.

sentence
—subject—
Shopping satisfies personal needs.
  noun

                            —object of preposition—
Malls are good at creating such needs.
                       noun phrase

■ Infinitive phrases

An **infinitive** is the plain form of a verb plus *to: to hide*. Infinitives and infinitive phrases serve as adjectives, adverbs, or nouns.

      sentence
—— subject ——   —————— subject complement ——————
To design a mall is to create an artificial environment.
  noun phrase   noun phrase

Malls are designed to make shoppers feel safe.
                    adverb phrase

The environment supports the impulse to shop.
                            adjective

CULTURE LANGUAGE Infinitives and gerunds may follow some verbs and not others and may differ in meaning after a verb: *The singer stopped to sing. The singer stopped singing*. (See pp. 221–23.)

EXERCISE 23.3   Identifying verbals and verbal phrases

The following sentences contain participles, gerunds, and infinitives as well as participial, gerund, and infinitive phrases. Identify each verbal or verbal phrase. (You can do this exercise online at *ablongman.com/ littlebrown*.)

Example:
<u>Laughing</u>, the talk-show host prodded her guest <u>to talk</u>.

1 Written in 1850 by Nathaniel Hawthorne, *The Scarlet Letter* tells the story of Hester Prynne. 2 Shunned by the community because of her adultery, Hester endures loneliness. 3 She is humble enough to withstand

her Puritan neighbors' cutting remarks. 4 Despite the cruel treatment, the determined young woman refuses to leave her home. 5 By living a life of patience and unselfishness, Hester eventually becomes the community's angel.

EXERCISE 23.4 Sentence combining: Verbals and verbal phrases

To practice writing sentences with verbals and verbal phrases, combine each of the following pairs of sentences into one sentence. You will have to add, delete, change, and rearrange words. Each item has more than one possible answer. (You can do this exercise online at *ablongman.com/littlebrown.*)

> *Example:*
> My father took pleasure in mean pranks. For instance, he hid the neighbor's cat.
>
> My father took pleasure in mean pranks such as <u>hiding the neighbor's cat</u>.

1 Air pollution is a health problem. It affects millions of Americans.
2 The air has been polluted mainly by industries and automobiles. It contains toxic chemicals.
3 Environmentalists pressure politicians. They think politicians should pass stricter laws.
4 Many politicians waver. They are not necessarily against environmentalism.
5 The problems are too complex. They cannot be solved easily.

---

3 Absolute phrases

An **absolute phrase** consists of a noun or pronoun and a participle, plus any modifiers. It modifies the entire rest of the sentence it appears in.

> ┌─── absolute phrase ───┐
> Their own place established, many ethnic groups are making way for new arrivals.

Unlike a participial phrase (p. 202), an absolute phrase always contains a noun that serves as a subject.

> participial
> ┌── phrase ──┐
> Learning English, many immigrants discover American culture.

> ┌─────── absolute phrase ───────┐
> Immigrants having learned English, their opportunities widen.

EXERCISE 23.5 Sentence combining: Absolute phrases

To practice writing sentences with absolute phrases, combine each pair of sentences below into one sentence that contains an absolute phrase. You will have to add, delete, change, and rearrange words. (You can do this exercise online at *ablongman.com/littlebrown.*)

Example:
The flower's petals wilted. It looked pathetic.
<u>Its petals wilted</u>, the flower looked pathetic.

1 Geraldine Ferraro's face beamed. She enjoyed the crowd's cheers after her nomination for Vice President.
2 A vacancy had occurred. Sandra Day O'Connor was appointed the first female Supreme Court justice.
3 Her appointment was confirmed. Condoleezza Rice became the first female national security adviser.
4 The midterm elections were over. Nancy Pelosi was elected the first female minority leader of the House of Representatives.
5 The election was won. Elizabeth Dole was a US senator from North Carolina.

4 Appositive phrases

An **appositive** is usually a noun that renames another noun. An appositive phrase includes modifiers as well.

↗⌐appositive phrase¬
Bizen ware, a dark stoneware, is produced in Japan.

Appositives and appositive phrases sometimes begin with *that is, such as, for example,* or *in other words.*

↗⌐——— appositive phrase———
Bizen ware is used in the Japanese tea ceremony, that is, the Zen Buddhist

observance that links meditation and art.

EXERCISE 23.6 Sentence combining: Appositive phrases

Combine each pair of sentences into one sentence that contains an appositive phrase. You will have to delete and rearrange words. Some items have more than one possible answer. (You can do this exercise online at *ablongman.com/littlebrown.*)

Example:
The largest land animal is the elephant. The elephant is also one of the most intelligent animals.

The largest land animal, <u>the elephant,</u> is also one of the most intelligent animals.

1 Some people perform amazing feats when they are very young. These people are geniuses from birth.
2 John Stuart Mill was a British philosopher. He had written a history of Rome by age seven.
3 Two great artists began their work at age four. They were Paul Klee and Gustav Mahler.
4 Mahler was a Bohemian composer of intensely emotional works. He was also the child of a brutal father.
5 Paul Klee was a Swiss painter. As a child he was frightened by his own drawings of devils.

EXERCISE 23.7 Identifying phrases

In the paragraphs below, identify every verbal and appositive and every verbal, appositive, prepositional, and absolute phrase. (All but one of the sentences includes two or more such words and phrases.) (You can do this exercise online at *ablongman.com/littlebrown*.)

1 Because of its many synonyms, or words with similar meanings, English can make choosing the right word a difficult task. 2 Borrowing words from early Germanic languages and from Latin, English acquired an unusual number of synonyms. 3 With so many choices, how does a writer decide between *motherly* and *maternal* or among *womanly, feminine,* and *female*?

4 Some people prefer longer and more ornate words to avoid the flatness of short words. 5 Indeed, during the Renaissance a heated debate occurred between the Latinists, favoring Latin words, and the Saxonists, preferring Anglo-Saxon words derived from Germanic roots. 6 Today, students in writing classes are often told to choose the shorter word, usually an Anglo-Saxon derivative. 7 Better advice, wrote William Hazlitt, is the principle of choosing "the best word in common use." 8 Keeping this principle in mind, a writer would choose either *womanly,* the Anglo-Saxon word, or *feminine,* a French derivative, according to meaning and situation. 9 Of course, synonyms rarely have exactly the same meaning, usage having created subtle but real differences over time. 10 To take another example, the Old English word *handbook* has a slightly different meaning from the French derivative *manual,* a close synonym.

23b Recognizing subordinate clauses

A **clause** is any group of words that contains both a subject and a predicate. There are two kinds of clauses, and the distinction between them is important.

- A *main clause* makes a complete statement and can stand alone as a sentence: *The sky darkened.*
- A *subordinate clause* is just like a main clause *except* that it begins with a subordinating word: *when the sky darkened; whoever calls.* The subordinating word reduces the clause from a complete statement to a single part of speech: an adjective, adverb, or noun. Use subordinate clauses to support the ideas in main clauses, as described in **3** pp. 148–50.

Note A subordinate clause punctuated as a sentence is a sentence fragment. (See pp. 279–80.)

■ Adjective clauses

An **adjective clause** modifies a noun or pronoun. It usually begins with the relative pronoun *who, whom, whose, which,* or *that.*

The relative pronoun is the subject or object of the clause it begins. The clause ordinarily falls immediately after the word it modifies.

┌─────adjective clause─┐
Parents who cannot read may have bad memories of school.

┌──── adjective clause ────┐
One school, which is open year-round, helps parents learn to read.

■ Adverb clauses

An **adverb clause** modifies a verb, an adjective, another adverb, or a whole word group. It always begins with a subordinating conjunction, such as *although, because, if,* or *when* (see p. 193 for a list).

┌────────── adverb clause ──────────┐
The school began teaching parents when adult illiteracy gained national attention.

┌────── adverb clause ──────┐ ┌──main clause──
Because it was directed at people who could not read, advertising had to be inventive.

■ Noun clauses

A **noun clause** replaces a noun in a sentence and serves as a subject, object, or complement. It begins with *that, what, whatever, who, whom, whoever, whomever, when, where, whether, why,* or *how.*

┌───── sentence subject ─────┐
Whether the program would succeed depended on door-to-door advertising.
        noun clause

┌───── object of verb─────┐
Teachers explained in person how the program would work.
                noun clause

EXERCISE 23.8   Identifying clauses

Underline the subordinate clauses in the following paragraphs and identify each one as adjective (ADJ), adverb (ADV), or noun (N) by determining how it functions in its sentence. (You can do this exercise online at *ablongman.com/littlebrown.*)

1 The Prophet Muhammad, who was the founder of Islam, was born about 570 CE in the city of Mecca. 2 He grew up in the care of his grandfather and an uncle because both of his parents had died when he was very young. 3 His extended family was part of a powerful Arab tribe that lived in western Arabia. 4 When Muhammad was about forty years old, he had a vision while in a cave outside Mecca. 5 He believed that God had selected him to be the prophet of a true religion for the Arab people. 6 Viewed as God's messenger, Muhammad attracted many followers before he lost the support of the clans of Mecca. 7 He and his followers moved to Medina, where they established an organized Muslim community that

sometimes clashed with the Meccans and with Jewish clans. **8** Through-out his life Muhammad continued as the religious, political, and military leader of Islam as it spread in Asia and Africa. **9** He continued to have rev-elations, which are recorded in the sacred book of Muslims, the Koran.

EXERCISE 23.9   Sentence combining: Subordinate clauses

To practice writing sentences with subordinate clauses, combine each pair of main clauses into one sentence. Use either subordinating con-junctions or relative pronouns as appropriate, referring to the lists on pp. 189 and 193 if necessary. You will have to add, delete, and rearrange words. Each item has more than one possible answer. (You can do this exercise online at *ablongman.com/littlebrown*.)

Example:

She did not have her tire irons with her. She could not change her bicycle tire.

<u>Because</u> she did not have her tire irons with her, she could not change her bicycle tire.

1 Moviegoers expect something. Movie sequels should be as exciting as the original films.
2 A few sequels are good films. Most are poor imitations of the origi-nals.
3 A sequel to a blockbuster film arrives in the theater. Crowds quickly line up to see it.
4 Viewers pay to see the same villains and heroes. They remember these characters fondly.
5 Afterward, viewers often grumble about filmmakers. The filmmakers rehash tired plots and characters.

24 Sentence Types

The four basic sentence structures vary in the number of main and subordinate clauses. Each structure gives different emphasis to the main and supporting information in a sentence.

24a   Recognizing simple sentences

A **simple sentence** consists of a single main clause and no sub-ordinate clause.

http://www.ablongman.com/littlebrown ▶

Visit the companion Web site for more help and an electronic exercise on sentence types.

┌────────── main clause ──────────┐
Last summer was unusually hot.

┌──────────────────────────── main clause ─────────────────────────────┐
The summer made many farmers leave the area for good or reduced them
┌────────────────────┐
to bare existence.

24b Recognizing compound sentences

A **compound sentence** consists of two or more main clauses and no subordinate clause.

┌── main clause──┐   ┌────── main clause ──────┐
Last July was hot, but August was even hotter.

┌────────── main clause ──────────┐   ┌────────── main clause ──────────┐
The hot sun scorched the earth, and the lack of rain killed many crops.

24c Recognizing complex sentences

A **complex sentence** consists of one main clause and one or more subordinate clauses.

┌── main clause──┐ ┌────────── subordinate clause ──────────┐
Rain finally came, although many had left the area by then.

┌────────────── main clause ──────────────┐ ┌── subordinate clause ──
Those who remained were able to start anew because the government
  └─ subordinate clause ─┘
┌─────────────────────┐
came to their aid.

24d Recognizing compound-complex sentences

A **compound-complex sentence** has the characteristics of both the compound sentence (two or more main clauses) and the complex sentence (at least one subordinate clause).

┌────────── subordinate clause ──────────┐ ┌────── main clause ──────┐
Even though government aid finally came, many people had already been
┌─────────────────────┐   ┌────── main clause ──────┐
reduced to poverty, and others had been forced to move.

EXERCISE 24.1 Identifying sentence structures

Mark the main clauses and subordinate clauses in the following paragraphs. Then identify each sentence as simple, compound, complex, or compound-complex. (You can do this exercise online at *ablongman .com/littlebrown*.)

Example:

```
┌──────────────── main clause ────────────────┐
The human voice is produced in the larynx, a section of the throat
┌────────── subordinate clause ──────────┐
that has two bands called vocal cords. [Complex.]
```

1 Our world has many sounds, but they all have one thing in common. 2 They are all produced by vibrations. 3 Vibrations make the air move in waves, and these sound waves travel to the ear. 4 When the waves enter the ear, the brain has to interpret them. 5 Some sounds are pleasant, and others, which we call noise, are not. 6 Pleasant sounds, such as music, are produced by regular vibrations at regular intervals. 7 Most noises are produced by irregular vibrations at irregular intervals; an example is the barking of a dog.

8 Sounds, both pleasant and unpleasant, have frequency and pitch. 9 When an object vibrates rapidly, it produces high-frequency, high-pitched sounds. 10 People can hear sounds over a wide range of frequencies; but many other animals, including dogs and cats, can hear high frequencies that humans can't.

─────────────────── **Verbs** ───────────────────

Verbs express actions, conditions, and states of being. The basic uses and forms of verbs are described on pp. 190–91. This section explains and solves the most common problems with verbs' forms (Chapter 25), tenses (26), mood (27), and voice (28) and shows how to make verbs match their subjects (29).

25 Verb Forms

25a Use the correct forms of *sing/sang/sung* and other irregular verbs.

Most verbs are **regular:** they form their past tense and past participle by adding *-d* or *-ed* to the plain form.

http://www.ablongman.com/littlebrown ▶

Visit the companion Web site for more help and electronic exercises on verb forms.

Plain form	Past tense	Past participle
live	lived	lived
act	acted	acted

About two hundred English verbs are **irregular:** they form their past tense and past participle in some irregular way. Check a dictionary under the verb's plain form if you have any doubt about its other forms. If the verb is irregular, the dictionary will list the plain form, the past tense, and the past participle in that order (*go, went, gone*). If the dictionary gives only two forms (as in *think, thought*), then the past tense and the past participle are the same.

Common irregular verbs

Plain form	Past tense	Past participle
arise	arose	arisen
become	became	become
begin	began	begun
bid	bid	bid
bite	bit	bitten, bit
blow	blew	blown
break	broke	broken
bring	brought	brought
burst	burst	burst
buy	bought	bought
catch	caught	caught
choose	chose	chosen
come	came	come
cut	cut	cut
dive	dived, dove	dived
do	did	done
dream	dreamed, dreamt	dreamed, dreamt
drink	drank	drunk
drive	drove	driven
eat	ate	eaten
fall	fell	fallen
find	found	found
flee	fled	fled
fly	flew	flown

(continued)

Key terms ─────────────────────────────

plain form The dictionary form of the verb: *I walk. You forget.* (See p. 190.)

past-tense form The verb form indicating action that occurred in the past: *I walked. You forgot.* (See p. 190.)

past participle The verb form used with *have, has,* or *had: I have walked.* It may serve as a modifier: *It is a forgotten book.* (See p. 190.)

Common irregular verbs

(continued)

Plain form	Past tense	Past participle
forget	forgot	forgotten, forgot
freeze	froze	frozen
get	got	got, gotten
give	gave	given
go	went	gone
grow	grew	grown
hang (suspend)	hung	hung
hear	heard	heard
hide	hid	hidden
hold	held	held
keep	kept	kept
know	knew	known
lay	laid	laid
lead	led	led
leave	left	left
lend	lent	lent
let	let	let
lie	lay	lain
lose	lost	lost
pay	paid	paid
prove	proved	proved, proven
ride	rode	ridden
ring	rang	rung
rise	rose	risen
run	ran	run
say	said	said
see	saw	seen
set	set	set
shake	shook	shaken
shrink	shrank, shrunk	shrunk, shrunken
sing	sang, sung	sung
sink	sank, sunk	sunk
sit	sat	sat
sleep	slept	slept
slide	slid	slid
speak	spoke	spoken
spring	sprang, sprung	sprung
stand	stood	stood
steal	stole	stolen
swim	swam	swum
swing	swung	swung
take	took	taken
tear	tore	torn
throw	threw	thrown
wear	wore	worn
write	wrote	written

CULTURE LANGUAGE ⬥ Some English dialects use distinctive verb forms that differ from those of standard American English: for instance, *drug* for *dragged, growed* for *grew, come* for *came,* or *went* for *gone.* In situations requiring standard American English, use the forms in the list here or in a dictionary.

Note A grammar and style checker may flag incorrect forms of irregular verbs, but it may also fail to do so. For example, a checker flagged *The runner stealed second base (stole* is correct) but not *The runner had steal second base (stolen* is correct). When in doubt about the forms of irregular verbs, refer to the list on these pages, consult a dictionary, or consult the links at *ablongman.com/littlebrown.*

EXERCISE 25.1 Using irregular verbs

For each irregular verb in brackets, supply either the past tense or the past participle, as appropriate, and identify the form you used. (You can do this exercise online at *ablongman.com/littlebrown.*)

1 The world population had [grow] by two-thirds of a billion people in less than a decade. 2 Recently it [break] the 6 billion mark. 3 Population experts have [draw] pictures of a crowded future, predicting that the world population may have [slide] up to as many 10 billion by the year 2050. 4 The supply of food, clean water, and land is of particular concern. 5 Even though the food supply [rise] in the last decade, the share to each person [fall]. 6 At the same time the water supply, which had actually [become] healthier in the twentieth century, [sink] in size and quality. 6 Changes in land use [run] nomads and subsistence farmers off their fields, while the overall number of species on earth [shrink] by 20 percent.

7 Yet not all the news is bad. 8 Recently some countries have [begin] to heed these and other problems and to explore how technology can be [drive] to help the earth and all its populations. 9 Population control has [find] adherents all over the world. 10 Crop management has [take] some pressure off lands with poor soil, allowing their owners to produce food, while genetic engineering promises to replenish food supplies that have [shrink]. 11 Some new techniques for waste processing have [prove] effective. 12 Land conservation programs have [give] endangered species room to reproduce and thrive.

25b Distinguish between *sit* and *set, lie* and *lay,* and *rise* and *raise.*

The forms of *sit* and *set, lie* and *lay,* and *rise* and *raise* are easy to confuse.

Plain form	Past tense	Past participle
sit	sat	sat
set	set	set

Plain form	Past tense	Past participle
lie	lay	lain
lay	laid	laid
rise	rose	risen
raise	raised	raised

In each of these confusing pairs, one verb is intransitive (it does not take an object) and one is transitive (it does take an object). (See pp. 198–200 for more on this distinction.)

Intransitive

The patients lie in their beds. [*Lie* means "recline" and takes no object.]

Visitors sit with them. [*Sit* means "be seated" or "be located" and takes no object.]

Patients' temperatures rise. [*Rise* means "increase" or "get up" and takes no object.]

Transitive

Orderlies lay the dinner trays on tables. [*Lay* means "place" and takes an object, here *trays*.]

Orderlies set the trays down. [*Set* means "place" and takes an object, here *trays*.]

Nursing aides raise the shades. [*Raise* means "lift" or "bring up" and takes an object, here *shades*.]

EXERCISE 25.2   Distinguishing between *sit/set, lie/lay, rise/raise*

Choose the correct verb from the pair given in brackets. Then supply the past tense or past participle, as appropriate. (You can do this exercise online at *ablongman.com/littlebrown*.)

Example:
After I washed all the windows, I [lie, lay] down the squeegee and then I [sit, set] the table.
After I washed all the windows, I laid down the squeegee and then I set the table.

1 Yesterday afternoon the child [lie, lay] down for a nap.
2 The child has been [rise, raise] by her grandparents.
3 Most days her grandfather has [sit, set] with her, reading her stories.
4 She has [rise, raise] at dawn most mornings.
5 Her toys were [lie, lay] on the floor.

25c   Use the -s and -ed forms of the verb when they are required. CULTURE LANGUAGE

Speakers of some English dialects and nonnative speakers of English sometimes omit the *-s* and *-ed* verb endings when they are required in standard American English.

Note A grammar and style checker will flag many omitted -s and -ed endings from verbs, as in *he ask* and *was ask*. But it will miss many omissions, too.

1 **Required -s ending**

Use the -s form of a verb when *both* of these situations hold:

- The subject is a singular noun (*boy*), an indefinite pronoun (*everyone*), or *he, she,* or *it*. These subjects are **third person,** used when someone or something is being spoken about.
- The verb's action occurs in the present.

The letter asks [not ask] for a quick response.
Delay costs [not cost] money.

Be especially careful with the -s forms of *be* (*is*), *have* (*has*), and *do* (*does, doesn't*). These forms should always be used to indicate present time with third-person singular subjects.

The company is [not be] late in responding.
It has [not have] problems.
It doesn't [not don't] have the needed data.
The contract does [not do] depend on the response.

In addition, *be* has an -s form in the past tense with *I* and third-person singular subjects:

The company was [not were] in trouble before.

I, you, and plural subjects do *not* take the -s form of verbs:

I am [not is] a student.
You are [not is] also a student.
They are [not is] students, too.

2 **Required -ed or -d ending**

The -ed or -d verb form is required in *any* of these situations:

- The verb's action occurred in the past:

The company asked [not ask] for more time.

- The verb form functions as a modifier:

The data concerned [not concern] should be retrievable.

- The verb form combines with a form of *be* or *have*:

The company is supposed [not suppose] to be the best.
It has developed [not develop] an excellent reputation.

Watch especially for a needed -ed or -d ending when it isn't pronounced clearly in speech, as in *asked, discussed, mixed, supposed, walked,* and *used*.

EXERCISE 25.3   Using -s and -ed verb endings

CULTURE LANGUAGE ⬚ Supply the correct form of each verb in brackets. Be careful to include -s and -ed (or -d) endings where they are needed for standard English. (You can do this exercise online at *ablongman.com/littlebrown.*)

Example:
Unfortunately, the roof on our new house already [leak].
Unfortunately, the roof on our new house already leaks.

1 A teacher sometimes [ask] too much of a student. 2 In high school I was once [punish] for being sick. 3 I had [miss] a week of school because of a serious case of the flu. 4 I [realize] that I would fail a test unless I had a chance to make up the class work, so I [discuss] the problem with the teacher. 5 He said I was [suppose] to make up the work while I was sick. 6 At that I [walk] out of the class. 7 I [receive] a failing grade then, but it did not change my attitude. 8 I [work] harder in the courses that have more understanding teachers. 9 Today I still balk when a teacher [make] unreasonable demands or [expect] miracles.

25d   Use helping verbs with main verbs appropriately. ⬚ CULTURE LANGUAGE ⬚

Helping verbs combine with main verbs in verb phrases: *The line should have been cut. Who was calling?*

Note Grammar and style checkers often spot omitted helping verbs and incorrect main verbs with helping verbs, but sometimes they do not. A checker flagged *Many been fortunate* and *She working* but overlooked other errors, such as *The conference will be occurred.*

1   Required helping verbs

Standard American English requires helping verbs in certain situations:

■ **The main verb ends in -ing:**

Researchers are conducting fieldwork all over the world. [Not Researchers conducting. . . .]

┌─ **Key terms** ───

helping verb A word such as *can, may, be, have,* or *do* that forms a verb phrase with another verb to show time, permission, and other meanings. (See p. 191.)

main verb The verb that carries the principal meaning in a verb phrase: *has walked, could be happening.* (See p. 191.)

verb phrase A helping verb plus a main verb: *will be singing, would speak.* (See p. 191.)

- The main verb is *been* or *be:*

    Many <u>have</u> been fortunate in their discoveries. [Not Many <u>been</u>. . . .]

    Some <u>could</u> be real-life Indiana Joneses. [Not Some <u>be</u>. . . .]

- The main verb is a past participle, such as *talked, begun,* or *thrown*.

    Their discoveries <u>were</u> covered in newspapers and magazines. [Not Their discoveries <u>covered</u>. . . .]

    The researchers <u>have</u> given interviews on TV. [Not The researchers <u>given</u>. . . .]

The omission of a helping verb may create an incomplete sentence, or **sentence fragment,** because a present participle (*conducting*), an irregular past participle (*been*), or the infinitive *be* cannot stand alone as the only verb in a sentence (see p. 279). To work as sentence verbs, these verb forms need helping verbs.

2 Combination of helping verb + main verb

Helping verbs and main verbs combine into verb phrases in specific ways.

Note The main verb in a verb phrase (the one carrying the main meaning) does not change to show a change in subject or time: *she has <u>sung</u>, you had <u>sung</u>.* Only the helping verb may change.

■ Form of *be* + present participle

The **progressive tenses** indicate action in progress. Create them with *be, am, is, are, was, were,* or *been* followed by the main verb's present participle, as in the following example.

    She <u>is working</u> on a new book.

Be and *been* always require additional helping verbs to form progressive tenses:

can	might	should	⎫	have	⎫
could	must	will	⎬ be working	has	⎬ <u>been</u> working
may	shall	would	⎭	had	⎭

When forming the progressive tenses, be sure to use the *-ing* form of the main verb, as in the following revised examples.

Key terms

present participle The *-ing* form of the verb: *flying, playing, writing.* (See p. 190.)

progressive tenses Verb tenses expressing action in progress—for instance, *I am flying* (present progressive), *I was flying* (past progressive), *I will be flying* (future progressive). (See p. 228.)

Faulty	Her ideas are <u>grow</u> more complex. She is <u>developed</u> a new approach to ethics.
Revised	Her ideas are <u>growing</u> more complex. She is <u>developing</u> a new approach to ethics.

■ Form of *be* + past participle

The **passive voice** of the verb indicates that the subject *receives* the action of the verb. Create the passive voice with a form of *be* (*be, am, is, are, was, were, being,* or *been*) followed by the main verb's past participle:

Her latest book <u>was completed</u> in four months.

Be, being, and *been* always require additional helping verbs to form the passive voice:

have ⎫   am   was ⎫
has ⎬ <u>been</u> completed   is   <u>were</u> ⎬ <u>being</u> completed
had ⎭   are

will <u>be</u> completed

Be sure to use the main verb's past participle for the passive voice:

Faulty	Her next book will be <u>publish</u> soon.
Revised	Her next book will be <u>published</u> soon.

Note Only transitive verbs may form the passive voice:

Faulty	A philosophy conference <u>will be occurred</u> in the same week. [*Occur* is not a transitive verb.]
Revised	A philosophy conference <u>will occur</u> in the same week.

See p. 235 for advice on when to use and when to avoid the passive voice.

■ Forms of *have*

Four forms of *have* serve as helping verbs: *have, has, had, having.* One of these forms plus the main verb's past participle creates

---

Key terms

past participle The *-d* or *-ed* form of a regular verb: *hedged, walked.* Most irregular verbs have distinctive past participles: *eaten, swum.* (See p. 190.)

passive voice The verb form when the subject names the receiver of the verb's action: *An essay <u>was written</u> by every student.* (See p. 234.)

transitive verb A verb that requires an object to complete its meaning: *Every student <u>completed</u> an essay* (*essay* is the object of *completed*). (See p. 198.)

one of the perfect tenses, those expressing action completed before another specific time or action:

> Some students <u>have complained</u> about the laboratory.
> Others <u>had complained</u> before.

Will and other helping verbs sometimes accompany forms of *have* in the perfect tenses:

> Several more students <u>will have complained</u> by the end of the week.

▨ Forms of *do*

Do, does, and *did* have three uses as helping verbs, always with the plain form of the main verb:

- **To pose a question:** *How <u>did</u> the trial <u>end</u>?*
- **To emphasize the main verb:** *It <u>did end</u> eventually.*
- **To negate the main verb, along with *not* or *never*:** *The judge <u>did not withdraw</u>.*

Be sure to use the main verb's plain form with any form of *do:*

| Faulty | The judge did <u>remained</u> in court. |
| Revised | The judge did <u>remain</u> in court. |

▨ Modals

The modal helping verbs include *can, could, may,* and *might,* along with several two- and three-word combinations, such as *have to* and *be able to.* (See p. 191 for a list of modals.) Use the plain form of the main verb with a modal unless the modal combines with another helping verb (usually *have*):

| Faulty | The equipment <u>can detects</u> small vibrations. It <u>should have detect</u> the change. |
| Revised | The equipment <u>can detect</u> small vibrations. It <u>should have detected</u> the change. |

Modals convey various meanings, with these being most common:

- **Ability:** *can, could, be able to*

The equipment <u>can detect</u> small vibrations. [Present.]

The equipment <u>could detect</u> small vibrations. [Past.]

The equipment <u>is able to detect</u> small vibrations. [Present. Past: *was able to.* Future: *will be able to.*]

Key term

perfect tenses Verb tenses expressing an action completed before another specific time or action: *We have eaten* (present perfect), *We had eaten* (past perfect), *We will have eaten* (future perfect). (See p. 227.)

- **Possibility:** *could, may, might, could/may/might have* + past participle

    The equipment could fail. [Present.]
    The equipment may fail. [Present and future.]
    The equipment might fail. [Present and future.]
    The equipment may have failed. [Past.]

- **Necessity or obligation:** *must, have to, be supposed to*

    The lab must purchase a backup. [Present or future.]
    The lab has to purchase a backup. [Present or future. Past: *had to.*]
    The lab will have to purchase a backup. [Future.]
    The lab is supposed to purchase a backup. [Present. Past: *was supposed to.*]

- **Permission:** *may, can, could*

    The lab may spend the money. [Present or future.]
    The lab can spend the money. [Present or future.]
    The lab could spend the money. [Present or future, more tentative.]
    The lab could have spent the money. [Past.]

- **Intention:** *will, shall, would*

    The lab will spend the money. [Future.]

    Shall we offer advice? [Future. Use *shall* for questions requesting opinion or consent.]

    We would have offered advice. [Past.]

- **Request:** *could, can, would*

    Could [or can or would] you please obtain a bid? [Present or future.]

- **Advisability:** *should, had better, ought to, should have* + past participle

    You should obtain three bids. [Present or future.]
    You had better obtain three bids. [Present or future.]
    You ought to obtain three bids. [Present or future.]
    You should have obtained three bids. [Past.]

- **Past habit:** *would, used to*

    In years past we would obtain five bids.
    We used to obtain five bids.

EXERCISE 25.4 Using helping verbs

⟐ **CULTURE LANGUAGE** ⟐ Add helping verbs to the following paragraph where they are needed for standard American English. If a sentence is correct as given, mark the number preceding it. (You can do this exercise online at *ablongman .com/littlebrown*.)

1 Each year thousands of new readers been discovering Agatha Christie's mysteries. 2 Christie, a well-loved writer who worked as a nurse during World War I, wrote more than sixty-five detective novels. 3 Christie never expected that her mysteries become as popular as they did. 4 Nor did she anticipate that her play, *The Mousetrap,* be performed for decades. 5 At her death in 1976, Christie been the best-selling English novelist for some time. 6 Her books still selling well to readers who like being baffled.

EXERCISE 25.5   Revising: Helping verbs plus main verbs

CULTURE LANGUAGE Revise the following paragraph so that helping verbs and main verbs are used correctly. If a sentence is correct as given, mark the number preceding it. (You can do this exercise online at *ablongman .com/littlebrown.*)

1 A report from the Bureau of the Census has confirm a widening gap between rich and poor. 2 As suspected, the percentage of people below the poverty level did increased over the last decade. 3 More than 17 percent of the population is make 5 percent of all the income. 4 About 1 percent of the population will keeping an average of $500,000 apiece after taxes. 5 The other 99 percent all together will may retain about $300,000.

25e   Use a gerund or an infinitive after a verb as appropriate.   CULTURE LANGUAGE

Nonnative speakers of English sometimes stumble over whether to use a gerund or an infinitive after a verb. Gerunds and infinitives may follow certain verbs but not others. And sometimes the use of a gerund or infinitive with the same verb changes the meaning.

Note A grammar and style checker will spot some but not all errors in matching gerunds or infinitives with verbs. For example, a checker failed to flag *I practice to swim* and *I promise helping out.* Use the lists given here and a dictionary of English as a second language to determine whether an infinitive or a gerund is appropriate. (See 3 p. 168 for a list of ESL dictionaries.)

1 Either gerund or infinitive

A gerund or an infinitive may come after the following verbs with no significant difference in meaning.

> **Key terms**
>
> **gerund** The *-ing* form of the verb used as a noun: *Smoking is unhealthful.* (See p. 203.)
>
> **infinitive** The plain form of the verb usually preceded by *to: to smoke.* An infinitive may serve as an adjective, adverb, or noun. (See p. 203.)

begin	continue	intend	prefer
can't bear	hate	like	start
can't stand	hesitate	love	

The pump began working.
The pump began to work.

2 Meaning change with gerund or infinitive

With four verbs, a gerund has quite a different meaning from an infinitive:

forget	stop
remember	try

The engineer stopped eating. [He no longer ate.]
The engineer stopped to eat. [He stopped in order to eat.]

3 Gerund, not infinitive

Do not use an infinitive after these verbs:

admit	discuss	mind	recollect
adore	dislike	miss	resent
appreciate	enjoy	postpone	resist
avoid	escape	practice	risk
consider	finish	put off	suggest
deny	imagine	quit	tolerate
detest	keep	recall	understand

Faulty   He finished to eat lunch.
Revised   He finished eating lunch.

4 Infinitive, not gerund

Do not use a gerund after these verbs:

agree	claim	manage	promise
appear	consent	mean	refuse
arrange	decide	offer	say
ask	expect	plan	wait
assent	have	prepare	want
beg	hope	pretend	wish

Faulty   He decided checking the pump.
Revised   He decided to check the pump.

5 Noun or pronoun + infinitive

Some verbs may be followed by an infinitive alone or by a noun or pronoun and an infinitive. The presence of a noun or pronoun changes the meaning.

ask	dare	need	wish
beg	expect	promise	would like
choose	help	want	

He expected to watch.
He expected his workers to watch.

Some verbs *must* be followed by a noun or pronoun before an infinitive:

advise	encourage	oblige	require
allow	forbid	order	teach
cause	force	permit	tell
challenge	hire	persuade	train
command	instruct	remind	urge
convince	invite	request	warn

He instructed his workers to watch.

Do not use *to* before the infinitive when it follows one of these verbs and a noun or pronoun:

feel	hear	make ("force")	watch
have	let	see	

He let his workers learn by observation.

EXERCISE 25.6   Revising: Verbs plus gerunds or infinitives

CULTURE LANGUAGE Revise the following paragraph so that gerunds or infinitives are used correctly with verbs. Mark the number preceding any sentence that is correct as given. (You can do this exercise online at *ablongman.com/littlebrown.*)

1 Without enough highly trained people to draw on, American businesses risk to lose their competitive edge. 2 In recent years, American business leaders have found that their workers need improving their math and science skills. 3 Some colleges have responded by encouraging more students to choose math or engineering as their major. 4 A program called HELP Wanted challenges students take action on behalf of American competitiveness. 5 Officials who work with this program hope increasing the number of math, science, and engineering majors and providing more job training.

25f   Use the appropriate particles with two-word verbs. **CULTURE LANGUAGE**

Standard American English includes some verbs that consist of two words: the verb itself and a **particle**, a preposition or adverb that affects the meaning of the verb.

> ┌─ **Key terms** ─────────────────────────────
> **preposition** A word such as *about, for,* or *to* that takes a noun or pronoun as its object: *at the house, in the woods.* (See p. 193 for a list of prepositions.)
>
> **adverb** A word that modifies a verb, adjective, other adverb, or whole word group. (See p. 192.)

Look up the answer. [Research the answer.]
Look over the answer. [Examine the answer.]

The meanings of these two-word verbs are often quite different from the meanings of the individual words that make them up. (There are some three-word verbs, too, such as *put up with* and *run out of*.) A dictionary of English as a second language will define two-word verbs and say whether the verbs may be separated in a sentence, as explained below. (See 3 p. 168 for a list of ESL dictionaries.) A grammar and style checker will recognize few if any misuses of two-word verbs.

Note Many two-word verbs are more common in speech than in more formal academic or business writing. For formal writing, consider using *research* instead of *look up, examine* or *inspect* instead of *look over.*

1 Inseparable two-word verbs

Verbs and particles that may not be separated by any other words include the following:

catch on	go over	play around	stay away
come across	grow up	run into	stay up
get along	keep on	run out of	take care of
give in	look into	speak up	turn up at

Faulty   Children grow quickly up.
Revised   Children grow up quickly.

2 Separable two-word verbs

Most two-word verbs that take direct objects may be separated by the object.

Parents help out their children.
Parents help their children out.

If the direct object is a pronoun, the pronoun *must* separate the verb from the particle.

Faulty   Parents help out them.
Revised   Parents help them out.

The separable two-word verbs include the following:

bring up	give back	make up	throw out
call off	hand in	point out	try on
call up	hand out	put away	try out
drop off	help out	put back	turn down
fill out	leave out	put off	turn on
fill up	look over	take out	turn up
give away	look up	take over	wrap up

EXERCISE 25.7 Revising: Verbs plus particles

CULTURE LANGUAGE The two- and three-word verbs in the paragraph below are underlined. Some are correct as given, and some are not because they should or should not be separated by other words. Revise the verbs and other words that are incorrect. Consult the lists opposite or an ESL dictionary if necessary to determine which verbs are separable. (You can do this exercise online at *ablongman.com/littlebrown*.)

1 American movies treat everything from <u>going out with</u> someone to <u>making up</u> an ethnic identity. 2 Some filmmakers like to address current topics, such as <u>getting</u> in today's world <u>along</u>. 3 Others, however, <u>stay</u> from serious topics <u>away</u> and choose lighter themes. 4 Whatever the topic, viewers <u>fill</u> theaters <u>up</u> when a movie is controversial. 5 It seems that filmmakers will <u>keep</u> creating controversy <u>on</u>, <u>trying</u> it <u>out</u> whenever they can. 6 They are always eager to make money and <u>point</u> their influence <u>out</u> to the public.

26 Verb Tenses

Tense shows the time of a verb's action. The table on the next page illustrates the tense forms for a regular verb. (Irregular verbs have different past-tense and past-participle forms. See pp. 210–13.)

Note Grammar and style checkers can provide little help with incorrect verb tenses and tense sequences because correctness usually depends on meaning.

CULTURE LANGUAGE In standard American English, a verb conveys time and sequence through its form. In some other languages and English dialects, various markers besides verb form may indicate the time of a verb. For instance, in African American dialect *I be attending class on Friday* means that the speaker attends class every Friday. To a speaker of standard American English, however, the sentence may be unclear: last Friday? this Friday? every Friday? The intended meaning must be indicated by verb tense. *I attended class on Friday. I will attend class on Friday. I attend class on Friday.*

26a Observe the special uses of the present tense (*sing*).

Most academic and business writing uses the past tense (*the rebellion occurred*), but the present tense has several distinctive uses.

http://www.ablongman.com/littlebrown ▶

Visit the companion Web site for more help and electronic exercises on verb tenses.

Tenses of a regular verb (active voice)

Present Action that is occurring now, occurs habitually, or is generally true

Simple present Plain form or -s form	**Present progressive** *Am, is,* or *are* plus *-ing* form
I <u>walk</u>. You/we/they <u>walk</u>. He/she/it <u>walks</u>.	I <u>am walking</u>. You/we/they <u>are walking</u>. He/she/it <u>is walking</u>.

Past Action that occurred before now

Simple past Past-tense form (*-d* or *-ed*)	**Past progressive** *Was* or *were* plus *-ing* form
I/he/she/it <u>walked</u>. You/we/they <u>walked</u>.	I/he/she/it <u>was walking</u>. You/we/they <u>were walking</u>.

Future Action that will occur in the future

Simple future Plain form plus *will*	**Future progressive** *Will be* plus *-ing* form
I/you/he/she/it/we/they <u>will</u> <u>walk</u>.	I/you/he/she/it/we/they <u>will be</u> <u>walking</u>.

Present perfect Action that began in the past and is linked to the present

Present perfect *Have* or *has* plus past participle (*-d* or *-ed*)	**Present perfect progressive** *Have been* or *has been* plus *-ing* form
I/you/we/they <u>have walked</u>. He/she/it <u>has walked</u>.	I/you/we/they <u>have been walking</u>. He/she/it <u>has been walking</u>.

Past perfect Action that was completed before another past action

Past perfect *Had* plus past participle (*-d* or *-ed*)	**Past perfect progressive** *Had been* plus *-ing* form
I/you/he/she/it/we/they <u>had</u> <u>walked</u>.	I/you/he/she/it/we/they <u>had been</u> <u>walking</u>.

Future perfect Action that will be completed before another future action

Future perfect *Will have* plus past participle (*-d* or *-ed*)	**Future perfect progressive** *Will have been* plus *-ing* form
I/you/he/she/it/we/they <u>will have</u> <u>walked</u>.	I/you/he/she/it/we/they <u>will have</u> <u>been walking</u>.

Action occurring now

She <u>understands</u> the problem.
We <u>define</u> the problem differently.

Habitual or recurring action

Banks regularly <u>undergo</u> audits.
The audits <u>monitor</u> the banks' activities.

A general truth

The mills of the gods <u>grind</u> slowly.
The earth <u>is</u> round.

Discussion of literature, film, and so on

Huckleberry Finn <u>has</u> adventures we all envy.
In that article the author <u>examines</u> several causes of crime.

Future time

Next week we <u>draft</u> a new budget.
Funding <u>ends</u> in less than a year.

(The present tense shows future time with expressions like those in the examples above: *next week, in less than a year.*)

26b Observe the uses of the perfect tenses (*have/had/will have sung*).

The **perfect tenses** consist of a form of *have* plus the verb's past participle (*closed, hidden*). They indicate an action completed before another specific time or action. The present perfect tense also indicates action begun in the past and continued into the present.

present perfect
The dancer <u>has performed</u> here only once. [The action is completed at the time of the statement.]

present perfect
Critics <u>have written</u> about the performance ever since. [The action began in the past and continues now.]

past perfect
The dancer <u>had trained</u> in Asia before his performance. [The action was completed before another past action.]

future perfect
He <u>will have danced</u> here again by next month. [The action begins now or in the future and will be completed by a specific time in the future.]

CULTURE LANGUAGE With the present perfect tense, the words *since* and *for* are followed by different information. After *since,* give a specific point in time: *The play has run <u>since 1999</u>.* After *for,* give a span of time: *It could run <u>for decades</u>.*

The **progressive tenses** indicate continuing (therefore progressive) action. In standard American English the progressive tenses consist of a form of *be* plus the verb's *-ing* form (present participle). (The words *be* and *been* must be combined with other helping verbs. See pp. 217–18.)

present progressive
The economy is improving.

past progressive
Last year the economy was stagnating.

future progressive
Economists will be watching for signs of growth.

present perfect progressive
The government has been expecting an upturn.

past perfect progressive
Various indicators had been suggesting improvement.

future perfect progressive
By the end of this year, investors will have been watching interest rates nervously for nearly a decade.

Note Verbs that express unchanging states (especially mental states) rather than physical actions do not usually appear in the progressive tenses. These verbs include *adore, appear, believe, belong, care, hate, have, hear, know, like, love, mean, need, own, prefer, remember, see, sound, taste, think, understand,* and *want.*

Faulty   She is wanting to study ethics.
Revised   She wants to study ethics.

26d Keep tenses consistent.

Within a sentence, the tenses of verbs and verb forms need not be identical as long as they reflect actual changes in time: *Ramon will graduate from college thirty years after his father arrived in America.* But needless shifts in tense will confuse or distract readers:

Inconsistent   Immediately after Booth shot Lincoln, Major Rathbone threw himself upon the assassin. But Booth pulls a knife and plunges it into the major's arm.

Revised   Immediately after Booth shot Lincoln, Major Rathbone threw himself upon the assassin. But Booth pulled a knife and plunged it into the major's arm.

Inconsistent	The main character in the novel suffers psychologically because he has a clubfoot, but he eventually triumphed over his disability.
Revised	The main character in the novel suffers psychologically because he has a clubfoot, but he eventually triumphs over his disability. [Use the present tense to discuss the content of literature, film, and so on.]

EXERCISE 26.1   Revising: Consistent past tense

In the paragraph below, change the tenses of the verbs as needed to maintain consistent simple past tense. If a sentence is correct as given, mark the number preceding it. (You can do this exercise online at *ablongman.com/littlebrown*.)

1 The 1960 presidential race between Richard Nixon and John F. Kennedy was the first to feature a televised debate. 2 Despite his extensive political experience, Nixon perspires heavily and looks haggard and uneasy in front of the camera. 3 By contrast, Kennedy was projecting cool poise and providing crisp answers that made him seem fit for the office of President. 4 The public responded positively to Kennedy's image. 5 His poll ratings shoot up immediately, while Nixon's take a corresponding drop. 6 Kennedy won the election by a close 118,564 votes.

EXERCISE 26.2   Revising: Consistent present tense

In the paragraph below, change the tenses of the verbs as needed to maintain consistent simple present tense. If a sentence is correct as given, mark the number preceding it. (You can do this exercise online at *ablongman.com/littlebrown*.)

1 E. B. White's famous children's novel *Charlotte's Web* is a wonderful story of friendship and loyalty. 2 Charlotte, the wise and motherly spider, decided to save her friend Wilbur, the young and childlike pig, from being butchered by his owner. 3 She made a plan to weave words into her web that described Wilbur. 4 She first weaves "Some Pig" and later presented "Terrific," "Radiant," and "Humble." 5 Her plan succeeded beautifully. 6 She fools the humans into believing that Wilbur was a pig unlike any other, and Wilbur lived.

26e   Use the appropriate sequence of verb tenses.

The **sequence of tenses** is the relation between the verb tense in a main clause and the verb tense in a subordinate clause. The tenses should change when necessary to reflect changes in actual or relative time. The main difficulties with tense sequence are discussed on the next two pages.

1 Past or past perfect tense in main clause

When the verb in the main clause is in the past or past perfect tense, the verb in the subordinate clause must also be past or past perfect:

main clause: subordinate clause:
past   past

The researchers <u>discovered</u> that people <u>varied</u> widely in their knowledge of public events.

main clause: subordinate clause:
past   past perfect

The variation <u>occurred</u> because respondents <u>had been born</u> in different decades.

main clause: subordinate clause:
past perfect   past

None of them <u>had been born</u> when Dwight Eisenhower <u>was</u> President.

Exception Always use the present tense for a general truth, such as *The earth is round.*

main clause: subordinate clause:
past   present

Most <u>understood</u> that popular Presidents <u>are</u> not necessarily good Presidents.

2 Conditional sentences

A **conditional sentence** states a factual relation between cause and effect, makes a prediction, or speculates about what might happen. Such a sentence usually contains a subordinate clause beginning with *if, when,* or *unless* and a main clause stating the result. The three kinds of conditional sentences use distinctive verbs.

■ Factual relation

Statements linking factual causes and effects use matched tenses in the subordinate and main clauses:

subordinate clause: main clause:
present   present

When a voter <u>casts</u> a ballot, he or she <u>has</u> complete privacy.

subordinate clause: main clause:
past   past

When voters <u>registered</u> in some states, they <u>had</u> to pay a poll tax.

┌ Key terms ──

main clause   A word group that contains a subject and a verb and does not begin with a subordinating word. *Books are valuable.* (See p. 206.)

subordinate clause   A word group that contains a subject and a verb, begins with a subordinating word such as *because* or *who,* and is not a question: *Books are valuable <u>when they enlighten</u>.* (See p. 206.)

■ Prediction

Predictions generally use the present tense in the subordinate clause and the future tense in the main clause:

subordinate clause: main clause:
present   future
Unless citizens <u>regain</u> faith in politics, they <u>will</u> not <u>vote</u>.

Sometimes the verb in the main clause consists of *may, can, should,* or *might* plus the verb's plain form: *If citizens <u>regain</u> faith, they <u>may vote</u>.*

■ Speculation

The verbs in speculations depend on whether the linked events are possible or impossible. For possible events in the present, use the past tense in the subordinate clause and *would, could,* or *might* plus the verb's plain form in the main clause:

subordinate clause: main clause:
past   *would* + verb
If voters <u>had</u> more confidence, they <u>would vote</u> more often.

Always use *were* instead of *was* in the subordinate clause, even when the subject is *I, he, she, it,* or a singular noun. (See pp. 232–33 for more on this distinctive verb form.)

subordinate clause: main clause:
past   *would* + verb
If the voter <u>were</u> more confident, he or she <u>would vote</u> more often.

For impossible events in the present—events that are contrary to fact—use the same forms as above (including the distinctive *were* when applicable):

subordinate clause: main clause:
past   *might* + verb
If Lincoln <u>were</u> alive, he <u>might inspire</u> confidence.

For impossible events in the past, use the past perfect tense in the subordinate clause and *would, could,* or *might* plus the present perfect tense in the main clause:

subordinate clause: main clause:
past perfect   *might* + present perfect
If Lincoln <u>had lived</u> past the Civil War, he <u>might have helped</u> stabilize the country.

EXERCISE 26.3   Using correct tense sequence

In the following paragraph, change the tense of each bracketed verb so that it is in correct sequence with other verbs. (You can do this exercise online at *ablongman.com/littlebrown*.)

1 Diaries that Adolph Hitler [be] supposed to have written surfaced in Germany. 2 Many people believed that the diaries [be] authentic

because a well-known historian [have] declared them so. 3 However, the historian's evaluation was questioned by other authorities, who [call] the diaries forgeries. 4 They claimed, among other things, that the paper [be] not old enough to have been used by Hitler. 5 Eventually, the doubters won the debate because they [have] the best evidence.

EXERCISE 26.4   Revising: Tense sequence with conditional sentences

In the following paragraph, use the forms of *be* that create correct tense sequence for all verbs. (You can do this exercise online at *ablongman.com/ littlebrown.*)

1 If you think you [be] exposed to the flu, you should get a flu shot. 2 You may avoid the illness altogether, and if you contract it your illness [be] milder. 3 Avoid the vaccine only if you [be] allergic to eggs. 4 If every person [be] willing and able to get the shot, there [be] very little serious flu each year. 5 But nearly universal vaccination [be] possible only if public outreach [be] improved and vaccine supplies [be] adequate.

---

27   Verb Mood

Mood in grammar is a verb form that indicates the writer's or speaker's attitude toward what he or she is saying. The **indicative mood** states a fact or opinion or asks a question: *The theater needs help.* The **imperative mood** expresses a command or gives a direction. It omits the subject of the sentence, *you: Help the theater.*

The **subjunctive mood** is trickier and requires distinctive verb forms described below.

Note A grammar and style checker may spot some errors in the subjunctive mood, but it may miss others. For example, a checker flagged *I wish I was home* (should be *were home*) but not *If I were home, I will not leave* (should be *would not leave*).

27a   Use the subjunctive verb forms appropriately, as in *I wish I were.*

The subjunctive mood expresses a suggestion, requirement, or desire, or it states a condition that is contrary to fact (that is, imaginary or hypothetical).

---

http://www.ablongman.com/littlebrown ▶

Visit the companion Web site for more help and an electronic exercise on verb mood.

- Verbs such as *ask, insist, urge, require, recommend,* and *suggest* indicate request or requirement. They often precede a subordinate clause beginning with *that* and containing the substance of the request or requirement. For all subjects, the verb in the *that* clause is the plain form:

  plain form
  Rules require that every donation be mailed.

- Contrary-to-fact clauses state imaginary or hypothetical conditions and usually begin with *if* or *unless* or follow *wish*. For present contrary-to-fact clauses, use the verb's past-tense form (for *be,* use the past-tense form *were*):

  past   past
  If the theater were in better shape and had more money, its future would be assured.

  past
  I wish I were able to donate money.

  For past contrary-to-fact clauses, use the verb's past perfect form (*had* + past participle):

  past perfect
  The theater would be better funded if it had been better managed.

Note Do not use the helping verb *would* or *could* in a contrary-to-fact clause beginning with *if:*

Not	Many people would have helped if they would have known.
But	Many people would have helped if they had known.

See also p. 231 on verb tenses in sentences like these.

27b   Keep mood consistent.

Shifts in mood within a sentence or among related sentences can be confusing. Such shifts occur most frequently in directions.

Inconsistent	Cook the mixture slowly, and you should stir it until the sugar is dissolved. [Mood shifts from imperative to indicative.]
Revised	Cook the mixture slowly, and stir it until the sugar is dissolved. [Consistently imperative.]

EXERCISE 27.1   Revising: Subjunctive mood

Revise the following paragraph with appropriate subjunctive verb forms. If a sentence is correct as given, mark the number preceding it. (You can do this exercise online at *ablongman.com/littlebrown.*)

1 If John Hawkins would have known of all the dangerous side effects of smoking tobacco, would he have introduced the plant to England in 1565? 2 In promoting tobacco, Hawkins noted that if a Florida Indian man was to travel for several days, he would have smoked tobacco to satisfy his hunger and thirst. 3 Early tobacco growers in the United States feared that their product would not gain acceptance unless it was perceived as healthful, so they spread Hawkins's story. 4 But local governments, more concerned about public safety and morality than health, passed laws requiring that colonists smoked tobacco only if they were five miles from any town. 5 To prevent decadence, in 1647 Connecticut passed a law mandating that one's smoking of tobacco was limited to once a day in one's own home.

28 Verb Voice

The **voice** of a verb tells whether the subject of the sentence performs the action (**active**) or is acted upon (**passive**). The actor in a passive sentence may be named in a prepositional phrase (as in *Rents are controlled by the city*), or the actor may be omitted (as in *Rents are controlled*).

Active and passive voice

Active voice The subject acts.

Subject = actor → Transitive verb in active voice → Direct object

The city — controls — rents.

Passive voice The subject is acted upon.

Subject = object of action ← Transitive verb in passive voice — (optional) by (actor)

Rents — are controlled — by the city.
Rents — are controlled.

http://www.ablongman.com/littlebrown ▶

Visit the companion Web site for more help and electronic exercises on verb voice.

 CULTURE
 LANGUAGE A passive verb always consists of a form of *be* plus the past participle of the main verb: *rents are controlled, people were inspired.* Other helping verbs must also be used with the words *be, being,* and *been: rents have been controlled, people would have been inspired.* Only a transitive verb (one that takes an object) may be used in the passive voice. (See p. 198.)

28a Generally, prefer the active voice. Use the passive voice when the actor is unknown or unimportant.

The active voice is usually clearer, more concise, and more forthright than the passive voice.

Weak passive	The Internet is used for research by many scholars, and its expansion to the general public has been criticized by some.
Strong active	Many scholars use the Internet for research, and some have criticized its expansion to the general public.

The passive voice is useful in two situations: when the actor is unknown and when the actor is unimportant or less important than the object of the action.

The Internet was established in 1969 by the US Department of Defense. The network has now been extended internationally to governments, universities, foundations, corporations, and private individuals. [In the first sentence the writer wishes to stress the Internet rather than the Department of Defense. In the second sentence the actor is unknown or too complicated to name.]

After the solution had been cooled to 10°C, the acid was added. [The person who cooled and added, perhaps the writer, is less important than the facts that the solution was cooled and acid was added. Passive sentences are common in scientific writing.]

Note Most grammar and style checkers can be set to spot the passive voice. But they will also flag appropriate uses of the passive voice (such as when the actor is unknown).

28b Keep voice consistent.

Shifts in voice that involve shifts in subject are usually unnecessary and confusing.

Inconsistent	Internet newsgroups cover an enormous range of topics for discussion. Forums for meeting people with like interests are provided in these groups.
Revised	Internet newsgroups cover an enormous range of topics for discussion and provide forums for meeting people with like interests.

A shift in voice is appropriate when it helps focus the reader's attention on a single subject, as in *The candidate campaigned vigorously and was nominated on the first ballot.*

EXERCISE 28.1 Converting between active and passive voices

Convert the verbs in the following sentences from active to passive or from passive to active. (In converting from passive to active, you may need to add a subject.) Which version of the sentence seems more effective and why? (You can do this exercise online at *ablongman.com/littlebrown.*)

> *Example:*
> The aspiring actor was discovered in a nightclub.
> A talent <u>scout</u> <u>discovered</u> the actor in a nightclub.

1 When the Eiffel Tower was built in 1889, it was thought by the French to be ugly.
2 At the time, many people still resisted industrial technology.
3 The tower's naked steel construction typified this technology.
4 Beautiful ornament was expected to grace fine buildings.
5 Further, a structure without solid walls could not even be called a building.

EXERCISE 28.2 Revising: Using the active voice

In the following paragraph, rewrite passive sentences into the active voice, adding new sentence subjects as needed. (You can do this exercise online at *ablongman.com/littlebrown.*)

1 Water quality is determined by many factors. 2 Suspended and dissolved substances are contained in all natural waters. 3 The amounts of the substances are controlled by the environment. 4 Some dissolved substances are produced by pesticides. 5 Other substances, such as sediment, are deposited in water by fields, livestock feedlots, and other sources. 6 The bottom life of streams and lakes is affected by sediment. 7 Light penetration is reduced by sediment, and bottom-dwelling organisms may be smothered. 8 The quality of water in city systems is measured frequently. 9 Some contaminants can be removed by treatment plants. 10 If the legal levels are exceeded by pollutants, the citizens must be notified by city officials.

29 Agreement of Subject and Verb

A subject and its verb should agree in number and person.

More Japanese Americans live in Hawaii and California than elsewhere.
subject   verb

Daniel Inouye was the first Japanese American in Congress.
subject   verb

Most problems of subject-verb agreement arise when endings are omitted from subjects or verbs or when the relation between sentence parts is uncertain.

Note A grammar and style checker will catch many simple errors in subject-verb agreement, such as *Addie and John is late*, and some more complicated errors, such as *Is Margaret and Tom going with us?* (should be *are* in both cases). But a checker failed to flag *The old group has gone their separate ways* (should be *have*) and offered a wrong correction for *The old group have gone their separate ways*, which is already correct.

29a The -s and -es endings work differently for nouns and verbs.

An -s or -es ending does opposite things to nouns and verbs: it usually makes a noun *plural*, but it always makes a present-tense verb *singular*. Thus a singular-noun subject will not end in -s, but its verb will. A plural-noun subject will end in -s, but its verb will not. Between them, subject and verb use only one -s ending.

Singular subject	Plural subject
The boy plays.	The boys play.
The bird soars.	The birds soar.

┌ **Key terms** ─────────────────────────────

	Number	
Person	**Singular**	**Plural**
First	I eat.	We eat.
Second	You eat.	You eat.
Third	He/she/it eats.	They eat.
	The bird eats.	Birds eat.

http://www.ablongman.com/littlebrown ▶

Visit the companion Web site for more help and electronic exercises on subject-verb agreement.

The only exceptions to these rules involve the nouns that form irregular plurals, such as *child/children, woman/women*. The irregular plural still requires a plural verb: *The children play. The women read.*

CULTURE LANGUAGE If your first language or dialect is not standard American English, subject-verb agreement may be problematic, especially for the following reasons:

- **Some English dialects follow different rules for subject-verb agreement,** such as omitting the *-s* ending for singular verbs or using the *-s* ending for plural verbs.

Nonstandard	The voter resist change.
Standard	The voter resists change.
Standard	The voters resist change.

  The verb *be* changes spelling for singular and plural in both present and past tense. (See also p. 191.)

Nonstandard	Taxes is high. They was raised just last year.
Standard	Taxes are high. They were raised just last year.

  Have also has a distinctive *-s* form, *has:*

Nonstandard	The new tax have little chance of passing.
Standard	The new tax has little chance of passing.

- **Some other languages change all verb phrases to match their subjects,** but in English only the helping verbs *be, have,* and *do* change for different subjects. The modal helping verbs—*can, may, should, will*, and others—do not change:

Nonstandard	The tax mays pass next year.
Standard	The tax may pass next year.

  The main verb in a verb phrase also does not change for different subjects:

Nonstandard	The tax may passes next year.
Standard	The tax may pass next year.

29b Subject and verb should agree even when other words come between them.

The catalog of course requirements often baffles [not baffle] students.

The requirements stated in the catalog are [not is] unclear.

Note Phrases beginning with *as well as, together with, along with,* and *in addition to* do not change a singular subject to plural:

The president, as well as the deans, has [not have] agreed.

29c Subjects joined by *and* usually take plural verbs.

Frost and Roethke were contemporaries.

Exceptions When the parts of the subject form a single idea or refer to a single person or thing, they take a singular verb:

Avocado and bean sprouts is a California sandwich.

When a compound subject is preceded by the adjective *each* or *every*, the verb is usually singular:

Each man, woman, and child has a right to be heard.

29d When parts of a subject are joined by *or* or *nor*, the verb agrees with the nearer part.

Either the painter or the carpenter knows the cost.

The cabinets or the bookcases are too costly.

When one part of the subject is singular and the other plural, avoid awkwardness by placing the plural part closer to the verb so that the verb is plural:

Awkward   Neither the owners nor the contractor agrees.

Revised   Neither the contractor nor the owners agree.

29e With *everyone* and other indefinite pronouns, use a singular or plural verb as appropriate.

Most indefinite pronouns are singular in meaning (they refer to a single unspecified person or thing), and they take a singular verb.

Key term

indefinite pronoun A pronoun that does not refer to a specific person or thing:

Singular			Singular or plural	Plural
anybody	everyone	no one	all	both
anyone	everything	nothing	any	few
anything	much	one	more	many
each	neither	somebody	most	several
either	nobody	someone	some	
everybody	none	something		

Something smells.   Neither is right.

The plural indefinite pronouns refer to more than one unspecified thing, and they take a plural verb:

Both are correct.   Several were invited.

The other indefinite pronouns take a singular or a plural verb depending on whether the word they refer to is singular or plural:

All of the money is reserved for emergencies.

All of the funds are reserved for emergencies.

CULTURE LANGUAGE See p. 270 for the distinction between *few* ("not many") and *a few* ("some").

29f Collective nouns such as *team* take singular or plural verbs depending on meaning.

Use a singular verb with a collective noun when the group acts as a unit:

The group agrees that action is necessary.

But when the group's members act separately, not together, use a plural verb:

The old group have gone their separate ways.

The collective noun *number* may be singular or plural. Preceded by *a*, it is plural; preceded by *the*, it is singular:

A number of people are in debt.

The number of people in debt is very large.

CULTURE LANGUAGE Some noncount nouns (nouns that don't form plurals) are collective nouns because they name groups: for instance, *furniture, clothing, mail, machinery, equipment, military, police*. These noncount nouns usually take singular verbs: *Mail arrives daily.* But some of these nouns take plural verbs, including *clergy, military, people, police,* and any collective noun that comes from an adjective, such as *the poor, the rich, the young, the elderly*. If you mean one representative of the group, use a singular noun such as *police officer* or *poor person*.

Key term

collective noun   A noun with singular form that names a group of individuals or things—for instance, *army, audience, committee, crowd, family*.

29g Who, which, and that take verbs that agree with their antecedents.

When used as subjects, *who, which,* and *that* refer to another word in the sentence, called the **antecedent.** The verb agrees with the antecedent.

Mayor Garber ought to listen to the people who work for her.

Bardini is the only aide who has her ear.

Agreement problems often occur with relative pronouns when the sentence includes *one of the* or *the only one of the:*

Bardini is one of the aides who work unpaid. [Of the aides who work unpaid, Bardini is one.]

Bardini is the only one of the aides who knows the community. [Of the aides, only one, Bardini, knows the community.]

CULTURE LANGUAGE In phrases beginning with *one of the,* be sure the noun is plural: *Bardini is one of the aides* [not *aide*] *who work unpaid.*

29h News and other singular nouns ending in -s take singular verbs.

Singular nouns ending in *-s* include *athletics, economics, linguistics, mathematics, measles, mumps, news, physics, politics,* and *statistics,* as well as place names such as *Athens, Wales,* and *United States.*

After so long a wait, the news has to be good.

Statistics is required of psychology majors.

A few of these words also take plural verbs, but only when they describe individual items rather than whole bodies of activity or knowledge: *The statistics prove him wrong.*

Measurements and figures ending in *-s* may also be singular when the quantity they refer to is a unit.

Three years is a long time to wait.

Three-fourths of the library consists of reference books.

29i The verb agrees with the subject even when the normal word order is inverted.

Inverted subject-verb order occurs mainly in questions and in constructions beginning with *there* or *it* and a form of *be.*

Is voting a right or a privilege?

Are a right and a privilege the same thing?

There are differences between them.

29j Is, are, and other linking verbs agree with their subjects, not subject complements.

Make a linking verb agree with its subject, usually the first element in the sentence, not with the noun or pronoun serving as a subject complement.

The child's sole support is her court-appointed guardians.

Her court-appointed guardians are the child's sole support.

29k Use singular verbs with titles and with words being defined.

Hakada Associates is a new firm.

Dream Days remains a favorite book.

Folks is a down-home word for *people*.

EXERCISE 29.1 Revising: Subject-verb agreement

Revise the verbs in the following paragraphs as needed to make subjects and verbs agree in number. If a sentence is correct as given, mark the number preceding it. (You can do this exercise online at *ablongman .com/littlebrown*.)

1 Statistics from recent research suggests that humor in the workplace relieves job-related stress. 2 Reduced stress in the workplace in turn reduce illness and absenteeism. 3 It can also ease friction within an employee group, which then work together more productively.

4 Weinstein Associates is a consulting firm that hold workshops designed to make businesspeople laugh. 5 In sessions held by one consultant, each of the participants practice making others laugh. 6 "Isn't

---

┌─ **Key terms** ───

linking verb A verb that connects or equates the subject and subject complement: for example, *seem, become, appear,* and forms of *be.* (See p. 199.)

subject complement A word that describes or renames the subject: *They became chemists.* (See p. 199.)

there enough laughs within you to spread the wealth?" the consultant asks the students. 7 She quotes Casey Stengel's rule that the best way to keep your management job is to separate the underlings who hate you from the ones who have not decided how they feel. 8 Such self-deprecating comments in public is uncommon among business managers, the consultant says. 9 Each of the managers in a typical firm takes the work much too seriously. 10 The humorous boss often feels like the only one of the managers who have other things in mind besides profits.

11 Another consultant from Weinstein Associates suggest cultivating office humor with practical jokes and cartoons. 12 When a manager or employees drops a rubber fish in the water cooler or posts cartoons on the bulletin board, office spirit usually picks up. 13 If the job of updating the cartoons is entrusted to an employee who has seemed easily distracted, the employee's concentration often improves. 14 Even the former sourpuss becomes one of those who hides a bad temper. 15 Every one of the consultants caution, however, that humor has no place in life-affecting corporate situations such as employee layoffs.

EXERCISE 29.2   Adjusting for subject-verb agreement

Rewrite the following paragraphs to change the underlined words from plural to singular. (You will sometimes need to add *a* or *the* for the singular, as in the example below.) Then change verbs as necessary so that they agree with their new subjects. (You can do this exercise online at *ablongman.com/littlebrown*.)

> *Example:*
> Siberian tigers are an endangered subspecies.
> The Siberian tiger is an endangered subspecies.

1 Siberian tigers are the largest living cats in the world, much bigger than their relative the Bengal tiger. 2 They grow to a length of nine to twelve feet, including their tails, and to a height of about three and a half feet. 3 They can weigh over six hundred pounds. 4 These carnivorous hunters live in northern China and Korea as well as in Siberia. 5 During the long winter of this Arctic climate, the yellowish striped coats get a little lighter in order to blend with the snow-covered landscape. 6 The coats also grow quite thick, since the tigers have to withstand temperatures as low as −50°F.

7 Siberian tigers sometimes have to travel great distances to find food. 8 They need about twenty pounds of food a day because of their size and the cold climate, but when they have fresh food they may eat as much as a hundred pounds at one time. 9 They hunt mainly deer, boars, and even bears, plus smaller prey such as fish and rabbits. 10 They pounce on their prey and grab them by the back of the neck. 11 Animals that are not killed immediately are thrown to the ground and suffocated with a bite to the throat. 12 Then the tigers feast.

Pronouns

Pronouns—words such as *she* and *who* that refer to nouns—merit special care because all their meaning comes from the other words they refer to. This section discusses pronoun case (Chapter 30), matching pronouns and the words they refer to (31), and making sure pronouns refer to the right nouns (32).

30 Pronoun Case

Case is the form of a noun or pronoun that shows the reader how it functions in a sentence.

- **The subjective case** indicates that the word is a subject or subject complement.
- **The objective case** indicates that the word is an object of a verb or preposition.
- **The possessive case** indicates that the word owns or is the source of a noun in the sentence.

Nouns change form only to show possession: *teacher's* (see **5** pp. 323–26). Most of the following pronouns change more frequently.

Subjective	Objective	Possessive
I	me	my, mine
you	you	your, yours

Key terms

subject Who or what a sentence is about: *Biologists often study animals. They often work in laboratories.* (See pp. 195–97.)

subject complement A word or words that rename or describe the sentence subject: *Biologists are scientists. The best biologists are she and Scoggins.* (See p. 199.)

object of verb The receiver of the verb's action (**direct object**): *Many biologists study animals. The animals teach them.* Or the person or thing the action is performed for (**indirect object**): *Some biologists give animals homes. The animals give them pleasure.* (See pp. 198–200.)

object of preposition The word linked by *with, for,* or another preposition to the rest of the sentence: *Many biologists work in a laboratory. For them the lab often provides a second home.* (See p. 201.)

---

http://www.ablongman.com/littlebrown ▶

Visit the companion Web site for more help and electronic exercises on pronoun case.

Subjective	Objective	Possessive
he	him	his
she	her	her, hers
it	it	its
we	us	our, ours
you	you	your, yours
they	them	their, theirs
who	whom	whose
whoever	whomever	—

Note Grammar and style checkers may flag some problems with pronoun case, but they will also miss a lot. For instance, one checker spotted the error in *We asked whom would come* (should be *who would come*), but it overlooked *We dreaded them coming* (should be *their coming*).

■ CULTURE LANGUAGE ■ In standard American English, *-self* pronouns do not change form to show function. Their only forms are *myself, yourself, himself, herself, itself, ourselves, yourselves, themselves.* Avoid nonstandard forms such as *hisself, ourself,* and *theirselves.*

30a   **Distinguish between compound subjects and compound objects: *she and I* vs. *her and me.***

Compound subjects or objects—those consisting of two or more nouns or pronouns—have the same case forms as they would if one noun or pronoun stood alone:

compound
subject
She and Novick discussed the proposal.

compound
object
The proposal disappointed her and him.

If you are in doubt about the correct form, try the test below:

A test for case forms in compound constructions

- **Identify a compound construction** (one connected by *and, but, or, nor*):

  [He, Him] and [I, me] won the prize.
  The prize went to [he, him] and [I, me].

- **Write a separate sentence for each part of the compound:**

  [He, Him] won the prize. [I, Me] won the prize.
  The prize went to [he, him]. The prize went to [I, me].

(continued)

A test for case forms in compound constructions
(continued)

- ■ **Choose the pronouns that sound correct:**

    <u>He</u> won the prize. <u>I</u> won the prize. [Subjective.]
    The prize went to <u>him</u>. The prize went to <u>me</u>. [Objective.]

- ■ **Put the separate sentences back together:**

    <u>He and I</u> won the prize.
    The prize went to <u>him and me</u>.

30b | Use the subjective case for subject complements:
It was she.

After a linking verb, a pronoun renaming the subject (a subject complement) should be in the subjective case:

subject complement
The ones who care most are <u>she and Novick</u>.

subject
complement
It was <u>they</u> whom the mayor appointed.

If this construction sounds stilted to you, use the more natural order: *<u>She and Novick</u> are the ones who care most. The mayor appointed <u>them</u>.*

EXERCISE 30.1 Choosing between subjective and objective pronouns

In the following paragraph, select the appropriate subjective or objective pronoun from the pairs in brackets. (You can do this exercise online at *ablongman.com/littlebrown*.)

1 Jody and [I, me] had been hunting for jobs. **2** The best employees at our old company were [she, her] and [I, me], so [we, us] expected to find jobs quickly. **3** Between [she, her] and [I, me] the job search had lasted two months, and still it had barely begun. **4** Slowly, [she, her] and [I, me] stopped sharing leads. **5** It was obvious that Jody and [I, me] could not be as friendly as [we, us] had been.

┌─ **Key term** ───

linking verb A verb, such as a form of *be,* that connects a subject and a word that renames or describes the subject (subject complement): *They <u>are</u> biologists.* (See p. 199.)

30c   The use of *who* vs. *whom* depends on the pronoun's function in its clause.

Use *who* where you would use *he* or *she*—all ending in vowels. Use *whom* where you would use *him* or *her*—all ending in consonants.

1   Questions

At the beginning of a question use *who* for a subject and *whom* for an object:

subject →
Who wrote the policy?

object ←
Whom does it affect?

To find the correct case of *who* in a question, follow the steps below.

- **Pose the question:**

  [Who, Whom] makes that decision?
  [Who, Whom] does one ask?

- **Answer the question, using a personal pronoun.** Choose the pronoun that sounds correct, and note its case:

  [She, Her] makes that decision. She makes that decision. [Subjective.]
  One asks [she, her]. One asks her. [Objective.]

- **Use the same case (*who* or *whom*) in the question:**

  Who makes that decision? [Subjective.]
  Whom does one ask? [Objective.]

2   Subordinate clauses

In subordinate clauses use *who* and *whoever* for all subjects, *whom* and *whomever* for all objects.

subject →
Give old clothes to whoever needs them.

object ←
I don't know whom the mayor appointed.

To determine which form to use, try the following test:

- **Locate the subordinate clause:**

  Few people know [who, whom] they should ask.
  They are unsure [who, whom] makes the decision.

┌ **Key term** ─────────────────────────────────
subordinate clause A word group that contains a subject and a verb and also begins with a subordinating word, such as *who, whom,* or *because.* (See pp. 206–07.)
└──

- Rewrite the subordinate clause as a separate sentence, substituting a personal pronoun for *who, whom.* Choose the pronoun that sounds correct, and note its case:

They should ask [she, her]. They should ask her. [Objective.]

[She, her] usually makes the decision. She usually makes the decision. [Subjective.]

- Use the same case (*who* or *whom*) in the subordinate clause:

Few people know whom they should ask. [Objective.]
They are unsure who makes the decision. [Subjective.]

Note Don't let expressions such as *I think* and *she says* mislead you into using *whom* rather than *who* for the subject of a clause.

subject ⟶
He is the one who I think is best qualified.

To choose between *who* and *whom* in such constructions, delete the interrupting phrase so that you can see the true relation between parts: *He is the one who is best qualified.*

EXERCISE 30.2   Choosing between *who* and *whom*

In the following paragraph, select the appropriate pronoun from the pairs in brackets. (You can do this exercise online at *ablongman.com/ littlebrown.*)

1 The school administrators suspended Jurgen, [who, whom] they suspected of setting the fire. 2 Jurgen had been complaining to other custodians, [who, whom] reported him. 3 He constantly complained of unfair treatment from [whoever, whomever] happened to be passing in the halls, including pupils. 4 "[Who, Whom] here has heard Mr. Jurgen's complaints?" the police asked. 5 "[Who, Whom] did he complain most about?"

EXERCISE 30.3   Sentence combining: *Who* versus *whom*

Combine each pair of sentences below into one sentence that contains a clause beginning with *who* or *whom.* Be sure to use the appropriate case form. You will have to add, delete, and rearrange words. Each item may have more than one possible answer. (You can do this exercise online at *ablongman.com/littlebrown.*)

Example:
David is the candidate. We think David deserves to win.
David is the candidate who we think deserves to win.

1 Some children have undetected hearing problems. These children may do poorly in school.
2 They may not hear important instructions and information from teachers. Teachers may speak softly.

3 Classmates may not be audible. The teacher calls on those classmates.
4 Some hearing-impaired children may work harder to overcome their disability. These children get a lot of encouragement at home.
5 Some hearing-impaired children may take refuge in fantasy friends. They can rely on these friends not to criticize or laugh.

30d Use the appropriate case in other constructions.

1 *We* or *us* with a noun

The choice of *we* or *us* before a noun depends on the use of the noun.

object of
preposition
Freezing weather is welcomed by us skaters.

subject
We skaters welcome freezing weather.

2 Pronoun in an appositive

In an appositive the case of a pronoun depends on the function of the word the appositive describes or identifies.

appositive
identifies object
The class elected two representatives, DeShawn and me.

appositive
identifies subject
Two representatives, DeShawn and I, were elected.

3 Pronoun after *than* or *as*

When a pronoun follows *than* or *as* in a comparison, the case of the pronoun indicates what words may have been omitted. A subjective pronoun must be the subject of the omitted verb.

subject
Some critics like Glass more than he [does].

An objective pronoun must be the object of the omitted verb:

object
Some critics like Glass more than [they like] him.

4 Subject and object of infinitive

Both the object *and* the subject of an infinitive are in the objective case.

Key term

appositive A noun or noun substitute that renames another noun immediately before it. (See p. 205.)
---

subject
of infinitive
The school asked <u>him</u> to speak.

object
of infinitive
Students chose to invite <u>him</u>.

5 Case before a gerund

Ordinarily, use the possessive form of a pronoun or noun immediately before a gerund:

The coach disapproved of <u>their</u> lifting weights.

The <u>coach's</u> disapproving was a surprise.

EXERCISE 30.4 Choosing between subjective and objective pronouns

In the following paragraph, select the appropriate pronoun from the pairs in brackets. (You can do this exercise online at *ablongman.com/littlebrown.*)

1 Obtaining enough protein is important to [we, us] vegetarians. 2 Instead of obtaining protein from meat, [we, us] vegetarians get our protein from other sources such as eggs, cheese, nuts, and beans. 3 Some of [we, us] vegetarians also eat fish, an excellent source of protein, but vegans avoid all animal products, including eggs and cheese. 4 My friend Jeff claims to know only two vegans, Helena and [he, him]. 5 He believes that [we, us] vegetarians who eat fish and dairy products are not as truly vegetarian as [he, him].

EXERCISE 30.5 Revising: Pronoun case

Revise all inappropriate case forms in the following paragraph. If a sentence is correct as given, mark the number preceding it. (You can do this exercise online at *ablongman.com/littlebrown.*)

1 Written four thousand years ago, *The Epic of Gilgamesh* tells the story of Gilgamesh and his friendship with Enkidu. 2 Gilgamesh was a bored king who his people thought was too harsh. 3 Then he met Enkidu, a wild man whom had lived with the animals in the mountains. 4 Immediately, him and Gilgamesh wrestled to see whom was more powerful. 5 After hours of struggle, Enkidu admitted that Gilgamesh was stronger than him. 6 Now the friends needed adventures worthy of them, the two strongest men on earth. 7 Gilgamesh said, "Between you

---

┌ **Key terms** ────────────────────────────────────

infinitive The plain form of the verb plus *to: to run.* (See p. 203.)

gerund The *-ing* form of a verb used as a noun: *Running is fun.* (See p. 203.)

and I, mighty deeds will be accomplished, and our fame will be everlasting." 8 Among their acts, Enkidu and him defeated a giant bull, Humbaba, cut down the bull's cedar forests, and brought back the logs to Gilgamesh's treeless land. 9 Their heroism won them great praise from the people. 10 When Enkidu died, Gilgamesh mourned his death, realizing that no one had been a better friend than him. 11 When Gilgamesh himself died many years later, his people raised a monument praising Enkidu and he for their friendship and their mighty deeds of courage.

31 Agreement of Pronoun and Antecedent

The **antecedent** of a pronoun is the noun or other pronoun to which the pronoun refers:

Homeowners fret over their tax bills.
    antecedent   pronoun

Its constant increases make the tax bill a dreaded document.
pronoun   antecedent

For clarity, a pronoun should agree with its antecedent in person, number, and gender.

Note Grammar and style checkers cannot help you with agreement between pronoun and antecedent because they cannot recognize the intended relation between the two.

CULTURE LANGUAGE The gender of a pronoun should match its antecedent, not a noun that the pronoun may modify: *Sara Young invited her* [not *his*] *son to join the company's staff.* Also, nouns in

---

Key terms

Person	Number	
	Singular	Plural
First	*I*	*we*
Second	*you*	*you*
Third	*he, she, it,*	*they,*
	indefinite pronouns,	plural nouns
	singular nouns	
Gender		
Masculine	*he,* nouns naming males	
Feminine	*she,* nouns naming females	
Neuter	*it,* all other nouns	

English have only neuter gender unless they specifically refer to males or females. Thus nouns such as *book, table, sun,* and *earth* take the pronoun *it*.

31a Antecedents joined by *and* usually take plural pronouns.

Mr. Bartos and I cannot settle our dispute.

The dean and my adviser have offered their help.

Exceptions When the compound antecedent refers to a single idea, person, or thing, then the pronoun is singular.

My friend and adviser offered her help.

When the compound antecedent follows *each* or *every*, the pronoun is singular.

Every girl and woman took her seat.

31b When parts of an antecedent are joined by *or* or *nor*, the pronoun agrees with the nearer part.

Tenants or owners must present their grievances.

Either the tenant or the owner will have her way.

When one subject is plural and the other singular, the sentence will be awkward unless you put the plural subject second.

Awkward Neither the tenants nor the owner has yet made her case.

Revised Neither the owner nor the tenants have yet made their case.

31c With *everyone, person,* and other indefinite words, use a singular or plural pronoun as appropriate.

Indefinite words—indefinite pronouns and generic nouns—do not refer to any specific person or thing. Most indefinite pronouns and all generic nouns are singular in meaning. When they serve as antecedents of pronouns, the pronouns should be singular:

Everyone on the women's team now has her own locker.
indefinite
pronoun

Every person on the women's team now has her own locker.
    generic noun

Five indefinite pronouns—*all, any, more, most, some*—may be singular or plural in meaning depending on what they refer to:

Few women athletes had changing spaces, so most had to change in their rooms.

Most of the changing space was dismal, its color a drab olive green.

Four indefinite pronouns—*both, few, many, several*—are always plural in meaning:

Few realize how their athletic facilities have changed.

Most agreement problems arise with the singular indefinite words. We often use these words to mean "many" or "all" rather than "one" and then refer to them with plural pronouns, as in *Everyone has their own locker*. Often, too, we mean indefinite words to include both masculine and feminine genders and thus resort to *they* instead of the **generic *he***—the masculine pronoun referring to both genders, as in *Everyone deserves his privacy*. (For more on the generic *he*, which many readers view as sexist, see **3** p. 165.) To achieve agreement in such cases, you have several options:

Ways to correct agreement with indefinite words

- **Change the indefinite word to a plural, and use a plural pronoun to match:**

    Faulty   Every athlete deserves their privacy.
    Revised   Athletes deserve their privacy.

(continued)

Key terms

indefinite pronoun A pronoun that does not refer to a specific person or thing:

Singular			Singular or plural	Plural
anybody	everyone	no one	all	both
anyone	everything	nothing	any	few
anything	much	one	more	many
each	neither	somebody	most	several
either	nobody	someone	some	
everybody	none	something		

generic noun A singular noun such as *person* and *student* when it refers to a typical member of a group, not to a particular individual.

Ways to correct agreement with indefinite words
(continued)

- **Rewrite the sentence to omit the pronoun:**

  Faulty   Everyone is entitled to their own locker.
  Revised   Everyone is entitled to a locker.

- **Use *he or she* (*him or her, his or her*) to refer to the indefinite word:**

  Faulty   Now everyone has their private space.
  Revised   Now everyone has his or her private space.

  However, used more than once in several sentences, *he or she* quickly becomes awkward. (Many readers do not accept the alternative *he/she*.) In most cases, using the plural or omitting the pronoun will not only correct agreement problems but also create more readable sentences.

31d   Collective nouns such as *team* take singular or plural pronouns depending on meaning.

Use a singular pronoun with a collective noun when referring to the group as a unit:

The committee voted to disband itself.

When referring to the individual members of the group, use a plural pronoun:

The old group have gone their separate ways.

CULTURE LANGUAGE   In standard American English, collective nouns that are noncount nouns (they don't form plurals) usually take singular pronouns: *The mail sits in its own basket.* A few noncount nouns take plural pronouns, including *clergy, military, police, the rich,* and *the poor: The police support their unions.*

EXERCISE 31.1   Revising: Pronoun-antecedent agreement

Revise the following sentences so that pronouns and their antecedents agree in person and number. Try to avoid the generic *he* (see the previous page). If you change the subject of a sentence, be sure to change the verb as necessary for agreement. Mark the number preceding any

Key term

collective noun A noun with singular form that names a group of individuals or things—for instance, *army, audience, committee, crowd, family, group, team.*

sentence that is correct as given. (You can do this exercise online at *ablongman.com/littlebrown.*)

> *Example:*
>
> Each of the Boudreaus' children brought their laundry home at Thanksgiving.
>
> <u>All</u> of the Boudreaus' children brought their laundry home at Thanksgiving. *Or:* Each of the Boudreaus' children brought <u>his or her</u> laundry home at Thanksgiving.

1 Each girl raised in a Mexican American family in the Rio Grande Valley of Texas hopes that one day they will be given a *quinceañera* party for their fifteenth birthday. 2 Such celebrations are very expensive because it entails a religious service followed by a huge party. 3 A girl's immediate family, unless they are wealthy, cannot afford the party by themselves. 4 The parents will ask each close friend or relative if they can help with the preparations. 5 Surrounded by her family and attended by her friends and their escorts, the *quinceañera* is introduced as a young woman eligible for Mexican American society.

EXERCISE 31.2   Revising: Pronoun-antecedent agreement

Revise the following sentences so that pronouns and their antecedents agree in person and number. Try to avoid the generic *he* (see p. 253). If you change the subject of a sentence, be sure to change the verb as necessary for agreement. Mark the number preceding any sentence that is correct as given. (You can do this exercise online at *ablongman.com/ littlebrown.*)

1 Despite their extensive research and experience, neither child psychologists nor parents have yet figured out how children become who they are. 2 Of course, the family has a tremendous influence on the development of a child in their midst. 3 Each member of the immediate family exerts their own unique pull on the child. 4 Other relatives, teachers, and friends can also affect the child's view of the world and of themselves. 5 The workings of genetics also strongly influence the child, but it may never be fully understood. 6 The psychology community cannot agree in its views of whether nurture or nature is more important in a child's development. 7 Another debated issue is whether the child's emotional development or their intellectual development is more central. 8 Just about everyone has their strong opinion on these issues, often backed up by evidence. 9 Neither the popular press nor scholarly journals devote much of their space to the wholeness of the child.

32 Reference of Pronoun to Antecedent

A **pronoun** should refer clearly to its **antecedent,** the noun it substitutes for. Otherwise, readers will have difficulty grasping the pronoun's meaning.

Note Grammar and style checkers are not sophisticated enough to recognize unclear pronoun reference. For instance, a checker did not flag any of the confusing examples on the next page.

🔲 CULTURE
  LANGUAGE In standard American English, a pronoun needs a clear antecedent nearby, but don't use both a pronoun and its antecedent as the subject of the same clause: *Jim* [not *Jim he*] *told Mark to go alone.* (See also p. 291.)

32a Make a pronoun refer clearly to one antecedent.

When either of two nouns can be a pronoun's antecedent, the reference will not be clear.

Confusing   Emily Dickinson is sometimes compared with Jane Austen,
            but she was quite different.

Revise such a sentence in one of two ways:

- **Replace the pronoun with the appropriate noun.**

    Clear   Emily Dickinson is sometimes compared with Jane Austen, but Dickinson [or Austen] was quite different.

- **Avoid repetition by rewriting the sentence.** If you use the pronoun, make sure it has only one possible antecedent.

    Clear   Despite occasional comparison, Emily Dickinson and Jane Austen were quite different.

    Clear   Though sometimes compared with her, Emily Dickinson was quite different from Jane Austen.

32b Place a pronoun close enough to its antecedent to ensure clarity.

A clause beginning with *who, which,* or *that* should generally fall immediately after the word to which it refers.

---

http://www.ablongman.com/littlebrown ▶

Visit the companion Web site for more help and electronic exercises on pronoun reference.

Confusing	Jody found a lamp in the attic that her aunt had used.
Clear	In the attic Jody found a lamp that her aunt had used.

32c Make a pronoun refer to a specific antecedent, not an implied one.

A pronoun should refer to a specific noun or other pronoun. A reader can only guess at the meaning of a pronoun when its antecedent is implied by the context, not stated outright.

1 Vague *this, that, which,* or *it*

This, that, which, or *it* should refer to a specific noun, not to a whole word group expressing an idea or situation.

Confusing	The British knew little of the American countryside, and they had no experience with the colonists' guerrilla tactics. This gave the colonists an advantage.
Clear	The British knew little of the American countryside, and they had no experience with the colonists' guerrilla tactics. This ignorance and inexperience gave the colonists an advantage.

2 Implied nouns

A noun may be implied in some other word or phrase, as *happiness* is implied in *happy, driver* is implied in *drive,* and *mother* is implied in *mother's.* But a pronoun cannot refer clearly to an implied noun, only to a specific, stated one.

Confusing	Cohen's report brought her a lawsuit.
Clear	Cohen was sued over her report.
Confusing	Her reports on psychological development generally go unnoticed outside it.
Clear	Her reports on psychological development generally go unnoticed outside the field.

32d Use *it* and *they* to refer to definite antecedents.

It and *they* should have definite noun antecedents. Rewrite the sentence if the antecedent is missing.

Confusing	In Chapter 4 of this book it describes the early flights of the Wright brothers.

Clear   Chapter 4 of this book describes the early flights of the Wright brothers.

Confusing   Even in reality TV shows, they present a false picture of life.

Clear   Even reality TV shows present a false picture of life.

EXERCISE 32.1   Revising: Pronoun reference

Rewrite the following paragraph to eliminate unclear pronoun reference. If you use a pronoun in your revision, be sure that it refers to only one antecedent and that it falls close enough to its antecedent to ensure clarity. (You can do this exercise online at *ablongman.com/littlebrown*.)

1 There is a difference between the heroes of modern times and the heroes of earlier times: they have flaws in their characters. 2 Despite their imperfections, sports fans still admire Pete Rose, Babe Ruth, and Joe Namath. 3 Fans liked Rose for having his young son serve as batboy when he was in Cincinnati. 4 The reputation Rose earned as a gambler and tax evader may overshadow his reputation as a ballplayer, but it will survive. 5 He amassed an unequaled record as a hitter, using his bat to do things no one has ever done, and it remains even though Rose was banned from baseball.

EXERCISE 32.2   Revising: Pronoun reference

Revise the following paragraph as needed so that pronouns refer to specific, appropriate antecedents. If a sentence is correct as given, mark the number preceding it. (You can do this exercise online at *ablongman.com/littlebrown*.)

1 In Charlotte Brontë's *Jane Eyre*, she is a shy young woman who takes a job as a governess. 2 Her employer, a rude, brooding man named Rochester, lives in a mysterious mansion on the English moors, which contributes a strange quality to Jane's experience. 3 Stranger still are the fires, eerie noises, and other unexplained happenings in the house; but Rochester refuses to discuss this. 4 Eventually, they fall in love, but the day they are to marry, she learns that he has a wife hidden in the house. 5 She is hopelessly insane and violent and must be guarded at all times, which explains his strange behavior. 6 Heartbroken, Jane leaves the moors, and many years pass before they are reunited.

32e   Use *you* only to mean "you, the reader."

You should clearly mean "you, the reader." The context must be appropriate for such a meaning:

Inappropriate   In the fourteenth century you had to struggle simply to survive.

Revised   In the fourteenth century one [or a person] had to struggle simply to survive.

Writers sometimes drift into *you* because *one, a person,* or a similar indefinite word can be difficult to sustain. Sentence after sentence, the indefinite word may sound stuffy, and it requires *he* or *he or she* for pronoun-antecedent agreement (see pp. 252–54). To avoid these problems, try using plural nouns and pronouns:

Original   In the fourteenth century <u>one</u> had to struggle simply to survive.

Revised   In the fourteenth century <u>people</u> had to struggle simply to survive.

32f   Keep pronouns consistent.

Within a sentence or a group of related sentences, pronouns should be consistent. Partly, consistency comes from making pronouns and their antecedents agree (see Chapter 31). In addition, the pronouns within a passage should match each other.

Inconsistent   <u>One</u> finds when reading that <u>your</u> concentration improves with practice, so that <u>I</u> now comprehend more in less time.

Revised   <u>I</u> find when reading that <u>my</u> concentration improves with practice, so that <u>I</u> now comprehend more in less time.

EXERCISE 32.3   Revising: Consistency in pronouns

Revise the following paragraph to make pronouns consistent. (You can do this exercise online at *ablongman.com/littlebrown.*)

1 When a taxpayer is waiting to receive a tax refund from the Internal Revenue Service, you begin to notice what time the mail carrier arrives. **2** If the taxpayer does not receive a refund check within six weeks of filing a return, they may not have followed the rules of the IRS. **3** For instance, if a taxpayer does not include a Social Security number on a return, you will have to wait for a refund. **4** If one makes errors on the tax form, they will certainly have to wait and they might be audited, delaying a refund for months or longer. **5** A refund may be held up even if you file on time, because returns received close to the April 15 deadline swamp the IRS.

EXERCISE 32.4   Revising: Pronoun reference

Revise the following paragraph as needed so that pronouns are consistent and refer to specific, appropriate antecedents. (You can do this exercise online at *ablongman.com/littlebrown.*)

1 "Life begins at forty" is a cliché many people live by, and this may or may not be true. **2** Whether one agrees or not with the cliché, you can cite many examples of people whose public lives began at forty. **3** For instance, when she was forty, Pearl Buck's novel *The Good Earth* won the Pulitzer Prize. 4 Kenneth Kanuda, past president of Zambia, was elected to it in 1964, when he was forty. 5 Catherine I became Empress of Russia at age forty, more feared than loved by them. 6 Paul Revere at forty made his famous ride to warn American revolutionary leaders that the British were going to arrest them, which gave the colonists time to prepare for battle. 7 Forty-year-old Nancy Astor joined the British House of Commons in 1919 as its first female member, though they did not welcome her. 8 In 610 CE, Muhammad, age forty, began to have visions that became the foundation of the Muslim faith and still inspire millions of people to practice it.

Modifiers

Modifiers describe or limit other words in a sentence. They are adjectives, adverbs, or word groups serving as adjectives or adverbs. This section shows how to solve problems in the forms of modifiers (Chapter 33) and in their relation to the rest of the sentence (34).

33 Adjectives and Adverbs

Adjectives modify nouns (*happy child*) and pronouns (*special someone*). **Adverbs** modify verbs (*almost see*), adjectives (*very happy*), other adverbs (*not very*), and whole word groups (*Otherwise, I'll go*). The only way to tell whether a modifier should be an adjective or an adverb is to determine its function in the sentence.

Note Grammar and style checkers will spot some but not all problems with misused adjectives and adverbs. For instance, a checker flagged *Some children suffer bad* and *Jenny did not feel nothing*. But it did not flag *Educating children good is everyone's focus.*

CULTURE LANGUAGE In standard American English, an adjective does not change along with the noun it modifies to show plural number: *square* [not *squares*] *spaces*. Only nouns form plurals.

33a Use adjectives only to modify nouns and pronouns.

Using adjectives instead of adverbs to modify verbs, adverbs, or other adjectives is nonstandard.

| Nonstandard | Educating children good is everyone's focus. |
| Standard | Educating children well is everyone's focus. |

| Nonstandard | Some children suffer bad. |
| Standard | Some children suffer badly. |

CULTURE LANGUAGE To negate a verb or an adjective, use the adverb *not:*

They are not learning. They are not stupid.

To negate a noun, use the adjective *no:*

No child should fail to read.

33b Use an adjective after a linking verb to modify the subject. Use an adverb to modify a verb.

Some verbs may or may not be linking verbs, depending on their meaning in the sentence. When the word after the verb modifies the subject, the verb is linking and the word should be an adjective: *He looked happy.* When the word modifies the verb, however, it should be an adverb: *He looked carefully.*

Two word pairs are especially tricky. One is *bad* and *badly:*

The weather grew bad.   She felt bad.
   linking adjective   linking adjective
    verb   verb

Flowers grow badly in such soil.
   verb   adverb

The other is *good* and *well. Good* serves only as an adjective. *Well* may serve as an adverb with a host of meanings or as an adjective meaning only "fit" or "healthy."

Decker trained well.   She felt well.   Her health was good.
  verb adverb   linking adjective   linking adjective
                 verb   verb

EXERCISE 33.1 Revising: Adjectives and adverbs

Revise the following paragraph to use adjectives and adverbs appropriately. Mark the number preceding any sentence that is correct as given. (You can do this exercise online at *ablongman.com/littlebrown.*)

Key term

linking verb A verb that connects a subject and a word that describes the subject: *They are golfers.* Linking verbs include *look, sound, feel, appear, seem, become,* and forms of *be.* (See p. 199.)

1 The eighteenth-century essayist Samuel Johnson fared bad in his early life. 2 His family was poor, his hearing was weak, and he received little formal education. 3 After failing as a schoolmaster, Johnson moved to London, where he was finally taken serious as a critic and dictionary maker. 4 Johnson was real surprised when he received a pension from King George III. 5 Thinking about his meeting with the king, Johnson felt proudly that he had not behaved badly in the presence of the king. 6 Now, after living cheap for over twenty years, Johnson finally had enough money to eat and dress good. 7 He spent his time writing and living stylish.

33c Use the comparative and superlative forms of adjectives and adverbs appropriately.

Adjectives and adverbs can show degrees of quality or amount with the endings -er and -est or with the words more and most or less and least. Most modifiers have three forms: positive, comparative, and superlative.

Positive The basic form listed in the dictionary	Comparative A greater or lesser degree of the quality	Superlative The greatest or least degree of the quality
Adjectives		
red	redder	reddest
awful	more/less awful	most/least awful
Adverbs		
soon	sooner	soonest
quickly	more/less quickly	most/least quickly

If sound alone does not tell you whether to use -er/-est or more/most, consult a dictionary. If the endings can be used, the dictionary will list them. Otherwise, use more or most.

1 Irregular adjectives and adverbs

The irregular modifiers change the spelling of their positive form to show comparative and superlative degrees.

Positive	Comparative	Superlative
Adjectives		
good	better	best
bad	worse	worst
little	littler, less	littlest, least
many		
some	more	most
much		
Adverbs		
well	better	best
badly	worse	worst

2 Double comparisons

A double comparative or double superlative combines the *-er* or *-est* ending with the word *more* or *most*. It is redundant.

Chang was the wisest [not most wisest] person in town.
He was smarter [not more smarter] than anyone else.

3 Logical comparisons

■ Absolute modifiers

Some adjectives and adverbs cannot logically be compared—for instance, *perfect, unique, dead, impossible, infinite*. These absolute words can be preceded by adverbs like *nearly* or *almost* that mean "approaching," but they cannot logically be modified by *more* or *most* (as in *most perfect*).

Not   He was the most unique teacher we had.

But   He was a unique teacher.

■ Completeness

To be logical, a comparison must also be complete in the following ways:

■ **The comparison must state a relation fully enough for clarity.**

Unclear   Carmakers worry about their industry more than environmentalists.

Clear   Carmakers worry about their industry more than environmentalists do.

Clear   Carmakers worry about their industry more than they worry about environmentalists.

■ **The items being compared should in fact be comparable.**

Illogical   The cost of an electric car is greater than a gasoline-powered car. [Illogically compares a cost and a car.]

Revised   The cost of an electric car is greater than the cost of [or that of] a gasoline-powered car.

See also **3** p. 154 on parallelism with comparisons.

■ *Any* versus *any other*

Use *any other* when comparing something with others in the same group. Use *any* when comparing something with others in a different group.

Illogical   Los Angeles is larger than any city in California. [Since Los Angeles is itself a city in California, the sentence seems to say that Los Angeles is larger than itself.]

Revised   Los Angeles is larger than any other city in California.

Illogical	Los Angeles is larger than <u>any other</u> city in Canada. [The cities in Canada constitute a group to which Los Angeles does not belong.]
Revised	Los Angeles is larger than <u>any</u> city in Canada.

EXERCISE 33.2   Using comparatives and superlatives

Write the comparative and superlative forms of each adjective or adverb below. Then use all three forms in your own sentences. (You can do this exercise online at *ablongman.com/littlebrown*.)

Example:

heavy: heavier (comparative), heaviest (superlative)

The barbells were too <u>heavy</u> for me. The trunk was <u>heavier</u> than I expected. Joe Clark was the <u>heaviest</u> person on the team.

1	badly	3	good	5	understanding
2	steady	4	well		

EXERCISE 33.3   Revising: Comparisons

Revise the following paragraph as needed to correct the forms of adjectives and adverbs and to make comparisons logical. Mark the number preceding any sentence that is correct as given. (You can do this exercise online at *ablongman.com/littlebrown*.)

1 The Brontë sisters—Charlotte, Emily, and Anne—are among the more interesting literary families in English history. 2 Of the three novelists, Charlotte was the older. 3 Critics sometimes dispute whether Charlotte or Emily was more talented. 4 For some readers, Emily's *Wuthering Heights* is among the most saddest stories ever written. 5 For other readers, Charlotte's *Jane Eyre* made more significant contributions to literature than Emily.

33d   Watch for double negatives.

A **double negative** is a nonstandard construction in which two negative words such as *no, not, none, neither, barely, hardly,* or *scarcely* cancel each other out. Some double negatives are intentional: for instance, *She was <u>not unhappy</u>* indicates with understatement that she was indeed happy. But most double negatives say the opposite of what is intended: *Jenny did <u>not feel nothing</u>* asserts that Jenny felt other than nothing, or something. For the opposite meaning, one of the negatives must be eliminated (*She felt <u>nothing</u>*) or one of them must be changed to a positive (*She did <u>not feel anything</u>*).

Faulty	The IRS <u>cannot hardly</u> audit all tax returns. <u>None</u> of its audits <u>never</u> touch many cheaters.
Revised	The IRS <u>cannot</u> audit all tax returns. Its audits <u>never</u> touch many cheaters.

EXERCISE 33.4 Revising: Double negatives

Identify and revise the double negatives in the following paragraph. Each error may have more than one correct revision. Mark the number preceding any sentence that is correct as given. (You can do this exercise online at *ablongman.com/littlebrown*.)

1 Interest in books about the founding of the United States is not hardly consistent among Americans: it seems to vary with the national mood. 2 Americans show barely any interest in books about the founders when things are going well in the United States. 3 However, when Americans can't hardly agree on major issues, sales of books about the Revolutionary War era increase. 4 During such periods, one cannot go to no bookstore without seeing several new volumes about John Adams, Thomas Jefferson, and other founders. 5 When Americans feel they don't have nothing in common, their increased interest in the early leaders may reflect a desire for unity.

33e Distinguish between present and past participles as adjectives. ⟨CULTURE LANGUAGE⟩

Both present participles and past participles may serve as adjectives: *a burning building, a burned building.* As in the examples, the two participles usually differ in the time they indicate.

But some present and past participles—those derived from verbs expressing feeling—can have altogether different meanings. The present participle modifies something that causes the feeling: *That was a frightening storm* (the storm frightens). The past participle modifies something that experiences the feeling: *They quieted the frightened horses* (the horses feel fright).

The following participles are among those likely to be confused:

amazing/amazed
amusing/amused
annoying/annoyed
astonishing/astonished
boring/bored
confusing/confused
depressing/depressed
embarrassing/embarrassed
exciting/excited
exhausting/exhausted

fascinating/fascinated
frightening/frightened
frustrating/frustrated
interesting/interested
pleasing/pleased
satisfying/satisfied
shocking/shocked
surprising/surprised
tiring/tired
worrying/worried

Key terms

present participle The *-ing* form of a verb: *flying, writing.* (See p. 190.)

past participle The *-d* or *-ed* form of a regular verb: *slipped, walked.* Most irregular verbs have distinctive past participles, such as *eaten* or *swum.* (See p. 190.)

EXERCISE 33.5 Revising: Present and past participles

CULTURE LANGUAGE Revise the adjectives in the following paragraph as needed to distinguish between present and past participles. Mark the number preceding any sentence that is correct as given. (You can do this exercise online at *ablongman.com/littlebrown*.)

1 Many critics found Alice Walker's novel *The Color Purple* to be a fascinated book, though the reviews were mixed. 2 One otherwise excited critic wished that Walker had deleted the scenes set in Africa. 3 Another critic argued that although the book contained many depressed episodes, the overall effect was pleased. 4 Responding to other readers who had found the book annoyed, this critic pointed out its many surprising qualities. 5 In the end most critics agreed that the book was a pleased novel about the struggles of an African American woman. 6 For many, the movie made from the book was less interested. 7 Some viewers found the entire movie irritated, criticizing it for relying on tired feelings. 8 Other viewers thought that Whoopi Goldberg did an amazed job of creating Celie, the central character. 9 Some critics congratulated Steven Spielberg, the director, for creating a fulfilling movie.

33f Use *a, an, the,* and other determiners appropriately. **CULTURE LANGUAGE**

Determiners are special kinds of adjectives that mark nouns because they always precede nouns. Some common determiners are *a, an,* and *the* (called **articles**) and *my, their, whose, this, these, those, one, some,* and *any.*

Native speakers of standard American English can rely on their intuition when using determiners, but speakers of other languages and dialects often have difficulty with them. In standard American English, the use of determiners depends on the context they appear in and the kind of noun they precede:

- A *proper noun* names a particular person, place, or thing and begins with a capital letter: *February, Joe Allen, Red River.* Most proper nouns are not preceded by determiners.

- A *count noun* names something that is countable in English and can form a plural: *girl/girls, apple/apples, child/children.* A singular count noun is always preceded by a determiner; a plural count noun sometimes is.

- A *noncount noun* names something not usually considered countable in English, and so it does not form a plural. A noncount noun is sometimes preceded by a determiner. Here is a sample of noncount nouns, sorted into groups by meaning:

Abstractions: confidence, democracy, education, equality, evidence, health, information, intelligence, knowledge, luxury, peace, pollution, research, success, supervision, truth, wealth, work

Food and drink: bread, candy, cereal, flour, meat, milk, salt, water, wine

Emotions: anger, courage, happiness, hate, joy, love, respect, satisfaction

Natural events and substances: air, blood, dirt, gasoline, gold, hair, heat, ice, oil, oxygen, rain, silver, smoke, weather, wood

Groups: clergy, clothing, equipment, furniture, garbage, jewelry, junk, legislation, machinery, mail, military, money, police, vocabulary

Fields of study: architecture, accounting, biology, business, chemistry, engineering, literature, psychology, science

A dictionary of English as a second language will tell you whether a noun is a count noun, a noncount noun, or both. (See **3** p. 168 for recommended dictionaries.)

Note Many nouns are sometimes count nouns and sometimes noncount nouns:

The library has a room for readers. [*Room* is a count noun meaning "walled area."]

The library has room for reading. [*Room* is a noncount noun meaning "space."]

Partly because the same noun may fall into different groups, grammar and style checkers are unreliable guides to missing or misused articles and other determiners. For instance, a checker flagged the omitted *a* before *Scientist* in *Scientist developed new processes;* it did not flag the omitted *a* before *new* in *A scientist developed new process;* and it mistakenly flagged the correctly omitted article *the* before *Vegetation* in *Vegetation suffers from drought.*

1 *A, an,* and *the*

■ With singular count nouns

A or *an* precedes a singular count noun when the reader does not already know its identity, usually because you have not mentioned it before:

A scientist in our chemistry department developed a process to strengthen metals. [*Scientist* and *process* are being introduced for the first time.]

The precedes a singular count noun that has a specific identity for the reader, for one of the following reasons:

■ You have mentioned the noun before:

A scientist in our chemistry department developed a process to strengthen metals. The scientist patented the process. [*Scientist* and *process* were identified in the preceding sentence.]

■ You identify the noun immediately before or after you state it:

The most productive laboratory is the research center in the chemistry department. [*Most productive* identifies *laboratory. In the chemistry department* identifies *research center*. And *chemistry department* is a shared facility—see below.]

- **The noun names something unique—the only one in existence:**

  The sun rises in the east. [*Sun* and *east* are unique.]

- **The noun names an institution or facility that is shared by the community of readers:**

  Many men and women aspire to the presidency. [*Presidency* is a shared institution.]

  The fax machine has changed business communication. [*Fax machine* is a shared facility.]

The is not used before a singular noun that names a general category:

Wordsworth's poetry shows his love of nature [not the nature].
General Sherman said that war is hell. [*War* names a general category.]
The war in Croatia left many dead. [*War* names a specific war.]

With plural count nouns

A or *an* never precedes a plural noun. *The* does not precede a plural noun that names a general category. *The* does precede a plural noun that names specific representatives of a category.

Men and women are different. [*Men* and *women* name general categories.]
The women formed a team. [*Women* refers to specific people.]

With noncount nouns

A or *an* never precedes a noncount noun. *The* does precede a noncount noun that names specific representatives of a general category.

Vegetation suffers from drought. [*Vegetation* names a general category.]
The vegetation in the park withered or died. [*Vegetation* refers to specific plants.]

With proper nouns

A or *an* never precedes a proper noun. *The* generally does not precede proper nouns.

Garcia lives in Boulder.

There are exceptions, however. For instance, we generally use *the* before plural proper nouns (*the Murphys, the Boston Celtics*) and before the names of groups and organizations (*the Department of Justice, the Sierra Club*), ships (*the Lusitania*), oceans (*the Pacific*), mountain ranges (*the Alps*), regions (*the Middle East*), rivers (*the Mississippi*), and some countries (*the United States, the Netherlands*).

EXERCISE 33.6 Revising: *A, an,* and *the*

CULTURE LANGUAGE In the following paragraph, identify and revise errors in the use of *a, an,* and *the* with count, noncount, and proper nouns. Mark the number preceding any sentence that is correct as given. (You can do this exercise online at *ablongman.com/littlebrown*.)

1 A recent court case has moved some Native Americans to observe that a lot of people want to be the Native Americans now that the tribes have something of the value—namely, gambling casinos. 2 The man named Stephen Jones claimed to be the Native American in order to open casino in the New York's Catskills region. 3 However, the documents Jones provided to support the claim were questioned by a US Bureau of Indian Affairs. 4 On death certificate for Jones's grandfather, the W for *white* had been changed to an I for *Indian* with the ballpoint pen. 5 The ballpoint pens had not been invented until after a grandfather's death. 6 In addition, Jones provided the 1845 census of Indians in New York, and someone had recently added Jones's great-grandfather's name to the list of Indian household heads. 7 Jones, who called himself the Chief Golden Eagle, pled guilty to filing false documents with Bureau of Indian Affairs.

2 Other determiners

The uses of English determiners besides articles also depend on context and kind of noun. The following determiners may be used as indicated with singular count nouns, plural count nouns, or noncount nouns.

■ **With any kind of noun (singular count, plural count, noncount)**

my, our, your, his, her, its, their, possessive nouns (*boy's, boys'*)
whose, which(ever), what(ever)
some, any, the other
no

Their account is overdrawn. [Singular count.]
Their funds are low. [Plural count.]
Their money is running out. [Noncount.]

■ **Only with singular nouns (count and noncount)**

this, that

This account has some money. [Count.]
That information may help. [Noncount.]

■ **Only with noncount nouns and plural count nouns**

most, enough, other, such, all, all of the, a lot of

Most funds are committed. [Plural count.]
Most money is needed elsewhere. [Noncount.]

■ **Only with singular count nouns**

one, every, each, either, neither, another

<u>One</u> car must be sold. [Singular count.]

■ **Only with plural count nouns**

these, those
both, many, few, a few, fewer, fewest, several
two, three, and so forth

<u>Two</u> cars are unnecessary. [Plural count.]

Note *Few* means "not many" or "not enough." *A few* means "some" or "a small but sufficient quantity."

<u>Few</u> committee members came to the meeting.
<u>A few</u> members can keep the committee going.

Do not use *much* with a plural count noun.

<u>Many</u> [not <u>Much</u>] members want to help.

■ **Only with noncount nouns**

much, more, little, a little, less, least, a large amount of

<u>Less</u> luxury is in order. [Noncount.]

Note *Little* means "not many" or "not enough." *A little* means "some" or "a small but sufficient quantity."

<u>Little</u> time remains before the conference.
The members need <u>a little</u> help from their colleagues.

Do not use *many* with a noncount noun.

<u>Much</u> [not <u>Many</u>] work remains.

EXERCISE 33.7   Revising: Determiners

⟪ CULTURE / LANGUAGE ⟫ In the following paragraph, identify and revise missing or incorrect determiners. Mark the number preceding any sentence that is correct as given. (You can do this exercise online at *ablongman.com/ littlebrown.*)

1 Much people love to swim for exercise or just plain fun. **2** Few swimmers, however, are aware of the possible danger of sharing their swimming spot with others. **3** These danger has increased in recent years because of dramatic rise in outbreaks of the parasite cryptosporidium. **4** Swallowing even little water containing cryptosporidium can make anyone sick. **5** Chlorine is used in nearly every public pools to kill parasites, but the chlorine takes six or seven days to kill cryptosporidium. **6** Most health authorities advise people to limit their swimming in public pools and to drink as little of the pool water as possible.

EXERCISE 33.8   Revising: Adjectives and adverbs

Revise the paragraph below to correct errors in the use of adjectives and adverbs. (You can do this exercise online at *ablongman.com/littlebrown*.)

1 Americans often argue about which professional sport is better: basketball, football, or baseball. 2 Basketball fans contend that their sport offers more action because the players are constant running and shooting. 3 Because it is played indoors in relative small arenas, basketball allows fans to be more closer to the action than the other sports. 4 Football fanatics say they don't hardly stop yelling once the game begins. 5 They cheer when their team executes a complicated play good. 6 They roar more louder when the defense stops the opponents in a goal-line stand. 7 They yell loudest when a fullback crashes in for a score. 8 In contrast, the supporters of baseball believe that it is the better sport. 9 It combines the one-on-one duel of pitcher and batter struggling valiant with the tight teamwork of double and triple plays. 10 Because the game is played slow and careful, fans can analyze and discuss the manager's strategy.

34 Misplaced and Dangling Modifiers

The arrangement of words in a sentence is an important clue to their relationships. Modifiers will be unclear if readers can't connect them to the words they modify.

Note Grammar and style checkers cannot recognize most problems with modifiers. For instance, a checker failed to flag the misplaced modifiers in *Gasoline high prices affect usually car sales* or the dangling modifier in *The vandalism was visible passing the building*.

34a Reposition misplaced modifiers.

A **misplaced modifier** falls in the wrong place in a sentence. It is usually awkward or confusing. It may even be unintentionally funny.

1 Clear placement

Readers tend to link a modifier to the nearest word it could modify. Any other placement can link the modifier to the wrong word.

---

http://www.ablongman.com/littlebrown   ▶

Visit the companion Web site for more help and electronic exercises on misplaced and dangling modifiers.

Confusing	He served steak to the men on paper plates.
Clear	He served the men steak on paper plates.

Confusing	According to the police, many dogs are killed by automobiles and trucks roaming unleashed.
Clear	According to the police, many dogs roaming unleashed are killed by automobiles and trucks.

2 *Only* and other limiting modifiers

Limiting modifiers include *almost, even, exactly, hardly, just, merely, nearly, only, scarcely,* and *simply.* For clarity place such a modifier immediately before the word or word group you intend it to limit.

Unclear	The archaeologist only found the skull on her last dig.
Clear	The archaeologist found only the skull on her last dig.
Clear	The archaeologist found the skull only on her last dig.

3 Adverbs with grammatical units

Adverbs can often move around in sentences, but some will be awkward if they interrupt certain grammatical units:

■ **A long adverb stops the flow from subject to verb:**

	subject ── adverb ── verb
Awkward	Kuwait, after the first Gulf War ended in 1991, began returning to normal.
	── adverb ── subject verb
Revised	After the first Gulf War ended in 1991, Kuwait began returning to normal.

■ **Any adverb is awkward between a verb and its direct object:**

	verb adverb object
Awkward	The war had damaged badly many of Kuwait's oil fields.
	verb object
Revised	The war had badly damaged many of Kuwait's oil fields.
	adverb

> ┌─ **Key terms** ──
>
> **adverb** A word or word group that describes a verb, adjective, other adverb, or whole word group, specifying how, when, where, or to what extent: *quickly see, solid like a boulder.*
>
> **direct object** The receiver of the verb's action: *The car hit a tree.* (See p. 198.)

■ A *split infinitive*—an adverb placed between *to* and the verb—
annoys many readers:

Awkward   The weather service expected temperatures to <u>not</u> rise.

(infinitive: *to not rise*)

Revised   The weather service expected temperatures <u>not</u> to rise.

(infinitive: *not to rise*)

A split infinitive may sometimes be natural and preferable,
though it may still bother some readers:

Several US industries expect to <u>more than</u> triple their use of robots.

(infinitive)

Here the split infinitive is more economical than the alternatives, such as *Several US industries expect to increase their use of
robots by more than three times.*

■ A long adverb is usually awkward inside a verb phrase:

Awkward   The spacecraft *Ulysses* will <u>after traveling near the sun</u>
report on the sun's energy fields.

(helping verb: *will*; adverb: *after traveling near the sun*; main verb: *report*)

Revised   <u>After traveling near the sun,</u> the spacecraft *Ulysses*
will report on the sun's energy fields.

(adverb; verb phrase: *will report*)

CULTURE LANGUAGE In a question, place a one-word adverb after the
first helping verb and subject:

Will spacecraft <u>ever</u> be able to leave the solar system?

(helping verb: *Will*; subject: *spacecraft*; adverb: *ever*; rest of verb phrase: *be able to leave*)

4 Other adverb positions **CULTURE LANGUAGE**

Placements of a few adverbs can be difficult for nonnative
speakers of English:

■ **Adverbs of frequency** include *always, never, often, rarely, seldom, sometimes,* and *usually.* They generally appear at the beginning of a sentence, before a one-word verb, or after the helping verb in a verb phrase.

Key terms

infinitive A verb form consisting of *to* plus the verb's plain (or dictionary)
form: *to produce, to enjoy.* (See p. 203.)

verb phrase A verb consisting of a helping verb and a main verb that carries the principal meaning: *will have begun, can see.* (See p. 191.)

helping   main
verb   adverb   verb
Robots have sometimes put humans out of work.

adverb   verb phrase
Sometimes robots have put humans out of work.

Adverbs of frequency always follow the verb *be*.

verb adverb
Robots are often helpful to workers.

verb adverb
Robots are seldom useful around the house.

- **Adverbs of degree** include *absolutely, almost, certainly, completely, definitely, especially, extremely, hardly,* and *only*. They fall just before the word modified (an adjective, another adverb, sometimes a verb):

adverb   adjective
Robots have been especially useful in making cars.

- **Adverbs of manner** include *badly, beautifully, openly, sweetly, tightly, well,* and others that describe how something is done. They usually fall after the verb:

verb   adverb
Robots work smoothly on assembly lines.

- **The position of the adverb *not* depends on what it modifies.** When it modifies a verb, place it after the helping verb (or the first helping verb if more than one):

helping   main
verb   verb
Robots do not think.

When *not* modifies another adverb or an adjective, place it before the other modifier:

adjective
Robots are not sleek machines.

5 Order of adjectives

English follows distinctive rules for arranging two or three adjectives before a noun. (A string of more than three adjectives before a noun is rare.) The order is shown in the following chart.

> **Key term**
>
> **adjective** A word that describes a noun or pronoun, specifying which one, what quality, or how many: *good one, three cars.* (See p. 192.)

Determiner	Opinion	Size or shape	Color	Origin	Material	Noun used as adjective	Noun
many						state	**laws**
	lovely		green	Thai			**birds**
a	fine			German			**camera**
a		square			wooden		**table**
all						business	**reports**
the			blue		litmus		**paper**

See **5** p. 309 on punctuating adjectives before a noun.

EXERCISE 34.1   Revising: Misplaced modifiers

Revise the following paragraph so that modifiers clearly and appropriately describe the intended words. (You can do this exercise online at *ablongman.com/littlebrown.*)

1 People dominate in our society who are right-handed. 2 Hand tools, machines, and doors even are designed for right-handed people. 3 However, nearly 15 percent may be left-handed of the population. 4 Children when they enter kindergarten generally prefer one hand or the other. 5 Parents and teachers should not try to deliberately change a child's preference for the left hand.

EXERCISE 34.2   Revising: Misplaced modifiers

Revise the following paragraph so that modifiers clearly and appropriately describe the intended words. Mark the number preceding any sentence that is correct as given. (You can do this exercise online at *ablongman .com/littlebrown.*)

1 Women have contributed much to American culture of significance. 2 For example, during the colonial era Elizabeth Pinckney introduced indigo, the source of a valuable blue dye. 3 Later, Emma Willard founded the Troy Female Seminary, the first institution to provide a college-level education for women in 1821. 4 Mary Lyon founded Mount Holyoke Female Seminary as the first true women's college with directors and a campus who would sustain the college even after Lyon's death. 5 Pauline Wright Davis founded in 1853 *Una*, the first US newspaper that was dedicated to gaining women's rights. 6 Maria Mitchell was the first American woman astronomer who lived from 1818 to 1889. 7 Mitchell's Comet was discovered in 1847, which was named for the astronomer.

EXERCISE 34.3   Arranging adjectives

CULTURE LANGUAGE A group of adjectives follows each sentence below. Arrange the adjectives as needed for appropriate order in English, and place them in the sentence. (You can do this exercise online at *ablongman.com/littlebrown.*)

Example:

Programs for computer graphics perform _____ chores. (*drafting, many, tedious*)

Programs for computer graphics perform <u>many tedious drafting</u> chores.

1   _____ researchers are studying image controls for computer graphics. (*several, university*)
2   The controls depend on _____ object connected by wires to the computer. (*T-shaped, hand-sized, a*)
3   The image allows a biochemist to walk into _____ display of a molecule. (*three-dimensional, gigantic, a*)
4   Using _____ gestures, the biochemist can rotate and change the entire image. (*simple, hand*)
5   _____ games also depend on computer graphics. (*computer, all, video*)
6   Even _____ games operate this way. (*sophisticated, flight, simulated*)

34b   Connect dangling modifiers to their sentences.

A **dangling modifier** does not sensibly modify anything in its sentence.

Dangling   Passing the building, the vandalism became visible.

Dangling modifiers usually introduce sentences, contain a verb form, and imply but do not name a subject: in the example above, the implied subject is the someone or something passing the building. Readers assume that this implied subject is the same as the subject of the sentence (*vandalism* in the example). When it is not, the modifier "dangles" unconnected to the rest of the sentence. Here is another example:

Dangling   Although intact, graffiti covered every inch of the walls and windows. [The walls and windows, not the graffiti, were intact.]

To revise a dangling modifier, you have to recast the sentence it appears in. (Revising just by moving the modifier will leave it dangling: *The vandalism became visible passing the building.*) Choose a revision method depending on what you want to emphasize in the sentence.

Identifying and revising dangling modifiers

- **Find a subject.** If the modifier lacks a subject of its own (e.g., *when in diapers*), identify what it describes.
- **Connect the subject and modifier.** Verify that what the modifier describes is in fact the subject of the main clause. If it is not, the modifier is probably dangling:

> ┌─── modifier ───┐   subject
> Dangling   When in diapers, my mother remarried.

- **Revise as needed.** Revise a dangling modifier (*a*) by recasting it with a subject of its own or (*b*) by changing the subject of the main clause:

> Revision *a*   When I was in diapers, my mother remarried.
> Revision *b*   When in diapers, I attended my mother's second wedding.

- **Rewrite the dangling modifier as a complete clause with its own stated subject and verb.** Readers can accept that the new subject and the sentence subject are different.

> Dangling   Passing the building, the vandalism became visible.
>
> Revised   As we passed the building, the vandalism became visible.

- **Change the subject of the sentence to a word the modifier properly describes.**

> Dangling   Trying to understand the causes, vandalism has been extensively studied.
>
> Revised   Trying to understand the causes, researchers have extensively studied vandalism.

EXERCISE 34.4   Revising: Dangling modifiers

Revise the sentences in the following paragraph to eliminate any dangling modifiers. Each item has more than one possible answer. Mark the number preceding any sentence that is correct as given. (You can do this exercise online at *ablongman.com/littlebrown*.)

1 Andrew Jackson's career was legendary in his day. 2 Starting with the American Revolution, service as a mounted courier was Jackson's choice. 3 Though not well educated, a successful career as a lawyer and judge proved Jackson's ability. 4 Earning the nicknames "Old Hickory" and "Sharp Knife," Jackson established his military prowess in the War of 1812. 5 Losing only six dead and ten wounded, the triumph of the Battle of New Orleans burnished Jackson's reputation. 6 After putting down raiding parties from Florida, Jackson's victories helped pressure Spain to cede that territory. 7 While Jackson was briefly governor of Florida, the

US presidency became his goal. 8 With so many skills and deeds of valor, Jackson's fame led to his election to the presidency in 1828 and 1832.

EXERCISE 34.5 Revising: Misplaced and dangling modifiers

Revise the following paragraph to eliminate any misplaced or dangling modifiers. (You can do this exercise online at *ablongman.com/littlebrown*.)

1 Central American tungara frogs silence several nights a week their mating croaks. 2 When not croaking, the chance that the frogs will be eaten by predators is reduced. 3 The frogs seem to fully believe in "safety in numbers." 4 They more than likely will croak along with a large group rather than by themselves. 5 By forgoing croaking on some nights, the frogs' behavior prevents the species from "croaking."

Sentence Faults

A word group punctuated as a sentence will confuse or annoy readers if it lacks needed parts, has too many parts, or has parts that don't fit together.

35 Sentence Fragments

A **sentence fragment** is part of a sentence that is set off as if it were a whole sentence by an initial capital letter and a final period or other end punctuation. Although writers occasionally use fragments deliberately and effectively (see p. 281), readers perceive most fragments as serious errors.

Note A grammar and style checker can spot many but not all sentence fragments, and it may flag sentences that are actually commands, such as *Continue reading.*

35a Test your sentences for completeness.

A word group punctuated as a sentence should pass *all three* of the following tests. If it does not, it is a fragment and needs revision.

---

http://www.ablongman.com/littlebrown ▶

Visit the companion Web site for more help and electronic exercises on sentence fragments.

Complete sentence versus sentence fragment

A complete sentence or main clause

1. contains a subject and a verb (*The wind blows*)
2. and is not a subordinate clause (beginning with a word such as *because* or *who*).

A sentence fragment

1. lacks a verb (*The wind blowing*),
2. or lacks a subject (*And blows*),
3. or is a subordinate clause not attached to a complete sentence (*Because the wind blows*).

■ **Test 1: Find the verb.**

Look for a verb in the group of words:

Fragment	Uncountable numbers of sites on the Web.
Revised	Uncountable numbers of sites make up the Web.

Any verb form you find must be a **finite verb,** one that changes form as indicated below. A verbal does not change; it cannot serve as a sentence verb without the aid of a helping verb.

	Finite verbs in complete sentences	Verbals in sentence fragments
Singular	The network grows.	The network growing.
Plural	Networks grow.	Networks growing.
Present	The network grows.	
Past	The network grew.	The network growing.
Future	The network will grow.	

CULTURE LANGUAGE Some languages allow forms of *be* to be omitted as helping verbs or linking verbs. But English requires stating forms of *be*, as shown in the following revised example.

Key terms

verb The part of a sentence that asserts something about the subject: *Ducks swim.* Also called **predicate.** (See pp. 190, 195–97.)

verbal A verb form that can serve as a noun, a modifier, or a part of a sentence verb, but not alone as the only verb of a sentence: *drawing, to draw, drawn.* (See p. 202.)

helping verb A verb such as *is, were, have, might,* and *could* that combines with various verb forms to indicate time and other kinds of meaning: for instance, *were drawing, might draw.* (See p. 191.)

Fragments	The network growing. It already larger than its developers anticipated.
Revised	The network <u>is</u> growing. It <u>is</u> already larger than its developers anticipated.

■ Test 2: Find the subject.

The subject of the sentence will usually come before the verb. If there is no subject, the word group is probably a fragment:

Fragment	And has enormous popular appeal.
Revised	And <u>the Web</u> has enormous popular appeal.

In one kind of complete sentence, a command, the subject *you* is understood: [*You*] *Experiment with the Web.*

◀ CULTURE LANGUAGE ▶ Some languages allow the omission of the sentence subject, especially when it is a pronoun. But in English, except in commands, the subject is always stated:

Fragment	Web commerce is expanding dramatically. Is threatening traditional stores.
Revised	Web commerce is expanding dramatically. <u>It</u> is threatening traditional stores.

■ Test 3: Make sure the clause is not subordinate.

A subordinate clause usually begins with a subordinating word, such as one of the following:

Subordinating conjunctions			Relative pronouns	
after	once	until	that	who/whom
although	since	when	which	whoever/whomever
as	than	where		
because	that	whereas		
if	unless	while		

Subordinate clauses serve as parts of sentences (nouns or modifiers), not as whole sentences:

Fragment	When the government devised the Internet.
Revised	The government devised the Internet.
Revised	When the government devised the Internet, <u>no expansive computer network existed.</u>

┌─ **Key terms** ────────────────────────────────

subject The part of a sentence that names who or what performs the action or makes the assertion of the verb: *Ducks swim.* (See pp. 195–97.)

subordinate clause A word group that contains a subject and a verb, begins with a subordinating word such as *because* or *who,* and is not a question: *Ducks can swim <u>when they are young.</u>* A subordinate clause may serve as a modifier or as a noun. (See pp. 206–07.)

| Fragment | The reason that the government devised the Internet. |
| Revised | The reason that the government devised the Internet <u>was to link departments and defense contractors</u>. |

Note Questions beginning with *how, what, when, where, which, who, whom, whose,* and *why* are not sentence fragments: *Who was responsible? When did it happen?*

35b Revise sentence fragments.

Correct sentence fragments in one of two ways depending on the importance of the information in the fragment and thus how much you want to stress it.

- **Rewrite the fragment as a complete sentence.** The information in the fragment will then have the same importance as that in other complete sentences.

| Fragment | A major improvement of the Internet occurred with the Web. <u>Which allows users to move easily between sites.</u> |
| Revised | A major improvement of the Internet occurred with the Web. <u>It</u> allows users to move easily between sites. |

| Fragment | The Web is a boon to researchers. <u>A vast and accessible library</u>. |
| Revised | The Web is a boon to researchers. <u>It forms</u> a vast and accessible library. |

- **Combine the fragment with the appropriate main clause.** The information in the fragment will then be subordinated to that in the main clause.

| Fragment | The Web is easy to use. <u>Loaded with links and graphics</u>. |
| Revised | The Web, loaded with links and graphics, is easy to use. |

| Fragment | With the links, users can move to other Web sites. <u>That they want to consult.</u> |
| Revised | With the links, users can move to other Web sites that they want to consult. |

35c Be aware of the acceptable uses of incomplete sentences.

A few word groups lacking the usual subject-predicate combination are incomplete sentences, but they are not fragments because they conform to the expectations of most readers. They include exclamations (*Oh no!*); questions and answers (*Where next? To Kansas.*); and commands (*Move along. Shut the window.*).

Experienced writers sometimes use sentence fragments when they want to achieve a special effect. Such fragments appear more in informal than in formal writing. Unless you are experienced and thoroughly secure in your own writing, you should avoid all fragments and concentrate on writing clear, well-formed sentences.

EXERCISE 35.1   Identifying and revising sentence fragments

Apply the tests for completeness to each of the word groups in the following paragraph. If a word group is a complete sentence, mark the number preceding it. If it is a sentence fragment, revise it in two ways: by making it a complete sentence, and by combining it with a main clause written from the information given in other items. (You can do this exercise online at *ablongman.com/littlebrown*.)

Example:

And could help. [The word group has a verb (*could . . . help*) but no subject.]

Revised into a complete sentence: And he could help.

Combined with a new main clause: He had money and could help.

1 In an interesting magazine article about vandalism against works of art. 2 The focus was on the vandals themselves. 3 The motives of the vandals varying widely. 4 Those who harm artwork are usually angry. 5 But not necessarily at the artist or the owner. 6 For instance, a man who hammered at Michelangelo's *Pietà*. 7 And knocked off the Virgin Mary's nose. 8 Because he was angry with the Roman Catholic Church. 9 Which knew nothing of his grievance. 10 Although many damaged works can be repaired. 11 Usually even the most skillful repairs are forever visible.

EXERCISE 35.2   Revising: Sentence fragments

Correct any sentence fragment below either by combining it with a complete sentence or by making it a complete sentence. If an item contains no sentence fragment, mark the number preceding it. (You can do this exercise online at *ablongman.com/littlebrown*.)

Example:

Jujitsu is good for self-protection. Because it enables one to overcome an opponent without the use of weapons.

Jujitsu is good for self-protection because it enables one to overcome an opponent without the use of weapons. *Or:* Jujitsu is good for self-protection. It enables one to overcome an opponent without the use of weapons.

1   Human beings who perfume themselves. They are not much different from other animals.

2   Animals as varied as insects and dogs release pheromones. Chemicals that signal other animals.

3   Human beings have a diminished sense of smell. And do not consciously detect most of their own species' pheromones.

4   The human substitute for pheromones may be perfumes. Most

common in ancient times were musk and other fragrances derived from animal oils.

5 Some sources say that people began using perfume to cover up the smell of burning flesh. During sacrifices to the gods.

6 Perfumes became religious offerings in their own right. Being expensive to make, they were highly prized.

7 The earliest historical documents from the Middle East record the use of fragrances. Not only in religious ceremonies but on the body.

8 In the nineteenth century, chemists began synthesizing perfume oils. Which previously could be made only from natural sources.

9 The most popular animal oil for perfume today is musk. Although some people dislike its heavy, sweet odor.

10 Synthetic musk oil would help conserve a certain species of deer. Whose gland is the source of musk.

EXERCISE 35.3 Revising: Sentence fragments

Revise the following paragraph to eliminate sentence fragments by combining them with main clauses or rewriting them as main clauses. (You can do this exercise online at *ablongman.com/littlebrown*.)

Baby red-eared slider turtles are brightly colored. With bold patterns on their yellowish undershells. Which serve as a warning to predators. The bright colors of skunks and other animals. They signal that the animals will spray nasty chemicals. In contrast, the turtle's colors warn largemouth bass. That the baby turtle will actively defend itself. When a bass gulps down a turtle. The feisty baby claws and bites. Forcing the bass to spit it out. To avoid a similar painful experience. The bass will avoid other baby red-eared slider turtles. The turtle loses its bright colors as it grows too big. For a bass's afternoon snack.

36 Comma Splices and Fused Sentences

When a sentence contains two main clauses in a row, readers need a signal that one main clause is ending and another beginning. The usual signal is a comma with a coordinating conjunction (*The*

Key terms

main clause A word group that contains a subject and a verb and does not begin with a subordinating word: *A dictionary is essential.*

coordinating conjunction *And, but, or, nor, for, so, yet.* (See p. 194.)

---

http://www.ablongman.com/littlebrown

Visit the companion Web site for more help and electronic exercises on comma splices and fused sentences.

ship was huge, and its mast stood eighty feet high) or a semicolon (*The ship was huge; its mast stood eighty feet high*).

Two problems in punctuating main clauses deprive readers of this signal. One is the **comma splice,** in which the clauses are joined (or spliced) *only* with a comma:

> Comma splice   The ship was huge, its mast stood eighty feet high.

The other is the **fused sentence** (or **run-on sentence**), in which no punctuation or conjunction appears between the clauses.

> Fused sentence   The ship was huge its mast stood eighty feet high.

Note Grammar and style checkers can detect many comma splices, but they will miss most fused sentences. For example, a checker flagged *Money is tight, we need to spend carefully* but not *Money is tight we need to spend carefully.* A checker may also question sentences that are actually correct, such as *Money being tighter now than before, we need to spend carefully.*

CULTURE LANGUAGE   In standard American English, a sentence may not include more than one main clause unless the clauses are separated by a comma and a coordinating conjunction or by a semicolon. If your native language does not have such a rule or has accustomed you to writing long sentences, you may need to edit your English writing especially for comma splices and fused sentences.

36a   Separate main clauses not joined by *and, but,* or another coordinating conjunction.

If your readers point out comma splices or fused sentences in your writing, you're not creating enough separation between main clauses in your sentences. Punctuate consecutive main clauses in the following ways.

▪ Separate sentences

Make the clauses into separate sentences when the ideas expressed are only loosely related:

> Comma splice   Chemistry has contributed much to our understanding of foods, many foods such as wheat and beans can be produced in the laboratory.
>
> Revised   Chemistry has contributed much to our understanding of foods. Many foods such as wheat and beans can be produced in the laboratory.

▪ Coordinating conjunction

Insert a coordinating conjunction in a comma splice when the ideas in the main clauses are closely related and equally important:

Punctuation of two or more main clauses

■ **Separate main clauses with periods.**

(Main clause) . (Main clause) .

The ship burned in 2001. Its lavish cabins and beautiful decks were destroyed.

■ **Link main clauses with a coordinating conjunction and a comma.**

(Main clause) , {for and or so but nor yet} (main clause) .

The ship burned in 2001, and its lavish cabins and beautiful decks were destroyed.

■ **Link main clauses with a semicolon.**

(Main clause) ; (main clause) .

The ship burned in 2001; its lavish cabins and beautiful decks were destroyed.

■ **Relate main clauses with a semicolon and a conjunctive adverb or transitional expression.**

(Main clause) ; {however, for example, etc.} , (main clause) .

The ship burned in 2001; as a result, its lavish cabins and beautiful decks were destroyed.

| Comma splice | Some laboratory-grown foods taste good, they are nutritious. |
| Revised | Some laboratory-grown foods taste good, and they are nutritious. |

In a fused sentence insert a comma and a coordinating conjunction:

| Fused sentence | Chemists have made much progress they still have a way to go. |
| Revised | Chemists have made much progress, but they still have a way to go. |

■ **Semicolon**

Insert a semicolon between clauses if the relation between the ideas is very close and obvious without a conjunction:

Comma splice	Good taste is rare in laboratory-grown vegetables, they are usually bland.
Revised	Good taste is rare in laboratory-grown vegetables; they are usually bland.

■ Subordination

Subordinate one clause to the other when one idea is less important than the other:

Comma splice	The vitamins are adequate, the flavor is deficient.
Revised	Even though the vitamins are adequate, the flavor is deficient.

36b Separate main clauses related by *however, for example,* and so on.

Two groups of words describe how one main clause relates to another: **conjunctive adverbs** and other **transitional expressions.** (See **1** pp. 44–45 for a longer list of transitional expressions.)

Common conjunctive adverbs and transitional expressions

accordingly	for instance	instead	on the contrary
anyway	further	in the meantime	otherwise
as a result	furthermore	in the past	similarly
at last	hence	likewise	still
besides	however	meanwhile	that is
certainly	incidentally	moreover	then
consequently	in contrast	namely	thereafter
even so	indeed	nevertheless	therefore
finally	in fact	nonetheless	thus
for all that	in other words	now	undoubtedly
for example	in short	of course	until now

When two main clauses are related by a conjunctive adverb or another transitional expression, they must be separated by a period or by a semicolon. The adverb or expression is also generally set off by a comma or commas.

Comma splice	Most Americans refuse to give up unhealthful habits, consequently our medical costs are higher than those of many other countries.
Revised	Most Americans refuse to give up unhealthful habits. Consequently, our medical costs are higher than those of many other countries.

Revised   Most Americans refuse to give up unhealthful habits;
                 consequently, our medical costs are higher than those
                 of many other countries.

Conjunctive adverbs and transitional expressions are different from coordinating conjunctions (*and, but,* and so on) and subordinating conjunctions (*although, because,* and so on):

- Unlike conjunctions, conjunctive adverbs and transitional expressions do not join two clauses into a grammatical unit. They merely describe the way two clauses relate in meaning.

- Unlike conjunctions, conjunctive adverbs and transitional expressions can be moved within a clause. No matter where in the clause an adverb or expression falls, though, the clause must be separated from another main clause by a period or semicolon:

Most Americans refuse to give up unhealthful habits; our medical costs, consequently, are higher than those of many other countries.

EXERCISE 36.1   Identifying and revising comma splices

Correct each comma splice below in *two* of the ways described on pp. 284–86. If a sentence contains no comma splice, mark the number preceding it. (You can do this exercise online at *ablongman.com/ littlebrown.*)

1 Money has a long history, it goes back at least as far as the earliest records. 2 Many of the earliest records concern financial transactions, indeed, early history must often be inferred from commercial activity. 3 Every known society has had a system of money, though the objects serving as money have varied widely. 4 Sometimes the objects had actual value for the society, examples include cattle and fermented beverages. 5 Today, in contrast, money may be made of worthless paper, or it may even consist of a bit of data in a computer's memory. 6 We think of money as valuable, only our common faith in it makes it valuable. 7 That faith is sometimes fragile, consequently, currencies themselves are fragile. 8 Economic crises often shake the belief in money, indeed, such weakened faith helped cause the Great Depression of the 1930s.

EXERCISE 36.2   Identifying and revising fused sentences

Revise each of the fused sentences in the paragraph below in *two* of the four ways shown on pp. 284–86. If a sentence is correct as given, mark the number preceding it. (You can do this exercise online at *ablongman .com/littlebrown.*)

1 Throughout history money and religion were closely linked there was little distinction between government and religion. 2 The head of state and the religious leader were often the same person so that all power rested in one ruler. 3 These powerful leaders decided what objects would serve as money their backing encouraged public faith in

the money. 4 Coins were minted of precious metals the religious over-
tones of money were then strengthened. 5 People already believed the
precious metals to be divine their use in money intensified its allure.

**EXERCISE 36.3   Sentence combining: Comma splices and
fused sentences**

Using the method suggested in parentheses, combine each pair of sentences below into one sentence without creating a comma splice
or fused sentence. (You can do this exercise online at *ablongman.com/
littlebrown*.)

Example:
The sun sank lower in the sky. The colors gradually faded.
(*Subordinate one clause to the other.*)

As the sun sank lower in the sky, the colors gradually faded.

1 The exact origin of paper money is unknown. It has not survived as
   coins, shells, and other durable objects have. (*Subordinate one clause
   to the other.*)
2 Scholars disagree over where paper money originated. Many believe
   it was first used in Europe. (*Subordinate one clause to the other.*)
3 Perhaps goldsmiths were also gold bankers. They held the gold of
   their wealthy customers. (*Supply a semicolon and a conjunctive adverb or transitional expression.*)
4 The goldsmiths probably gave customers receipts for their gold.
   These receipts were then used in trade. (*Supply a comma and coordinating conjunction.*)
5 The goldsmiths were something like modern-day bankers. Their
   receipts were something like modern-day money. (*Supply a semicolon.*)

EXERCISE 36.4   Revising: Comma splices and fused sentences

Revise each comma splice and fused sentence in the following paragraphs using the technique that seems most appropriate for the meaning. (You can do this exercise online at *ablongman.com/littlebrown*.)

What many call the first genocide of modern times occurred during
World War I, the Armenians were deported from their homes in Anatolia,
Turkey. The Turkish government assumed that the Armenians were sympathetic to Russia, with whom the Turks were at war. Many Armenians
died because of the hardships of the journey, many were massacred. The
death toll was estimated at between 600,000 and 1 million.

Many of the deported Armenians migrated to Russia, in 1918 they
established the Republic of Armenia, they continued to be attacked by
Turkey, in 1920 they became the Soviet Republic of Armenia rather than
surrender to the Turks. Like other Soviet republics, Armenia became
independent in 1991, about 3.4 million Armenians live there now.

37   Mixed Sentences

A **mixed sentence** contains parts that do not fit together. The misfit may be in grammar or in meaning.

Note Grammar and style checkers may recognize a simple mixed construction such as *reason is because,* but they will fail to flag most mixed sentences.

37a   Match subjects and predicates in meaning.

In a sentence with mixed meaning, the subject is said to do or be something illogical. Such a mixture is sometimes called **faulty predication** because the predicate conflicts with the subject.

1   Illogical equation with *be*

When a form of *be* connects a subject and a word that describes the subject (a complement), the subject and complement must be logically related:

Mixed   A compromise between the city and the country would be the ideal place to live.

Revised   A community that offered the best qualities of both city and country would be the ideal place to live.

2   *Is when, is where*

Definitions require nouns on both sides of *be.* Clauses that define and begin with *when* or *where* are common in speech but should be avoided in writing:

Mixed   An examination is when you are tested on what you know.

Revised   An examination is a test of what you know.

Key terms

subject The part of a sentence that names who or what performs the action or makes the assertion of the verb: *Geese fly.* (See pp. 195–97.)

predicate The part of a sentence containing the verb and asserting something about the subject: *Geese fly.* (See pp. 195–97.)

---

http://www.ablongman.com/littlebrown ▶

Visit the companion Web site for more help and an electronic exercise on mixed sentences.

Reason is because

The commonly heard construction *reason is because* is redundant since *because* means "for the reason that":

Mixed   The <u>reason</u> the temple requests donations <u>is because</u> the school needs expansion.

Revised   The <u>reason</u> the temple requests donations <u>is that</u> the school needs expansion.

Revised   The temple requests donations <u>because</u> the school needs expansion.

4 Other mixed meanings

Faulty predications are not confined to sentences with *be:*

Mixed   The <u>use</u> of emission controls <u>was created</u> to reduce air pollution.

Revised   Emission <u>controls were created</u> to reduce air pollution.

37b Untangle sentences that are mixed in grammar.

Many mixed sentences start with one grammatical plan or construction but end with a different one:

        ⌐————————— modifier (prepositional phrase) —————————⌐ verb
Mixed   By paying more attention to impressions than facts leads us to misjudge others.

        ⌐————————— modifier (prepositional phrase) —————————⌐ subject
Revised   By paying more attention to impressions than facts, <u>we</u>
        verb
        <u>misjudge</u> others.

        subject ⌐————————— modifier (prepositional phrase) —————————
Mixed   The fact that someone may be considered guilty just for associating with someone guilty.

        subject + verb
Revised   The <u>fact is</u> that someone may be considered guilty just for associating with someone guilty.

Mixed sentences are especially likely on a computer when you connect parts of two sentences or rewrite half a sentence but not the other half. Mixed sentences may also occur when you don't make the subject and verb of a sentence carry the principal meaning. (See **3** p. 141.)

EXERCISE 37.1 Revising: Mixed sentences

Revise the following paragraph so that sentence parts fit together both in grammar and in meaning. Each item has more than one possible answer. If a sentence is correct as given, mark the number preceding it. (You can do this exercise online at *ablongman.com/littlebrown*.)

1 A hurricane is when the winds in a tropical depression rotate counterclockwise at more than seventy-four miles per hour. **2** People fear hurricanes because they can destroy lives and property. **3** Through storm surge, high winds, floods, and tornadoes is how hurricanes have killed thousands of people. **4** Storm surge is where the hurricane's winds whip up a tide that spills over seawalls and deluges coastal islands. **5** The winds themselves are also destructive, uprooting trees and smashing buildings. **6** By packing winds of 150 to 200 miles per hour is how a hurricane inflicts terrible damage even on inland towns. **7** However, the worst damage to inland areas occurs when tornadoes and floods strike. **8** Many scientists observe that hurricanes in recent years they have become more ferocious and destructive. **9** However, in the last half-century, with improved communication systems and weather satellites have made hurricanes less deadly. **10** The reason is because people have more time to escape. **11** The emphasis on evacuation is in fact the best way for people to avoid a hurricane's force. **12** Simply boarding up a house's windows will not protect a family from wind, water surges, and flying debris.

37c State parts of sentences, such as subjects, only once. CULTURE LANGUAGE

In some languages other than English, certain parts of sentences may be repeated. These include the subject in any kind of clause or an object or adverb in an adjective clause. In English, however, these parts are stated only once in a clause.

1 Repetition of subject

You may be tempted to restate a subject as a pronoun before the verb. But the subject needs stating only once in its clause:

Faulty   The liquid it reached a temperature of 180°F.
Revised   The liquid reached a temperature of 180°F.

Faulty   Gases in the liquid they escaped.
Revised   Gases in the liquid escaped.

2 Repetition in an adjective clause

Adjective clauses begin with *who, whom, whose, which, that, where,* and *when* (see also p. 206). The beginning word replaces another word: the subject (*He is the person who called*), an object of a verb or preposition (*He is the person whom I mentioned*), or a preposition and pronoun (*He knows the office where* [*in which*] *the conference will occur*).

Do not state the word being replaced in an adjective clause:

Faulty   The technician whom the test depended on her was burned.
[*Whom* should replace *her*.]

Revised   The technician whom the test depended on was burned.

Adjective clauses beginning with *where* or *when* do not need an adverb such as *there* or *then*:

Faulty   Gases escaped at a moment when the technician was unprepared then.

Revised   Gases escaped at a moment when the technician was unprepared.

Note *Whom, which,* and similar words are sometimes omitted but are still understood by the reader. Thus the word being replaced should not be stated.

Faulty   Accidents rarely happen to technicians the lab has trained *them*. [*Whom* is understood: . . . *technicians whom the lab has trained.*]

Revised   Accidents rarely happen to technicians the lab has trained.

EXERCISE 37.2   Revising: Repeated subjects and other parts

◖ CULTURE LANGUAGE ◗ Revise the sentences in the following paragraph to eliminate any unneeded words. If a sentence is correct as given, mark the number preceding it. (You can do this exercise online at *ablongman.com/littlebrown.*)

1 Archaeologists and other scientists they can often determine the age of their discoveries by means of radiocarbon dating. 2 This technique is based on the fact that all living organisms contain carbon. 3 The most common isotope is carbon 12, which it contains six protons and six neutrons. 4 A few carbon atoms are classified as the isotope carbon 14, where the nucleus consists of six protons and eight neutrons there. 5 Because of the extra neutrons, the carbon 14 atom it is unstable. 6 What is significant about the carbon 14 atom is its half-life of 5700 years. 7 Scientists they measure the proportion of carbon 14 to carbon 12 and estimate the age of the specimen. 8 Radiocarbon dating it can be used on any material that was once living, but it is most accurate with specimens between 500 and 50,000 years old.

PART 5

Punctuation

sed on love but on the understa

hing to do. Illych finds that his

e wants and life becomes unple

after the birth of their child Illy

self-involvement. He blames h

ngs and disappointments, belie

cial success can make him happ

PLEASE FASTEN
THIS GATE
PROPERLY
AS THE CATTLE
GET OUT ?
THANK YOU

PART **5**

Punctuation

38 End Punctuation

End a sentence with one of three punctuation marks: a period (.), a question mark (?), or an exclamation point (!).

Note A grammar and style checker may flag missing question marks after direct questions or incorrect combinations of marks (such as a question mark and a period at the end of a sentence), but it cannot do much else.

38a Use a period after most sentences and with some abbreviations.

1 Statements, mild commands, and indirect questions

Statement

The airline went bankrupt.   It no longer flies.

Mild command

Think of the possibilities.   Please consider others.

Indirect question

An **indirect question** reports what someone asked but not in the exact form or words of the original question:

The judge asked why I had been driving with my lights off.
No one asked how we got home.

CULTURE LANGUAGE In standard American English, an indirect question uses the wording and subject-verb order of a statement: *The reporter asked why the negotiations failed* [not *why did the negotiations fail*].

2 Abbreviations

Use periods with abbreviations that consist of or end in small letters. Otherwise, omit periods from abbreviations.

Dr.	Mr., Mrs.	e.g.	Feb.	ft.
St.	Ms.	i.e.	p.	a.m., p.m.
PhD	BC, BCE	USA	IBM	AM, PM
BA	AD, CE	US	USMC	AIDS

http://www.ablongman.com/littlebrown ▶

Visit the companion Web site for more help and an electronic exercise on end punctuation.

Note When a sentence ends in an abbreviation with a period, don't add a second period: *My first class is at 8 a.m.*

EXERCISE 38.1 Revising: Periods

Revise the following sentences so that periods are used correctly. (You can do this exercise online at *ablongman.com/littlebrown*.)

1 The instructor asked when Plato wrote *The Republic*?
2 Give the date within one century
3 The exact date is not known, but it is estimated at 370 BCE
4 Dr Arn will lecture on Plato at 7:30 p.m..
5 The area of the lecture hall is only 1600 sq ft

38b Use a question mark after a direct question and sometimes to indicate doubt.

1 Direct questions

Who will follow her?
What is the difference between these two people?

After indirect questions, use a period: *We wondered who would follow her.* (See the preceding page.)

Questions in a series are each followed by a question mark:

The officer asked how many times the suspect had been arrested. Three times? Four times? More than that?

Note Do not combine question marks with other question marks, periods, commas, or other punctuation.

2 Doubt

A question mark within parentheses can indicate doubt about a number or date.

The Greek philosopher Socrates was born in 470 (?) BC and died in 399 BC from drinking poison. [Socrates's birthdate is not known for sure.]

Use sentence structure and words, not a question mark, to express sarcasm or irony.

Not Stern's friendliness (?) bothered Crane.
But Stern's insincerity bothered Crane.

EXERCISE 38.2 Revising: Question marks

Add, delete, or replace question marks as needed in the following sentences. (You can do this exercise online at *ablongman.com/littlebrown*.)

1 In Homer's *Odyssey*, Odysseus took several years to travel from Troy to Ithaca. Or was it eight years. Or more?
2 Odysseus must have wondered whether he would ever make it home?
3 "What man are you and whence?," asks Odysseus's wife Penelope.
4 Why does Penelope ask, "Where is your city? Your family?"?
5 Penelope does not recognize Odysseus and asks who this stranger is?

38c Use an exclamation point after an emphatic statement, interjection, or command.

No! We must not lose this election!
Come here immediately!

Follow mild interjections and commands with commas or periods, as appropriate: *Oh,* *call whenever you can.*

Note Do not combine exclamation points with periods, commas, or other punctuation marks. And use exclamation points sparingly, even in informal writing. Overused, they'll fail to impress readers, and they may make you sound overemphatic.

EXERCISE 38.3 Revising: Exclamation points

Add or replace exclamation points as needed in the following sentences. (You can do this exercise online at *ablongman.com/littlebrown*.)

1 As the firefighters moved their equipment into place, the police shouted, "Move back!".
2 A child's cries could be heard from above: "Help me. Help."
3 When the child was rescued, the crowd called "Hooray."
4 The rescue was the most exciting event of the day!
5 The neighbors talked about it for days!

EXERCISE 38.4 Revising: End punctuation

Insert appropriate end punctuation (periods, question marks, or exclamation points) where needed in the following paragraph. (You can do this exercise online at *ablongman.com/littlebrown*.)

When visitors first arrive in Hawaii, they often encounter an unexpected language barrier Standard English is the language of business and government, but many of the people speak Pidgin English Instead of

---

Key term

interjection A word that expresses feeling or commands attention, either alone or within a sentence: *Oh! Hey! Wow!*

an excited "Aloha" the visitors may be greeted with an excited Pidgin "Howzit" or asked if they know "how fo' find one good hotel" Many Hawaiians question whether Pidgin will hold children back because it prevents communication with *haoles*, or Caucasians, who run businesses Yet many others feel that Pidgin is a last defense of ethnic diversity on the islands To those who want to make standard English the official language of the state, these Hawaiians may respond, "Just 'cause I speak Pidgin no mean I dumb" They may ask, "Why you no listen" or, in standard English, "Why don't you listen"

39 The Comma

The comma (,) is the most common punctuation mark inside sentences. Its main uses are shown in the box opposite.

Note Grammar and style checkers will ignore many comma errors. For example, a checker failed to catch the missing commas in *We cooked lasagna spinach and apple pie* and the misused commas in *The trip was short but, the weather was perfect* and *The travelers were tempted by, the many shops.*

39a Use a comma before *and, but,* or another coordinating conjunction linking main clauses.

When a coordinating conjunction links words or phrases, do not use a comma: *Dugain plays and sings Irish and English folk songs*. However, *do* use a comma when a coordinating conjunction joins main clauses, as in the next examples.

Caffeine can keep coffee drinkers alert, and it may elevate their mood.

Caffeine was once thought to be safe, but now researchers warn of harmful effects.

Coffee drinkers may suffer sleeplessness, for the drug acts as a stimulant to the nervous system.

Key terms

coordinating conjunctions *And, but, or, nor,* and sometimes *for, so, yet.* (See 4 p. 194.)

main clause A word group that contains a subject and a verb and does not begin with a subordinating word: *Water freezes at temperatures below 32°F.* (See 4 p. 206.)

---

http://www.ablongman.com/littlebrown ▶

Visit the companion Web site for more help and electronic exercises on the comma.

Main uses of the comma

- **Separate main clauses linked by a coordinating conjunction** (facing page):

The building is finished**,** but it has no tenants.

- **Set off most introductory elements** (p. 301).

Unfortunately**,** the only tenant pulled out.

- **Set off nonessential elements** (p. 303).

The empty building symbolizes a weak local economy**,** which affects everyone.

The primary cause**,** the decline of local industry**,** is not news.

- **Separate items in a series** (p. 308).

The city needs healthier businesses**,** new schools**,** and improved housing.

- **Separate coordinate adjectives** (p. 309).

A tall**,** sleek skyscraper is not needed.

Other uses of the comma:

Separate parts of dates, addresses, long numbers (p. 310).
Separate quotations and signal phrases (p. 311).

See also p. 313 for when *not* to use the comma.

Note The comma goes *before,* not after, a coordinating conjunction that links main clauses: *Caffeine increases heart rate, and it* [not *and, it*] *constricts blood vessels.*

Exception Some writers omit the comma between main clauses that are very short and closely related in meaning: *Caffeine helps but it also hurts.* If you are in doubt about whether to use the comma in such a sentence, use it. It will always be correct.

EXERCISE 39.1 Revising: Comma with linked main clauses

In the following paragraph, insert a comma before each coordinating conjunction that links main clauses. Do not insert commas between words, phrases, or subordinate clauses. If a sentence is correct as given, mark the number preceding it. (You can do this exercise online at *ablongman.com/littlebrown.*)

1 Parents once automatically gave their children the father's last name but some no longer do. 2 In fact, parents were once legally required to give their children the father's last name but these laws have been contested in court. 3 Parents may now give their children any last name they choose and some parents opt for the mother's last name. 4 Those parents who choose the mother's last name may do so because they believe the mother's importance should be recognized or because the mother's name is easier to pronounce.

EXERCISE 39.2 Sentence combining: Linked main clauses

Combine each group of sentences below into one sentence that contains only two main clauses connected by the coordinating conjunction in parentheses. Use commas only to separate the main clauses. You will have to add, delete, and rearrange words. (You can do this exercise online at *ablongman.com/littlebrown.*)

Example:

The circus had come to town. The children wanted to see it. Their parents wanted to see it. (*and*)

The circus had come to town, and the children and their parents wanted to see it.

1 The arguments for bestowing the mother's surname on children are often strong. They are often convincing. They are not universally accepted. (*but*)
2 Some parents have combined their last names. They have created a new surname. They have given that name to their children. (*and*)
3 Critics sometimes question the effects of unusual surnames on children. They wonder how confusing the new surnames will be. They wonder how fleeting the surnames will be. (*or*)
4 Children with surnames different from their parents' may suffer embarrassment. They may suffer identity problems. Giving children their father's surname is still very much the norm. (*for*)
5 Hyphenated names are awkward. They are also difficult to pass on. Some observers think they will die out in the next generation. Or they may die out before. (*so*)

39b Use a comma to set off most introductory elements.

An **introductory element** begins a sentence and modifies a word or words in the main clause. It is usually followed by a comma.

Subordinate clause

Even when identical twins are raised apart, they grow up very like each other.

Verbal or verbal phrase

Explaining the similarity, some researchers claim that one's genes are one's destiny.

Concerned, other researchers deny the claim.

Prepositional phrase

In a debate that has lasted centuries, scientists use identical twins to argue for or against genetic destiny.

Transitional expression

Of course, scientists can now look directly at the genes themselves to answer questions.

You may omit the comma after a short subordinate clause or prepositional phrase if its omission does not create confusion: *When snow falls the city collapses. By the year 2000 the world population had topped 6 billion.* But the comma is never wrong.

Note Take care to distinguish *-ing* words used as modifiers from *-ing* words used as subjects. The former almost always take a comma; the latter never do.

⎡————— modifier —————⎤   subject   verb

Studying identical twins, geneticists learn about inheritance.

⎡————— subject —————⎤   verb

Studying identical twins helps geneticists learn about inheritance.

Key terms

subordinate clause A word group that contains a subject and a verb, begins with a subordinating word such as *because* or *who,* and is not a question: *When water freezes, crystals form.* (See **4** pp. 206–07.)

verbal A verb form used as an adjective, adverb, or noun. A verbal plus any object or modifier is a **verbal phrase:** *frozen water, ready to freeze, rapid freezing.* (See **4** pp. 202–03.)

prepositional phrase A word group consisting of a preposition, such as *for* or *in,* followed by a noun or pronoun plus any modifiers: *in a jar, with a spoon.* (See **4** p. 201.)

transitional expression A word or phrase that shows the relationship between sentences: *for example, however, in fact, of course.* (See **1** pp. 44–45.)

EXERCISE 39.3 Revising: Comma with introductory elements

In the following paragraph, insert commas wherever they are needed after introductory elements. If a sentence is correct as given, mark the number preceding it. (You can do this exercise online at *ablongman.com/littlebrown*.)

1 Veering sharply to the right a large flock of birds neatly avoids a high wall. 2 Moving in a fluid mass is typical of flocks of birds and schools of fish. 3 With the help of complex computer simulations zoologists are learning more about this movement. 4 Because it is sudden and apparently well coordinated the movement of flocks and schools has seemed to be directed by a leader. 5 Almost incredibly the group could behave with more intelligence than any individual seemed to possess. 6 However new studies have discovered that flocks and schools are leaderless. 7 As it turns out evading danger is really an individual response. 8 When each bird or fish senses a predator it follows individual rules for fleeing. 9 To keep from colliding with its neighbors each bird or fish uses other rules for dodging. 10 Multiplied over hundreds of individuals these responses look as if they have been choreographed.

EXERCISE 39.4 Sentence combining: Introductory elements

Combine each pair of sentences below into one sentence that begins with an introductory modifier as specified in parentheses. Follow the introductory element with a comma. You will have to add, delete, change, and rearrange words. (You can do this exercise online at *ablongman.com/littlebrown*.)

Example:

The girl was humming to herself. She walked upstairs. (*Modifier beginning Humming.*)

Humming to herself, the girl walked upstairs.

1 Scientists have made an effort to explain the mysteries of flocks and schools. They have proposed bizarre magnetic fields and telepathy. (*Modifier beginning In.*)

2 Scientists developed computer models. They have abandoned earlier explanations. (*Modifier beginning Since.*)

3 The movement of a flock or school starts with each individual. It is rapidly and perhaps automatically coordinated among individuals. (*Modifier beginning Starting.*)

4 One zoologist observes that human beings seek coherent patterns. He suggests that investigators saw purpose in the movement of flocks and schools where none existed. (*Modifier beginning Observing.*)

5 One may want to study the movement of flocks or schools. Then one must abandon a search for purpose or design. (*Modifier beginning To.*)

39c Use a comma or commas to set off nonessential elements.

Commas around part of a sentence often signal that the element is not essential to the meaning. This **nonessential element** may modify or rename the word it refers to, but it does not limit the word to a particular individual or group. The meaning of the word would still be clear if the element were deleted:

Nonessential element
The company, which is located in Oklahoma, has a good reputation.

(Because it does not restrict meaning, a nonessential element is also called a **nonrestrictive element**.)

In contrast, an **essential** (or **restrictive**) element *does* limit the word it refers to: the element cannot be omitted without leaving the meaning too general. Because it is essential, such an element is *not* set off with a comma or commas.

Essential element
The company rewards employees who work hard.

Omitting the underlined words would distort the meaning: the company doesn't necessarily reward *all* employees, only the hardworking ones.

A test for nonessential and essential elements

1. **Identify the element:**

   Hai Nguyen who emigrated from Vietnam lives in Dallas.
   Those who emigrated with him live elsewhere.

2. **Remove the element.** Does the fundamental meaning of the sentence change?

   Hai Nguyen lives in Dallas.   *No.*
   Those live elsewhere.   *Yes.* [Who are *Those?*]

3. **If *no*, the element is *nonessential* and *should* be set off with punctuation:**

   Hai Nguyen, who emigrated from Vietnam, lives in Dallas.

   If *yes*, the element is *essential* and should *not* be set off with punctuation:

   Those who emigrated with him live elsewhere.

The same element in the same sentence may be essential or nonessential depending on your meaning and the context:

Essential

Not all the bands were equally well received, however. The band playing old music held the audience's attention. The other groups created much less excitement. [*Playing old music* identifies a particular band.]

Nonessential

A new band called Fats made its debut on Saturday night. The band, playing old music, held the audience's attention. If this performance is typical, the group has a bright future. [*Playing old music* adds information about a band already named.]

Note When a nonessential element falls in the middle of a sentence, be sure to set it off with a pair of commas, one *before* and one *after* the element.

1 Nonessential phrases and clauses

Most nonessential phrases and subordinate clauses function as adjectives or, less commonly, as adverbs. In each of the following examples, the underlined words could be omitted with no loss of clarity.

Elizabeth Blackwell was the first woman to graduate from an American medical school, in 1849. [Phrase.]

She was a medical pioneer, helping to found the first medical college for women. [Phrase.]

She taught at the school, which was affiliated with the New York Infirmary. [Clause.]

Blackwell, who published books and papers on medicine, practiced pediatrics and gynecology. [Clause.]

Note Use *that* only in an essential clause, never in a nonessential clause: . . . *school, which* [not *that*] *was affiliated.* . . . Many writers reserve *which* for nonessential clauses.

2 Nonessential appositives

A nonessential appositive merely adds information about the word it refers to.

┌─ **Key terms** ─────────────────────────────

phrase A word group lacking a subject or a verb or both: *in Duluth, carrying water.* (See **4** p. 201.)

subordinate clause A word group that contains a subject and a verb, begins with a subordinating word such as *who* or *although,* and is not a question: *Samson, who won a gold medal, coaches in Utah.* (See **4** p. 206.)

appositive A noun that renames another noun immediately before it: *His wife, Kyra Sedgwick, is also an actor.* (See **4** p. 205.)

Toni Morrison's fifth novel, *Beloved,* won the Pulitzer Prize in 1988. [The word *fifth* identifies the novel, while the title adds a detail.]

In contrast, an essential appositive limits or defines the word it refers to:

Morrison's novel *The Bluest Eye* is about an African American girl who longs for blue eyes. [Morrison has written more than one novel, so the title is essential to identify the intended one.]

3 Other nonessential elements

Like nonessential modifiers or appositives, many other elements contribute to texture, tone, or overall clarity but are not essential to the meaning. Unlike nonessential modifiers or appositives, these other nonessential elements generally do not refer to any specific word in the sentence.

Note Use a pair of commas—one before, one after—when any of these elements falls in the middle of a sentence.

Absolute phrases

Household recycling having succeeded, the city now wants to extend the program to businesses.

Many businesses, their profits already squeezed, resist recycling.

Parenthetical and transitional expressions

Generally, set off parenthetical and transitional expressions with commas:

The world's most celebrated holiday is, perhaps surprisingly, New Year's Day. [Parenthetical expression.]

Interestingly, Americans have relatively few holidays. [Parenthetical expression.]

American workers, for example, receive fewer holidays than European workers do. [Transitional expression.]

(Dashes and parentheses may also set off parenthetical expressions. See pp. 336–38.)

Key terms

absolute phrase A phrase modifying a whole main clause and consisting of a participle and its subject: *Their homework completed,* the children watched TV. (See **4** p. 204.)

parenthetical expression An explanatory or supplemental word or phrase, such as *all things considered, to be frank,* or a brief example or fact. (See p. 338.)

transitional expression A word or phrase that shows the relationship between sentences: *for example, however, in fact, of course.* (See **1** pp. 44–45.)

When a transitional expression links main clauses, precede it with a semicolon and follow it with a comma (see p. 317):

> European workers often have long paid vacations; indeed, they may receive a full month after just a few years with a company.

Note The conjunctions *and* and *but,* sometimes used as transitional expressions, are not followed by commas (see pp. 313–14). Nor are commas required after some transitional expressions that we read without pauses, such as *also, hence, next, now,* and *thus.* A few transitional expressions, notably *therefore* and *instead,* do not need commas when they fall inside or at the ends of clauses.

> American workers thus put in more work days. But the days themselves may be shorter.

Phrases of contrast

> The substance, not the style, is important.
> Substance, unlike style, cannot be faked.

Tag questions

> Jones should be allowed to vote, should he not?
> They don't stop to consider others, do they?

Yes and *no*

> Yes, the editorial did have a point.
> No, that can never be.

Words of direct address

> Cody, please bring me the newspaper.
> With all due respect, sir, I will not.

Mild interjections

> Well, you will never know who did it.
> Oh, they forgot all about the baby.

EXERCISE 39.5   Revising: Punctuation of nonessential and essential elements

Insert commas as needed in the following paragraph to set off nonessential elements, and delete any commas that incorrectly set off essential elements. If a sentence is correct as given, mark the number preceding it. (You can do this exercise online at *ablongman.com/littlebrown.*)

   1 Anesthesia which is commonly used during medical operations once made patients uncomfortable and had serious risks. 2 But new

---

Key terms

tag question A question at the end of a statement, consisting of a pronoun, a helping verb, and sometimes *not: It isn't wet, is it?*

interjection A word that expresses feeling or commands attention: *Oh, must we?*

drugs and procedures, that have been developed in recent years, allow patients under anesthesia to be comfortable and much safer. 3 Twenty years ago, any patient, undergoing anesthesia, would have had to stay overnight in a hospital, probably feeling sick and very confused. 4 Today, many patients can have general anesthesia, which renders them completely unconscious, and still go home the same day. 5 Another form of anesthesia, monitored anesthesia or conscious sedation, allows the patient to be awake while feeling sleepy with no pain. 6 A surgeon may also suggest regional or local anesthesia which numbs only a specific part of the body and leaves the patient completely awake. 7 Sometimes, patients must choose among local, regional, and general anesthesia whether or not they want to make the choice. 8 In that case, patients should ask which type the anesthesiologist would choose if his or her child or spouse were having the surgery.

EXERCISE 39.6 Revising: Punctuation of nonessential and essential elements

Insert commas as needed in the following paragraphs to set off nonessential elements, and delete any commas that incorrectly set off essential elements. If a sentence is correct as given, mark the number preceding it. (You can do this exercise online at *ablongman.com/littlebrown*.)

1 Italians insist that Marco Polo the thirteenth-century explorer did not import pasta from China. 2 Pasta which consists of flour and water and often egg existed in Italy long before Marco Polo left for his travels. 3 A historian who studied pasta says that it originated in the Middle East in the fifth century. 4 Most Italians dispute this account although their evidence is shaky. 5 Wherever it originated, the Italians are now the undisputed masters, in making and cooking pasta.

6 Marcella Hazan, who has written several books on Italian cooking, insists that homemade and hand-rolled pasta is the best. 7 However, most cooks buy dried pasta lacking the time to make their own. 8 Homemade or dried, the finest pasta is made from semolina, a flour from hard durum wheat. 9 Pasta manufacturers choose hard durum wheat, because it makes firmer cooked pasta than common wheat does. 10 Pasta, made from common wheat, gets soggy in boiling water.

EXERCISE 39.7 Sentence combining: Essential and nonessential elements

Combine each pair of sentences below into one sentence that uses the element described in parentheses. Insert commas as appropriate. You will have to add, delete, change, and rearrange words. Some items have more than one possible answer. (You can do this exercise online at *ablongman.com/littlebrown*.)

Example:
Mr. Ward's oldest sister helped keep him alive. She was a nurse in the hospital. (*Nonessential clause beginning* who.)

Mr. Ward's oldest sister, who was a nurse in the hospital, helped keep him alive.

1 American colonists first imported pasta from the English. The English had discovered it as tourists in Italy. (*Nonessential clause beginning* who.)

2 The English returned from their grand tours of Italy. They were called *macaronis* because of their fancy airs. (*Essential phrase beginning* returning.)

3 A hair style was also called *macaroni*. It had elaborate curls. (*Essential phrase beginning* with.)

4 The song "Yankee Doodle" refers to this hairdo. It reports that Yankee Doodle "stuck a feather in his cap and called it macaroni." (*Essential clause beginning* when.)

5 The song was actually intended to poke fun at unrefined American colonists. It was a creation of the English. (*Nonessential appositive beginning* a creation.)

39d Use commas between items in a series.

A **series** consists of three or more items of equal importance. The items may be words, phrases, or clauses.

> Anna Spingle married at the age of seventeen, had three children by twenty-one, and divorced at twenty-two.
> She worked as a cook, a baby-sitter, and a crossing guard.

Some writers omit the comma before the coordinating conjunction in a series (*Breakfast consisted of coffee, eggs and kippers*). But the final comma is never wrong, and it always helps the reader see the last two items as separate.

EXERCISE 39.8 Revising: Commas with series items

In the following paragraph, insert commas as needed to punctuate items in series. If a sentence is correct as given, mark the number preceding it. (You can do this exercise online at *ablongman.com/littlebrown*.)

1 Photographers who take pictures of flowers need to pay special attention to lighting composition and focal point. 2 Many photographers prefer to shoot in the early morning, when the air is calm, the dew is still on the flowers, and the light is soft. 3 Some even like to photograph in light rain because water helps flowers to look fresh colorful and especially lively. 4 In composing a picture, the photographer can choose to show several flowers, just one flower or even a small part of a flower. 5 One effective composition leads the viewer's eye in from an edge of the photo devotes a large amount of the photo to the primary subject and then leads the eye out of the photo. 6 The focus changes as the eye moves away from the subject: the primary subject is in sharp focus, elements near the primary subject are in sharp focus and elements in the background are deliberately out of focus.

39e Use commas between two or more adjectives that equally modify the same word.

Adjectives that equally modify the same word—**coordinate adjectives**—may be separated either by *and* or by a comma.

Spingle's scratched and dented car is old, but it gets her to work.
She has dreams of a sleek, shiny car.

Adjectives are not coordinate—and should not be separated by commas—when the one nearer the noun is more closely related to the noun in meaning.

Spingle's children work at various part-time jobs.
They all expect to go to a nearby community college.

Tests for commas with adjectives

1. **Identify the adjectives:**

   She was a faithful sincere friend.
   They are dedicated medical students.

2. **Can the adjectives be reversed without changing meaning?**

   She was a sincere faithful friend.   *Yes.*
   They are medical dedicated students.   *No.*

3. **Can the word *and* be inserted between the adjectives without changing meaning?**

   She was a faithful and sincere friend.   *Yes.*
   They are dedicated and medical students.   *No.*

4. **If *yes* to both questions, the adjectives *should* be separated by a comma:**

   She was a faithful, sincere friend.

5. **If *no* to both questions, the adjectives should *not* be separated by a comma:**

   They are dedicated medical students.

EXERCISE 39.9 Revising: Commas with adjectives

In the following paragraph, insert commas as needed between adjectives, and delete any unneeded commas. If a sentence is correct as given, mark the number preceding it. (You can do this exercise online at *ablongman.com/littlebrown*.)

1 Most people have seen a blind person being aided by a patient observant guide dog. 2 What is not commonly known is how normal

untrained dogs become these special, highly skilled dogs. 3 An organization called the Seeing Eye breeds dogs to perform this specific, guide job. 4 Enthusiastic affectionate volunteers raise the dogs until they are about seventeen months old. 5 Each dog then undergoes a thorough health examination. 6 Dogs who pass the health exam go through a rigorous, four-month, training program. 7 The trained dog is then matched with a blind person, and the two of them undergo their own intensive communication training before graduating to their life together.

EXERCISE 39.10   Revising: Punctuation of series and adjectives

Insert commas as needed in the following paragraph to separate series items or adjectives. If a sentence is correct as given, mark the number preceding it. (You can do this exercise online at *ablongman.com/ littlebrown.*)

1 Shoes with high heels were originally designed to protect the wearer's feet from mud garbage and animal waste in the streets. 2 The first high heels worn strictly for fashion, however, appeared in the sixteenth century. 3 They were made popular when the short powerful King Louis XIV of France began wearing them. 4 At first, high heels were worn by men and were made of colorful silk fabrics soft suedes or smooth leathers. 5 But Louis's influence was so strong that men and women of the court priests and cardinals and even household servants wore high heels. 6 By the seventeenth and eighteenth centuries, only wealthy fashionable French women wore high heels. 7 At that time, French culture represented the one true standard of elegance and refinement. 8 High-heeled shoes for women spread to other courts of Europe among the Europeans of North America and to all social classes. 9 Now high heels are common, though depending on the fashion they range from short squat thick heels to tall skinny spikes. 10 A New York boutique recently showed a pair of purple satin pumps with tiny jeweled bows and four-inch stiletto heels.

39f   Use commas in dates, addresses, place names, and long numbers.

Within a sentence, any date, address, or place name that contains a comma should also end with a comma.

Dates

July 4, 1776, is the date the Declaration was signed.

The bombing of Pearl Harbor on Sunday, December 7, 1941, prompted American entry into World War II.

Do not use commas between the parts of a date in inverted order (*15 December 1992*) or in dates consisting of a month or season and a year (*December 1941*).

Addresses and place names

Use the address 220 Cornell Road, Woodside, California 94062, for all correspondence. [Do not use a comma between a state name and a zip code.]

Columbus, Ohio, is the location of Ohio State University.

Long numbers

Use the comma to separate the figures in long numbers into groups of three, counting from the right. With numbers of four digits, the comma is optional.

The new assembly plant cost $7,525,000.
A kilometer is 3,281 feet [*or* 3281 feet].

CULTURE LANGUAGE Usage in standard American English differs from that in some other languages and dialects, which use a period, not a comma, to separate the figures in long numbers.

EXERCISE 39.11 Revising: Punctuation of dates, addresses, place names, numbers

Insert commas as needed in the following paragraph. (You can do this exercise online at *ablongman.com/littlebrown*.)

1 The festival will hold a benefit dinner and performance on March 10 2007 in Asheville. 2 The organizers hope to raise more than $100000 from donations and ticket sales. 3 Performers are expected from as far away as Milan Italy and Kyoto Japan. 4 All inquiries sent to Mozart Festival PO Box 725 Asheville North Carolina 28803 will receive a quick response. 5 The deadline for ordering tickets by mail is Monday December 3 2006.

39g Use commas with quotations according to standard practice.

The words *she said, he writes,* and so on identify the source of a quotation. These **signal phrases** should be separated from the quotation by punctuation, usually a comma or commas.

"Knowledge is power," writes Francis Bacon.

"The shore has a dual nature," observes Rachel Carson, "changing with the swing of the tides." [The signal phrase interrupts the quotation at a comma and thus ends with a comma.]

Exceptions When a signal phrase interrupts a quotation between main clauses, follow the signal phrase with a semicolon or a period. The choice depends on the punctuation of the original.

Not	"That part of my life was over," she wrote, "his words had sealed it shut."
But	"That part of my life was over," she wrote. "His words had sealed it shut." [*She wrote* interrupts the quotation at a period.]
Or	"That part of my life was over," she wrote; "his words had sealed it shut." [*She wrote* interrupts the quotation at a semicolon.]

Do not use a comma when a signal phrase follows a quotation ending in an exclamation point or a question mark:

"Claude!" Mrs. Harrison called.
"Why must I come home?" he asked.

Do not use a comma with a quotation that is integrated into your sentence structure, including one introduced by *that*:

James Baldwin insists that "one must never, in one's life, accept . . . injustices as commonplace."

Baldwin thought that the violence of a riot "had been devised as a corrective" to his own violence.

Do not use a comma with a quoted title unless it is a nonessential appositive:

The Beatles recorded "She Loves You" in 1963.
The Beatles' first huge US hit, "She Loves You," appeared in 1963.

EXERCISE 39.12 Revising: Punctuation of quotations

In the following sentences, insert commas or semicolons as needed to correct punctuation with quotations. If a sentence is correct as given, mark the number preceding it. (You can do this exercise online at *ablongman.com/littlebrown.*)

1 The writer and writing teacher Peter Elbow proposes an "open-ended writing process" that "can change you, not just your words."
2 "I think of the open-ended writing process as a voyage in two stages" Elbow says.
3 "The sea voyage is a process of divergence, branching, proliferation, and confusion" Elbow continues "the coming to land is a process of convergence, pruning, centralizing, and clarifying."
4 "Keep up one session of writing long enough to get loosened up and tired" advises Elbow "long enough in fact to make a bit of a voyage."
5 "In coming to new land" Elbow says "you develop a new conception of what you are writing about."

Key term

nonessential appositive A word or words that rename an immediately preceding noun but do not limit or define the noun: *The author's first story, "Biloxi," won a prize.* (See pp. 304–05.)

39h Delete commas where they are not required.

Commas can make sentences choppy and even confusing if they are used more often than needed.

1 Not between subject and verb, verb and object, or preposition and object

Not The returning <u>soldiers, received</u> a warm welcome. [Separated subject and verb.]

But The returning <u>soldiers received</u> a warm welcome.

Not They had <u>chosen, to fight</u> for their country <u>despite, the risks.</u> [Separated verb *chosen* and its object; separated preposition *despite* and its object.]

But They had <u>chosen to fight</u> for their country <u>despite the risks.</u>

2 Not in most compound constructions

Compound constructions consisting of two elements almost never require a comma. The only exception is the sentence consisting of two main clauses linked by a coordinating conjunction: *The computer failed, but employees kept working* (see p. 298).

┌────────── compound subject ──────────┐
Not <u>Banks, and other financial institutions</u> have helped older people
┌──── compound object of preposition ────┐
with <u>money management, and investment.</u>

But <u>Banks and other financial institutions</u> have helped older people with <u>money management and investment.</u>

┌─────────────── compound predicate ───────────────┐
Not One bank <u>created</u> special accounts for older people, <u>and held</u>
┌compound object of verb┐
<u>classes, and workshops.</u>

But One bank <u>created</u> special accounts for older <u>people and held</u> <u>classes and workshops.</u>

3 Not after a conjunction

Not Parents of adolescents notice increased conflict at puberty, <u>and,</u> they complain of bickering.

┌─ Key terms ─────────────────────────────────────

compound construction Two or more words, phrases, or clauses connected by a coordinating conjunction, usually *and, but, or, nor: man and woman, old or young, leaking oil and spewing steam.*

conjunction A connecting word such as a **coordinating conjunction** (*and, but, or,* and so on) or a **subordinating conjunction** (*although, because, when,* and so on). (See **4** pp. 193–94.)

But   Parents of adolescents notice increased conflict at puberty, and they complain of bickering.

Not   Although, other primates leave the family at adolescence, humans do not.

But   Although other primates leave the family at adolescence, humans do not.

4 Not around essential elements

Not   Hawthorne's work, *The Scarlet Letter*, was the first major American novel. [The title is essential to distinguish the novel from the rest of Hawthorne's work.]

But   Hawthorne's work *The Scarlet Letter* was the first major American novel.

Not   The symbols, that Hawthorne uses, have influenced other novelists. [The clause identifies which symbols have been influential.]

But   The symbols that Hawthorne uses have influenced other novelists.

5 Not around a series

Commas separate the items *within* a series (p. 308) but do not separate the series from the rest of the sentence.

Not   The skills of, hunting, herding, and agriculture, sustained the Native Americans.

But   The skills of hunting, herding, and agriculture sustained the Native Americans.

6 Not before an indirect quotation

Not   The report concluded, that dieting could be more dangerous than overeating.

But   The report concluded that dieting could be more dangerous than overeating.

EXERCISE 39.13   Revising: Needless and misused commas

Revise the following paragraph to eliminate needless or misused commas. If a sentence is correct as given, mark the number preceding it. (You can do this exercise online at *ablongman.com/littlebrown*.)

1 One of the largest aquifers in North America, the Ogallala aquifer, is named after the Ogallala Indian tribe, which once lived in the region and hunted buffalo there. 2 The Ogallala aquifer underlies a region from

---

┌─ **Key term** ──────────────────────────────
essential element Limits the word it refers to and thus can't be omitted without leaving the meaning too general. (See p. 303.)

western Texas through northern Nebraska, and has a huge capacity of fresh water, that is contained in a layer of sand and gravel. 3 But, the water in the Ogallala is being removed faster than it is being replaced. 4 Water is pumped from the aquifer for many purposes, such as, drinking and other household use, industrial use, and, agricultural use. 5 The Great Plains area above the Ogallala, often lacks enough rainfall for the crops, that are grown there. 6 As a consequence, the crops in the Great Plains are watered by irrigation systems, that pump water from the Ogallala, and distribute it from half-mile-long sprinkler arms. 7 Ogallala water is receding between six inches and three feet a year, the amount depending on location. 8 Some areas are experiencing water shortages already, and the pumping continues. 9 A scientific commission recently estimated that, "at the present consumption rate, the Ogallala will be depleted in forty years."

EXERCISE 39.14 Revising: Commas

Insert commas as needed in the following paragraphs, and delete any misused commas. If a sentence is correct as given, mark the number preceding it. (You can do this exercise online at *ablongman.com/littlebrown.*)

1 Ellis Island New York reopened for business in 1990 but now the customers are tourists not immigrants. 2 This spot which lies in New York Harbor was the first American soil seen, or touched by many of the nation's immigrants. 3 Though other places also served as ports of entry for foreigners none has the symbolic power of, Ellis Island. 4 Between its opening in 1892 and its closing in 1954, over 20 million people about two-thirds of all immigrants were detained there before taking up their new lives in the United States. 5 Ellis Island processed over 2000 newcomers a day when immigration was at its peak between 1900 and 1920.

6 As the end of a long voyage and the introduction to the New World Ellis Island must have left something to be desired. 7 The "huddled masses" as the Statue of Liberty calls them indeed were huddled. 8 New arrivals were herded about kept standing in lines for hours or days yelled at and abused. 9 Assigned numbers they submitted their bodies to the pokings and proddings of the silent nurses and doctors, who were charged with ferreting out the slightest sign, of sickness disability or insanity. 10 That test having been passed, the immigrants faced interrogation by an official through an interpreter. 11 Those, with names deemed inconveniently long or difficult to pronounce, often found themselves permanently labeled with abbreviations, of their names, or with the names, of their hometowns. 12 But, millions survived the examination humiliation and confusion, to take the last short boat ride to New York City. 13 For many of them and especially for their descendants Ellis Island eventually became not a nightmare but the place where a new life began.

40 The Semicolon

The semicolon (;) separates equal and balanced sentence elements—usually main clauses (below and opposite) and occasionally items in series (p. 318).

Note A grammar and style checker can spot a few errors in the use of semicolons. For example, a checker suggested using a semicolon after *perfect* in *The set was perfect, the director had planned every detail,* thus correcting a comma splice. But it missed the incorrect semicolon in *The set was perfect; deserted streets, dark houses, and gloomy mist* (a colon would be correct).

40a **Use a semicolon between main clauses not joined by *and, but,* or another coordinating conjunction.**

When no coordinating conjunction links two main clauses, the clauses should be separated by a semicolon.

> A new ulcer drug arrived on the market with a mixed reputation; doctors find that the drug works but worry about its side effects.

> The side effects are not minor; some leave the patient quite uncomfortable or even ill.

Note This rule prevents the errors known as comma splice and fused sentence. (See **4** pp. 283–87.)

EXERCISE 40.1   Revising: Punctuation between main clauses

In the following paragraph, insert semicolons as needed to separate main clauses. If a sentence is correct as given, mark the number preceding it. (You can do this exercise online at *ablongman.com/littlebrown*.)

1 More and more musicians are playing computerized instruments more and more listeners are worrying about the future of acoustic instruments. 2 The computer is not the first technology in music the pipe organ and saxophone were also technological breakthroughs in

---

Key terms

main clause A word group that contains a subject and a verb and does not begin with a subordinating word: *Parks help cities breathe.*

coordinating conjunctions *And, but, or, nor,* and sometimes *for, so, yet.*

---

http://www.ablongman.com/littlebrown ▶

Visit the companion Web site for more help
and an electronic exercise on the semicolon.

their day. 3 Musicians have always experimented with new technology while audiences have always resisted the experiments. 4 Most computer musicians are not merely following the latest fad they are discovering new sounds and new ways to manipulate sound. 5 Few musicians have abandoned acoustic instruments most value acoustic sounds as much as electronic sounds.

40b Use a semicolon between main clauses related by *however, for example,* and so on.

When a conjunctive adverb or another transitional expression relates two main clauses in a single sentence, the clauses should be separated with a semicolon:

> An American immigrant, Levi Strauss, invented blue jeans in the 1860s; eventually, his product clothed working men throughout the West.

The position of the semicolon between main clauses never changes, but the conjunctive adverb or transitional expression may move around within the second clause. Wherever the adverb or expression falls, it is usually set off with a comma or commas. (See p. 305.)

> Blue jeans have become fashionable all over the world; however, the American originators still wear more jeans than anyone else.

> Blue jeans have become fashionable all over the world; the American originators, however, still wear more jeans than anyone else.

> Blue jeans have become fashionable all over the world; the American originators still wear more jeans than anyone else, however.

Note This rule prevents the errors known as comma splice and fused sentence. (See **4** pp. 283–87.)

> **EXERCISE 40.2 Revising: Punctuation between main clauses with conjunctive adverbs or transitional expressions**
>
> In the following paragraph, insert semicolons as needed to separate main clauses related by a conjunctive adverb or transitional expression.

Key terms

conjunctive adverb A modifier that describes the relation of the ideas in two clauses, such as *consequently, hence, however, indeed, instead, nonetheless, otherwise, still, then, therefore, thus.* (See **4** p. 286.)

transitional expression A word or phrase that shows the relationship between ideas. Transitional expressions include conjunctive adverbs as well as *for example, in fact, of course,* and many other words and phrases. (See **1** pp. 44–45.)

Also insert a comma or commas as needed to set off the adverb or expression. (You can do this exercise online at *ablongman.com/littlebrown*.)

1 Music is a form of communication like language the basic elements however are not letters but notes. 2 Computers can process any information that can be represented numerically as a result they can process musical information. 3 A computer's ability to process music depends on what software it can run it must moreover be connected to a system that converts electrical vibration into sound. 4 Computers and their sound systems can produce many different sounds indeed the number of possible sounds is infinite. 5 The powerful music computers are very expensive therefore they are used only by professional musicians.

EXERCISE 40.3   Sentence combining: Related main clauses

Combine each set of three sentences below into one sentence containing only two main clauses. As indicated in parentheses, connect the clauses with a semicolon alone or with a semicolon plus a conjunctive adverb or transitional expression followed by a comma. You will have to add, delete, change, and rearrange words. Each item has more than one possible answer. (You can do this exercise online at *ablongman.com/littlebrown*.)

Example:

The Albanians censored their news. We got little news from them. And what we got was unreliable. (*Therefore and semicolon.*)

The Albanians censored their news; therefore, the little news we got from them was unreliable.

1   Electronic instruments are prevalent in jazz. They are also prevalent in rock music. They are less common in classical music. (*However and semicolon.*)
2   Jazz and rock change rapidly. They nourish experimentation. They nourish improvisation. (*Semicolon alone.*)
3   The notes and instrumentation of traditional classical music were established by a composer. The composer was writing decades or centuries ago. Such music does not change. (*Therefore and semicolon.*)
4   Contemporary classical music not only can draw on tradition. It can also respond to innovations. These are innovations such as jazz rhythms and electronic sounds. (*Semicolon alone.*)
5   Much contemporary electronic music is more than just one type of music. It is more than just jazz, rock, or classical. It is a fusion of all three. (*Semicolon alone.*)

40c   Use semicolons between main clauses or series items containing commas.

Normally, commas separate main clauses linked by coordinating conjunctions (*and, but, or, nor*) and separate items in a series.

But when the clauses or series items contain commas, a semicolon between them makes the sentence easier to read.

> Lewis and Clark led the men of their party with consummate skill, inspiring and encouraging them, doctoring and caring for them; and they kept voluminous journals.   —Page Smith

> The custody case involved Amy Dalton, the child; Ellen and Mark Dalton, the parents; and Ruth and Hal Blum, the grandparents.

EXERCISE 40.4   Revising: Punctuation of main clauses and series items containing commas

Substitute semicolons for commas in the following paragraph to separate main clauses or series items that contain commas. (You can do this exercise online at *ablongman.com/littlebrown.*)

1 The Indian subcontinent is separated from the rest of the world by clear barriers: the Bay of Bengal and the Arabian Sea to the east and west, respectively, the Indian Ocean to the south, and 1600 miles of mountain ranges to the north. 2 In the north of India are the world's highest mountains, the Himalayas, and farther south are fertile farmlands, unpopulated deserts, and rain forests. 3 India is a nation of ethnic and linguistic diversity, with numerous religions, including Hinduism, Islam, and Christianity, with distinct castes and ethnic groups, and with sixteen languages, including the official Hindi and the "associate official" English.

40d   Delete or replace unneeded semicolons.

Too many semicolons can make writing choppy. And semicolons are often misused in certain constructions that call for other punctuation or no punctuation.

1   Not between a main clause and a subordinate clause or phrase

The semicolon does not separate unequal parts, such as main clauses and subordinate clauses or phrases.

Not   Pygmies are in danger of extinction; because of encroaching development.

But   Pygmies are in danger of extinction because of encroaching development.

Not   According to African authorities; only about 35,000 Pygmies exist today.

But   According to African authorities, only about 35,000 Pygmies exist today.

2 Not before a series or explanation

Colons and dashes, not semicolons, introduce series, explanations, and so forth. (See opposite and p. 337.)

Not Teachers have heard all sorts of reasons why students do poorly; psychological problems, family illness, too much work; too little time.

But Teachers have heard all sorts of reasons why students do poorly: psychological problems, family illness, too much work, too little time.

EXERCISE 40.5 Revising: Semicolons

In the following paragraph, insert semicolons as needed and eliminate any misused semicolons, substituting other punctuation as appropriate. If a sentence is correct as given, mark the number preceding it. (You can do this exercise online at *ablongman.com/littlebrown*.)

1 The set, sounds, and actors in the movie captured the essence of horror films. 2 The set was ideal; dark, deserted streets, trees dipping their branches over the sidewalks, mist hugging the ground and creeping up to meet the trees, looming shadows of unlighted, turreted houses. 3 The sounds, too, were appropriate, especially terrifying was the hard, hollow sound of footsteps echoing throughout the film. 4 But the best feature of the movie was its actors; all of them tall, pale, and thin to the point of emaciation. 5 With one exception, they were dressed uniformly in gray and had gray hair. 6 The exception was an actress who dressed only in black as if to set off her pale yellow, nearly white, long hair; the only color in the film. 7 The glinting black eyes of another actor stole almost every scene, indeed, they were the source of the film's mischief.

---

41 The Colon

The colon (:) is mainly a mark of introduction: it signals that the words following will explain or amplify (below). The colon also has several conventional uses, such as in expressions of time.

Note Many grammar and style checkers cannot recognize missing or misused colons and instead simply ignore them.

---

http://www.ablongman.com/littlebrown ▶

Visit the companion Web site for more help and an electronic exercise on the colon.

:

41a Use a colon to introduce a concluding explanation, series, appositive, or long or formal quotation.

As an introducer, a colon is always preceded by a complete main clause. It may or may not be followed by a main clause. This is one way the colon differs from the semicolon, which generally separates main clauses only. (See pp. 316–17.)

Explanation
Soul food has a deceptively simple definition**:** the ethnic cooking of African Americans.

Sometimes a concluding explanation is preceded by *the following* or *as follows* and a colon:

A more precise definition might be the following**:** soul food draws on ingredients, cooking methods, and dishes originating in Africa, brought to the New World by slaves, and modified or supplemented in the Caribbean and the American South.

Note A complete sentence *after* a colon may begin with a capital letter or a small letter (as in the preceding example). Just be consistent throughout an essay.

Series
At least three soul food dishes are familiar to most Americans**:** fried chicken, barbecued spareribs, and sweet potatoes.

Appositive
Soul food has only one disadvantage**:** fat.

Namely, that is, and other expressions that introduce appositives *follow* the colon: *Soul food has only one disadvantage**:** namely, fat.*

Long or formal quotation
One soul food chef has a solution**:** "Soul food doesn't have to be greasy to taste good. Instead of using ham hocks to flavor beans, I use smoked turkey wings. The soulful, smoky taste remains, but without all the fat of pork."

┌─ **Key terms** ─────────────────────────────

main clause A word group that contains a subject and a verb and does not begin with a subordinating word: *Soul food is a varied cuisine.* (See **4** p. 206.)

appositive A noun or noun substitute that renames another noun immediately before it: *my brother, Jack.* (See **4** p. 205.)

41b Use a colon after the salutation of a business letter, between a title and subtitle, and between divisions of time.

Salutation of business letter
Dear Ms. Burak**:**

Title and subtitle
*Charles Dickens***:** *An Introduction to His Novels*

Time
12**:**26 AM   6**:**00 PM

41c Delete or replace unneeded colons.

Use the colon only at the end of a main clause, not in the following situations:

- Delete a colon after a verb:

    Not   The best-known soul food dish is: fried chicken.
    But   The best-known soul food dish is fried chicken.

- Delete a colon after a preposition:

    Not   Soul food recipes can be found in: mainstream cookbooks as well as specialized references.
    But   Soul food recipes can be found in mainstream cookbooks as well as specialized references.

- Delete a colon after *such as* or *including:*

    Not   Many Americans have not tasted delicacies such as: chitlins and black-eyed peas.
    But   Many Americans have not tasted delicacies such as chitlins and black-eyed peas.

EXERCISE 41.1 Revising: Colons

In the following paragraph, insert colons as needed and delete misused colons. If a sentence is correct as given, mark the number preceding it. (You can do this exercise online at *ablongman.com/littlebrown*.)

1 In remote areas of many developing countries, simple signs mark human habitation a dirt path, a few huts, smoke from a campfire. 2 However, in the built-up sections of industrialized countries, nature is

---

┌─ **Key term** ───

preposition *In, on, outside,* or another word that takes a noun or pronoun as its object: *in the house.* (See 4 p. 193.)

all but obliterated by signs of human life, such as: houses, factories, sky-scrapers, and highways. 3 The spectacle makes many question the words of Ecclesiastes 1.4 "One generation passeth away, and another cometh; but the earth abideth forever." 4 Yet many scientists see the future differently: they hold that human beings have all the technology necessary to clean up the earth and restore the cycles of nature. 5 All that is needed is: a change in the attitudes of those who use technology.

EXERCISE 41.2   Revising: Colons and semicolons

In the following paragraphs, insert colons and semicolons as needed and delete or replace them where they are misused. If a sentence is correct as given, mark the number preceding it. (You can do this exercise online at *ablongman.com/littlebrown.*)

1 Sunlight is made up of three kinds of radiation: visible rays; infrared rays, which we cannot see; and ultraviolet rays, which are also invisible. 2 Infrared rays are the longest; measuring 700 nanometers and longer; while ultraviolet rays are the shortest; measuring 400 nano-meters and shorter. 3 Especially in the ultraviolet range; sunlight is harm-ful to the eyes. 4 Ultraviolet rays can damage the retina: furthermore, they can cause cataracts on the lens.

5 The lens protects the eye by: absorbing much of the ultraviolet radiation and thus protecting the retina. 6 Protecting the retina, how-ever, the lens becomes a victim; growing cloudy and blocking vision. 7 The best way to protect your eyes is: to wear hats that shade the face and sunglasses that screen out ultraviolet rays. 8 Many sunglass lenses have been designed as ultraviolet screens; many others are extremely ineffective. 9 If sunglass lenses do not screen out ultraviolet rays and if people can see your eyes through them, they will not protect your eyes, and you will be at risk for cataracts later in life. 10 People who spend much time outside in the sun; owe it to themselves to buy and wear sunglasses that shield their eyes.

42   The Apostrophe

The apostrophe (') appears as part of a word to indicate posses-sion (next page), the omission of one or more letters (p. 328), or sometimes plural number (p. 329).

Note Grammar and style checkers have mixed results in recog-nizing apostrophe errors. For instance, most flag missing apos-trophes in contractions (as in *isnt*), but many cannot distinguish between *its* and *it's*, *their* and *they're*, *your* and *you're*, *whose* and

http://www.ablongman.com/littlebrown ▶

Visit the companion Web site for more help and electronic exercises on the apostrophe.

who's. The checkers can identify some apostrophe errors in possessives but will overlook others and may flag correct plurals. Instead of relying on your checker, try using your computer's Search or Find function to hunt for all words you have ended in *-s.* Then check them to ensure that apostrophes are used correctly.

42a   Use the apostrophe and sometimes *-s* to form possessive nouns and indefinite pronouns.

A noun or indefinite pronoun shows possession with an apostrophe and, usually, an *-s: the dog's hair, everyone's hope.*

Note Apostrophes are easy to misuse. Always check your drafts to be sure that all words ending in *-s* neither omit needed apostrophes nor add unneeded ones. Also, remember that the apostrophe or apostrophe-plus-*s* is an *addition.* Before this addition, always spell the name of the owner or owners without dropping or adding letters.

1 Singular words: Add -'s.

Bill Boughton's skillful card tricks amaze children.

Anyone's eyes would widen.

Most tricks will pique an adult's curiosity, too.

The -'s ending for singular words pertains also to singular words ending in *-s,* as the next examples show.

Henry James's novels reward the patient reader.

The business's customers filed suit.

Exception An apostrophe alone may be added to a singular word ending in *-s* when another *s* would make the word difficult to say: *Moses' mother, Joan Rivers' jokes.* But the added *-s* is never wrong (*Moses's, Rivers's*).

2 Plural words ending in -s: Add -' only.

Workers' incomes have fallen slightly over the past year.

Many students benefit from several years' work after high school.

The Jameses' talents are extraordinary.

Note the difference in the possessives of singular and plural words ending in *-s.* The singular form usually takes *-'s: James's.* The plural takes only the apostrophe: *Jameses'.*

Key term

indefinite pronoun A pronoun that does not refer to a specific person or thing, such as *anyone, each, everybody, no one,* or *something.* (See 4 p. 253.)

Uses and misuses of the apostrophe

Uses of the apostrophe

- **Use an apostrophe to form the possessives of nouns and indefinite pronouns** (opposite).

Singular	Plural
Ms. Park's	the Parks'
lawyer's	lawyers'
everyone's	two weeks'

- **Use an apostrophe to form contractions** (p. 328).

it's a girl	shouldn't
you're	won't

- **The apostrophe is optional for plurals of abbreviations, dates, and words or characters named as words** (p. 329).

MAs or MA's	Cs or C's
1960s or 1960's	ifs or if's

Misuses of the apostrophe

- **Do not use an apostrophe plus -s to form the possessives of plural nouns ending in -s** (see opposite). Instead, use an apostrophe alone after the -s that forms the plural.

Not	But
the Kim's car	the Kims' car
boy's fathers	boys' fathers
babie's care	babies' care

- **Do not use an apostrophe to form plurals of nouns** (p. 326).

Not	But
book's are	books are
the Freed's	the Freeds

- **Do not use an apostrophe with verbs ending in -s** (p. 326).

Not	But
swim's	swims

- **Do not use an apostrophe to form the possessives of personal pronouns** (p. 326).

Not	But
it's toes	its toes
your's	yours

3 | **Plural words not ending in -s: Add -'s.**

Children's educations are at stake.

We need to attract the media's attention.

4 **Compound words: Add -'s only to the last word.**

The brother-in-law's business failed.

Taxes are always somebody else's fault.

5 **Two or more owners: Add -'s depending on possession.**

Individual possession

Zimbale's and Mason's comedy techniques are similar. [Each comedian has his own technique.]

Joint possession

The child recovered despite her mother and father's neglect. [The mother and father were jointly neglectful.]

EXERCISE 42.1 Forming possessives

Form the possessive of each word or word group in brackets. (You can do this exercise online at *ablongman.com/littlebrown*.)

Example:

The [men] blood pressures were higher than the [women].
The men's blood pressures were higher than the women's.

1 In the myths of ancient Greeks, the [goddesses] roles vary widely. 2 [Demeter] responsibility is the fruitfulness of the earth. 3 [Athena] role is to guard the city of Athens. 4 [Artemis] function is to care for wild animals and small children. 5 [Athena and Artemis] father, Zeus, is the king of the gods.

6 Even a single [goddess] responsibilities are often varied. 7 For instance, over several [centuries] time Athena changes from a [mariner] goddess to the patron of crafts. 8 She is also concerned with fertility and with [children] well-being, since the strength of Athens depended on a large and healthy population. 9 Athena often changes into [birds] forms, and in [Homer] *Odyssey*, she assumes a [sea eagle] form.

10 In ancient Athens the myths of Athena were part of [everyone] knowledge and life. 11 A cherished myth tells how she fights to retain possession of her [people] land when the god Poseidon wants it. 12 [Athena and Poseidon] skills are different, and each promises a special gift to the Athenians. 13 At the [contest] conclusion, Poseidon has given water and Athena has given an olive tree, for sustenance. 14 The other gods decide that the [Athenians] lives depend more on Athena than on Poseidon.

EXERCISE 42.2 Revising: Apostrophes with possessives

In the following paragraph, insert or reposition apostrophes as needed and delete any needless apostrophes. If a sentence is correct as given, mark the number preceding it. (You can do this exercise online at *ablongman.com/littlebrown*.)

1 The eastern coast of Belize was once a fishermans paradise, but overfishing caused the fishing industrys sharp decline in this Central American country. 2 The country's government is now showing the world that leaders' foresight can turn a problem into an opportunity. 3 Belize is capitalizing on something that can capture tourists interest: whale sharks. 4 Huge but harmless to people, whale sharks regularly visit Belizes coast to feed on smaller fishes eggs. 5 The predictable gatherings of the shark's attract large numbers of scuba diver's and snorkeler's, so that the fishs' fascinating beauty has become an economic treasure. 6 A tourists eagerness to spend money for an up-close view of whale sharks is Belizes renewable and reliable resource.

42b Delete or replace any apostrophe in a plural noun, a singular verb, or a possessive personal pronoun.

1 Plural nouns

The plurals of nouns are generally formed by adding -s or -es, never with an apostrophe: *boys, families, Joneses, Murphys.*

Not   The Jones' controlled the firm's until 2001.
But   The Joneses controlled the firms until 2001.

2 Singular verbs

Verbs ending in -s never take an apostrophe:

Not   The subway break's down less often now.
But   The subway breaks down less often now.

3 Possessives of personal pronouns

His, hers, its, ours, yours, theirs, and *whose* are possessive forms of *he, she, it, we, you, they,* and *who.* They do not take apostrophes:

Not   The house is her's. It's roof leaks.
But   The house is hers. Its roof leaks.

Don't confuse possessive pronouns with contractions. See the next page.

EXERCISE 42.3 Distinguishing between plurals and possessives

Supply the appropriate form—possessive or plural—of each word given in brackets. Some words require apostrophes, and some do not. (You can do this exercise online at *ablongman.com/littlebrown*.)

Example:
A dozen Hawaiian [shirt], each with [it] own loud design, hung in the window.
A dozen Hawaiian shirts, each with its own loud design, hung in the window.

1 Demeter may be the oldest of the ancient Greek [god], older than Zeus. 2 In myth she is the earth mother, which means that the responsibility for the fertility of both [animal] and [plant] is [she]. 3 Many prehistoric [culture] had earth [goddess] like Demeter. 4 In Greek culture the [goddess] festival came at harvest time, with [it] celebration of bounty. 5 The [people] [prayer] to Demeter thanked her for grain and other [gift].

EXERCISE 42.4   Revising: Misuses of the apostrophe

Revise the following paragraph by deleting or repositioning apostrophes or by repairing incorrect possessive pronouns or contractions. If a sentence is correct as given, mark the number preceding it. (You can do this exercise online at *ablongman.com/littlebrown*.)

1 Research is proving that athlete's who excel at distance running have physical characteristics that make them faster than most people. 2 For example, they're hearts are larger. 3 An average adult's heart pump's about fifteen liters of blood per minute, but a competitive distance runner's heart circulate's twice as much. 4 Elite runners are also more efficient: they're able to run with less work than less talented runners must exert. 5 In addition, competitive runner's are able to keep running for long time's at high levels of exertion. 6 Although these abilities can be honed in training, they cannot be acquired by a runner: they are his' or her's from birth.

EXERCISE 42.5   Revising: Contractions and personal pronouns

Revise the following paragraph to correct mistakes in the use of contractions and personal pronouns. If a sentence is correct as given, mark the number preceding it. (You can do this exercise online at *ablongman.com/littlebrown*.)

1 Roald Dahl's children's novel *James and the Giant Peach* has been enjoyed by each generation of readers since its first publication in 1961. 2 Its a magical story of adventure and friendship. 3 James, a lonely boy whose being raised by his two nasty aunts, accidentally drops some mysterious crystals by an old peach tree in the yard. 4 The peach at the very top grows to an enormous size, and when James crawls inside, he finds friendly, oversized bugs ready to welcome him into there family. 5 As the peach breaks from the tree and rolls into the ocean, their plunged into an adventure that takes them to the top of the Empire State Building.

42c   Use the apostrophe to form contractions.

A **contraction** replaces one or more letters, numbers, or words with an apostrophe, as in the following examples:

it is, it has	it's	you are	you're
they are	they're	who is, who has	who's

cannot	can't		were not	weren't
does not	doesn't		class of 2009	class of '09

Note Don't confuse contractions with personal pronouns:

Contractions	Personal pronouns
It's a book.	Its cover is green.
They're coming.	Their car broke down.
You're right.	Your idea is good.
Who's coming?	Whose party is it?

EXERCISE 42.6 Forming contractions

Form contractions from each set of words below. Use each contraction in a complete sentence. (You can do this exercise online at *ablongman.com/littlebrown.*)

Example:
we are: we're
We're open to ideas.

1 she would
2 could not
3 they are
4 he is
5 do not

6 she will
7 hurricane of 1962
8 is not
9 it is
10 will not

EXERCISE 42.7 Revising: Contractions and personal pronouns

Revise the following paragraph to correct mistakes in the use of contractions and personal pronouns. If a sentence is correct as given, mark the number preceding it. (You can do this exercise online at *ablongman.com/littlebrown.*)

1 In Greek myth the goddess Demeter has a special fondness for Eleusis, near Athens, and it's people. 2 She finds rest among the people and is touched by their kindness. 3 As a reward Demeter gives the Eleusians the secret for making they're land fruitful. 4 The Eleusians begin a cult in honor of Demeter, whose worshiped in secret ceremonies. 5 Its unknown what happened in the ceremonies, for no participant ever revealed there rituals.

42d Increasingly, the apostrophe does not mark plural abbreviations, dates, and words or characters named as words.

You'll sometimes see apostrophes used to form the plurals of abbreviations (BA's), dates (1900's), and words or characters named as words (*but*'s). However, most current style guides recommend against the apostrophe in these cases.

BAs   PhDs
1990s   2000s

The sentence has too many *buts* [or <u>buts</u>].
Two *3s* [or <u>3s</u>] end the zip code.

Note Underline or italicize a word or character named as a word (see **6** p. 361), but not the added -*s*.

EXERCISE 42.8   Revising: Apostrophes

Revise the following paragraph to correct mistakes in the use of apostrophes or any confusion between contractions and possessive personal pronouns. If a sentence is correct as given, mark the number preceding it. (You can do this exercise online at *ablongman.com/littlebrown*.)

1 Landlocked Chad is among the worlds most troubled countries. 2 The people's of Chad are poor: they're average per capita income equals $1000 per year. 3 Less than half of Chads population is literate, and every five hundred people must share only two teacher's. 4 The natural resources of the nation have never been plentiful, and now, as it's slowly being absorbed into the growing Sahara Desert, even water is scarce. 5 Chads political conflicts go back to the nineteenth century, when the French colonized the land by brutally subduing it's people. 6 The rule of the French—who's inept government of the colony did nothing to ease tensions among racial, tribal, and religious group's—ended with independence in 1960. 7 But since then the Chadians experience has been one of civil war and oppression, and their also threatened with invasions from they're neighbors.

---

43 Quotation Marks

Quotation marks—either double (" ") or single (' ')—mainly enclose direct quotations from speech or writing, enclose certain titles, and highlight words used in a special sense. These are the uses covered in this chapter, along with placing quotation marks outside or inside other punctuation marks. Additional information on using quotations appears elsewhere in this book:

- Using commas with signal phrases introducing quotations. See pp. 311–12.

---

http://www.ablongman.com/littlebrown ▶

Visit the companion Web site for more help and an electronic exercise on quotation marks.

- Using brackets and the ellipsis mark to indicate changes in quotations. See pp. 339–41.
- Quoting sources versus paraphrasing or summarizing them. See 7 pp. 411–12.
- Integrating quotations into your text. See 7 pp. 413–18.
- Acknowledging the sources of quotations to avoid plagiarism. See 7 pp. 422–23.
- Formatting long prose quotations and poetry quotations. See MLA pp. 497–98 and APA p. 525.

Note Always use quotation marks in pairs, one at the beginning of a quotation and one at the end. Some grammar and style checkers will help you use quotation marks in pairs by flagging a lone mark. Most checkers can also be set to ignore other punctuation with quotations or to look for punctuation inside or outside quotation marks, but they may not detect errors when punctuation should actually fall outside quotation marks.

43a Use double quotation marks to enclose direct quotations.

A **direct quotation** reports what someone said or wrote, in the exact words of the original:

> "Life," said the psychoanalyst Karen Horney, "remains a very efficient therapist."

Note Do not use quotation marks with a direct quotation that is set off from your text. See MLA pp. 497–98 and APA p. 525. Also do not use quotation marks with an **indirect quotation**, which reports what someone said or wrote but not in the exact words.

> The psychoanalyst Karen Horney claimed that life is a good therapist.

43b Use single quotation marks to enclose a quotation within a quotation.

> "In formulating any philosophy," Woody Allen writes, "the first consideration must always be: What can we know? Descartes hinted at the problem when he wrote, 'My mind can never know my body, although it has become quite friendly with my leg.'"

Notice that two different quotation marks appear at the end of the sentence—one single (to finish the interior quotation) and one double (to finish the main quotation).

EXERCISE 43.1   Revising: Double and single quotation marks

Insert double and single quotation marks as needed in the following sentences. Mark the number preceding any sentence that is already correct. (You can do this exercise online at *ablongman.com/littlebrown*.)

1 Why, the lecturer asked, do we say Bless you! or something else when people sneeze but not acknowledge coughs, hiccups, and other eruptions?

2 She said that sneezes have always been regarded differently.

3 Sneezes feel more uncontrollable than some other eruptions, she said.

4 Unlike coughs and hiccups, she explained, sneezes feel as if they come from inside the head.

5 She concluded, People thus wish to recognize a sneeze, if only with a Gosh.

43c   Set off quotations of dialog according to standard practice.

When quoting conversations, begin a new paragraph for each speaker.

"What shall I call you? Your name?" Andrews whispered rapidly, as with a high squeak the latch of the door rose.

"Elizabeth," she said. "Elizabeth."

—Graham Greene, *The Man Within*

When you quote a single speaker for more than one paragraph, put quotation marks at the beginning of each paragraph but at the end of only the last paragraph.

43d   Put quotation marks around the titles of works that are parts of other works.

Use quotation marks to enclose the titles of works that are published or released within larger works. (See the following box.) Use single quotation marks for a quotation within a quoted title, as in the article title and essay title in the box. And enclose all punctuation in the title within the quotation marks, as in the article title.

Titles to be enclosed in quotation marks

Other titles should be underlined or italicized. (See 6 p. 360.)

Song
"The Star-Spangled Banner"

Short poem
"Mending Wall"

Short story
"The Gift of the Magi"

Article in periodical
"Does 'Scaring' Work?"

Essay	Episode of a television or radio program
"Joey: A 'Mechanical Boy'"	"The Mexican Connection" (on 60 Minutes)
Page or document on a Web site	**Subdivision of a book**
"Readers' Page" (on the site Friends of Prufrock)	"The Mast Head" (Chapter 35 of Moby-Dick)

Note Some academic disciplines do not require quotation marks for titles within source citations. See APA pp. 512–22 and CSE pp. 546–50.

EXERCISE 43.2   Revising: Quotation marks for titles

Insert quotation marks as needed for titles and words in the following sentences. If quotation marks should be used instead of underlining, insert them. (You can do this exercise online at *ablongman.com/littlebrown.*)

1 In Chapter 8, titled How to Be Interesting, the author explains the art of conversation.
2 The Beatles' song Let It Be reminds Martin of his uncle.
3 The article that appeared in Mental Health was titled Children of Divorce Ask, "Why?"
4 In the encyclopedia the discussion under Modern Art fills less than a column.
5 One prizewinning essay, Cowgirls on Wall Street, first appeared in Entrepreneur magazine.

43e Quotation marks may enclose words being used in a special sense.

On movie sets movable "wild walls" make a one-walled room seem four-walled on film.

Note Use underlining or italics for defined words. (See 6 p. 361.)

43f Delete quotation marks where they are not required.

Title of your paper
Not   "The Death Wish in One Poem by Robert Frost"
But   The Death Wish in One Poem by Robert Frost
Or   The Death Wish in "Stopping by Woods on a Snowy Evening"

Common nickname

Not   As President, "Jimmy" Carter preferred to use his nickname.

But   As President, Jimmy Carter preferred to use his nickname.

Slang or trite expression

Quotation marks will not excuse slang or a trite expression that is inappropriate to your writing. If slang is appropriate, use it without quotation marks.

Not   We should support the President in his "hour of need" rather than "wimp out on him."

But   We should give the President the support he needs rather than turn away like cowards.

43g Place other punctuation marks inside or outside quotation marks according to standard practice.

1 Commas and periods: Inside quotation marks

Swift uses irony in his essay "A Modest Proposal."

Many first-time readers are shocked to see infants described as "delicious."

"'A Modest Proposal,'" writes one critic, "is so outrageous that it cannot be believed."

Exception When a parenthetical source citation immediately follows a quotation, place any period or comma *after* the citation.

One critic calls the essay "outrageous" (Olms 26).

Partly because of "the cool calculation of its delivery" (Olms 27), Swift's satire still chills a modern reader.

2 Colons and semicolons: Outside quotation marks

A few years ago the slogan in elementary education was "learning by playing"; now educators are concerned with basic skills.

We all know what is meant by "inflation": more money buys less.

3 Dashes, question marks, and exclamation points: Inside quotation marks only if part of the quotation

When a dash, question mark, or exclamation point is part of the quotation, place it *inside* quotation marks. Don't use any other punctuation, such as a period or comma:

"But must you—" Marcia hesitated, afraid of the answer.

"Go away!" I yelled.

Did you say, "Who is she?" [When both your sentence and the quotation would end in a question mark or exclamation point, use only the mark in the quotation.]

When a dash, question mark, or exclamation point applies only to the larger sentence, not to the quotation, place it *outside* quotation marks—again, with no other punctuation:

One evocative line in English poetry—"After many a summer dies the swan"—comes from Alfred, Lord Tennyson.

Who said, "Now cracks a noble heart"?

The woman called me "stupid"!

EXERCISE 43.3 Revising: Quotation marks

Some of the underlined words in the following paragraph are direct quotations or should be quoted titles. Remove incorrect underlining, and insert quotation marks. Be sure that other marks of punctuation are correctly placed inside or outside the quotation marks. (You can do this exercise online at *ablongman.com/littlebrown.*)

1 In the title essay of her book The Death of the Moth and Other Essays, Virginia Woolf describes the last moments of a frail and diminutive body. 2 An insect's death may seem insignificant, but the moth is, in Woolf's words, life, a pure bead. 3 The moth's struggle against death, indifferent, impersonal, is heroic. 4 Where else but in such a bit of life could one see a protest so superb? 5 At the end of The Death of the Moth, Woolf sees the insect lying most decently and uncomplainingly composed; in death it finds dignity.

EXERCISE 43.4 Revising: Quotation marks

Insert quotation marks as needed in the following paragraph. If a sentence is correct as given, mark the number preceding it. (You can do this exercise online at *ablongman.com/littlebrown.*)

1 In one class we talked about a passage from I Have a Dream, the speech delivered by Martin Luther King, Jr., on the steps of the Lincoln Memorial on August 28, 1963:

2 When the architects of our republic wrote the magnificent words of the Constitution and the Declaration of Independence, they were signing a promissory note to which every American was to fall heir. 3 This note was a promise that all men would be guaranteed the unalienable rights of life, liberty, and the pursuit of happiness.

4 What did Dr. King mean by this statement? the teacher asked. 5 Perhaps we should define promissory note first. 6 Then she explained that a person who signs such a note agrees to pay a specific sum of money on a particular date or on demand by the holder of the note. 7 One student suggested, Maybe Dr. King meant that the writers of the Constitution and Declaration promised that all people in America should be equal. 8 He and over 200,000 people had gathered in Washington, DC, added another student. 9 Maybe their purpose was to demand payment, to demand those rights for African Americans. 10 The whole discussion was an eye-opener for those of us (including me) who had never considered that those documents make promises that we should expect our country to fulfill.

44 Other Marks

The other marks of punctuation are the dash (below), parentheses (opposite), the ellipsis mark (p. 339), brackets (p. 341), and the slash (p. 342).

Note Many grammar and style checkers will flag a lone parenthesis or bracket so that you can match it with another parenthesis or bracket. But most checkers cannot recognize other misuses of the marks covered here and instead simply ignore the marks.

44a   Use the dash or dashes to indicate shifts and to set off some sentence elements.

The dash (—) is mainly a mark of interruption: it signals a shift, insertion, or break. In your papers, form a dash with two hyphens (--) or use the character called an em dash on your word processor. Do not add extra space around or between the hyphens or around the em dash.

Note When an interrupting element starting with a dash falls in the middle of a sentence, be sure to add the closing dash to signal the end of the interruption. See the first example below.

1 Shifts in tone or thought

The novel—if one can call it that—appeared in 2005.
If the book had a plot—but a plot would be conventional.

2 Nonessential elements

Dashes may be used instead of commas to set off and emphasize modifiers, parenthetical expressions, and other nonessential elements, especially when these elements are internally punctuated:

The qualities Monet painted—sunlight, rich shadows, deep colors— abounded near the rivers and gardens he used as subjects.

Key term

nonessential element Gives added information but does not limit the word it refers to. (See pp. 303–06.)

---

http://www.ablongman.com/littlebrown ▶

Visit the companion Web site for more help and electronic exercises on the dash, parentheses, the ellipsis mark, brackets, and the slash.

Though they are close together—separated by only a few blocks—the two neighborhoods could be in different countries.

3 Introductory series and concluding series and explanations

Shortness of breath, skin discoloration or the sudden appearance of moles, persistent indigestion, the presence of small lumps—all these may signify cancer. [Introductory series.]

The patient undergoes a battery of tests—CAT scan, bronchoscopy, perhaps even biopsy. [Concluding series.]

Many patients are disturbed by the CAT scan—by the need to keep still for long periods in an exceedingly small space. [Concluding explanation.]

A colon could be used instead of a dash in the last two examples. The dash is more informal.

4 Overuse

Too many dashes can make writing jumpy or breathy:

Not   In all his life—eighty-seven years—my great-grandfather never allowed his picture to be taken—not even once. He claimed the "black box"—the camera—would steal his soul.

But   In all his eighty-seven years, my great-grandfather did not allow his picture to be taken even once. He claimed the "black box"—the camera—would steal his soul.

EXERCISE 44.1   Revising: Dashes

Insert dashes as needed in the following paragraph. (You can do this exercise online at *ablongman.com/littlebrown.*)

1 The movie-theater business is undergoing dramatic changes changes that may affect what movies are made and shown. 2 The closing of independent theaters, the control of theaters by fewer and fewer owners, and the increasing ownership of theaters by movie studios and distributors these changes may reduce the availability of noncommercial films. 3 Yet at the same time the number of movie screens is increasing primarily in multiscreen complexes so that smaller films may find more outlets. 4 The number of active movie screens that is, screens showing films or booked to do so is higher now than at any time since World War II. 5 The biggest theater complexes seem to be something else as well art galleries, amusement arcades, restaurants, spectacles.

44b   Use parentheses to enclose parenthetical expressions and labels for lists within sentences.

Note Parentheses *always* come in pairs, one before and one after the punctuated material.

1 Parenthetical expressions

Parenthetical expressions include explanations, facts, digressions, and examples that may be helpful or interesting but are not essential to meaning. Parentheses de-emphasize parenthetical expressions. (Commas emphasize them more than parentheses do, and dashes emphasize them still more.)

> The population of Philadelphia (now about 1.5 million) has declined since 1950.

Note Don't put a comma before a parenthetical expression enclosed in parentheses. Punctuation after the parenthetical expression should be placed outside the closing parenthesis.

> Not   Philadelphia's population compares with Houston's, (just over 1.6 million.)
> But   Philadelphia's population compares with Houston's (just over 1.6 million).

When it falls between other complete sentences, a complete sentence enclosed in parentheses begins with a capital letter and ends with a period.

> In general, coaches will tell you that scouts are just guys who can't coach. (But then, so are brain surgeons.)
>   —Roy Blount

2 Labels for lists within sentences

> Outside the Middle East, the countries with the largest oil reserves are (1) Venezuela (63 billion barrels), (2) Russia (57 billion barrels), and (3) Mexico (51 billion barrels).

When you set a list off from your text, do not enclose such labels in parentheses.

EXERCISE 44.2   Revising: Parentheses

Insert parentheses around parenthetical expressions in the following paragraph. (You can do this exercise online at *ablongman.com/littlebrown*.)

1 Many of those involved in the movie business agree that multiscreen complexes are good for two reasons: 1 they cut the costs of exhibitors, and 2 they offer more choices to audiences. 2 However, those who produce and distribute films and not just the big studios argue that the multiscreen theaters give exhibitors too much power. 3 The major studios are buying movie theaters to gain control over important parts of the distribution process what gets shown and for how much money. 4 For twelve years 1938–50 the federal government forced the studios to sell all their movie theaters. 5 But because they now have more competition television and DVD players, for instance, the studios are permitted to own theaters.

44c Use the ellipsis mark to indicate omissions from quotations.

The ellipsis mark, consisting of three spaced periods (. . .), generally indicates an omission from a quotation. All the following examples quote from this passage about environmentalism:

Original quotation

"At the heart of the environmentalist world view is the conviction that human physical and spiritual health depends on sustaining the planet in a relatively unaltered state. Earth is our home in the full, genetic sense, where humanity and its ancestors existed for all the millions of years of their evolution. Natural ecosystems—forests, coral reefs, marine blue waters—maintain the world exactly as we would wish it to be maintained. When we debase the global environment and extinguish the variety of life, we are dismantling a support system that is too complex to understand, let alone replace, in the foreseeable future."

—Edward O. Wilson, "Is Humanity Suicidal?"

1. Omission of the middle of a sentence

"Natural ecosystems . . . maintain the world exactly as we would wish it to be maintained."

2. Omission of the end of a sentence, without source citation

"Earth is our home. . . ." [The sentence period, closed up to the last word, precedes the ellipsis mark.]

3. Omission of the end of a sentence, with source citation

"Earth is our home . . ." (Wilson 27). [The sentence period follows the source citation.]

4. Omission of parts of two or more sentences

Wilson writes, "At the heart of the environmentalist world view is the conviction that human physical and spiritual health depends on sustaining the planet . . . where humanity and its ancestors existed for all the millions of years of their evolution."

5. Omission of one or more sentences

As Wilson puts it, "At the heart of the environmentalist world view is the conviction that human physical and spiritual health depends on sustaining the planet in a relatively unaltered state. . . . When we debase the global environment and extinguish the variety of life, we are dismantling a support system that is too complex to understand, let alone replace, in the foreseeable future."

6. Omission from the middle of a sentence through the end of another sentence

"Earth is our home. . . . When we debase the global environment and extinguish the variety of life, we are dismantling a support system that is too complex to understand, let alone replace, in the foreseeable future."

7. Omission of the beginning of a sentence, leaving a complete sentence

a. Bracketed capital letter

"[H]uman physical and spiritual health," Wilson writes, "depends on sustaining the planet in a relatively unaltered state." [No ellipsis mark is needed because the brackets around the *H* indicate that the letter was not capitalized originally and thus that the beginning of the sentence has been omitted.]

b. Small letter

According to Wilson, "human physical and spiritual health depends on sustaining the planet in a relatively unaltered state." [No ellipsis mark is needed because the small *h* indicates that the beginning of the sentence has been omitted.]

c. Capital letter from the original

Hami comments, ". . . Wilson argues eloquently for the environmentalist world view." [An ellipsis mark *is* needed because the quoted part of the sentence begins with a capital letter and it is not clear that the beginning of the original sentence has been omitted.]

8. Use of a word or phrase

Wilson describes the earth as "our home." [No ellipsis mark needed.]

Note these features of the examples:

- **Use an ellipsis mark when it is not otherwise clear that you have left out material from the source,** as when you omit one or more sentences (examples 5 and 6) or when the words you quote form a complete sentence that is different in the original (examples 1–4 and 7c).

- **You don't need an ellipsis mark when it is obvious that you have omitted something,** such as when capitalization indicates omission (examples 7a and 7b) or when a phrase clearly comes from a larger sentence (example 8).

- **Place an ellipsis mark after a sentence period** *except* **when a parenthetical source citation follows the quotation,** as in example 3. Then the sentence period falls after the citation.

If you omit one or more lines of poetry or paragraphs of prose from a quotation, use a separate line of ellipsis marks across the full width of the quotation to show the omission.

In "Song: Love Armed" from 1676, Aphra Behn contrasts two lovers' experiences of a romance:

> Love in fantastic triumph sate,
>   Whilst bleeding hearts around him flowed,
>
> . . . .

> But my poor heart alone is harmed,
>> Whilst thine the victor is, and free. (lines 1-2, 15-16)

(See **MLA** pp. 497–98 for the format of displayed quotations like this one.)

EXERCISE 44.3 Using ellipsis marks

Use ellipsis marks and any other needed punctuation to follow the numbered instructions for quoting from the following paragraph. (You can do this exercise online at *ablongman.com/littlebrown*.)

> Women in the sixteenth and seventeenth centuries were educated in the home and, in some cases, in boarding schools. Men were educated at home, in grammar schools, and at the universities. The universities were closed to female students. For women, "learning the Bible," as Elizabeth Joceline puts it, was an impetus to learning to read. To be able to read the Bible in the vernacular was a liberating experience that freed the reader from hearing only the set passages read in the church and interpreted by the church. A Protestant woman was expected to read the scriptures daily, to meditate on them, and to memorize portions of them. In addition, a woman was expected to instruct her entire household in "learning the Bible" by holding instructional and devotional times each day for all household members, including the servants.
> —Charlotte F. Otten, *English Women's Voices, 1540–1700*

1 Quote the fifth sentence, but omit everything from *that freed the reader* to the end.
2 Quote the fifth sentence, but omit the words *was a liberating experience that.*
3 Quote the first and sixth sentences.

44d Use brackets to indicate changes in quotations.

Brackets have specialized uses in mathematical equations, but their main use for all kinds of writing is to indicate that you have altered a quotation to explain, clarify, or correct it.

> "That Texaco station [just outside Chicago] is one of the busiest in the nation," said a company spokesperson.

The word *sic* (Latin for "in this manner") in brackets indicates that an error in the quotation appeared in the original and was not made by you. Do not underline or italicize *sic* in brackets.

> According to the newspaper report, "The car slammed thru [sic] the railing and into oncoming traffic."

Do not use *sic* to make fun of a writer or to note errors in a passage that is clearly nonstandard.

44e Other marks

44e Use the slash between options, between lines of poetry run into the text, and in electronic addresses.

Option
Some teachers oppose pass/fail courses.

Poetry
Many readers have sensed a reluctant turn away from death in Frost's lines "The woods are lovely, dark and deep, / But I have promises to keep" (13–14).

When separating lines of poetry in this way, leave a space before and after the slash. (See **MLA** pp. 497–98 for more on quoting poetry.)

Electronic addresses
http://www.stanford.edu/depts/spc/spc.html

EXERCISE 44.4   Revising: Dashes, parentheses, ellipsis marks, brackets, slashes

Insert dashes, parentheses, ellipsis marks, brackets, or slashes as needed in the following paragraph. In some cases, two or more different marks could be correct. (You can do this exercise online at *ablongman.com/littlebrown.*)

1 "Let all the learned say what they can, 'Tis ready money makes the man." 2 These two lines of poetry by the Englishman William Somerville 1645–1742 may apply to a current American economic problem. 3 Non-American investors with "ready money" pour some of it as much as $1.3 trillion in recent years into the United States. 4 Stocks and bonds, savings deposits, service companies, factories, artworks, political campaigns the investments of foreigners are varied and grow more numerous every day. 5 Proponents of foreign investment argue that it revives industry, strengthens the economy, creates jobs more than 3 million, they say, and encourages free trade among nations. 6 Opponents caution that the risks associated with heavy foreign investment namely decreased profits at home and increased political influence from outside may ultimately weaken the economy. 7 On both sides, it seems, "the learned say, 'Tis ready money makes the man or country." 8 The question is, whose money theirs or ours?

PART **6**

Spelling and Mechanics

PART **6**

Spelling and Mechanics

45 Spelling and the Hyphen

You can train yourself to spell better, and this chapter will tell you how. But you can improve instantly by acquiring three habits:

- Carefully proofread your writing.
- Cultivate a healthy suspicion of your spellings.
- Check a dictionary *every time* you doubt a spelling.

Note A spelling checker can help you find and track spelling errors in your papers. But its usefulness is limited, mainly because it can't spot the confusion of words with similar spellings, such as *now/not, to/too,* and *their/they're/there.* See 1 pp. 31–32 for more on spelling checkers.

45a   Anticipate typical spelling problems.

Certain situations, such as misleading pronunciation, commonly lead to misspelling.

1 Pronunciation

In English, pronunciation of words is an unreliable guide to how they are spelled. Pronunciation is especially misleading with **homonyms,** words pronounced the same but spelled differently. Some homonyms and near-homonyms appear in the following box.

Words commonly confused

accept (to receive)
except (other than)

affect (to have an influence on)
effect (result)

all ready (prepared)
already (by this time)

allusion (indirect reference)
illusion (erroneous belief or
    perception)

ascent (a movement up)
assent (agreement)

bare (unclothed)
bear (to carry, or an animal)

board (a plane of wood)
bored (uninterested)

brake (stop)
break (smash)

(continued)

http://www.ablongman.com/littlebrown

Visit the companion Web site for more help and electronic exercises on spelling and the hyphen.

Words commonly confused

(continued)

buy (purchase)
by (next to)

cite (to quote an authority)
sight (the ability to see)
site (a place)

desert (to abandon)
dessert (after-dinner course)

discreet (reserved, respectful)
discrete (individual, distinct)

fair (average, or lovely)
fare (a fee for transportation)

forth (forward)
fourth (after *third*)

hear (to perceive by ear)
here (in this place)

heard (past tense of *hear*)
herd (a group of animals)

hole (an opening)
whole (complete)

its (possessive of *it*)
it's (contraction of *it is* or *it has*)

know (to be certain)
no (the opposite of *yes*)

loose (not attached)
lose (misplace)

meat (flesh)
meet (encounter)

passed (past tense of *pass*)
past (after, or a time gone by)

patience (forbearance)
patients (persons under medical
    care)

peace (the absence of war)
piece (a portion of something)

plain (clear)
plane (a carpenter's tool, or an
    airborne vehicle)

presence (the state of being at
    hand)
presents (gifts)

principal (most important, or the
    head of a school)
principle (a basic truth or law)

rain (precipitation)
reign (to rule)
rein (a strap for an animal)

right (correct)
rite (a religious ceremony)
write (to make letters)

road (a surface for driving)
rode (past tense of *ride*)

scene (where an action occurs)
seen (past participle of *see*)

stationary (unmoving)
stationery (writing paper)

their (possessive of *they*)
there (opposite of *here*)
they're (contraction of *they are*)

to (toward)
too (also)
two (following *one*)

waist (the middle of the body)
waste (discarded material)

weak (not strong)
week (Sunday through Saturday)

weather (climate)
whether (*if*, or introducing a
    choice)

which (one of a group)
witch (a sorcerer)

who's (contraction of *who is* or
    who has)
whose (possessive of *who*)

your (possessive of *you*)
you're (contraction of *you are*)

2 Different forms of the same word

Often, the noun form and the verb form of the same word are spelled differently: for example, *advice* (noun) and *advise* (verb). Sometimes the noun and the adjective forms of the same word differ: *height* and *high*. Similar changes occur in the parts of some irregular verbs (*know, knew, known*) and the plurals of irregular nouns (*man, men*).

3 American vs. British spellings ⟨ CULTURE LANGUAGE ⟩

If you learned English outside the United States, you may be accustomed to British rather than American spellings. Here are the chief differences:

American	British
color, humor	colour, humour
theater, center	theatre, centre
canceled, traveled	cancelled, travelled
judgment	judgement
realize, civilize	realise, civilise
connection	connexion

Your dictionary may list both spellings, but it will specially mark the British one with *chiefly Brit* or a similar label.

45b Follow spelling rules.

1 *ie* vs. *ei*

To distinguish between *ie* and *ei*, use the familiar jingle:

I before *e*, except after *c*, or when pronounced "ay" as in *neighbor* and *weigh*.

i before *e*	believe	thief	hygiene
ei after *c*	ceiling	conceive	perceive
ei sounded as "ay"	sleigh	eight	beige

Exceptions For some exceptions, remember this sentence:

The weird foreigner neither seizes leisure nor forfeits height.

EXERCISE 45.1 Distinguishing between *ie* and *ei*

Insert *ie* or *ei* in the words below. Check doubtful spellings in a dictionary. (You can do this exercise online at *ablongman.com/littlebrown*.)

1 br__f	5 for__gn	9 l__surely	13 h__ght
2 dec__ve	6 pr__st	10 ach__ve	14 fr__ght
3 rec__pt	7 gr__vance	11 pat__nce	15 f__nt
4 s__ze	8 f__nd	12 p__rce	16 s__ve

EXERCISE 45.2 Revising: *ie* and *ei*

In the following paragraph, revise any incorrect spellings of words with *ie* or *ei*. If a sentence is correct as given, mark the number preceding it. (You can do this exercise online at *ablongman.com/littlebrown.*)

1 Many people perceive donating blood as a rewarding experience. 2 Giving blood is niether painful nor wierd, although many people beleive it is both. 3 It takes a leisurely half hour or so, and it gives one a feeling of having acheived something. 4 In truth, there is a slight sting when the needle is inserted into the vien, so the best thing to do then is to focus on something else, like the cieling. 5 After donating blood once, you can expect to receive regular invitations from the blood center to give blood again.

2 Final *e*

When adding an ending to a word with a final *e*, drop the *e* if the ending begins with a vowel:

advise + able = advisable   surprise + ing = surprising

Keep the *e* if the ending begins with a consonant:

care + ful = careful   like + ly = likely

Exceptions Retain the *e* after a soft *c* or *g*, to keep the sound of the consonant soft rather than hard: *courageous, changeable.* And drop the *e* before a consonant when the *e* is preceded by another vowel: *argue + ment = argument, true + ly = truly.*

EXERCISE 45.3 Keeping or dropping a final *e*

Combine the following words and endings, keeping or dropping a final *e* as necessary to make correctly spelled words. Check doubtful spellings in a dictionary. (You can do this exercise online at *ablongman.com/littlebrown.*)

1 malice + ious   4 retire + ment   7 note + able
2 love + able   5 sue + ing   8 battle + ing
3 service + able   6 virtue + ous   9 suspense + ion

EXERCISE 45.4 Revising: Final *e*

In the following paragraph, revise any incorrect changes in words with a final *e*. If a sentence is correct as given, mark the number preceding it. (You can do this exercise online at *ablongman.com/littlebrown.*)

1 For decades scientists have been secureing metal and plastic bands to the flippers of penguins and useing the numbered bands to observe the birds' behavior. 2 Recently, a five-year study produced truely convinceing evidence that the bands themselves are influenceing the penguins' behavior. 3 For instance, banded penguins are less likly to produce offspring. 4 The researchers recommended replacing the bands with tiny electronic devices implanted under the birds' skin.

3 Final *y*

When adding an ending to a word with a final *y*, change the *y* to *i* if it follows a consonant:

beauty, beaut<u>i</u>es   worry, worried   supply, suppl<u>i</u>es

But keep the *y* if it follows a vowel, if it ends a proper name, or if the ending is *-ing:*

day, da<u>y</u>s   Minsky, Minsk<u>y</u>s   cry, cr<u>y</u>ing

---

EXERCISE 45.5   Keeping or dropping a final *y*

Combine the following words and endings, changing or keeping a final *y* as necessary to make correctly spelled words. Check doubtful spellings in a dictionary. (You can do this exercise online at *ablongman.com/ littlebrown.*)

1 imply + s	4 delay + ing	7 solidify + s
2 messy + er	5 defy + ance	8 Murphy + s
3 apply + ing	6 say + s	9 supply + ed

EXERCISE 45.6   Revising: Final *y*

In the following paragraph, revise any incorrect changes in words with a final *y*. If a sentence is correct as given, mark the number preceding it. (You can do this exercise online at *ablongman.com/littlebrown.*)

1 My neighbor, Mr. Sorsky, often says he is worryed about his job. 2 However, today's harryed white-collar workers, like Mr. Sorsky, have a much easyer situation than did workers of a hundred years ago. 3 Most men used to work in such industrys as farming, mining, and steelworking, in which job loss and injurys were common. 4 Women often worked in low-paying jobs as domestics or millworkers. 5 Many of today's working poor still labor in such triing situations. 6 Perhaps the middle-class Mr. Sorskies of the world should count their blessings instead of complaining about their troubles.

4 Final consonants

When adding an ending to a one-syllable word ending in a consonant, double the final consonant when it follows a single vowel. Otherwise, don't double the consonant.

slap, slap<u>p</u>ing   park, parking   pair, paired

In words of more than one syllable, double the final consonant when it follows a single vowel *and* when it ends a stressed syllable once the new ending is added. Otherwise, don't double the consonant.

refer, refer<u>r</u>ing   refer, reference   relent, relent<u>ed</u>

EXERCISE 45.7 Doubling consonants

Combine the following words and endings, doubling final consonants as necessary to make correctly spelled words. Check doubtful spellings in a dictionary. (You can do this exercise online at a*blongman.com/littlebrown.*)

1 repair + ing
2 admit + ance
3 benefit + ed
4 shop + ed
5 conceal + ed
6 allot + ed
7 drip + ing
8 declaim + ed
9 parallel + ing

EXERCISE 45.8 Revising: Consonants

In the following paragraph, revise any incorrect changes in words ending in consonants. If a sentence is correct as given, mark the number preceding it. (You can do this exercise online at a*blongman.com/littlebrown.*)

1 People have always been charmmed by the idea of walking on water. 2 A new device, the W Boat, finaly allows just that. 3 By pairring two connected, buoyant platforms, the inventor of the W Boat created something like long, floatting snowshoes for use on water. 4 Fiting the W Boat technology to everyday use, the inventor also developped a "paddle-skiing" device, which allows a person to paddle while standing. 5 Now strolling on water, as many have dreamed of doing, is an actuality.

5 Prefixes

When adding a prefix, do not drop a letter from or add a letter to the original word:

unnecessary   disappoint   misspell

EXERCISE 45.9 Attaching prefixes

Combine the following prefixes and words to make correctly spelled words. Check doubtful spellings in a dictionary. (You can do this exercise online at *ablongman.com/littlebrown.*)

1 mis + place
2 self + conscious
3 dis + service
4 pre + conception
5 anti + American
6 un + fold
7 dis + charge
8 mis + shape
9 under + run

EXERCISE 45.10 Revising: Prefixes

In the following paragraph, revise any incorrect spellings of words with prefixes. If a sentence is correct as given, mark the number preceding it. (You can do this exercise online at *ablongman.com/littlebrown.*)

1 People often seem to regard bacteria as somehow unatural intruders in human biology. 2 This notion is missinformed, however. 3 Even though it seems ilogical, most bacteria in fact improve health and prolong life. 4 The health benefits of antibacterial soaps and cleaners are overrated. 5 In most situations such products are unecessary to fight disease, and they can kill bacteria we require. 6 The best yet most underated way to kill harmful bacteria is simple, thorough, and frequent handwashing.

6 Plurals

Most nouns form plurals by adding *s* to the singular form. Add *es* for the plural of nouns ending in *s, sh, ch,* or *x*.

boy, boy<u>s</u>   kiss, kiss<u>es</u>   church, church<u>es</u>

Nouns ending in *o* preceded by a vowel usually form the plural with *s*. Those ending in *o* preceded by a consonant usually form the plural with *es*.

ratio, ratio<u>s</u>   hero, hero<u>es</u>

Some very common nouns form irregular plurals.

child, child<u>ren</u>   woman, wom<u>en</u>   mouse, m<u>ice</u>

Some English nouns that were originally Italian, Greek, Latin, or French form the plural according to their original language:

analysis, analyse<u>s</u>	criterion, criteri<u>a</u>	piano, piano<u>s</u>
basis, base<u>s</u>	datum, dat<u>a</u>	thesis, these<u>s</u>
crisis, crise<u>s</u>	medium, medi<u>a</u>	

A few such nouns may form irregular *or* regular plurals: for instance, *index, ind<u>ices</u>, index<u>es</u>; curriculum, curricul<u>a</u>, curriculum<u>s</u>.* The regular plural is more contemporary.

With compound nouns, add *s* to the main word of the compound. Sometimes this main word is not the last word.

city-state<u>s</u>   fathers-in-law   passersby

❝ CULTURE LANGUAGE ❞ Noncount nouns do not form plurals, either regularly (with an added *s*) or irregularly. Examples of noncount nouns include *equipment, intelligence,* and *wealth*. See **4** pp. 266–67.

EXERCISE 45.11 Forming plurals

Make correct plurals of the following singular words. Check doubtful spellings in a dictionary. (You can do this exercise online at *ablongman.com/littlebrown*.)

1 pile	5 mile per hour	9 Bales	13 thief
2 donkey	6 box	10 cupful	14 goose
3 beach	7 switch	11 libretto	15 hiss
4 summary	8 sister-in-law	12 video	16 appendix

EXERCISE 45.12 Revising: Plurals

In the following paragraph, revise any incorrect spellings of plural nouns. (You can do this exercise online at *ablongman.com/littlebrown*.)

1 Fewer original video games are available these dayes, but sales and production of sequeles to popular games are strong. 2 Mainstream game

publishers follow formulaes that have proved profitable, and sequeles are cheaper to produce than original games. 3 What's more, many video game enthusiastes tend to buy new versions of games they already know. 4 Many players crave original games and think of publishers as thiefs because they merely trade on previous successs. 5 But publishers have found that trying to be heros by following their hunchs often results in low profits.

EXERCISE 45.13 Using correct spellings

In the following paragraph, select the correct spellings from the choices in brackets. Refer as needed to the list of words on pp. 345–46, the preceding rules, or a dictionary. (You can do this exercise online at *ablongman.com/littlebrown*.)

1 Science [affects, effects] many [important, importent] aspects of our lives, though many people have a [pore, poor] understanding of the [role, roll] of scientific breakthroughs in [their, they're] health. 2 Many people [beleive, believe] that [docters, doctors], more than science, are [responsable, responsible] for [improvements, improvments] in health care. 3 But scientists in the [labratory, laboratory] have made crucial steps in the search for [knowlege, knowledge] about health and [medecine, medicine]. 4 For example, one scientist [who's, whose] discoveries have [affected, effected] many people is Ulf Von Euler. 5 In the 1950s Von Euler's discovery of certain hormones [lead, led] to the invention of the birth control pill. 6 Von Euler's work was used by John Rock, who [developed, developped] the first birth control pill and influenced family [planing, planning]. 7 Von Euler also discovered the [principal, principle] neurotransmitter that controls the heartbeat. 8 Another scientist, Hans Selye, showed what [affect, effect] stress can have on the body. 9 His findings have [lead, led] to methods of [baring, bearing] stress.

EXERCISE 45.14 Working with a spelling checker

Try your computer's spelling checker on the following paragraph. Type the paragraph or download it from *ablongman.com/littlebrown*, and run it through your spelling checker. Then proofread it to correct the errors missed by the checker. (Hint: There are fourteen errors in all.)

1 The whether effects all of us, though it's affects are different for different people. 2 Some people love a fare day with warm temperatures and sunshine. 3 They revel in spending a hole day outside without the threat of rein. 4 Other people prefer dark, rainy daze. 5 They relish the opportunity to slow down and here they're inner thoughts. 6 Most people agree, however, that to much of one kind of whether—reign, sun, snow, or clouds—makes them board.

45c Use the hyphen to form or divide words.

The hyphen is used either to form compound words or to divide words at the ends of lines.

1 Compound adjectives

When two or more words serve together as a single modifier before a noun, a hyphen forms the modifying words clearly into a unit.

She is a well-known actor.
Some Spanish-speaking students work as translators.

When such a compound adjective follows the noun, the hyphen is unnecessary.

The actor is well known.
Many students are Spanish speaking.

The hyphen is also unnecessary in a compound modifier containing an -*ly* adverb, even before the noun: *clearly defined terms.*

When part of a compound adjective appears only once in two or more parallel compound adjectives, hyphens indicate which words the reader should mentally join with the missing part.

School-age children should have eight- or nine-o'clock bedtimes.

2 Fractions and compound numbers

Hyphens join the numerator and denominator of fractions: *one-half, three-fourths.* Hyphens also join the parts of the whole numbers *twenty-one* to *ninety-nine.*

When a hyphenated number is part of a compound adjective before a noun, join all parts of the modifier with hyphens: *sixty-three-foot wall.*

3 Prefixes and suffixes

Do not use hyphens with prefixes except as follows:

- With the prefixes *self-, all-,* and *ex-: self-control, all-inclusive, ex-student.*
- With a prefix before a capitalized word: *un-American.*
- With a capital letter before a word: *T-shirt.*
- To prevent misreading: *de-emphasize, re-create a story.*

The only suffix that regularly requires a hyphen is -*elect,* as in *president-elect.*

EXERCISE 45.15 Using hyphens in compound words

Insert hyphens as needed in the following compounds, consulting a dictionary as needed. If a compound is correct as given, mark the number preceding it. (You can do this exercise online at *ablongman.com/ littlebrown.*)

1 reimburse	6 seventy eight	11 two and six
2 deescalate	7 happy go lucky	person cars
3 forty odd soldiers	8 preexisting	12 ex songwriter
4 little known bar	9 senator elect	13 V shaped
5 seven eighths	10 postwar	14 reeducate

EXERCISE 45.16 Revising: Hyphens

Insert hyphens as needed in the following paragraph, and delete them where they are not needed. If a sentence is correct as given, mark the number preceding it. (You can do this exercise online at *ablongman.com/ littlebrown.*)

1 The African elephant is well known for its size. 2 A male elephant weighs five and one half to six tons, and a female weighs up to four tons. 3 Even with the difference in weight, both male and female elephants can grow to a ten-foot height. 4 A newborn elephant calf weighs two to three hundred pounds and stands about thirty three inches high. 5 A two hundred pound, thirty three inch baby is quite a big baby! 6 African elephants reach maturity at the age of fourteen or fifteen and often live for sixty five or seventy years.

4 Words at the ends of lines

You can avoid occasional short lines in your documents by setting your word processor to divide words automatically at appropriate breaks. (In the Tools menu, select Language and then Hyphenation.) To divide words manually, follow these guidelines:

- **Divide words only between syllables**—for instance, *win-dows,* not *wi-ndows.* Check a dictionary for correct syllable breaks.
- **Never divide a one-syllable word.**
- **Leave at least two letters on the first line and three on the second line.** If a word cannot be divided to follow this rule (for instance, *a-bus-er*), don't divide it.

If you must break an electronic address—for instance, in a source citation—do so only after a slash. Do not hyphenate, because readers may perceive any added hyphen as part of the address.

Not   http://www.library.miami.edu/staff/lmc/soc-
      race.html
But   http://www.library.miami.edu/staff/lmc/
      socrace.html

46 Capital Letters

Generally, capitalize a word only when a dictionary or conventional use says you must. Consult one of the style guides listed in **8** pp. 451–52 and 456 for special uses of capitals in the social, natural, and applied sciences.

Note A grammar and style checker will flag overused capital letters and missing capitals at the beginnings of sentences. It will also spot missing capitals at the beginnings of proper nouns and adjectives—*if* the nouns and adjectives are in the checker's dictionary. For example, a checker caught *christianity* and *europe* but not *china* (for the country) or *Stephen king*.

⟨ **CULTURE LANGUAGE** ⟩ Conventions of capitalization vary from language to language. English, for instance, is the only language to capitalize the first-person singular pronoun (*I*), and its practice of capitalizing proper nouns but not most common nouns also distinguishes it from some other languages.

46a Capitalize the first word of every sentence.

Every writer should own a good dictionary.

When quoting other writers, you should reproduce the capital letters beginning their sentences or indicate that you have altered the source's capitalization. Whenever possible, integrate the quotation into your own sentence so that its capitalization coincides with yours:

"Psychotherapists often overlook the benefits of self-deception," the author argues.

The author argues that "the benefits of self-deception" are not always recognized by psychotherapists.

If you need to alter the capitalization in the source, indicate the change with brackets:

"[T]he benefits of self-deception" are not always recognized by psychotherapists, the author argues.

The author argues that "[p]sychotherapists often overlook the benefits of self-deception."

http://www.ablongman.com/littlebrown ▶

Visit the companion Web site for more help and an electronic exercise on capital letters.

Note Capitalization of questions in a series is optional. Both of the following examples are correct:

> Is the population a hundred? Two hundred? More?
> Is the population a hundred? two hundred? more?

Also optional is capitalization of the first word in a complete sentence after a colon.

46b   Capitalize proper nouns, proper adjectives, and words used as essential parts of proper nouns.

1 Proper nouns and proper adjectives

Proper nouns name specific persons, places, and things: *Shakespeare, California, World War I.* **Proper adjectives** are formed from some proper nouns: *Shakespearean, Californian.* Capitalize all proper nouns and proper adjectives but not the articles (*a, an, the*) that precede them:

Proper nouns and adjectives to be capitalized

Specific persons and things
Stephen King
Napoleon Bonaparte
Boulder Dam
the Empire State Building

Specific places and geographical regions
New York City
China
the Mediterranean Sea
the Northeast, the South
But: northeast of the city, going south

Days of the week, months, holidays
Monday
May
Yom Kippur
Christmas

Historical events, documents, periods, movements
the Vietnam War
the Constitution
the Renaissance
the Romantic Movement

Government offices or departments and institutions
House of Representatives
Department of Defense
Polk Municipal Court
Northeast High School

Political, social, athletic, and other organizations and associations and their members
Democratic Party, Democrats
Sierra Club
B'nai B'rith
League of Women Voters
Boston Celtics
Chicago Symphony Orchestra

Races, nationalities, and their languages

Native American	Germans
African American	Swahili
Caucasian	Italian

But: blacks, whites

Religions, their followers, and terms for the sacred

Christianity, Christians	God
Catholicism, Catholics	Allah
Judaism, Orthodox Jews	the Bible [*but* biblical]
Islam, Muslims	the Koran, the Qur'an

2 Common nouns used as essential parts of proper nouns

Capitalize the common nouns *street, avenue, park, river, ocean, lake, company, college, county,* and *memorial* when they are part of proper nouns naming specific places or institutions:

Main Street	Lake Superior
Central Park	Ford Motor Company
Mississippi River	Madison College
Pacific Ocean	George Washington Memorial

3 Compass directions

Capitalize compass directions only when they name a specific region instead of a general direction:

Students from the West often melt in eastern humidity.

4 Relationships

Capitalize the names of relationships only when they precede or replace proper names:

Our aunt scolded us for disrespecting Father and Uncle Jake.

5 Titles with persons' names

Before a person's name, capitalize his or her title. After or apart from the name, do not capitalize the title.

Professor Otto Osborne	Otto Osborne, a professor
Doctor Jane Covington	Jane Covington, a doctor
Governor Ella Moore	Ella Moore, the governor

Note Many writers capitalize a title denoting very high rank even when it follows a name or is used alone: *Ronald Reagan, past President of the United States.*

46c Capitalize most words in titles and subtitles of works.

Within your text, capitalize all the words in a title *except* the following: articles (*a, an, the*); *to* in infinitives; and connecting words (prepositions and conjunctions) of fewer than five letters. Capitalize even these short words when they are the first or last word in a title or when they fall after a colon or semicolon.

"Courtship Through the Ages"   *Management: A New Theory*
A Diamond Is Forever   "Once More to the Lake"
"Knowing Whom to Ask"   *An End to Live For*
Learning from Las Vegas   *File Under Architecture*

Note The style guides of the academic disciplines have their own rules for capitals in titles. For instance, MLA style for English and some other humanities capitalizes all subordinating conjunctions but no prepositions. In addition, APA style for the social sciences and CSE style for the sciences capitalize only the first word and proper names in book and article titles within source citations (see **APA** pp. 512–22 and **CSE** pp. 546–50).

46d Use capitals according to convention in online communication.

Online messages written in all-capital letters or with no capital letters are difficult to read. Further, messages in all-capital letters may be taken as rude (see also **2** p. 117). Use capital letters according to rules 46a–46c in all your online communication.

EXERCISE 46.1 Revising: Capitals

Revise the following paragraph to correct errors in capitalization, consulting a dictionary as needed. If a sentence is correct as given, mark the number preceding it. (You can do this exercise online at *ablongman .com/littlebrown.*)

1 San Antonio, texas, is a thriving city in the southwest that has always offered much to tourists interested in the roots of spanish settlement in the new world. 2 Most visitors stop at the Alamo, one of five Catholic Missions built by Priests to convert native americans and to maintain spain's claims in the area. 3 The Alamo is famous for being the site of an 1836 battle that helped to create the republic of Texas. 4 San Antonio has grown tremendously in recent years. 5 The Hemisfair plaza and the San Antonio river link tourist and convention facilities. 6 Restaurants, Hotels, and shops line the River. 7 the haunting melodies of "Una paloma blanca" and "malagueña" lure passing tourists into Casa rio and other mexican restaurants. 8 The university of Texas at San Antonio has

expanded, and a Medical Center lies in the Northwest part of the city.
9 Sea World, on the west side of San Antonio, entertains grandparents,
fathers and mothers, and children with the antics of dolphins and seals.
10 The City has attracted high-tech industry, creating a corridor between san antonio and austin.

47 Underlining or Italics

<u>Underlining</u> and *italic type* indicate the same thing: the word or
words are being distinguished or emphasized. If you underline two
or more words in a row, underline the space between the words,
too: <u>Criminal Statistics: Misuses of Numbers</u>.

Note A grammar and style checker cannot recognize problems
with underlining or italics. Check your own work to ensure that you
have used highlighting appropriately.

47a Use underlining or italics consistently and appropriately for your writing situation.

Italic type is now used almost universally in business and academic writing. Still, some academic style guides, notably the *MLA
Handbook*, continue to prefer underlining, especially in source citations. Other styles discussed in this book—APA and Chicago—call
for italics. Ask your instructor for his or her preference. (Underlining is used for the examples in this chapter because it is easier to
see than italics.)

Use either italics or underlining consistently throughout a document. For instance, if you are writing an English paper and following MLA style for underlining in source citations, use underlining in
the body of your paper as well.

47b Underline or italicize the titles of works that appear independently.

Within your text, underline or italicize the titles of works that
are published, released, or produced separately from other works.
(See the box on the next page.) Use quotation marks for all other
titles. (See **5** pp. 332–33.)

http://www.ablongman.com/littlebrown ▶

Visit the companion Web site for more help
and an electronic exercise on underlining or
italics.

Titles to be underlined or italicized

Other titles should be placed in quotation marks. (See 5 pp. 332–33.)

Books	**Television and radio programs**
War and Peace	The Shadow
And the Band Played On	NBC Sports Hour
Plays	**Long poems**
Hamlet	Beowulf
The Phantom of the Opera	Paradise Lost
Computer software	**Periodicals**
Microsoft Internet Explorer	Time
Acrobat Reader	Philadelphia Inquirer
Web sites	**Published speeches**
Google	Lincoln's Gettysburg Address
Friends of Prufrock	**Movies, DVDs, and videos**
Pamphlets	Schindler's List
The Truth About Alcoholism	How to Relax
Long musical works	**Works of visual art**
Tchaikovsky's Swan Lake	Michelangelo's David
But: Symphony in C	Picasso's Guernica

Exceptions Legal documents, the Bible, the Koran, and their parts are generally not underlined or italicized:

Not   We studied the Book of Revelation in the Bible.

But   We studied the Book of Revelation in the Bible.

47c   Underline or italicize the names of ships, aircraft, spacecraft, and trains.

Challenger	Orient Express	Queen Elizabeth 2
Apollo XI	Montrealer	Spirit of St. Louis

47d   Underline or italicize foreign words that are not part of the English language.

Underline or italicize a foreign expression that has not been absorbed into English. A dictionary will say whether a word is still considered foreign to English.

The scientific name for the brown trout is Salmo trutta. [The Latin scientific names for plants and animals are always underlined or italicized.]

The Latin De gustibus non est disputandum translates roughly as "There's no accounting for taste."

47e Underline or italicize words or characters named as words.

Use underlining or italics to indicate that you are citing a character or word as a word rather than using it for its meaning. Words you are defining fall under this convention.

The word syzygy refers to a straight line formed by three celestial bodies, as in the alignment of the earth, sun, and moon.

Some people say th, as in thought, with a faint s or f sound.

47f Occasionally, underlining or italics may be used for emphasis.

Underlining or italics can stress an important word or phrase, especially in reporting how someone said something. But use such emphasis very rarely, or your writing may sound immature or hysterical.

47g In online communication, use alternatives for underlining or italics.

Electronic mail and other forms of online communication often do not allow conventional highlighting such as underlining or italics for the purposes described in this chapter. (On Web sites, for instance, underlining often indicates a link to another site.)

To distinguish book titles and other elements that usually require underlining or italics, type an underscore before and after the element: *Measurements coincide with those in _Joule's Handbook_.* You can also emphasize words with asterisks before and after: *I *will not* be able to attend.*

Don't use all-capital letters for emphasis; they yell too loudly. (See also p. 358.)

EXERCISE 47.1   Revising: Underlining or italics

Underline or italicize words and phrases as needed in the following paragraph, or delete the underlining from any words or phrases that are highlighted unnecessarily. If a sentence is correct as given, mark the number preceding it. (You can do this exercise online at *ablongman.com/littlebrown*.)

1 A number of veterans of the war in Vietnam have become prominent writers. 2 Oliver Stone is perhaps the most famous for writing and directing the films Platoon and Born on the Fourth of July. 3 The fiction

writer Tim O'Brien has published short stories about the war in Esquire, GQ, and Massachusetts Review. 4 His dreamlike novel Going After Cacciato is about the horrors of combat. 5 Typically for veterans' writing, the novel uses words and phrases borrowed from Vietnamese, such as di di mau ("go quickly") or dinky dau ("crazy"). 6 Another writer, Philip Caputo, provides a gripping account of his service in Vietnam in the book A Rumor of War. 7 Caputo's book was made into a television movie, also titled A Rumor of War. 8 The playwright David Rabe—in such dramas as The Basic Training of Pavlo Hummel, Streamers, and Sticks and Bones—depicts the effects of war not only on the soldiers but on their families. 9 Steve Mason, called the poet laureate of the Vietnam war, has published two collections of poems on the war: Johnny's Song and Warrior for Peace. 10 And Rod Kane wrote an autobiography about the war, Veterans Day, that received rave reviews in the Washington Post.

48 Abbreviations

The following guidelines on abbreviations pertain to the text of a nontechnical document. All academic disciplines use abbreviations in source citations, and much technical writing, such as in the sciences and engineering, uses many abbreviations in the document text. For the in-text requirements of the discipline you are writing in, consult one of the style guides listed in 8 pp. 447 (humanities), 451–52 (social sciences), and 456 (natural and applied sciences).

Usage varies, but writers increasingly omit periods from abbreviations that consist of or end in capital letters: *US, BA, USMC, PhD*. See 5 pp. 295–96 on punctuating abbreviations.

Note A grammar and style checker may flag some abbreviations, such as *ft.* (for *foot*) and *st.* (for *street*). A spelling checker will flag abbreviations it does not recognize. But neither checker can tell you whether an abbreviation is appropriate for your writing situation or will be clear to your readers.

48a Use standard abbreviations for titles immediately before and after proper names.

Before the name	After the name
Dr. James Hsu	James Hsu, MD
Mr., Mrs., Ms., Hon.,	DDS, DVM, PhD,
St., Rev., Msgr., Gen.	EdD, OSB, SJ, Sr., Jr.

http://www.ablongman.com/littlebrown ▶

Visit the companion Web site for more help and an electronic exercise on abbreviations.

Do not use abbreviations such as *Rev., Hon., Prof., Rep., Sen., Dr.,* and *St.* (for *Saint*) unless they appear before a proper name.

48b   Familiar abbreviations and acronyms are acceptable in most writing.

An **acronym** is an abbreviation that spells a pronounceable word, such as WHO, NATO, and AIDS. These and other abbreviations using initials are acceptable in most writing as long as they are familiar to readers.

Institutions	LSU, UCLA, TCU
Organizations	CIA, FBI, YMCA, AFL-CIO
Corporations	IBM, CBS, ITT
People	JFK, LBJ, FDR
Countries	US, USA

Note If a name or term (such as *operating room*) appears often in a piece of writing, then its abbreviation (*OR*) can cut down on extra words. Spell out the full term at its first appearance, indicate its abbreviation in parentheses, and then use the abbreviation.

48c   Use *BC, BCE, AD, CE, AM, PM, no.,* and *$* only with specific dates and numbers.

44 BC	44 BCE	11:26 AM (*or* a.m.)	no. 36 (*or* No. 36)
AD 1492	1492 CE	8:05 PM (*or* p.m.)	$7.41

The abbreviations BC ("before Christ"), BCE ("before the common era"), and CE ("common era") always follow a date. In contrast, AD (*anno Domini,* Latin for "in the year of the Lord") precedes a date.

48d   Generally reserve Latin abbreviations for source citations and comments in parentheses.

Latin abbreviations are generally not italicized or underlined.

i.e.	*id est:* that is
cf.	*confer:* compare
e.g.	*exempli gratia:* for example
et al.	*et alii:* and others
etc.	*et cetera:* and so forth
NB	*nota bene:* note well

He said he would be gone a fortnight (i.e., two weeks).
Bloom et al., editors, *Anthology of Light Verse*
Trees, too, are susceptible to disease (e.g., Dutch elm disease).

Some writers avoid these abbreviations in formal writing, even within parentheses.

48e Use *Inc., Bros., Co.,* or & (for *and*) only in official names of business firms.

Not   The Santini <u>bros.</u> operate a large moving firm in New York City <u>&</u> environs.

But   The Santini <u>brothers</u> operate a large moving firm in New York City <u>and</u> environs.

Or   Santini <u>Bros.</u> is a large moving firm in New York City <u>and</u> environs.

48f Generally spell out units of measurement and names of places, calendar designations, people, and courses.

In most academic, general, and business writing, the types of words listed below should always be spelled out. (In source citations and technical writing, however, these words are more often abbreviated.)

Units of measurement
The dog is thirty <u>inches</u> [not <u>in.</u>] high.

Geographical names
The publisher is in <u>Massachusetts</u> [not <u>Mass.</u> or <u>MA</u>].

Names of days, months, and holidays
The truce was signed on <u>Tuesday</u> [not <u>Tues.</u>], <u>April</u> [not <u>Apr.</u>] 16.

Names of people
<u>Robert</u> [not <u>Robt.</u>] Frost writes accessible poems.

Courses of instruction
I'm majoring in <u>political science</u> [not <u>poli. sci.</u>].

EXERCISE 48.1 Revising: Abbreviations

Revise the following paragraph as needed to correct inappropriate use of abbreviations for nontechnical writing. If a sentence is correct as given, mark the number preceding it. (You can do this exercise online at *ablongman.com/littlebrown*.)

   1 In an issue of *Science* magazine, Dr. Virgil L. Sharpton discusses a theory that could help explain the extinction of dinosaurs. 2 According to the theory, a comet or asteroid crashed into the earth about 65 mill. yrs. ago. 3 The result was a huge crater about 10 km. (6.2 mi.) deep in the Gulf of Mex. 4 Sharpton's measurements suggest that the

crater is 50 pct. larger than scientists had previously believed. 5 Indeed, 20-yr.-old drilling cores reveal that the crater is about 186 mi. wide, roughly the size of Conn. 6 The space object was traveling more than 100,000 miles per hour and hit earth with the impact of 100 to 300 megatons of TNT. 7 On impact, 200,000 cubic km. of rock and soil were vaporized or thrown into the air. 8 That's the equivalent of 2.34 bill. cubic ft. of matter. 9 The impact would have created 400-ft. tidal waves across the Atl. Ocean, temps. higher than 20,000 degs., and powerful earthquakes. 10 Sharpton theorizes that the dust, vapor, and smoke from this impact blocked the sun's rays for mos., cooled the earth, and thus resulted in the death of the dinosaurs.

49 Numbers

This chapter addresses the use of numbers (numerals versus words) in the text of a document. All disciplines use many more numerals in source citations.

Note Grammar and style checkers will flag numerals beginning sentences and can be customized to ignore or to look for numerals. But they can't tell you whether numerals or spelled-out numbers are appropriate for your writing situation.

49a Use numerals according to standard practice in the field you are writing in.

Always use numerals for numbers that require more than two words to spell out:

The leap year has <u>366</u> days.
The population of Minot, North Dakota, is about <u>32,800</u>.

In nontechnical academic writing, spell out numbers of one or two words:

<u>Twelve</u> nations signed the treaty.
The ball game drew <u>forty-two thousand</u> people. [A hyphenated number may be considered one word.]

In much business writing, use numerals for all numbers over ten: *five reasons, 11 participants.* In technical academic and business writing, such as in science and engineering, use numerals for all

http://www.ablongman.com/littlebrown ▶

Visit the companion Web site for more help and an electronic exercise on numbers.

numbers over ten, and use numerals for zero through nine when they refer to exact measurements: *2 liters, 1 hour.* (Consult one of the style guides listed in **8** pp. 451–52 and 456 for more details.)

Note Use a combination of numerals and words for round numbers over a million: *26 million, 2.45 billion.* And use either all numerals or all words when several numbers appear together in a passage, even if convention would require a mixture.

CULTURE LANGUAGE In standard American English, a comma separates the numerals in long numbers (*26,000*), and a period functions as a decimal point (*2.06*).

49b **Use numerals according to convention for dates, addresses, and other information.**

Days and years
June 18, 1985   AD 12
456 BCE   2010

The time of day
9:00 AM   3:45 PM

Addresses
355 Clinton Avenue
Washington, DC 20036

Exact amounts of money
$3.5 million $4.50

Decimals, percentages, and fractions
22.5   3½
48% (*or* 48 percent)

Scores and statistics
21 to 7   a ratio of 8 to 1
a mean of 26

Pages, chapters, volumes, acts, scenes, lines
Chapter 9, page 123
Hamlet, act 5, scene 3

Exceptions Round dollar or cent amounts of only a few words may be expressed in words: *seventeen dollars; sixty cents.* When the word *o'clock* is used for the time of day, also express the number in words: *two o'clock* (not *2 o'clock*).

49c **Spell out numbers that begin sentences.**

For clarity, spell out any number that begins a sentence. If the number requires more than two words, reword the sentence so that the number falls later and can be expressed as a numeral.

Not   3.5 billion people live in Asia.
But   The population of Asia is 3.5 billion.

EXERCISE 49.1 Revising: Numbers

Revise the following paragraphs so that numbers are used appropriately for nontechnical writing. If a sentence is correct as given, mark the number preceding it. (You can do this exercise online at *ablongman.com/littlebrown.*)

1 The planet Saturn is nine hundred million miles, or nearly one billion five hundred million kilometers, from the sun. 2 Saturn orbits the sun only two and four-tenths times during the average human life span. 3 As a result, a year on Saturn equals almost thirty of our years. 4 The planet travels in its orbit at about twenty-one thousand six hundred miles per hour.

5 Saturn is huge: more than seventy-two thousand miles in diameter, compared to Earth's eight-thousand-mile diameter. 6 Saturn is also very cold, with an average temperature of minus two hundred and eighteen degrees Fahrenheit, compared to Earth's fifty-nine degrees Fahrenheit. 7 Saturn is cold because of its great distance from the sun and because its famous rings reflect almost 70 percent of the sunlight that approaches the planet. 8 The ring system is almost forty thousand miles wide, beginning 8800 miles from the planet's visible surface and ending forty-seven thousand miles from that surface.

Research Writing

Research Writing

50   Research Strategy

Research writing gives you a chance to work like a detective solving a case. The mystery is the answer to a question you care about. The search for the answer leads you to consider what others think about your subject, but you do more than simply report their views. You build on them to develop and support your own opinion, and ultimately you become an expert in your own right.

Your investigation will be more productive and enjoyable if you take some steps described in this chapter: plan your work (below), keep a research journal (next page), find an appropriate subject and research question (p. 373), set goals for your sources (p. 374), and keep a working, annotated bibliography (p. 377).

50a   Planning your work

Research writing is a *writing* process:

- You work within a particular situation of subject, purpose, audience, and other factors (see 1 pp. 3–8).
- You gather ideas and information about your subject (1 pp. 8–13).
- You focus and arrange your ideas (1 pp. 14–21).
- You draft to explore your meaning (1 pp. 22–24).
- You revise and edit to develop, shape, and polish (1 pp. 24–33).

Although the process seems neatly sequential in this list, you know from experience that the stages overlap—that, for instance, you may begin drafting before you've gathered all the information you expect to find, and then while drafting you may discover a source that causes you to rethink your approach. Anticipating the process of research writing can free you to be flexible in your search and open to discoveries.

A thoughtful plan and systematic procedures can help you follow through on the diverse activities of research writing. One step is to make a schedule like the one on the next page that apportions the available time to the necessary work. You can estimate that each segment marked off by a horizontal line will occupy *roughly* one-quarter of the total time—for example, a week in a four-week

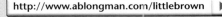

http://www.ablongman.com/littlebrown ▶

Visit the companion Web site for more help and an electronic exercise on research strategy.

assignment or two weeks in an eight-week assignment. The most unpredictable segments are the first two, so get started early enough to accommodate the unexpected.

Complete
by:

_____ 1. Setting a schedule and beginning a research journal (here and below)
_____ 2. Finding a researchable subject and question (facing page)
_____ 3. Setting goals for sources (p. 374)
_____ 4. Finding print and electronic sources (p. 379), and making a working, annotated bibliography (p. 377)

_____ 5. Evaluating and synthesizing sources (pp. 397, 406)
_____ 6. Gathering information from sources (p. 408), often using summary, paraphrase, and direct quotation (p. 409)
_____ 7. Taking steps to avoid plagiarism (p. 418)

_____ 8. Developing a thesis statement and creating a structure (p. 427)
_____ 9. Drafting the paper (p. 428), integrating summaries, paraphrases, and direct quotations into your ideas (p. 413)

_____ 10. Revising and editing the paper (p. 428)
_____ 11. Citing sources in your text (p. 425)
_____ 12. Preparing the list of works cited or references (p. 425)
_____ 13. Preparing the final manuscript (p. 428)
_____   Final paper due

(You can download the schedule from *ablongman.com/littlebrown*. Use a duplicate to plan and time the specific steps of each research project you work on.)

50b   Keeping a research journal

While working on a research project, carry a notebook or a computer with you at all times to use as a **research journal,** a place to record your activities and ideas. (See 1 p. 9 on journal keeping.) In the journal's dated entries, you can write about the sources you consult, the leads you want to pursue, any difficulties you encounter, and, most important, your thoughts about sources, leads, difficulties, new directions, relationships, and anything else that strikes you. The very act of writing in the journal can expand and clarify your thinking.

Note The research journal is the place to track and develop your own ideas. To avoid mixing up your thoughts and those of others, keep separate notes on what your sources actually say, using one of the methods discussed on pp. 408–09.

50c Finding a researchable subject and question

Before reading this section, review the suggestions given in Chapter 1 for finding and narrowing a writing subject (1 pp. 5–6). Generally, the same procedure applies to writing any kind of research paper. However, selecting and limiting a subject for a research paper can present special opportunities and problems. And before you proceed with your subject, you'll want to transform it into a question that can guide your search for sources.

1 Appropriate subject

Seek a research subject that interests you and that you care about. (It may be a subject you've already written about without benefit of research.) Starting with your own views will motivate you, and you will be a participant in a dialog when you begin examining sources.

When you settle on a subject, ask the following questions about it. For each requirement, there are corresponding pitfalls.

- **Are ample sources of information available on the subject?**

  Avoid very recent subjects, such as a newly announced medical discovery or a breaking story in today's newspaper.

- **Does the subject encourage research in the kinds and number of sources required by the assignment?**

  Avoid (a) subjects that depend entirely on personal opinion and experience, such as the virtues of your hobby, and (b) subjects that require research in only one source, such as a straight factual biography.

- **Will the subject lead you to an objective assessment of sources and to defensible conclusions?**

  Avoid subjects that rest entirely on belief or prejudice, such as when human life begins or why women (or men) are superior. Your readers are unlikely to be swayed from their own beliefs.

- **Does the subject suit the length of paper assigned and the time given for research and writing?**

  Avoid broad subjects that have too many sources to survey adequately, such as a major event in history.

2 Research question

Asking a question about your subject can give direction to your research by focusing your thinking on a particular approach. To discover your question, consider what about your subject intrigues or perplexes you, what you'd like to know more about. (See below for suggestions on using your own knowledge.)

Try to narrow your research question so that you can answer it in the time and space you have available. The question *How will the Internet affect business?* is very broad, encompassing issues as diverse as electronic commerce, information management, and employee training. In contrast, the question *How will Internet commerce benefit consumers?* or *How, if at all, should Internet commerce be taxed?* is much narrower. Each question also requires more than a simple *yes* or *no* answer, so that answering, even tentatively, demands thought about pros and cons, causes and effects.

As you read and write, your question will probably evolve to reflect your increasing knowledge of the subject, and eventually its answer will become your main idea, or thesis statement (see p. 427).

50d   Setting goals for sources

Before you start looking for sources, consider what you already know about your subject and where you are likely to find information on it.

1 Your own knowledge

Discovering what you already know about your topic will guide you in discovering what you don't know. Take some time to spell out facts you have learned, opinions you have heard or read elsewhere, and of course your own opinions. Use one of the discovery techniques discussed in **1** pp. 9–13 to explore and develop your ideas: keeping a journal, observing your surroundings, freewriting, brainstorming, clustering, and asking questions.

When you've explored your thoughts, make a list of questions for which you don't have answers, whether factual (*What laws govern taxes in Internet commerce?*) or more open-ended (*Who benefits from a tax-free Internet? Who doesn't benefit?*). These questions will give you clues about the sources you need to look for first.

2 Kinds of sources

For many research projects, you'll want to consult a mix of sources, as described on the next two pages. You may start by seeking the outlines of your topic—the range and depth of opinions about it—in reference works and articles in popular periodicals or through a Web search. Then, as you refine your views and your research question, you'll move on to more specialized sources, such as scholarly books and periodicals and your own interviews or surveys. (See pp. 383–97 for more on each kind of source.)

■ Library and Internet sources

The print and electronic sources available through your library—mainly reference works, periodicals, and books—have two big advantages over most of what you'll find on the Internet: they are cataloged and indexed for easy retrieval; and they are generally reliable, having been screened first by their publishers and then by the library's staff. In contrast, the Internet's retrieval systems are more difficult to use effectively, and Internet sources tend to be less reliable because most do not pass through any screening before being posted. (There are many exceptions, such as online scholarly journals and reference works. But these sources are generally available through your library's Web site as well.)

Most instructors expect research writers to consult library sources. But they'll accept Internet sources, too, if you have used them judiciously. Even with its disadvantages, the Internet can be a valuable resource for primary sources, current information, and a diversity of views. For guidelines on evaluating both library and Internet sources, see pp. 397–405.

■ Primary and secondary sources

As much as possible, you should rely on **primary sources,** or firsthand accounts: historical documents (letters, speeches, and so on), eyewitness reports, works of literature, reports on experiments or surveys conducted by the writer, or your own interviews, experiments, observations, or correspondence.

In contrast, **secondary sources** report and analyze information drawn from other sources, often primary ones: a reporter's summary of a controversial issue, a historian's account of a battle, a critic's reading of a poem, a physicist's evaluation of several studies. Secondary sources may contain helpful summaries and interpretations that direct, support, and extend your own thinking. However, most research-writing assignments expect your ideas to go beyond those in such sources.

■ Scholarly and popular sources

The scholarship of acknowledged experts is essential for depth, authority, and specificity. Most instructors expect you to emphasize scholarly sources in your research. But the general-interest views and information of popular sources can help you apply more scholarly approaches to daily life.

- **Check the title.** Is it technical, or does it use a general vocabulary?
- **Check the publisher.** Is it a scholarly journal (such as *Education Forum*) or a publisher of scholarly books (such as Harvard University Press), or is it a popular magazine (such as *Time* or *Newsweek*) or a publisher of popular books (such as Little, Brown)?
- **Check the length of periodical articles.** Scholarly articles are generally much longer than magazine and newspaper articles.
- **Check the author.** Have you seen the name elsewhere, which might suggest that the author is an expert?
- **Check the electronic address.** Addresses, or URLs, for Internet sources often include an abbreviation that tells you something about the origin of the source: *edu* means the source comes from an educational institution, *gov* from a government body, *org* from a nonprofit organization, *com* from a commercial organization such as a corporation. The abbreviation is not a firm guide to the kind of source—*edu* sites, for instance, may include student papers and Web logs as well as works by scholars—but it can indicate the context. (See pp. 389–94 for more on types of online sources.)

■ **Older and newer sources**

Check the publication date. For most subjects a combination of older, established sources (such as books) and current sources (such as newspaper articles, interviews, or Web sites) will provide both background and up-to-date information. Only historical subjects or very current subjects require an emphasis on one extreme or another.

■ **Impartial and biased sources**

Seek a range of viewpoints. Sources that attempt to be impartial can offer an overview of your subject and trustworthy facts. Sources with clear biases can offer a diversity of opinion. Of course, to discover bias, you may have to read the source carefully (see pp. 397–405); but even a bibliographical listing can be informative.

- **Check the author.** You may have heard of the author as a respected researcher (thus more likely to be objective) or as a leading proponent of a certain view (less likely to be objective).
- **Check the title.** It may reveal something about point of view. (Consider these contrasting titles: "Keep the Internet Tax-Free" and "Taxation of Commerce on the Internet: Issues and Questions.")

Note Sources you find on the Internet must be approached with particular care. See pp. 399–405.

■ **Sources with helpful features**

Depending on your topic and how far along your research is, you may want to look for sources with features such as illustrations (which can clarify important concepts), bibliographies (which can direct you to other sources), and indexes (which can help you develop keywords for electronic searches; see p. 381).

50e Keeping a working, annotated bibliography

To track where sources are, compile a **working bibliography** as you uncover possibilities. When you have a substantial file—say, ten to thirty sources—you can decide which ones seem most promising and look them up first.

1 Source information

When you turn in your paper, you will be expected to attach a list of the sources you have used. So that readers can check or follow up on your sources, your list must include all the information needed to find the sources, in a format readers can understand. (See pp. 425–26.) The box on the next page shows the information you should record for each type of source so that you will not have to retrace your steps later.

Note Whenever possible, record source information in the correct format for the documentation style you will be using. Then you will be less likely to omit needed information or to confuse numbers, dates, and other data when it's time to write your citations. This book describes four styles: MLA (see **MLA** p. 460), APA (see **APA** p. 507), Chicago (see **Chic** p. 533), and CSE (see **CSE** p. 544). For others, consult one of the guides listed in **8** pp. 451–52 and 456.

2 Annotations

Creating annotations for a working bibliography converts it from a simple list into a tool for assessing sources. When you discover a possible source, record not only its publication information but also the following:

■ **What you know about the content of the source.** Periodical databases and book catalogs generally include abstracts, or summaries, of sources that can help with this part of the annotation.

Information for a working bibliography

For books

Library call number

Name(s) of author(s), editor(s), translator(s), or others listed

Title and subtitle

Publication data:
  Place of publication
  Publisher's name
  Date of publication

Other important data, such as edition or volume number

For periodical articles

Name(s) of author(s)

Title and subtitle of article

Title of periodical

Publication data:
  Volume number and issue number (if any) in which article appears
  Date of issue
  Page numbers on which article appears

For electronic sources

Name(s) of author(s)

Title and subtitle

Publication data for books and articles (see above)

Date of release, online posting, or latest revision

Medium (online, CD-ROM, etc.)

Format of online source (Web site, Web page, e-mail, etc.)

Date you consulted the source

Complete URL (unless source was obtained through a subscription service and has no permanent address)

For sources obtained through a subscription service
  Name of database
  Name of service
  Electronic address of the service's home page *or* search terms used to reach the source

For other sources

Name(s) of author(s), creator(s), government department, recording artist, photographer, or others listed

Title of the work

Format, such as unpublished letter, live performance, or photograph

Publication title or production data:
  Publisher's or producer's name
  Date of publication, release, or production
  Identifying numbers (if any)

You can download these lists from *ablongman.com/littlebrown*. Copy the appropriate list for each source you're using, and fill in the required information.

- **How you think the source may be helpful in your research.** Does it offer expert opinion, statistics, an important example, or a range of views? Does it place your subject in a historical, social, or economic context?

Taking the time with your annotations can help you discover gaps that may remain in your sources and will later help you decide which sources to pursue in depth. One student annotated a bibliography entry on his computer with a summary and a note on the source features he thought would be most helpful to him:

Entry for an annotated working bibliography

United States. Dept. of Education. National Center for Education
  Statistics. <u>Internet Access in US Public Schools and Class-</u>
  <u>rooms</u>. 24 Feb. 2005. 12 Mar. 2005 <http://nces.ed.gov/
  pubsearch/pubsinfo.asp?pubid=2005015>.

Report on the annual NCES survey of the quantity and quality
of technology used in K-12 classrooms. Includes important
statistics on trends—student-to-computer ratios, teacher training, computer availability to students in different socio-
economic brackets.

> Publication and access
> information for source

> Summary of source

> Ideas on use of source

As you become more familiar with your sources, you can use
your initial annotated bibliography to record your evaluations of
them and more detailed thoughts on how they fit into your research.

51 Finding Sources

This chapter discusses conducting electronic searches (below)
and taking advantage of the range of sources, both print and electronic, that you have access to: reference works (p. 383), books
(p. 384), periodicals (p. 384), the Web (p. 389), other online sources
(p. 393), government publications (p. 394), images (p. 394), and
your own interviews, surveys, and other primary sources (p. 396).

51a Searching electronically

1 Your library's Web site

As you conduct research, the World Wide Web will be your
gateway to ideas and information. Always start with your library's
Web site, not with a public search engine such as *Google*. (*Google
Scholar*, a new tool that searches for scholarly articles, is discussed
on p. 386.) The library site will lead you to vast resources, including
books, periodical articles, and reference works. More important,
every source you find on the library site will have passed through

http://www.ablongman.com/littlebrown

Visit the companion Web site for more help
and an electronic exercise on finding sources.

A tip for researchers

Take advantage of two valuable resources offered by your library:

- **An orientation,** which introduces the library's resources and explains how to reach and use the Web site and the print holdings.
- **Reference librarians,** whose job it is to help you and others navigate the library's resources. Even very experienced researchers often consult reference librarians.

filters to ensure its value. A scholarly journal article, for instance, undergoes at least three successive reviews: subject-matter experts first deem it worth publishing in the journal; then a database vendor deems the journal worth including in the database; and finally your school's librarians deem the database worth subscribing to.

Google and other search engines may seem more user-friendly than the library's Web site and may seem to return plenty of sources for you to work with. Many of the sources may indeed be reliable and relevant to your research, but many more will not be. In the end, a library Web search will be more efficient and more effective than a direct Web search. (For help with evaluating sources from any resource, see pp. 397–405.)

Note Start with the library's Web site, but don't stop there. Many books, periodicals, and other excellent sources are available only on library shelves, not online, and most instructors expect research papers to be built to some extent on these resources. When you spot promising print sources while browsing the library's online databases, make records of them and then look them up at the library.

2 Kinds of electronic sources

Your school's library and the Web offer several kinds of electronic resources that are suitable for academic research:

- **The library's catalog of holdings** is a database that lists all the resources that the library owns or subscribes to: books, journals, magazines, newspapers, reference works, and more. The catalog may also include the holdings of other school libraries nearby or in your state.
- **Online databases** include indexes, bibliographies, and other reference works. They are your main route to articles in periodicals, providing publication information, summaries, and often full text. Your library subscribes to the databases and makes them available through its Web site. (You may also discover

databases directly on the Web, but, again, the library is a more productive starting place.)

- **Databases on CD-ROM** include the same information as online databases, but they must be read at a library computer terminal. Increasingly, libraries are providing CD-ROM databases through their Web sites or are moving away from CD-ROMs in favor of online databases.
- **Full-text resources** contain the entire contents of articles, book chapters, even whole books. The library's databases provide access to the full text of many listed sources. In addition, the Web sites of many periodicals and organizations, such as government agencies, offer the full text of articles, reports, and other publications.

3 Keyword searches

Probably the most important element in an electronic search is appropriate **keywords,** or **descriptors,** that name your subject for databases and Web search engines.

■ Databases vs. the Web

To develop keywords it helps to understand an important difference in how library databases and the open Web work:

- **A database indexes sources by authors, titles, publication years, and its own subject headings.** The subject headings reflect the database's directory of terms and are assigned by people who have read the sources. You can find these subject headings by using your own keywords until you locate a promising source. The information for the source will list the headings under which the database indexes it and other sources like it. (See p. 387 for an illustration.) You can then use those headings for further searches.
- **A Web search engine seeks your keywords in the titles and texts of sites.** The process is entirely electronic, so the performance of a search engine depends on how well your keywords describe your subject and anticipate the words used in sources. If you describe your subject too broadly or describe it specifically but don't match the vocabulary in relevant sources, your search will turn up few relevant sources and probably many that aren't relevant.

■ Keyword refinement

Every database and search engine provides a system that you can use to refine your keywords for a productive search. The basic operations appear in the box on the next two pages, but resources do differ. For instance, some assume that *AND* should link two or more keywords, while others provide options specifying "Must contain all the words," "May contain any of the words," and other equivalents for the operations in the box. You can learn a search engine's system by consulting its Advanced Search page.

Ways to refine keywords

Most databases and many search engines work with **Boolean operators**, terms or symbols that allow you to expand or limit your keywords and thus your search.

- Use *AND* or + to narrow the search by including only sources that use all the given words. The keywords *Internet AND tax* request only the sources in the shaded area.

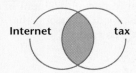

- Use *NOT* or – ("minus") to narrow the search by excluding irrelevant words. *Internet AND tax NOT access* excludes sources that use the word *access*.

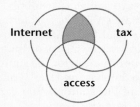

- Use *OR* to broaden the search by giving alternate keywords. *Internet OR (electronic commerce) AND tax* allows for sources that use *Internet* or *electronic commerce* (or both) along with *tax*.

- Use parentheses or quotation marks to form search phrases. For instance, *(electronic commerce)* requests the exact phrase, not the separate words.

- Use *NEAR* to narrow the search by requiring the keywords to be close to each other—for instance, *Internet NEAR tax.* Depending on the resource you're using, the words could be directly next to each other or many words apart. Some resources use *WITHIN* __ so that you can specify the exact number of words apart—for instance, *Internet WITHIN 10 tax.*
- Use wild cards to permit different versions of the same word. In *child**, for instance, the wild card * indicates that sources may include *child, children, childcare, childhood, childish, childlike,* and *childproof.* The example suggests that you have to consider all the variations allowed by a wild card and whether it opens up your search too much. If you seek only two or three from many variations, you may be better off using *OR: child OR children.* (Note that some systems use ?, :, or + for a wild card instead of *.)
- Be sure to spell your keywords correctly. Some search tools will look for close matches or approximations, but correct spelling gives you the best chance of finding relevant sources.

■ Trial and error

You will probably have to use trial and error in developing your keywords, sometimes running dry (turning up few or no sources) and sometimes hitting uncontrollable gushers (turning up hundreds or thousands of mostly irrelevant sources). But the process is not busywork—far from it. Besides leading you eventually to worthwhile sources, it can also teach you a great deal about your subject: how you can or should narrow it, how it is and is not described by others, what others consider interesting or debatable about it, and what the major arguments are.

See pp. 391–92 for an example of a student's keyword search of the Web.

51b Finding reference works

Reference works, often available online or on CD-ROM, include encyclopedias, dictionaries, digests, bibliographies, indexes, atlases, almanacs, and handbooks. Your research *must* go beyond these sources, but they can help you decide whether your topic really interests you and whether it meets the requirements for a research paper (p. 373). Preliminary research in reference works can also help you develop keywords for electronic searches and can direct you to more detailed sources on your topic.

You'll find many reference works through your library and directly on the Web. The following list gives general Web references for all disciplines:

Internet Public Library
http://www.ipl.org
Library of Congress
http://lcweb.loc.gov
LSU Libraries Webliography
http://www.lib.lsu.edu/weblio.html
World Wide Web Virtual Library
http://vlib.org/Overview.html

For Web sites in specific academic disciplines, see **8** pp. 440–41 (literature), 446–47 (other humanities), 451 (social sciences), and 455 (natural and applied sciences). Visit *ablongman.com/littlebrown* for additional print and Web references.

51c | Finding books

Your library's catalog is searchable either at a terminal in the library or via the library's Web site. You can search the catalog by author or title, of course, and by your own keywords or the headings found in *Library of Congress Subject Headings* (*LCSH*). The screen shot below shows the complete record for a book, including the *LCSH* headings that can be used to find similar sources.

Book catalog full record

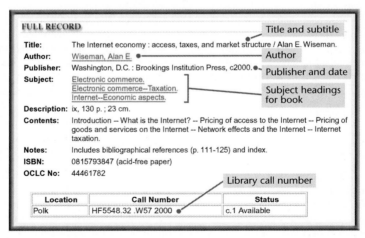

51d | Finding periodicals

Periodicals include newspapers, journals, and magazines. Newspapers, the easiest to recognize, are useful for detailed accounts of past and current events. Journals and magazines can be harder to distinguish, but their differences are important. Most college instructors expect students' research to rely more on journals than on magazines.

Journals	Magazines
Examples: *American Anthropologist, Journal of Black Studies, Journal of Chemical Education*	Examples: *The New Yorker, Time, Rolling Stone, People*
Available mainly through college and university libraries.	Available in public libraries, on newsstands, and in bookstores.
Articles are intended to advance knowledge in a particular field.	Articles are intended to express opinion, inform, or entertain.
Writers and readers are specialists in the field.	Writers may or may not be specialists in their subjects. Readers are members of the general public or a subgroup with a particular interest.
Articles always include source citations.	Articles rarely include source citations.
Articles are usually long, ten pages or more.	Articles are usually short, fewer than ten pages.
Appearance is bland, with black-only type, little or no decoration, and only illustrations that directly amplify the text, such as graphs.	Appearance varies but is generally lively, with color, decoration (headings, sidebars, and other elements), and illustrations (drawings, photographs).
Issues may appear quarterly or less often.	Issues may appear weekly, biweekly, or monthly.
Issues may be paged separately (like a magazine) or may be paged sequentially throughout an annual volume, so that issue number 3 (the third issue of the year) could open on page 327. (The paging method affects source citations. See pp. MLA 475–77.)	Issues are paged separately, each beginning on page 1.

1 Indexes to periodicals

■ How indexes work

Periodical databases index the articles in journals, magazines, and newspapers. Often these databases include abstracts, or summaries, of the articles, and they may offer the full text of the articles as well. Your library subscribes to many periodical databases and to services that offer multiple databases. (See p. 388 for a list.) Most databases and services will be searchable through the library's Web site.

Note The search engine *Google* is developing *Google Scholar*, an engine at *scholar.google.com* that seeks out scholarly articles. Although it could eventually prove a valuable research tool, at this point *Google Scholar* produces results that are far from complete and include more from science and engineering than from the humanities and social sciences. If you find an article through *Google Scholar*, search for it specifically on your library's site.

■ **Selection of databases**

To decide which databases to consult, you'll need to consider what you're looking for:

- **How broadly and deeply should you search?** Periodical databases vary widely in what they index. Some, such as *ProQuest Research Library*, cover many subjects but don't index the full range of periodicals in each subject. Others, such as *Historical Abstracts*, cover a single subject but then include most of the available periodicals. If your subject ranges across disciplines, then start with a broad database. If your subject focuses on a particular discipline, then start with a narrower database.

- **Which databases most likely include the kinds of resources you need?** The Web sites of most libraries allow you to narrow a database search to a particular kind of periodical (such as newspapers or journals) or to a particular discipline. You can then discover each database's focus by checking the description of the database (sometimes labeled "Help" or "Guide") or the

---

1. Initial keyword search of periodical database

list of indexed resources (sometimes labeled "Publications" or "Index"). The description will also tell you the time period the database covers, so you'll know whether you also need to consult older print indexes at the library.

■ Database searches

When you first search a database, use your own keywords to locate sources. The procedure is illustrated in the three screen shots shown here. Your goal is to find at least one source that seems just

2. Partial keyword search results

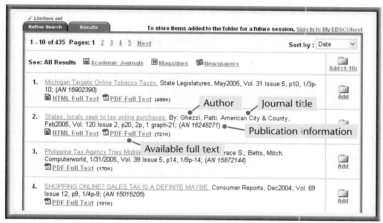

3. Full article record with abstract

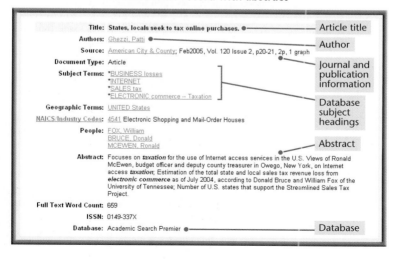

right for your subject, so that you can then see what subject headings the database itself uses for such sources. Using one or more of those headings will focus and speed your search.

Note Many databases allow you to limit your search to so-called peer-reviewed or refereed journals—that is, scholarly journals whose articles have been reviewed before publication by experts in the field and then revised by the author. Limiting your search to peer-reviewed journals can help you navigate huge databases that might otherwise return scores of unusable articles.

■ **The use of abstracts**

In screen 3 on the previous page, the full article record shows a key feature of many databases' periodical listings: an **abstract** that summarizes the article. By describing research methods, conclusions, and other information, an abstract can tell you whether you want to pursue an article and thus save you time. However, the abstract cannot replace the actual article. If you want to use the work as a source, you must consult the full text.

■ **Helpful databases**

The list below includes databases to which academic libraries commonly subscribe. Some of these databases cover much the same material, so your library may subscribe to several of them but not all.

EBSCOhost Academic Search. A periodical index covering magazines and journals in the social sciences, sciences, arts, and humanities. Many articles are available full-text.

InfoTrac Expanded Academic. The Gale Group's general periodical index covering the social sciences, sciences, arts, and humanities as well as national news periodicals. It includes full-text articles.

LexisNexis Academic. An index of news and business, legal, and reference information, with full-text articles. *LexisNexis* includes international, national, and regional newspapers, news magazines, legal and business publications, and court cases.

Nineteenth-Century Masterfile. Perhaps the only electronic database for periodicals from the nineteenth century.

ProQuest Research Library. A periodical index covering the sciences, social sciences, arts, and humanities, including many full-text articles.

Wilson Databases. A collection of indexes, often provided in a package, including *Business Periodicals Index, Education Index, General Science Index, Humanities Index, Readers' Guide to Periodical Literature,* and *Social Sciences Index.*

2 **Locations of periodicals**

If an index listing does not include or link directly to the full text of an article, you'll need to consult the periodical itself. Recent issues of periodicals are probably held in the library's periodical room. Back issues are usually stored elsewhere, either in bound volumes or on film that requires a special machine to read. A librarian will show you how to operate the machine.

51e Finding sources on the Web

As an academic researcher, you enter the World Wide Web in two ways: through your library's Web site, and through public search engines such as *Yahoo!* and *Google*. The library entrance, covered in the preceding sections, is your main path to the books and periodicals that, for most subjects, should make up most of your sources. The public entrance, discussed here, can lead to a wealth of information and ideas, but it also has a number of disadvantages:

- **The Web is a wide-open network.** Anyone with the right hardware and software can place information on the Internet, and even a carefully conceived search can turn up sources with widely varying reliability: journal articles, government documents, scholarly data, term papers written by high school students, sales pitches masked as objective reports, wild theories. You must be especially diligent about evaluating Internet sources (see pp. 399–405).
- **The Web changes constantly.** No search engine can keep up with the Web's daily additions and deletions, and a source you find today may be different or gone tomorrow. You should not put off consulting an online source that you think you may want to use.
- **The Web provides limited information on the past.** Sources dating from before the 1980s or even more recently probably will not appear on the Web.
- **The Web is not all-inclusive.** Most books and many periodicals are available only via the library, not directly via the Web.

Clearly, the Web warrants cautious use. It should not be the only resource you work with.

1 Search engines

To find sources on the Web, you use a **search engine** that catalogs Web sites in a series of directories and conducts keyword searches. Generally, use a directory when you haven't yet refined your topic or you want a general overview. Use keywords when you have refined your topic and you seek specific information.

■ **Current search engines**

The box below lists the currently most popular search engines. To reach any one of them, enter its address in the Address or Location field of your Web browser.

Note For a good range of reliable sources, try out more than a single search engine, perhaps as many as four or five. No search engine can catalog the entire Web—indeed, even the most powerful engine may not include half the sites available at any given time, and most engines include only a fifth or less. In addition, most search engines accept paid placements, giving higher billing to sites that pay a fee. These so-called sponsored links are usually marked as such, but they can compromise a search engine's method for arranging sites in response to your keywords.

Web search engines

The features of search engines change often, and new ones appear constantly. For the latest on search engines, see the links collected by Search Engine Watch at *searchenginewatch.com/links*.

Directories that review sites
BUBL Link (*bubl.ac.uk*)
Internet Public Library (*ipl.org/div/subject*)
Internet Scout Project (*scout.wisc.edu/archives*)
Librarians' Index to the Internet (*lii.org*)

Most advanced and efficient engines
AlltheWeb (*alltheweb.com*)

One of the fastest and most comprehensive engines, *AlltheWeb* updates its database frequently so that it returns more of the Web's most recent sites. It allows searches for news, pictures, and audio and video files.

Google (*google.com*)

Also fast and comprehensive, *Google* ranks a site based not only on its content but also on the other sites that are linked to it, thus providing a measure of a site's usefulness. *Google* also allows searches for news, discussion groups, and images.

Other engines
AltaVista (*altavista.com*)
Ask Jeeves (*ask.com*)
Dogpile (*dogpile.com*)
Excite (*excite.com*)
Lycos (*lycos.com*)
MetaCrawler (*metacrawler.com*)
Yahoo! (*yahoo.com*)

■ A sample search engine

The screen shot below from *Google* shows the features common to most search engines.

Google home page

A search engine's Advanced Search option allows you to customize your search (for instance, by selecting a date range, a language, or a number of results to see) and to limit or expand your keywords (for instance, by using *AND, NOT*, and other operators). It may also tell you how the search engine determines the order in which it presents results. (Criteria include the number of times your keywords appear on a site, whether the terms appear in the site's title or address, and, in *Google*'s case, which other sites link to the site.)

■ Search records

The screen shot above shows two features of your Web browser that allow you to keep track of Web sources and your search:

- *Favorites* or *Bookmarks* **save site addresses as links.** Click one of these terms near the top of the browser screen to add a site you want to return to. A favorite or bookmark remains on file until you delete it.

- *History* **records the sites you visited over a certain period,** such as a single online session or a week's sessions. (After that period, the history is deleted.) If you forgot to bookmark a site, you can click History or Go to locate your search history and recover the site.

2 A sample search

The following sample Web search illustrates how the refinement of keywords can narrow a search to maximize the relevant hits and minimize the irrelevant ones. Kisha Alder, a student researching taxes on Internet commerce, first used the keywords

Internet taxes on *Google*. But, as shown in the screen shot below, the search produced more than 13 *million* hits, an unusably large number and a sure sign that Alder's keywords needed revision.

1. First *Google* search results

After several tries, Alder arrived at *"sales tax" Internet states reform* to describe her subject more precisely. Narrowed in this way, Alder's search still produced 5,000 hits, but this large number included many potential sources on the first few screens, as shown below.

2. *Google* results with refined keywords

51f Finding other online sources

Several online sources can put you directly in touch with experts and others whose ideas and information may inform your research. Because these sources, like Web sites, are unfiltered, you must always evaluate them carefully. (See pp. 399–405.)

1 Using electronic mail

As a research tool, e-mail allows you to communicate with others who are interested in your topic. You may, for instance, carry on an e-mail conversation with a teacher at your school or interview an expert in another state to follow up on a scholarly article he or she published. (See **2** pp. 114–17 for more on using e-mail.)

2 Using discussion lists

A **discussion list** (sometimes called a **listserv** or just a **list**) uses e-mail to connect individuals who are interested in a common subject, often with a scholarly or technical focus. By sending a question to an appropriate list, you may be able to reach scores of people who know something about your topic. For an index of discussion lists, see *tile.net/lists*.

When conducting research on a discussion list, follow the guidelines for e-mail etiquette (**2** pp. 116–17) as well as these:

- *Lurk* for a while—read without posting messages. Make sure the discussion is relevant to your topic, and get a sense of how the group interacts.

- **Don't ask for information you can find elsewhere.** Most list members are glad to help with legitimate questions but resent messages that rehash familiar debates or that ask them to do someone else's work.

- **Evaluate messages carefully.** Many list subscribers are passionate experts with fair-minded approaches to their topics, but almost anyone with an Internet connection can post a message to a list. See pp. 399–405 on evaluating online sources.

3 Using Web forums and newsgroups

Web forums and newsgroups are more open and less scholarly than discussion lists, so their messages require even more diligent evaluation. **Web forums** allow participants to join a conversation simply by selecting a link on a Web page. For a directory of forums, see *delphiforums.com*. **Newsgroups** are organized under subject headings such as *soc* for social issues and *biz* for business. For a directory of newsgroups, see *groups.google.com*.

4 Using Web logs

Web logs, or **blogs,** are personal sites on which an author posts time-stamped comments, generally centering on a common theme, in a format that allows readers to respond to the author and to each other. You can find a directory of blogs at *bloglines.com* and *blogwise.com*.

Like all other online media discussed in this section, Web logs consulted as potential sources must be evaluated carefully. Some are reliable sources of opinion, news, or evolving scholarship, and many refer to worthy books, articles, Web sites, and other resources. But lots of blogs are little more than outlets for their authors' gripes and prejudices. See pp. 404–05 for tips on telling the good from the bad.

5 Using synchronous communication

Synchronous (or simultaneous) **communication** allows conversation in real time, the way you talk on the phone. Synchronous programs include instant-messaging applications, Web courseware, Internet relay chat (IRC), and virtual environments called MOOs.

Synchronous communication can be used to conduct interviews or hold debates. Your instructor may ask you to use it for your coursework or research and will provide the software and instructions to get you started. You can also find out more about synchronous communication at *du.org/cybercomp.html* or *Internet101.org/chat.html*.

51g Using government publications

Government publications provide a vast array of data, compilations, reports, policy statements, public records, and other historical and contemporary information. For US government publications, consult the Government Printing Office's *GPO Access* at *gpoaccess .gov/index.html*. Many federal, state, and local government agencies post important publications—legislation, reports, press releases—on their own Web sites. You can find lists of sites for various federal agencies by using the keywords *United States federal government* with a search engine. In addition, several Web sites are useful resources: *fedstats.gov* (government statistics) and *infoplease.com/us.html* (links to information on federal, state, and local governments).

51h Finding images

The use of images to support an argument is discussed in **2** pp. 104–10. To find images, you have a number of options. (The Web links in the following lists are available online at *ablongman.com/ littlebrown.*)

- **Scout for images while reading sources.** Your sources may include charts, graphs, photographs, and other images that can support your ideas. When you find an image you may want to use, photocopy or download it so you'll have it available later.
- **Create your own images,** such as photographs or charts. See 1 pp. 62–65 for examples.
- **Use an image search engine.** *Google, Yahoo!, AlltheWeb,* and some other search engines conduct specialized image searches. They can find scores of images, but the results may be inaccurate or incomplete because the sources surveyed often do not include descriptions of the images. (The engines will search file names and any text accompanying the images.)
- **Use a public image database.** The following sites generally conduct accurate searches because their images are filed with information such as a description of the image, the artist's name, and the image's date:

    Adflip (*adflip.com*): Historical and contemporary print advertisements
    Duke University, *Ad*Access* (*scriptorium.lib.duke.edu/adaccess*): Print advertisements spanning 1911–55
    Library of Congress, *American Memory* (*memory.loc.gov/ammem*): Maps, photographs, and prints documenting the American experience
    Library of Congress, *Prints and Photographs Online Catalog* (*loc.gov/rr/ print/catalog.html*): Images from the library's collection, including those available through *American Memory*
    New York Public Library Digital Gallery (*digitalgallery.nypl.org/nypldigital*): Maps, drawings, photographs, and paintings from the library's collection
    Political Cartoons (*politicalcartoons.com*): Cartoons on contemporary issues and events

- **Use a public image directory.** The following sites collect links to image sources:

    Art Source (*ilpi.com/artsource/general.html*): Sources on art and architecture
    ARTstor (*artstor.org*): Museum collections and a database of images typically used in art history courses
    Museum Computer Network (*mcn.edu/resources/sitesonline.htm*): Museum collections
    Washington State University, *Popular Culture: Resources for Critical Analysis* (*wsu.edu/%7Eamerstu/pop/tvrguide.html*): Sources on advertising, fashion, magazines, toys, and other artifacts of popular culture
    Yale University Arts Library, *Image Resources* (*library.yale.edu/art/ imageresources.html*): Sources on the visual and performing arts

- **Use a subscription database.** Your library may subscribe to the following resources:

Associated Press, *AccuNet/AP Multimedia Archives*: Historical and contemporary news images
Grove Art Online: Art images and links to museum sites

Many images you find will be available for free, but some sources do charge a fee for use. Before paying for an image, check with a librarian to see if it is available elsewhere for free.

Note You must cite every image source fully in your paper, just as you cite text sources, with author, title, and publication information. In addition, some sources will require that you seek permission from the copyright holder, either the source itself or a third party such as a photographer. Permission is especially likely to be required if you are submitting your paper on the public Web. See p. 425 for more about online publication.

51i   Generating your own sources

Academic writing will often require you to conduct primary research for information of your own. For instance, you may need to analyze a poem, conduct an experiment, or interview an expert.

An interview can be especially helpful for a research project because it allows you to ask questions precisely geared to your topic. You can conduct an interview in person, over the telephone, or online using electronic mail (p. 393) or a form of synchronous communication (p. 394). A personal interview is preferable if you can arrange it, because you can see the person's expressions and gestures as well as hear his or her tone and words.

Here are a few guidelines for interviews:

- **Call or write for an appointment.** Tell the person exactly why you are calling, what you want to discuss, and how long you expect the interview to take. Be true to your word on all points.

- **Prepare a list of open-ended questions to ask**—perhaps ten or twelve for a one-hour interview. Plan on doing some research for these questions to discover background on the issues and your subject's published views on the issues.

- **Give your subject time to consider your questions.** Don't rush into silences with more questions.

- **Pay attention to your subject's answers** so that you can ask appropriate follow-up questions and pick up on unexpected but worthwhile points.

- **Take care in interpreting answers,** especially if you are online and thus can't depend on facial expressions, gestures, and tone of voice to convey the subject's attitudes.

- **Keep thorough notes.** Take notes during an in-person or telephone interview, or tape-record the interview if you have the equipment and your subject agrees. For online interviews, save the discussion in a file of its own.

- **Verify quotations.** Before you quote your subject in your paper, check with him or her to ensure that the quotations are accurate.

- **Send a thank-you note immediately after the interview.** Promise your subject a copy of your finished paper, and send the paper promptly.

52 Working with Sources

Research writing is much more than finding sources and reporting their contents. The challenge and interest come from *interacting* with sources, reading them critically to discover their meanings, judge their relevance and reliability, and create relationships among them. This chapter shows you how to use the sources you find to extend and support your own ideas, to make your subject your own.

CULTURE LANGUAGE Making a subject your own requires thinking critically about sources and developing independent ideas. These goals may at first be uncomfortable if your native culture emphasizes understanding and respecting established authority more than questioning and enlarging it. The information here will help you work with sources so that you can become an expert in your own right and convincingly convey your expertise to others.

52a Evaluating sources

Before you gather information and ideas from sources, scan them to evaluate what they have to offer and how you might use them.

1 Judging relevance and reliability

Not all the sources you find will prove worthwhile: some may be irrelevant to your subject, and others may be unreliable. Gauging the relevance and reliability of sources is the essential task of evaluating them. If you haven't already done so, read this book's chapter

http://www.ablongman.com/littlebrown ▶

Visit the companion Web site for more help and electronic exercises on working with sources.

on critical thinking and reading (**2** pp. 82–95). It provides a foundation for answering the questions in the box below.

Questions for evaluating sources

For online sources, supplement these guidelines with those opposite and on p. 404.

Relevance

- **Does the source devote some attention to your subject?** Check whether the source focuses on your subject or covers it marginally, and compare the source's coverage to that in other sources.
- **Is the source appropriately specialized for your needs?** Check the source's treatment of a topic you know something about, to ensure that it is neither too superficial nor too technical.
- **Is the source up to date enough for your subject?** Check the publication date. If your subject is current, your sources should be, too.

Reliability

- **Where does the source come from?** It matters whether you found the source through your library or directly on the Internet. (If the latter, see opposite and p. 404.) Check whether a library source is popular or scholarly. Scholarly sources, such as refereed journals and university press books, are generally deeper and more reliable.
- **Is the author an expert in the field?** The authors of scholarly publications tend to be experts. To verify expertise, check an author's credentials in a biography (if the source includes one), in a biographical reference, or by a keyword search of the Web.
- **What is the author's bias?** Every author has a point of view that influences the selection and interpretation of evidence. How do the author's ideas relate to those in other sources? What areas does the author emphasize, ignore, or dismiss? When you're aware of sources' biases, you can attempt to balance them.
- **Is the source fair and reasonable?** Even a strongly biased work should present sound reasoning, adequate evidence, and a fair picture of opposing views—all in an objective, calm tone. The absence of any of these qualities should raise a warning flag.
- **Is the source well written?** A logical organization and clear, error-free sentences indicate a careful author.

You can download these questions from *ablongman.com/littlebrown* and use a copy of the file for each source you are evaluating, providing written answers between the questions.

Note In evaluating sources, you need to consider how they come to you. The sources you find through the library, both print and online, have been previewed for you by their publishers and by the library's staff. They still require your critical reading, but you can have some confidence in the information they contain. With online sources you reach directly, however, you can't assume similar pre-viewing, so your critical reading must be especially rigorous. Special tips for evaluating Web sites and other online sources appear below and on the following pages.

2 Evaluating a Web site

To a great extent, the same critical reading that helps you evaluate library sources will help you evaluate Web sites. But most Web sites have not undergone prior screening by editors and librarians. On your own, you must distinguish scholarship from corporate promotion, valid data from invented statistics, well-founded opinion from clever propaganda.

The strategy summarized in the box below can help you make such distinctions. We'll apply the strategy to the Web site shown on p. 401, *Global Warming Information Center,* which turned up in a search for views and data on global warming.

Questions for evaluating Web sites

Supplement these questions with those on the facing page.

- **What type of site are you viewing?** What does the type lead you to expect about the site's purpose and content?
- **Who is the author or sponsor?** How credible is the person or group responsible for the site?
- **What is the purpose of the site?** What does the site's author or sponsor intend to achieve?
- **What does context tell you?** What do you already know about the site's subject that can inform your evaluation? What kinds of support or other information do the site's links provide?
- **What does presentation tell you?** Is the site's design well thought out and effective? Is the writing clear and error-free?
- **How worthwhile is the content?** Are the site's claims well supported by evidence? Is the evidence from reliable sources?

You can download these questions from *ablongman.com/littlebrown.* Use a copy of the file for each source you are evaluating, providing written answers between the questions.

Note To evaluate a Web document, you'll often need to travel to the site's home page to discover the author or sponsoring organization, date of publication, and other relevant information. The page you're reading may include a link to the home page. If it doesn't, you can find it by editing the URL in the Address or Location field of your browser. Working backward, delete the end of the URL up to the last slash and hit Enter. Repeat this step until you reach the home page. There you may also find a menu option, often labeled

"About," that will lead you to a description of the site's author or sponsor.

■ Determine the type of site.

When you search the Web, you're likely to encounter various types of sites. Although they overlap—a primarily informational site may include scholarship as well—the types can usually be identified by their content and purposes. Here are the main types:

- **Sites focusing on scholarship:** These sites have a knowledge-building interest and include research reports with supporting data and extensive documentation of scholarly sources. The URLs of the sites generally end in *edu* (originating from an educational institution), *org* (a nonprofit organization), or *gov* (a government department or agency). Such sites are more likely to be reliable than the others described below.

- **Sites with an informational purpose:** Individuals, nonprofit organizations, schools, corporations, and government bodies all produce sites intended to centralize information on subjects as diverse as astronomy, hip-hop music, and zoo design. The sites' URLs may end in *edu, org, gov,* or *com* (originating from a commercial organization). Such sites generally do not have the knowledge-building focus of scholarly sites and may omit supporting data and documentation, but they can provide useful information and often include links to scholarly sources.

- **Sites focusing on advocacy:** Many sites present the views of individuals or organizations that advocate certain policies or actions. Their URLs usually end in *org*, but they may end in *edu* or *com*. Some advocacy sites include serious, well-documented research to support their positions, but others select or distort evidence.

- **Sites with a commercial purpose:** Corporations and other businesses maintain Web sites to explain or promote themselves or to sell goods and services. The URLs of commercial sites end in *com*. The information on such a site furthers the sponsor's profit-making purpose, but it can include reliable data.

- **Personal sites:** The sites maintained by individuals range from diaries of a family's travels to opinions on political issues to reports on evolving scholarship. The sites' URLs usually end in *com* or *edu*. Personal sites are only as reliable as their authors, but some do provide valuable eyewitness accounts, links to worthy sources, and other usable information. A particular kind of personal site, the Web log, is discussed on pp. 404–05.

The home page of the *Global Warming Information Center* gives some information that can be used to tell what type of site it is:

1. Home page of the *Global Warming Information Center*

URL including *org:* a nonprofit organization

Site title implying an informational purpose

Sponsor's name

■ Identify the author or sponsor.

A reputable site will list the author or group responsible for the site and will provide information or a link for contacting the author or group. If none of this information is provided, you should not use the source. If you have only the author or group name, you may be able to discover more in a biographical dictionary or through a keyword search. You should also look for mentions of the author or group in your other sources.

As the screen shot shows, the Web site *Global Warming Information Center* names its sponsor right up front: the John P. McGovern M.D. Center for Environmental and Regulatory Affairs. The bottom of this home page gives links to information about the McGovern Center and its parent organization, the National Center for Public Policy Research. Their names imply that both groups are involved in research, so the site does indeed seem to be informational or possibly even scholarly.

■ Gauge purpose.

A Web site's purpose determines what ideas and information it offers. Inferring that purpose tells you how to interpret what you see on the site. If a site is intended to sell a product or an opinion, it will likely emphasize favorable ideas and information while ignoring or even distorting what is unfavorable. In contrast, if a site is intended to build knowledge—for instance, a scholarly project or journal—it will likely acknowledge diverse views and evidence.

Determining the purpose of a site often requires looking beneath the surface of words and images and beyond the first page. The elements of the *Global Warming* page—the title, the green color, the photo of a child carrying a globe through a field of grass—suggest an environmentalist purpose of informing readers about the theory and consequences of rising earth temperatures caused by pollution. The site's purpose is actually different, though. The home-page links lead to statements about the aims of the McGovern Center and its parent, the National Center. The McGovern Center states that it was launched in the 1900s "to counter misinformation being spread to the public and policymakers by the environmental left." The National Center states its purpose more broadly:

> The National Center for Public Policy Research is a communications and research foundation supportive of a strong national defense and dedicated to providing free market solutions to today's public policy problems. We believe that the principles of a free market, individual liberty, and personal responsibility provide the greatest hope for meeting the challenges facing America in the 21st century.

These two statements imply that the purpose of the McGovern Center's *Global Warming* site is to inform readers about the evidence against global warming in the interest of reducing or overturning environmental regulations.

■ Consider context.

Your evaluation of a Web site should be informed by considerations outside the site itself. Chief among these is your own knowledge: What do you already know about the site's subject and the prevailing views of it? In addition, you can follow some of the site's links to see how they support, or don't support, the site's credibility. For instance, links to scholarly sources lend authority to a site—but *only if* the scholarly sources actually relate to and back up the site's claims.

The *Global Warming* site has a clear anti-regulatory bias, but this view is a significant one in the debates over global warming. That is, the bias does not necessarily disqualify the site as a source on global warming. The question is how reliable its information is: does it come from trustworthy, less-biased sources? All the site's links lead to publications of the McGovern Center or the National Center, so the question can be answered only by looking more deeply at these publications.

■ Look at presentation.

Considering both the look of a site and the way it's written can illuminate its intentions and reliability. Are the site's elements all functional and well integrated, or is the site cluttered with irrelevant material and graphics? Does the site seem carefully constructed and well maintained, or is it sloppy and outdated? Does the design reflect the apparent purpose of the site, or does it undercut or conceal that purpose in some way? Is the text clearly written, or is it difficult to understand? Is it error-free, or does it contain typos and grammatical errors?

At first glance, as noted earlier, the *Global Warming* site casts a pro-environmentalist image that turns out not to coincide with its purpose. Otherwise, the site is cleanly designed, with minimal elements laid out clearly. The text on other pages is straightforward and readable. Apparently, the sponsor takes its purpose seriously and has thought out its presentation.

■ Analyze content.

With information about a site's author, purpose, and context, you're in a position to evaluate its content. Are the ideas and information slanted and, if so, in what direction? Are the views and data authoritative, or do you need to balance them—or even reject them? These questions require close reading of the text and its sources.

The *Global Warming* site links to a wealth of reports and prominently features "Questions and Answers on Global Warming." The following screen shots show two of the items from this page and the footnotes citing sources for the answers.

---

2. Content and documentation from the site

Questions and Answers on Global Warming

1. Is global warming occurring? Have the forecasts of global warming been confirmed by actual measurements?

There is no serious evidence that man-made global warming is taking place. The computer models used in U.N. studies say the first area to heat under the "greenhouse gas effect" should be the lower atmosphere - known as the troposphere. 1 Highly accurate, carefully checked satellite data have shown absolutely no such tropospheric warming. There has been surface warming of about half a degree Celsius, but this is far below the customary natural swings in surface temperatures. 2

Assertions about the validity and causes of global warming, citing data and expert opinion as evidence

2. Are carbon dioxide emissions from burning fossil fuels the primary cause of climate change? Can the Earth's temperature be expected to rise between 2.5 and 10.4 degrees Fahrenheit in this century as has been reported?

There are many indications that carbon dioxide does not play a significant role in global warming. Richard Lindzen, Ph.D., professor at the Massachusetts Institute of Technology and one of the 11 scientists who prepared a 2001 National Academy of Sciences (NAS) report on climate change, estimates that a doubling of carbon dioxide in the atmosphere would produce a temperature increase of only one degree Celsius. 3 In fact, clouds and water vapor appear to be far more important factors related to global temperature. According to Dr. Lindzen and NASA scientists, clouds and water vapor may play a significant role in regulating the Earth's temperature to keep it more constant. 4

Footnotes

1 James K. Glassman and Sallie Baliunas, *The Weekly Standard*, June 25, 2001.
2 *Ibid*.
3 Richard Lindzen, professor of meteorology, Massachusetts Institute of Technology and member of the National Academy of Sciences, "Scientists' Report Doesn't Support The Kyoto Treaty," *The Wall Street Journal*, June 11, 2001.
4 Glassman and Baliunas.

Footnotes citing an article in the conservative magazine *The Weekly Standard* and a newspaper report, not scholarly publications that explain methods of gathering and interpreting the data used as evidence

The source mix shown in the preceding screen shot is similar in the other publications found through the *Global Warming* site. Scholars do disagree over whether the earth's temperatures are rising significantly, whether human-made pollution is an important cause, how serious the consequences may be, and how to solve the problem. Because the *Global Warming* site does not offer or refer to the scholarly research, its claims and evidence must be viewed suspiciously and probably rejected for use in a research paper. A usable source need not be less biased, but it must be more substantial.

3 Evaluating other online sources

Web logs and the postings to online discussions require the same critical scrutiny as Web sites do. Web logs can be sources of in-depth information and informed opinion, but they can also be virtually useless. Web forums and newsgroups are similarly suspect. Even if a reliable blog or discussion-group message provides very current information or eyewitness testimony, it will not have the authority of a scholarly publication. An e-mail discussion list may be more trustworthy if its subscribers are professionals in the field, but you will still find wrong or misleading data and skewed opinions.

Use the following strategy for evaluating blogs and messages in online discussions.

Questions for evaluating Web logs and online discussions

Supplement these questions with those on p. 398.

- **Who is the author?** How credible is the person writing?
- **What is the author's purpose?** What can you tell about why the author is writing?
- **What does the context reveal?** What do others' responses on a blog or the other messages in a discussion thread indicate about the source's balance and reliability?
- **How worthwhile is the content?** Are the author's claims supported by evidence? Is the evidence from reliable sources?
- **How does the blog or message compare with other sources?** Do the author's claims seem accurate and fair given what you've seen in sources you know to be reliable?

You can download these questions from *ablongman.com/littlebrown*. Use a copy of the file for each source you are evaluating, providing written answers between the questions.

- **Identify the author.**

Checking out the author of a blog or online message can help you judge the reliability of the posting. If the author uses a screen name, write directly to him or her requesting full name and credentials. Do not use the message as a source if the author fails to respond. Once you know an author's name, you may be able to obtain background information from a keyword search of the Web or a biographical dictionary.

■ Analyze the author's purpose.

As with Web sites, you can use cues in the author's writing to figure out *why* he or she is writing and thus how to position the blog or message among your other sources. The claims, use (or not) of evidence, and treatment of opposing views all convey the author's stand on the subject and general fairness.

■ Consider the context.

Web logs and discussion-group postings are often difficult to evaluate in isolation. Looking outside a particular contribution to the responses of others will give you a sense of how the author's view is regarded. On a blog, look at the comments others have posted. Do the same with discussion-group messages, going back to the initial posting in the discussion thread and reading forward.

■ Analyze content.

A reliable source will offer evidence for claims and sources for evidence. If you don't see such supporting information, ask the author for it. (If he or she fails to respond, don't use the source.) Then verify the sources with your own research: are they reputable?

The tone of the writing can also be a clue to its purpose and reliability. Blogs and online discussions tend to be more informal and often more heated than other kinds of dialog, but look askance at writing that's contemptuous, dismissive, or shrill.

■ Compare with other sources.

Always consider blogs and discussion-group messages in comparison to other sources so that you can distinguish singular, untested views from more mainstream views that have been subject to verification. Don't assume that a blog author's information and opinions are mainstream just because you see them on other blogs. The technology allows content to be picked up instantly on other blogs, so widespread distribution indicates only popularity, not reliability.

Be wary of blogs or messages that reproduce periodical articles, reports, or other publications. Try to locate the original version of the publication to be sure it has been reproduced fully and accurately, not quoted selectively or distorted. If you can't locate the original version, then don't use the publication as a source.

52b Synthesizing sources

When you begin to locate the differences and similarities among sources, you move into the most significant part of research writing: forging relationships for your own purpose. This **synthesis** is an essential step in reading sources critically, and it continues through the drafting and revision of a research paper. As you infer connections—say, between one writer's opinions and another's or between two works by the same author—you create new knowledge.

Your synthesis of sources will grow more detailed and sophisticated as you proceed through the research-writing process. Unless you are analyzing primary sources such as the works of a poet, at first read your sources quickly and selectively to obtain an overview of your subject and a sense of how the sources approach it. Don't get bogged down in gathering detailed information, but *do* record your ideas about sources in your research journal (p. 372) or your annotated bibliography (p. 377).

▥ Respond to sources.

Write down what your sources make you think. Do you agree or disagree with the author? Do you find his or her views narrow, or do they open up new approaches for you? Is there anything in the source that you need to research further before you can understand it? Does the source prompt questions that you should keep in mind while reading other sources?

▥ Connect sources.

When you notice a link between sources, jot it down. Do two sources differ in their theories or their interpretations of facts? Does one source illuminate another—perhaps commenting or clarifying or supplying additional data? Do two or more sources report studies that support a theory you've read about or an idea of your own?

▥ Heed your own insights.

Apart from ideas prompted by your sources, you are sure to come up with independent thoughts: a conviction, a point of confusion that suddenly becomes clear, a question you haven't seen anyone else ask. These insights may occur at unexpected times, so it's good practice to keep a notebook or computer handy to record them.

▥ Use sources to support your own ideas.

As your research proceeds, the responses, connections, and insights you form through synthesis will lead you to answer your starting research question with a statement of your thesis (see

p. 427). They will also lead you to the main ideas supporting your thesis—conclusions you have drawn from your synthesis of sources, forming the main divisions of your paper. When drafting the paper, make sure each paragraph focuses on an idea of your own, with the support for the idea coming from your sources. In this way, your paper will synthesize others' work into something wholly your own.

EXERCISE 52.1 Synthesizing sources

The three passages below address the same issue, the legalization of drugs. What similarities do you see in the authors' ideas? What differences? Write a paragraph of your own in which you use these authors' views as a point of departure for your own view about drug legalization. (You can do this exercise online at *ablongman.com/littlebrown*.)

Perhaps the most unfortunate victims of drug prohibition laws have been the residents of America's ghettos. These laws have proved largely futile in deterring ghetto-dwellers from becoming drug abusers, but they do account for much of what ghetto residents identify as the drug problem. Aggressive, gun-toting drug dealers often upset law-abiding residents far more than do addicts nodding out in doorways. Meanwhile other residents perceive the drug dealers as heroes and successful role models. They're symbols of success to children who see no other options. At the same time the increasingly harsh criminal penalties imposed on adult drug dealers have led drug traffickers to recruit juveniles. Where once children started dealing drugs only after they had been using them for a few years, today the sequence is often reversed. Many children start using drugs only after working for older drug dealers for a while. Legalization of drugs, like legalization of alcohol in the 1930s, would drive the drug-dealing business off the streets and out of apartment buildings and into government-regulated, tax-paying stores. It also would force many of the gun-toting dealers out of the business and convert others into legitimate businessmen.
—Ethan A. Nadelmann, "Shooting Up"

Statistics argue against legalization. The University of Michigan conducts an annual survey of twelfth graders, asking the students about their drug consumption. In 1980, 56.4 percent of those polled said they had used marijuana in the past twelve months, whereas in 2004 only 45.7 percent had done so. Cocaine use was also reduced in the same period (22.6 percent to 15.4 percent). At the same time, twelve-month use of legally available drugs—alcohol and nicotine-containing cigarettes—remained constant at about 75 percent and 55 percent, respectively. The numbers of illegal drug users haven't declined nearly enough: those teenaged marijuana and cocaine users are still vulnerable to addiction and even death, and they threaten to infect their impressionable peers. But clearly the prohibition of illegal drugs has helped, while the legal status of alcohol and cigarettes has not made them less popular.
—Sylvia Runkle, "The Case Against Legalization"

I have to laugh at the debate over what to do about the drug problem. Everyone is running around offering solutions—from making drug use a more serious criminal offense to legalizing it. But there isn't a real solution. I know that. I used and abused drugs, and people, and society, for two decades. Nothing worked to get me to stop all that behavior except just plain being sick and tired. Nothing. Not threats, not ten-plus years in prison, not anything that was said to me. I used until I got through. Period. And that's when you'll win the war. When all the dope fiends are done. Not a minute before.

—Michael W. Posey, "I Did Drugs Until They Wore Me Out. Then I Stopped."

52c   Gathering information from sources

You can accomplish a great deal of synthesis while gathering information from your sources. This information gathering is not a mechanical process. Rather, as you read you assess and organize the information in your sources.

Researchers vary in their methods for working with sources, but all methods share the same goals:

- **Keep accurate records of what sources say.** Accuracy helps prevent misrepresentation and plagiarism.
- **Keep accurate records of how to find sources.** These records are essential for retracing steps and for citing sources in the final paper. (See pp. 377–79 on keeping a working bibliography.)
- **Interact with sources.** Reading sources critically leads to an understanding of them, the relationships among them, and their support for one's own ideas.

To achieve these goals, you can take handwritten notes, type notes into your computer, annotate photocopies or printouts of sources, or annotate downloaded documents. On any given project, you may use all the methods. Each has advantages and disadvantages.

- **Handwritten notes:** Taking notes by hand is especially useful if you come across a source with no computer or photocopier handy. But handwritten notes can be risky. It's easy to introduce errors as you work from source to note card. And it's possible to copy source language and then later mistake and use it as your own, thus plagiarizing the source. Always take care to make accurate notes and to place big quotation marks around any passage you quote.
- **Notes on computer:** Taking notes on a computer can streamline the path of source to note to paper, because you can import the notes into your draft as you write. However, computer

notes have the same disadvantages as handwritten notes: the risk of introducing errors and the risk of plagiarizing. As with handwritten notes, strive for accuracy, and use quotation marks for quotations.

- **Photocopies and printouts:** Photocopying from print sources or printing out online sources each has the distinct advantages of convenience and reduction in the risks of error and plagiarism during information gathering. But each method has disadvantages, too. The busywork of copying or printing can distract you from the crucial work of interacting with sources. And you have to make a special effort to annotate copies and printouts with the publication information for sources. If you don't have this information for your final paper, you can't use the source.

- **Downloads:** Researching online, you can usually download full-text articles, Web pages, discussion-group messages, and other materials onto your computer. While drafting, you can import source information from one file into another. Like photocopies and printouts, though, downloads can distract you from interacting with sources and can easily become separated from the publication information you must have in order to use the sources. Even more important, directly importing source material creates a high risk of plagiarism. You must keep clear boundaries between your own ideas and words and those of others.

52d Using summary, paraphrase, and quotation

As you take notes from sources or work source material into your draft, you can summarize, paraphrase, quote, or combine methods. The choice should depend on why you are using a source.

Note Summaries, paraphrases, and quotations all require source citations. A summary or paraphrase without a source citation or a quotation without quotation marks and a source citation is plagiarism. (See pp. 418–25 for more on plagiarism.)

1 Summary

When you **summarize,** you condense an extended idea or argument into a sentence or more in your own words. Summary is most useful when you want to record the gist of an author's idea without the background or supporting evidence. Following is a passage from a government report on the so-called digital divide between US residents with and without access to the Internet. Then a sample computer note shows a summary of the passage.

Original quotation

The following examples highlight the breadth of the digital divide today:

- Those with a college degree are more than *eight times* as likely to have a computer at home, and nearly *sixteen times* as likely to have home Internet access, as those with an elementary school education.
- A high-income household in an urban area is more than *twenty times* as likely as a rural, low-income household to have Internet access.
- A child in a low-income white family is *three times* as likely to have Internet access as a child in a comparable black family, and *four times* as likely to have access as children in a comparable Hispanic household.

—US Department of Commerce, *Falling Through the Net: Toward Digital Inclusion*, p. 7

Summary of source

Digital divide

Dept. of Commerce 7

US residents who are urban, white, college educated, and affluent are <u>much</u> more likely to be connected to the Internet than those who are rural, black or Hispanic, not educated past elementary school, and poor.

---

2 Paraphrase

When you **paraphrase,** you follow much more closely the author's original presentation, but you still restate it in your own words and sentence structures. Paraphrase is most useful when you want to present or examine an author's line of reasoning but don't feel the original words merit direct quotation. Here is a paraphrase of the above quotation from the Department of Commerce report.

Paraphrase of source

Digital divide

Dept. of Commerce 7

Likelihood of being connected to the Internet among US groups:

Home connection, elementary education vs. college education: 1/16 as likely.

Any access, rural setting and low-income household vs. urban setting and affluent household: 1/20 as likely.

Any access, low-income black child vs. low-income white child: 1/3 as likely.

Any access, low-income Hispanic child vs. low-income white child: 1/4 as likely.

Paraphrasing a source

- **Read the relevant material several times to be sure you understand it.**
- **Restate the source's ideas in your own words and sentence structures.** You need not put down in new words the whole passage or all the details. Select what is relevant to your topic, and restate only that. If complete sentences seem too detailed or cumbersome, use phrases, as in the example on the preceding page.
- **Be careful not to distort meaning.** Don't change the source's emphasis or omit connecting words, qualifiers, and other material whose absence will confuse you later or cause you to misrepresent the source.

Notice that the paraphrase follows the original but uses different words and different sentence structures. In contrast, an unsuccessful paraphrase—one that plagiarizes—copies the author's words or sentence structures or both *without quotation marks*. (See p. 423 for examples.)

CULTURE LANGUAGE If English is not your native language and you have difficulty paraphrasing the ideas in sources, try this. Before attempting a paraphrase, read the original passage several times. Then, instead of "translating" line by line, try to state the gist of the passage without looking at it. Check your effort against the original to be sure you have captured the source author's meaning and emphasis without using his or her words and sentence structures. If you need a synonym for a word, look it up in a dictionary.

3 | Direct quotation

Your notes from sources may include many quotations, especially if you rely on photocopies, printouts, or downloads. Whether to use a quotation in your draft, instead of a summary or paraphrase, depends on whether the source is primary or secondary and on how important the exact words are:

- **Quote extensively when you are analyzing primary sources,** such as literary works and historical documents. The quotations will often be both the target of your analysis and the chief support for your ideas.
- **Quote selectively when you are drawing on secondary sources.** Favor summaries and paraphrases over quotations, and put every quotation to both tests in the box on the next page. Most papers of ten or so pages should not need more than two or three quotations that are longer than a few lines each.

Tests for direct quotations from secondary sources

The author's original satisfies one of these requirements:

- The language is unusually vivid, bold, or inventive.
- The quotation cannot be paraphrased without distortion or loss of meaning.
- The words themselves are at issue in your interpretation.
- The quotation represents and emphasizes a body of opinion or the view of an important expert.
- The quotation emphatically reinforces your own idea.
- The quotation is an illustration, such as a graph, diagram, or table.

The quotation is as short as possible:

- It includes only material relevant to your point.
- It is edited to eliminate examples and other unneeded material, using ellipsis marks and brackets (5 pp. 339–41).

When you quote a source, either in your notes or in your draft, take precautions to avoid plagiarism or misrepresentation of the source:

- **Copy the material carefully.** Take down the author's exact wording, spelling, capitalization, and punctuation.
- **Proofread every direct quotation at least twice.**
- **Use quotation marks around the quotation** so that later you won't confuse it with a paraphrase or summary. Be sure to transfer the quotation marks into your draft as well, unless the quotation is long and is set off from your text. For advice on handling long quotations, see **MLA** pp. 497–98 and **APA** p. 525.
- **Use brackets** to add words for clarity or to change the capitalization of letters (see 5 p. 341 and 6 p. 355).
- **Use ellipsis marks** to omit irrelevant material (see 5 pp. 339–41).
- **Cite the source of the quotation in your draft.** See pp. 425–26 on documentation.

EXERCISE 52.2 Summarizing and paraphrasing

Prepare two source notes, one summarizing the entire paragraph below and the other paraphrasing the first four sentences (ending with the word *autonomy*). Use the format for a note illustrated on p. 410, omitting only the subject heading. (You can do this exercise online at *ablongman .com/littlebrown*.)

Federal organization [of the United States] has made it possible for the different states to deal with the same problems in many different ways. One consequence of federalism, then, has been that people are treated differently, by law, from state to state. The great strength of this system is that differences from state to state in cultural preferences, moral standards, and levels of wealth can be accommodated. In contrast to a unitary system in which the central government makes all important decisions (as in France), federalism is a powerful arrangement for maximizing regional freedom and autonomy. The great weakness of our federal system, however, is that people in some states receive less than the best or the most advanced or the least expensive services and policies that government can offer. The federal dilemma does not invite easy solution, for the costs and benefits of the arrangement have tended to balance out.   —Peter K. Eisinger et al., *American Politics*, p. 44

EXERCISE 52.3   Combining summary, paraphrase, and direct quotation

Prepare a source note containing a combination of paraphrase or summary and direct quotation that states the main idea of the passage below. Use the format for a note illustrated on p. 410, omitting only the subject heading. (You can do this exercise online at *ablongman.com/littlebrown.*)

Most speakers unconsciously duel even during seemingly casual conversations, as can often be observed at social gatherings where they show less concern for exchanging information with other guests than for asserting their own dominance. Their verbal dueling often employs very subtle weapons like mumbling, a hostile act which defeats the listener's desire to understand what the speaker claims he is trying to say (but is really not saying because he is mumbling!). Or the verbal dueler may keep talking after someone has passed out of hearing range— which is often an aggressive challenge to the listener to return and acknowledge the dominance of the speaker.

—Peter K. Farb, *Word Play*, p. 107

52e   Integrating sources into your text

The evidence of others' information and opinions should back up, not dominate, your own ideas. To synthesize evidence, you need to smooth the transitions between your ideas and words and those of your sources, and you need to give the reader a context for interpreting the borrowed material.

Note The examples in this section use the MLA syle of source documentation and also present-tense verbs (such as *disagrees* and *claims*). See pp. 416–18 for specific variations in documentation style and verb tense within the academic disciplines. Several other conventions governing quotations are discussed elsewhere in this book:

■ Using commas to punctuate signal phrases (5 pp. 311–12).

- Placing other punctuation marks with quotation marks (**5** pp. 334–35).
- Using brackets and the ellipsis mark to indicate changes in quotations (**5** pp. 339–41).
- Punctuating and placing parenthetical citations (**MLA** pp. 465–67).
- Formatting long prose quotations and poetry quotations (**MLA** pp. 497–98 and **APA** p. 525).

1 Introduction of borrowed material

Readers will be distracted from your point if borrowed material does not fit into your sentence. In the passage below, the writer has not meshed the structures of her own and her source's sentences:

> Awkward   One editor disagrees with this view and "a good reporter does not fail to separate opinions from facts" (Lyman 52).

In the following revision the writer adds words to integrate the quotation into her sentence:

> Revised   One editor disagrees with this view, <u>maintaining that</u> "a good reporter does not fail to separate opinions from facts" (Lyman 52).

To mesh your own and your source's words, you may sometimes need to make a substitution or addition to the quotation, signaling your change with brackets:

> Words added   "The tabloids [of England] are a journalistic case study in bad reporting," claims Lyman (52).
>
> Verb form changed   A bad reporter, Lyman implies, is one who "[fails] to separate opinions from facts" (52). [The bracketed verb replaces *fail* in the original.]
>
> Capitalization changed   "[T]o separate opinions from facts" is the work of a good reporter (Lyman 52). [In the original, *to* is not capitalized.]
>
> Noun supplied for pronoun   The reliability of a news organization "depends on [reporters'] trustworthiness," says Lyman (52). [The bracketed noun replaces *their* in the original.]

2 Interpretation of borrowed material

Even when it does not conflict with your own sentence structure, borrowed material will be ineffective if you merely dump it in readers' laps without explaining how you intend it to be understood. Reading the following passage, we must figure out for ourselves that the writer's sentence and the quotation state opposite points of view:

Dumped   Many news editors and reporters maintain that it is impossi-
          ble to keep personal opinions from influencing the selection
          and presentation of facts. "True, news reporters, like every-
          one else, form impressions of what they see and hear. How-
          ever, a good reporter does not fail to separate opinions from
          facts" (Lyman 52).

In the revision, the underlined additions tell us how to interpret the
quotation:

Revised   Many news editors and reporters maintain that it is impossi-
          ble to keep personal opinions from influencing the selection
          and presentation of facts. Yet not all authorities agree with
          this view. One editor grants that "news reporters, like every-
          one else, form impressions of what they see and hear." But,
          he insists, "a good reporter does not fail to separate opinions
          from facts" (Lyman 52).

■ Signal phrases

The words *One editor grants* and *he insists* in the revised passage above are **signal phrases:** they tell readers who the source is
and what to expect in the quotations that follow. Signal phrases
usually contain (1) the source author's name (or a substitute for it,
such as *One editor* and *he*) and (2) a verb that indicates the source
author's attitude or approach to what he or she says.

Some verbs for signal phrases appear in the list below. These
verbs are in the present tense, typical of writing in the humanities.
But in the social and natural sciences, the present perfect or past
tense is more common. See pp. 417–18.

Author is neutral	Author infers or suggests	Author argues	Author is uneasy or disparaging
comments	analyzes	claims	belittles
describes	asks	contends	bemoans
explains	assesses	defends	complains
illustrates	concludes	holds	condemns
notes	considers	insists	deplores
observes	finds	maintains	deprecates
points out	predicts		derides
records	proposes	Author agrees	disagrees
relates	reveals		laments
reports	shows	admits	warns
says	speculates	agrees	
sees	suggests	concedes	
thinks	supposes	grants	
writes			

Vary your signal phrases to suit your interpretation of borrowed
material and also to keep readers' interest. A signal phrase may precede, interrupt, or follow the borrowed material:

Precedes	Lyman insists that "a good reporter does not fail to separate opinions from facts" (52).
Interrupts	"However," Lyman insists, "a good reporter does not fail to separate opinions from facts" (52).
Follows	"[A] good reporter does not fail to separate opinions from facts," Lyman insists (52).

■ Background information

You can add information to a quotation to integrate it into your text and inform readers why you are using it. In most cases, provide the author's name in the text, especially if the author is an expert or if readers will recognize the name:

Author named	Harold Lyman grants that "news reporters, like everyone else, form impressions of what they see and hear." But, Lyman insists, "a good reporter does not fail to separate opinions from facts" (52).

If the source title contributes information about the author or the context of the quotation, you can provide it in the text:

Title given	Harold Lyman, in his book *The Conscience of the Journalist*, grants that "news reporters, like everyone else, form impressions of what they see and hear." But, Lyman insists, "a good reporter does not fail to separate opinions from facts" (52).

If the quoted author's background and experience reinforce or clarify the quotation, you can provide these credentials in the text:

Credentials given	Harold Lyman, a newspaper editor for more than forty years, grants that "news reporters, like everyone else, form impressions of what they see and hear." But, Lyman insists, "a good reporter does not fail to separate opinions from facts" (52).

You need not name the author, source, or credentials in your text when you are simply establishing facts or weaving together facts and opinions from varied sources. In the following passage, the information is more important than the source, so the name of the source is confined to a parenthetical acknowledgment:

> To end the abuses of the British, many colonists were urging three actions: forming a united front, seceding from Britain, and taking control of their own international relations (Wills 325–36).

3 Discipline styles for integrating sources

The preceding guidelines for introducing and interpreting borrowed material apply generally across academic disciplines, but there are differences in verb tenses and documentation style.

- **English and some other humanities**

Writers in English, foreign languages, and related disciplines use MLA style for documenting sources and generally use the present tense of verbs in signal phrases. In discussing sources other than works of literature, the present perfect tense is also sometimes appropriate:

> Lyman insists . . . [present].
> Lyman has insisted . . . [present perfect].

In discussing works of literature, use only the present tense to describe both the work of the author and the action in the work:

> Kate Chopin builds irony into every turn of "The Story of an Hour." For example, Mrs. Mallard, the central character, finds joy in the death of her husband, whom she loves, because she anticipates "the long procession of years that would belong to her absolutely" (23).

Avoid shifting tenses in writing about literature. You can, for instance, shorten quotations to avoid their past-tense verbs.

Shift	Her freedom elevates her, so that "she carried herself unwittingly like a goddess of victory" (24).
No shift	Her freedom elevates her, so that she walks "unwittingly like a goddess of victory" (24).

- **History and other humanities**

Writers in history, art history, philosophy, and related disciplines generally use the present perfect tense or present tense of verbs in signal phrases.

> Lincoln persisted, as Haworth has noted, in "feeling that events controlled him."[3]

> What Miller calls Lincoln's "severe self-doubt"[6] undermined his effectiveness on at least two occasions.

The raised numbers after the quotations are part of the Chicago documentation style, used in history and other disciplines.

- **Social and natural sciences**

Writers in the sciences generally use a verb's present tense just for reporting the results of a study (*The data suggest . . .*). Otherwise, they use a verb's past tense or present perfect tense in a signal phrase, as when introducing an explanation, interpretation, or other commentary. (Thus when you are writing for the sciences, generally convert the list of signal-phrase verbs on p. 415 from the present to the present perfect tense or past tense.)

> Lin (1999) has suggested that preschooling may significantly affect children's academic performance through high school (pp. 22–23).

In an exhaustive survey of the literature published between 1990 and 2000, Walker (2001) <u>found</u> "no proof, merely a weak correlation, linking place of residence and rate of illness" (p. 121).

These passages conform to APA documentation style. APA style, or one quite similar to it, is also used in sociology, education, nursing, biology, and many other sciences.

EXERCISE 52.4 Introducing and interpreting borrowed material

Drawing on the ideas in the following paragraph and using examples from your own observations and experiences, write a paragraph about anxiety. Integrate at least one direct quotation and one paraphrase from the following paragraph into your own sentences. In your paragraph identify the author by name and give his credentials: he is a professor of psychiatry and a practicing psychoanalyst. (You can do this exercise on-line at *ablongman.com/littlebrown*.)

> There are so many ways in which human beings are different from all the lower forms of animals, and almost all of them make us uniquely susceptible to feelings of anxiousness. Our imagination and reasoning powers facilitate anxiety; the anxious feeling is precipitated not by an absolute impending threat—such as the worry about an examination, a speech, travel—but rather by the symbolic and often unconscious representations. We do not have to be experiencing a potential danger. We can experience something related to it. We can recall, through our incredible memories, the original symbolic sense of vulnerability in childhood and suffer the feeling attached to that. We can even forget the original memory and be stuck with the emotion—which is then compounded by its seemingly irrational quality at this time. It is not just the fear of death which pains us, but the anticipation of it; or the anniversary of a specific death; or a street, a hospital, a time of day, a color, a flower, a symbol associated with death.
>
> —Willard Gaylin, "Feeling Anxious," p. 23

---

53 Avoiding Plagiarism and Documenting Sources

The knowledge building that is the focus of academic writing rests on participants' integrity in using sources. This standard of integrity derives from the idea that the work of an author is his or her intellectual property: if you use that work, you must acknowledge

http://www.ablongman.com/littlebrown ▶

Visit the companion Web site for more help and an electronic exercise on avoiding plagiarism and documenting sources.

the author's ownership. At the same time, source acknowledgments tell readers what your own writing is based on, creating the trust that knowledge building requires.

Plagiarism (from a Latin word for "kidnapper") is the presentation of someone else's ideas or words as your own. Whether deliberate or accidental, plagiarism is a serious offense.

- *Deliberate* plagiarism:

  Copying or downloading a phrase, a sentence, or a longer passage from a source and passing it off as your own by omitting quotation marks and a source citation.

  Summarizing or paraphrasing someone else's ideas without acknowledging your debt in a source citation.

  Handing in as your own work a paper you have bought, copied off the Web, had a friend write, or accepted from another student.

- *Accidental* plagiarism:

  Forgetting to place quotation marks around another writer's words.

  Carelessly omitting a source citation for a paraphrase.

  Omitting a source citation for another's idea because you are unaware of the need to acknowledge the idea.

In most schools a code of academic honesty calls for severe consequences for deliberate or accidental plagiarism: a failing grade, suspension from school, or even expulsion.

The way to avoid plagiarism is to acknowledge your sources by documenting them. This chapter discusses plagiarism and the Internet, shows how to distinguish what doesn't require acknowledgment from what does, and provides an overview of source documentation.

CULTURE LANGUAGE The concept of intellectual property and thus the rules governing plagiarism are not universal. In some other cultures, for instance, students may be encouraged to copy the words of scholars without acknowledgment, in order to demonstrate their mastery of or respect for the scholars' work. In the United States, however, using an author's work without a source citation is considered theft. When in doubt about the guidelines in this chapter, ask your instructor for advice.

53a Committing and detecting plagiarism on the Internet

The Internet has made it easier to plagiarize than ever before, but it has also made plagiarism easier to catch.

Checklist for avoiding plagiarism

Type of source

Are you using
- your own independent material,
- common knowledge, or
- someone else's independent material?

You must acknowledge someone else's material.

Quotations

- Do all quotations exactly match their sources? Check them.
- Have you inserted quotation marks around quotations that are run into your text?
- Have you shown omissions with ellipsis marks and additions with brackets?
- Does every quotation have a source citation?

Paraphrases and summaries

- Have you used your own words and sentence structures for every paraphrase and summary? If not, use quotation marks around the original author's words.
- Does every paraphrase and summary have a source citation?

The Web

- Have you obtained any necessary permission to use someone else's material on the Web?

Source citations

- Have you acknowledged every use of someone else's material in the place where you use it?
- Does your list of works cited include all the sources you have used?

You can download this checklist from *ablongman.com/littlebrown*. Working with a copy of the list, question every use you make of someone else's material.

Even honest students risk accidental plagiarism by downloading sources and importing portions into their drafts. Dishonest students may take advantage of downloading to steal others' work. They may also use the term-paper businesses on the Web, which offer both ready-made research and complete papers, usually for a fee. **Paying for research or a paper does not make it the buyer's work.** Anyone who submits someone else's work as his or her own is a plagiarist.

Students who plagiarize from the Internet both deprive themselves of an education in honest research and expose themselves to detection. Teachers can use search engines to locate specific phrases or sentences anywhere on the Web, including among scholarly publications, all kinds of Web sites, and term-paper collections. They can search the term-paper sites as easily as students can, looking for similarities with papers they've received. Increasingly, teachers can use special detection programs that compare students' work with other work anywhere on the Internet, seeking matches as short as a few words.

Some instructors suggest that their students use plagiarism-detection programs to verify that their own work does not include accidental plagiarism from the Internet. Links to such programs appear in this book's Web site at *ablongman.com/littlebrown*.

53b Knowing what you need not acknowledge

1 Your independent material

Your own observations, thoughts, compilations of facts, or experimental results—expressed in your words and format—do not require acknowledgment. You should describe the basis for your conclusions so that readers can evaluate your thinking, but you need not cite sources for them.

2 Common knowledge

Common knowledge consists of the standard information on a subject as well as folk literature and commonsense observations.

- **Standard information** includes the major facts of history, such as the dates during which Charlemagne ruled as emperor of Rome (800–14). It does *not* include interpretations of facts, such as a historian's opinion that Charlemagne was sometimes needlessly cruel in extending his power.

- **Folk literature,** such as the fairy tale "Snow White," is popularly known and cannot be traced to a particular writer. Literature traceable to a writer is *not* folk literature, even if it is very familiar.

- **Commonsense observations** are things most people know, such as that inflation is most troublesome for people with low and fixed incomes. However, a particular economist's argument about the effects of inflation on Chinese immigrants is *not* a commonsense observation.

If you do not know a subject well enough to determine whether a piece of information is common knowledge, make a record of the source as you would for any other quotation, paraphrase, or summary. As you read more about the subject, the information may come up repeatedly without acknowledgment, in which case it is probably common knowledge. But if you are still in doubt when you finish your research, always acknowledge the source.

53c   Knowing what you *must* acknowledge

You must always acknowledge other people's independent material—that is, any facts or ideas that are not common knowledge or your own. The source may be anything, including a book, an article, a movie, an interview, a microfilmed document, a Web page, a newsgroup posting, or an opinion expressed on the radio. You must acknowledge summaries or paraphrases of ideas or facts as well as quotations of the language and format in which ideas or facts appear: wording, sentence structures, arrangement, and special graphics (such as a diagram). You must acknowledge another's material no matter how you use it, how much of it you use, or how often you use it.

1   Using copied language: Quotation marks and a source citation

The following example baldly plagiarizes the original quotation from Jessica Mitford's *Kind and Usual Punishment*, p. 9. Without quotation marks or a source citation, the example matches Mitford's wording (underlined) and closely parallels her sentence structure:

Original	"The character and mentality of the keepers may be of more importance in understanding prisons than the character and mentality of the kept."
Plagiarism	But the character of prison officials (the keepers) is more important in understanding prisons than the character of prisoners (the kept).

To avoid plagiarism, the writer can paraphrase and cite the source (see the revised examples opposite) or use Mitford's actual words *in quotation marks* and *with a source citation* (here, in MLA style):

Revision (quotation)	According to one critic of the penal system, "The character and mentality of the keepers may be of more importance in understanding prisons than the character and mentality of the kept" (Mitford 9).

Even with a source citation and with a different sentence structure, the next example is still plagiarism because it uses some of Mitford's words (underlined) without quotation marks:

Plagiarism	According to one critic of the penal system, the psychology of the kept may say less about prisons than the psychology of the keepers (Mitford 9).
Revision (quotation)	According to one critic of the penal system, the psychology of "the kept" may say less about prisons than the psychology of "the keepers" (Mitford 9).

2 Using a paraphrase or summary: Your own words and sentence structure and a source citation

The example below changes the sentence structure of the original Mitford quotation opposite, but it still uses Mitford's words (underlined) without quotation marks and without a source citation:

Plagiarism | In understanding prisons, we should know more about the character and mentality of the keepers than of the kept.

To avoid plagiarism, the writer can use quotation marks and cite the source (see opposite) or *use his or her own words* and still *cite the source* (because the idea is Mitford's, not the writer's):

Revision (paraphrase) | Mitford holds that we may be able to learn more about prisons from the psychology of the prison officials than from that of the prisoners (9).

Revision (paraphrase) | We may understand prisons better if we focus on the personalities and attitudes of the prison workers rather than those of the inmates (Mitford 9).

In the next example, the writer cites Mitford and does not use her words but still plagiarizes her sentence structure:

Plagiarism | One critic of the penal system maintains that the psychology of prison officials may be more informative about prisons than the psychology of prisoners (Mitford 9).

Revision (paraphrase) | One critic of the penal system maintains that we may be able to learn less from the psychology of prisoners than from the psychology of prison officials (Mitford 9).

EXERCISE 53.1 Recognizing plagiarism

The following numbered items show various attempts to quote or paraphrase the passage below. Carefully compare each attempt with the original passage. Which attempts are plagiarized, inaccurate, or both, and which are acceptable? Why? (You can do this exercise online at *ablongman.com/littlebrown.*)

I would agree with the sociologists that psychiatric labeling is dangerous. Society can inflict terrible wounds by discrimination, and by confusing health with disease and disease with badness.
—George E. Vaillant, *Adaptation to Life,* p. 361

1 According to George Vaillant, society often inflicts wounds by using psychiatric labeling, confusing health, disease, and badness (361).

2 According to George Vaillant, "psychiatric labeling [such as 'homosexual' or 'schizophrenic'] is dangerous. Society can inflict terrible wounds by . . . confusing health with disease and disease with badness" (361).

3 According to George Vaillant, when psychiatric labeling discriminates between health and disease or between disease and badness, it can inflict wounds on those labeled (361).

4 Psychiatric labels can badly hurt those labeled, says George Vaillant, because they fail to distinguish among health, illness, and immorality (361).

5 Labels such as "homosexual" and "schizophrenic" can be hurtful when they fail to distinguish among health, illness, and immorality.

6 "I would agree with the sociologists that society can inflict terrible wounds by discrimination, and by confusing health with disease and disease with badness" (Vaillant 361).

53d Using and acknowledging online sources

Online sources are so accessible and so easy to download into your own documents that it may seem they are freely available, exempting you from the obligation to acknowledge them. They are not. Acknowledging online sources is somewhat trickier than acknowledging print sources, but no less essential. Further, if you are publishing your work on the Web, you need to take account of sources' copyright restrictions as well.

1 Online sources in an unpublished project

When you use material from an online source in a print or online document to be distributed just to your class, your obligation to cite sources does not change: you must acknowledge someone else's independent material in whatever form you find it. With online sources, that obligation can present additional challenges:

- **Record complete publication information each time you consult an online source.** Online sources may change from one day to the next or even disappear entirely. See p. 378 for the information to record, such as the electronic address and the publication date. Without the proper information, you *may not* use the source.

- **Acknowledge linked sites.** If you use not only a Web site but also one or more of its linked sites, you must acknowledge the linked sites as well. The fact that one person has used a second person's work does not release you from the responsibility to cite the second work.

- **Seek the author's permission before using an e-mail message, discussion-group posting, or Web log contribution.** Obtaining permission advises the author that his or her ideas are about to be distributed more widely and lets the author verify that you have not misrepresented the ideas.

2 Print and online sources in a Web composition

When you use material from print or online sources in a composition for the Web, you must not only acknowledge your sources but also take the additional precaution of observing copyright restrictions.

A Web site is a medium of publication just as a book or magazine is and so involves the same responsibility to obtain reprint permission from copyright holders. The exception is a password-protected site (such as a course site), which many copyright holders regard as private. You can find information about copyright holders and permissions on the copyright page of a print publication (following the title page) and on a page labeled something like "Terms of Use" on a Web site. If you don't see an explicit release for student use or publication on private Web sites, assume you must seek permission.

The legal convention of fair use allows an author to reprint a small portion of copyrighted material without obtaining the copyright holder's permission, as long as the author acknowledges the source. The online standards of fair use differ for print and online sources and are not fixed in either case. The guidelines below are conservative:

- **Print sources:** Quote without permission fewer than fifty words from an article or fewer than three hundred words from a book. You'll need permission to use any longer quotation from an article or book; any quotation at all from a play, poem, or song; and any use of an entire work, such as a photograph, chart, or other illustration.

- **Online sources:** Quote without permission text that represents just a small portion of the whole—say, forty words out of three hundred. Follow the print guidelines above for plays, poems, songs, and illustrations, adding multimedia elements (audio or video clips) to the list of works that require reprint permission for any use.

- **Links:** You may need to seek permission to link your site to another one—for instance, if you rely on the linked site to substantiate your claims or to provide a multimedia element.

53e Documenting sources

Every time you borrow the words, facts, or ideas of others, you must **document** the source—that is, supply a reference (or document) telling readers that you borrowed the material and where you borrowed it from.

Editors and teachers in most academic disciplines require special documentation formats (or styles) in their scholarly journals and in students' papers. All the styles use a citation in the text that serves two purposes: it signals that material is borrowed, and it refers readers to detailed information about the source so that they can locate both the source and the place in the source where the borrowed material appears. The detailed source information appears either in footnotes or at the end of the paper.

Aside from these essential similarities, the disciplines' documentation styles differ markedly in citation form, arrangement of source information, and other particulars. Each discipline's style reflects the needs of its practitioners for certain kinds of information presented in certain ways. For instance, the currency of a source is important in the social sciences, where studies build on and correct each other; thus in-text citations in the social sciences include a source's date of publication. In the humanities, however, currency is less important, so in-text citations do not include date of publication.

The disciplines' documentation formats are described in style guides listed in **8** pp. 441–42 (literature), 447 (other humanities), 451–52 (social sciences), and 456 (natural and applied sciences). This book discusses and illustrates four common documentation styles:

- MLA style, used in English, foreign languages, and some other humanities (**MLA** p. 460).
- APA style, used in psychology and some other social sciences (**APA** p. 507).
- Chicago style, used in history, art history, philosophy, religion, and some other humanities (**Chic** p. 533).
- CSE style, used in the biological and some other sciences (**CSE** p. 544).

Always ask your instructor which documentation style you should use. If your instructor does not require a particular style, use the one in this book that's most appropriate for the discipline in which you're writing. Do follow a single system for citing sources so that you provide all the necessary information in a consistent format.

Note Bibliography software—*Biblio, Refworks, Endnote, Procite,* and others—can help you format your source citations in the style of your choice. Always ask your instructors if you may use such software for your papers. The programs prompt you for needed information (author's name, book title, and so on) and then arrange, capitalize, underline, and punctuate the information as required by the style. But no program can anticipate all the varieties of source information, nor can it substitute for your own care and attention in giving your sources complete acknowledgment using the required form.

54 Writing the Paper

This chapter complements and extends the detailed discussion of the writing situation and the writing process in Chapters 1–5 (**1** pp. 3–38), which also include many tips for using a word processor. If you haven't already done so, you may want to read those chapters before this one.

54a Focusing and organizing the paper

Before you begin using your source notes in a draft, give some thought to your main idea and your organization.

1 Thesis statement

You began research with a question about your subject (see p. 374). Though that question may have evolved during research, you should be able to answer it once you've consulted most of your sources. Try to state that answer in a **thesis statement,** a claim that narrows your subject to a single idea. Here, for example, are the research question and thesis statement of Kisha Alder, whose final paper appears later in this book (**MLA** pp. 500–05):

Research question
How, if at all, should the Internet be taxed?

Thesis statement
To improve equity between online and traditional stores and between consumers with and without Internet access, tax laws should be revised to allow collection of sales taxes on Internet purchases.

A precise thesis statement will give you a focus as you organize and draft your paper. For more on thesis statements, see **1** pp. 14–16.

2 Organization

To structure your paper, you'll need to synthesize, or forge relationships among ideas (see pp. 406–07). Here is one approach:

- **Arrange source information in categories.** Each group should correspond to a main section of your paper: a key idea of your own that supports the thesis.
- **Review your research journal** for connections between sources and other thoughts that can help you organize your paper.

http://www.ablongman.com/littlebrown ▶

Visit the companion Web site for more help on writing and revising a research paper.

- **Look objectively at your categories.** If some are skimpy, with little information, consider whether you should drop the categories or conduct more research to fill them out. If most of your information falls into one or two categories, consider whether they are too broad and should be divided. (If any of this rethinking affects your thesis statement, revise it accordingly.)
- **Within each group, distinguish between the main idea and the supporting ideas and evidence.** Only the support should come from your sources. The main idea should be your own.

See **1** pp. 17–21 for more on organizing a paper, including samples of both informal and formal outlines.

54b Drafting, revising, and formatting the paper

1 First draft

In drafting your paper, you do not have to proceed methodically from introduction to conclusion. Instead, draft in sections, beginning with the one you feel most confident about. Each section should center on a principal idea contributing to your thesis, a conclusion you have drawn from reading and responding to sources. Start the section by stating the idea; then support it with information, summaries, paraphrases, and quotations from your notes. Remember to insert source information from your notes as well.

2 Revision and editing

For a complex project like a research paper, you'll certainly want to revise in at least two stages—first for thesis, structure, and other whole-paper issues, and then for clarity, grammar, and other sentence-level issues. Chapter 5 supports this two-stage approach with checklists for revision (**1** pp. 25–26) and editing (**1** p. 30). The box on the facing page provides additional steps to take when revising a research paper.

3 Format

The final draft of your paper should conform to the document format recommended by your instructor or by the style guide of the discipline in which you are writing. This book details two common formats: Modern Language Association (**MLA** pp. 496–98) and American Psychological Association (**APA** pp. 523–26).

In any discipline you can use a word processor to present your ideas effectively and attractively with readable typefonts, headings, illustrations, and other elements. See **1** pp. 56–66 for ideas.

Checklist for revising a research paper

Assignment

How does the draft satisfy all of the criteria stated in your instructor's assignment?

Thesis statement

How well does your thesis statement describe your subject and your perspective as they emerged during drafting?

Structure

(Outlining your draft can help you see structure at a glance. See 1 p. 25.)

How consistently does borrowed material illuminate and support—not lead and dominate—your own ideas? How well is the importance of ideas reflected in the emphasis they receive? Will the arrangement of ideas be clear to readers?

Evidence

Where might evidence seem weak or irrelevant to readers?

Reasonableness and clarity

How reasonable will readers find your argument? (See 2 pp. 98–103.) Where do you need to define terms or concepts that readers may not know or may dispute?

You can download this checklist from *ablongman.com/littlebrown*. Copy the checklist for each research paper, answering the questions in writing.

PART 8

Writing in the Disciplines

Writing in the Disciplines

55 Working with the Goals and Requirements of the Disciplines

Chapter 8 (2 p. 69) outlines the general concerns of subject, purpose, and audience that figure in most academic writing situations. The disciplines have more in common as well: methods of gathering evidence, kinds of assignments, scholarly tools, language conventions, and styles for source citations and document format. This chapter introduces these common goals and requirements. The following chapters then distinguish the disciplines along the same lines, focusing on literature (Chapter 56), and on other humanities, the social sciences, and the natural and applied sciences (Chapter 57).

55a   Using methods and evidence

The **methodology** of a discipline is the way its practitioners study their subjects—that is, how they proceed when investigating the answers to questions. Methodology relates to the way practitioners analyze evidence and ideas. For instance, a literary critic and a social historian would probably approach Shakespeare's *Hamlet* quite differently: the literary critic might study the play for a theme among its poetic images; the historian might examine the play's relation to Shakespeare's context, England at the turn of the seventeenth century.

Whatever their approach, academic writers do not compose entirely out of their personal experience. Rather, they combine the evidence of their experience with that appropriate to the discipline, drawing well-supported conclusions about their subjects. The evidence of the discipline comes from research using primary or secondary sources.

- **Primary sources** are firsthand or original accounts, such as historical documents, works of art, and reports on experiments that the writer has conducted. When you use primary sources, you conduct original research, generating your own evidence. You might use your analysis of a painting as evidence for an interpretation of the painting. Or you might use data from your own survey of students to support your conclusions about students' attitudes.
- **Secondary sources** are books and articles written *about* primary sources. Much academic writing requires that you use

http://www.ablongman.com/littlebrown   ▶

Visit the companion Web site for more help
with writing in the disciplines.

Guidelines for academic writers

- **Become familiar with the methodology and the kinds of evidence for the discipline in which you are writing.**
- **Analyze the special demands of each assignment.** The questions you set out to answer, the assertions you wish to support, will govern how you choose your sources and evidence.
- **Become familiar with the discipline's specialized tools and language.**
- **Use the discipline's style for source citations and document format.**

such sources to spark, extend, or support your own ideas, as when you review the published opinions on your subject before contributing conclusions from your original research.

55b   Understanding writing assignments

For most academic writing, your primary purpose will be either to explain something to your readers or to persuade them to accept your conclusions. To achieve your purpose, you will adapt your writing process to the writing situation, particularly to your reader's likely expectations for evidence and how you use it. Most assignments will contain keywords that imply some of these expectations —words such as *compare, define, analyze,* and *illustrate* that express customary ways of thinking about and organizing a vast range of subjects. (See 1 p. 8 for more on these so-called patterns of development.) You should be aware of them and alert to the wording in assignments that directs you to use them.

55c   Using tools and language

When you write in an academic discipline, you use the scholarly tools of that discipline, particularly its periodical indexes. In addition, you may use the aids developed by practitioners of the discipline for efficiently and effectively approaching research, conducting it, and recording the findings. Many of these aids, such as a system for recording evidence from sources, are discussed in 7 pp. 371–426 and can be adapted to any discipline. Other aids are discussed in the next two chapters.

Pay close attention to the texts assigned in a course and any materials given out in class, for these items may introduce you to valuable references and other research aids, and they will use the specialized language of the discipline. This specialized language allows practitioners to write to each other both efficiently and precisely. It also furthers certain concerns of the discipline, such as accuracy and objectivity. Scientists, for example, try to interpret their data objectively, so they avoid *undoubtedly, obviously,* and other words that slant conclusions. Some of the language conventions like this one are discussed in the following chapters. As you gain experience in a particular discipline, keep alert for such conventions and train yourself to follow them.

55d   Following styles for source citations and document format

Most disciplines publish journals that require authors to use a certain style for source citations and a certain format for documents. In turn, most instructors in a discipline require the same of students writing papers for their courses.

When you cite your sources, you tell readers which ideas and information you borrowed and where they can find your sources. Thus source citations indicate how much knowledge you have and how broad and deep your research was. They also help you avoid **plagiarism,** the serious offense of presenting the words, ideas, and data of others as if they were your own. (See **7** pp. 418–25 on avoiding plagiarism.)

Document format includes such features as margins and the placement of the title. But it also extends to special elements of the manuscript, such as tables or an abstract, that may be required by the discipline.

The style guides for various disciplines are listed on pp. 447 (humanities), 451–52 (social sciences), and 456 (natural and applied sciences). If your instructor does not require a particular style, use that of the Modern Language Association, which is described and illustrated at length in **MLA** pp. 460–98.

56   Reading and Writing About Literature

By Sylvan Barnet

Writers of literature—stories, novels, poems, and plays—are concerned with presenting human experience concretely, with *showing* rather than *telling*, with giving a sense of the feel of life. Reading

---

http://www.ablongman.com/littlebrown ▶

Visit the companion Web site for more help with reading and writing about literature.

and writing about literature thus require extremely close attention to the feel of the words. For instance, the word *woods* in Robert Frost's "Stopping by Woods on a Snowy Evening" has a rural, folksy quality that *forest* doesn't have, and many such small distinctions contribute to the poem's effect.

When you read literature, you interpret distinctions like these, forming an idea of the work. When you write about literature, you state your idea as your thesis, and you support the thesis with evidence from the work. (See 1 pp. 14–16 for more on thesis statements.)

Note Writing about literature is not merely summarizing literature. Your thesis is a claim about the meaning or effect of the literary work, not a statement of its plot. And your paper is a demonstration of your thesis, not a retelling of the work's changes or events.

56a Using the methods and evidence of literary analysis

1 Reading literature

Reading literature critically involves interacting with a text, not in order to make negative judgments but in order to understand the work and evaluate its significance or quality. Such interaction is not passive, like scanning a newspaper or watching television. Instead, it is a process of engagement, of diving into the words themselves.

You will become more engaged if you write while you read. If you own the book you're reading, don't hesitate to underline or highlight passages that especially interest you. Don't hesitate to annotate the margins, indicating your pleasures, displeasures, and uncertainties with remarks such as *Nice detail* or *Do we need this long description?* or *Not believable.* If you don't own the book, make these notes on separate sheets or on your computer.

An effective way to interact with a text is to keep a **reading journal.** A journal is not a diary in which you record your doings; instead, it is a place to develop and store your reflections on what you read, such as an answer to a question you may have posed in the margin of the text or a response to something said in class. You may, for instance, want to reflect on why your opinion is so different from that of another student. You may even make an entry in the form of a letter to the author or from one character to another. (See 1 p. 9 for more on journal keeping.)

2 Meaning in literature

In analyzing literature, you face right off the question of *meaning.* Readers disagree all the time over the meanings of works of literature, partly because (as noted earlier) literature *shows* rather than *tells:* it gives concrete images of imagined human experiences, but it usually does not say how we ought to understand the images. Further, readers bring different experiences to their reading and thus understand images differently. In writing about literature, then, we can offer only our *interpretation* of the meaning rather than *the* meaning. Still, most people agree that there are limits to interpretation: it must be supported by evidence that a reasonable person finds at least plausible if not totally convincing.

3 Questions for a literary analysis

One reason interpretations of meaning differ is that readers approach literary works differently, focusing on certain elements and interpreting those elements distinctively. For instance, some critics look at a literary work mainly as an artifact of the particular time and culture in which it was created, while other critics stress the work's effect on its readers.

This chapter emphasizes so-called formalist criticism, which sees a literary work primarily as something to be understood in itself. This critical framework engages the reader immediately in the work of literature, without requiring extensive historical or cultural background, and it introduces the conventional elements of literature that all critical approaches discuss, even though they view the elements differently. The list below poses questions for each element that can help you think constructively and imaginatively about what you read.

- *Plot:* **the relationships and patterns of events.** Even a poem has a plot—for instance, a change in mood from grief to resignation.

  What actions happen?
  What conflicts occur?
  How do the events connect to each other and to the whole?

- *Characters:* **the people the author creates,** including the narrator of a story or the speaker of a poem.

  Who are the principal people in the work?
  How do they interact?
  What do their actions, words, and thoughts reveal about their personalities and the personalities of others?
  Do the characters stay the same, or do they change? Why?

- *Point of view:* **the perspective or attitude of the speaker in a poem or the voice who tells a story.** The point of view may be **first person** (a participant, using *I*) or **third person** (an outsider, using *he, she, it, they*). A first-person narrator may be a major or a minor character in the narrative and may be **reliable** or **unreliable** (unable to report events wholly or accurately). A third-person narrator may be **omniscient** (knows what goes on in all characters' minds), **limited** (knows what goes on in the mind of only one or two characters), or **objective** (knows only what is external to the characters).

Who is the narrator (or the speaker of a poem)?
How does the narrator's point of view affect the narrative?

■ *Tone:* **the narrator's or speaker's attitude,** perceived through the words (for instance, joyful, bitter, or confident).

What tone (or tones) do you hear? If there is a change, how do you account for it?
Is there an ironic contrast between the narrator's tone (for instance, confidence) and what you take to be the author's attitude (for instance, pity for human overconfidence)?

■ *Imagery:* **word pictures or details involving the senses of sight, sound, touch, smell, and taste.**

What images does the writer use? What senses do they draw on?
What patterns are evident in the images (for instance, religious or commercial images)?
What is the significance of the imagery?

■ *Symbolism:* **concrete things standing for larger and more abstract ideas.** For instance, the American flag may symbolize freedom, or a dead flower may symbolize mortality.

What symbols does the author use? What do they seem to signify?
How does the symbolism relate to the theme of the work?

■ *Setting:* **the place where the action happens.**

What does the locale contribute to the work?
Are scene shifts significant?

■ *Form:* **the shape or structure of the work.**

What *is* the form? (For example, a story might divide sharply in the middle, moving from happiness to sorrow.)
What parts of the work does the form emphasize, and why?

■ *Theme:* **the central idea, a conception of human experience suggested by the work as a whole.** Theme is neither plot (what happens) nor subject (such as mourning or marriage). Rather it is what the author says with that plot about that subject.

Can you state the theme in a sentence? For instance, you might state the following about Gwendolyn Brooks's poem "The

Bean Eaters" (p. 442): *People can live contentedly despite old age and poverty.*

Do certain words, passages of dialog or description, or situations seem to represent the theme most clearly?

How do the work's elements combine to develop the theme?

- *Appeal:* the degree to which the work pleases you.

  What do you especially like or dislike about the work? Why?

  Do you think your responses are unique, or would they be common to most readers? Why?

4 Using evidence in writing about literature

The evidence for a literary analysis always comes from at least one primary source (the work or works being discussed) and may come from secondary sources (critical and historical works). For example, in the paper on pp. 442–44 about Gwendolyn Brooks's "The Bean Eaters," the primary material is the poem itself, and the secondary material is the three critical studies of the poem. The bulk of the evidence is usually quotations from the work, although summaries and paraphrases can be useful as well.

Your instructor will probably tell you if you are expected to consult secondary sources for an assignment. They can help you understand a writer's work, but your primary concern should always be the work itself, not what critics A, B, and C say about it. In general, then, quote or summarize secondary material sparingly. And always cite your sources.

56b Understanding writing assignments in literature

A literature instructor may ask you to write one or more of the following types of papers. The first two are the most common.

Key terms

primary source A firsthand account: for instance, a historical document, a work of literature, or your own observations. (See also p. 433.)

secondary source A report on or analysis of other sources, often primary ones: for instance, a historian's account of a battle or a critic's view of a poem. (See also pp. 433–34.)

quotation An exact repetition of an author's words, placed in quotation marks. (See also 7 pp. 411–12.)

paraphrase A restatement of an author's words, closely following the author's line of thought but using different words and sentence structures. (See also 7 pp. 410–11.)

summary A condensation of an extended passage into a sentence or more. (See also 7 pp. 409–10.)

- **A literary analysis paper:** your ideas about a work of literature—your interpretation of its meaning, context, or representations based on specific words, passages, characters, and events.
- **A literary research paper:** analysis of a literary work combined with research about the work and perhaps its author. A literary research paper draws on both primary and secondary sources.
- **A personal response or reaction paper:** your thoughts and feelings about a work of literature.
- **A book review:** a summary of a book and a judgment about the book's value.
- **A theater review:** your reactions to and opinions about a theatrical performance.

56c Using the tools and language of literary analysis

1 Writing tools

The fundamental tool for writing about literature is reading critically. Asking analytical questions such as those on pp. 437–39 can help you focus your ideas. In addition, keeping a reading journal can help you develop your thoughts. Make careful, well-organized notes on any research materials. Finally, discuss the work with others who have read it. They may offer reactions and insights that will help you shape your own ideas.

2 Language considerations

Use the present tense of verbs to describe both the action in a literary work and the writing of an author: *The old people live a meager existence. Brooks emphasizes how isolated the couple is. The critic Harry Shaw reads the lines as perhaps despairing.* Use the past tense to describe events that actually occurred in the past: *Brooks was born in 1917.*

Some instructors discourage students from using the first-person *I* (as in *I felt sorry for the character*) in writing about literature. At least use *I* sparingly to avoid sounding egotistical. Rephrase sentences to avoid using *I* unnecessarily—for instance, *The character evokes the reader's sympathy.*

3 Research sources

In addition to the following resources on literature, you may also want to consult some on other humanities (pp. 446–47).

■ Specialized encyclopedias, dictionaries, and bibliographies

Bibliographical Guide to the Study of the Literature of the USA
Cambridge Bibliography of English Literature
Cambridge Encyclopedia of Language

Cambridge Guide to Literature in English
Dictionary of Literary Biography
Handbook to Literature
Literary Criticism Index
McGraw-Hill Encyclopedia of World Drama
MLA International Bibliography of Books and Articles on the Modern Languages and Literatures
New Princeton Encyclopedia of Poetry and Poetics
Oxford Companion to American Literature
Oxford Companion to the Theatre
Schomburg Center Guide to Black Literature from the Eighteenth Century to the Present

■ **Indexes**

Abstracts of Folklore Studies
Dissertation Abstracts International (doctoral dissertations)
Humanities Index
Literary Criticism Index
MLA International Bibliography of Books and Articles on the Modern Languages and Literatures

■ **Book reviews**

Book Review Digest
Book Review Index
Index to Book Reviews in the Humanities

■ **Web sources**

For updates of these sources and URLs, visit *ablongman.com/littlebrown.*

Alex Catalog of Electronic Texts (*infomotions.com/alex*)
EServer (*eserver.org*)
Internet Public Library: Online Literary Criticism (*ipl.org/div/litcrit*)
Key Sites on American Literature (*usinfo.state.gov/products/pubs/oal/amlitweb.htm*)
Literary Index (*galenet.com/servlet/LitIndex*)
Literary Resources on the Net (*andromeda.rutgers.edu/~jlynch/Lit*)
Online Books Page (*online.books.library.upenn.edu/books*)
Voice of the Shuttle: Drama, Theater, and Performance Art Studies (*vos.ucsb.edu/browse.asp?id=782*)
Voice of the Shuttle: Literature (in English) (*vos.ucsb.edu/browse.asp?id=3*)
Voice of the Shuttle: Literatures (Other than English) (*vos.ucsb.edu/browse.asp?id=2719*)

56d Documenting sources and formatting papers in literary analysis

Unless your instructor specifies otherwise, use the style of the Modern Language Association, detailed in **MLA** pp. 460–98 and in *MLA Handbook for Writers of Research Papers*, 6th edition, 2003. In

MLA style, parenthetical citations in the text of the paper refer to a list of works cited at the end. Sample papers illustrating this style appear opposite and in **2** pp. 110–14 and **MLA** pp. 500–05.

Use MLA format for headings, margins, long quotations, and other elements, as detailed in **MLA** pp. 496–98.

56e Examining a sample literary analysis

The following pages reprint a poem and a student paper on the work. The author develops a thesis about the poem, supporting this main idea with quotations, paraphrases, and summaries from the work being discussed, a primary source. The author also draws sparingly on secondary sources (other critics' views), which further support his own views.

Note the following features of the student's paper:

- **The writer does not merely summarize the literary work.** He summarizes briefly to make his meaning clear, but his essay consists mostly of his own analysis.

- **The writer uses many quotations from the literary work.** The quotations provide evidence for his ideas and let readers hear the voice of the work.

- **The writer integrates quotations smoothly into his own sentences.** See **7** pp. 413–17.

- **The writer uses the present tense of verbs** to describe both the author's work and the action in the work.

- **Poem**

Gwendolyn Brooks

The Bean Eaters

They eat beans mostly, this old yellow pair.
Dinner is a casual affair.
Plain chipware on a plain and creaking wood,
Tin flatware.

Two who are Mostly Good.   5
Two who have lived their day,
But keep on putting on their clothes
And putting things away.

And remembering . . .
Remembering, with twinklings and twinges,   10
As they lean over the beans in their rented back room that
      is full of beads and receipts and dolls and cloths,
         tobacco crumbs, vases and fringes.

■ **An essay on poetry with secondary sources**

Marking Time Versus Enduring in

Gwendolyn Brooks's "The Bean Eaters"

Gwendolyn Brooks's poem "The Bean Eaters" runs only eleven lines. It is written in plain language about very plain people. Yet its meaning is ambiguous. One critic, George E. Kent, says the old couple who eat beans "have had their day and exist now as time-markers" (141). However, another reader, D. H. Melhem, perceives not time marking but "endurance" in the old couple (123). Is this poem a despairing picture of old age or a more positive portrait?

"The Bean Eaters" describes an "old yellow pair" who "eat beans mostly" (line 1) off "Plain chipware" (3) with "Tin flatware" (4) in "their rented back room" (11). Clearly, they are poor. Their existence is accompanied not by friends or relatives—children or grandchildren are not mentioned—but by memories and a few possessions (9-11). They are "Mostly Good" (5), words Brooks capitalizes at the end of a line, perhaps to stress the old people's adherence to traditional values as well as their lack of saintliness. They are unexceptional, whatever message they have for readers.

The isolated routine of the couple's life is something Brooks draws attention to with a separate stanza:

> Two who are Mostly Good.
> Two who have lived their day,
> But keep on putting on their clothes
> And putting things away. (5-8)

Brooks emphasizes how isolated the couple is by repeating "Two who." Then she emphasizes how routine their life is by repeating "putting."

A pessimistic reading of this poem seems justified. The critic Harry B. Shaw reads the lines just quoted as perhaps despairing: "they are putting things away as if winding down an operation and readying for withdrawal from activity" (80). However, Shaw observes, the word "But" also indicates that the couple resist slipping away, that they intend to hold on (80). This dual meaning is at the heart of Brooks's poem: the old people live a meager existence, yes, but their will, their self-control, and their connection with another person—their essential humanity—are unharmed.

The truly positive nature of the poem is revealed in the last stanza. In Brooks's words, the old couple remember with some "twinges" perhaps, but also with "twinklings" (10), a cheerful image. As Melhem says, these people are "strong in mutual affection and shared memories" (123). And the final line, which is much longer than all the rest and which catalogs the evidence of the couple's long life together, is almost musically affirmative: "As they lean over the beans in their rented back room that is full of beads and receipts and dolls and cloths, tobacco crumbs, vases and fringes" (11).

What these people have is not much, but it is something.

Works Cited

Brooks, Gwendolyn. "The Bean Eaters." Literature: Fiction, Poetry, and Drama. Ed. Sylvan Barnet, William Burto, and William E. Cain. 13th ed. New York: Longman, 2004. 807.

Kent, George E. A Life of Gwendolyn Brooks. Lexington: UP of Kentucky, 1990.

Melhem, D. H. Gwendolyn Brooks: Poetry and the Heroic Voice. Lexington: UP of Kentucky, 1987.

Shaw, Harry B. Gwendolyn Brooks. Twayne's United States Authors Ser. 395. Boston: Twayne, 1980.

—Kenneth Scheff (student)

57 Writing in Other Disciplines

57a Writing in the humanities

The humanities include literature, the visual arts, music, film, dance, history, philosophy, and religion. The preceding chapter discusses the particular requirements of reading and writing about literature. This section concentrates on history. Although the arts, religion, and other humanities have their own concerns, they share many important goals and methods with literature and history.

1 Methods and evidence in the humanities

Writers in the humanities record and speculate about the growth, ideas, and emotions of human beings. Based on the evidence of written words, artworks, and other human traces and creations, humanities writers explain, interpret, analyze, and reconstruct the human experience.

The discipline of history focuses particularly on reconstructing the past. In Greek the word for history means "to inquire": historians inquire into the past to understand the events of the past. Then

http://www.ablongman.com/littlebrown ►

Visit the companion Web site for more help with writing in the disciplines.

they report, explain, analyze, and evaluate those events in their context, asking such questions as what happened before or after the events or how the events were related to then existing political and social structures.

Historians' reconstructions of the past—their conclusions about what happened and why—are always supported with reference to the written record. The evidence of history is mainly primary sources, such as eyewitness accounts and contemporary documents, letters, commercial records, and the like. For history papers, you might also be asked to support your conclusions with those in secondary sources.

In reading historical sources, you need to weigh and evaluate their evidence. If, for example, you find conflicting accounts of the same event, you need to consider the possible biases of the authors. In general, the more a historian's conclusions are supported by public records such as deeds, marriage licenses, and newspaper accounts, the more reliable the conclusions are likely to be.

2 Writing assignments in the humanities

Papers in the humanities generally perform one or more of the following operations:

- **Explanation:** for instance, showing how a painter developed a particular technique or clarifying a general's role in a historical battle.
- **Analysis:** examining the elements of a philosophical argument or breaking down the causes of a historical event.
- **Interpretation:** inferring the meaning of a film from its images or the significance of a historical event from contemporary accounts of it.
- **Synthesis:** finding a pattern in a historical period or in a composer's works.
- **Evaluation:** judging the quality of an architect's design or a historian's conclusions.

Most likely, you will use these operations in combination—say, interpreting and explaining the meaning of a painting and then evaluating it. (These operations are discussed in more detail in **2** pp. 86–89.)

3 Tools and language in the humanities

The tools and language of the humanities vary according to the discipline. Major reference works in each field, such as those listed on the next pages, can clarify specific tools you need and language you should use.

■ **Writing tools**

A useful tool for the arts is to ask a series of questions to analyze and evaluate a work. (A list of such questions for reading literature appears on pp. 437–39.) In any humanities discipline, a journal—a log of questions, reactions, and insights—can help you discover and record your thoughts.

In history the tools are those of any thorough and efficient researcher: a system for finding and tracking sources; a methodical examination of sources, including evaluating and synthesizing them; a system for gathering source information; and a separate system, such as a research journal, for tracking one's own evolving thoughts.

■ **Language considerations**

Historians strive for precision and logic. They do not guess about what happened or speculate about "what if." They avoid trying to influence readers' opinions with words having strongly negative or positive connotations, such as *stupid* or *brilliant*. Instead, historians show the evidence and draw conclusions from that. Generally, they avoid using *I* because it tends to draw attention away from the evidence and toward the writer.

Writing about history demands some attention to the tenses of verbs to maintain consistency. Generally, historians use the past tense to refer to events that occurred in the past. They reserve the present tense only for statements about the present or statements of general truths. For example:

> Franklin Delano Roosevelt died in 1945. Many of Roosevelt's economic reforms persist in programs such as Social Security, unemployment compensation, and farm subsidies.

■ **Research sources on the Web**

The following lists give resources in the humanities. (Resources for literature appear on pp. 440–41.) For updates of these sources and URLs, visit *ablongman.com/littlebrown*.

General
BUBL Information Service (bubl.ac.uk/link)
EDSITEment (edsitement.neh.gov)
Voice of the Shuttle (vos.ucsb.edu)

Art
Artnet (artnet.com)
World Wide Arts Resources (wwar.com/browse.html)

Dance
BUBL Link: Dance (bubl.ac.uk/link/d/dance.htm)

Google Directory: Dance Links (directory.google.com/Top/Arts/
    Performing_Arts/Dance)

Film

Film Studies on the Internet (www.ualberta.ca/~slis/guides/films/film.htm)
Internet Movie Database (imdb.com)

History

Best of History Web Sites (besthistorysites.net)
Librarians' Index to the Internet: History (lii.org/search/file/history)

Music

American Music Resource (amrhome.net)
Web Resources Research in Music (music.ucc.ie/wrrm)

Philosophy

Guide to Philosophy on the Internet (www.earlham.edu/~peters/gpi)
Social Science Information Gateway: Philosophy (sosig.ac.uk/philosophy)

Religion

Academic Info: Religion Gateway (academicinfo.net/religindex.html)
Virtual Religion Index (religion.rutgers.edu/vri)

Theater

McCoy's Brief Guide to Internet Resources in Theatre and Performance
    Studies (stetson.edu/departments/csata/thr_guid.html)
Theater Connections (uncc.edu/jvanoate/theater)

4 Documentation and format in the humanities

Writers in the humanities generally rely on one of the following
guides for source-citation style:

The Chicago Manual of Style, 15th ed., 2003
Joseph Gibaldi, MLA Handbook for Writers of Research Papers, 6th ed.,
    2003
Kate L. Turabian, A Manual for Writers of Term Papers, Theses, and Disser-
    tations, 6th ed., rev. John Grossman and Alice Bennett, 1996

See **MLA** pp. 460–98 for the recommendations of the *MLA
Handbook.* Unless your instructor specifies otherwise, use these recommendations for papers in English and foreign languages. In history, art history, and many other disciplines, however, writers rely
on *The Chicago Manual of Style* or the student reference adapted
from it, *A Manual for Writers.* Both books detail two documentation
styles. One, used mainly by scientists and social scientists, closely
resembles the style of the American Psychological Association (see
APA pp. 507–26). The other style, used more in the humanities, calls
for footnotes or endnotes and an optional bibliography. This style is
described in **Chic** pp. 533–43.

57b Writing in the social sciences

The social sciences—including anthropology, economics, education, management, political science, psychology, and sociology—focus on the study of human behavior. As the name implies, the social sciences examine the way human beings relate to themselves, to their environment, and to one another.

1 Methods and evidence in the social sciences

Researchers in the social sciences systematically pose a question, formulate a **hypothesis** (a generalization that can be tested), collect data, analyze those data, and draw conclusions to support, refine, or disprove their hypothesis. This is the scientific method developed in the natural sciences (see p. 452).

Social scientists gather data in several ways:

- **They make firsthand observations of human behavior,** recording the observations in writing or on audio- or videotape.
- **They interview subjects about their attitudes and behavior,** recording responses in writing or on tape. (See 7 pp. 396–97 for guidelines on conducting an interview.)
- **They conduct broader surveys using questionnaires,** asking people about their attitudes and behavior. (See the box on the facing page.)
- **They conduct controlled experiments,** structuring an environment in which to encourage and measure a specific behavior.

In their writing, social scientists explain their own research or analyze and evaluate others' research.

The research methods of social science generate two kinds of data:

- *Quantitative data* **are numerical,** such as statistical evidence based on surveys, polls, tests, and experiments. When public-opinion pollsters announce that 47 percent of US citizens polled approve of the President's leadership, they are offering quantitative data gained from a survey. Social science writers present quantitative data in graphs, charts, and other illustrations that accompany their text.
- *Qualitative data* **are not numerical but more subjective:** they are based on interviews, firsthand observations, and inferences, taking into account the subjective nature of human experience. Examples of qualitative data include an anthropologist's description of the initiation ceremonies in a culture she is studying or a psychologist's interpretation of interviews he conducted with a group of adolescents.

Conducting a survey

- **Decide what you want to find out—what your hypothesis is.** The questions you ask should be dictated by your purpose.
- **Define your population.** Think about the kinds of people your hypothesis is about—for instance, college men, or five-year-old children. Plan to sample this population so that your findings will be representative.
- **Write your questions.** Surveys may contain closed questions that direct the respondent's answers (checklists and multiple-choice, true/false, or yes/no questions) or open-ended questions allowing brief, descriptive answers. Avoid loaded questions that reveal your own biases or make assumptions about subjects' answers, such as "Do you want the United States to support democracy in China?" or "How much more money does your father make than your mother?"
- **Test your questions.** Use a few respondents with whom you can discuss the answers. Eliminate or recast questions that respondents find unclear, discomforting, or unanswerable.
- **Tally the results.** Count the actual numbers of answers, including any nonanswers.
- **Seek patterns in the raw data.** Such patterns may confirm or contradict your hypothesis. Revise the hypothesis or conduct additional research if necessary.

2 Writing assignments in the social sciences

Depending on what social science courses you take, you may be asked to complete a variety of assignments:

- **A summary or review of research** reports on the available research literature on a subject, such as infants' perception of color.
- **A case analysis** explains the components of a phenomenon, such as a factory closing.
- **A problem-solving analysis** explains the elements of a problem, such as unreported child abuse, and suggests ways to solve it.
- **A research paper** interprets and sometimes analyzes and evaluates the writings of other social scientists about a subject, such as the effect of national appeals in advertising.
- **A research report** explains the author's own original research or the author's attempt to replicate someone else's research. (See **APA** pp. 526–29 for an example of a research report.)

Many social science disciplines have special requirements for the content and organization of each kind of paper. The requirements appear in the style guides of the disciplines, listed on pp. 451–52. For instance, the American Psychological Association specifies the outline for research reports that is illustrated in **APA** pp. 523–25. Because of the differences among disciplines and even among different kinds of papers in the same discipline, you should always ask your instructor what he or she requires for an assignment.

3 Tools and language in the social sciences

The following guidelines for tools and language apply to most social sciences. However, the particular discipline you are writing in, or an instructor in a particular course, may have additional requirements.

■ Writing tools

Many social scientists rely on a **research journal** or **log**, in which they record their ideas throughout the research-writing process. Even if a research journal is not required in your courses, you may want to use one. As you begin formulating a hypothesis, you can record preliminary questions. Then when you are in the field conducting research, you can use the journal to react to the evidence you are collecting, to record changes in your perceptions and ideas, and to assess your progress.

To avoid confusing your reflections on the evidence with the evidence itself, keep records of actual data—notes from interviews, observations, surveys, and experiments—separately from the journal.

■ Language considerations

Each social science discipline has specialized terminology for concepts basic to the discipline. In sociology, for example, the words *mechanism, identity,* and *deviance* have specific meanings different from those of everyday usage. And *identity* means something different in sociology, where it applies to groups of people, than in psychology, where it applies to the individual. Social scientists also use precise terms to describe or interpret research. For instance, they say *The subject expressed a feeling of* rather than *The subject felt* because human feelings are not knowable for certain; or they say *These studies indicate* rather than *These studies prove* because conclusions are only tentative.

Just as social scientists strive for objectivity in their research, so they strive to demonstrate their objectivity through language in their writing. They avoid expressions such as *I think* in order to focus attention on what the evidence shows rather than on the researcher's opinions. (However, many social scientists prefer *I* to the artificial *the researcher* when they refer to their own actions, as in *I then interviewed the subjects.* Ask your instructor for his or her preferences.) Social scientists also avoid direct or indirect expression of their personal biases or emotions, either in discussions of other researchers' work or in descriptions of research subjects. Thus one social scientist does not call another's work *sloppy* or *immaculate* and does not refer to his or her own subjects as *drunks* or *innocent victims*. Instead, the writer uses neutral language and ties conclusions strictly to the data.

■ **Research sources on the Web**

For updates of these sources and URLs, visit *ablongman.com/ littlebrown*.

General

Data on the Net (odwin.ucsd.edu/idata)
Social Science Information Gateway (sosig.ac.uk)
WWW Virtual Library: Social and Behavorial Sciences (vlib.org/SocialSciences)

Anthropology

Anthro.Net (anthro.net)
Anthropology Resources on the Internet (anthropologie.net)

Business and economics

Resources for Economics on the Internet (rfe.org)
Virtual International Business and Economic Sources (library.uncc.edu/ display/?dept=reference&format=open&page=68)

Education

Educator's Reference Desk (eduref.org)
US Department of Education (ed.gov)

Ethnic and gender studies

Diversity and Ethnic Studies (public.iastate.edu/~savega/divweb2.htm)
Voice of the Shuttle: Gender Studies (vos.ucsb.edu/browse.asp?id=2711)

Political science and law

Librarians' Index to the Internet: Law (lii.org/search/file/law)
Political Science Resources (psr.keele.ac.uk)

Psychology

Psychology Online Resource Central (psych-central.com)
PsychWeb (psywww.com)

Sociology

SocioWeb (socioweb.com)
WWW Virtual Library: Sociology (socserv2.mcmaster.ca/w3virtsoclib)

4 **Documentation and format in the social sciences**

Some of the social sciences publish style guides that advise practitioners how to organize, document, and type papers. The following is a partial list:

American Anthropological Association, *AAA Style Guide*, 2002, *http://www .aaanet.org/pubs/style_guide.htm*

American Political Science Association, *Style Manual for Political Science*, 2001
American Psychological Association, *Publication Manual of the American Psychological Association*, 5th ed., 2001
American Sociological Association, *ASA Style Guide*, 2nd ed., 1997
Linguistic Society of America, "LSA Style Sheet," published every December in *LSA Bulletin*
A Uniform System of Citation (law), 17th ed., 2001

By far the most widely used style is that of the American Psychological Association, detailed in **APA** pp. 507–26. Always ask your instructor in any discipline what style you should use.

57c   Writing in the natural and applied sciences

The natural and applied sciences include biology, chemistry, physics, mathematics, engineering, computer science, and their branches. Their purpose is to understand natural and technological phenomena. (A *phenomenon* is a fact or event that can be known by the senses.) Scientists conduct experiments and write to explain the step-by-step processes in their methods of inquiry and discovery.

1   Methods and evidence in the sciences

Scientists investigate phenomena by the **scientific method**, a process of continual testing and refinement.

The scientific method

- **Observe carefully.** Accurately note all details of the phenomenon being researched.
- **Ask questions about the observations.**
- **Formulate a *hypothesis*,** or preliminary generalization, that explains the observed facts.
- **Test the hypothesis** with additional observations or controlled experiments.
- **If the hypothesis proves accurate, formulate a *theory*,** or unified model, that explains *why.*
- **If the hypothesis is disproved, revise it or start anew.**

Scientific evidence is almost always quantitative—that is, it consists of numerical data obtained from the measurement of phenomena. These data are called **empirical** (from a Greek word for "experience"): they result from observation and experience, generally in a controlled laboratory setting but also (as sometimes in astronomy or biology) in the natural world. Often the empirical evidence for scientific writing comes from library research into other people's reports of their investigations. Surveys of known data or existing literature are common in scientific writing.

2 Writing assignments in the sciences

No matter what your assignment, you will be expected to document and explain your evidence carefully so that anyone reading can check your sources and replicate your research. It is important for your reader to know the context of your research—both the previous experimentation and research on your particular subject (acknowledged in the survey of the literature) and the physical conditions and other variables surrounding your own work.

Assignments in the natural and applied sciences include the following:

- **A summary** distills a research article to its essence in brief, concise form. (Summary is discussed in detail in **2** pp. 79–80.)
- **A critique** summarizes and critically evaluates a scientific report.
- **A laboratory report** explains the procedure and results of an experiment conducted by the writer.
- **A research report** explains the experimental research of other scientists and the writer's own methods, findings, and conclusions.
- **A research proposal** reviews the relevant literature and explains a plan for further research.

A laboratory report has four or five major sections:

1. **"Abstract"**: a summary of the report.
2. **"Introduction"** or **"Objective"**: a review of why the study was undertaken, a summary of the background of the study, and a statement of the problem being studied.
3. **"Method"** or **"Procedure"**: a detailed explanation of how the study was conducted, including any statistical analysis.
4. **"Results"**: an explanation of the major findings (including unexpected results) and a summary of the data presented in graphs and tables.
5. **"Discussion"**: an interpretation of the results and an explanation of how they relate to the goals of the experiment. This section also describes new hypotheses that might be tested as a result of the experiment. If the discussion is brief, it may be combined with the results in a single section labeled "Conclusions."

In addition, laboratory or research reports may include a list of references (if other sources were consulted). They almost always include tables and figures (graphs and charts) containing the data from the research.

3 Tools and language in the sciences

Tools and language concerns vary from discipline to discipline in the sciences. Consult your instructor for specifics about the field in which you are writing.

■ Writing tools

In the sciences a **lab notebook** or **scientific journal** is almost indispensable for accurately recording the empirical data from observations and experiments. Use such a notebook or journal for these purposes:

- **Record observations** from reading, from class, or from the lab.
- **Ask questions and refine hypotheses.**
- **Record procedures.**
- **Record results.**
- **Keep an ongoing record of ideas and findings** and how they change as data accumulate.
- **Sequence and organize your material** as you compile your findings and write your report.

Make sure that your records of data are clearly separate from your reflections on the data so that you don't mistakenly confuse the two in drawing your conclusions.

■ Language considerations

Science writers prefer to use objective language that removes the writer as a character in the situation and events being explained, except as the impersonal agent of change, the experimenter. Although usage is changing, scientists still rarely use *I* in their reports and evaluations, and they often resort to the passive voice of verbs, as in *The mixture was then subjected to centrifugal force.* This conscious objectivity focuses attention (including the writer's) on the empirical data and what they show. It discourages the writer from, say, ascribing motives and will to animals and plants. For instance, instead of asserting that the sea tortoise *evolved* its hard shell *to protect* its body, a scientist would write only what could be observed: that the hard shell *covers and thus protects* the tortoise's body.

Science writers typically change verb tenses to distinguish between established information and their own research. For established information, such as that found in journals and other reliable sources, use the present tense: *Baroreceptors monitor blood pressure.* For your own and others' research, use the past tense: *The bacteria died within three hours. Marti reported some success.*

Each discipline in the natural and applied sciences has a specialized vocabulary that permits precise, accurate, and efficient communication. Some of these terms, such as *pressure* in physics, have different meanings in the common language and must be handled carefully in science writing. Others, such as *enthalpy* in chemistry, have no meanings in the common language and must simply be learned and used correctly.

■ Research sources on the Web

For updates of these sources and URLs, visit *ablongman.com/littlebrown*.

General

Google Directory: Science Links (*directory.google.com/Top/Science*)
Librarians' Index to the Internet: Science (*lii.org/search/file/scitech*)
WWW Virtual Library: Natural Sciences and Mathematics (*vlib.org/Science .html*)

Biology

Biology Online (*biology-online.org*)
National Biological Information Infrastructure (*nbii.gov*)

Chemistry

Chemistry.org (*chemistry.org/portal/a/c/s/1/home.html*)
WWW Virtual Library: Links for Chemists (*liv.ac.uk/Chemistry/Links/links .html*)

Computer science

IEEE Computer Society (*computer.org*)
University of Texas Virtual Computer Library (*utexas.edu/computer/vcl*)

Engineering

BUBL: Technology (*bubl.ac.uk*)
Internet Guide to Engineering, Mathematics, and Computing (*eevl.ac.uk*)

Environmental science

EE-link: Environmental Education on the Internet (*eelink.net*)
EnviroLink (*envirolink.org*)

Geology

American Geological Institute (*agiweb.org*)
US Geological Survey Library (*usgs.gov*)

Health sciences

Hardin MD (*lib.uiowa.edu/hardin/md*)
World Health Organization (*who.int*)

Mathematics

Math on the Web (*www.ams.org*)
BUBL: Natural Sciences and Mathematics (*bubl.ac.uk/mathematics*)

Physics and astronomy

American Institute of Physics (*aip.org*)
PhysicsWeb (*physicsweb.org*)

4 Documentation and format in the sciences

Within the natural and applied sciences, practitioners use one of two styles of documentation, varying slightly from discipline to discipline. Following are some of the style guides most often consulted:

> American Chemical Society, *ACS Style Guide: A Manual for Authors and Editors*, 2nd ed., 1997
>
> American Institute of Physics, *Style Manual for Guidance in the Preparation of Papers*, 4th ed., 1990
>
> American Mathematical Society, *The AMS Author Handbook: General Instructions for Preparing Manuscripts*, rev. ed., 1996
>
> *American Medical Association Manual of Style*, 9th ed., 1998
>
> Council of Biology Editors, *Scientific Style and Format: The CBE Manual for Authors, Editors, and Publishers*, 6th ed., 1994

The most thorough and widely used of these guides is the last one, *Scientific Style and Format*. Its sponsoring organization, the Council of Science Editors, was until 2000 called the Council of Biology Editors, so the style is abbreviated either CSE or CBE. See CSE pp. 544–50 for a description of the style.

MLA Documentation
and Format

MLA Documentation and Format

58 MLA Documentation and Format

The style guide for English, foreign languages, and some other humanities is the *MLA Handbook for Writers of Research Papers,* 6th ed., 2003, published by the Modern Language Association. In the documentation system of the *MLA Handbook,* you twice acknowledge the sources of borrowed material:

- In your text, a brief parenthetical citation adjacent to the borrowed material directs readers to a complete list of all the works you cite.
- At the end of your paper, the list of works cited includes complete bibliographical information for every source.

Every entry in the list of works cited has at least one corresponding citation in the text, and every in-text citation has a corresponding entry in the list of works cited.

This chapter describes MLA documentation: writing text citations (below), placing citations (p. 465), using supplementary notes (p. 467), and preparing the list of works cited (p. 468). A detailed discussion of MLA document format (p. 496) and a sample MLA paper (p. 498) conclude the chapter.

58a Writing MLA parenthetical text citations

1 Citation formats

In-text citations of sources must include just enough information for the reader to locate the following:

- The *source* in your list of works cited.
- The *place in the source* where the borrowed material appears.

For any kind of source, you can usually meet both these requirements by providing the author's last name and (if the source uses them) the page numbers where the borrowed material appears. The reader can find the source in your list of works cited and find the borrowed material in the source itself.

The following models illustrate the basic text-citation forms and also forms for more unusual sources, such as those with no named

http://www.ablongman.com/littlebrown ▶

Visit the companion Web site for more help and an electronic exercise on MLA documentation and format.

author or no page numbers. See the **MLA** divider for an index to all the models.

Note Models 1 and 2 below show the direct relationship between what you include in your text and what you include in a parenthetical citation. If you do *not* name the author in your text, you include the name in parentheses before the page reference (model 1). If you *do* name the author in your text, you do not include the name in parentheses (model 2).

1. Author not named in your text

When you have not already named the author in your sentence, provide the author's last name and the page number(s), with no punctuation between them, in parentheses:

> One researcher concludes that "women impose a distinctive construction on moral problems, seeing moral dilemmas in terms of conflicting responsibilities" (Gilligan 105-06).

2. Author named in your text

If the author's name is already given in your text, you need not repeat it in the parenthetical citation. The citation gives just the page number(s):

> Carol Gilligan concludes that "women impose a distinctive construction on moral problems, seeing moral dilemmas in terms of conflicting responsibilities" (105-06).

3. A work with two or three authors

If the source has two or three authors, give all their last names in the text or in the citation. Separate two authors' names with and:

> As Frieden and Sagalyn observe, "The poor and the minorities were the leading victims of highway and renewal programs" (29).

> According to one study, "The poor and the minorities were the leading victims of highway and renewal programs" (Frieden and Sagalyn 29).

With three authors, add commas and also and before the final name:

> The textbook by Wilcox, Ault, and Agee discusses the "ethical dilemmas in public relations practice" (125).

> One textbook discusses the "ethical dilemmas in public relations practice" (Wilcox, Ault, and Agee 125).

4. A work with more than three authors

If the source has more than three authors, you may list all their last names or use only the first author's name followed by et al. (the abbreviation for the Latin "and others"). The choice depends on what you do in your list of works cited (see p. 470).

> It took the combined forces of the Americans, Europeans, and Japanese to break the rebel siege of Beijing in 1900 (Lopez et al. 362).

> It took the combined forces of the Americans, Europeans, and Japanese to break the rebel siege of Beijing in 1900 (Lopez, Blum, Cameron, and Barnes 362).

5. A work with numbered paragraphs or screens instead of pages

Some electronic sources number each paragraph or screen instead of each page. In citing passages in these sources, give the paragraph or screen number(s) and distinguish them from page numbers: after the author's name, put a comma, a space, and the abbreviation par. (one paragraph), pars. (more than one paragraph), screen, or screens.

> Twins reared apart report similar feelings (Palfrey, pars. 6-7).

6. An entire work or a work with no page or other reference numbers

When you cite an entire work rather than a part of it, the citation will not include any page or paragraph number. Try to work the author's name into your text, in which case you will not need a parenthetical citation. But remember that the source must appear in the list of works cited.

> Boyd deals with the need to acknowledge and come to terms with our fear of nuclear technology.

Use the same format when you cite a specific passage from a work that has no page, paragraph, or other reference numbers, such as an online source.

If the author's name does not appear in your text, put it in a parenthetical citation:

> Almost 20 percent of commercial banks have been audited for the practice (Friis).

7. A multivolume work

If you consulted only one volume of a multivolume work, your list of works cited will say so (see pp. 472–73), and you can treat the volume as any book.

If you consulted two or more volumes of a multivolume work, your citation must indicate which one you are referring to. In the example the number 5 indicates the volume from which the quotation was taken; the number 438 indicates the page number in that volume.

> After issuing the Emancipation Proclamation, Lincoln said, "What I did, I did after very full deliberations, and under a very heavy and solemn sense of responsibility" (5: 438).

8. A work by an author of two or more cited works

If your list of works cited includes two or more works by the same author, then your citation must tell the reader which of the author's works you are referring to. Give the title either in the text or in a parenthetical citation. In a parenthetical citation, give the full title only if it is brief; otherwise, shorten the title to the first one, two, or three main words (excluding *A*, *An*, or *The*). For the following source, the full book title is *The Arts and Human Development:*

> At about age seven, most children begin to use appropriate gestures to reinforce their stories (Gardner, Arts 144-45).

9. An anonymous work

Anonymous works are alphabetized by title in the list of works cited. In the text they are referred to by full or shortened title. The next citation refers to an unsigned article titled "The Right to Die." (A page number is omitted because the article is only one page.)

> One article notes that a death-row inmate may demand his own execution to achieve a fleeting notoriety ("Right").

If two or more anonymous works have the same title, distinguish them with additional information in the text citation, such as the publication date.

10. A government publication or a work with a corporate author

Some works list as author a government body, association, committee, company, or other group. Cite such a work by that organization's name. If the name is long, work it into the text to avoid an intrusive citation.

> A 2005 report by the Hawaii Department of Education predicts an increase in enrollments (6).

11. An indirect source

When you want to use a quotation that is already in quotation marks—indicating that the author you are reading is quoting someone else—try to find the original source and quote directly from it. If you can't find the original source, then your citation must indicate that your quotation of it is indirect. In the following citation, qtd. in ("quoted in") says that Davino was quoted by Boyd:

> George Davino maintains that "even small children have vivid ideas about nuclear energy" (qtd. in Boyd 22).

The list of works cited then includes only Boyd (the work consulted), not Davino.

12. A literary work

Novels, plays, and poems are often available in many editions, so your instructor may ask you to provide information that will help readers find the passage you cite no matter what edition they consult.

- **Novels:** the page number comes first, followed by a semicolon and then information on the appropriate part or chapter of the work.

  > Toward the end of James's novel, Maggie suddenly feels "the thick breath of the definite—which was the intimate, the immediate, the familiar, as she hadn't had them for so long" (535; pt. 6, ch. 41).

- **Poems that are not divided into parts:** You may omit the page number and supply the line number(s) for the quotation. To prevent confusion with page numbers, precede the number(s) with line or lines in the first citation; then use just the number(s).

  > In Shakespeare's Sonnet 73 the speaker identifies with the trees of late autumn, "Bare ruined choirs, where late the sweet birds sang" (line 4). "In me," Shakespeare writes, "thou seest the glowing of such fire / That on the ashes of his youth doth lie . . ." (9-10).

- **Verse plays and poems that are divided into parts:** Omit a page number and cite the appropriate part—act (and scene, if any), canto, book, and so on—plus the line number(s). Use Arabic numerals for parts, including acts and scenes (3.4 in the example).

  > Later in King Lear the disguised Edgar says, "The prince of darkness is a gentleman" (3.4.147).

- **Prose plays:** Provide the page number followed by the act and scene, if any (see the citation of *Death of a Salesman* on p. 467).

13. The Bible

When you cite passages of the Bible in parentheses, abbreviate the title of any book longer than four letters—for instance, Gen. (Genesis), 1 Sam. (1 Samuel), Ps. (Psalms), Matt. (Matthew). Then give the chapter and verse(s) in Arabic numerals.

> According to the Bible, at Babel God "did . . . confound the language of all the earth" (Gen. 11.9).

14. An electronic source

Cite an electronic source as you would any other source: usually by author's name or, if there is no author, by title.

> Business forecasts for the fourth quarter tended to be optimistic (White 4).

This example cites a source with page numbers. For a source with paragraph or screen numbers or no numbering, see models 5 and 6 (p. 462).

15. Two or more works in the same citation

If you use a single parenthetical citation to refer to more than one work, separate the references with a semicolon.

> Two recent articles point out that a computer badly used can be less efficient than no computer at all (Gough and Hall 201; Richards 162).

Since long citations in the text can distract the reader, you may choose to cite several or more works in an endnote or footnote rather than in the text. See p. 467.

2 Placement and punctuation of parenthetical citations

The following guidelines will help you place and punctuate text citations to distinguish between your and your sources' ideas and to make your own text readable. See also 7 pp. 413–18 on editing quotations and using signal phrases to integrate source material into your sentences.

■ Where to place citations

Position text citations to accomplish two goals: (1) make it clear exactly where your borrowing begins and ends; (2) keep the citation as unobtrusive as possible. You can accomplish both goals by placing the parenthetical citation at the end of the sentence element containing the borrowed material. This sentence element may be a phrase or a clause, and it may begin, interrupt, or conclude the sentence. Usually, as in the examples below, the element ends with a punctuation mark.

> The inflation rate might climb as high as 30 percent (Kim 164), an increase that could threaten the small nation's stability.

> The inflation rate, which might climb as high as 30 percent (Kim 164), could threaten the small nation's stability.

> The small nation's stability could be threatened by its inflation rate, which, one source predicts, might climb as high as 30 percent (Kim 164).

In the last example the addition of *one source predicts* clarifies that Kim is responsible only for the inflation-rate prediction, not for the statement about stability.

When your paraphrase or summary of a source runs longer than a sentence, clarify the boundaries by using the author's name in the first sentence and placing the parenthetical citation at the end of the last sentence.

> Juliette Kim studied the effects of acutely high inflation in several South American and African countries since World War II. She discovered that a major change in government accompanied or followed the inflationary period in 56 percent of cases (22-23).

When you cite two or more sources in the same paragraph, position authors' names and parenthetical citations so that readers can see who said what. In the following example, the beginnings and ends of sentences clearly mark the different sources:

> For some time, schools have been using computers extensively for drill-and-practice exercises, in which students repeat specific skills such as spelling words or using the multiplication facts. But many education experts criticize such exercises for boring students and failing to engage their critical thinking and creativity. Jane M. Healy, a noted educational psychologist and teacher, takes issue with "interactive" software for children as well as drill-and-practice software, arguing that "some of the most popular 'educational' software . . . may be damaging to independent thinking, attention, and motivation" (20). Another education expert, Harold Wenglinsky of the Educational Testing Service, found in a well-regarded 1998 study that fourth and eighth graders who used computers frequently, including for drill and practice, actually did worse on tests than their peers who used computers less often (Does It Compute? 21). In a later article, Wenglinsky concludes that "the quantity of use matters far less than the quality of use." In schools, he says, high-quality computer work, involving critical thinking, is still rare ("In Search" 17).

■ How to punctuate citations

Generally place a parenthetical citation *before* any punctuation required by your sentence, as in the preceding examples. If the borrowed material is a quotation, place the citation *between* the closing quotation mark and the punctuation.

> Spelling argues that during the 1970s American automobile manufacturers met consumer needs "as well as could be expected" (26).

The exception is a quotation ending in a question mark or exclamation point. Then use the appropriate punctuation inside the closing quotation mark, and follow the quotation with the text citation and a period.

> "Of what use is genius," Emerson asks, "if the organ . . . cannot find a focal distance within the actual horizon of human life?" ("Experience" 60). Mad genius is no genius.

When a citation appears at the end of a quotation set off from the text, place it one space *after* the punctuation ending the quotation. Do not use additional punctuation with the citation or quotation marks around the quotation.

> In Arthur Miller's <u>Death of a Salesman</u>, the most poignant defense of Willie Loman comes from his wife, Linda:
>
> > He's not the finest character that ever lived. But he's a human being, and a terrible thing is happening to him. So attention must be paid. He's not to be allowed to fall into his grave like an old dog. Attention, attention must finally be paid to such a person. (56; act 1)

(This citation of a play includes the act number as well as the page number. See p. 464.)

3 Footnotes or endnotes in special circumstances

Footnotes or endnotes may replace parenthetical citations when you cite several sources at once, when you comment on a source, or when you provide information that does not fit easily in the text. Signal a footnote or endnote in your text with a numeral raised above the appropriate line. Then write a note with the same numeral.

> Text   At least five studies have confirmed these results.[1]
>
> Note   [1] Abbott and Winger 266-68; Casner 27; Hoyenga 78-79; Marino 36; Tripp, Tripp, and Walk 179-83.

In a note, the raised numeral is indented one-half inch or five spaces and is followed by a space. If the note appears as a footnote, place it at the bottom of the page on which the citation appears, set it off from the text with quadruple spacing, and single-space the note itself. If the note appears as an endnote, place it in numerical order with the other endnotes on a page between the text and the list of works cited. Double-space all the endnotes.

58b   Preparing the MLA list of works cited

At the end of your paper, a list titled Works Cited includes all the sources you quoted, paraphrased, or summarized in your paper. (If your instructor asks you to include sources you examined but did not cite, title the list Works Consulted.)

The list of works cited always begins a new page, numbered in sequence with the preceding pages. Format the list as in the sample below. Arrange all your sources in alphabetical order by the last name of the author—or by the last name of the first author if there is more than one. If a source has no named author, alphabetize it by the first main word of the title (excluding *A, An,* or *The*). Use *only* alphabetical order to arrange sources, not another principle such as type of source or date of publication.

MLA works-cited page

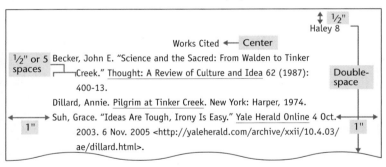

An index to all the following models appears at the **MLA** divider. Use your best judgment in adapting the models to your particular sources. If you can't find a model that exactly matches a source you used, locate and follow the closest possible match. You will certainly need to combine formats—for instance, drawing on model 2 ("A book with two or three authors") and model 26 ("An article in a daily newspaper") for a newspaper article with two authors.

1   Books

The facing page shows the basic format for a book and the location of the required information in a book. When other information is required for a reference, it generally falls either between the author's name and the title or between the title and the publication information, as in the following models.

Information for a book

①
Gilligan, Carol. In a Different Voice: Psychological Theory and Women's Development.
③   ④   ⑤
    Cambridge: Harvard UP, 1982.

Title page

In a Different Voice

Psychological Theory and Women's Development

Carol Gilligan

Harvard University Press
Cambridge, Massachusetts, and London, England

② **Title,** underlined. Give the full title and any subtitle, separating them with a colon. End the title with a period.

① **Author.** Give the full name —last name first, a comma, first name, and any middle name or initial. Omit *Dr., PhD,* or any other title. End the name with a period.

④ **Publisher's name.** Shorten most publishers' names ("UP" for University Press, "Little" for Little, Brown). Give both imprint and publisher's names when they appear on the title page: e.g., "Vintage-Random" for Vintage Books and Random House.

③ **City of publication.** Precede the publisher's name with its city, followed by a colon. Use only the first city if the title page lists more than one.

Copyright page

Copyright © 1982 by Carol Gilligan
All rights reserved
Printed in the United States of America

⑤ **Date of publication.** If the date doesn't appear on the title page, look for it on the next page. End the date with a period.

1. A book with one author

Gilligan, Carol. <u>In a Different Voice: Psychological Theory and Women's Devel-
opment</u>. Cambridge: Harvard UP, 1982.

2. A book with two or three authors

Lifton, Robert Jay, and Greg Mitchell. <u>Who Owns Death: Capital Punishment,
the American Conscience, and the End of Executions</u>. New York: Morrow,
2000.

Wilcox, Dennis L., Phillip H. Ault, and Warren K. Agee. <u>Public Relations:
Strategies and Tactics</u>. 6th ed. New York: Irwin, 2005.

Give the authors' names in the order provided on the title page. Reverse the first and last names of the first author *only*, not of any other authors. Separate two authors' names with a comma and and; separate three authors' names with commas and with and before the third name.

3. A book with more than three authors

Lopez, Geraldo, Judith P. Salt, Anne Ming, and Henry Reisen. <u>China and the
West</u>. Boston: Little, 2004.

Lopez, Geraldo, et al. <u>China and the West</u>. Boston: Little, 2004.

You may, but need not, give all authors' names if the work has more than three authors. If you choose not to give all names, provide the name of the first author only, and follow the name with a comma and the abbreviation et al. (for the Latin *et alii*, meaning "and others").

4. Two or more works by the same author(s)

Gardner, Howard. <u>The Arts and Human Development</u>. New York: Wiley, 1973.

---. <u>The Quest for Mind: Piaget, Lévi-Strauss, and the Structuralist Movement</u>.
New York: Knopf, 1973.

Give the author's name only in the first entry. For the second and any subsequent works by the same author, substitute three hyphens for the author's name, followed by a period. (If you are citing two or more works by the same editor, editors, or translator, follow the hyphens with a comma and ed., eds., or trans. as appropriate. See models 5, 6, and 7.) Note that the three hyphens stand for *exactly* the same name or names. If the second source above were by Gardner and somebody else, both names would have to be given in full.

Place an entry or entries using three hyphens immediately after the entry that names the author. Within the set of entries by the same author, arrange the sources alphabetically by the first main word of the title, as in the preceding examples (Arts, then Quest).

5. A book with an editor

Holland, Merlin, and Rupert Hart-Davis, eds. The Complete Letters of Oscar
Wilde. New York: Holt, 2000.

Handle editors' names like authors' names (models 1–3), but add a
comma and the abbreviation ed. (one editor) or eds. (two or more
editors) after the last editor's name.

6. A book with an author and an editor

Mumford, Lewis. The City in History. Ed. Donald L. Miller. New York: Pantheon,
1986.

When citing the work of the author, give his or her name first, and
give the editor's name after the title, preceded by Ed. (singular only,
meaning "Edited by"). When citing the work of the editor, use model
5 for a book with an editor, adding By and the author's name after
the title: Miller, Donald L., ed. The City in History. By Lewis Mumford.

7. A translation

Alighieri, Dante. The Inferno. Trans. John Ciardi. New York: NAL, 1971.

When citing the work of the author, give his or her name first, and
give the translator's name after the title, preceded by Trans. ("Translated by"). When citing the work of the translator, give his or her
name first, followed by a comma and trans.; then follow the
title with By and the author's name: Ciardi, John, trans. The Inferno. By
Dante Alighieri.

When a book you cite by author has a translator and an editor,
give the translator's *and* editor's names in the order used on the
book's title page.

8. A book with a corporate author

Lorenz Research, Inc. Research in Social Studies Teaching. Baltimore: Arrow,
2000.

Corporate authors include associations, committees, institutions,
government bodies, companies, and other groups. List the name of
the group as author when a source gives only that name and not an
individual's.

9. An anonymous book

The Dorling Kindersley World Reference Atlas. London: Dorling, 2005.

List a book that names no author—neither an individual nor a
group—by its full title. Alphabetize the book by the title's first main
word (here Dorling), excluding *A*, *An*, or *The*.

10. The Bible

The Bible. King James Version.

The New English Bible. London: Oxford UP and Cambridge UP, 1970.

When citing a standard version of the Bible (first example), do not underline the title or the name of the version, and you need not provide publication information. For an edition of the Bible (second example), underline the title and give full publication information.

11. A later edition

Bolinger, Dwight L. Aspects of Language. 3rd ed. New York: Harcourt, 1981.

For any edition after the first, place the edition number after the title. (If an editor's name follows the title, place the edition number after the name. See model 18.) Use the appropriate designation for editions that are named or dated rather than numbered—for instance, Rev. ed. for "Revised edition."

12. A republished book

James, Henry. The Golden Bowl. 1904. London: Penguin, 1966.

Republished books include paperbound editions of books originally released in hard bindings and books reissued under new titles. Place the original date of publication (but not the place of publication or the publisher's name) after the title, and then provide the full publication information for the source you are using. If the book was originally published under a different title, add this title at the end of the entry and move the original publication date to follow the title—for example, Rpt. of Thomas Hardy: A Life. 1941.

13. A book with a title in its title

Eco, Umberto. Postscript to The Name of the Rose. Trans. William Weaver. New
    York: Harcourt, 1983.

When a book's title contains another book title (as here: *The Name of the Rose*), do not underline the second title. When a book's title contains a quotation or the title of a work normally placed in quotation marks, keep the quotation marks and underline both titles: Critical Response to Henry James's "The Beast in the Jungle." (Note that the underlining extends under the closing quotation mark.)

14. A work in more than one volume

Lincoln, Abraham. The Collected Works of Abraham Lincoln. Ed. Roy P. Basler.
    8 vols. New Brunswick: Rutgers UP, 1953.

Lincoln, Abraham. <u>The Collected Works of Abraham Lincoln</u>. Ed. Roy P. Basler.
Vol. 5. New Brunswick: Rutgers UP, 1953. 8 vols.

If you use two or more volumes of a multivolume work, give the work's total number of volumes before the publication information (8 vols. in the first example). Your text citation will indicate which volume you are citing (see pp. 462–63). If you use only one volume, give that volume number before the publication information (Vol. 5 in the second example). You may add the total number of volumes to the end of the entry (8 vols. in the second example).

If you cite a multivolume work published over a period of years, give the inclusive years as the publication date: for instance, Cambridge: Harvard UP, 1978-90.

15. A work in a series

Bergman, Ingmar. <u>The Seventh Seal</u>. Mod. Film Scripts Ser. 12. New York: Simon,
1995.

Place the name of the series (not quoted or underlined) just before the publication information. Abbreviate common words such as *modern* and *series*. Add any series number after the series title.

16. Published proceedings of a conference

<u>Watching Our Language: A Conference Sponsored by the Program in Architec-
ture and Design Criticism</u>. 6-8 May 2005. New York: Parsons School of
Design, 2005.

Whether in or after the title of the conference, supply information about who sponsored the conference, when it was held, and who published the proceedings. Treat a particular presentation at the conference like a selection from an anthology (model 18).

17. An anthology

Kennedy, X. J., and Dana Gioia, eds. <u>Literature: An Introduction to Fiction,
Poetry, and Drama</u>. 9th ed. New York: Longman, 2005.

Cite an entire anthology only when citing the work of the editor or editors or when your instructor permits cross-referencing like that shown in model 19. Give the name of the editor or editors (followed by ed. or eds.) and then the title of the anthology.

18. A selection from an anthology

Mason, Bobbie Ann. "Shiloh." <u>Literature: An Introduction to Fiction, Poetry, and
Drama</u>. Ed. X. J. Kennedy and Dana Gioia. 9th ed. New York: Longman,
2005. 643-54.

The essentials of this listing are these: author of selection; title of selection (in quotation marks); title of anthology (underlined); editors' names preceded by Ed. (meaning "Edited by"); publication information for the anthology; and inclusive page numbers for the selection (without the abbreviation "pp."). In addition, this source requires an edition number for the anthology. If you wish, you may also supply the original date of publication for the work you are citing, after its title. See model 12 on p. 472.

If the work you cite comes from a collection of works by one author and with no editor, use the following form:

> Auden, W. H. "Family Ghosts." The Collected Poetry of W. H. Auden. New York: Random, 1945. 132-33.

If the work you cite is a scholarly article that was previously printed elsewhere, provide the complete information for the earlier publication of the piece, followed by Rpt. in ("Reprinted in") and the information for the source in which you found the piece:

> Molloy, Francis C. "The Suburban Vision in John O'Hara's Short Stories." Critique: Studies in Modern Fiction 25.2 (1984): 101-13. Rpt. in Short Story Criticism: Excerpts from Criticism of the Works of Short Fiction Writers. Ed. David Segal. Vol. 15. Detroit: Gale, 1989. 287-92.
>
> San Juan, E. "Theme Versus Imitation: D. H. Lawrence's 'The Rocking-Horse Winner.'" D. H. Lawrence Review 3 (1970): 136-40. Rpt. in From Fiction to Film: D. H. Lawrence's "The Rocking-Horse Winner." Ed. Gerald R. Barrett and Thomas L. Erskine. Dickenson Literature and Film Ser. Encino: Dickenson, 1974. 70-74.

19. Two or more selections from the same anthology

> Chopin, Kate. "The Storm." Kennedy and Gioia 127-31.
>
> Kennedy, X. J., and Dana Gioia, eds. Literature: An Introduction to Fiction, Poetry, and Drama. 9th ed. New York: Longman, 2005.
>
> O' Connor, Flannery. "Revelation." Kennedy and Gioia 443-58.

When you are citing more than one selection from the same source, your instructor may allow you to avoid repetition by giving the source in full (as in the Kennedy and Gioia entry) and then simply cross-referencing it in entries for the works you used. Thus, instead of full information for the Chopin and O'Connor works, give Kennedy and Gioia and the appropriate pages in that book. Each entry appears in its proper alphabetical place among other works cited.

20. An introduction, preface, foreword, or afterword

> Donaldson, Norman. Introduction. The Claverings. By Anthony Trollope. New York: Dover, 1977. vii-xv.

An introduction, foreword, or afterword is often written by someone other than the book's author. When citing such a piece, give its name without quotation marks or underlining. (If the piece has a title of its own, provide it, in quotation marks, between the name of the author and the name of the piece.) Follow the title of the book with By and its author's name. Give the inclusive page numbers of the part you cite. (In the preceding example, the small Roman numerals refer to the front matter of the book, before page 1.)

When the author of a preface or introduction is the same as the author of the book, give only the last name after the title:

> Gould, Stephen Jay. Prologue. The Flamingo's Smile: Reflections in Natural History. By Gould. New York: Norton, 1985. 13-20.

21. An article in a reference work

> Mark, Herman F. "Polymers." The New Encyclopaedia Britannica: Macropaedia. 15th ed. 1991.

> "Reckon." Merriam-Webster's Collegiate Dictionary. 11th ed. 2003.

List an article in a reference work by its title (second example) unless the article is signed (first example). For works with entries arranged alphabetically, you need not include volume or page numbers. For well-known works like those listed above, you may also omit the editors' names and all publication information except any edition number and the year of publication. For works that are not well known, give full publication information:

> "Hungarians in America." The Ethnic Almanac. Ed. Stephanie Bernardo. New York: Doubleday, 2001. 109-11.

2 Periodicals: Journals, magazines, and newspapers

The next page shows the basic format for an article in a periodical (a journal) and the location of the required information in a journal.

Note The treatment of volume and issue numbers and publication dates varies depending on the kind of periodical being cited, as the models indicate. For the distinction between journals and magazines, see 7 p. 385.

22. An article in a journal with continuous pagination throughout the annual volume

> Lever, Janet. "Sex Differences in the Games Children Play." Social Problems 23 (1996): 478-87.

Some journals number the pages of issues consecutively throughout a year, so that each issue after the first in a year begins numbering where the previous issue left off—say, at page 132 or 416. For this

Information for a journal article

Selwyn, Neil. "The Social Processes of Learning to Use Computers." Social Science
Computer Review 23.1 (2005): 122-35.

(Labeled with numbered markers: ① Selwyn, Neil. ② "The Social Processes of Learning to Use Computers." ③ Social Science Computer Review ④ 23.1 ⑤ (2005): ⑥ 122-35.)

Journal cover

④ Volume and/or issue number, in Arabic numerals.

SPRING 2005 VOLUME 23 NUMBER I

⑤ Year of publication, in parentheses and followed by a colon.

③ Title of periodical, underlined. Omit any *A, An,* or *The* from the beginning of the title. Do not end with a period.

SOCIAL SCIENCE COMPUTER REVIEW

First page of article

② Title of article, in quotation marks. Give the full title and any subtitle, separating them with a colon. End the title with a period inside the final quotation mark.

The Social Processes of Learning to Use Computers

NEIL SELWYN
Cardiff School of Social Sciences

① Author. Give the full name—last name first, a comma, first name, and any middle name or initial. Omit *Dr., PhD,* or any other title. End the name with a period.

The ability to use a computer is assumed to be a cornerstone of effective citizenship in the Information Age, with a range of initiatives and educational provisions being introduced to encourage people to become competent with information technology (IT). Despite such provision, levels of computer use and competence have been found to vary widely throughout the general population, and we know little of how different ways of learning to use computers contribute to people's eventual use of IT. Based on data from in-depth interviews with 100 adults in the United Kingdom, this article examines the range and social stratification of formal and informal learning about computers that is taking place, suggesting that formal computer instruction orientated toward the general public may inadvertently widen the digital knowledge gap. In particular, the data highlight the importance of informal learning about IT and of encouraging such learning, especially in the home.

AUTHOR'S NOTE: This article is based on a project funded by the Economic and Social Research Council (R000239518). I would like to thank the other members of the Adults Learning@Home project (Stephen Gorard and John Furlong) as well as the individuals who took part in the in-depth interviews. Correspondence concerning this article may be addressed to Neil Selwyn, School of Social Sciences, Cardiff University, Glamorgan Building, King Edward VII Avenue, Cardiff CF10 3WT, UK; e-mail: selwynnc@cardiff.ac.uk.

⑥ Inclusive page numbers of article, without "pp." Go to the end of the article for the last page number. Provide only as many digits in the last number as needed for clarity, usually two.

122

kind of journal, give the volume number after the title (23 in the preceding example) and place the year of publication in parentheses. The page numbers will be enough to guide readers to the issue you used.

23. An article in a journal that pages issues separately or that numbers only issues, not volumes

Selwyn, Neil. "The Social Processes of Learning to Use Computers." Social
Science Computer Review 23.1 (2005): 122-35.

Some journals page each issue separately (starting each issue at page 1). For these journals, give the volume number, a period, and the issue number (as in 23.1 in the Selwyn entry above and opposite). When citing an article in a journal that numbers only issues, not annual volumes, treat the issue number as if it were a volume number, as in model 22.

24. An article in a monthly or bimonthly magazine

Garber, Marjorie. "Our Genius Problem." Atlantic Monthly Dec. 2002: 46-53.

Follow the magazine title with the month and the year of publication. (Abbreviate all months except May, June, and July.) Don't place the date in parentheses, and don't provide a volume or issue number.

25. An article in a weekly or biweekly magazine

Talbot, Margaret. "The Bad Mother." New Yorker 5 Aug. 2004: 40-46.

Follow the magazine title with the day, the month, and the year of publication. (Abbreviate all months except May, June, and July.) Don't place the date in parentheses, and don't provide a volume or issue number.

26. An article in a daily newspaper

Zeller, Tom, Jr. "To Go Global, Do You Ignore Censorship?" New York Times 24
Oct. 2005, natl. ed.: C3+.

Give the name of the newspaper as it appears on the first page (but without A, An, or The). If the name of the city is not in the title of a local newspaper, add the city name in brackets after the title, without underlining: Gazette [Chicago]. Then follow model 25, with two differences: (1) If the newspaper lists an edition at the top of the first page, include that information after the date and a comma. (See natl. ed. above.) (2) If the newspaper is divided into lettered or numbered sections, provide the section designation before the page number when the newspaper does the same (as in C3+ above);

otherwise, provide the section designation before the colon—for instance, sec. 1: 1+. The plus sign here and with C3+ in the preceding model indicates that the articles do not run on consecutive pages but start on page 1 or C3 and continue later.

27. An anonymous article

"The Right to Die." Time 11 Oct. 1996: 101.

For an article with no named author, begin the entry with the title of the article. In the list of works cited, alphabetize an anonymous source by the first main word of the title ("Right" in this model).

28. An editorial or letter to the editor

"Dualing Power Centers." Editorial. New York Times 14 Jan. 2005, natl. ed.:
    A16.

Add the word Editorial or Letter after the title if there is one or after the author's name, as follows:

Dowding, Michael. Letter. Economist 5-11 Jan. 2005: 4.

(The numbers 5-11 in this entry are the publication days of the periodical: the issue spans January 5 through 11.)

29. A review

Nelson, Cary. "Between Anonymity and Celebrity." Rev. of Anxious Intellects:
    Academic Professionals, Public Intellectuals, and Enlightenment Values,
    by John Michael. College English 64 (2002): 710-19.

Rev. is an abbreviation for "Review." The name of the author of the work being reviewed follows the title of the work, a comma, and by. If the review has no title of its own, then Rev. of and the title of the reviewed work immediately follow the name of the reviewer.

30. An abstract of a dissertation or article

Steciw, Steven K. "Alterations to the Pessac Project of Le Corbusier." Diss. U of
    Cambridge, England, 1986. DAI 46 (1986): 565C.

For an abstract appearing in *Dissertation Abstracts* (*DA*) or *Dissertation Abstracts International* (*DAI*), give the author's name and the title, Diss. (for "Dissertation"), the institution granting the author's degree, the date of the dissertation, and the publication information. See model 58, pp. 491–92, for listing an entire dissertation rather than an abstract.

For an abstract of an article, first provide the publication information for the article itself, followed by the information for the abstract. If the abstract publisher lists abstracts by item rather than page number, add item before the number.

> Lever, Janet. "Sex Differences in the Games Children Play." <u>Social Problems</u> 23
> (1996): 478-87. <u>Psychological Abstracts</u> 63 (1996): item 1431.

3 Electronic sources

Electronic sources include those you find online (either through the library Web site or directly over the Internet) and those you find on CD-ROM (see p. 490). The following list, adapted from the *MLA Handbook*, itemizes the possible elements of an online source, in order of their appearance in a works-cited entry. *No source will include all the elements.*

1. **Name of author, editor, compiler, or translator,** arranged and punctuated as in models 1–3, p. 470. Use ed., comp., or trans. after the name as appropriate, as shown in models 5 and 7, p. 471.
2. **Title of a short work,** in quotation marks. Short works include poems, articles, documents or pages on a Web site, Web log entries, and postings to discussion groups. (Follow the last with Online posting.)
3. **Title of a book,** underlined.
4. **Name of editor, compiler, or translator of the source,** if not cited before, preceded by Ed., Comp., or Trans. as appropriate. See models 6 and 7, p. 471.
5. **Publication information for any print version of the source,** following earlier models for books and periodical articles. For a periodical article, the publication information includes the periodical title.
6. **Title of the online site,** underlined. The title might be that of a periodical (if not already given), a scholarly project, a database, a Web log, and so on. For a site with no title, add Home page, Course home page, or another description.
7. **Name of site editor,** if any, preceded by Ed.
8. **Version number, if any, or volume/issue numbers for an online journal.** See models 22–23, pp. 475–77, for journals.
9. **Date of electronic publication, latest revision, or posting.**
10. **Title of a subscription database, name of the subscription service, and name and location of the subscriber.**
11. **Title of a discussion group.**
12. **Inclusive page numbers, number of paragraphs, or other identifying numbers,** if any.
13. **Name of site sponsor,** such as an institution or organization, if not cited before.

14. **Date you consulted the source.**
15. **URL of the source.** To ensure the accuracy of URLs, use Copy and Paste to duplicate them in a file or an e-mail to yourself. In the list of works cited, break URLs *only* after slashes—do not hyphenate. Unless you are submitting your paper online, use the Tools menu of your word processor to eliminate hyperlinks in works-cited entries (click on AutoCorrect in *Microsoft Word*, Settings in *WordPerfect*).

> **Note** A URL does not always provide a usable route to a source, especially with subscription services. See models 31 and 32.

31. A work from an online service to which your library subscribes

Gorski, Paul C. "Privilege and Repression in the Digital Era: Rethinking the Sociopolitics of the Digital Divide." <u>Race, Gender and Class</u> 10.4 (2003): 145-76. <u>Ethnic NewsWatch</u>. ProQuest. U of Minnesota, Twin Cities, Wilson Lib. 24 July 2005 <http://proquest.umi.com>.

See the facing page for an analysis of the preceding entry and the location of the required information on the subscription service.

> **Note** Many subscription services provide source URLs that are temporary, specific to the library, or too long to copy with certain accuracy. If any of these applies to the URL of the source you're consulting, you can use the service's home page URL instead or omit a URL. Some services provide a "Permanent link" or "Document URL" on each source record: a URL for finding the source from within the library's system (not from the open Web). You can see such a link on the database page opposite. Like the one in the example, permanent links are often unmanageably long and complex. In that case, use the service's home-page URL, which runs through *com* in the permanent link.

32. A work from an online service to which you subscribe

"China–Dragon Kings." The Encyclopedia Mythica. America Online. 6 Jan. 2005. Path: Research and Learn; Encyclopedia; More Encyclopedias; Encyclopedia Mythica.

If you find a source through America Online, MSN, or another personal online service, you may not see a usable URL or any URL for the source. In that case, provide the path you used to get to the source, as in the example above: ① Title of source, in quotation marks, and title of larger work, underlined. ② Name of the service,

Information for an article from a subscription service

Gorski, Paul C. "Privilege and Repression in the Digital Era: Rethinking the Sociopoli-

tics of the Digital Divide." Race, Gender and Class 10.4 (2003): 145-76. Ethnic

NewsWatch. ProQuest. U of Minnesota, Twin Cities, Wilson Lib. 24 July 2005

<http://proquest.umi.com>.

⑤ **Name of the service,** not underlined, ending with a period.

④ **Name of the database,** underlined, ending with a period.

⑥ **Names of the subscribing institution and library,** separated by a comma and ending with a period.

② **Title of the article,** in quotation marks. End the title with a period inside the final quotation mark.

③ **Publication information for any print version.** If the site gives information for a print version of the source, give it after the source title, following an appropriate model on pp. 468–79.

① **Author.** Give the full name—last name first, a comma, first name, and any middle name or initial. Omit Dr., PhD, or any other title. End with a period.

⑧ **URL,** enclosed in angle brackets. But if the source URL is temporary, unique to your search, or too long (as in the example), use the URL of the site's home page. See the note on the facing page.

⑦ **Date of your access.** Give the day first, then month, then year. Abbreviate all months except May, June, and July. Do not end the date with a period. (Since this date does not appear on the site, record it separately.)

neither underlined nor quoted. ③ Date of your access, followed by a period. ④ Path: and the sequence of topics required to reach the source, with the topics separated by semicolons.

If you used a keyword instead of a path to reach the source, give that information instead: Keyword: Chinese dragon kings.

33. An entire online site (scholarly project, professional site, personal site, etc.)

A scholarly project or professional site:

American Verse Project. 16 May 2001. U of Michigan Humanities Text Initiative.
21 July 2005 <http://www.hti.umich.edu/a/amverse>.

When citing a scholarly project or professional site, include the following: ① Title of the site, underlined. ② Date of publication or most recent update. ③ Name of any organization or institution that sponsors the site. ④ Date of your access. ⑤ URL. If the project or site has an editor or compiler, add the name, preceded by Ed. or Comp., between the site title and the publication date. See the Conrad entry on p. 484.

A personal site:

Lederman, Leon. Topics in Modern Physics—Lederman. 28 Aug. 2005.
12 Dec. 2005 <http://www-ed.fnal.gov/samplers/hsphys/people/
lederman.html>.

Cite a personal site with this information: ① Author's name, if any. ② Title, if any, underlined. If the site has no title, describe it with a label such as Home page, without quotation marks or underlining. ③ Date of last revision. ④ Date of your access. ⑤ URL.

A business site:

Prius. 2006. Toyota Motor Corp. 2 Feb. 2006 <http://www.toyota.com/
prius>.

For the site of a corporation or other business, give the following: ① Site title, underlined. ② Date of site. ③ Name of sponsoring business. ④ Date of your access. ⑤ URL.

34. A poem, essay, or other short work from an online site

Wheatley, Phillis. "On Virtue." Poems on Various Subjects, Religious and Moral.
London: A. Bell, 1773. American Verse Project. 16 May 2001. U of Michigan Humanities Text Initiative. 21 July 2005 <http://
name.umdl.umich.edu/BAP5379>.

See the model and screen shots on the facing page for an analysis of this entry and the location of the required information on the Web site.

Information for a short work from an online site

①   ②   ③
Wheatley, Phillis. "On Virtue." Poems on Various Subjects, Religious and Moral. Lon-

                        ④   ⑤   ⑥
    don: A. Bell, 1773. American Verse Project. 16 May 2001. U of Michigan Human-

            ⑦   ⑧
    ities Text Initiative. 21 July 2005 <http://name.umdl.umich.edu/BAP5379>.

Home page of site

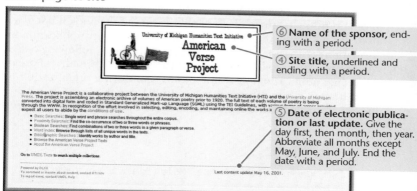

⑥ Name of the sponsor, ending with a period.

④ Site title, underlined and ending with a period.

⑤ Date of electronic publication or last update. Give the day first, then month, then year. Abbreviate all months except May, June, and July. End the date with a period.

Source record for poem

③ Publication information for any print version. If the site gives information for a print version of the source, as here, provide it after the source title, following an appropriate model on pp. 468–79.

Poem

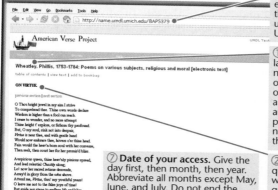

⑧ URL of the short work, enclosed in angle brackets. If the URL is long, temporary, or unique to your search, use the URL of the site's home page.

① Author. Give the full name—last name first, a comma, first name, and any middle name or initial. Omit *Dr.*, *PhD*, or any other title. End the name with a period. If you don't see the author's name at the top of the page, look at the bottom. If no author is listed, begin with the title.

⑦ Date of your access. Give the day first, then month, then year. Abbreviate all months except May, June, and July. Do not end the date with a period. (Since this date does not appear on the site, record it separately.)

② Title of the short work, in quotation marks. End the title with a period inside the final quotation mark.

35. An online book

An entire book:

Austen, Jane. *Emma*. 1816. Ed. R. W. Chapman. Oxford: Clarendon, 1926. *Oxford Text Archive*. 2004. Oxford U. 15 Dec. 2005 <http://ota.ahds.ac.uk/ Austen/Emma.1519>.

(annotations above, numbered ① Author, ② 1816, ③ Ed. R. W. Chapman, ④ Oxford: Clarendon, 1926, ⑤ Oxford Text Archive, ⑥ 2004, ⑦ Oxford U., ⑧ 15 Dec. 2005, ⑨ <http://ota.ahds.ac.uk/Austen/Emma.1519>.)

For a book published online, give the following information: ① Author and title. ② Date of original publication of the book if not given in item 4. ③ Name of any editor or translator. ④ Any publication information for the original print version of the book, following one of models 1–17 (pp. 469–73). ⑤ Title of the site, underlined. ⑥ Date of electronic publication. ⑦ Name of any sponsoring organization or institution. ⑧ Date of your access. ⑨ URL for the book. If the site has an editor, add the name after the site's title (see the following model).

A part of a book:

Conrad, Joseph. "A Familiar Preface." *Modern Essays*. Ed. Christopher Morley. New York: Harcourt, 1921. *Bartleby.com: Great Books Online*. Ed. Steven van Leeuwan. Nov. 2000. 16 Feb. 2006 <http://www.bartleby.com/237/ 8.html>.

(annotations: ① Conrad, Joseph, ② "A Familiar Preface.", ③ Modern Essays. Ed. Christopher Morley. New York: Harcourt, 1921., ④ Bartleby.com: Great Books Online. Ed. Steven van Leeuwan., ⑤ Nov. 2000, ⑥ 16 Feb. 2006, ⑦ <http://www.bartleby.com/237/8.html>.)

For a part of a book published online, provide this information: ① Author of the part. ② Title of the part, in quotation marks. (Do not use quotation marks for Introduction, Foreword, or another standard part.) ③ Title of the book (underlined), editor of the book (if any), and publication information for the print version of the book. ④ Title of the site (underlined) and editor of the site (if any). ⑤ Date of electronic publication. ⑥ Date of your access. ⑦ URL for the part of the book. If the site as a whole has a sponsoring organization, give the name between the date of electronic publication and the date of your access (see the Austen model above).

36. An article in an online journal

Palfrey, Andrew. "Choice of Mates in Identical Twins." *Modern Psychology* 4.1 (2003): 26-40. 25 Feb. 2006 <http://www.liasu.edu/modpsy/ palfrey4(1).htm>.

(annotations: ① Palfrey, Andrew. "Choice of Mates in Identical Twins." Modern Psychology 4.1, ② (2003): 26-40., ③ 25 Feb. 2006, ④ <http://www.liasu.edu/modpsy/palfrey4(1).htm>.)

Give the following information for an online scholarly article that you reach directly: ① Author, article title, journal title, volume and any issue numbers, and publication date, as in model 22 or 23 (pp. 475–77). ② Page numbers in the journal or total number of pages, paragraphs, or sections, if any of these are given. Omit reference numbers if the source does not use them. ③ Date of your access. ④ URL for the article.

For a journal article reached through a subscription service, see model 31 (p. 480).

37. An online abstract

Palfrey, Andrew. "Choice of Mates in Identical Twins." Modern Psychology 4.1

(2003): 26-40. Abstract. 25 Feb. 2006 <http://www.liasu.edu/modpsy/

abstractpalfrey4(1).htm>.

Treat an online abstract like an online journal article (model 36), but add Abstract (without quotation marks or underlining) between the publication information and the date of your access.

38. An article in an online newspaper or on a newswire

Still, Lucia. "On the Battlefields of Business, Millions of Casualties." New York
Times on the Web 3 Mar. 2005. 17 Aug. 2005 <http://www.nytimes.com/
specials/downsize/05down1.html>.

Provide the following information for an online newspaper article that you reach directly: ① Author, article title, newspaper title, and publication date as in model 26 (p. 477). Give section, page, or paragraph numbers if the newspaper does. ② Date of your access. ③ URL for the article.

Treat a newswire article similarly, substituting the title of the wire service for the newspaper title (this article is anonymous):

"Film, Fashion Asked to Stop Glamorizing Smoking." Reuters 18 Feb.

2003. 28 Feb. 2003 <http://www.reuters.com/

newsArticle.jhtml?type=industryNewsID2246811>.

See model 31 (p. 480) when citing a newspaper or newswire article that you reached through a subscription service.

39. An article in an online magazine

Lewis, Ricki. "The Return of Thalidomide." Scientist 22 Jan. 2001: 5. 24 Jan.
2006 <http://www.the-scientist.com/yr2001/jan/lewis_pl_010122.html>.

Provide the following information for an online magazine article that you reach directly: ① Author's name, article title, magazine title, and publication date, as in model 24 or 25 on p. 477. ② Any page, paragraph, or other reference numbers. ③ Date of your access. ④ URL for the article.

See model 31 (p. 480) when citing a magazine article that you reached through a subscription service.

40. An online review

Detwiler, Donald S., and Chu Shao-Kang. Rev. of Important Documents of the
Republic of China, ed. Tan Quon Chin. Journal of Military History 56.4
(1992): 669-84. 16 Sept. 2005 <http://www.jstor.org/fcgi-bin/jstor/
viewitem.fcg/08993718/96p0008x>.

Cite an online review as follows: ① Author, any review title, Rev. of and the title of the reviewed book, author or editor of the reviewed book, and publication information—all as in model 29 (p. 478). ② Date of your access. ③ URL for the review.

See model 31 (p. 480) when citing a review that you reached through a subscription service.

41. An online government publication

United States. Dept. of Commerce. National Telecommunications and Information Admin. A Nation Online: Entering the Broadband Age. Feb. 2005.
1 Mar. 2005 <http://www.ntia.doc.gov/reports/anol/index.html>.

See p. 491 for models of government publications in print. Provide the same information for online publications, and add facts of electronic publication. The model above includes the following: ① Names of government, department, and agency. ② Title of publication, underlined. ③ Date of publication. ④ Date of your access. ⑤ URL for the publication.

42. An article in an online encyclopedia or other information database

Dull, Jack L. "Wu-ti." Encyclopaedia Britannica Online. 2004 Encyclopaedia
Britannica. 23 Dec. 2005 <http://www.britannica.com/eb/
article?tocid:9077599>.

For an article in an encyclopedia or other information database, provide the following: ① Author's name, if any is given. ② Title of the article, in quotation marks. ③ Title of the database, underlined. ④ Date of electronic publication. ⑤ Name of sponsoring organization or publisher. ⑥ Date of your access. ⑦ URL for the article.

See models 31 and 32 (pp. 480–81) when citing an information database that you reached through a library or personal subscription service. For encyclopedias and other reference works that you find in print or on CD-ROM, see pp. 475 and 490, respectively.

43. An online image (artwork, advertisement, graph, etc.)

In general, you can base citations of online images on the examples in model 59 (pp. 492–93), adding information for the online source, particularly site title, date of your access, and URL. The following examples show a range of possibilities:

A work of art:

> Pollock, Jackson. Shimmering Substance. 1946. Museum of Modern Art,
> New York. WebMuseum. 12 Mar. 2003 <http://www.ibiblio.org/
> wm/paint/auth/Pollock/pollock.shimmering.jpg>.

A photograph:

> Curtis, Edward S. Canyon de Chelly—Navaho. 1904. Lib. of Congress. American
> Memory. 21 July 2005 <http://hdl.loc.gov/loc.award/iencurt.cp01028>.

An advertisement:

> Absolut Vodka. Advertisement. Vanity Fair Jan. 2003. Adflip. 18 Nov. 2005
> <http://adflip.com/php?adID=14714>.

A cartoon or comic strip:

> Keefe, Mike. "Suspicious Package." Cartoon. Denver Post 21 July 2005.
> PoliticalCartoons.com. 6 Jan. 2006 <http://
> www.politicalcartoons.com>.

A map, chart, graph, or diagram:

> Hamilton, Calvin J. "Components of Comets." Diagram. Space Art. 2003.
> 20 Dec. 2005 <http://solarviews.com/eng/comet.htm>.

44. An online television or radio program

Base citations of online television and radio programs on model 60, p. 493, adding your access date and the URL.

> Gross, Terry, host. Fresh Air. National Public Radio. 11 Feb. 2006. 12 Feb. 2006
> <http://discover.npr.org/freshair/day_fa.html?display=February/
> 11/2006>.

45. An online sound recording or clip

Base citations of online sound recordings or clips on model 61, p. 493, adding your access date and the URL.

Reagan, Ronald W. State of the Union Address. 26 Jan. 1982. Vincent Voice Library. Digital and Multimedia Center, U of Michigan. 6 May 2005 <http://www.lib.msu.edu/vincent/presidents/reagan.htm>.

46. An online film or film clip

Base citations of online films or film clips on model 62, p. 493, adding your access date and the URL.

Stewart, Leslie J. 96 Ranch Rodeo and Barbecue. 1951. Lib. of Congress. American Memory. 7 Jan. 2006 <http://lcweb2.loc.gov/ammem/afc96ran_v034>.

47. The home page for a course or department

Anderson, Daniel. Business Communication. Course home page. Jan.-June 2003. Dept. of English, U of North Carolina. 16 Feb. 2003 <http://sites.unc.edu/daniel/eng32/index.html>.

For the home page of a course, provide this information: ① Instructor's name. ② Course title, without quotation marks or underlining. ③ The description Course home page. ④ Inclusive dates of the course. ⑤ Names of the department and the school, separated by a comma. ⑥ Date of your access. ⑦ URL for the home page.

For a department home page, give the department name first, followed by Dept. home page, the name of the school, your access date, and the URL:

Computer Engineering. Dept. home page. Santa Clara U School of Engineering. 12 Oct. 2005 <http://www.cse.scu.edu>.

48. An entry on a Web log

Daswani, Susheel. "Hollywood vs. Silicon Valley." Berkeley Intellectual Property Weblog. 16 Mar. 2005. 22 Aug. 2005 <http://www.biplog.com/archive/cat_hollywood.html>.

To cite an entry on a Web log, give the following: ① Author's name. ② Title of the entry, in quotation marks. ③ Title of the Web log, underlined. ④ Date of the entry. ⑤ Date of your access. ⑥ URL for the entry.

49. Electronic mail

Millon, Michele. "Re: Grief Therapy." E-mail to the author. 4 May 2005.

For e-mail, give the following: ① Writer's name. ② Title, if any, from the e-mail's subject heading, in quotation marks. ③ Description of the transmission, including to whom it was sent. ④ Date of posting.

50. A posting to an e-mail discussion list

Tourville, Michael. "European Currency Reform." Online posting. 6 Jan. 2006.

International Finance Discussion List. 12 Jan. 2006 <http://

www.weg.isu.edu/finance-dl/archive/46732>.

Whenever possible, cite an archived version of a posting to an e-mail discussion list so that readers can find it without difficulty. Give this information for the posting: ① Author's name. ② Title, if any, from the e-mail's subject heading, in quotation marks. ③ Online posting. ④ Date of posting. ⑤ Name of the discussion list, without quotation marks or underlining. ⑥ Date of your access. ⑦ URL, if known, or e-mail address for the list's moderator or supervisor.

51. A posting to a newsgroup or Web forum

A newsgroup:

Cramer, Sherry. "Recent Investment Practices in US Business." Online posting.

26 Mar. 2005. Young Entrepreneurs. 3 Apr. 2005 <http://

finance.groups.yahoo.com/group/youngentrepreneurs3>.

For a posting to a newsgroup that you read on the Web, give the following: ① Author's name. ② Title from the subject heading, in quotation marks. ③ Online posting. ④ Date of posting. ⑤ Name of the newsgroup, without quotation marks or underlining. ⑥ Date of your access. ⑦ URL for the group. If you read the posting on a news server instead of on the Web, omit the group name before your access date and give the group name in the URL, preceded by news: (<news:biz.startups.youngentrepreneurs.2700>).

A Web forum:

Razi, N. M. "Hypothyroidism." Online posting. 6 July 2005. Homeopathy

Forum. 28 Jan. 2006 <http://www.hpathy.com/homeopathy/forums/

forum_topics.asp?FID=328>.

For a posting to a Web forum, provide this information: ① Author's name. ② Title, if any, in quotation marks. ③ Online posting. ④ Date of posting. ⑤ Name of the forum, without quotation marks or underlining. ⑥ Date of your access. ⑦ URL for the forum.

52. A synchronous communication

Bruckman, Amy. MediaMOO Symposium: Virtual Worlds for Business? 20 Jan.
2006. MediaMOO. 26 Feb. 2006 <http://www.co.gatech.edu/fac/
Amy.Bruckman/MediaMOO/cscw-symposium-06.html>.

Whenever possible, cite an archived version of a synchronous communication so that readers can find it without difficulty. Provide this information: ① Speaker's name. ② Description of the event, without quotation marks or underlining. ③ Date of the event. ④ Forum, without quotation marks or underlining. ⑤ Date of your access. ⑥ URL for the archive.

53. A source on a periodical CD-ROM database

Hakim, Danny. "Iacocca, Away from the Grind, Still Has a Lot to Say." New York
Times 19 July 2005, natl. ed.: C1+. New York Times Ondisc. CD-ROM.
UMI-ProQuest. Sept. 2005.

Databases on CD-ROM are issued periodically—for instance, every six months or every year. The journals, newspapers, and other publications included in such a database are generally available in print as well, so your works-cited entry should give the information for both formats: ① Information for the print version, following models on pp. 475–79. ②Title of the CD-ROM, underlined. ③ Medium, CD-ROM. ④ Name of the vendor (or distributor) of the CD-ROM. ⑤ Date of electronic publication.

54. A source on a nonperiodical CD-ROM

Nunberg, Geoffrey. "Usage in the Dictionary." The American Heritage Dictionary of the English Language. 4th ed. CD-ROM. Boston: Houghton,
2005.

Single-issue CD-ROMs may be encyclopedias, dictionaries, books, and other resources that are published just once, like printed books. Use this format: ① Author's name, if any. ② Title of the source. Use quotation marks for short works, such as an article. Underline the title if it is a book. ③ Title of the entire CD-ROM, underlined. Note that this CD-ROM also includes an edition number. ④ Medium, CD-ROM. ⑤ CD-ROM's place of publication, publisher, and date of publication.

See also pp. 475 and 486, respectively, for models of print and online reference works.

55. Computer software

Project Scheduler 9000. Vers. 5.1. Orlando: Scitor, 2006.

For software, provide the following: ① Title, underlined. ② Version number. ③ Publication information, including place of publication, publisher, and date. If the software has a listed author, give his or her name first in the entry. If you consulted or obtained the software online, replace the publication information with the date of your access and the URL, as in earlier examples.

4 Other print and nonprint sources

56. A government publication

Board of Governors. US Federal Reserve System. Federal Reserve Bulletin Aug. 2005: 20-21.

Hawaii. Dept. of Education. Kauai District Schools, Profile 2004-05. Honolulu: Hawaii Dept. of Education, 2005.

Stiller, Ann. Historic Preservation and Tax Incentives. US Dept. of Interior. Washington: GPO, 2002.

United States. Cong. House. Committee on Ways and Means. Medicare Payment for Outpatient Occupational Therapy Services. 108th Cong., 1st sess. Washington: GPO, 2003.

If an author is not listed for a government publication, give the appropriate agency as author, as in the first, second, and last examples. Provide information in the order illustrated, separating elements with a period: the name of the government, the name of the agency (which may be abbreviated), and the title and publication information. For a congressional publication (last example), give the house and committee involved before the title, and give the number and session of Congress after the title. In the last two examples, GPO stands for the US Government Printing Office.

57. A pamphlet

Medical Answers About AIDS. New York: Gay Men's Health Crisis, 2006.

Most pamphlets can be treated as books. In the example above, the pamphlet has no listed author, so the title comes first. If the pamphlet has an author, list his or her name first, followed by the title and publication information as given here.

58. An unpublished dissertation or thesis

Wilson, Stuart M. "John Stuart Mill as a Literary Critic." Diss. U of Michigan, 1990.

The title is quoted rather than underlined. Diss. stands for "Dissertation." U of Michigan is the institution that granted the author's degree.

59. An image (artwork, advertisement, graph, etc.)

A work of art:

> Hockney, David. Place Furstenberg, Paris. 1985. College Art Gallery, New Paltz,
>   New York. David Hockney: A Retrospective. Ed. Maurice Tuchman and
>   Stephanie Barron. Los Angeles: Los Angeles County Museum of Art,
>   1988. 247.

For a work of art, name the artist and give the title (underlined), the date of creation, and the name and location of the owner. For a work you see only in a reproduction, provide the complete publication information, too, as in the Hockney model. Omit such information only if you examined the actual work.

A photograph:

> Heinz, Thomas A. Fallingwater: Exterior Detail. Frank Lloyd Wright: Architect.
>   Ed. Terence Riley. New York: Museum of Modern Art, 2000. 236.

Treat a photograph you find in a collection or book like a work of art, with photographer's name (if known), photograph title (underlined), and date. Add the owner's name (as in the Hockney entry above) if the photograph is an artwork and not an illustration. Give the publication information unless you examined an actual print of the photograph.

For a personal photograph by you or someone else, describe the subject (without quotation marks or underlining), say who took the photograph, and add the date:

> Children in Central Park. Personal photograph by the author. 16 Mar. 2006.

An advertisement:

> Jetta by Volkswagen. Advertisement. New Yorker 25 July 2005: 31.

Cite an advertisement with the name of the product or company advertised, the description Advertisement, and the publication information.

A cartoon or comic strip:

> Trudeau, Garry. "Doonesbury." Comic strip. San Francisco Chronicle 28 Aug.
>   2005: E6.

Cite a cartoon or comic strip with the artist's name, the title (in quotation marks), the description Cartoon or Comic strip, and the publication information.

A map, chart, graph, or diagram:

> Women in the Armed Forces. Map. Women in the World: An International Atlas.
>   By Joni Seager and Ann Olson. New York: Touchstone, 2006. 44-45.

List the image by its title (underlined) unless its creator is credited on the source. Provide a description (Map, Chart, and so on) and then the publication information.

60. A television or radio program

> "I'm Sorry, I'm Lost." By Alan Ball. Dir. Jill Soloway. Six Feet Under. HBO.
>   2 July 2005.

Start with the title unless you are citing the work of a person or persons. The example here includes an episode title (in quotation marks), the writer's and director's names, the program title (underlined), the name of the network, and the date. If the program aired on a local TV station, identify the station between the network and the date—for example, WGBH, Boston.

61. A sound recording

> Brahms, Johannes. Piano Concerto no. 2 in B-flat, op. 83. Perf. Artur Rubin-
>   stein. Cond. Eugene Ormandy. Philadelphia Orch. LP. RCA, 1972.
> Springsteen, Bruce. "Empty Sky." The Rising. Columbia, 2002.

Begin with the name of the individual whose work you are citing. If you're citing a song or song lyrics, give the title in quotation marks. Then provide the title of the recording, not underlined if it identifies a composition by form, number, and key (first example). After the title, provide the names of any other artists it seems appropriate to mention, the manufacturer of the recording, and the date of release. If the medium is other than compact disk, provide it immediately before the manufacturer's name—for instance, LP (as in the first example) or Audiocassette.

62. A film, DVD, or video recording

> The Lord of the Rings: The Return of the King. Dir. Peter Jackson. New Line,
>   2003.

Start with the title of the work you are citing, unless you are citing the contribution of a particular individual (as in the next model). Give additional information (director, writer, lead performers, and so on) as you judge appropriate. For a film, end with the distributor and date.

For a DVD or videocassette, include the original release date (if any) and the medium (DVD, videocassette) before the distributor's name:

George Balanchine, chor. <u>Serenade</u>. Perf. San Francisco Ballet. Dir. Hilary Bean.

    1991. Videocassette. PBS Video, 1997.

63. A musical composition

Fauré, Gabriel. Sonata for Violin and Piano no. 1 in A Major, op. 15.

Don't underline musical compositions, such as the one above, that are identified only by form, number, and key. Do underline titled operas, ballets, and compositions (<u>Carmen</u>, <u>Sleeping Beauty</u>).

64. A performance

Barenboim, Daniel, cond. Chicago Symphony Orch. Symphony Center, Chicago.

    22 Jan. 2005.

<u>The English Only Restaurant</u>. By Silvio Martinez Palau. Dir. Susana Tubert.

    Puerto Rican Traveling Theater, New York. 27 July 2005.

As with films and television programs, place the title first unless you are citing the work of an individual (first example). Provide additional information about participants after the title, as well as the theater, city, and date. Note that the orchestra name in the first example is neither quoted nor underlined.

65. A letter

Buttolph, Mrs. Laura E. Letter to Rev. and Mrs. C. C. Jones. 20 June 1857. In

    <u>The Children of Pride: A True Story of Georgia and the Civil War</u>. Ed.

    Robert Manson Myers. New Haven: Yale UP, 1972. 334-35.

List a published letter under the writer's name. Specify that the source is a letter and to whom it was addressed, and give the date on which it was written. Treat the remaining information like that for a selection from an anthology (model 18, pp. 473–74). (See also p. 478 for the format of a letter to the editor of a periodical.)

    For a letter in the collection of a library or archive, specify the writer, recipient, and date, as in the previous example, and give the name and location of the archive as well:

James, Jonathan E. Letter to his sister. 16 Apr. 1970. Jonathan E. James

    Papers. South Dakota State Archive, Pierre.

    For a letter you receive, give the name of the writer, note the fact that the letter was sent to you, and provide the date of the letter:

Packer, Ann E. Letter to the author. 15 June 2005.

Use the form above for personal e-mail as well, substituting E-mail for Letter: E-mail to the author (see model 49, p. 488).

66. A lecture or address

Carlone, Dennis. "Architecture for the City of the Twenty-First Century." Symposium on the City. Urban Issues Group. Cambridge City Hall, Cambridge. 22 May 2005.

Give the speaker's name, the title (in quotation marks), the title of the meeting, the name of the sponsoring organization, the location of the lecture, and the date. If the lecture has no title, use Lecture, Address, or another description instead.

Although the *MLA Handbook* does not provide a specific style for classroom lectures in your courses, you can adapt the preceding format for this purpose:

Chang, Julia. Class lecture on the realist novel. Homans College. 20 Jan. 2006.

67. An interview

Graaf, Vera. Personal interview. 19 Dec. 2005.

Rumsfeld, Donald. Interview. Frontline. PBS. WGBH, Boston. 10 Oct. 2005.

Begin with the name of the person interviewed. For an interview you conducted, specify Personal interview or the medium (such as Telephone interview or E-mail interview), and then give the date. For an interview you read, heard, or saw, provide the title if any or Interview if there is no title, along with other bibliographic information and the date.

EXERCISE 58.1   Writing works-cited entries

Prepare works-cited entries from the following information. Follow the models of the *MLA Handbook* given in this chapter unless your instructor specifies a different style. For titles, use underlining (as here) unless your instructor requests italics. Arrange the finished entries in alphabetical order, not numbered. (You can do this exercise online at *ablongman.com/littlebrown*.)

1 A journal article titled "Networking the Classroom" by Christopher Conte. The article appears in volume 5 of CQ Researcher, a journal that pages issues continuously throughout each annual volume. Volume 5 is dated 2004. The article runs from page 923 to page 943.

2 A magazine article on a database that is also available in print. The author is Larry Irving. The title is "The Still Yawning Divide." The article appears in the March 12, 2005, issue of Newsweek, a weekly magazine, and starts on page 64. You consulted the article on November 14, 2005, through the database Expanded Academic ASAP from the service InfoTrac (http://www.galegroup.com). You reached the database through Southeast State University's Polk Library.

3 A government document you consulted on November 12, 2005, over the Internet. The author is the National Center for Education

Statistics, an agency within the United States Department of Education. The title of the document is Internet Access in Public Schools. It was published February 24, 2005, and can be accessed at http://www.ed.gov/nces/edstats.

4 A book called Failure to Connect: How Computers Affect Our Children's Minds—For Better and Worse, written by Jane M. Healy and published in 2000 by Simon & Schuster in New York.

5 An article in the October 9, 2004, issue of the magazine The Nation titled "The Threat to the Net." The article is by Jeff Chester and appears on pages 6 to 7 of the magazine. You found it through Polk Library at Southeast State University on November 14, 2005, using the database Expanded Academic ASAP from the service InfoTrac. The home page URL for the database is http://www.galegroup.com.

6 A pamphlet titled Bridging the Digital Divide, with no named author. It was published in 2005 by the ALA in Chicago.

7 An article titled "MyPyramid.gov: Achieving E-Health for All?" on the Web site Digital Divide Network at http://www.digitaldivide.net/articles. The Web site is sponsored by the Benton Foundation. The article is by Andy Carvin and is dated February 22, 2005. You found it on November 10, 2005.

8 An e-mail interview you conducted with Mary McArthur on October 31, 2005.

58c Formatting a paper in MLA style

The document format recommended by the *MLA Handbook* is fairly simple, with just a few elements. See also 1 pp. 56–66 for guidelines on type fonts, headings, lists, and other features that are not specified in MLA style.

The following illustrations show the formats for the first page and a later page of a paper. For the format of the list of works cited, see p. 468.

First page of MLA paper

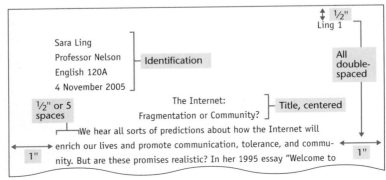

Later page of MLA paper

Margins Use minimum one-inch margins on all sides of every page.

Spacing and indentions Double-space throughout. Indent paragraphs one-half inch or five spaces. (See the next page for indention of set-off quotations.)

Paging Begin numbering on the first page, and number consecutively through the end (including the list of works cited). Type Arabic numerals (1, 2, 3) in the upper right about one-half inch from the top. Place your last name before the page number in case the pages later become separated.

Identification and title MLA style does not require a title page for a paper. Instead, give your name, your instructor's name, the course title, and the date on separate lines in the upper left of the first page—one inch from the top and the left of the paper. (See the sample on the facing page.) Double-space between all lines of this identification.

Double-space also around the title, and center it. If the title runs two lines, center both lines and double-space between them. Use capital and small letters for the title, capitalizing according to the guidelines in **6** p. 358. Don't type the title in all-capital letters, underline it, or enclose it in quotation marks. (See the sample on the facing page.)

Poetry and long prose quotations Treat a single line of poetry like any other quotation, running it into your text and enclosing it in quotation marks. You may run in two or three lines of poetry as well, separating the lines with a slash surrounded by space.

> An example of Robert Frost's incisiveness is in two lines from "Death of the Hired Man": "Home is the place where, when you have to go there **/** They have to take you in" (119-20).

Always set off quotations of more than three lines of poetry and more than four typed lines of prose. (See **7** pp. 411–12 for guidelines on when to use such long quotations.) Use double spacing above and below the quotation and for the quotation itself. Indent the quotation one inch or ten spaces from the left margin. *Do not add quotation marks to set-off quotations.*

Emily Dickinson stripped ideas to their essence, as in this description of "A narrow Fellow in the Grass," a snake:

> I more than once at Noon
> Have passed, I thought, a Whip lash
> Unbraiding in the Sun
> When stopping to secure it
> It wrinkled, and was gone and – (12-16)

In Talley's Corner, his influential 1967 study of the urban poor, Elliot Liebow observes that "unskilled" construction work requires more experience and skill than is generally assumed:

> A healthy, sturdy, active man of good intelligence requires from two to four weeks to break in on a construction job. . . . It frequently happens that his foreman or the craftsman he services is not willing to wait that long for him to get into condition or to learn at a glance the difference in size between a rough 2 x 8 and a finished 2 x 10. (62)

Do not use a paragraph indention for a quotation of a single complete paragraph or a part of a paragraph. Use paragraph indentions of one-quarter inch or three spaces only for a quotation of two or more paragraphs.

58d Examining a sample paper in MLA style

The sample paper beginning on p. 500 follows the guidelines of the *MLA Handbook* for overall format, parenthetical citations, and the list of works cited. Marginal annotations highlight features of the paper.

Note Because the sample paper addresses a current Internet controversy, many of its sources come from the Internet and do not use page or other reference numbers. Thus the in-text citations of these sources do not give reference numbers. In a paper relying solely on printed journals, books, and other traditional sources, most if not all in-text citations would include page numbers.

■ A note on outlines

Some instructors ask students to submit an outline of the final paper. For advice on constructing a formal or topic outline, see pp. 19–20. Below is an outline of the sample paper following, written in complete sentences. Note that the thesis statement precedes either a topic or a sentence outline.

Thesis statement

To improve equity between online and traditional stores and between consumers with and without Internet access, tax laws should be revised to allow collection of sales taxes on Internet purchases.

I. A Supreme Court ruling and congressional legislation presently govern Internet taxation.

   A. A 1992 Supreme Court decision frees vendors from collecting sales taxes from customers in states where the vendors have no physical presence.

   B. A 1998 law, extended in 2000, placed a moratorium on Internet taxes.

II. A tax-free Internet is unfair to traditional bricks-and-mortar stores.

   A. Sales taxes can make bricks-and-mortar purchases significantly more expensive than online purchases.

   B. Sales taxes exceed online merchants' shipping charges.

III. A tax-free Internet is unfair to consumers who lack Internet access.

   A. A government report shows a huge "digital divide" among US residents.

      1. The affluent are much more likely to have Internet access than the poor.

      2. Whites who are college educated are much more likely to have Internet access than nonwhites with elementary educations.

   B. The digital divide means the poor must pay sales taxes while the affluent can avoid the taxes by shopping online.

IV. The three main arguments against Internet taxation do not rebut the issue of fairness.

   A. Taxes on Internet commerce would not, as claimed, undermine the freedom of the Internet.

   B. Internet commerce does not, as claimed, deserve special protection and encouragement that is not given to traditional commerce.

   C. The very real complexities of Internet taxation do not, as claimed, justify a permanent ban on taxation.

Alder 1

Identification: writer's name, instructor's name, course title, date.

Kisha Alder

Ms. Savarro

English 101

15 December 2005

Title centered.

Double-space throughout.

Introduction: gives background to establish the issue.

Citation form: shortened title for anonymous source; online source has no page number.

Thesis statement.

Who Pays the Bill for Internet Shopping?

Going to the mall may soon go out of style. These days more and more people are shopping from home over the Internet. In 2002 electronic commerce (e-commerce) took in approximately $40 billion from shoppers; by 2007 that amount is expected to be $105 billion or more ("Sales Tax"). These numbers are good news for the online stores and for online shoppers, who can anticipate increasing variety in e-commerce offerings. But because taxes are not collected on Internet sales as they are on purchases in almost all states, online stores compete unfairly with traditional "bricks-and-mortar" stores, and shoppers with Internet access have an unfair advantage over shoppers with no such access. To improve equity between online and traditional stores and between consumers with and without Internet access, tax laws should be revised to allow collection of sales taxes on Internet purchases.

Background on Internet taxation (next two paragraphs).

Citation form: law case; case name underlined in the text citation.

Citation form: source with two authors.

Internet commerce is regulated by the same tax laws that govern other commerce. However, in 1992 the Supreme Court ruled that vendors do not have to collect taxes on behalf of states where they do not have a physical presence, because such collection would place an unconstitutional burden on interstate commerce (Quill Corp. v. North Dakota 5-8). Buyers are supposed to send the correct taxes to their state governments voluntarily, but they rarely do and states currently have no way to collect (Zimmerman and Hoover 45). In a decision addressing mail-order sales but considered applicable to Internet sales, the Court's majority urged Congress to reexamine the tax laws governing interstate commerce:

Quotation over four lines set off without quotation marks. See p. 498.

Ellipsis mark signals omission from quotation.

Citation form: after displayed quotation, citation follows sentence period and one space.

> The underlying issue is not only one that Congress may be better qualified to resolve, but also one that Congress has the ultimate power to resolve. . . . Accordingly, Congress is now free to decide whether, when, and to what extent the States may burden interstate mail-order concerns with a duty to collect use taxes. (Quill Corp. v. North Dakota 18-19)

Alder 2

Because of this decision, Congress has been wrestling with whether and how to tax Internet commerce.

Congress did take some action in 1998, when e-commerce was blossoming, by placing a temporary moratorium on new Internet taxes and by creating the Advisory Commission on Electronic Commerce to study the taxation issue and recommend solutions. A majority of the commission recommended extending the moratorium for another five years, through 2006, so that the taxation issue could be studied further and the state and local taxing authorities could simplify their complex and overlapping tax systems (US Advisory Commission). Congress agreed and voted in 2002 to extend the moratorium. Meanwhile, the debate over taxing e-commerce continues to heat up. On one side are state and local governments that are attempting to regain lost revenue with a uniform tax rate that would apply to Internet purchases. On the other side are those who would transform the moratorium on Internet sales taxes into a permanent ban ("E-Commerce").

As long as the moratorium is in effect, Internet shopping is essentially tax-free. Yet in almost all states, traditional shopping is subject to sales tax. Bricks-and-mortar stores that are required by law to charge and collect sales taxes are at a distinct disadvantage compared to the online stores with no such burden. The local bookstore, music store, and drugstore must charge sales tax; their competitors Barnes&Noble.com, CDNOW.com, and PlanetRx.com do not, though some, like Amazon.com, have begun voluntarily collecting sales tax under pressure from the states. The tax burden can be significant: for instance, California and New York State charge residents at least 7 percent to shop in their own neighborhoods (Wiseman 60).

Some online merchants claim that the shipping costs they charge offset the sales taxes they don't charge (Granfield 57). However, many online companies offer free shipping and handling as an incentive to online shoppers. And even without such promotions, state and local sales taxes far exceed most shipping costs. As one frequent online consumer said, "If I buy more than three CDs . . . , the shipping cost is less than the sales tax would have been" (James). On balance, the traditional purchase just costs more.

Common knowledge of congressional votes does not require source citations.

Source: corporate author. Citation form: corporate author only, because online source has no page or other reference numbers.

Citation form: shortened title for anonymous source; no page number for one-page source.

Contrast between online and traditional commerce (next two paragraphs).

Selective use of data, with summary of source acknowledged.

Paragraph integrates evidence from two sources.

Primary source: e-mail interview. Citation form: source name only, because interview has no page or other reference numbers.

Alder 3

The Internet's tax-free shopping is also damaging to equality
among groups of people. Governments, scholars, and businesspeople
express concern about the "digital divide" between the affluent who
have Internet access and the poor who do not. According to A Nation
Online, the most recent US Department of Commerce study of Internet access, "Households with incomes of $75,000 and higher are
more than twice as likely to have access to the Internet as those at
the lowest income levels [below $15,000]" (24; emphasis added).
The same study shows that Internet access is two times more common among whites than among African Americans or Latinos (72)
and twelve times more common among those with college educations
than among those with elementary school educations (71).

The digital divide has implications for the relative abilities of
people in different groups to function effectively in an increasingly
electronic world. But where sales taxes are concerned, it does further
harm to the disadvantaged. For the most part, white, educated, and
affluent consumers can shop tax-free because they can shop on the
Internet, whereas nonwhite, uneducated, and poor consumers have
no choice but to shop locally and pay the required taxes.

Equity thus requires sales taxes on e-commerce, but there are
many who argue strongly against such taxes. The writing about Internet taxation (in articles and discussion groups and on Web sites) reveals three major arguments against it. (A fourth, against any new
taxes of any kind, is not specifically relevant to Internet commerce.)

The first argument holds that Internet freedom is sacred and
should be protected. "To me," writes one discussion participant, "the
Internet is . . . freedom of thought. We can't have the government
meddling in the ability of its citizens to read, speak, and, yes, conduct free enterprise online" (Angeles). But Internet commerce is
commerce, after all. Even if the network often serves as a site for free
thought and communication, when it serves as a place of business it
should be subject to the same rules as other businesses.

The second major argument against Internet taxes, related to
the first, is expressed in this statement by a major opponent of the
taxes, US Senator Ron Wyden: "State and local taxes could do ir-
reparable harm to the Internet, killing the goose that could lay bil-
lions of dollars in golden eggs." But this argument, like the first one,
assumes that Internet commerce deserves special protection and

encouragement—even at the expense of bricks-and-mortar commerce. In fact, both kinds of commerce contribute to the health of the economy, and they should be protected, or taxed, equally.

Finally, the third major argument against Internet taxes holds that the issue is too complex to be resolved, a "logistical nightmare," in the words of a taxation opponent (Granfield 57). As outlined by more neutral observers—members of the respected accounting firm of Deloitte Touche Tohmatsu—the main complexities are very real: the existence of more than 3000 state and local taxing authorities in the United States, each with its own regulations and rates; the need to bring these jurisdictions into agreement on how to rationalize and simplify their systems; the concern that any federally imposed solution might violate states' rights; and finally the uncertainty about whether an online vendor conducts taxable business where its office, its server, its customer, or all three are located (67-72).

The complexities do seem nightmarish, as tax opponents claim, but change is underway. In October 2005 eighteen states launched a voluntary program, the Streamlined Sales Tax Project, to tax Internet transactions using a uniform tax system. Online merchants who participate receive free collection and remittance software and services (Krebs). Stephen Kranz of the Council on State Taxation says that "states, local governments, and businesses interested in reducing the complexity of sales taxes have created a plan that might work nationwide" (qtd. in Krebs). The states hope that the success of the pilot will lead Congress to pass into law a mandatory national sales tax program.

The Internet has introduced many improvements in our lives, including the ability to make purchases with the click of a mouse. But at the same time the tax-free status of Internet commerce has allowed it to compete unfairly with traditional businesses and given an unfair financial advantage to those who most likely already have plenty of advantages. Congress and Internet businesses must recognize these inequities and must work with state and local taxing authorities to remedy them.

Citation form: author not named in the text.

Citation form (here and end of paragraph): corporate author named in the text.

Summary reduces six pages in the source to a list of four points.

Position of citation indicates that all preceding information comes from the Deloitte source.

Citation form: author's name only, because online source has no page or other reference numbers.

Citation form: indirect source (Kranz quoted by Krebs).

Conclusion: summary and a call for action.

Works Cited

Angeles, Lemuel. "Internet Freedom." Online posting. 8 Oct. 2005.
    ZDNet Talkback. 18 Nov. 2005 <http://www.zdnet.com/
    tklbck/comment/22/0,7056.html>.

Deloitte Touche Tohmatsu. Establishing a Framework to Evaluate
    E-Commerce Tax Options. Berkeley: U of California P, 2004.

"E-Commerce: Congress to Consider Extending Internet Tax Morato-
    rium." New York Times 9 Jan. 2004, late ed.: C4. LexisNexis
    Academic. LexisNexis. Southeast State U, Polk Lib. 14 Jan.
    2003 <http://www.lexisnexis.com>.

Granfield, Anne. "Taxing the Internet." Forbes 17 Dec. 2004: 56-58.

James, Nora. E-mail interview. 26 Nov. 2005.

Krebs, Brian. "States Move Forward on Internet Sales Tax."
    washingtonpost.com 1 July 2005. 18 Nov. 2005 <http://
    www.washingtonpost.com/wp-dyn/content/article/2005/
    07/01>.

Quill Corp. v. North Dakota. 504 US 298. 1992.

"Sales Tax on Internet Buys Could Help Fill Budget Gaps." Associated
    Press State and Local Wire. 26 Aug. 2005. LexisNexis Academic.
    LexisNexis. Southeast State U, Polk Lib. 18 Nov. 2005
    <http://www.lexisnexis.com>.

United States. Advisory Commission on Electronic Commerce. Report
    to Congress. Apr. 2000. 25 Nov. 2005 <http://
    www.ecommercecommission.org/report.htm>.

---. Dept. of Commerce. National Telecommunications and Informa-
    tion Admin. A Nation Online: Entering the Broadband Age.
    Sept. 2004. 22 Nov. 2005 <http://www.ntia.doc.gov/reports/
    anol/index./html>.

Wiseman, Alan E. The Internet Economy: Access, Taxes, and Market
    Structure. Washington: Brookings, 2005.

Wyden, Ron. "Statement on the Internet Tax Non-Discrimination Act."
    Ron Wyden Online. 7 Jan. 2003. 16 Nov. 2005 <http://
    wyden.senate.gov/media/speeches/2003/
    01072003_internettax_statement.html>.

Zimmerman, Malai, and Kent Hoover. "Use of Third Parties to Collect
    State and Local Taxes on Internet Sales." Pacific Business Jour-
    nal 26.2 (2004): 45-48.

APA Documentation and Format

APA Documentation and Format

APA parenthetical text citations

APA references

Books

Periodicals

59 APA Documentation and Format

The style guide for psychology and some other social sciences is the *Publication Manual of the American Psychological Association* (5th ed., 2001). In the APA documentation style, you acknowledge each of your sources twice:

- In your text, a brief parenthetical citation adjacent to the borrowed material directs readers to a complete list of all the works you refer to.
- At the end of your paper, the list of references includes complete bibliographical information for every source.

http://www.ablongman.com/littlebrown

Visit the companion Web site for more help and an electronic exercise on APA documentation and format.

Every entry in the list of references has at least one corresponding citation in the text, and every in-text citation has a corresponding entry in the list of references.

This chapter describes APA text citations (below) and references (p. 511), details APA document format (p. 523), and concludes with a sample APA paper (p. 526).

59a Writing APA parenthetical text citations

In the APA documentation style, parenthetical citations within the text refer the reader to a list of sources at the end of the text. See the **APA** divider for an index to the models for various kinds of sources.

Note Models 1 and 2 below show the direct relationship between what you include in your text and what you include in a parenthetical citation. The citation always includes a publication date and may include a page number. It also includes the author's name if you do *not* name the author in your text (model 1). It does not include the author's name if you *do* name the author in your text (model 2).

1. Author not named in your text

One critic of Milgram's experiments said that the subjects "should have been fully informed of the possible effects on them" (Baumrind, 1988, p. 34).

When you do not name the author in your text, place in parentheses the author's last name and the date of the source. Separate the elements with commas. Position the reference so that it is clear what material is being documented *and* so that the reference fits as smoothly as possible into your sentence structure. (See **MLA** pp. 465–66 for guidelines.) The following would also be correct:

In the view of one critic of Milgram's experiments (Baumrind, 1988), the subjects "should have been fully informed of the possible effects on them" (p. 34).

Unless none is available, the APA requires a page or other identifying number for a direct quotation (as in the preceding examples) and recommends an identifying number for a paraphrase. Use an appropriate abbreviation or symbol before the number—for instance, p. for *page* and ¶ for *paragraph* (or para. if you do not have the symbol). The identifying number may fall with the author and date (first example above) or by itself in a separate pair of parentheses (second example). See also model 11, p. 511.

2. Author named in your text

Baumrind (1988) said that the subjects in Milgram's study "should have been fully informed of the possible effects on them" (p. 34).

When you use the author's name in the text, do not repeat it in the reference. Place the source date in parentheses after the author's name. Place any page or paragraph reference either after the borrowed material (as in the example) or with the date: (1988, p. 34). If you cite the same source again in the paragraph, you need not repeat the reference as long as it is clear that you are using the same source.

3. A work with two authors

Pepinsky and DeStefano (1997) demonstrated that a teacher's language often reveals hidden biases.

One study (Pepinsky & DeStefano, 1997) demonstrated hidden biases in teachers' language.

When given in the text, two authors' names are connected by and. In a parenthetical citation, they are connected by an ampersand, &.

4. A work with three to five authors

Pepinsky, Dunn, Rentl, and Corson (1999) further demonstrated the biases evident in gestures.

In the first citation of a work with three to five authors, name all the authors, as in the example above. In the second and subsequent references to the work, generally give only the first author's name, followed by et al. (Latin abbreviation for "and others"):

In the work of Pepinsky et al. (1999), the loaded gestures included head shakes and eye contact.

However, two or more sources published in the same year could shorten to the same form—for instance, two references shortening to Pepinsky et al., 1999. In that case, cite the last names of as many authors as you need to distinguish the sources, and then give et al.: for instance, Pepinsky, Dunn, et al., 1999 and Pepinsky, Bradley, et al., 1999.

5. A work with six or more authors

One study (Rutter et al., 2003) attempted to explain these geographical differences in adolescent experience.

For six or more authors, even in the first citation of the work, give only the first author's name, followed by et al. If two or more sources published in the same year shorten to the same form, follow the instructions for model 4.

6. A work with a group author

An earlier prediction was even more somber (Lorenz Research, 2003).

For a work that lists an institution, agency, corporation, or other group as author, treat the name of the group as if it were an individual's name. If the name is long and has a familiar abbreviation, you may use the abbreviation in the second and subsequent citations. For example, you might abbreviate American Psychological Association as APA.

7. A work with no author or an anonymous work

One article ("Right to Die," 1996) noted that a death-row inmate may crave notoriety.

For a work with no named author, use the first two or three words of the title in place of an author's name, excluding an initial *The, A,* or *An.* Italicize book and journal titles, place quotation marks around article titles, and capitalize the significant words in all titles cited in the text. (In the reference list, however, do not use quotation marks for article titles, and capitalize only the first word in all but periodical titles. See p. 512.)

For a work that lists "Anonymous" as the author, use this word in the citation: (Anonymous, 1999).

8. One of two or more works by the same author(s)

At about age seven, most children begin to use appropriate gestures to reinforce their stories (Gardner, 1973a).

If your reference list includes two or more works published by the same author(s) *in the same year,* the works should be lettered in the reference list (see pp. 514–15). Then your parenthetical citation should include the appropriate letter, as in 1973a in the example.

9. Two or more works by different authors

Two studies (Herskowitz, 1989; Marconi & Hamblen, 1999) found that periodic safety instruction can dramatically reduce employees' accidents.

List the sources in alphabetical order by their first authors' names. Insert a semicolon between sources.

10. An indirect source

Supporting data appeared in a study by Wong (cited in Marconi & Hamblen, 1999).

The phrase cited in indicates that the reference to Wong's study was found in Marconi and Hamblen. Only Marconi and Hamblen then appears in the list of references.

11. An electronic source

Ferguson and Hawkins (1998) did not anticipate the "evident hostility" of participants (¶ 6).

Electronic sources can be cited like printed sources, usually with the author's last name and the publication date. When quoting or paraphrasing electronic sources that number paragraphs instead of pages, provide the paragraph number preceded by the symbol ¶ if you have it, or by para. Even if the source does not number its paragraphs, you can still direct readers to a specific location by listing the heading under which the quotation appears and then (counting paragraphs yourself) the number of the paragraph in which the quotation appears—for example, (Morrison & Lee, 2004, Method section, ¶ 4). When the source does not number pages or paragraphs or provide frequent headings, omit any reference number.

59b Preparing the APA reference list

In APA style, the in-text parenthetical citations refer to the list of sources at the end of the text. This list, titled References, includes full publication information on every source cited in the paper. The list falls at the end of the paper, numbered in sequence with the preceding pages. The sample below shows the elements and their spacing.

APA reference list

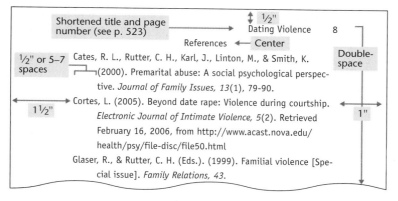

Arrangement Arrange sources alphabetically by the author's last name. If there is no author, alphabetize by the first main word of the title. Do *not* group sources by type (books, journals, and so on).

Spacing Double-space everything in the references, as shown in the sample, unless your instructor requests single spacing. (If you do single-space the entries themselves, always double-space *between* them.)

Indention As illustrated in the sample on the previous page, begin each entry at the left margin, and indent the second and subsequent lines five to seven spaces or one-half inch.

Punctuation Separate the parts of the reference (author, date, title, and publication information) with a period and one space. Do not use a final period in references to electronic sources, which conclude with an electronic address (see pp. 517–20).

Authors For works with up to six authors, list all authors with last name first, separating names and parts of names with commas. Use initials for first and middle names. Use an ampersand (&) before the last author's name. See model 3 (opposite) for the treatment of seven or more authors.

Publication date Place the publication date in parentheses after the author's or authors' names, followed by a period. Generally this date is the year only, though for some sources (such as magazine and newspaper articles) it includes month and sometimes day as well.

Titles In titles of books and articles, capitalize only the first word of the title, the first word of the subtitle, and proper nouns; all other words begin with small letters. In titles of journals, capitalize all significant words. Italicize the titles of books and journals. Do not italicize or use quotation marks around the titles of articles.

City of publication For print sources that are not periodicals (such as books or government publications), give the city of publication. The following US cities do not require state names as well: Baltimore, Boston, Chicago, Los Angeles, New York, Philadelphia, and San Francisco. Follow their names with a colon. For most other cities, add a comma after the city name, give the two-letter postal abbreviation of the state, and then add a colon. (You may omit the state if the publisher is a university whose name includes the state name, such as University of Arizona.)

Publisher's name For nonperiodical print sources, give the publisher's name after the place of publication and a colon. Use shortened names for many publishers (such as Morrow for William Morrow), and omit "Co.," "Inc.," and "Publishers." However, give full names for associations, corporations, and university presses (such as Harvard University Press), and do not omit "Books" or "Press" from a publisher's name.

Page numbers Use the abbreviation p. or pp. before page numbers in books and in newspapers. Do *not* use the abbreviation for journals and magazines. For inclusive page numbers, include all figures: 667-668.

An index to the following models appears at the **APA** divider. If you don't see a model listed for the kind of source you used, try to find one that comes close, and provide ample information so that readers can trace the source. Often you will have to combine models to provide the necessary information on a source—for instance, combining "A book with two to six authors" (model 2) and "An article in a journal" (model 12) for a journal article with two or more authors.

1 Books

1. A book with one author

Rodriguez, R. (1982). *A hunger of memory: The education of Richard Rodriguez.* Boston: Godine.

The initial R appears instead of the author's first name, even though the author's full first name appears on the source. In the title, only the first words of title and subtitle and the proper name are capitalized.

2. A book with two to six authors

Nesselroade, J. R., & Baltes, P. B. (1999). *Longitudinal research in the study of behavioral development.* New York: Academic Press.

An ampersand (&) precedes the last author's name.

3. A book with seven or more authors

Wimple, P. B., Van Eijk, M., Potts, C. A., Hayes, J., Obergau, W. R., Zimmer, S., et al. (2001). *Case studies in moral decision making among adolescents.* San Francisco: Jossey-Bass.

Substitute et al. (Latin abbreviation for "and others") for all authors' names after the first six.

4. A book with an editor

Dohrenwend, B. S., & Dohrenwend, B. P. (Eds.). (1999). *Stressful life events: Their nature and effects*. New York: Wiley.

List the editors' names as if they were authors, but follow the last name with (Eds.)—or (Ed.) with only one editor. Note the periods inside and outside the final parenthesis.

5. A book with a translator

Trajan, P. D. (1927). *Psychology of animals* (H. Simone, Trans.). Washington, DC: Halperin.

The name of the translator appears in parentheses after the title, followed by a comma, Trans., and a closing parenthesis, and a final period. Note also the absence of periods in DC.

6. A book with a group author

Lorenz Research (2003). *Research in social studies teaching*. Baltimore: Arrow Books.

For a work with a group author—such as a research group, government agency, institution, or corporation—begin the entry with the group name. In the reference list, alphabetize the work as if the first main word (excluding *The*, *A*, and *An*) were an author's last name.

7. A book with no author or an anonymous book

Merriam-Webster's collegiate dictionary (11th ed.). (2003). Springfield, MA: Merriam-Webster.

When no author is named, list the work under its title, and alphabetize it by the first main word (excluding *The*, *A*, *An*).

For a work whose author is actually given as "Anonymous," use this word in place of the author's name and alphabetize it as if it were a name:

Anonymous. (2006). *Teaching research, researching teaching*. New York: Alpine Press.

8. Two or more works by the same author(s) published in the same year

Gardner, H. (1973a). *The arts and human development*. New York: Wiley.

Gardner, H. (1973b). *The quest for mind: Piaget, Lévi-Strauss, and the structuralist movement*. New York: Knopf.

When citing two or more works by exactly the same author(s), published in the same year—as in the preceding examples—arrange them alphabetically by the first main word of the title (here *arts*, then *quest*) and distinguish the sources by adding a letter to the date. Both the date *and* the letter are used in citing the source in the text (see p. 510).

When citing two or more works by exactly the same author(s) but *not* published in the same year, arrange the sources in order of their publication dates, earliest first.

9. A later edition

Bolinger, D. L. (1981). *Aspects of language* (3rd ed.). New York: Harcourt Brace
    Jovanovich.

The edition number in parentheses follows the title and is followed by a period.

10. A work in more than one volume

Lincoln, A. (1953). *The collected works of Abraham Lincoln* (R. P. Basler, Ed.).
    (Vol. 5). New Brunswick, NJ: Rutgers University Press.
Lincoln, A. (1953). *The collected works of Abraham Lincoln* (R. P. Basler, Ed.).
    (Vols. 1-8). New Brunswick, NJ: Rutgers University Press.

The first entry cites a single volume (5) in the eight-volume set. The second cites all eight volumes. Use the abbreviation Vol. or Vols. in parentheses, and follow the closing parenthesis with a period. In the absence of an editor's name, the description of volumes would follow the title directly: *The collected works of Abraham Lincoln* (Vol. 5).

11. An article or chapter in an edited book

Paykel, E. S. (1999). Life stress and psychiatric disorder: Applications of the
    clinical approach. In B. S. Dohrenwend & B. P. Dohrenwend (Eds.),
    Stressful life events: Their nature and effects (pp. 239-264). New York:
    Wiley.

Give the publication date of the collection (1999 above) as the publication date of the article or chapter. After the article or chapter title and a period, write In and then provide the editors' names (in normal order), (Eds.) and a comma, the title of the collection, and the page numbers of the article in parentheses.

2 Periodicals: Journals, magazines, newspapers

12. An article in a journal with continuous pagination throughout the annual volume

Emery, R. E. (2005). Marital turmoil: Interpersonal conflict and the children of
    discord and divorce. *Psychological Bulletin, 92*, 310-330.

See **7** p. 385 for an explanation of journal pagination. Note that you do not place the article title in quotation marks and that you capitalize only the first words of the title and subtitle. In contrast, you italicize the journal title and capitalize all significant words. Separate the volume number from the title with a comma, and italicize the number. Do not add "pp." before the page numbers.

13. An article in a journal that pages issues separately

Dacey, J. (1998). Management participation in corporate buy-outs. *Management Perspectives, 7*(4), 20-31.

Consult **7** p. 385 for an explanation of journal pagination. In this case, place the issue number in parentheses after the volume number without intervening space. Do *not* italicize the issue number.

14. An abstract of a journal article

Emery, R. E. (2005). Marital turmoil: Interpersonal conflict and the children of discord and divorce. *Psychological Bulletin, 92*, 310-330. Abstract obtained from *Psychological Abstracts*, 2005, *69*, Item 1320.

When you cite the abstract of an article, rather than the article itself, give full publication information for the article, followed by Abstract obtained from and the information for the collection of abstracts, including title, date, volume number, and either page number or other reference number (Item 1320 above).

15. An article in a magazine

William, N. (2005, October 24). Beethoven's late quartets. *The New York Review of Books*, 16-19.

If a magazine has volume and issue numbers, give them as in models 12 and 13. Also give the full date of the issue: year, followed by a comma, month, and day (if any). Give all page numbers even when the article appears on discontinuous pages, without "pp."

16. An article in a newspaper

Kolata, G. (2006, January 7). Kill all the bacteria! *The New York Times*, pp. B1, B6.

Give month *and* date along with year of publication. Use *The* in the newspaper name if the paper itself does. Precede the page number(s) with p. or pp.

17. An unsigned article

The right to die. (1996, October 11). *Time, 121*, 101.

List and alphabetize the article under its title, as you would a book with no author (model 7, p. 514).

18. A review

Dinnage, R. (1987, November 29). Against the master and his men [Review of the book *A mind of her own: The life of Karen Horney*]. *The New York Times Book Review,* 10-11.

If the review is not titled, use the bracketed information as the title, keeping the brackets.

3 Electronic sources

In general, the APA's electronic-source references begin as those for print references do: author(s), date, title. Then you add information on when and how you retrieved the source. For example, an online source might end Retrieved January 8, 2006, from http://www.isu.edu/finance-dl/46732 (in APA style, no period follows a URL at the end of the reference).

Using the following models for electronic sources, you may have to improvise to match your source to a model. Try to locate all the information required by a model, referring to the samples in **MLA** pp. 481 and 483 for help. However, if you search for and still cannot find some information, then give what you can find. If a source has no publication date, use n.d. (for *no date*) in place of a publication date (see model 28, p. 519).

Note When you need to divide a URL from one line to the next, APA style calls for breaking *only* after a slash or before a period. Do not hyphenate a URL.

19. A journal article that is published online and in print

Palfrey, A. (2003). Choice of mates in identical twins [Electronic version]. *Modern Psychology, 4*(1), 26-40.

If you consulted the online version of a journal article that appears the same way both online and in print, follow model 12 or 13 (pp. 515–16) for a print journal article, and insert [Electronic version] between the article title and the following period.

If you believe that the online version you consulted differs in some way from the print version, omit the bracketed insert and provide a retrieval statement with the date of your access and the complete URL for the article:

Grady, G. F. (2003). The here and now of hepatitis B immunization. *Today's Medicine, 13,* 145-151. Retrieved December 27, 2005, from http://www.fmrt.org/todaysmedicine/Grady050203.html

20. An article in an online journal

Wissink, J. A. (2004). Techniques of smoking cessation among teens and
adults. *Adolescent Medicine, 2*. Retrieved August 16, 2005, from
http://www.easu.edu/AdolescentMedicine/2-Wissink.html

If the article has an identifying number, give it after the volume
number and a comma.

21. A journal article retrieved from an electronic database

Wilkins, J. M. (1999). The myths of the only child. *Psychology Update, 11*(1),
16-23. Retrieved December 20, 2005, from ProQuest Direct database.

Many reference works and periodicals are available full-text from
electronic databases to which your library subscribes, such as
ProQuest Direct or LexisNexis Academic. Your reference need not
specify how you reached the database—for instance, through a
Web site or on a CD-ROM. However, it should provide the appropriate information for the source itself—in the example above, for
a journal article—and it should conclude with a retrieval statement giving the date of your access and the name of the database.

22. An abstract retrieved from an electronic database

Wilkins, J. M. (1999). The myths of the only child. *Psychology Update, 11*(1),
16-23. Abstract retrieved December 20, 2005, from ProQuest Direct
database.

23. An article in an online newspaper

Pear, R. (2006, January 23). Gains reported for children of welfare to work
families. *The New York Times on the Web*. Retrieved January 23, 2006,
from http://www.nytimes.com/2006/01/23/national/23/WELF.html

24. An entire Web site (text citation)

The APA's Web site provides answers to frequently asked questions about style
(http://www.apa.org).

Cite an entire Web site (rather than a specific page or document) by
giving the URL in your text.

25. An independent document on the Web

Anderson, D. (2005, May 1). *Social constructionism and MOOs*. Retrieved
August 6, 2005, from http://sites.unc.edu/~daniel/social_constructionism

Treat the title of an independent Web document like the title of a book. If the document has no named author, begin with the title and place the publication date after the title.

26. A document from the Web site of a university or government agency

McConnell, L. M., Koenig, B. A., Greeley, H. T., & Raffin, T. A. (2004, August 17). *Genetic testing and Alzheimer's disease: Has the time come?* Retrieved September 1, 2005, from Stanford University, Project in Genomics, Ethics, and Society Web site: http://sebe.stanford.edu/pges

Provide the name of the host organization and any sponsoring program as part of the retrieval statement.

27. An online government report

U.S. Department of Commerce, National Telecommunications and Information Administration. (2005, February). *A nation online: Entering the broadband age.* Retrieved January 22, 2006, from http://www.ntia.doc.gov/reports/anol/index.html

28. A multipage online document

Elston, C. (n.d.). *Multiple intelligences.* Retrieved June 6, 2002, from http://education.com/teachspace/intelligences

For an Internet document with multiple pages, each with its own URL, give the URL of the document's home page. Note the use of n.d. after the author's name to indicate that the document provides no publication date.

29. A part of an online document

Elston, C. (n.d.). Logical/math intelligence. In *Multiple intelligences.* Retrieved June 6, 2005, from http://education.com/teachspace/intelligences/logical.jsp

If the part of a document you cite has a label (such as "chapter 6" or "section 4"), provide that in parentheses after the document title: *Multiple intelligences* (chap. 6).

30. An entry on a Web log

Daswani, S. (2005, March 16). Hollywood vs. Silicon Valley. *Berkeley intellectual property Weblog.* Retrieved October 22, 2005, from http://www.biplog.com/archive/cat_hollywood.html

31. A retrievable online posting

Tourville, M. (2006, January 6). European currency reform. Message posted to International Finance electronic mailing list, archived at http://www .isu.edu/finance-dl/46732

Include postings to discussion lists and newsgroups in your list of references *only* if they are retrievable by others. The source above is archived (as the reference makes plain) and is thus retrievable at the address given.

32. Electronic mail or a nonretrievable online posting (text citation)

At least one member of the research team has expressed reservations about the design of the study (L. Kogod, personal communication, February 6, 2006).

Personal electronic mail and other online postings that are not retrievable by others should be cited only in your text, as in the preceding example.

33. Software

Project scheduler 9000 [Computer software]. (2006). Orlando, FL: Scitor.

Provide an author's name for the software if an individual has the rights to the program. If you obtain the software online, you can generally replace the producer's city and name with a retrieval statement that includes the URL.

4 Other sources

34. A report

Gerald, K. (2003). *Medico-moral problems in obstetric care* (Report No. NP-71). St. Louis, MO: Catholic Hospital Association.

Treat a report like a book, but provide any report number in parentheses immediately after the title, with no punctuation between them.

For a report from the Educational Resources Information Center (ERIC), provide the ERIC document number in parentheses at the end of the entry:

Jolson, M. K. (2001). *Music education for preschoolers* (Report No. TC-622). New York: Teachers College, Columbia University. (ERIC Document Reproduction Service No. ED 264488)

35. A government publication

Hawaii. Department of Education. (2005). *Kauai district schools, profile 2004-05.* Honolulu, HI: Author.

Stiller, A. (2002). *Historic preservation and tax incentives.* Washington, DC: U.S. Department of the Interior.

U.S. House. Committee on Ways and Means. (2003). *Medicare payment for out-patient physical and occupational therapy services.* 108th Cong., 1st Sess. Washington, DC: U.S. Government Printing Office.

If no individual is given as the author, list the publication under the name of the sponsoring agency. When the agency is both the author and the publisher, use Author in place of the publisher's name.

36. A doctoral dissertation

A dissertation abstracted in DAI *and obtained from UMI:*

Steciw, S. K. (1986). Alterations to the Pessac project of Le Corbusier. *Dissertation Abstracts International, 46,* 565C. (UMI No. 6216202)

A dissertation abstracted in DAI *and obtained from the university:*

Chang, J. K. (2003). Therapeutic intervention in treatment of injuries to the hand and wrist (Doctoral dissertation, University of Michigan, 2003). *Dissertation Abstracts International, 50,* 162.

An unpublished dissertation:

Delaune, M. L. (2005). *Child care in single-mother and single-father families: Differences in time, activity, and stress.* Unpublished doctoral dissertation, University of California, Davis.

37. An interview

Brisick, W. C. (2005, July 1). [Interview with Ishmael Reed]. *Publishers Weekly,* 41-42.

List a published interview under the interviewer's name. Provide the publication information for the kind of source the interview appears in (here, a magazine). Immediately after the date, in brackets, specify that the piece is an interview and give the subject's name if necessary. For an interview with a title, add the title (with an initial capital letter, no quotation marks, and no closing period) before the bracketed information.

An interview you conduct yourself should not be included in the list of references. Instead, use an in-text parenthetical citation, as shown in model 32 (opposite).

38. A motion picture

American Psychological Association (Producer). (2001). *Ethnocultural psy-
chotherapy* [Motion picture]. (Available from the American Psychological
Association, 750 First Street, NE, Washington, DC 20002-4242, or online
from http://www.apa.org/videos/4310240.html)

Spielberg, S. (Director). (1993). *Schindler's list* [Motion picture]. United
States: Viacom.

A motion picture may be a film, DVD, or video. Depending on whose
work you are citing, begin with the name or names of the creator, director, producer, or primary contributor, followed by the function in
parentheses. (The second model above would begin with the producer's name if you were citing the motion picture as a whole, not
specifically the work of the director.) Add [Motion picture] after the title.
For a motion picture in wide circulation (second example), give the
country of origin and the name of the organization that released the
picture. For a motion picture that is not widely circulated (first example), give the distributor's name and address in parentheses.

39. A musical recording

Springsteen, B. (2002). My city of ruins. *The rising* [CD]. New York:
Columbia.

Begin with the name of the writer or composer. (If you cite another
artist's recording of the work, provide this information after the title
of the work—for example, [Recorded by E. Davila].) Give the medium in
brackets ([CD], [Cassette recording], and so on). Finish with the city and
name of the recording label.

40. A television series or episode

Cleveland, R., Andries, L., & Taylor, C. (Producers). (2005). *Six feet under*
[Television series]. New York: HBO.

Cleveland, R. (Writer), & Engler, M. (Director). (2005). Dillon Michael Cooper
[Television series episode]. In R. Cleveland, L. Andries, & C. Taylor (Producers), *Six feet under*. New York: HBO.

For a television series, begin with the producers' names and identify
their function in parentheses. Add [Television series] after the series title, and give the city and name of the network. For an episode, begin with the writer and then the director, identifying the function
of each in parentheses, and add [Television series episode] after the
episode title. Then provide the series information, beginning with In
and the producers' names and function, giving the series title, and
ending with the city and name of the network.

59c   Formatting a paper in APA style

The APA *Publication Manual* distinguishes between documents intended for publication (which will be set in type) and those submitted by students (which are the final copy). The following guidelines apply to most undergraduate papers. Check with your instructor for any modifications to this format.

Note See p. 511 for the APA format of a reference list. And see pp. 56–66 for guidelines on type fonts, lists, tables and figures, and other elements of document design.

Margins Use one-inch margins on the top, bottom, and right side. Add another half-inch on the left to accommodate a binder.

Spacing and indentions Double-space your text and references. (See p. 525 for spacing of displayed quotations.) Indent paragraphs and displayed quotations one-half inch or five to seven spaces.

Paging Begin numbering on the title page, and number consecutively through the end (including the reference list). Type Arabic numerals (1, 2, 3) in the upper right, about one-half inch from the top.

Place a shortened version of your title five spaces to the left of the page number.

Title page Include the full title, your name, the course title, the instructor's name, and the date. Type the title on the top half of the page, followed by the identifying information, all centered horizontally and double-spaced. Include a shortened form of the title along with the page number at the top of this and all other pages.

APA title page

‡ ½"   5 spaces
Dating Violence⌐⌐1

An Assessment of
Dating Violence on Campus
Karen M. Tarczyk
Sociology 213
Mr. Durkan
March 6, 2006

Center horizontally
and double-space

Abstract Summarize (in a maximum of 120 words) your subject, research method, findings, and conclusions. Put the abstract on a page by itself. (See the sample below.)

Body Begin with a restatement of the paper's title and then an introduction (not labeled). The introduction concisely presents the

---

APA abstract

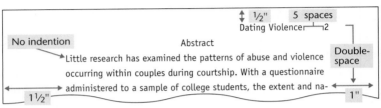

No indention

Abstract

Little research has examined the patterns of abuse and violence occurring within couples during courtship. With a questionnaire administered to a sample of college students, the extent and na-

½"   Dating Violence   2

5 spaces

Double-space

1½"   1"

First page of APA body

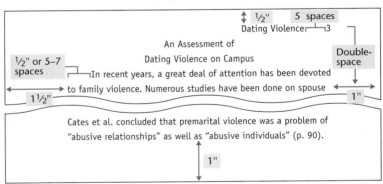

½"   Dating Violence   3

5 spaces

Double-space

An Assessment of
Dating Violence on Campus

½" or 5-7 spaces   In recent years, a great deal of attention has been devoted to family violence. Numerous studies have been done on spouse

1½"   1"

Cates et al. concluded that premarital violence was a problem of "abusive relationships" as well as "abusive individuals" (p. 90).

1"

Later page of APA body

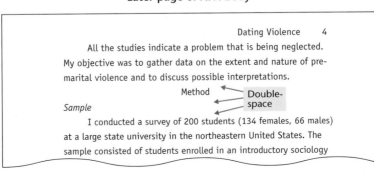

Dating Violence   4

All the studies indicate a problem that is being neglected. My objective was to gather data on the extent and nature of premarital violence and to discuss possible interpretations.

Method   Double-space

Sample

I conducted a survey of 200 students (134 females, 66 males) at a large state university in the northeastern United States. The sample consisted of students enrolled in an introductory sociology problem you researched, your research method, the relevant background (such as related studies), and the purpose of your research.

The next section, labeled Method, provides a detailed discussion of how you conducted your research, including a description of the research subjects, any materials or tools you used (such as questionnaires or surveys), and the procedure you followed. In the last illustration on the facing page, the labels Method and *Sample* are first-level and second-level headings, respectively. When you need one, two, or three levels of headings, use the following formats, always double-spacing above and below:

First-Level Heading

Second-Level Heading

  Third-level heading. Run this heading into the text paragraph.

The Results section (labeled with a first-level heading) summarizes the data you collected, explains how you analyzed them, and presents them in detail, often in tables, graphs, or charts.

The Discussion section (labeled with a first-level heading) interprets the data and presents your conclusions. (When the discussion is brief, you may combine it with the previous section under the heading Results and Discussion.)

The References section, beginning a new page, includes all your sources. See pp. 511–12 for an explanation and sample.

Long quotations Run into your text all quotations of forty words or less, and enclose them in quotation marks. For quotations of more than forty words, set them off from your text by indenting all lines one-half inch or five to seven spaces, double-spacing above and below. For student papers, the APA allows single-spacing of displayed quotations:

Echoing the opinions of other Europeans at the time, Freud (1961) had a poor view of Americans:

> The Americans are really too bad. . . . Competition is much more pungent with them, not succeeding means civil death to every one, and they have no private resources apart from their profession, no hobby, games, love or other interests of a cultured person. And success means money. (p. 86)

Do not use quotation marks around a quotation displayed in this way.

Illustrations Present data in tables and figures (graphs or charts), as appropriate. (See p. 528 and 1 pp. 62–65 for examples.) Begin each illustration on a separate page. Number each kind of illustration consecutively and separately from the other (Table 1, Table 2, etc., and Figure 1, Figure 2, etc.). Refer to all illustrations in your text—for instance, (see Figure 3). Generally, place illustrations immediately after the text references to them.

59d Examining a sample paper in APA style

The following excerpts from a sociology paper illustrate elements of a research paper using the APA style of documentation and format.

[Title page.]

Dating Violence   1

Shortened title and page number.

An Assessment of

Dating Violence on Campus

Karen M. Tarczyk

Sociology 213

Mr. Durkan

March 6, 2006

Double-space all information: title, name, course title, instructor, date.

[New page.]

Dating Violence   2

Abstract

Little research has examined the patterns of abuse and violence occurring within couples during courtship. With a questionnaire administered to a sample of college students, the extent and nature of such abuse and violence were investigated. The results, interpretations, and implications for further research are discussed.

Abstract: summary of subject, research method, conclusions.

Double-space throughout.

[New page.]

Dating Violence   3

An Assessment of

Dating Violence on Campus

In recent years, a great deal of attention has been devoted to family violence. Numerous studies have been done on spouse and child abuse. However, violent behavior occurs in dating relationships as well, yet the problem of dating violence has been relatively ignored by sociological research. It should be examined further since the premarital relationship is one context in which individuals learn and adopt behaviors that surface in marriage.

Title repeated on first text page.

Introduction: presentation of the problem researched by the writer.

Dating Violence   4

The sociologist James Makepeace (1989) contended that courtship violence is a "potential mediating link" between violence in one's family of orientation and violence in one's later family of procreation (p. 103). Studying dating behaviors at Bemidji State University in Minnesota, Makepeace reported that one-fifth of the respondents had had at least one encounter with dating violence. He then extended these percentages to students nationwide, suggesting the existence of a major hidden social problem.

More recent research supports Makepeace's. Cates, Rutter, Karl, Linton, and Smith (2000) found that 22.3% of respondents at Oregon State University had been either the victim or the perpetrator of premarital violence. Another study (Cortes, 2005) found that so-called date rape, while much more publicized and discussed, was reported by many fewer woman respondents (2%) than was other violence during courtship (21%).

[The introduction continues.]

All these studies indicate a problem that is being neglected. My objective was to gather data on the extent and nature of premarital violence and to discuss possible interpretations.

Method

Sample

I conducted a survey of 200 students (134 females, 66 males) at a large state university in the northeastern United States. The sample consisted of students enrolled in an introductory sociology course.

[The explanation of method continues.]

The Questionnaire

A questionnaire exploring the personal dynamics of relationships was distributed during regularly scheduled class. Questions were answered anonymously in a 30-minute period. The survey consisted of three sections.

[The explanation of method continues.]

Section 3 required participants to provide information about their current dating relationships. Levels of stress and frustration, communication between partners, and patterns of decision making were examined. These variables were expected to influence the amount of violence in a relationship. The next part of the survey was adopted from Murray Strauss's Conflict Tactics Scales (1992). These scales contain 19 items

---

Citation form: author named in the text.

Citation form: page number given for quotation.

Citation form: source with three to five authors, named in the text.

Citation form: author not named in the text.

First- and second-level headings.

"Method" section: discussion of how research was conducted.

designed to measure conflict and the means of conflict resolution, including reasoning, verbal aggression, and actual violence. The final page of the questionnaire contained general questions on the couple's use of alcohol, sexual activity, and overall satisfaction with the relationship.

Results

The questionnaire revealed significant levels of verbal aggression and threatened and actual violence among dating couples. A high number of students, 50% (62 of 123 subjects), reported that they had been the victim of verbal abuse, either being insulted or sworn at. In addition, almost 14% (17 of 123) of respondents admitted being threatened with some type of violence, and more than 14% (18 of 123) reported being pushed, grabbed, or shoved. (See Table 1.)

[The explanation of results continues.]

[Table on a page by itself.]

Table 1

Incidence of Courtship Violence

Type of violence	Number of students reporting	Percentage of sample
Insulted or swore	62	50.4
Threatened to hit or throw something	17	13.8
Threw something	8	6.5
Pushed, grabbed, or shoved	18	14.6
Slapped	8	6.5
Kicked, bit, or hit with fist	7	5.7
Hit or tried to hit with something	2	1.6
Threatened with a knife or gun	1	0.8
Used a knife or gun	1	0.8

Discussion

Violence within premarital relationships has been relatively ignored. The results of the present study indicate that abuse and force do occur in dating relationships. Although the percentages are small, so was the sample. Extending them to the entire campus population of 5,000 would mean significant numbers. For example, if the nearly 6%

Margin notes:

"Results" section: summary and presentation of data.

Reference to table.

Table presents data in clear format.

"Discussion" section: interpretation of data and presentation of conclusions.

incidence of being kicked, bitten, or hit with a fist is typical, then 300 students might have experienced this type of violence.

[The discussion continues.]

If the courtship period is characterized by abuse and violence, what accounts for it? The other sections of the survey examined some variables that appear to influence the relationship. Level of stress and frustration, both within the relationship and in the respondent's life, was one such variable. The communication level between partners, both the frequency of discussion and the frequency of agreement, was another.

[The discussion continues.]

The method of analyzing the data in this study, utilizing frequency distributions, provided a clear overview. However, more tests of significance and correlation and a closer look at the social and individual variables affecting the relationship are warranted. The courtship period may set the stage for patterns of married life. It merits more attention.

[New page.]

New page for reference list.

References

Cates, R. L., Rutter, C. H., Karl, J., Linton, M., & Smith, K. (2000). Premarital abuse: A social psychological perspective. *Journal of Family Issues, 13*(1), 79-90.

Cortes, L. (2005). Beyond date rape: Violence during courtship. *Electronic Journal of Intimate Violence, 5*(2). Retrieved February 16, 2006, from http://www.acast.nova.edu/health/psy/file-disc/file50.html

Glaser, R., & Rutter, C. H. (Eds.). (1999). Familial violence [Special issue]. *Family Relations, 43*.

Makepeace, J. M. (1989). Courtship violence among college students. *Family Relations, 28*, 97-103.

Strauss, M. L. (1992). *Conflict Tactics Scales*. New York: Sociological Tests.

An article in a print journal.

An article in an online journal.

A book. ("Tactics Scales" is part of a proper name and so is capitalized.)

Chicago and CSE Documentation

Chicago and CSE Documentation

Chicago note and works-cited models

CSE references

60 Chicago Documentation

History, art history, philosophy, and some other humanities use endnotes or footnotes to document sources, following one style recommended by *The Chicago Manual of Style* (15th ed., 2003) and the student guide adapted from it, Kate L. Turabian's *A Manual for Writers of Term Papers, Theses, and Dissertations* (6th ed., revised by John Grossman and Alice Bennett, 1996).

60a Using Chicago notes and works-cited entries

In the Chicago note style, raised numerals in the text refer to footnotes (bottoms of pages) or endnotes (end of paper). These notes

http://www.ablongman.com/littlebrown

Visit the companion Web site for more help with Chicago documentation.

533

contain complete source information. A separate list of works cited is optional: ask your instructor for his or her preference.

Whether providing footnotes or endnotes, single-space each note and double-space between notes, as shown in the samples below. Separate footnotes from the text with a short line. Place endnotes directly after the text, beginning on a new page. For the list of sources at the end of the paper, use the format on the facing page. Arrange the sources alphabetically by the authors' last names.

The note and works-cited entry on the facing page illustrate the essentials of each type of reference.

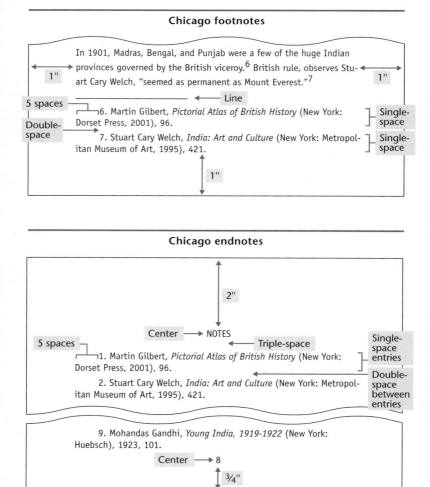

Chicago footnotes

In 1901, Madras, Bengal, and Punjab were a few of the huge Indian provinces governed by the British viceroy.[6] British rule, observes Stuart Cary Welch, "seemed as permanent as Mount Everest."[7]

1"   1"

Line

5 spaces

Double-space

6. Martin Gilbert, *Pictorial Atlas of British History* (New York: Dorset Press, 2001), 96.

Single-space

7. Stuart Cary Welch, *India: Art and Culture* (New York: Metropolitan Museum of Art, 1995), 421.

Single-space

1"

Chicago endnotes

2"

Center → NOTES

Triple-space

5 spaces

1. Martin Gilbert, *Pictorial Atlas of British History* (New York: Dorset Press, 2001), 96.

Single-space entries

2. Stuart Cary Welch, *India: Art and Culture* (New York: Metropolitan Museum of Art, 1995), 421.

Double-space between entries

9. Mohandas Gandhi, *Young India, 1919-1922* (New York: Huebsch), 1923, 101.

Center → 8

3/4"

Chicago list of works cited

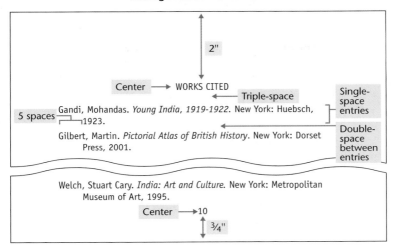

Note

6. Martin Gilbert, *Pictorial Atlas of British History* (New York: Dorset Press, 2001), 96.

Works-cited entry

Gilbert, Martin. *Pictorial Atlas of British History*. New York: Dorset Press, 2001.

Notes and works-cited entries share certain features:

- Single-space each note or entry, and double-space between them.
- Italicize or underline the titles of books and periodicals. Ask your instructor for his or her preference.
- Enclose in quotation marks the titles of parts of books or articles in periodicals.
- Do not abbreviate publishers' names, but omit "Inc.," "Co.," and similar abbreviations.
- Do not use "p." or "pp." before page numbers.

Notes and works-cited entries also differ in important ways:

Note	Works-cited entry
Start with a number that corresponds to the note number in the text.	Do not begin with a number.
Indent the first line five spaces.	Indent the second and subsequent lines five spaces.

Note	Works-cited entry
Give the author's name in normal order.	Begin with the author's last name.
Use commas between elements.	Use periods between elements.
Enclose publication information in parentheses, with no preceding punctuation.	Precede the publication information with a period, and don't use parentheses.
Include the specific page number(s) you borrowed from, omitting "p." or "pp."	Omit page numbers except for parts of books or articles in periodicals.

You can instruct your word processor to position footnotes at the bottoms of appropriate pages. It will also automatically number notes and even renumber them if you add or delete one or more.

60b Models of Chicago notes and works-cited entries

In the following models for common sources, notes and works-cited entries appear together for easy reference. (An index to the models appears at the **Chicago** divider.) Be sure to use the numbered note form for notes and the unnumbered works-cited form for works-cited entries.

1 Books

1. A book with one, two, or three authors

1. Carol Gilligan, *In a Different Voice: Psychological Theory and Women's Development* (Cambridge: Harvard University Press, 1982), 27.

Gilligan, Carol. *In a Different Voice: Psychological Theory and Women's Development.* Cambridge: Harvard University Press, 1982.

1. Dennis L. Wilcox, Phillip H. Ault, and Warren K. Agee, *Public Relations: Strategies and Tactics,* 6th ed. (New York: Irwin, 2005), 182.

Wilcox, Dennis L., Phillip H. Ault, and Warren K. Agee. *Public Relations: Strategies and Tactics.* 6th ed. New York: Irwin, 2005.

2. A book with more than three authors

2. Geraldo Lopez and others, *China and the West* (Boston: Little, Brown, 2000), 461.

Lopez, Geraldo, Judith P. Salt, Anne Ming, and Henry Reisen. *China and the West.* Boston: Little, Brown, 2000.

3. A book with an editor

3. Hendrick Ruitenbeek, ed., *Freud as We Knew Him* (Detroit: Wayne State University Press, 1973), 64.

Ruitenbeek, Hendrick, ed. *Freud as We Knew Him*. Detroit: Wayne State University Press, 1973.

4. A book with an author and an editor

4. Lewis Mumford, *The City in History,* ed. Donald L. Miller (New York: Pantheon, 1986), 216-17.

Mumford, Lewis. *The City in History*. Edited by Donald L. Miller. New York: Pantheon, 1986.

5. A translation

5. Dante Alighieri, *The Inferno,* trans. John Ciardi (New York: New American Library, 1971), 51.

Alighieri, Dante. *The Inferno*. Translated by John Ciardi. New York: New American Library, 1971.

6. An anonymous work

6. *The Dorling Kindersley World Reference Atlas* (London: Dorling Kindersley, 2005), 150-51.

The Dorling Kindersley World Reference Atlas. London: Dorling Kindersley, 2005.

7. A later edition

7. Dwight L. Bolinger, *Aspects of Language,* 3rd ed. (New York: Harcourt Brace Jovanovich, 1981), 20.

Bolinger, Dwight L. *Aspects of Language*. 3rd ed. New York: Harcourt Brace Jovanovich, 1981.

8. A work in more than one volume

Citation of one volume without a title:

8. Abraham Lincoln, *The Collected Works of Abraham Lincoln,* ed. Roy P. Basler (New Brunswick: Rutgers University Press, 1953), 5:426-28.

Lincoln, Abraham. *The Collected Works of Abraham Lincoln*. Edited by Roy P. Basler. Vol. 5. New Brunswick: Rutgers University Press, 1953.

Citation of one volume with a title:

8. Linda B. Welkin, *The Age of Balanchine,* vol. 3 of *The History of Ballet* (New York: Columbia University Press, 1999), 56.

Welkin, Linda B. *The Age of Balanchine*. Vol. 3 of *The History of Ballet*. New York: Columbia University Press, 1999.

9. A selection from an anthology

9. Rosetta Brooks, "Streetwise," in *The New Urban Landscape,* ed. Richard Martin (New York: Rizzoli, 2005), 38-39.

Brooks, Rosetta. "Streetwise." In *The New Urban Landscape,* ed. Richard Martin, 37-60. New York: Rizzoli, 2005.

10. A work in a series

10. Ingmar Bergman, *The Seventh Seal,* Modern Film Scripts, no. 12 (New York: Simon and Schuster, 1995), 27.

Bergman, Ingmar. *The Seventh Seal.* Modern Film Scripts, no. 12. New York: Simon and Schuster, 1995.

11. An article in a reference work

11. *Merriam-Webster's Collegiate Dictionary,* 11th ed., s.v. "reckon."

Merriam-Webster's Collegiate Dictionary. 11th ed. S.v. "reckon."

As in the example, use the abbreviation s.v. (Latin *sub verbo,* "under the word") for reference works that are alphabetically arranged. Well-known works like the one listed here do not need publication information except for edition number.

2 Periodicals: Journals, magazines, newspapers

12. An article in a journal

12. Janet Lever, "Sex Differences in the Games Children Play," *Social Problems* 23 (1996): 482.

Lever, Janet. "Sex Differences in the Games Children Play." *Social Problems* 23 (1996): 478-87.

Provide the issue number if the journal numbers issues. The issue number is required for any journal that pages each issue separately or that numbers only issues, not volumes:

12. June Dacey, "Management Participation in Corporate Buy-Outs," *Management Perspectives* 7, no. 4 (1998): 22.

Dacey, June. "Management Participation in Corporate Buy-Outs." *Management Perspectives* 7, no. 4 (1998): 20-31.

13. An article in a magazine

13. Mark Stevens, "Low and Behold," *New Republic,* December 24, 2005, 28.

Stevens, Mark. "Low and Behold." *New Republic,* December 24, 2005, 27-33.

Chicago works-cited style does not require inclusive page numbers for magazine articles, so 27-33 could be omitted from the preceding example.

14. An article in a newspaper

14. Gina Kolata, "Kill All the Bacteria!" *New York Times,* January 7, 2006, national edition, B1.

Kolata, Gina. "Kill All the Bacteria!" *New York Times,* January 7, 2006, national edition, B1, B6.

Chicago style does not require page numbers for newspaper citations, whether in notes or in works-cited entries. Thus B1 and B1, B6 could be omitted from the preceding examples.

15. A review

15. John Gregory Dunne, "The Secret of Danny Santiago," review of *Famous All over Town,* by Danny Santiago, *New York Review of Books,* August 16, 1994, 25.

Dunne, John Gregory. "The Secret of Danny Santiago." Review of *Famous All over Town,* by Danny Santiago. *New York Review of Books,* August 16, 1994, 17-27.

3 Electronic sources

The Chicago Manual's models for documenting electronic sources derive mainly from those for print sources, with the addition of a URL or other indication of the medium along with any other information that may help readers locate the source. Chicago requires the date of your access to an online source only if the source could change significantly (for instance, a report on medical research). However, your instructor may require access dates for a broader range of online sources, so they are included in the following models (in parentheses at the end).

Note Chicago style allows many ways to break URLs between the end of one line and the beginning of the next: after slashes, before most punctuation marks (periods, commas, question marks, and so on), and before or after equal signs and ampersands (&). *Do not* break after a hyphen or add any hyphens.

16. A work on CD-ROM or DVD-ROM

16. *The American Heritage Dictionary of the English Language,* 4th ed., CD-ROM (Boston: Houghton Mifflin, 2000).

The American Heritage Dictionary of the English Language. 4th ed. CD-ROM. Boston: Houghton Mifflin, 2000.

17. A work from an online database

17. Irina Netchaeva, "E-Government and E-Democracy," *International Journal for Communication Studies* 64 (2002): 470-71, http://www.epnet.com (accessed December 20, 2005).

Netchaeva, Irina. "E-Government and E-Democracy." *International Journal for Communication Studies* 64 (2002): 467-78. http://www.epnet.com (accessed December 20, 2005).

For news and journal databases, including those to which your library subscribes, you may omit the name of the database. Give its main URL (as in the examples) unless the work has a usable URL of its own. (See **MLA** p. 480 for more on database URLs.)

18. An online book

18. Jane Austen, *Emma*, ed. R. W. Chapman (1816; Oxford: Clarendon, 1926; Oxford Text Archive, 2004), chap. 1, http://ota.ahds.ac.uk/Austen/ Emma.1519 (accessed December 15, 2005).

Austen, Jane. *Emma*. Edited by R. W. Chapman. 1816. Oxford: Clarendon, 1926. Oxford Text Archive, 2004. http://ota.ahds.ac.uk/Austen/Emma.1519 (accessed December 15, 2005).

19. An article in an online journal

19. Andrew Palfrey, "Choice of Mates in Identical Twins," *Modern Psychology* 4, no. 1 (2003): 28, http://www.liasu.edu/modpsy/palfrey4(1).htm (accessed February 25, 2006).

Palfrey, Andrew. "Choice of Mates in Identical Twins." *Modern Psychology* 4, no. 1 (2003): 26-40. http://www.liasu.edu/modpsy/palfrey4(1).htm (accessed February 25, 2006).

20. An article in an online magazine

20. Ricki Lewis, "The Return of Thalidomide," *Scientist,* January 22, 2001, http://www.the-scientist.com/yr2001/jan/lewis_pl_010122.html (accessed January 24, 2006).

Lewis, Ricki. "The Return of Thalidomide." *Scientist,* January 22, 2001. http://www.the-scientist.com/yr2001/jan/lewis_pl_010122.html (accessed January 24, 2006).

21. An article in an online newspaper

21. Lucia Still, "On the Battlefields of Business, Millions of Casualties," *New York Times on the Web,* March 3, 2005, http://www.nytimes.com/specials/ downsize/03down1.html (accessed August 17, 2005).

Still, Lucia. "On the Battlefields of Business, Millions of Casualties." *New York Times on the Web,* March 3, 2005. http://www.nytimes.com/specials/ downsize/03down1.html (accessed August 17, 2005).

22. An article in an online reference work

22. *Encyclopaedia Britannica Online,* s.v. "Wu-ti," http://www.eb.com:80 (accessed December 23, 2005).

Encyclopaedia Britannica Online. S.v. "Wu-ti." http://www.eb.com:80 (accessed December 23, 2005).

23. An online audio or visual source

A work of art:

23. Jackson Pollock, *Shimmering Substance,* oil on canvas, 1946, Museum of Modern Art, New York, WebMuseum, http://www.ibiblio.org/ wm/paint/auth/Pollock/pollock.shimmering.jpg (accessed March 12, 2006).

Pollock, Jackson. *Shimmering Substance.* Oil on canvas, 1946. Museum of Modern Art, New York. WebMuseum. http://www.ibiblio.org/wm/paint/auth/Pollock/pollock.shimmering.jpg (accessed March 12, 2006).

A sound recording:

23. Ronald W. Reagan, State of the Union Address, January 26, 1982, Vincent Voice Library, Digital and Multimedia Center, University of Michigan, http://www.lib.msu.edu/vincent/presidents/reagan.html (accessed May 6, 2005).

Reagan, Ronald W. State of the Union Address. January 26, 1982. Vincent Voice Library. Digital and Multimedia Center, University of Michigan. http://www.lib.msu.edu/vincent/presidents/reagan.html (accessed May 6, 2005).

A film or film clip:

23. Leslie J. Stewart, *96 Ranch Rodeo and Barbecue* (1951), 16mm, from Library of Congress, *Buckaroos in Paradise: Ranching Culture in Northern Nevada, 1945-1982,* MPEG, http://lcweb2.loc.gov/ammem/afc96ran_v034 (accessed January 7, 2006).

Stewart, Leslie J. *96 Ranch Rodeo and Barbecue.* 1951, 16mm. From Library of Congress, *Buckaroos in Paradise: Ranching Culture in Northern Nevada, 1945-1982.* MPEG. http://lcweb2.loc.gov/ammem/afc96ran_v034 (accessed January 7, 2006).

24. An entry on a Web log or a posting to a discussion group

24. Susheel Daswani, "Hollywood vs. Silicon Valley," Berkeley Intellectual Property Weblog, March 16, 2005, http://www.biplog.com/archive/cat_hollywood.html (accessed August 22, 2005).

Daswani, Susheel. "Hollywood vs. Silicon Valley." Berkeley Intellectual Property Weblog. March 16, 2005. http://www.biplog.com/archive/cat_hollywood.html (accessed August 22, 2005).

24. Michael Tourville, "European Currency Reform," e-mail to International Finance Discussion List, January 6, 2006, http://www.weg.isu.edu/finance-dl/archive/46732 (accessed January 12, 2006).

Tourville, Michael. "European Currency Reform." E-mail to International Finance Discussion List. January 6, 2006. http://www.weg.isu.edu/finance-dl/archive/46732 (accessed January 12, 2006).

25. Electronic mail

25. Michele Millon, "Re: Grief Therapy," e-mail message to author, May 4, 2005.

Millon, Michele. "Re: Grief Therapy." E-mail message to author. May 4, 2005.

4 Other sources

26. A government publication

26. House Committee on Ways and Means, *Medicare Payment for Out-patient Physical and Occupational Therapy Services,* 108th Cong., 1st sess., 2003, H. Doc. 409, 12-13.

U.S. Congress. House. Committee on Ways and Means. *Medicare Payment for Outpatient Physical and Occupational Therapy Services.* 108th Cong., 1st sess., 2003. H. Doc. 409.

26. Hawaii Department of Education, *Kauai District Schools, Profile 2004-05* (Honolulu, 2005), 27.

Hawaii. Department of Education. *Kauai District Schools, Profile 2004-05.* Honolulu, 2005.

27. A published letter

27. Mrs. Laura E. Buttolph to Rev. and Mrs. C. C. Jones, June 20, 1857, in *The Children of Pride: A True Story of Georgia and the Civil War,* ed. Robert Manson Myers (New Haven, CT: Yale University Press, 1972), 334.

Buttolph, Laura E. Mrs. Laura E. Buttolph to Rev. and Mrs. C. C. Jones, June 20, 1857. In *The Children of Pride: A True Story of Georgia and the Civil War,* edited by Robert Manson Myers. New Haven, CT: Yale University Press, 1972.

28. A published or broadcast interview

28. Donald Rumsfeld, interview by William Lindon, *Frontline,* PBS, October 13, 2005.

Rumsfeld, Donald. Interview by William Lindon. *Frontline.* PBS, October 13, 2005.

29. A personal letter or interview

29. Ann E. Packer, letter to author, June 15, 2005.

Packer, Ann E. Letter to author. June 15, 2005.

29. Vera Graaf, interview by author, December 19, 2005.

Graaf, Vera. Interview by author. December 19, 2005.

30. A work of art

30. John Singer Sargent, *In Switzerland,* watercolor, 1908, Metropolitan Museum of Art, New York.

Sargent, John Singer. *In Switzerland.* Watercolor, 1908. Metropolitan Museum of Art, New York.

31. A film, DVD, or video recording

31. George Balanchine, *Serenade,* DVD, San Francisco Ballet (New York: PBS Video, 2003).

Balanchine, George. *Serenade*. DVD. San Francisco Ballet. New York: PBS Video, 2003.

32. A sound recording

32. Johannes Brahms, Piano Concerto no. 2 in B-flat, Artur Rubinstein, Philadelphia Orchestra, Eugene Ormandy, compact disc, RCA BRC4-6731.

Brahms, Johannes. Piano Concerto no. 2 in B-flat. Artur Rubinstein. Philadelphia Orchestra. Eugene Ormandy. Compact disc. RCA BRC4-6731.

5 Shortened notes

To streamline documentation, Chicago style recommends shortened notes for sources that are fully cited elsewhere, either in a complete list of works cited or in previous notes. Ask your instructor whether your paper should include a list of works cited and, if so, whether you may use shortened notes for first references to sources as well as for subsequent references.

A shortened note contains the author's last name, the work's title (minus any initial *A*, *An*, or *The*), and the page number. Reduce long titles to four or fewer key words.

Complete note

8. Janet Lever, "Sex Differences in the Games Children Play," *Social Problems* 23 (1996): 482.

Complete works-cited entry

Lever, Janet. "Sex Differences in the Games Children Play." *Social Problems* 23 (1996): 478-87.

Shortened note

12. Lever, "Sex Differences," 483.

You may use the Latin abbreviation "ibid." (meaning "in the same place") to refer to the same source cited in the preceding note. Give a page number if it differs from that in the preceding note.

12. Lever, "Sex Differences," 483.

13. Gilligan, *In a Different Voice,* 92.

14. Ibid., 93.

15. Lever, "Sex Differences," 483.

Chicago style allows for in-text parenthetical citations when you cite one or more works repeatedly. In the following example, the raised number 2 refers to the source information in a note; the number in parentheses is a page number in the same source.

British rule, observes Stuart Cary Welch, "seemed as permanent as Mount Everest."[2] Most Indians submitted, willingly or not, to British influence in every facet of life (42).

61 CSE Documentation

Writers in the life sciences, physical sciences, and mathematics rely for documentation style on *Scientific Style and Format: The CBE Style Manual for Authors, Editors, and Publishers* (6th ed., 1994). Its sponsoring organization, the Council of Science Editors, was until 2000 called the Council of Biology Editors, so you will see the style abbreviated both CSE (as here) and CBE.

Scientific Style and Format details both styles of scientific documentation: one using author and date and one using numbers. Both types of text citation refer to a list of references at the end of the paper. Ask your instructor which style you should use.

61a Writing CSE name-year text citations

In the CSE name-year style, parenthetical text citations provide the last name of the author being cited and the source's year of publication. At the end of the paper, a list of references, arranged alphabetically by authors' last names, provides complete information on each source. (See opposite.)

The CSE name-year style closely resembles the APA name-year style detailed in **APA** pp. 508–11. You can follow the APA examples for in-text citations, making several notable changes for CSE:

- **Do not use a comma to separate the author's name and the date:** (Baumrind 1968, p. 34).
- **Separate two authors' names with and (not "&"):** (Pepinsky and DeStefano 1997).
- **Use and others (not "et al.") for three or more authors:** (Rutter and others 1996).
- **List unnamed or anonymous authors as Anonymous, both in the citation and in the list of references:** (Anonymous 1976).

61b Writing CSE numbered text citations

In the CSE number style, raised numbers in the text refer to a numbered list of references at the end of the paper.

http://www.ablongman.com/littlebrown ▶

Visit the companion Web site for more help with CSE documentation.

Two standard references[1,2] use this term.

These forms of immunity have been extensively researched.[3]

Hepburn and Tatin[2] do not discuss this project.

Assignment of numbers The number for each source is based on the order in which you cite the source in the text: the first cited source is 1, the second is 2, and so on.

Reuse of numbers When you cite a source you have already cited and numbered, use the original number again (see the last example above, which reuses the number 2 from the first example). This reuse is the key difference between the CSE numbered citations and numbered references to footnotes or endnotes. In the CSE style, each source has only one number, determined by the order in which the source is cited. With notes, in contrast, the numbering proceeds in sequence, so that each source has as many numbers as it has citations in the text.

Citation of two or more sources When you cite two or more sources at once, arrange their numbers in sequence and separate them with a comma and no space, as in the first example above.

61c Preparing the CSE reference list

For both the name-year and the number styles of in-text citation, provide a list, titled References, of all sources you have cited. Format the page as shown for APA references in **APA** p. 511, except that CSE entries are single-spaced.

The following examples show the differences and similarities between the name-year and number styles:

Name-year style

Hepburn PX, Tatin JM. 2005. Human physiology. New York: Columbia Univ Pr. 1026 p.

Number style

2. Hepburn PX, Tatin JM. Human physiology. New York: Columbia Univ Pr; 2005. 1026 p.

Spacing In both styles, single-space each entry and double-space between entries.

Arrangement In the name-year style, arrange entries alphabetically by authors' last names. In the number style, arrange entries in numerical order—that is, in order of their citation in the text.

Format In both styles, begin the first line of each entry at the left margin and indent subsequent lines.

Authors In both styles, give each author's last name and then initials for first and middle names. Do not use a comma between an author's last name and initials, and do not use periods or space with the initials. Do use a comma to separate authors' names.

Placement of dates In the name-year style, the date follows the author's or authors' names. In the number style, the date follows the publication information (for a book) or the periodical title (for a journal, magazine, or newspaper).

Journal titles In both styles, do not underline or italicize journal titles. For titles of two or more words, abbreviate words of six or more letters (without periods) and omit most prepositions, articles, and conjunctions. Capitalize each word. For example, *Journal of Chemical and Biochemical Studies* becomes J Chem Biochem Stud.

Book and article titles In both styles, do not underline, italicize, or use quotation marks around a book or an article title. Capitalize only the first word and any proper nouns.

Publication information for journal articles The name-year and number styles differ in the placement of the publication date (see above). However, both styles end with the journal's volume number, any issue number in parentheses, a colon, and the inclusive page numbers of the article, run together without space: 28:329-30 or 62(2):26-40.

The following examples show both a name-year reference and a number reference for each type of source. An index to all the models appears at the CSE divider.

1 Books

1. A book with one author

Gould SJ. 1987. Time's arrow, time's cycle. Cambridge: Harvard Univ Pr. 222 p.

1. Gould SJ. Time's arrow, time's cycle. Cambridge: Harvard Univ Pr; 1987. 222 p.

2. A book with two to ten authors

Hepburn PX, Tatin JM. 2005. Human physiology. New York: Columbia Univ Pr. 1026 p.

2. Hepburn PX, Tatin JM. Human physiology. New York: Columbia Univ Pr; 2005. 1026 p.

3. A book with more than ten authors

Evans RW, Bowditch L, Dana KL, Drummond A, Wildovitch WP, Young SL, Mills P, Mills RR, Livak SR, Lisi OL, and others. 2004. Organ transplants: ethical issues. Ann Arbor: Univ of Michigan Pr. 498 p.

10 IF ENGLISH IS NOT YOUR FIRST LANGUAGE

If you are not a native speaker of English, the idea of writing academically and professionally in English may be intimidating. The challenges, however, are not insurmountable, especially if you understand what is involved in writing in a second language and make conscious and continuous efforts to develop your literacy.

Common ESL Errors Workbook

If English is not your first language, you may need an occasional review of some of the more difficult areas of English usage. Visit the Common ESL Errors Workbook at **www.ablongman.com/faigley274** for explanations, examples, and practices on the following topics:

- Differences among languages
- Writing for diverse audiences
- Using your native language as a resource
- Verb tenses and forms
- Passive voice
- Troublesome words

 Visit *The Brief Penguin Handbook* Companion Website at
www.ablongman.com/faigley/

CHAPTER 48

Writing in a Second Language

Writing well takes hard work and years of practice even in your native language; writing in a second language is harder still. If you are not a native speaker of English, the idea of writing academically and professionally in English may be intimidating. The challenges, however, are not insurmountable, especially if you understand what is involved in writing in a second language and make conscious and continuous efforts to develop your literacy.

48a UNDERSTAND HOW LANGUAGES DIFFER

Many writers say that the main challenges of writing in a second language are grammar and vocabulary. While grammar and vocabulary are important, sometimes too much focus on the details of writing can take your attention away from other issues that affect your ability to communicate effectively. If English is not your first language, you may have noticed some differences between writing in English and in your native language. Some of the differences are relatively easy to identify, such as the direction of writing (left to right instead of right to left or top to bottom), the uses of punctuation (€ 2,500.00 instead of € 2.500,00), or conventions of capitalization and spelling. Other differences are more subtle and complex, such as the citation of sources, uses of persuasive appeals, and the level of directness expected in a given situation. Readers of business correspondence in English, for example, expect communication to be direct, concise, and explicit, and they often become impatient with the indirect style of address sometimes preferred in business writing in other languages.

Since the sources of the differences are often varied, complex, and constantly changing, it is not always possible to make generalized statements such as "people in the United States write this way while people in China write in that way." Such generalizations can even lead to unproductive stereotypes about different languages, cultures, and ways of thinking.

When you write in an unfamiliar situation, it may be helpful to find a few examples of the type of writing you are trying to produce. If you are writing a cover letter to accompany a résumé, for example, ask your friends to share similar cover letters with you and look for the various ways they

WRITING IN THE WORLD

Differences within and between languages

Good writing is not a simple concept because the effectiveness of writing depends on the context and audience. Even within the same language, the clear and concise style of writing preferred in business letters may not be the top priority in legal writing, where being precise is more important. When you move from one language community to another, differences in the rhetorical situation and your readers' expectations may be even greater. In Japanese, for example, it is customary to begin a business letter with a paragraph-long seasonal greeting, while in English, business letter writers are encouraged to state the main point in the first paragraph.

While different conventions have evolved in different communities of writers, these conventions do not remain the same forever or in all contexts. Partly because of the influence of U.S. business conventions, simplified Japanese business letters that do not have seasonal greetings are becoming more common. Similarly, within the United States, business letters in some situations—such as letters of rejection—do not necessarily state the main point in the first paragraph.

present themselves in writing in that situation. Ask them to read their letters out loud, and to explain the decisions they made as they wrote and revised their letters. In talking with them about how and why they wrote their cover letters, you will develop a better understanding of the ways writers in English respond to a given writing situation than you may be able to get from simply studying the format of a cover letter in a textbook.

Throughout the process of writing, try to focus on the overall effectiveness of your writing. If you find your concerns about grammar and vocabulary to be interfering with your writing process, consider setting aside some time at the end of the writing process to address these concerns. Many of the revision and editing strategies discussed in Chapter 5 may be applied to writing in a second language. The writing classroom and the writing center provide practical and handy settings for peer review. Ask a peer to respond to your first draft by focusing on your main ideas and purpose. If your reader can summarize your main idea and purpose, then you can move on to consider the organization and content of your draft. Issues of grammar, vocabulary, and mechanics are best addressed in editing and proofreading after you are comfortable that your main ideas are clear (see Sections 5c and 5d).

48b USE YOUR NATIVE LANGUAGE AS A RESOURCE

As you continue to develop your ability to write in English, you will find that many of the strategies you developed in your native language are useful in English as well. The ability to think critically, for example, is important in any language, although what it means to be "critical" may differ from one context to another. You probably have developed the ability to tell stories and to organize your ideas in your native language. Imagery, metaphors, and expressions adapted from your native language may give your writing originality and uniqueness. It may make your writing culturally richer and more interesting to read.

You can also use your native language to develop your texts. While some writers find it more efficient to draft directly in English, others find it easier to develop an outline or even a rough draft in their native language first. Many people, when they cannot find an appropriate word in English, write down a word, a phrase, or even a sentence in their native language and consult a dictionary or a handbook later; it helps to avoid interrupting the flow of thought in the process of writing. Incorporating key terms from your native language is also a possible strategy. Here, for example, is the way a term from Japanese may be used to add flavor and perspective to a sentence: "Some political leaders need to have *wakimae*—a realistic idea of one's own place in the world."

Some people believe that using your own native language may interfere with your ability to write sentences that sound natural to native English speakers. Some readers may find words, concepts, or lines of arguments from your native language distracting, especially when there are too many of them. To avoid miscommunication, incorporate non-English elements sparingly, revise and edit rigorously, and ask your classmates or writing tutors for feedback when possible and appropriate.

48c USE DICTIONARIES

You can use regular English dictionaries for definitions, but most English dictionaries designed for native English speakers do not include all of the information that many nonnative English speakers find useful. For example, you may know the word *audience* but not whether and when *audience* can function as a count noun. Learner's dictionaries, such as the *Longman Dictionary of American English*, include information about count/noncount nouns and transitive/intransitive verbs (see Chapters 49 and 50). Many of them also provide sample sentences to help you understand how the word is used.

Some nonnative English speakers also find a bilingual dictionary useful. Bilingual dictionaries are especially useful when you want to check your understanding of an English word or when you want to find equivalent words for culture-specific concepts and technical terms. Some bilingual dictionaries also provide sample sentences. When sample sentences are not provided, check the usage in another dictionary or by searching the word or phrase on the Web (see Section 17c).

CHAPTER 49

Nouns and Articles

Hurdlers in track races try to clear every hurdle, yet it is not unusual to see even the most experienced runners clip one or two—and sometimes several—in a single race. If English is not your native language, you have probably "clipped" some of the rules governing English more than once. Throughout Chapters 49 through 51, you will see references to a Web site that is designed to help nonnative speakers with some of the more difficult customs of English language usage. There, in addition to explanatory text, you will find many practice exercises to reinforce the guidelines in Chapters 49–51.

Perhaps the most troublesome conventions for nonnative speakers are those that guide usage of the common articles *the, a,* and *an.* To understand how articles work in English, you must first understand how the language uses **nouns.**

49a KINDS OF NOUNS

There are two basic kinds of nouns. A **proper noun** begins with a capital letter and names a unique person, place, or thing: *George W. Bush, Russia, Eiffel Tower.* In the following list, note that each word refers to someone or something so specific that it bears a name.

PROPER NOUNS

Beethoven	Michael Jordan	South Korea
Concorde	New York Yankees	Africa
Empire State Building	Picasso	Stockholm
Honda	Queen Elizabeth	Lake Michigan
Thanksgiving	Virginia Woolf	New Hampshire

The other basic kind of noun is called a **common noun.** Common nouns do not name a unique person, place, or thing: *man, country, tower.* Note that the words in the following list are not names and so are not capitalized.

COMMON NOUNS

composer	athlete	country
airplane	baseball team	continent
building	painter	city
company	queen	lake
holiday	writer	state

Common nouns can also refer to abstractions, such as *grace, love,* and *power.* In English, proper nouns are names and are always capitalized while common nouns are not names and are not capitalized.

49b COUNT AND NONCOUNT NOUNS

Common nouns can be classified as either *count* or *noncount.* **Count nouns** can be made plural, usually by adding *-s* (*finger, fingers*) or by using their plural forms (*person, people; datum, data*). **Noncount nouns** cannot be counted directly and cannot take the plural form (*information,* but not *informations; garbage,* but not *garbages*). Some nouns can be either count or noncount, depending on how they are used. *Hair* can refer to either a strand of hair, when it serves as a count noun, or a mass of hair, when it becomes a noncount noun.

CORRECT USAGE OF *HAIR* AS COUNT NOUN

I carefully combed my few hairs across my mostly bald scalp.

CORRECT USAGE OF *HAIR* AS NONCOUNT NOUN

My roommate spent an hour this morning combing his hair.

In the same way, *space* can refer to a particular, quantifiable area (as in *two parking spaces*) or to unspecified open area (as in *there is some space left*).

If you are not sure whether a particular noun is count or noncount, consult a learner's dictionary. Count nouns are usually indicated as [C] (for "countable") and noncount nouns as [U] (for "uncountable").

49c SINGULAR AND PLURAL FORMS

Count nouns usually take both singular and plural forms, while noncount nouns usually do not take plural forms and are not counted directly. A count noun can have a number before it (as in *two books, three oranges*) and can be qualified with adjectives such as many (as in *many books*), some (as in *some schools*), a lot of (as in *a lot of people*), a few (several, as in *I ate a few apples*), and few (almost none, as in *few people volunteered*).

WRITING IN THE WORLD

Noncount nouns in English

In some languages, all nouns can take singular and plural forms. In English, noncount nouns refer to a collective mass that, taken as a whole, does not have a particular or regular shape. Think of the noncount noun as a mass that can be subdivided into smaller parts without losing its identity. Noncount nouns like *information, garbage, bread,* and *sand* can be broken down into smaller units and remain unchanged in essence: *bits* of information, *piles* of garbage, *slices* of bread, *grains* of sand. Count nouns like *train, finger,* and *ocean* cannot be subdivided without becoming something else: a wheel on a train, a knuckle on a finger, but no longer simply a train or a finger.

Noncount nouns can be counted or quantified in only two ways: either by general adjectives that treat the noun as a mass (*much* information, *little* garbage, *some* news) or by placing another noun between the quantifying word and the noncount noun (two *kinds* of information, three *piles* of garbage, a *piece* of news).

COMMON ERRORS

Singular and plural forms of count nouns

Count nouns are simpler to quantify than noncount nouns. But remember that English requires you to state both singular and plural forms of nouns consistently and explicitly. Look at the following sentences.

INCORRECT   The three bicyclist shaved their leg before the big race.

CORRECT   The three bicyclists shaved their legs before the big race.

In the first sentence, readers would understand that the plural form of *bicyclist* is implied by the quantifier *three* and that the plural form of *leg* is implied by the fact that bicyclists have two legs. (If they didn't, you would hope that the writer would have made that clear already!) Nevertheless, correct form in English is to indicate the singular or plural nature of a count noun explicitly, in every instance.

Remember: English requires you to use plural forms of count nouns even if a plural number is otherwise indicated.

 For more help using count and noncount nouns, see the exercises at **www.ablongman.com/faigley257**.

49d ARTICLES

Articles indicate that a noun is about to appear, and they clarify what the noun refers to. There are only two kinds of articles in English, definite and indefinite:

1. **the:** *The* is a **definite article**, meaning that it refers to (1) a specific object already known to the reader, (2) one about to be made known to the reader, or (3) a unique object.

2. **a, an:** The **indefinite articles** *a* and *an* refer to an object whose specific identity is not known to the reader. The only difference between *a* and *an* is that *a* is used before a consonant sound (*man, friend, yellow*), while *an* is used before a vowel sound (*animal, enemy, orange*).

Look at these sentences, identical except for their articles, and imagine that each is taken from a different newspaper story:

Rescue workers lifted the man to safety.

Rescue workers lifted a man to safety.

By use of the definite article *the*, the first sentence indicates that the reader already knows something about the identity of this man and his needing to be rescued. The news story has already referred to him. The sentence also suggests that this was the only man rescued, at least in this particular part of the story.

The indefinite article *a* in the second sentence indicates that the reader does not know anything about this man. Either this is the first time the news story has referred to him, or there are other men in need of rescue. When deciding whether to use the definite or indefinite article, ask yourself whether the noun refers to something specific or unique, or whether it refers to something general. *The* is used for specific or unique nouns; *a* and *an* are used for nonspecific or general nouns.

A small number of conditions determine when and how count and noncount nouns are preceded by articles.

1. *A* or *an* is not used with noncount nouns.

INCORRECT   The crowd hummed with an excitement.

CORRECT   The crowd hummed with excitement.

2. *A* or *an* is used with singular count nouns whose particular identity is unknown to the reader or writer.

The security guard was reading a book.

3. *The* is used with most count and noncount nouns whose particular identity is known to the reader. The noun may be known for one of several reasons:

- The noun has already been mentioned.

    I bought a book yesterday. The book is about Iraq.

- The noun is accompanied by a superlative such as *highest, lowest, best, worst, least interesting*, or *most beautiful* that makes its specific identity clear.

  This is **the most interesting book** about Iraq.

- The noun's identity is made clear by its context in the sentence.

  The book I bought yesterday is about Iraq.

- The noun has a unique identity, such as *the moon*.

  This book has as many pages as **the Bible**.

4. *The* is not used with noncount nouns meaning "in general."

INCORRECT   The war is hell.

CORRECT   War is hell.

COMMON ERRORS

Articles with count and noncount nouns

Knowing how to distinguish between count and noncount nouns can help you decide which article to use. Noncount nouns are never used with the indefinite articles *a* or *an*.

INCORRECT   Maria jumped into a water.

CORRECT   Maria jumped into the water.

No articles are used with noncount and plural count nouns when you wish to state something that has a general application.

INCORRECT   The water is a precious natural resource.

CORRECT   Water is a precious natural resource.

INCORRECT   The soccer players tend to be quick and agile.

CORRECT   Soccer players tend to be quick and agile.

Remember:

1. Noncount nouns are never used with *a* and *an*.
2. Noncount and plural nouns used to make general statements do not take articles.

 For more help using articles, see the exercises at **www.ablongman.com/faigley258.**

Verbs

You cannot write a complete sentence in English without using a verb. As the heart animates the body, verbs animate sentences: Without them, nothing—either real or imagined, past or present—happens. Though both native and nonnative speakers of English encounter problems with verbs, this chapter focuses on the conventions of the verb system that are particularly challenging to nonnative English speakers. See also Chapters 34 and 35.

50a TYPES OF VERBS

The verb system in English can be divided between simple verbs like *run, speak,* and *look,* and verb phrases like *may have run, have spoken,* and *will be looking.* In the examples of verb phrases, the words that appear before the main verbs—*may, have, will,* and *be*—are called **auxiliary verbs** (also called **helping verbs**). Helping verbs, as their name suggests, exist to help express something about the action of main verbs: for example, when the action occurs (tense), whether the subject acted or was acted upon (voice), or whether or not an action occurred.

50b *BE* VERBS

Indicating tense and voice with *be* verbs

Like the other auxiliary verbs *have* and *do, be* changes form to signal tense. In addition to *be* itself, the **be verbs** are *is, am, are, was, were,* and *been.* To show ongoing action, *be* verbs are followed by the present participle, which is a verb with an *-ing* ending:

| INCORRECT | I am think of all the things I'd rather be do. |
| CORRECT | I am thinking of all the things I'd rather be doing. |

| INCORRECT | He was run as fast as he could. |
| CORRECT | He was running as fast as he could. |

To show that an action is being done to, rather than by, the subject, follow *be* verbs with the past participle (a verb usually ending in *-ed, -en,* or *-t*):

INCORRECT	The movie **was direct** by John Woo.
CORRECT	The movie **was directed** by John Woo.
INCORRECT	The complaint **will be file** by the victim.
CORRECT	The complaint **will be filed** by the victim.

WRITING IN THE WORLD

Verbs that express cognitive activity

English, unlike Chinese, Arabic, and several other languages, requires a form of *be* before the present or past participle. As you have probably discovered, however, English has many exceptions to its rules. Verbs that express some form of cognitive activity rather than a direct action are not used as present participles with *be* verbs. Examples of such words include *know, like, see,* and *believe.*

INCORRECT	You **were knowing** that I would be late.
CORRECT	You **knew** that I would be late.

But here's an exception to an exception: A small number of these verbs, such as *considering, thinking,* and *pondering,* can be used as present participles with *be* verbs.

> I am considering whether to finish my homework first.

50c MODAL AUXILIARY VERBS

Modal auxiliary verbs—*will, would, can, could, may, might, shall, must,* and *should*—are helping verbs that express conditions like possibility, permission, speculation, expectation, obligation, and necessity. Unlike the helping verbs *be, have,* and *do,* modal verbs do not change form based on the grammatical subject of the sentence (*I, you, she, he, it, we, they*).

Two basic rules apply to all uses of modal verbs. First, modal verbs are always followed by the simple form of the verb. The simple form is the verb by itself, in the present tense, such as *have,* but not *had, having,* or *to have.*

INCORRECT	She should **studies** harder to pass the exam.
CORRECT	She should **study** harder to pass the exam.

The second rule is that you should not use modals consecutively.

INCORRECT	If you work harder at writing, you **might could** improve.
CORRECT	If you work harder at writing, you **might** improve.

50d VERBS AND INFINITIVES

Several verbs are followed by particular verb forms. An **infinitive** is *to* plus the simple form of the verb. Here are some common verbs that are followed by an infinitive:

afford	expect	promise
agree	fail	refuse
ask	hope	seem
attempt	intend	struggle
claim	learn	tend
consent	need	wait
decide	plan	want
demand	prepare	wish

INCORRECT   You **learn playing** the guitar by practicing.

CORRECT   You **learn to play** the guitar by practicing.

Some verbs require that a noun or pronoun come after the verb and before the infinitive:

advise	instruct	require
cause	order	tell
command	persuade	warn

INCORRECT   I would **advise to watch** where you step.

CORRECT   I would **advise you to watch** where you step.

A few verbs, when followed by a noun or pronoun, take an *unmarked infinitive*, which is an infinitive without *to*.

have	let	make

INCORRECT   I will **let** her **to plan** the vacation.

CORRECT   I will **let** her **plan** the vacation.

50e VERBS AND –*ING* VERBALS

Other verbs are followed by **gerunds**, which are verbs ending in -*ing* that are used as nouns. Here are some of the more common verbs that are followed by a gerund.

admit	discuss	quit
advise	enjoy	recommend
appreciate	finish	regret
avoid	imagine	risk
consider	practice	suggest

INCORRECT	She will **finish to grade** papers by noon.
CORRECT	She will **finish grading** papers by noon.

A smaller number of verbs can be followed by either gerunds or infinitives (see Section 50d).

begin	hate	love
continue	like	start

WITH GERUND	She **likes working** in the music store.
WITH INFINITIVE	She **likes to work** in the music store.

 For more help using gerunds and infinitives, see the exercises at www.ablongman.com/faigley259.

50f CONDITIONAL SENTENCES

Conditional sentences express *if-then* relationships: They consist of a **subordinate clause** beginning with *if, unless,* or *when* that expresses a condition, and a **main clause** that expresses a result. The tense and mood of the verb in the main clause and the type of conditional sentence determine the tense and mood of the verb in the subordinate clause.

┌─SUBORDINATE CLAUSE─┐ ┌──────MAIN CLAUSE──────┐
When the wind stops, the sea becomes calm.

Conditional sentences fall into three categories: **factual, predictive,** and **hypothetical.**

Factual conditionals

Factual conditional sentences express factual relationships: If this happens, that will follow. The tense of the verb in the conditional clause is the same as the tense of the verb in the result clause:

INCORRECT	If it rains, the ground **would become** wet.
CORRECT	If it rains, the ground **becomes** wet.

Predictive conditionals

Predictive conditional sentences express predicted consequences from possible conditions. The verb in the conditional clause is present tense, and the verb in the result clause is formed with a modal (*will, would, can, could, may, might, shall, must,* and *should*) plus the base form of the verb.

| INCORRECT | If you **take** the long way home, you enjoy the ride more. |
| CORRECT | If you **take** the long way home, you will enjoy the ride more. |

Hypothetical conditionals

Hypothetical conditional sentences express events that are either not factual or unlikely to happen. For hypothetical events in the past, the conditional clause verb takes the past perfect tense. The main clause verb is formed from *could have, would have,* or *might have* plus the past participle.

| INCORRECT | If we **had fed** the dog last night, he would not run away. |
| CORRECT | If we **had fed** the dog last night, he would not have run away. |

For hypothetical events in the present or future, the conditional clause verb takes the past tense and the main clause verb is formed from *could, would,* or *might* and the base form.

| INCORRECT | If we **paid** off our credit cards, we can buy a house. |
| CORRECT | If we **paid** off our credit cards, we could buy a house. |

For more help using conditionals, see the exercises at
www.ablongman.com/faigley260.

50g PARTICIPIAL ADJECTIVES

The present participle always ends in *-ing* (*boring, exciting*), while most past participles end in *-ed* (*bored, excited*). Both participle forms can be used as adjectives.

When participles are used as adjectives, they can either precede the nouns they modify or they can come after a connecting verb.

It was a **thrilling** book. [*Thrilling* modifies *book.*]

Stephanie was **thrilled**. [*Thrilled* modifies *Stephanie.*]

Present participles like *thrilling* describe a thing or person causing an experience, while past participles like *thrilled* describe a thing or person receiving the experience.

| INCORRECT | Students were **exciting** by the lecture. |
| CORRECT | Students were **excited** by the lecture. |

English Sentence Structure

Performing musicians are not judged by the number of songs they know. Likewise, multilingual speakers understand that a good vocabulary is not enough to communicate effectively. Words derive much of their meaning from context, and the basic contextual unit is the **sentence**. Your ability to understand and convey information accurately in English depends largely on your understanding of how sentences are put together.

51a SUBJECTS

With the exception of **imperatives** (commands such as *Be careful!* and *Jump!*) and informal expressions (such as *Got it?*), sentences in English usually contain a subject and a predicate. A **subject** names who or what the sentence is about; the **predicate** contains information about the subject.

⌐SUBJECT¬ ⌐PREDICATE¬
The lion is asleep.

Many languages allow the writer to omit the subject if it's implied, but formal written English requires that each sentence include a subject, even when the meaning of the sentence would be clear without it. In some cases, you must supply an **expletive** (also known as *a dummy subject*), such as *it* or *there*, to stand in for the subject.

INCORRECT	Is snowing in Alaska.
CORRECT	It is snowing in Alaska.

INCORRECT	Won't be enough time to climb that mountain.
CORRECT	There won't be enough time to climb that mountain.

Both main and subordinate clauses within sentences require a subject and a predicate. A main clause can stand alone as a sentence, while subordinate clauses can only be understood in the context of the sentence of which they're a part. Still, even subordinate clauses must contain a subject. Look at the underlined subordinate clauses in the following two correct sentences.

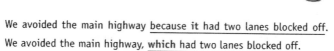

We avoided the main highway <u>because it had two lanes blocked off.</u>

We avoided the main highway, <u>which had two lanes blocked off.</u>

In the first example, the subject of the subordinate clause is *it*, a pronoun representing the highway. In the second sentence, the relative pronoun *which*—also representing the highway—becomes the subject. When you use a relative pronoun, do not repeat the subject within the same clause.

INCORRECT   We avoided the highway, which it had two lanes blocked off.

In this sentence, *it* repeats the subject *which* unnecessarily.

51b ENGLISH WORD ORDER

All languages have their own rules for sentence structure. In English, correct word order often determines whether or not you succeed in saying what you mean. The basic sentence pattern in English is subject + predicate. A **predicate** consists of at least one main verb (see Section 32a). Although it is possible to write single-verb sentences such as *Stop!* most English sentences consist of a combination of several words. A simple English sentence can be formed with a noun and a verb.

Birds fly.

In the above sentence, the subject (birds) is taking the action *and* receiving the action. There is no other object after the verb. The type of verb that can form a sentence without being followed by an object is called an **intransitive verb.** If the verb is intransitive, like *exist*, it does not take a direct object.

Some verbs are **transitive**, which means they require a **direct object** to complete their meaning. The direct object receives the action described by the verb.

INCORRECT   The bird saw.

CORRECT   The bird saw a cat.

In this sentence, the subject (the bird) is doing the action (saw) while the direct object (a cat) is receiving the action. A sentence with a transitive verb can be transformed into a passive sentence (*A cat was seen by the bird.*). See Chapter 26 for active and passive sentences.

Some verbs (*write, learn, read*, and others) can be both transitive and intransitive, depending on how they are used.

INTRANSITIVE   Pilots fly.

TRANSITIVE   Pilots fly airplanes.

Most learners' dictionaries and bilingual dictionaries indicate whether a particular verb is transitive or intransitive. See Section 48c on the use of dictionaries.

In another simple pattern, the transitive verb is replaced by a linking verb that joins its subject to a following description.

> The tallest player was the goalie.

Linking verbs like *was, become, sound, look*, and *seem* precede a *subject complement* (in this example, *the goalie*) that refers back to the subject.

At the next level of complexity, a sentence combines a subject with a verb, direct object, and indirect object.

> INDIRECT   DIRECT
> OBJ   OBJ
> The goalie passed her the ball.

Passed is a transitive verb, *ball* is the direct object of the verb, and *her* is the indirect object, the person for whom the action was taken. The same idea can be expressed with a prepositional phrase instead of an indirect object:

> DIRECT   PREP
> OBJ   PHRASE
> The goalie passed the ball to her.

Other sentence patterns are possible in English. (See Chapter 32.) However, it is important to remember that altering the basic subject + verb + object word order often changes the meaning of a sentence. If the meaning survives, the result may still be awkward. As a general rule, try to keep the verb close to its subject, and the direct or indirect object close to its verb.

51c PLACEMENT OF MODIFIERS

The proximity of a modifier—an adjective or adverb—to the noun or verb it modifies provides an important clue to their relationship. Modifiers, even more than verbs, will be unclear if your reader can't connect them to their associated words. Both native and nonnative speakers of English often have difficulty with misplaced modifiers.

Clarity should be your first goal when using a modifier. Readers usually link modifiers with the nearest word. In the following examples, the highlighted words are adjective clauses that modify nouns.

UNCLEAR   Many pedestrians are killed each year by motorists **not using sidewalks.**

CLEAR   Many pedestrians **not using sidewalks** are killed each year by motorists.

UNCLEAR   He gave an apple to his girlfriend **on a silver platter.**

CLEAR   He gave an apple **on a silver platter** to his girlfriend.

An **adverb**—a word or group of words that modifies a verb, adjective, or another adverb—should not come between a verb and its direct object.

AWKWARD	The hurricane destroyed **completely** the city's tallest building.
BETTER	The hurricane **completely** destroyed the city's tallest building.

While single-word adverbs can come between a subject and its verb, you should avoid placing adverbial phrases in this position.

AWKWARD	Galveston, **following the 1900 hurricane that killed thousands**, built a seawall to prevent a future catastrophe.
BETTER	**Following the 1900 hurricane that killed thousands**, Galveston built a seawall to prevent a future catastrophe.

As a general rule, try to avoid placing an adverb between *to* and its verb. This is called a **split infinitive**.

AWKWARD	The water level was predicted **to not rise.**
BETTER	The water level was predicted **not to rise.**

Sometimes, though, a split infinitive will read more naturally than the alternative. Note also how the sentence with the split infinitive is more concise:

WITHOUT SPLIT INFINITIVE	Automobile emissions in the city are expected to **increase by more than two times** over the next five years.
WITH SPLIT INFINITIVE	Automobile emissions in the city are expected to **more than double** over the next five years.

Certain kinds of adverbs have special rules for placement. Adverbs that describe how something is done—called **adverbs of manner**—usually follow the verb.

The student listened **closely** to the lecture.

These adverbs may also be separated from the verb by a direct object:

She threw the ball **well.**

Adverbs of frequency usually are placed at the head of a sentence, before a single verb, or after an auxiliary verb in a verb phrase.

Often, politicians have underestimated the intelligence of voters.

Politicians have **often** underestimated the intelligence of voters.

It's common practice in English to combine two or more nouns to form a compound noun. Where two or more adjectives or nouns are strung together, the main noun is always positioned at the end of the string:

12-speed road **bike**, tall oak **tree**, computer **table**

COMMON ERRORS

Dangling modifiers

A dangling modifier does not seem to modify anything in a sentence; it dangles, unconnected to the word or words it presumably is intended to modify. Frequently, it produces some funny results:

When still a girl, my father joined the army.

It sounds like *father* was once a girl. The problem is that the subject, *I*, is missing:

When I was still a girl, my father joined the army.

Dangling modifiers usually occur at the head of a sentence in the form of adjective clauses, with a subject that is implied but never stated.

INCORRECT   After lifting the heavy piano up the stairs, the apartment door was too small to get it through.

CORRECT   After lifting the heavy piano up the stairs, we discovered the apartment door was too small to get it through.

Whenever you use a modifier, ask yourself whether its relationship to the word it modifies will be clear to your reader. What is clear to you may not be clear to your audience. Writing, like speaking, is an exercise in making your own thoughts explicit. The solution for the dangling modifier is to recast it as a complete clause with its own explicit subject and verb.

Remember: Modifiers should be clearly connected to the words they modify, especially at the beginning of sentences.

 For more help with modifiers, see the exercises at **www.ablongman.com/faigley261.**

3. Evans RW, Bowditch L, Dana KL, Drummond A, Wildovitch WP, Young SL, Mills P, Mills RR, Livak SR, Lisi OL, and others. Organ transplants: ethical issues. Ann Arbor: Univ of Michigan Pr; 2004. 498 p.

4. A book with an editor

Jonson P, editor. 2006. Anatomy yearbook. Los Angeles: Anatco. 628 p.

4. Jonson P, editor. Anatomy yearbook. Los Angeles: Anatco; 2006. 628 p.

5. A selection from a book

Krigel R, Laubenstein L, Muggia F. 2005. Kaposi's sarcoma. In: Ebbeson P, Biggar RS, Melbye M, editors. AIDS: a basic guide for clinicians. 2nd ed. Philadelphia: WB Saunders. p 100-26.

5. Krigel R, Laubenstein L, Muggia F. Kaposi's sarcoma. In: Ebbeson P, Biggar RS, Melbye M, editors. AIDS: a basic guide for clinicians. 2nd ed. Philadelphia: WB Saunders; 2005. p 100-26.

6. An anonymous work

[Anonymous]. 2006. Health care for multiple sclerosis. New York: US Health Care. 86 p.

6. [Anonymous]. Health care for multiple sclerosis. New York: US Health Care; 2006. 86 p.

7. Two or more cited works by the same author published in the same year

Gardner H. 1973a. The arts and human development. New York: J Wiley. 406 p.

Gardner H. 1973b. The quest for mind: Piaget, Lévi-Strauss, and the structuralist movement. New York: AA Knopf. 492 p.

(The number style does not require such forms.)

2 Periodicals: Journals, magazines, newspapers

8. An article in a journal with continuous pagination throughout the annual volume

Ancino R, Carter KV, Elwin DJ. 2004. Factors contributing to viral immunity: a review of the research. Dev Biol 30:156-9.

8. Ancino R, Carter KV, Elwin DJ. Factors contributing to viral immunity: a review of the research. Dev Biol 2004;30:156-9.

9. An article in a journal that pages issues separately

Kim P. 2001 Feb. Medical decision making for the dying. Milbank Quar 64(2):26-40.

9. Kim P. Medical decision making for the dying. Milbank Quar 2001 Feb;64(2):26-40.

10. An article in a newspaper

Kolata G. 2006 Jan 7. Kill all the bacteria! New York Times;Sect B:1(col 3).

10. Kolata G. Kill all the bacteria! New York Times 2006 Jan 7;Sect B:1(col 3).

11. An article in a magazine

Scheiber N. 2004 June 24. Finger tip: why fingerprinting won't work. New Republic:15-6.

11. Scheiber N. Finger tip: why fingerprinting won't work. New Republic 2004 June 24:15-6.

3 Electronic sources

Scientific Style and Format includes a few formats for citing electronic sources, derived from *National Library of Medicine Recommended Formats for Bibliographic Citation*. For additional formats, the CSE Web site recommends the NLM 2001 supplement for Internet sources. The following models adapt these NLM formats to CSE name-year and number styles.

Note Since neither the CSE nor the NLM specifies how to break URLs, follow APA style: break only after slashes or before periods, and do not hyphenate.

12. A source on CD-ROM

Reich WT, editor. 2005. Encyclopedia of bioethics [CD-ROM]. New York: Co-Health.

12. Reich WT, editor. Encyclopedia of bioethics [CD-ROM]. New York: Co-Health; 2005.

13. An online journal article

Grady GF. 2005. The here and now of hepatitis B immunization. Today's Med [Internet] [cited 2005 Dec 7];6(2):39-41. Available from: http://www.fmrt.org/todaysmedicine/Grady050293.pdf6

13. Grady GF. The here and now of hepatitis B immunization. Today's Med [Internet] 2005 [cited 2005 Dec 7];6(2):39-41. Available from: http://www.fmrt.org/todaysmedicine/Grady050293.pdf6

Give the date of your access, preceded by cited, in brackets: [cited 2005 Dec 7] in the models above. If the article has no reference numbers (pages, paragraphs, and so on), estimate the length in brackets —for instance, [about 15 p.] or [about 6 screens]. (See below.)

14. An online book

Ruch BJ, Ruch DB. 2004. Homeopathy and medicine: resolving the conflict [Internet]. New York: Albert Einstein Coll of Medicine [cited 2006 Jan 28]. [about 50 p.]. Available from: http://www.einstein.edu/medicine/books/ruch.html

14. Ruch BJ, Ruch DB. Homeopathy and medicine: resolving the conflict [Internet]. New York: Albert Einstein Coll of Medicine; 2004 [cited 2006 Jan 28]. [about 50 p.]. Available from: http://www.einstein.edu/medicine/books/ruch.html

As with an online journal article, give the date of your access, preceded by cited, in brackets. If the source uses page or other reference numbers, provide the total as in model 1 on p. 546. If no reference numbers are provided, you may estimate them in brackets, as in the preceding examples.

15. A source retrieved from an online database

McAskill MR, Anderson TJ, Jones RD. 2005. Saccadic adaptation in neurological disorders. Prog Brain Res 140:417-31. In: PubMed [Internet]. Bethesda (MD): National Library of Medicine; [cited 2005 Mar 6]. Available from: http://www.ncbi.nlm.nih.gov/PubMed; PMID: 12508606.

15. McAskill MR, Anderson TJ, Jones RD. Saccadic adaptation in neurological disorders. Prog Brain Res 2005;140:417-31. In: PubMed [Internet]. Bethesda (MD): National Library of Medicine; [cited 2005 Mar 6]. Available from: http://www.ncbi.nlm.nih.gov/PubMed; PMID: 12508606.

After In: provide information on the database: title, place of publication, and publisher. (If the database author is different from the publisher, give the author's name before the title.) If you see a date of publication or copyright date for the database, give it after the publisher's name. Add the date of your access, preceded by cited, in brackets. After the availability statement, add any identifying number the database uses for the source.

16. A Web site

American Medical Association [Internet]. 2006. Chicago: American Medical Association; [cited 2006 Jan 26]. Available from: http://ama-assn.org

16. American Medical Association [Internet]. Chicago: American Medical Association; 2006 [cited 2006 Jan 26]. Available from: http://ama-assn.org

17. Electronic mail

Millon M. 2005 May 4. Grief therapy [Internet]. Message to: Naomi Sakai. 3:16 pm [cited 2005 May 4]. [about 2 screens].

17. Millon M. Grief therapy [Internet]. Message to: Naomi Sakai. 2005 May 4, 3:16 pm [cited 2005 May 4]. [about 2 screens].

18. A posting to a discussion list

Stalinsky Q. 2005 Aug 16. The hormone-replacement study. In: Women Physicians Congress [Internet]. [Chicago: American Medical Association]; 9:26 am [cited 2005 Aug 17]. [about 8 paragraphs]. Available from: ama-wpc@ama-assn.org

18. Stalinsky Q. The hormone-replacement study. In: Women Physicians Congress [Internet]. [Chicago: American Medical Association]; 2005 Aug 16, 9:26 am [cited 2005 Aug 17]. [about 8 paragraphs]. Available from: ama-wpc@ama-assn.org

19. Computer software

Project scheduler 9000 [computer program]. 2006. Version 5.1. Orlando (FL): Scitor. CD-ROM. System requirements: IBM PC or compatible; Windows 98 or higher; 32 MB RAM; minimum 50 MB of free disk space.

19. Project scheduler 9000 [computer program]. Version 5.1. Orlando (FL): Scitor; 2003. CD-ROM. System requirements: IBM PC or compatible; Windows 98 or higher; 32 MB RAM; minimum 50 MB of free disk space.

4 Other sources

20. A government publication

Committee on Science and Technology, House (US). 2003. Hearing on procurement and allocation of human organs for transplantation. 108th Cong., 1st Sess. House Doc. nr 409.

20. Committee on Science and Technology, House (US). Hearing on procurement and allocation of human organs for transplantation. 108th Cong., 1st Sess. House Doc. nr 409; 2003.

21. A nongovernment report

Warnock M. 2004. Report of the Committee on Fertilization and Embryology. Baylor University, Department of Embryology. Waco (TX): Baylor Univ. Report nr BU/DE.4261.

21. Warnock M. Report of the Committee on Fertilization and Embryology. Baylor University, Department of Embryology. Waco (TX): Baylor Univ; 2004. Report nr BU/DE.4261.

22. A sound recording, video recording, DVD, or film

Teaching Media. 2005. Cell mitosis [DVD]. White Plains (NY): Teaching Media. 40 min, sound, color.

22. Cell mitosis [DVD]. White Plains (NY): Teaching Media; 2005. 40 min, sound, color.

Glossary of Usage
Index

Glossary of Usage
Index

Glossary of Usage

This glossary provides notes on words or phrases that often cause problems for writers. The recommendations for standard American English are based on current dictionaries and usage guides. Items labeled **nonstandard** should be avoided in academic and business settings. Those labeled **colloquial** and **slang** occur in speech and in some informal writing but are best avoided in formal college and business writing. (Words and phrases labeled *colloquial* include those labeled by many dictionaries with the equivalent term *informal.*)

a, an Use *a* before words beginning with consonant sounds, including those spelled with an initial pronounced *h* and those spelled with vowels that are sounded as consonants: *a historian, a one-o'clock class, a university.* Use *an* before words that begin with vowel sounds, including those spelled with an initial silent *h: an orgy, an L, an honor.*

The article before an abbreviation depends on how the abbreviation is to be read: *She was once an AEC undersecretary* (*AEC* is to be read as three separate letters). *Many Americans opposed a SALT treaty* (*SALT* is to be read as one word, *salt*).

See also **4** pp. 267–68 on the uses of *a/an* versus *the.*

accept, except *Accept* is a verb meaning "receive." *Except* is usually a preposition or conjunction meaning "but for" or "other than"; when it is used as a verb, it means "leave out." *I can accept all your suggestions except the last one. I'm sorry you excepted my last suggestion from your list.*

advice, advise *Advice* is a noun, and *advise* is a verb: *Take my advice; do as I advise you.*

affect, effect Usually *affect* is a verb, meaning "to influence," and *effect* is a noun, meaning "result": *The drug did not affect his driving; in fact, it seemed to have no effect at all.* But *effect* occasionally is used as a verb meaning "to bring about": *Her efforts effected a change.* And *affect* is used in psychology as a noun meaning "feeling or emotion": *One can infer much about affect from behavior.*

agree to, agree with *Agree to* means "consent to," and *agree with* means "be in accord with": *How can they agree to a treaty when they don't agree with each other about the terms?*

all ready, already *All ready* means "completely prepared," and *already* means "by now" or "before now": *We were all ready to go to the movie, but it had already started.*

all right *All right* is always two words. *Alright* is a common misspelling.

all together, altogether *All together* means "in unison" or "gathered in one place." *Altogether* means "entirely." *It's not altogether true that our family never spends vacations all together.*

allusion, illusion An *allusion* is an indirect reference, and an *illusion* is a deceptive appearance: *Paul's constant allusions to Shakespeare created the illusion that he was an intellectual.*

almost, most *Almost* means "nearly"; *most* means "the greater number (or part) of." In formal writing, *most* should not be used as a substitute for *almost: We see each other almost* [not *most*] *every day.*

a lot *A lot* is always two words, used informally to mean "many." *Alot* is a common misspelling.

among, between In general, use *among* for relationships involving more than two people or for comparing one thing to a group to which it belongs. *The four of them agreed among themselves that the choice was between New York and Los Angeles.*

amount, number Use *amount* with a singular noun that names something not countable (a noncount noun): *The amount of food varies.* Use *number* with a plural noun that names more than one of something countable (a plural count noun): *The number of calories must stay the same.*

and/or *And/or* indicates three options: one or the other or both (*The decision is made by the mayor and/or the council*). If you mean all three options, *and/or* is appropriate. Otherwise, use *and* if you mean both, *or* if you mean either.

ante-, anti- The prefix *ante-* means "before" (*antedate, antebellum*); *anti-* means "against" (*antiwar, antinuclear*). Before a capital letter or *i*, *anti-* takes a hyphen: *anti-Freudian, anti-isolationist.*

anxious, eager *Anxious* means "nervous" or "worried" and is usually followed by *about. Eager* means "looking forward" and is usually followed by *to. I've been anxious about getting blisters. I'm eager* [not *anxious*] *to get new running shoes.*

anybody, any body; anyone, any one *Anybody* and *anyone* are indefinite pronouns; *any body* is a noun modified by *any; any one* is a pronoun or adjective modified by *any. How can anybody communicate with any body of government? Can anyone help Amy? She has more work than any one person can handle.*

any more, anymore *Any more* means "no more"; *anymore* means "now." Both are used in negative constructions. *He doesn't want any more. She doesn't live here anymore.*

apt, liable, likely *Apt* and *likely* are interchangeable. Strictly speaking, though, *apt* means "having a tendency to": *Horace is apt to forget his lunch in the morning. Likely* means "probably going to": *Horace is leaving so early today that he's likely to catch the first bus.*

Liable normally means "in danger of" and should be confined to situations with undesirable consequences: *Horace is liable to trip over that hose.* Strictly, *liable* means "responsible" or "exposed to": *The owner will be liable for Horace's injuries.*

are, is Use *are* with a plural subject (*books are*), *is* with a singular subject (*a book is*).

as   Substituting for *because, since,* or *while, as* may be vague or ambiguous: *As the researchers asked more questions, their money ran out.* (Does *as* mean "while" or "because"?) *As* should never be used as a substitute for *whether* or *who. I'm not sure whether* [not *as*] *we can make it. That's the man who* [not *as*] *gave me directions.*

as, like   In formal speech and writing, *like* should not introduce a full clause (with a subject and a verb) because it is a preposition. The preferred choice is *as* or *as if: The plan succeeded as* [not *like*] *we hoped. It seemed as if* [not *like*] *it might fail. Other plans like it have failed.*

as, than   In comparisons, *as* and *than* precede a subjective-case pronoun when the pronoun is a subject: *I love you more than he* [*loves you*]. *As* and *than* precede an objective-case pronoun when the pronoun is an object: *I love you as much as* [*I love*] *him.* (See also **4** p. 249.)

assure, ensure, insure   *Assure* means "to promise": *He assured us that we would miss the traffic. Ensure* and *insure* often are used interchangeably to mean "make certain," but some reserve *insure* for matters of legal and financial protection and use *ensure* for more general meanings: *We left early to ensure that we would miss the traffic. It's expensive to insure yourself against floods.*

at   The use of *at* after *where* is wordy and should be avoided: *Where are you meeting him?* is preferable to *Where are you meeting him at?*

awful, awfully   Strictly speaking, *awful* means "awe-inspiring." As intensifiers meaning "very" or "extremely" (*He tried awfully hard*), *awful* and *awfully* should be avoided in formal speech or writing.

a while, awhile   *Awhile* is an adverb; *a while* is an article and a noun. *I will be gone awhile* [not *a while*]. *I will be gone for a while* [not *awhile*].

bad, badly   In formal speech and writing, *bad* should be used only as an adjective; the adverb is *badly. He felt bad because his tooth ached badly.* In *He felt bad*, the verb *felt* is a linking verb and the adjective *bad* describes the subject. See also **4** p. 261.

being as, being that   Colloquial for *because*, the preferable word in formal speech or writing: *Because* [not *Being as*] *the world is round, Columbus never did fall off the edge.*

beside, besides   *Beside* is a preposition meaning "next to." *Besides* is a preposition meaning "except" or "in addition to" as well as an adverb meaning "in addition." *Besides, several other people besides you want to sit beside Dr. Christensen.*

better, had better   *Had better* (meaning "ought to") is a verb modified by an adverb. The verb is necessary and should not be omitted: *You had better* [not just *better*] *go.*

between, among   See *among, between.*

bring, take   Use *bring* only for movement from a farther place to a nearer one and *take* for any other movement. *First take these books to the library for renewal; then take them to Mr. Daniels. Bring them back to me when he's finished.*

but, hardly, scarcely These words are negative in their own right; using *not* with any of them produces a double negative (see **4** p. 264). *We have but* [not *haven't got but*] *an hour before our plane leaves. I could hardly* [not *couldn't hardly*] *make out her face.*

but, however, yet Each of these words is adequate to express contrast. Don't combine them. *He said he had finished, yet* [not *but yet*] *he continued.*

can, may Strictly, *can* indicates capacity or ability, and *may* indicates permission or possibility: *If I may talk with you a moment, I believe I can solve your problem.*

censor, censure To *censor* is to edit or remove from public view on moral or some other grounds; to *censure* is to give a formal scolding. *The lieutenant was censured by Major Taylor for censoring the letters her soldiers wrote home from boot camp.*

center around *Center on* is more logical than, and preferable to, *center around.*

cite, sight, site *Cite* is a verb usually meaning "quote," "commend," or "acknowledge": *You must cite your sources. Sight* is both a noun meaning "the ability to see" or "a view" and a verb meaning "perceive" or "observe": *What a sight you see when you sight Venus through a strong telescope. Site* is a noun meaning "place" or "location" or a verb meaning "situate": *The builder sited the house on an unlikely site.*

climatic, climactic *Climatic* comes from *climate* and refers to the weather: *Last winter's temperatures may indicate a climatic change. Climactic* comes from *climax* and refers to a dramatic high point: *During the climactic duel between Hamlet and Laertes, Gertrude drinks poisoned wine.*

complement, compliment To *complement* something is to add to, complete, or reinforce it: *Her yellow blouse complemented her black hair.* To *compliment* something is to make a flattering remark about it: *He complimented her on her hair. Complimentary* can also mean "free": *complimentary tickets.*

conscience, conscious *Conscience* is a noun meaning "a sense of right and wrong"; *conscious* is an adjective meaning "aware" or "awake." *Though I was barely conscious, my conscience nagged me.*

contact Often used imprecisely as a verb instead of a more exact word such as *consult, talk with, telephone,* or *write to.*

continual, continuous *Continual* means "constantly recurring": *Most movies on television are continually interrupted by commercials. Continuous* means "unceasing": *Some cable channels present movies continuously without commercials.*

could of See *have, of.*

credible, creditable, credulous *Credible* means "believable": *It's a strange story, but it seems credible to me. Creditable* means "deserving of credit" or "worthy": *Steve gave a creditable performance. Credulous* means "gullible": *The credulous Claire believed Tim's lies.* See also *incredible, incredulous.*

criteria The plural of *criterion* (meaning "standard for judgment"): *Our criteria are strict. The most important criterion is a sense of humor.*

data The plural of *datum* (meaning "fact"). Though *data* is often used as a singular noun, most careful writers still treat it as plural: *The data fail* [not *fails*] *to support the hypothesis.*

device, devise *Device* is the noun, and *devise* is the verb: *Can you devise some device for getting his attention?*

different from, different than *Different from* is preferred: *His purpose is different from mine.* But *different than* is widely accepted when a construction using *from* would be wordy: *I'm a different person now than I used to be* is preferable to *I'm a different person now from the person I used to be.*

differ from, differ with To *differ from* is to be unlike: *The twins differ from each other only in their hairstyles.* To *differ with* is to disagree with: *I have to differ with you on that point.*

discreet, discrete *Discreet* (noun form *discretion*) means "tactful": *What's a discreet way of telling Maud to be quiet?* *Discrete* (noun form *discreteness*) means "separate and distinct": *Within a computer's memory are millions of discrete bits of information.*

disinterested, uninterested *Disinterested* means "impartial": *We chose Pete, as a disinterested third party, to decide who was right.* *Uninterested* means "bored" or "lacking interest": *Unfortunately, Pete was completely uninterested in the question.*

don't *Don't* is the contraction for *do not,* not for *does not: I don't care, you don't care, and he doesn't* [not *don't*] *care.*

due to the fact that Wordy for *because.*

eager, anxious See *anxious, eager.*

effect See *affect, effect.*

elicit, illicit *Elicit* is a verb meaning "bring out" or "call forth." *Illicit* is an adjective meaning "unlawful." *The crime elicited an outcry against illicit drugs.*

emigrate, immigrate *Emigrate* means "to leave one place and move to another": *The Chus emigrated from Korea. Immigrate* means "to move into a place where one was not born": *They immigrated to the United States.*

ensure See *assure, ensure, insure.*

enthused Used colloquially as an adjective meaning "showing enthusiasm." The preferred adjective is *enthusiastic: The coach was enthusiastic* [not *enthused*] *about the team's victory.*

et al., etc. Use *et al.,* the Latin abbreviation for "and other people," only in source citations: *Jones et al.* Avoid *etc.,* the Latin abbreviation for "and other things," in formal writing, and do not use it to refer to people or to substitute for precision, as in *The government provides health care, etc.*

everybody, every body; everyone, every one *Everybody* and *everyone* are indefinite pronouns: *Everybody* [*everyone*] *knows Tom steals. Every one* is a pronoun modified by *every*, and *every body* a noun modified by *every*. Both refer to each thing or person of a specific group and are typically followed by *of*: *The game commissioner has stocked every body of fresh water in the state with fish, and now every one of our rivers is a potential trout stream.*

everyday, every day *Everyday* is an adjective meaning "used daily" or "common"; *every day* is a noun modified by *every*: *Everyday problems tend to arise every day.*

everywheres Nonstandard for *everywhere*.

except See *accept, except.*

except for the fact that Wordy for *except that.*

explicit, implicit *Explicit* means "stated outright": *I left explicit instructions. Implicit* means "implied, unstated": *We had an implicit understanding.*

farther, further *Farther* refers to additional distance (*How much farther is it to the beach?*), and *further* refers to additional time, amount, or other abstract matters (*I don't want to discuss this any further*).

fewer, less *Fewer* refers to individual countable items (a plural count noun), *less* to general amounts (a noncount noun, always singular). *Skim milk has fewer calories than whole milk. We have less milk left than I thought.*

flaunt, flout *Flaunt* means "show off": *If you have style, flaunt it. Flout* means "scorn" or "defy": *Hester Prynne flouted convention and paid the price.*

flunk A colloquial substitute for *fail.*

fun As an adjective, *fun* is colloquial and should be avoided in most writing: *It was a pleasurable* [not *fun*] *evening.*

further See *farther, further.*

get This common verb is used in many slang and colloquial expressions: *get lost, that really gets me, getting on. Get* is easy to overuse: watch out for it in expressions such as *it's getting better* (substitute *improving*) and *we got done* (substitute *finished*).

good, well *Good* is an adjective, and *well* is nearly always an adverb: *Larry's a good dancer. He and Linda dance well together. Well* is properly used as an adjective only to refer to health: *You look well. (You look good*, in contrast, means "Your appearance is pleasing.")

good and Colloquial for "very": *I was very* [not *good and*] *tired.*

had better See *better, had better.*

had ought The *had* is unnecessary and should be omitted: *He ought* [not *had ought*] *to listen to his mother.*

hanged, hung Though both are past-tense forms of *hang, hanged* is used to refer to executions and *hung* is used for all other meanings: *Tom Dooley was hanged* [not *hung*] *from a white oak tree. I hung* [not *hanged*] *the picture you gave me.*

hardly See *but, hardly, scarcely.*

have, of Use *have,* not *of,* after helping verbs such as *could, should, would, may,* and *might: You should have* [not *should of*] *told me.*

he, she; he/she Convention has allowed the use of *he* to mean "he or she": *After the infant learns to creep, he progresses to crawling.* However, many writers today consider this usage inaccurate and unfair because it seems to exclude females. The construction *he/she,* one substitute for *he,* is awkward and objectionable to most readers. The better choice is to make the pronoun plural, to rephrase, or, sparingly, to use *he or she.* For instance: *After infants learn to creep, they progress to crawling. After learning to creep, the infant progresses to crawling. After the infant learns to creep, he or she progresses to crawling.* See also **3** p. 165 and **4** p. 253.

herself, himself See *myself, herself, himself, yourself.*

hisself Nonstandard for *himself.*

hopefully *Hopefully* means "with hope": *Freddy waited hopefully for a glimpse of Eliza.* The use of *hopefully* to mean "it is to be hoped," "I hope," or "let's hope" is now very common; but since many readers continue to object strongly to the usage, try to avoid it. *I hope* [not *Hopefully*] *the law will pass.*

idea, ideal An *idea* is a thought or conception. An *ideal* (noun) is a model of perfection or a goal. *Ideal* should not be used in place of *idea: The idea* [not *ideal*] *of the play is that our ideals often sustain us.*

if, whether For clarity, use *whether* rather than *if* when you are expressing an alternative: *If I laugh hard, people can't tell whether I'm crying.*

illicit See *elicit, illicit.*

illusion See *allusion, illusion.*

immigrate, emigrate See *emigrate, immigrate.*

implicit See *explicit, implicit.*

imply, infer Writers or speakers *imply,* meaning "suggest": *Jim's letter implies he's having a good time.* Readers or listeners *infer,* meaning "conclude": *From Jim's letter I infer he's having a good time.*

incredible, incredulous *Incredible* means "unbelievable"; *incredulous* means "unbelieving": *When Nancy heard Dennis's incredible story, she was frankly incredulous.* See also *credible, creditable, credulous.*

individual, person, party *Individual* should refer to a single human being in contrast to a group or should stress uniqueness: *The US Constitution places strong emphasis on the rights of the individual.* For other meanings *person* is preferable: *What person* [not *individual*] *wouldn't want the security promised in that advertisement? Party* means "group" (*Can you seat a party of four for dinner?*) and should not be used to refer to an individual except in legal documents. See also *people, persons.*

infer See *imply, infer.*

in regards to Nonstandard for *in regard to, as regards,* or *regarding.*

inside of, outside of The *of* is unnecessary when *inside* and *outside* are used as prepositions: *Stay inside* [not *inside of*] *the house. The decision is outside* [not *outside of*] *my authority. Inside of* may refer colloquially to time, though in formal English *within* is preferred: *The law was passed within* [not *inside of*] *a year.*

insure See *assure, ensure, insure.*

irregardless Nonstandard for *regardless.*

is, are See *are, is.*

is because See *reason is because.*

is when, is where These are faulty constructions in sentences that define: *Adolescence is a stage* [not *is when a person is*] *between childhood and adulthood. Socialism is a system in which* [not *is where*] *government owns the means of production.* See also 4 p. 289.

its, it's *Its* is the pronoun *it* in the possessive case: *That plant is losing its leaves. It's* is a contraction for *it is* or *it has: It's* [*It is*] *likely to die. It's* [*It has*] *got a fungus.* Many people confuse *it's* and *its* because possessives are most often formed with *-'s;* but the possessive *its,* like *his* and *hers,* never takes an apostrophe.

-ize, -wise The suffix *-ize* changes a noun or adjective into a verb: *revolutionize, immunize.* The suffix *-wise* changes a noun or adjective into an adverb: *clockwise, otherwise, likewise.* Avoid the two suffixes except in established words: *I'm highly sensitive* [not *sensitized*] *to that kind of criticism. Financially* [not *Moneywise*], *it's a good time to buy real estate.*

kind of, sort of, type of In formal speech and writing, avoid using *kind of* or *sort of* to mean "somewhat": *He was rather* [not *kind of*] *tall.*

Kind, sort, and *type* are singular and take singular modifiers and verbs: *This kind of dog is easily trained.* Agreement errors often occur when these singular nouns are combined with the plural adjectives *these* and *those: These kinds* [not *kind*] *of dogs are easily trained. Kind, sort,* and *type* should be followed by *of* but not by *a: I don't know what type of* [not *type* or *type of a*] *dog that is.*

Use *kind of, sort of,* or *type of* only when the word *kind, sort,* or *type* is important: *That was a strange* [not *strange sort of*] *statement.*

lay, lie *Lay* means "put" or "place" and takes a direct object: *We could lay the tablecloth in the sun.* Its main forms are *lay, laid, laid. Lie* means "recline" or "be situated" and does not take an object: *I lie awake at night. The town lies east of the river.* Its main forms are *lie, lay, lain.* (See also 4 pp. 213–14.)

leave, let *Leave* and *let* are interchangeable only when followed by *alone; leave me alone* is the same as *let me alone.* Otherwise, *leave* means "depart" and *let* means "allow": *Jill would not let Sue leave.*

less See *fewer, less.*

liable See *apt, liable, likely.*

lie, lay See *lay, lie.*

like, as See *as, like.*

like, such as Strictly, *such as* precedes an example that represents a larger subject, whereas *like* indicates that two subjects are comparable. *Steve has recordings of many great saxophonists such as Ben Webster and Lee Konitz. Steve wants to be a great jazz saxophonist like Ben Webster and Lee Konitz.*

likely   See *apt, liable, likely.*

literally   This word means "actually" or "just as the words say," and it should not be used to qualify or intensify expressions whose words are not to be taken at face value. The sentence *He was literally climbing the walls* describes a person behaving like an insect, not a person who is restless or anxious. For the latter meaning, *literally* should be omitted.

lose, loose   *Lose* means "mislay": *Did you lose a brown glove? Loose* means "unrestrained" or "not tight": *Ann's canary got loose. Loose* also can function as a verb meaning "let loose": *They loose the dogs as soon as they spot the bear.*

lots, lots of   Colloquial substitutes for *very many, a great many,* or *much.* Avoid *lots* and *lots of* in college or business writing.

may, can   See *can, may.*

may be, maybe   *May be* is a verb, and *maybe* is an adverb meaning "perhaps": *Tuesday may be a legal holiday. Maybe we won't have classes.*

may of   See *have, of.*

media   *Media* is the plural of *medium* and takes a plural verb: *All the news media are increasingly visual.* The singular verb is common, even in the media, but many readers prefer the plural verb and it is always correct.

might of   See *have, of.*

moral, morale   As a noun, *moral* means "ethical conclusion" or "lesson": *The moral of the story escapes me. Morale* means "spirit" or "state of mind": *Victory improved the team's morale.*

most, almost   See *almost, most.*

must of   See *have, of.*

myself, herself, himself, yourself   The *-self* pronouns refer to or intensify another word or words: *Paul helped himself; Jill herself said so.* The *-self* pronouns are often used colloquially in place of personal pronouns, but that use should be avoided in formal speech and writing: *No one except me* [not *myself*] *saw the accident. Our delegates will be Susan and you* [not *yourself*]. See also 4 p. 245 on the unchanging forms of the *-self* pronouns in standard American English.

nowheres   Nonstandard for *nowhere.*

number   See *amount, number.*

of, have   See *have, of.*

off of   *Of* is unnecessary. Use *off* or *from* rather than *off of*: *He jumped off* [or *from,* not *off of*] *the roof.*

OK, O.K., okay   All three spellings are acceptable, but avoid this colloquial term in formal speech and writing.

on account of   Wordy for *because of.*

on the other hand   This transitional expression of contrast should be preceded by its mate, *on the one hand: On the one hand, we hoped for snow. On the other hand, we feared that it would harm the animals.* However, the two combined can be unwieldy, and a simple *but,* *however, yet,* or *in contrast* often suffices: *We hoped for snow.* *Yet we feared that it would harm the animals.*

outside of See *inside of, outside of.*

owing to the fact that Wordy for *because.*

party See *individual, person, party.*

people, persons In formal usage, *people* refers to a general group: *We the people of the United States.* . . . *Persons* refers to a collection of individuals: *Will the person or persons who saw the accident please notify.* . . . Except when emphasizing individuals, prefer *people* to *persons.* See also *individual, person, party.*

per Except in technical writing, an English equivalent is usually preferable to the Latin *per: $10 an* [not *per*] *hour; sent by* [not *per*] *parcel post; requested in* [not *per* or *as per*] *your letter.*

percent (per cent), percentage Both these terms refer to fractions of one hundred. *Percent* always follows a numeral (*40 percent of the voters*), and the word should be used instead of the symbol (%) in general writing. *Percentage* stands alone (*the percentage of voters*) or follows an adjective (*a high percentage*).

person See *individual, person, party.*

persons See *people, persons.*

phenomena The plural of *phenomenon* (meaning "perceivable fact" or "unusual occurrence"): *Many phenomena are not recorded. One phenomenon is attracting attention.*

plenty A colloquial substitute for *very: The reaction occurred very* [not *plenty*] *fast.*

plus *Plus* is standard as a preposition meaning "in addition to": *His income plus mine is sufficient.* But *plus* is colloquial as a conjunctive adverb: *Our organization is larger than theirs; moreover* [not *plus*], *we have more money.*

precede, proceed The verb *precede* means "come before": *My name precedes yours in the alphabet.* The verb *proceed* means "move on": *We were told to proceed to the waiting room.*

prejudice, prejudiced *Prejudice* is a noun; *prejudiced* is an adjective. Do not drop the *-d* from *prejudiced: I was fortunate that my parents were not prejudiced* [not *prejudice*].

pretty Overworked as an adverb meaning "rather" or "somewhat": *He was somewhat* [not *pretty*] *irked at the suggestion.*

previous to, prior to Wordy for *before.*

principal, principle *Principal* is an adjective meaning "foremost" or "major," a noun meaning "chief official," or, in finance, a noun meaning "capital sum." *Principle* is a noun only, meaning "rule" or "axiom." *Her principal reasons for confessing were her principles of right and wrong.*

proceed, precede See *precede, proceed.*

question of whether, question as to whether Wordy substitutes for *whether.*

raise, rise *Raise* means "lift" or "bring up" and takes a direct object: *The Kirks raise cattle.* Its main forms are *raise, raised, raised. Rise* means "get up" and does not take an object: *They must rise at dawn.* Its main forms are *rise, rose, risen.* (See also 4 pp. 213–14.)

real, really In formal speech and writing, *real* should not be used as an adverb; *really* is the adverb and *real* an adjective. *Popular reaction to the announcement was really* [not *real*] *enthusiastic.*

reason is because Although colloquially common, this expression should be avoided in formal speech and writing. Use a *that* clause after *reason is: The reason he is absent is that* [not *is because*] *he is sick.* Or: *He is absent because he is sick.* (See also 4 p. 290.)

respectful, respective *Respectful* means "full of (or showing) respect": *Be respectful of other people. Respective* means "separate": *The French and the Germans occupied their respective trenches.*

rise, raise See *raise, rise.*

scarcely See *but, hardly, scarcely.*

sensual, sensuous *Sensual* suggests sexuality; *sensuous* means "pleasing to the senses." *Stirred by the sensuous scent of meadow grass and flowers, Cheryl and Paul found their thoughts growing increasingly sensual.*

set, sit *Set* means "put" or "place" and takes a direct object: *He sets the pitcher down.* Its main forms are *set, set, set. Sit* means "be seated" and does not take an object: *She sits on the sofa.* Its main forms are *sit, sat, sat.* (See also 4 pp. 213–14.)

shall, will *Will* is the future-tense helping verb for all persons: *I will go, you will go, they will go.* The main use of *shall* is for first-person questions requesting an opinion or consent: *Shall I order a pizza? Shall we dance? Shall* can also be used for the first person when a formal effect is desired (*I shall expect you around three*), and it is occasionally used with the second or third person to express the speaker's determination (*You shall do as I say*).

should of See *have, of.*

sight, site, cite See *cite, sight, site.*

since *Since* mainly relates to time: *I've been waiting since noon.* But *since* is also often used to mean "because": *Since you ask, I'll tell you.* Revise sentences in which the word could have either meaning, such as *Since you asked, I've researched the question.*

sit, set See *set, sit.*

site, cite, sight See *cite, sight, site.*

so Avoid using *so* alone or as a vague intensifier: *He was so late. So* needs to be followed by *that* and a clause that states a result: *He was so late that I left without him.*

somebody, some body; someone, some one *Somebody* and *someone* are indefinite pronouns; *some body* is a noun modified by *some;* and *some one* is a pronoun or an adjective modified by *some. Somebody ought to invent a shampoo that will give hair some body. Someone told Janine she should choose some one plan and stick with it.*

sometime, sometimes, some time   *Sometime* means "at an indefinite time in the future": *Why don't you come up and see me sometime? Sometimes* means "now and then": *I still see my old friend Joe sometimes. Some time* means "a span of time": *I need some time to make the payments.*

somewheres   Nonstandard for *somewhere.*

sort of, sort of a   See *kind of, sort of, type of.*

such   Avoid using *such* as a vague intensifier: *It was such a cold winter. Such* should be followed by *that* and a clause that states a result: *It was such a cold winter that Napoleon's troops had to turn back.*

such as   See *like, such as.*

supposed to, used to   In both these expressions, the *-d* is essential: *I used to* [not *use to*] *think so. He's supposed to* [not *suppose to*] *meet us.*

sure   Colloquial when used as an adverb meaning *surely: James Madison sure was right about the need for the Bill of Rights.* If you merely want to be emphatic, use *certainly: Madison certainly was right.* If your goal is to convince a possibly reluctant reader, use *surely: Madison surely was right.*

sure and, sure to; try and, try to   *Sure to* and *try to* are the correct forms: *Be sure to* [not *sure and*] *buy milk. Try to* [not *Try and*] *find some decent tomatoes.*

take, bring   See *bring, take.*

than, as   See *as, than.*

than, then   *Than* is a conjunction used in comparisons, *then* an adverb indicating time: *Holmes knew then that Moriarty was wilier than he had thought.*

that, which   *That* introduces an essential clause: *We should use the lettuce that Susan bought* (*that Susan bought* limits the lettuce to a particular lettuce). *Which* can introduce both essential and nonessential clauses, but many writers reserve *which* only for nonessential clauses: *The leftover lettuce, which is in the refrigerator, would make a good salad* (*which is in the refrigerator* simply provides more information about the lettuce we already know of). Essential clauses (with *that* or *which*) are not set off by commas; nonessential clauses (with *which*) are. See also 5 pp. 303–05.

that, which, who   Use *that* for animals, things, and sometimes collective or anonymous people: *The rocket that failed cost millions. Infants that walk need constant tending.* Use *which* only for animals and things: *The river, which flows south, divides two countries.* Use *who* only for people and for animals with names: *Dorothy is the girl who visits Oz. Her dog, Toto, who accompanies her, gives her courage.*

their, there, they're   *Their* is the possessive form of *they: Give them their money. There* indicates place (*I saw her standing there*) or functions as an expletive (*There is a hole behind you*). *They're* is a contraction for *they are: They're going fast.*

theirselves   Nonstandard for *themselves.*

them   In standard American English, *them* does not serve as an adjective: *Those* [not *them*] *people want to know.*

then, than   See *than, then.*

these kind, these sort, these type, those kind   See *kind of, sort of, type of.*

this, these   *This* is singular: *this car* or *This is the reason I left. These* is plural: *these cars* or *These are not valid reasons.*

thru   A colloquial spelling of *through* that should be avoided in all academic and business writing.

to, too, two   *To* is a preposition; *too* is an adverb meaning "also" or "excessively"; and *two* is a number. *I too have been to Europe two times.*

too   Avoid using *too* as a vague intensifier: *Monkeys are too mean.* If you do use *too,* explain the consequences of the excessive quality: *Monkeys are too mean to make good pets.*

toward, towards   Both are acceptable, though *toward* is preferred. Use one or the other consistently.

try and, try to   See *sure and, sure to; try and, try to.*

type of   See *kind of, sort of, type of.* Don't use *type* without *of: It was a family type of* [not *type*] *restaurant.* Or better: *It was a family restaurant.*

uninterested   See *disinterested, uninterested.*

unique   *Unique* means "the only one of its kind" and so cannot sensibly be modified with words such as *very* or *most: That was a unique* [not *a very unique* or *the most unique*] *movie.*

usage, use   *Usage* refers to conventions, most often those of a language: *Is "hadn't ought" proper usage? Usage* is often misused in place of the noun *use: Wise use* [not *usage*] *of insulation can save fuel.*

use, utilize   *Utilize* can be used to mean "make good use of": *Many teachers utilize computers for instruction.* But for all other senses of "place in service" or "employ," prefer *use.*

used to   See *supposed to, used to.*

wait for, wait on   In formal speech and writing, *wait for* means "await" (*I'm waiting for Paul*) and *wait on* means "serve" (*The owner of the store herself waited on us*).

ways   Colloquial as a substitute for *way: We have only a little way* [not *ways*] *to go.*

well   See *good, well.*

whether, if   See *if, whether.*

which, that   See *that, which.*

which, who, that   See *that, which, who.*

who's, whose   *Who's* is the contraction of *who is* or *who has: Who's* [*Who is*] *at the door? Jim is the only one who's* [*who has*] *passed. Whose* is the possessive form of *who: Whose book is that?*

will, shall   See *shall, will.*

-wise   See *-ize, -wise.*

would have   Avoid this construction in place of *had* in clauses that begin *if* and state a condition contrary to fact: *If the tree had* [not *would* *have*] *withstood the fire, it would have been the oldest in town.* See also 4 p. 233.

would of See *have, of.*

you In all but very formal writing, *you* is generally appropriate as long as it means "you, the reader." In all writing, avoid indefinite uses of *you,* such as *In one ancient tribe your first loyalty was to your parents.* See also 4 pp. 258–59.

your, you're *Your* is the possessive form of *you: Your dinner is ready. You're* is the contraction of *you are: You're bound to be late.*

yourself See *myself, herself, himself, yourself.*

Credits

Text and Illustrations

American Society for Aesthetic Plastic Surgery: "Cosmetic Surgery Trends" from *Statistics: 2004.* Reprinted by permission.

American Verse Project: Screen images from HTI American Verse Project. Copyright © 2005 by the University of Michigan Press. Reprinted by permission.

Brooks: "The Bean Eaters" from *Blacks* by Gwendolyn Brooks. Copyright © 1991 by Gwendolyn Brooks. Reprinted by consent of Brooks Permissions.

Campbell: Excerpt from *Biology*, 7th Edition by Neil A. Campbell and Jane B. Reece. Copyright © 2005 by Pearson/Benjamin Cummings. Reprinted with permission.

CNN: "War Against Terror." Copyright © 2001 Cable News Network, LP, LLLP. Reprinted courtesy of CNN.

Davies: "Unemployment Rates of High School Graduates and College Graduates, 1984–2004," from "The Economics of College Tuition" by Antony Davies. Copyright © 2005. Reprinted by permission.

Drucker: Excerpt from "How Best to Protect the Environment" by Peter Drucker. *Harper's*, January 1972. Copyright © 1971 by Minneapolis Star and Tribune Co.

Dyson: Excerpt from *Disturbing the Universe* by Freeman J. Dyson. Copyright © 1979 by Freeman J. Dyson. Reprinted by permission of Basic Books, a member of Perseus Books, LLC.

EBSCOhost Publishing: Screen images of EBSCOhost database used with permission from EBSCOhost publishing.

Eisinger: Excerpt from *American Politics: The People and the Polity* by Peter Eisinger et al. Copyright © 1978 by Little, Brown and Company. Reprinted by permission of the author.

Farb: Excerpt from *Word Play: What Happens When People Talk* by Peter Farb. Copyright © 1973 by Peter Farb. Random House.

Gastner: "Electoral College Vote in the 2004 US Presidential Election" by Michael Gastner, Cosma Shalizi, and Mark Newman. Reprinted with permission.

Gaylin: Excerpt from "Feeling Anxious" in *Feelings: Our Vital Signs* by Willard Gaylin. Copyright © 1979 by Willard Gaylin. Reprinted by permission of William Morris Agency, LLC on behalf of the Author.

Gilligan: From *In a Different Voice: Psychological Theory and Women's Development* by Carol Gilligan. Copyright © 1982, 1993 by Carol Gilligan. Reprinted by permission of Harvard University Press.

Google: Screen images used by permission from Google.

Goreau: Excerpt from "Worthy Women Revisited" by Angeline Goreau. *The New York Times*, December 11, 1986. Copyright © 1986 by *The New York Times*. Reprinted by permission.

Ik: Excerpt from "A Book-Writing Venture" by Kim Yong Ik. Originally published in *The Writer*, October 1965. Copyright © Kim Yong Ik. Reprinted by permission of Faith M. Leigh.

Kuralt: From *Dateline America* by Charles Kuralt. Text copyright © 1979 by CBS, Inc. Reprinted by permission of Harcourt, Inc.

Mayer: Excerpt from "The Confounding Enemy of Sleep" by Lawrence A. Mayer. *Fortune*, June 1974. Copyright © 1975 Time Inc. All rights reserved. Reprinted by permission.

Nadelman: Excerpt from "Shooting Up" by Ethan A. Nadelman. *The New Republic*, June 1988. Copyright © 1988, The New Republic, Inc. Reprinted by permission of *The New Republic*.

Ouchi: Excerpt from *Theory Z: How American Business Can Meet the Japanese Challenge* by William G. Ouchi. Addison Wesley Publishing Company, Inc., 1981.

ProQuest: Screen image produced by ProQuest Information and Learning Company. Published with permission. Further reproduction is prohibited without

Photos

Index

discipline specific, **8** 434
documenting: Chicago style, Chic 539; MLA style, **MLA** 490
in the humanities, **8** 441
keyword searches of, **7** 381, 387–88
for literature and literary analysis, **8** 441
searching, **7** 387–88
selecting, **8** 434
using, **7** 385–88
Periodicals
documentation of. *See* Articles in periodicals
electronic, **7** 381, 385–88
finding and using, **7** 380–81, 385–88
journals vs. magazines, **7** 385
kinds of, **7** 385
peer-reviewed or refereed, **7** 388
quotation marks for titles of articles in, **5** 332
as research sources, **7** 385–88
titles of, underlining or italics for, **6** 360
Periodic sentences, **3** 145
Periods
correcting comma splices or fused sentences with, **4** 284–85, 286
ending sentences with, **5** 295
with quotation marks, **5** 334
in some abbreviations, **5** 295–96
space with, **5** 339–41
used in ellipsis marks, **5** 339, **7** 412
Permission
for material used in a Web composition, **7** 425
for postings on e-mail, discussion groups, or Web logs, **7** 424
for use of images, **7** 396, 425
person
pronouns with, **4** 252–54
vs. *you*, **4** 258–59
person, party, individual, Gl 559
Personal online sites, MLA style, **MLA** 482
Personal pronouns
agreement with antecedents, **4** 251–54
cases of, **4** 244–50
contractions vs., **5** 329
defined, **4** 189
list of, **4** 244–45
no apostrophes with possessives of, **5** 329

Person (first, second, third)
in academic writing, **2** 73, **8** 440, 446, 451, 454
defined, **4** 237
grammar/style checkers for, **1** 43
and point of view, in literary works, **8** 437–38
pronoun-antecedent agreement in, **4** 251–54
shifts in, **1** 43
subject-verb agreement in, **4** 237–40
persons, people, Gl 562
phenomena, Gl 562
Phenomena, in scientific research, **8** 452
Philosophy, research sources on, **8** 447
Photocopying sources, advantages and disadvantages of, **7** 409
Photographs. *See also* Illustrations and artworks
documenting, MLA style, **MLA** 487, 492
using, **1** 64–65
Phrases
absolute, **4** 204, **5** 305
appositive, **4** 205, **5** 304–05
conciseness of, **3** 179–80
defined, **4** 201–05
essential vs. nonessential, **5** 303–06, 314
as modifiers, **4** 202–03
prepositional. *See* Prepositional phrases
punctuation of: coordinate, **5** 309–10, 313–14; modifying, **5** 303–06
subordination with, **3** 148–50
types of, **4** 201–05
verb, **4** 191, 216–20
verbal. *See* Verbals and verbal phrases
Physics, research sources on, **8** 455
piece, peace, **6** 346
Place names
abbreviation of, **6** 364
capitalization of, **6** 356
commas in, **5** 311
Plagiarism
vs. academic integrity, **7** 418
accidental, **7** 419
avoiding, **7** 418–26
checklist for avoiding , **7** 420
with computer notes, **7** 408–09
defined, **7** 419
deliberate, **7** 419

Plagiarism (*continued*)
  detecting, on the Internet, **7**
    419–21
  with downloaded sources, **7** 409
  during information gathering, **7**
    408–09
  with handwritten notes, **7** 408
  and intellectual property, **7** 418
  with Internet sources, **7** 419–21
  with paraphrases, **7** 423
  with photocopied or printed-out
    sources, **7** 409
  with quotations, **7** 422
  with summaries, **2** 86, **7** 423
  vs. using common knowledge, **7**
    421
  vs. using your own independent
    material, **7** 421
plain, plane, **6** 346
Plain form, of verbs
  defined, **4** 190
  in forming past tense and past
    participles, **4** 210
  in forming simple present tense, **4**
    190
  forms of *do* with, **4** 219
plane, plain, **6** 346
Plays
  MLA style: list of works cited,
    MLA 494; parenthetical cita-
    tions, **MLA** 464, 466
  reading and writing about, **8**
    435–42
  research sources on, **8** 447
  titles of, underlining or italics for,
    6 360
plenty, GI 562
Plots, of literary works, **8** 437
Plurals. *See also* Agreement of pronouns and antecedents; Agreement of subjects and verbs
  of abbreviations, dates, and char-
    acters or words named as
    words, **5** 325, 329–30
  apostrophes misused to form, **5**
    325, 327
  apostrophes with possessives of, **5**
    324–25
  defined, **4** 189
  determiners with, **4** 266
  formation of, **6** 351
  grammar/style checkers for, **5**
    323–24
  of nouns, **4** 189, **5** 327
  in pronoun-antecedent agree-
    ment, **4** 251–54

  in subject-verb agreement, **4**
    237–40
plus, GI 562
PM, AM, **6** 363
Poetry
  MLA style: formatting quotations
    from, **MLA** 497–98; parentheti-
    cal citations for, **MLA** 464;
    works-cited entry for, **MLA**
    482–83
  omission of lines of, **5** 340–41
  reading and writing about, **8**
    435–44
  slashes between lines of, **5** 342
  titles of: quotation marks for
    short, **5** 332; underlining or ital-
    ics for long, **6** 360
Point-by-point comparison and contrast, **1** 48–49
Point of view
  in illustrations, **2** 91, 92
  in literary works, **8** 437–38
Point size (type fonts), **1** 57–58
Political Cartoons, **7** 395
Political science, research sources
  on, **8** 451
Popular Culture directory, **7** 395
Portfolios, writing, **1** 38
Positive form, of adjectives and adverbs, **4** 192, 262
Possessive case
  apostrophes to indicate, **4** 189, **5**
    324–26
  defined, **4** 244
  forming, **4** 189, 244–45, **5** 324–26
  before gerunds, **4** 250
  grammar/style checkers for, **5**
    323–24
  of nouns and indefinite pronouns,
    4 189, **5** 324–26
  of personal pronouns, **4** 244–45, **5**
    327
Post hoc fallacy, **2** 102–03
PowerPoint, **2** 125–27
precede, proceed, GI 562
Predicate adjective. *See* Subject
  complements
Predicate noun. *See* Subject complements
Predicates. *See also* Objects; Subject
  complements; Verbs
  agreement of subjects with, **4**
    237–40
  complete, **4** 196–97
  compound, **4** 196, **5** 313–14
  defined, **4** 195–96

Guide

Throughout this handbook, the symbol signals topics for students whose first language or dialect is not standard American English. These topics can be tricky because they arise from rules in standard English that are quite different in other languages and dialects. Many of the topics involve significant cultural assumptions as well.

No matter what your language background, as a college student you are learning the culture of US higher education and the language that is used and shaped by that culture. The process is challenging, even for native speakers of standard American English. It requires not just writing clearly and correctly but also mastering conventions of developing, presenting, and supporting ideas. The challenge is greater if, in addition, you are trying to learn standard American English and are accustomed to other conventions. Several habits can help you succeed:

- **Read.** Besides course assignments, read newspapers, magazines, and books in English. The more you read, the more fluently and accurately you'll write.
- **Write.** Keep a journal in which you practice writing in English every day.
- **Talk and listen.** Take advantage of opportunities to hear and use English.
- **Ask questions.** Your instructors, tutors in the writing lab, and fellow students can clarify assignments and help you identify and solve writing problems.
- **Don't try for perfection.** No one writes perfectly, and the effort to do so can prevent you from expressing yourself fluently. View mistakes not as failures but as opportunities to learn.
- **Revise first; then edit.** Focus on each essay's ideas, support, and organization before attending to grammar and vocabulary. See the revision and editing checklists in **1** pp. 25–26 and 30.
- **Set editing priorities.** Concentrate first on any errors that interfere with clarity, such as problems with word order or subject-verb agreement. The following index can help you identify the topics you need to work on and can lead you to appropriate text discussions. The pages marked * include exercises for self-testing.

Contents

◄———— " CULTURE LANGUAGE ➤ Guide" on reverse